edition 14

Corrections in America

An Introduction

Harry E. Allen, Ph.D.
San Jose State University

Edward J. Latessa, Ph.D.
University of Cincinnati

Bruce S. Ponder
Allen Ponder Associates

PEARSON

Boston Columbus Indianapolis New York San Francisco Hoboken
Amsterdam Cape Town Dubai London Madrid Milan Munich Paris Montréal Toronto
Delhi Mexico City São Paulo Sydney Hong Kong Seoul Singapore Taipei Tokyo

Editorial Director: Andrew Gilfillan
Senior Acquisitions Editor: Gary Bauer
Editorial Assistant: Lynda Cramer
Director of Marketing: David Gesell
Marketing Manager: Mary Salzman
Senior Marketing Coordinator: Alicia Wozniak
Marketing Assistant: Les Roberts
Senior Managing Editor: JoEllen Gohr
Project Manager: Susan Hannahs
Program Manager: Tara Horton
Senior Operations Supervisor: Vince Scelta
Operations Specialist: Deidra Skahill
Creative Director: Andrea Nix
Art Director: Diane Ernsberger
Cover Designer: Studio Montage
Cover Photo: Fotolia/Les Cunliffe and Shutterstock/Elnur
Full-Service Project Management: Vinolia Benedict Fernando, S4Carlisle Publishing Services
Composition: S4Carlisle Publishing Services
Printer/Binder: RR Donnelley/Roanoke
Cover Printer: Lehigh Phoenix Color
Text Font: Minion Pro

Library of Congress Cataloging-in-Publication Data

Allen, Harry E.
Corrections in America: an introduction / Harry E. Allen, Ph.D., San Jose State University, Edward J. Latessa, Ph.D., University of Cincinnati, Bruce S. Ponder, Allen Ponder Associates. — Edition 14.
pages cm
Includes bibliographical references and index.
ISBN 978-0-13-359121-7
ISBN 0-13-359121-2
1. Corrections—United States. I. Latessa, Edward J. II. Ponder, Bruce S. III. Title.
HV9304.A63 2016
364.60973—dc23

2014033400

10 9 8 7 6 5 4 3 2 1

ISBN-10: 0-13-359121-2
ISBN-13: 978-0-13-359121-7

dedication

To brother Joseph Hunter Allen, Bishop, and his sons

Harry Allen

To my family—Sally, Amy, Jennifer, Michael, Allison, and Denise, for always being there for me

Edward Latessa

To James and Gertrude Watts and my grandfather Warren White for providing the intellectual guidance to excel

Bruce S. Ponder

brief contents

contents

new to this edition

The field of corrections is undergoing rapid and significant changes, occasioned by court decisions, changes in correctional populations, the fiscal crises in many states, and legislative demands. Sentencing smarter and introducing evidence-based practices have exerted important impacts on practice, policies, and personnel. The results are problems unforeseen in the history of corrections. In this edition, we identify those major change factors and the effects they are having on the field. In addition, we have attempted to provide projections through the next three years. These improvements are designed to enhance student understanding and learning about this dynamic field. They include the following:

- About 25 percent of the research cited is new.
- Photographs have been updated.
- New or expanded coverage is included on such issues as prison recidivism rates, effects of court decisions on correctional practices, new techniques to improve community supervision, a leveling off of prison populations, strategies and innovative solutions for decreasing prison overpopulation, what works in corrections, and institutional threat groups.
- An extensive examination of the California Realignment effort, which will have major impacts on the field in the coming decades, is included.
- Approximately 80 percent of the charts, graphs, and figures are new or updated, and many are projected to 2015.
- More detailed biographical data are provided on major actors in the field of corrections.
- Almost 40 new Policy Position, Correctional Practice, and Correctional Profile features have been added to provide in-depth coverage of selected topics.
- Chapter objectives have been updated and enhanced.
- The Glossary has grown to include definitions and descriptions of all key words in this edition.
- Two new chapters have been included: *Security Threat Groups and Prison Gangs* (Chapter 8) and *Facilities for Juveniles* (Chapter 20).
- Correctional careers have been identified and described in a new appendix.

MyCJLab

Personalize learning with MyCJLab MyCJLab is an online homework, tutorial, and assessment program designed to work with this text to engage students and improve results. This powerful homework and test manager lets you create, import, and manage online homework assignments, quizzes, and tests that are automatically graded. You can choose from a wide range of assignment options, including time limits, proctoring, and maximum number of attempts allowed. The bottom line: MyLab means less time grading and more time teaching.

Assess and test using pre-loaded content in the Class/Quiz Prep Assignments and Pre-Built Chapter Quizzes. Assess what your students know before they come to class with **Class Prep** assignments. Students get specific, automatic feedback to help improve their performance, while instructors get an accurate view of their students' knowledge level of the chapter before they come to class. Students can prepare for an upcoming quiz with **Quiz Prep** assignments that test their knowledge of the text and classroom experience. These homework assignments are pre-built with automatic feedback and grade tracking. Now you can cover each of the objectives featured in your textbook using the Pre-Built Chapter Quizzes. Composed of multiple-choice questions, instructors can choose to either customize each quiz or assign as is, and simply pick the due date.

End of Chapter Questions and Critical Thinking Exercises. These essay-style questions can be assigned and used to measure students' understanding of the chapter material on a deeper level and challenge their writing skills. The Critical Thinking exercises will require students to compare and contrast, reference newspapers, conduct interviews, as well as look at articles and websites.

Assign discussion questions on the most recent current events videos, articles, and educational media with CJ Search. Designed for quick and easy access in and out of the classroom, our media search tool, CJ Search, organizes current CJ-related videos, news articles and other media from the Internet. Critical-thinking questions have been created for each of these media resources, allowing you to assign current videos to your students for assessment.

Help students investigate controversial issues in CJ with Point/CounterPoint Videos. In these video assignments, 2 individuals present opposing cases for or against 21 issues such as marijuana legalization, violent video games, death penalty, three strikes laws, etc. A writing space research assignment prompt and grading rubric for each issue asks the student to take a position on the issue and support it. For each assignment, the pro/con scripts and a list of references are included to assist student research.These videos can also be accessed for in class use from the Multimedia Library.

Help students explore key concepts and issues using Myths and Issues Videos. In these videos, CJ professors around the nation discuss concepts presented in the text providing insight regarding real world application. A short essay writing prompt and grading rubric is provided making these easily assignable within the MyLab. These videos can also be accessed for in class use from the Multimedia Library.

NEW: Foster better writing, all in one place with Writing Space. Better writers make great learners—who perform better in their courses. To help you develop and assess concept mastery and critical thinking through writing, we created the Writing Space. It's a single place to assign, track, and grade writing assignments, provide writing resources, and exchange meaningful, personalized feedback with students, quickly and easily. And thanks to integration with Turnitin®, Writing Space can check students' work for improper citation or plagiarism. Two writing assignments per chapter are available, as well as writing assignments for Point/CounterPoint and Myths & Issues videos. Instructors also have the ability to create their own writing assignments, as well as edit and create their own grading rubrics.

Review and assign multimedia assets for your textbook using the Multimedia Library. To help you build assignments, or add an extra engaging element to your lectures, each MyCJLab course comes with a Multimedia Library. Resources include videos such as Myths & Issues, flashcards, simulations, chapter PowerPoints, and summary.

NEW: Keep students on track with the Reporting Dashboard. View, analyze, and report learning outcomes clearly and easily, and get the information you need to keep your students on track throughout the course, with the new Reporting Dashboard. Available via the Gradebook and fully mobile-ready, the Reporting Dashboard presents student performance data.

INSTRUCTOR SUPPLEMENTS

Instructor's Manual with Test Bank Includes content outlines for classroom discussion, teaching suggestions, and answers to selected end-of-chapter questions from the text; also contains a Word document version of the test bank.

TestGen This computerized test generation system gives you maximum flexibility in creating and administering tests on paper, electronically, or online. It provides state-of-the-art features for viewing and editing test bank questions, dragging a selected question into a test you are creating, and printing sleek, formatted tests in a variety of layouts. Select test items from test banks included with TestGen for quick test creation, or write your own questions from scratch. TestGen's random generator provides the option to display different text or calculated number values each time questions are used.

PowerPoint Presentations Our presentations offer clear, straightforward outlines and notes to use for class lectures or study materials. Photos, illustrations, charts, and tables from the book are included in the presentations when applicable.

To access supplementary materials online, instructors need to request an instructor access code. Go to **www.pearsonhighered.com/irc**, where you can register for an instructor access code. Within 48 hours after registering, you will receive a confirming e-mail, including an instructor access code. Once you have received your code, go to the site and log on for full instructions on downloading the materials you wish to use.

PEARSON ONLINE COURSE SOLUTIONS

Corrections in America is supported by online course solutions that include interactive learning modules, a variety of assessment tools, videos, simulations, and current event features. Go to **www.pearsonhighered.com/irc** or contact your local representative for the latest information.

ALTERNATE VERSIONS

eBooks This text is also available in multiple eBook formats, including Adobe Reader and *CourseSmart*. *CourseSmart* is an exciting new choice for students looking to save money. As an alternative to purchasing the printed textbook, students can purchase an electronic version of the same content. With a *CourseSmart* eTextbook, students can search the text, make notes online, print out reading assignments that incorporate lecture notes, and bookmark important passages for later review. For more information or to purchase access to the *CourseSmart* eTextbook, visit **www.coursesmart.com**.

acknowledgments

We would like to acknowledge the great assistance of the people who merit special recognition in the 14th edition of *Corrections in America*. Instructors, former students, colleagues, and doctoral graduates were generous in pointing out the strengths and weaknesses of the 13th edition, and they made considerable suggestions for improving the textbook. Fortunately, we took them seriously and have benefited from their expertise. Our formal reviewers heaped praise where there might be praise and uniformly agreed on subjects deserving more attention, such as the chapters on security threat groups and facilities for juveniles. We would like to thank these conscientious reviewers: Lisa Cason, Columbia College; Scott Chenault, University of Central Missouri; Dana C. De Witt, Mount Marty College; Thomas A. Dreffein, Triton College; Lisa A. Hoston, Allegany College of Maryland; Patricia Nunally, Southwest Tennessee Community College; Patrick Patterson, Eastfield College; Mari Pierce, Penn State University; Russ Pomrenke, Gwinnett Technical College; and Jason Smith, New Hampshire Technical Institute.

We are also very pleased to welcome Gary Bauer as our new editor. He was very responsive to our needs and is a great editor with whom to work. A special thanks as well goes to Elisa Rogers, who took on the job of assisting with the original manuscript, tables, charts, and figures and manuscript preparation chores, and to Susan Hannahs at Pearson and Vinolia Benedict Fernando at S4Carlisle Publishing Services, who handled the production of the work. Gary's team contributed in many ways to the improvement of the 14th edition of this work, the longest continuously published textbook on corrections in the nation.

We wish to thank and acknowledge the recently deceased Clifford Simonsen, on whose shoulders we stand. Finally, we acknowledge our families, who endured our absences, humored us, handled our human needs, bolstered us in despondency, and were there when we needed them. We could not have done it without you.

Harry E. Allen

Edward J. Latessa

Bruce S. Ponder

about the authors

Harry E. Allen is Professor Emeritus in the Justice Studies Department at San Jose State University. Before joining San Jose State University in 1978, he served as director of the Program for the Study of Crime and Delinquency at The Ohio State University. Previously, he served as executive secretary of the Governor's Task Force on Corrections for the State of Ohio after teaching at Florida State University in the Department of Criminology and Corrections.

Professor Allen is the author or coauthor of numerous articles, chapters in books, essays, and textbooks, including the first 10 editions of *Corrections in America* with Clifford E. Simonsen, the 11th edition with Drs. Simonsen and Edward J. Latessa, and the last three with Professor Latessa and Bruce S. Ponder. He also coauthored the first three editions of *Corrections in the Community* with Edward J. Latessa. He has been very active in professional associations and was the first criminologist to serve as president of both the American Society of Criminology (1982) and the Academy of Criminal Justice Sciences (1994). He received the Herbert Block Award for service to the American Society of Criminology and the Founder's Award for contributions to the Academy of Criminal Justice Sciences. He is a fellow in both the Western and the American Society of Criminology and was the most frequently cited criminologist in the field of correctional textbooks. He was a Humana Scholar at the University of Louisville (2001) and for the past 14 years has been designing and instructing online courses for the University of Louisville in the areas of corrections, ethics, substance abuse, community corrections, terrorism, alternatives to incarceration, and capital punishment.

Edward J. Latessa received his Ph.D. from The Ohio State University in 1979 and is a professor and director of the School of Criminal Justice at the University of Cincinnati. Dr. Latessa has published over 140 works in the area of criminal justice, corrections, and juvenile justice. He is coauthor of eight books, including *Corrections in the Community* and *Corrections in America*. Professor Latessa has directed over 150 funded research projects, including studies of day reporting centers, juvenile justice programs, drug courts, prison programs, intensive supervision programs, halfway houses, and drug programs. He and his staff have also assessed over 600 correctional programs throughout the United States, and he has provided assistance and workshops in over 45 states. Dr. Latessa served as president of the Academy of Criminal Justice Sciences (1989–1990). He has also received several awards, including the Marguerite Q. Warren and Ted B. Palmer Differential Intervention Award presented by the Division of Corrections and Sentencing of the American Society of Criminology (2010); the Outstanding Community Partner Award from the Arizona Department of Juvenile Corrections (2010); the Maud Booth Correctional Services Award in recognition of dedicated service and leadership presented by the Volunteers of America (2010); the Community Hero Award presented by Community Resources for Justice (2010); the Bruce Smith Award for outstanding contributions to criminal justice by the Academy of Criminal Justice Sciences (2010); the George Beto Scholar, College of Criminal Justice, Sam Houston State University (2009); the Mark Hatfield Award for Contributions in public policy research by the Hatfield School of Government at Portland State University (2008); the Outstanding Achievement Award by the National Juvenile Justice Court Services Association (2007); the August Vollmer Award from the American Society of Criminology (2004); the Simon Dinitz Criminal Justice Research Award from the Ohio Department of Rehabilitation and Correction (2002); the Margaret Mead Award for dedicated service to the causes of social justice and humanitarian advancement by the International Community Corrections Association (2001); the Peter P. Lejins Award for Research from the American Correctional Association (1999); the ACJS Fellow Award (1998); the ACJS Founders Award (1992); and the

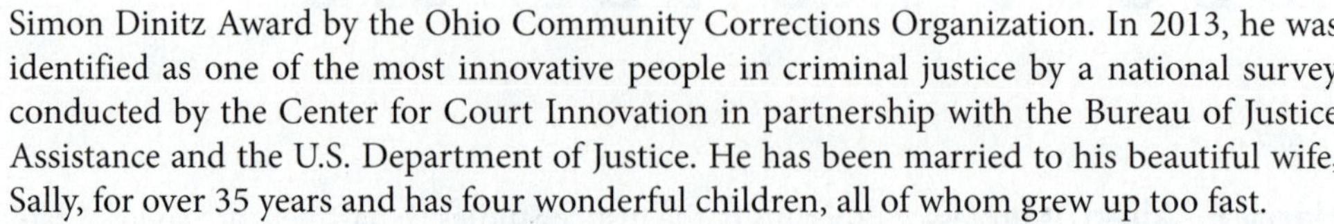

Simon Dinitz Award by the Ohio Community Corrections Organization. In 2013, he was identified as one of the most innovative people in criminal justice by a national survey conducted by the Center for Court Innovation in partnership with the Bureau of Justice Assistance and the U.S. Department of Justice. He has been married to his beautiful wife, Sally, for over 35 years and has four wonderful children, all of whom grew up too fast.

Bruce S. Ponder grew up in part on the raj of the Maharaja of Dharbhanaga and in Europe. He was a professional race car driver in the 1970s, winning major competitions including the "12 Hours of Sebring" (1972). He was formally trained in political science, computer information systems, and computer sciences. He also studied terrorism extensively and team-taught in-service training programs at the Southern Police Institute. Currently, he is Internet coordinator/online course developer and team instructor in a variety of courses at the Justice Administration Department at the University of Louisville, particularly in terrorism, intelligence and homeland security, and corrections.

part 1

Historical Perspectives

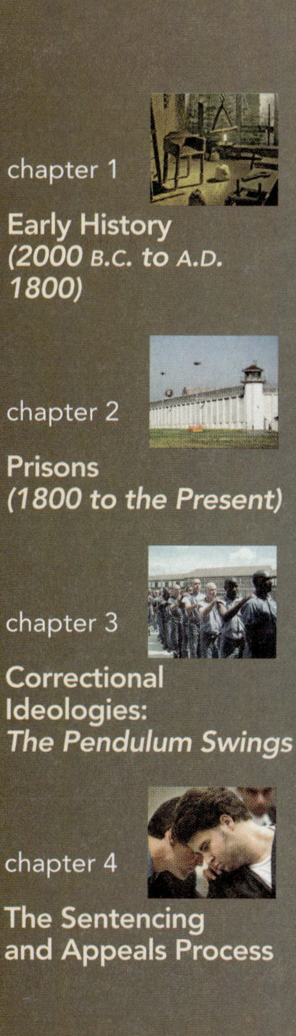

Overview

A crucial question in corrections is, "Who are offenders and what shall we do with them?" Part 1 deals with the process by which punishment originated as a private matter between an offending party and the victim but later came to be an official state function. Significant changes over time are examined, starting with 2000 B.C. and continuing through contemporary efforts to construct places of punishment and reform. Behind each of the four major answers to the crucial question lay assumptions about the nature of offenders and what to do with them. Part 1 details these perceptions, assumptions, and answers, as well as corresponding correctional practices and fads that have emerged during the last 4,000 years.

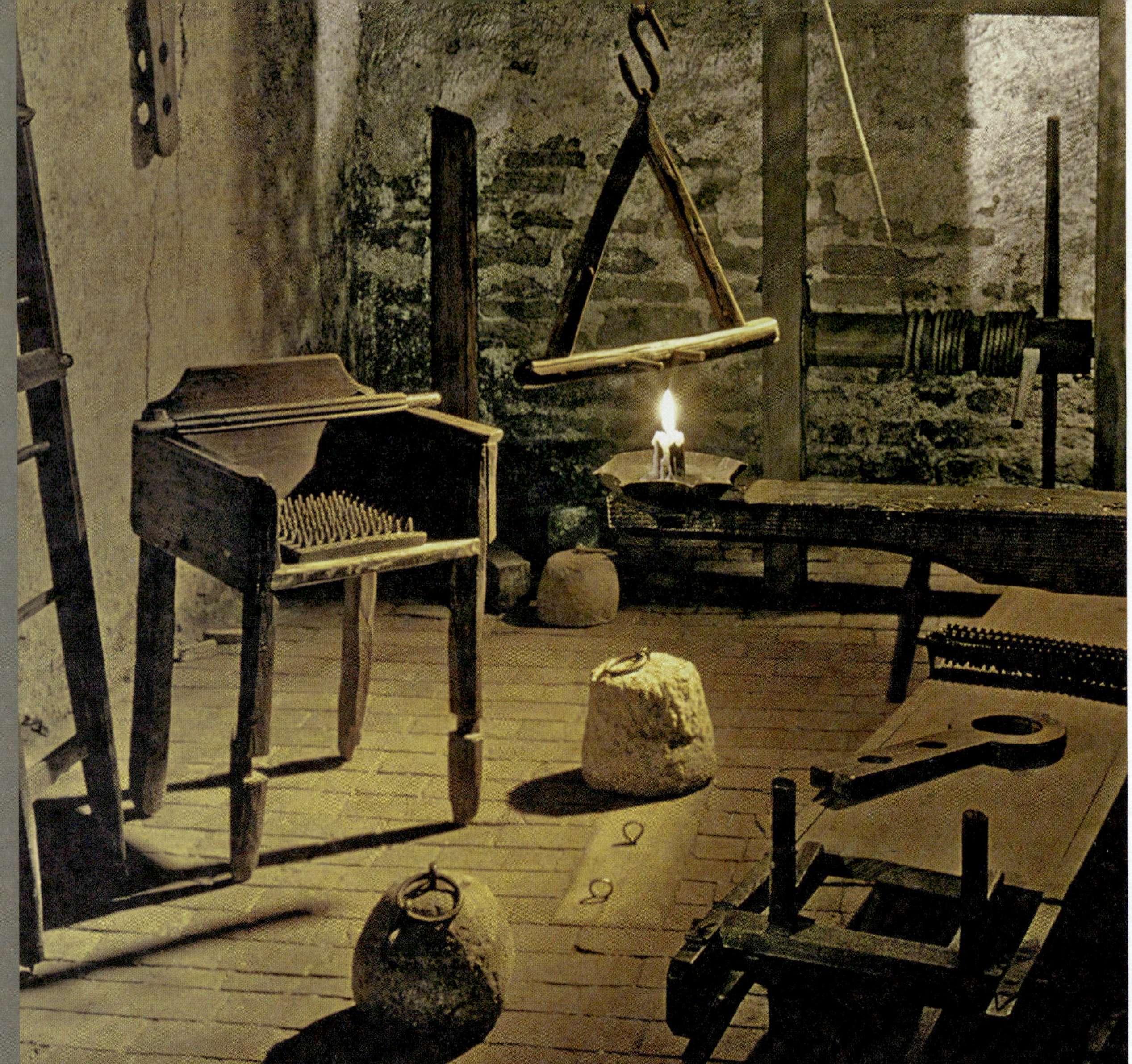

Erich Lessing/Art Resource

Objectives

- Summarize the definition, mission, and role of corrections.
- Summarize early responses to crime prior to the development of prisons.
- Describe how secular law emerged.
- Summarize sentencing goals and primary punishment philosophies.
- Outline the development of the prison.

chapter 1 Early History (*2000 B.C. to A.D. 1800*)

Outline

Redress of Wrongs

- Retaliation
- Fines and Punishments

Early Codes

- Babylonian and Sumerian Codes
- Crime and Sin
- Roman and Greek Codes
- The Middle Ages

Punishment

- Capital and Corporal Punishment
- Deterrence
- Emergence of Secular Law
- Early Prisons
- Workhouses

The Age of Enlightenment and Reform

- Montesquieu and Voltaire: The French Humanists
- Bentham and the Hedonistic Calculus
- John Howard

Houses of Correction, Workhouses, and Gaols

Transportation Systems

- Deportation to the American Colonies and Australia
- Hulks: A Sordid Episode

Early Cellular Prisons

- The Maison de Force at Ghent and the Hospice of San Michele
- William Penn and the "Great Law"
- The Walnut Street Jail

"The descent to hell is easy. The gates stand open day and night. But to reclimb the slope and escape to the upper air: this is labor."

—Virgil,
Aeneid, Book 6

Overview

This textbook is not intended to be an in-depth history of corrections nor a dissertation on its legal aspects. It is helpful, however, to know at least a little of the fascinating historical background (legal and social) to gain an improved understanding of the concepts, practices, and operations that we will discuss later and how we got to where corrections is today as we progress into the twenty-first century. In describing this background, we avoid technical jargon to keep misunderstanding to a minimum. Where appropriate, specific individuals and events that have influenced the history of corrections are detailed in the chapter.

It is important to study the growing field of corrections for a variety of reasons. This dynamic field is undergoing rapid, mind-boggling change. In the interest of reducing crime, protecting children, salvaging redeemable offenders, and increasing citizen and society safety, the nation has invested unprecedented amounts of time and money in the correctional system. Between 1972 and 2008, the number of state inmates grew 705 percent before beginning to drop in 2009. The growth of corrections has not been limited to prisons; the number of offenders reentering society as well as the jail and probation populations have never been higher.

Corrections is a major industry, annually costing over $75 billion recently,[1] and as such needs to be able to find and hire competent, educated, and motivated persons.

Never have so many Americans been in the arms of the law and under correctional control; never has the percentage of the citizenry incarcerated been as high as it is today (although U.S. Supreme Court decisions have recently forced some states to reduce their prison population). The size of corrections is rapidly increasing and—measured by the number of employees, offenders, and budgets—still undergoing significant growth.

Corrections affects the lives of ordinary people almost daily. Employees of prisons (as well as probation and parole officers) are in immediate contact with frequently violent and aggressive offenders, much more so than the typical municipal police officer who, in a busy week, may interact once with such an offender. The populace in general and students of corrections in particular must understand the dynamics that affect all forms of correctional work. They also must understand criminal behavior to better cope with the variety of offenders and to deal effectively with problematic clients. These factors are explored throughout this textbook, and your instructor will help you gain the necessary knowledge to begin your journey into this fascinating field. We begin now by tracing the roots of corrections back to the early beginnings of civilization as we know it.

REDRESS OF WRONGS

Retaliation

The earliest remedy for wrongs done to one's person or property was simply to retaliate against the wrongdoer. In early primitive societies, personal **retaliation** was accepted and even encouraged by members of the tribal group. This ancient concept of personal revenge could hardly be considered "law." Yet it has influenced the development of most legal systems, especially English criminal law, from which most American criminal law derives.

The practice of personal retaliation was later augmented by the **blood feud**, in which the victim's family or tribe took revenge on the offender's family or tribe. Because this form of retaliation could easily escalate and result in an endless battle or **vendetta** between the injured factions, some method of control had to be devised to make blood feuds less costly and damaging.

The practice of retaliation usually begins to develop into a system of criminal law when it becomes customary for the victim of the wrongdoing to accept money or property in place of blood vengeance. This custom, when established, is usually dictated by tribal tradition and the relative positions of power between the injured party and the wrongdoer. Custom has always exerted great force among primitive societies. The acceptance of vengeance in the form of a payment (such as cattle, food, or personal services) was usually not compulsory, however, and victims were still free to take whatever vengeance they wished. Legal historians Albert Kocourek and John Wigmore described this pressure to retaliate:

> It must not be forgotten that the right of personal revenge was also in many cases a duty. A man was bound by all the force of religion to avenge the death of his kinsman. This duty was by universal practice imposed upon the nearest male relative—the avenger of blood, as he is called in the Scripture accounts.[2]

The custom of atonement for wrongs by payment to appease the victim's family or tribe became known as ***lex salica*** (or ***wergeld*** in Europe). It is still in effect in many Middle Eastern and Far Eastern countries, with the amount of payment based on the injured person's rank and position in the social group. The practice of paying restitution for crimes to the Crown, in addition to victims, was known as **friedensgeld**. With fines, the victim disappeared from

key term

Retaliation
Act designed to repay (as an injury) in kind or to return like for like, *especially* "to get revenge."

key term

Blood feud or **vendetta**
An often-prolonged series of retaliatory, vengeful, or hostile acts or exchange of such acts.

key term

Lex salica
The custom of atonement for wrongs against a victim by payment to appease the victim's family.

key term

Wergeld
The European word denoting *lex salica*.

key term

Friedensgeld
The practice of paying restitution for crime to both the victim and the Crown.

the criminal justice system, becoming the ignored component of the crime. The victim has reappeared in the restorative justice movement, described in Chapter 5.

Fines and Punishments

How did these simple, voluntary programs become part of an official system of fines and punishments? As tribal leaders, elders, and (later) kings came into power,[3] they began to exert their authority on the negotiations. Wrongdoers could choose to stay away from the proceedings; this was their right. But if they refused to abide by the imposed sentence, they were declared to be outside the law of the tribe (nation, family), or an **outlaw**. There is little doubt that outlawry, or exile, was the first punishment imposed by society,[4] and it heralded the beginning of criminal law as we now know it.

key term

Outlaw
Declared to be outside the law of the tribe (nation, family).

Criminal law, even primitive criminal law, requires an element of public action against the wrongdoer—as in a pronouncement of outlawry. Before this element of public action, the backgrounds of criminal law and sanctions seem to have been parallel in most legal systems. The subsequent creation of legal codes and sanctions for different crimes either stressed or refined the vengeance factor, according to the particular society's values.

EARLY CODES

Babylonian and Sumerian Codes

Even primitive ethics demanded that a society express its vengeance within a system of regulations and rules. Moses was advised to follow the "eye for eye and tooth for tooth" doctrine stated in Exodus 21:24, but this concept of ***lex talionis*** is far older than the Bible; it appears in the Sumerian codes (1860 B.C.) and in the 1750 B.C. code of King Hammurabi of Babylon, compiled more than 500 years before the *Book of the Covenant* (1250 B.C.).

key term

Lex talionis
The act of repaying in kind, such as "an eye for an eye, a tooth for a tooth."

As early societies developed language and writing skills, they began attempting to record the laws of their nations. While most historians view the Hammurabic Code as the first comprehensive attempt at codifying social interaction, the Sumerian codes preceded it by about a century, and the principle of *lex talionis* was evident in both. The punishments handed out under these codes were harsh and based on vengeance (or *talion*), in many cases being inflicted by the injured party. In the Babylonian code, more than 24 offenses called for the penalty of death. Both codes also prescribed mutilation, whipping, or forced labor as punishments for numerous crimes.

The kinds of punishments applied to slaves and bonded servants have been cited by many scholars[5] as the origin of the punishments that in later law applied to all offenders. As stated by historian Gustav Radbruch,

> Applied earlier almost exclusively to slaves, [the mutilating penalties] became used more and more on freemen during the Carolingian period [A.D. 640–1012] and especially for offenses that betokened a base and servile mentality. Up to the end of the Carolingian era, punishments "to hide and hair" were overwhelmingly reserved for slaves. Even death penalties occurred as slave punishments and account for the growing popularity of such penalties in Carolingian times. The aggravated death penalties, combining corporal and capital punishments, have their roots in the penal law governing slaves.[6]

The early punishments were considered synonymous with slavery; those punished even had their heads shaved, indicating the "mark of the slave."[7] In Roman days, the extensive use of penal servitude was spurred by the need for workers to perform hard labor in the great public works. The sentence to penal servitude was generally reserved for the lower classes; it usually meant life in chains, working in the mines or rowing in the galleys or ships, or building the public works planned by the government. The sentences carried with them the complete loss of citizenship and liberty until they died and were classed, along with exile

key term

Civil death
The status of a living person equivalent in its legal consequences to natural death; loss of all rights and powers as if dead.

and death, as capital punishment. Penal servitude, or **civil death**, meant that the offender's property was confiscated in the name of the state and that his wife was declared a widow, eligible to remarry. To society, the criminal sentenced to penal servitude was, in effect, "dead."

Crime and Sin

key term

"Get right with God"
Directive that the offender must make peace with God through repentance and atonement.

Punishment of the individual in the name of the state also included the concept of superstitious revenge. Here crime was entangled with sin, and punishment in the form of *wergeld* (payment to the victim) or *friedensgeld* (payment to the state) was not sufficient. If society believed the crime might have offended a divinity, the accused had to undergo a long period of progressively harsher punishment to appease the gods. As time passed, the zone between church law and state law became more blurred, and the concept of personal responsibility for one's act was combined with the need to **"get right with God."**[8] The early codes, even the Ten Commandments, were designed to make the offender's punishment acceptable to both society and God.

Roman and Greek Codes

In the sixth century A.D., Emperor Justinian of Rome wrote his code of laws, one of the most ambitious early efforts to match a desirable amount of punishment with all possible crimes. Roman art of the period depicts the "scales of justice," a metaphor demanding that the punishment balance the crime. Justinian's effort, as might be expected, bogged down in the far-flung empire's morass of administrative details that were required to enforce it. The Code of Justinian did not survive the fall of the Roman Empire, but it left the foundation on which most of the Western world's legal codes were eventually built.

In Greece, the harsh Code of Draco provided the same penalties for both citizens and slaves, incorporating many of the concepts used in primitive societies (for example, vengeance, outlawry, and blood feuds). The Greeks were the first society to allow any of their citizens to prosecute an offender in the name of the injured party. This clearly illustrates that during the Greek period, public interest and protection of the social order were becoming more important than individual injury and individual vengeance.

The Middle Ages

The Middle Ages was a long period of general social disorder. Vast changes in the social structure and the growing influence of the church on everyday life resulted in a divided system of justice. Reformation was viewed as a process of religious, not secular, redemption. As in early civilizations, the sinner had to pay two debts, one to society and another to God. The "ordeal" was the church's substitute for a trial by the leadership of the secular group, until the practice was abolished in A.D. 1215. In trials by ordeal, the accused were subjected to impossible, dangerous, or painful tests, in the belief that those who were truly innocent would emerge unscathed, whereas the guilty would suffer agonies and die; this process determined guilt or innocence. The brutality of most trials by ordeal ensured a very high percentage of convictions.

key term

Inquisition
A former Roman Catholic tribunal for the discovery and punishment of heresy; an investigation conducted with little regard for individual rights through a severe questioning.

The church expanded the concept of crime to include some new areas, still reflected in modern codes. During the Middle Ages, sexual activity other than for the purpose of procreation was seen as especially sinful. Sexual offenses usually involved either public or "unnatural" acts, and they provoked horrible punishments, as did heresy and witchcraft. The church justified cruel reprisals as a means of saving the unfortunate sinner from the clutches of Satan. The zealous movement to stamp out heresy brought on the **Inquisition** and its use of the most vicious tortures imaginable to gain "confessions" and "repentance" from alleged heretics. Thousands upon thousands of persons died at the hands of the Inquisition in Spain and Holland, where these sometimes inhumane methods were the most extensively used. Punishment was viewed not as an end in itself but as the offender's only hope of pacifying a wrathful God.

The Inquisition was a tribunal, established by the Catholic Church in the Middle Ages, with very wide powers for the suppression of heresy. The tribunal searched out heretics and other offenders rather than waiting for charges to be brought forward. Emperor Frederick II made the Inquisition a formal institution in 1224, and it lasted until 1834. The main contribution of the medieval church to our study of corrections is the concept of free will. This idea assumes that individuals choose their actions, good or bad, and thus can be held fully responsible for them. The religious doctrines of eternal punishment, atonement, and spiritual conversion rest on the assumption that individuals who commit sins could have acted differently if they had chosen to do so.

The early codes and their administration were usually based on the belief that punishment was necessary to avenge the victim, or to satisfy God. In early, small tribal groups and less complex societies, direct compensation to the victim was used in place of revenge to prevent disintegration of the social structure through extended blood feuds. When those groups concentrated their power in a king or similar ruler with another title, the concept of crime as an offense against the victim gave way to the idea that crime (however lowly the victim) was an offense against the state and society in general. In the process, *wergeld* was replaced by *friedensgeld*, and the administration of punishment became the responsibility of the king. Concentrating that power also led to a tendency to ignore victims and their losses while concentrating on the crime and the criminal.

PUNISHMENT

Capital and Corporal Punishment

The most common forms of state punishment over the centuries have been death, torture, mutilation, branding, public humiliation, fines, forfeiture of property, banishment, imprisonment, and transportation.[9] These acts and numerous variations on them have always symbolized retribution for crimes. (Imprisonment and transportation are relatively modern penal practices and will be discussed in later chapters.)

The death penalty (killing the offender) was the most universal form of punishment among early societies. There was little knowledge of behavior modification and other modern techniques to control violent persons, and often the feared offenders were condemned to death by hanging, crucifixion, burning at the stake, drowning, being drawn and quartered, and any other cruel and unusual method the human mind could conceive. As technology advanced, methods for killing offenders became more sophisticated. In the belief that punishment, especially capital punishment, would act as a deterrent to others, societies carried out executions and lesser punishments in public.

Torture, mutilation, and branding fall in the general category of **corporal punishment** (any physical pain inflicted short of death). Many tortures were used to extract a "confession" from the accused, often resulting in the death penalty for an innocent person. Mutilation was often used in an attempt to match the crime with an "appropriate" punishment. (A liar's tongue was ripped out, a rapist's genitals were removed, and a thief's hands were cut off.) Branding was still practiced as late as the nineteenth century in many countries, including America. Corporal punishment was considered to be an example and a deterrent to other potential offenders.

key term

Corporal punishment
Any physical pain inflicted short of death; common methods include crucifixion, whipping, torture, mutilation, branding, and caning.

The public humiliation of offenders was a popular practice in early America, utilizing such devices as the stocks, the pillory, ducking stools, the brank, and branding. The most significant aspect of those punishments was their public nature. Offenders were placed in the stocks (sitting down, hands and feet fastened into a locked frame) or in the pillory (standing, with head and hands fastened into a locked frame) and then flogged, spat upon, heaped with garbage, and reviled by passersby.

The ducking stool and the brank were used as common public punishments for gossips. The ducking stool was a chair or platform placed at the end of a long lever, allowing the operator on the bank of a stream to dunk the victim. The **brank** was a birdcage-like

key term

Brank
A birdcage-like instrument placed on the offender's head with sharp-edged iron plates that would cut tongues and mouths of the gossipers.

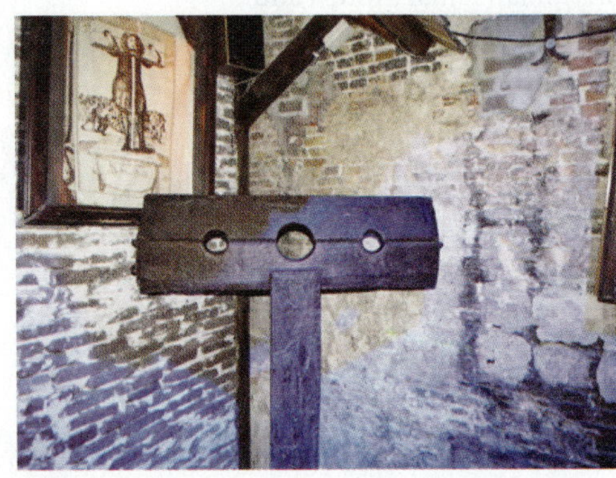

photo 1.1

The pillory was a way to provide public humiliation.
Michael Latessa

photo 1.2

The skull cracker was used for interrogations.
Harry Allen

key term

Cat-o'-nine-tails
Torture device for whipping or flogging.

instrument placed over the offender's head, containing a plate of iron with sharp spikes in it that extended into the subject's mouth. Any movement of the mouth or tongue would result in painful injury.

Flogging (or whipping) became a common punishment in almost all Western civilizations. The method was used particularly to preserve discipline in domestic, military, and academic settings. It was usually administered by a short lash at the end of a solid handle about three feet long or by a whip made of nine knotted wires, lines, or cords fastened to a handle (the famed **cat-o'-nine-tails**), sometimes with barbed-wire spikes worked into the knots. Flogging was a popular method of inducing confessions at heresy trials because few victims could stand up long under the tongue of the lash. Caning remains a legal punishment in the modern world in countries such as Malaysia, Saudi Arabia, Singapore, and South Africa.[10]

photo 1.3

The pear was used for interrogations and was inserted into an orifice of both men and women.
Michael Latessa

Deterrence

The extensive use of capital and corporal punishment during the Middle Ages reflected, in part, a belief that public punishment would deter potential wrongdoers—a belief that the passing years have refuted: "It is plain that, however futile it may be, social revenge is the only honest, straightforward, and logical justification for punishing criminals. The claim for deterrence is belied by both history and logic." No matter how society tried to "beat the devil" out of offenders, the only criminals who seemed to be deterred were the ones who had been tortured to death. Later, enlightened thinkers began to seek more rational deterrents for crime by investigating its cause.

Emergence of Secular Law

The problem of drawing up a set of laws that applied to the actions of men and women in earthly communities was compounded by Christian philosophers who insisted that law was made in heaven. In the fourth century A.D., St. Augustine recognized the need for justice, but only as decreed by God. The issue was somewhat clarified by Thomas Aquinas in the thirteenth century, when he distinguished among three laws: eternal law (***lex eterna***), natural law (***lex naturalis***), and human law (***lex humana***), all intended for the common good. The last was considered valid only if it did not conflict with the other two.

key term

Lex eterna
One of the major terms describing eternal law, intended for the common good. It cannot be changed by humans.

key term

Lex naturalis
Legal theory that there are laws that occur naturally and across all cultures.

key term

Lex humana
Laws that are enacted by human beings.

key term

Criminology
Looks at the reasons for and consequences of crime.

As time passed and the secular leaders (kings and other types of monarchs) became more powerful, they wanted to detach themselves from the divine legal order and its restrictions on their power. In the early fourteenth century, many scholars advocated the independence of the monarchy from the pope. England's lord chancellor Sir Thomas More opposed the forces advocating the unification of church and state and died on the executioner's block as a result. He refused to bend ecclesiastical law to suit the marital whims of his king, the fickle King Henry VIII. Sir Thomas More was out of step with his times in another sense as well. As an advocate of the seemingly radical theory that punishment could not prevent crime, he was one of the first to see that prevention might require a close look at the social conditions that gave rise to crime. In the sixteenth century, unfortunately, this line of thought was too far ahead of its time, but Sir Thomas More's ideas persisted and eventually contributed much to the foundation of modern theories in **criminology** and penology.

The early background of law and punishment points up the significance of social revenge as a justification for individual or societal punishment against an offender. This rationale allowed the development of penal slavery and civil death as retaliation for wrongs against the Crown. The idea of correcting an offender was entirely incidental to punishment. Imprisonment served purely for detention. Offenders who were condemned to the galleys or the sulfur mines suffered a form of social vengeance, often including the lash and other physical abuse, far more painful than was the loss of freedom alone. The offender

photo 1.4
The "rack" was used for punishment.
Harry Allen

correctional **practice 1.1**

Caning in the Modern World

Early in the development of criminal law for punishment of offenders, most countries used caning as a punishment. It was also used widely in the schools, military and religious institutions, prisons, and courts. Caning is a corporal punishment that directly inflicts serious and long-lasting medical and psychological damage to the offender.

Caning (sometimes known as "whipping") utilizes a four-foot-long wooden paddle (of varying widths) to tear the flesh of prisoners with rattan canes and intentionally inflict both severe pain and bodily trauma. The stroke rips off stripes of the offender's naked buttocks and emulsifies under-the-skin fats. Both blood and fats spurt out of the criminal's body, immediately followed by discharge of feces and urine. Some offenders, depending on their crime, could receive 21 strokes in some countries.

Until about the end of the 20th century, caning was popular in many English-speaking countries, such as Northern Ireland, the Republic of Ireland, Scotland, Wales, England, and Australia. Most of these countries have abandoned caning since about 1996.

Caning is still practiced in many other countries, and a large percentage of caning countries' citizens approve of its use. It is a frequent corporal punishment in Malaysia, Singapore, Zimbabwe, Botswana, Tanzania, Trinidad and Tobago, and other jurisdictions.

Caning is generally used as punishment for serious criminal violations such as rape, aggravated rape, incestuous rape, causing death while attempting to create rape, incest, extortion, gang robbery, possession and control of any dangerous drug, and (in Malaysia) drinking beer if the offender is Muslim. This list varies across countries using caning as punishment and deterrence. In some jurisdictions, prison staff solicit bribes from inmates sentenced to caning and may solicit other bribes from the family of the offender. The bribes are intended to persuade caning officers to miss a stroke, lessening the punishment. Some countries have correctional staff whose main duties are caning of offenders (sometimes up to 60 are caned on a single day) and are paid bonuses for the act of caning as well as the number of strokes inflicted.

Under international human rights law, corporal punishment in any form constitutes torture (or other cruel, degrading, or inhumane punishment), which in all circumstances is prohibited.

SOURCES: Amnesty International (2010). A Blow to Humanity: Torture by Judicial Caning in Malaysia. Published by The International Secretariat, Amnesty International. London, United Kingdom; USATODAY (August 8, 2009), "Muslim model spared from punishment, but just for now," at malaysia_ N.htm?FORM=ZZNB3.

Correctional Practice original from authors of the textbook.

was placed in dungeons, galleys, or mines to receive punishment, not *as* punishment in and of itself.

The idea of punishment to repay society and expiate one's transgressions against God explains in part why most punishments remained cruel and barbarous. Presumably, the hardships of physical torture, social degradation, exile, or financial loss (the four fundamental types of punishment)[11] would be rewarded by eternal joy in heaven. Ironically, those punishments did little to halt the spread of crime: "Even in the era when extremely severe punishment was imposed for crimes of minor importance, no evidence can be found to support the view that punitive measures materially curtailed the volume of crime."[12]

Early Prisons

What kinds of facilities for imprisonment existed during earlier ages? It is important to examine some aspects of the first institutions as they are related to later correctional practices. Some form of detention for offenders, whether temporary or permanent, has been a social institution from the earliest times. Offenders were, of course, always detained against their will, but the concept of imprisonment as a punishment in and of itself is a fairly recent thought. Formerly, imprisonment was primarily a means of holding the accused until the authorities had decided on his or her real punishment, chosen from the variety just described. Even those condemned to penal servitude in the Roman public works must surely have been kept in some special place at night, regardless of how primitive. Unfortunately, little is known about this form of imprisonment. Most places of confinement were basically cages. Later,

correctional **practice 1.2**

The Mamertine Prison

The Mamertine was a prison (in Italian, a "*carcer*") located near the heart of ancient Rome. This *carcer* was constructed between 640 and 616 B.C. and was a place of detention for the accused before trial and the guilty but important state prisoners who would be executed there. It was not intended as a place of long-term incarceration but functioned more like a contemporary jail with short-term detention and an execution chamber.

Captured generals, royalty, and kings would be forced to march in a triumphant procession when the conquering general returned home and would then be quickly executed in the *carcer*.

The Mamertine prison had two vaulted chambers, one atop the other. The lower chamber was originally intended to be a water cistern. It is important to note that the *carcer* was reserved for important state persons, such as captured kings, traitors, those who plotted the overthrow of Rome, prominent Roman citizens, and the dastardly. Executions were sudden, unannounced, and unheralded. The accused could be thrown or lowered into the lowest level of the *carcer* and executed at "ground zero," frequently by strangulation. Still others would be mistreated as if slaves and lived in misery and pain until death.

Higher-status offenders, both foreign and Roman, were typically held in the custody of ranking Roman citizens, sometimes on their country estates or homes. Some were hostages held lawfully under treaty with Rome; others were captives paraded as dinner guests at banquets. In this sense, there were two classes of offenders: the poor and loathsome and high-ranking citizens.

The church of San Giuseppe dei Falegnami now stands above the Mamertine.

SOURCES: Tour of Rome (2013). Mamertine Prison, *http://www.rometour.co.uk/mamertine_prison.htm*, and Richard Bauman (1996), *Crime and Punishment in Ancient Rome* (New York: Routledge, p. 23).

Correctional Practice written by textbook authors.

stone quarries and similar places designed for other purposes were used to house prisoners. The only early Roman place of confinement we know much about is the **Mamertine Prison**, a vast system of primitive cells built under the main sewer of Rome in 64 B.C.[13]

In the Middle Ages, after the fall of Rome, fortresses, castles, bridge abutments, and town gates were strongly and securely built to defend against roving bands of raiders. With the advent of gunpowder, however, those fortress cities lost much of the deterrent power of their walls and towers. The massive structures were then used as places of confinement. Many became famous as places to house political prisoners.[14] It was not until the twelfth century that prison chambers were specifically included in castle plans.

The Christian church had followed the custom of **sanctuary** or asylum[15] since the time of Constantine, placing the wrongdoer in seclusion to create an atmosphere conducive to penitence. This form of imprisonment was modified into more formalized places of punishment within the walls of monasteries and abbeys. Long periods in solitary confinement for alleged transgressions against canon law were common. The prisons built during the Inquisition were similar in concept, if not in operation, to later cellular prisons in America.[16] The idea of reformation through isolation and prayer had some influence on our first penitentiaries, but, in general, the impact of such practices in this respect remains hard to evaluate.

key term

Mamertine prison
An early place of confinement in Rome using primitive dungeons built under the main sewer.

key term

Sanctuary
Asylum that placed the wrongdoer in seclusion or arrest in cities.

Workhouses

Bridewell, a workhouse, was created for the employment and housing of London's "riff-raff" in 1557 and was based on the work ethic that followed the breakup of feudalism and the increased migration of the rural populations to urban areas (*http://www.workhouses.org.uk/CityOfLondon/corporation.shtml*). The workhouse was so successful that by 1576, Parliament required the construction of a Bridewell in every county in England. The same unsettled social conditions prevailed in Holland, and the Dutch began building workhouses in 1596 that were soon to be copied all over Europe.

Unfortunately, workhouses did not typify the places of confinement used for minor offenders and other prisoners in the seventeenth and eighteenth centuries. Most cities had

key term

Bridewell
A workhouse created for the employment and housing of London's unemployed or underemployed working classes.

to make prisons out of buildings erected for some other purpose. No attempt was made to keep the young from the old, the well from the sick, or even the males from the females. No food was provided for those without money, and sanitary conditions were usually deplorable. Exploitation of inmates by other inmates and jailers resulted in the most vicious acts of violence and degradation. "**Jail fever**" (a common term for typhus), which was spread easily in such conditions, soon traveled to surrounding cities and became the main method of keeping the country's population down. By the beginning of the eighteenth century, workhouses, prisons, and houses of correction in England and the rest of Europe had deteriorated into shocking conditions. Forcing criminals to exist in such miserable prisons became perhaps the most ruthless—if abstract—social revenge of all the punishments thus far described. "Out of sight, out of mind" was the watchword of that period, with the public seldom being aware of what happened behind the walls (ironically, a condition not unknown at the beginning of the last millennium).

key term

Jail fever

Typhus frequently concentrated in places of detention that caused large-scale death of inmates and local citizens.

THE AGE OF ENLIGHTENMENT AND REFORM

As suggested, the underlying principle of public revenge for private wrongs invariably tipped the scales of justice in favor of the state. Corporal and capital punishment were the rule. Executioners in sixteenth- and seventeenth-century Europe had at least 30 different methods of death from which to choose. These ranged from hanging and burning at the stake to more creative forms such as stretching the prisoner to death on the rack. Public punishment and degradation were commonly prescribed for even minor offenses. Imprisonment served only as a preface to the imposition of some gory punishment, carried out in the name of justice. With over 200 crimes in England punishable by death, that nation witnessed some 800 public executions a year. As the seventeenth century drew to a close, the concept of retributive punishment by the state (with its implication that pity and justice are forever locked in opposition) was firmly entrenched in the laws of England and many other European countries.[17]

The events of the eighteenth century are especially important to the student of corrections. For it was during this period, later known as the **Age of Enlightenment**, that some of the most brilliant philosophers of our history recognized humanity's essential dignity and imperfection. Such giants as Charles Montesquieu, Voltaire, Cesare Beccaria, Jeremy Bentham, John Howard, and William Penn led the movement for reform. The impact of their work, though not confined to any one area, was particularly constructive with regard to the treatment of criminals. Let us consider the contribution made by each.

key term

Age of Enlightenment

A philosophic movement of the eighteenth century marked by a rejection of traditional social, religious, and political ideas and an emphasis on rationalism.

Montesquieu and Voltaire: The French Humanists

The French philosophical thinkers Montesquieu (1689–1755) and Voltaire (1694–1778), along with Denis Diderot (1713–1784), epitomized the Age of Enlightenment's concern for the rights of humanity. In his essay *Persian Letters,*[18] Montesquieu used his mighty pen to bring the abuses of criminal law to public attention. Voltaire became involved in a number of trials that challenged the old ideas of legalized torture, criminal responsibility, and justice. The humanitarian efforts of those men paralleled the work of the most influential criminal law reformer of the era, **Cesare Beccaria** (1738–1794), founder of the **Classical School**. The best-known work of Beccaria is *An Essay on Crimes and Punishment,* a primary influence in the transition from punishment to corrections. It was the most exciting essay on law of the eighteenth century. It proposed a reorientation of criminal law toward humanistic goals and established the following principles:

1. The basis of all social action must be the utilitarian conception of the greatest happiness for the greatest number.

profile

Cesare Beccaria

The founder of the Classical School of Criminology.

key term

Classical School

Approach to understanding crime and social policy for offenders.

2. Crime must be considered an injury to society, and the only rational measure of crime is the extent of that injury.
3. Prevention of crime is more important than punishment for crimes; indeed, punishment is justifiable only on the supposition that it helps to prevent criminal conduct. In preventing crime, it is necessary to improve and publish the laws so that the nation can understand and support them, to reward virtue, and to improve the public's education both in regard to legislation and to life.
4. In criminal procedure, secret accusations and torture should be abolished. There should be speedy trials. The accused should be treated humanely before trial and must have every right and facility to bring forward evidence on his or her behalf. Turning state's evidence should be done away with, as it amounts to no more than the public authorization of treachery.
5. The purpose of punishment is to deter persons from the commission of crime and not to provide social revenge. Not severity but certainty and swiftness in punishment best secure this result. Punishment must be sure and swift and penalties determined strictly in accordance with the social damage wrought by the crime. Crimes against property should be punished solely by fines or by imprisonment when the person is unable to pay the fine. Banishment is an excellent punishment for crimes against the state. There should be no capital punishment. Life imprisonment is a better deterrent. Capital punishment is irreparable and hence makes no provision for possible mistakes and the desirability of later rectification.
6. Imprisonment should be more widely employed, but its mode of application should be greatly improved through providing better physical quarters and by separating and classifying the prisoners as to age, sex, and degree of criminality.[19]

Although Beccaria himself did not seek or receive great personal fame, his small volume was praised as one of the most significant books produced during the Age of Enlightenment.[20] Four of his newer ideas were incorporated into the French Code of Criminal Procedure in 1808 and into the French Penal Code of 1810:

1. An individual should be regarded as innocent until proven guilty.
2. An individual should not be forced to testify against himself or herself.
3. An individual should have the right to employ counsel and to cross-examine the state's witnesses.
4. An individual should have the right to a prompt and public trial and, in most cases, a trial by jury.

Among the philosophers inspired by Beccaria's ideas were the authors of the U.S. Constitution. It seems we owe a great deal to this shy Italian writer of the eighteenth century.[21]

Bentham and the Hedonistic Calculus

Jeremy Bentham (1748–1832) was the leading reformer of the British criminal law system during the late eighteenth and early nineteenth centuries. He believed that if punishments were designed to negate whatever pleasure or gain the criminal derived from crime, the crime rate would go down. He strongly advocated a system of graduated penalties to tie more closely the punishment to the crime. As political equality became a dominant philosophy, new penal policies were required to accommodate this change in emphasis. As Thorsten Sellin stated,

> Older penal law had reflected the views dominant in societies where slavery or serfdom flourished, political inequality was the rule, and sovereignty was assumed to be resting in absolute monarchs. Now the most objectionable features of that law, which had favored the upper classes and had provided often arbitrary, brutal, and revolting corporal and capital punishments for the lower classes, were to be removed and equality before the law established. Judicial torture for the purpose of extracting evidence was to be abolished, other

profile

Jeremy Bentham

Argued that the crime rate would go down if the amount of punishment were carefully calibrated to deter potential offenders and maximize pleasure.

> than penal measures used to control some conduct previously punished as crime, and punishments made only severe enough to outweigh the gains expected by the criminal from his crime. This meant a more humane law, no doubt, applied without discrimination to all citizens alike in harmony with the new democratic ideas.[22]

key term

Hedonistic calculus
Jeremy Bentham's argument that the main objective of an intelligent person is to maximize pleasure while minimizing pain; it was believed that individual's behavior could be influenced in a scientific manner.

Bentham believed that an individual's conduct could be influenced in a scientific manner. Asserting that the main objective of an intelligent person is to achieve the most pleasure while experiencing the least amount of pain, he developed his famous "**hedonistic calculus**,"[23] which he applied to his efforts to reform the criminal law. He, like Beccaria, believed punishment could act as a deterrent, but only if it were made appropriately relevant to the crime. This line of thought, adopted by active reformers Samuel Romilly (1757–1818) and Robert Peel (1788–1850) in the early nineteenth century, has been instrumental in the development of the modern prison.

John Howard

profile

John Howard
An English high sheriff who was so appalled by jail conditions that he undertook a crusade to improve places of detention.

John Howard (1726–1790) gave little thought to prisons or prison reform until he was appointed sheriff of Bedfordshire in 1773. The appointment opened his eyes to horrors he had never imagined. He was appalled by the conditions he found in the hulks and gaols (jails) and pressed for legislation to alleviate some of the abuses and improve sanitary conditions. He also traveled extensively on the European continent to examine prisons in other countries. He saw similarly deplorable conditions in most areas but was most impressed by some of the institutions in France and Italy. In 1777, he described those conditions and suggested reforms in his *State of Prisons*. In 1779, Parliament passed the Penitentiary Act, providing four principles for reform: secure and sanitary structures, systematic inspection, abolition of fees, and a reformatory regime.[24]

The Penitentiary Act resulted in the first penitentiary, located at Wyndomham in Norfolk, England, and operated by Sir Thomas Beever, the sheriff of Wyndomham. As we will see later, the principles contained in the act, though lofty in concept, were hard to implement in the prevailing atmosphere of indifference. It is ironic that this great advocate for better prison conditions did himself die of jail fever in the Russian Ukraine in 1790. John Howard's name has become synonymous with prison reform, and the John Howard Society has carried his ideas forward to this day.[25]

HOUSES OF CORRECTION, WORKHOUSES, AND GAOLS

key term

Workhouse
A house of correction for persons guilty of minor law violations; sometimes referred to as a "poorhouse."

key term

Gaols
Places of confinement in England for persons held in lawful custody, *specifically*, such a place under the jurisdiction of a local government (as a county) for the confinement of persons awaiting trial or those convicted of minor crimes.

The proliferation of Bridewell-style houses of correction in England was originally intended as a humanitarian move. As a result, in 1576, Parliament ordered that each county in England construct such an institution. They were not merely extensions of almshouses or poorhouses but were actually penal institutions for all sorts of misdemeanants. Although the bloody penalties for major offenses were growing in number, not even the most callous would advocate harsh physical punishment for every offender. All sorts of rogues, from idlers to whores, were put into the Bridewells, where they were compelled to work under strict discipline at the direction of hard taskmasters. Today, the house of correction and the **workhouse** are regarded as synonymous. The workhouse, however, was actually intended not as a penal institution but as a place for the training and care of the poor. In practice, however, the two soon became indistinguishable, first in England and later in America. Conditions and practices in such institutions were no better than those in the gaols by the turn of the eighteenth century.

The use of **gaols** ("jails") to detain prisoners has a grim and unsavory history. As the eighteenth century began, gaol administration was usually left up to the whim of the gaoler (jailer), who was usually under the control of the sheriff. Gaols were often used to extort

correctional **profile 1.1**

John Howard

John Howard (1726–1790) was a deeply humanitarian champion of bettering the handling and care of prison inmates and was born into a prosperous middle-class family in England. His father was a strict disciplinarian, and John became a difficult and lonely man. Because he was a Calvinist, he chose not to live an extravagant life. He was a complex, lonely, opinionated, self-righteous, and narrow-minded man but well deserving of the accolade of being the father of prison reform. He failed miserly as a father, and his only son was dismissed from a major university, declared insane, and imprisoned some 13 years before he died in a mental institution. His first two marriages were terminated by his spouses' deaths. Yet he was a generous and compassionate man who spent his inheritance from his father and a behest from his sister (her home and about 15,000 pounds of silver) in pursuit of his career.

To understand his contribution to prison reform, you must know that he was appointed high sheriff in Bedfordshire in 1773, originally for a one-year term. As that time, the post was mostly ceremonial and other high sheriffs had very little interest in inspecting and managing the gaol (jail), which was left in the hands of an undersheriff. Howard inspected the county prison himself and was shocked and repelled by the practices and conditions of jail management in his jail. He found no separation of women from men, felons from misdemeanants, boys from adults, or debtors from murderers. The jail at this time period was a storage facility for the accused until convicted and (usually) executed. During this time, the undersheriff took bribes, favors, and profits that were detrimental to prisoners. Many prisoners were forced to pay for their food for the term of their incarceration. The undersheriff typically charged inmates for bedding, food, and other services. The "going rate" in Howard's institution was two shillings and six pence a week for the sole use of bedding and sheets. Inmates could cost-share at half that cost (each). If the jailer had to transport an offender, the charge was six pounds (£6).

Conditions were worse than deplorable. There was no running water; the straw on the floor was dust, inmates were charged for drinking water, and food was not otherwise available. Even when declared innocent, the prisoner could not leave confinement without paying the jailer for all charges. There was no medical treatment. In some institutions, typhus fever would kill all inmates, a fate to which John Howard fell. Howard openly criticized his inherited jailer and ordered certain humanitarian changes.

John Howard wanted to find other English and Welsh institutions that would serve as an example for his jail to follow. He began an international tour of cells, dungeons, and torture centers and interviewed prisoners, staff ("turnkeys"), and jailers. His conclusion was that such malpractices were widespread over all jurisdictions. He began to seek better examples in France, Holland, Russia, and Ukraine. He spent £30,000 of his own money in his determination to improve prison conditions. In 1777, he published *The State of Prisons*, a well-received recitation of the ills of jails and what could be done to improve them. While in Ukraine, John Howard inspected a jail and came down with typhus fever. He is buried in a walled field in Stepanovka, Ukraine.

In about 1868, some 80 years after his death, the Howard Association was formed in London. The American, Canadian, and New Zealand associations were created shortly thereafter. Correctional reform organizations work to improve the conditions and services to prisoners' families, providing parenting classes, managing contractual reentry programs, and educating the general public of the challenges prisoners' families and children face. The Howard associations also generate extensive reports provided to legislatures about prison security and funding for programs and prisons designed to reintegrate adult and juvenile inmates. Finally, the Howard associations address issues with long-term prisoners by working to change sentencing policies that extend incarceration in jail longer that the offenders' original sentences.

SOURCES:

JHA Prison Report, Vandalia Correctional Center, "Prison Monitoring Project," at dhoffman@thejha.org.

John Howard Society of Niagara, "History of John Howard," at *http://www.jhs-niagara.com/history/history-of-jhs/*.

huge fines from those who had the means by holding those people indefinitely in pretrial confinement until they gave in and paid. The lot of the common "gaolbirds" (detained suspects and criminals) was surely not a happy one. Many of the prisoners perished long before their trial dates. The squalid and unhealthy conditions gave rise to epidemics of jail fever that spread to all levels of English life. John Howard claimed that more people died from this malady between 1773 and 1774 than were executed by the Crown.[26] Ironically, prisoners, not prison conditions, were blamed for the spread of the deadly disease, and even more sanguinary penalties for offenses were devised. Robert Caldwell describes the typical English gaol:

> Devoid of privacy and restrictions, its contaminated air heavy with the stench of unwashed bodies, human excrement, and the discharge of loathsome sores, the gaol bred the basest thoughts and the foulest deeds. The inmates made their own rules, and the weak and the

> innocent were exposed to the tyranny of the strong and the vicious. Prostitutes plied their trade with ease, often with the connivance and support of the gaolers, who thus sought to supplement their fees. Even virtuous women sold themselves to obtain food and clothing, and frequently the worst elements of the town used the gaol as they would a brothel. Thus, idleness, vice, perversion, profligacy, shameless exploitation, and ruthless cruelty were compounded in hotbeds of infection and cesspools of corruption. These were the common gaols of England.[27]

It is depressing to think that John Howard, shocked into humanitarian reform efforts when he found himself responsible for one of those human cesspools, was the only sheriff to undertake action against such institutions.

TRANSPORTATION SYSTEMS

Deportation to the American Colonies and Australia

key term

Banishment

To remove by authority from a state or country; the sentence to cast out of a local residence or country due to criminal behavior on the offender's part.

key term

Transportation

Legal sentence requiring the banishment of the offender to a different location; the act of transporting that offender to another country.

As noted, one of the earliest forms of social vengeance was **banishment**. In primitive societies, the offender was cast out into the wilderness, usually to be eaten by wild beasts or to succumb to the elements. As we have discovered, imprisonment and capital punishment were later substituted for banishment. Banishment to penal servitude was, in effect, civil death. Banishment to the gaols, however, more often than not ended in physical death.

The wandering and jobless lower classes, in the period following the breakup of feudalism, were concentrated mostly in high-crime slums in the major cities. As economic conditions worsened, the number of imprisonable crimes increased to the point that the available prisons were filled. In England, from 1596 to 1776, the pressure was partially relieved by the deportation or **transportation** of malefactors to the colonies in America. Estimates vary greatly of how many original American settlers arrived in chains. Margaret Wilson estimates between 300 and 400 annually;[28] other authorities put the figure as high as 2,000 a year. The use of convict labor was widespread before the adoption of slavery in the colonies. And even though the entering flow of dangerous felons was somewhat slowed by the introduction of slavery, the poor and the misdemeanant continued to come in great numbers.

The American Revolution brought transportation to America to an abrupt halt in 1776, but England and Ireland[29] still needed somewhere to send the criminals overloading their crowded institutions. Captain James Cook had discovered Australia in 1770, and soon the system of transportation was transferred to that continent. It was planned that the criminals would help tame that new and wild land. More than 135,000 felons were sent to Australia between 1787 and 1875, when the British finally abandoned the system.

Transportation ships were hired transports employed to convey convicts from England to New South Wales. Private business entrepreneurs carried offenders to another country for a fee, essentially making a pound off the backs of offenders. Contractors received between 20 and 30 pounds of silver per head. The more convicts carried, the greater the profit would be; thus, overcrowding on the ships was the rule, not the exception. As a result of such a state of confinement, the most loathsome diseases were common, and the death rate was extremely high: 158 of 502 who were placed on the *Neptune* in 1790 for conveyance to Australia died en route, and 95 of the 300 placed into the holds of the *Hillsborough* in 1799 died during the voyage. Those who did arrive were so near dead that they could not stand, and it was necessary to sling them like goods and hoist them out of the ships, and when first landed, they died at the rate of 10 to 12 a day. The government attempted in 1802 to correct these evils by sending convicts twice a year in ships specially fitted for the purpose that were under the direction of a transport board and commanded by naval officers.[30] Although the transports continued to be crowded, health conditions apparently improved greatly because Sir T. B. Martin, head of the transport board, reported in 1819 that "within

photo 1.5

Example of an old British hulk (ship) used to house convicts.
Image Asset Management Ltd/ SuperStock

the past three years, only 53 out of 6,409 convicts (a rate of 1 in 112) had died. Out of the 10 transports that had recently sailed, only one or two had died" (*http://scholarlycommons.law.northwestern.edu/cgi/viewcontent.cgi?article=1864&context=jclc.*).

Hulks: A Sordid Episode

From 1776 to 1875, even with limited transportation to Australia, the increased prisoner loads wreaked havoc in England's few available facilities. The immediate solution to that problem created one of the most odious episodes in the history of penology and corrections: the use of old **hulks**, abandoned or unusable transport ships anchored in rivers and harbors throughout the British Isles, to confine criminal offenders. The brutal and degrading conditions found in the gaols, houses of correction, and workhouses paled in comparison with the conditions found in those fetid and rotting human garbage dumps.

key term

Hulks
Abandoned or unusable transport ships anchored in rivers and harbors that confined criminal offenders.

Those responsible for the hulks made no attempt to segregate young from old, hardened criminals from poor misdemeanants, or even men from women. Brutal flogging and degrading labor soon bred moral degeneration in both inmates and keepers. The hulks were originally intended only as a temporary solution to a problem, but they were not completely abandoned until 1858, 80 years later. (Hulks were used in California in the nineteenth century, and one state, Washington, considered the use of decommissioned U.S. Navy warships in 1976. New York used a floating jail for some time in the 1980s.) This episode in penal history becomes especially relevant when the problems of overcrowding in our maximum-security prisons are examined.

EARLY CELLULAR PRISONS

The Maison de Force at Ghent and the Hospice of San Michele

key term

Maison de Force
A Belgian workhouse for beggars and miscreants, designed to make a profit by an enforced pattern of hard work and both discipline and silence. An important rule: "If a man will not work, neither let him eat."

In his travels through Europe, John Howard was most impressed by Jean-Jacques Vilain's **Maison de Force** (stronghouse) at Ghent, Belgium, and by the Hospice (hospital) of San Michele in Rome. Although those institutions had developed along individually different lines, both made lasting impressions on Howard. Both served as workhouses, but otherwise they had little in common. Their differences were more important than their similarities.

Predecessors of the Belgian workhouses were those in neighboring Amsterdam, constructed around 1596. Most were intended to make a profit,[31] not to exemplify humanitarian ideals, and were seen as a place to put rogues and able-bodied beggars to work. The workhouses were modeled after the Bridewell institution in England and followed a similar pattern of hard work and cruel punishment. By the eighteenth century, Belgium, too, was faced with increasing numbers of beggars and vagrants, and the government called on administrator and disciplinarian Jean-Jacques Vilain for help. His solution—the Maison de Force built in Ghent in 1773—followed the basic workhouse pattern established in Holland and England, but in many respects it was far more just and humane.

Vilain's efforts at improving the administration of the workhouse earned him an honored place in penal history. He was one of the first to develop a system of classification to separate women and children from hardened criminals and felons from minor offenders. Although he was a stern disciplinarian, he was opposed to life imprisonment and cruel punishment. Rather, he defined discipline by the rule, "If any man will not work, neither let him eat." Vilain's use of individual cells and a system of silence while working resembled the procedures observed at the Hospice of San Michele in Rome. His far-reaching concepts of fair and just treatment, when viewed against the harsh backdrop of that era, mark Vilain as a true visionary in the correctional field.

key term

Hospice of San Michele
A corrections facility designed for incorrigible boys and youth that included silence, large work areas, and separate sleeping cells. Both expiation and reform were intended goals.

The **Hospice of San Michele** was designed for incorrigible boys and youths under age 20. As such, it is generally recognized as one of the first institutions to handle juvenile offenders exclusively. Prisoners were administered massive doses of Scripture and hard work in hopes that this regimen would reform them. The rule of strict silence was enforced through the flogging of violators. (The use of separate cells for sleeping and a large central hall for working became the model for penal institutions in the nineteenth century.) This concept of expiation and penance, as applied to corrections, was new and exciting to John Howard, and his Puritan ethic enabled him to see the value of repentance and hard work as demonstrated by the program at San Michele. Under somewhat different policies, the Hospice of San Michele is still used today as a reformatory for delinquent boys.

The main concepts that carried over from the early cellular institutions were the monastic regimen of silence and expiation, the central community work area, and individual cells for sleeping. The philosophy of penitence and monastic contemplation of past wrongs espoused by those institutions was reflected in the Quakers' early prison efforts in America.

William Penn and the "Great Law"

profile

William Penn
Quaker leader who created the state of Pennsylvania and a system of justice that required compensation of victims and repentance to restore the offender to God's grace.

key term

The Great Law
Body of laws of the Quakers that saw hard labor as a more effective punishment than death for crimes and one that demanded compensation to victims.

The American colonies were governed by the British under codes established by the Duke of York in 1676 and part of the older Hampshire Code established in 1664. These codes were similar to those followed in England, and the use of capital and corporal punishment was the rule of the day. Branding, flogging, the stocks, the pillory, and the brank were also used extensively.

William Penn (1644–1718), the founder of Pennsylvania and leader of the Quakers, brought the concept of more humanitarian treatment of offenders to America. The Quaker movement was the touchstone of penal reform not only in America but also in Italy and England through its influence on such advocates as Beccaria and Howard. Compared with the other harsh colonial codes in force at the time, the **Great Law** of the Quakers was quite humane. This body of laws envisioned hard labor as a more effective punishment than death for serious crimes, and capital punishment was eliminated from the original codes. Later, in supplementary acts, murder and manslaughter were included as social crimes. Only premeditated murder was punishable by death, with other criminal acts treated according to the circumstances.

It is interesting to note that the Quakers' Great Law did away with most religious offenses and stuck to strictly secular criminal jurisprudence, a departure from the codes of other colonies and the earlier European codes. Under the Great Law, a "house of corrections" institution was established where most punishment was meted out in the form of hard labor. This was the first time that correctional confinement at hard labor was used as a punishment for serious crimes and not merely as a preface to punishment scheduled for a later date.

The Quaker Code of 1682 was in force until 1718, when it was repealed, ironically, only one day after the death of William Penn. The English Anglican Code replaced the Great Law, and the mild Quaker philosophy gave way to harsh punishments. The new code was even worse than the previous codes of the Duke of York. Capital punishment was prescribed for 13 offenses,[32] and mutilation, branding, and other corporal punishments were restored for many others.

The influence of Montesquieu, Voltaire, Beccaria, Bentham, Howard, and Penn was felt throughout colonial America. Much of the idealism embodied in the U.S. Constitution reflects the writings of those progressive eighteenth-century leaders. With their philosophies in mind, we can consider some of the major developments in correctional practice in that era of reform.

The Walnut Street Jail

As we have seen, the world of the eighteenth century had prisons, but they were generally used as places of detention for minor offenders and for pretrial confinement. One of the earliest American attempts to operate a state prison for felons was located in an abandoned copper mine in Simsbury, Connecticut.[33] This underground prison began operation in 1773 and quickly became the site of America's first prison riots in 1774. Although some have called it the first state prison, it was really not much more than a throwback to the sulfur pits of ancient Rome, and it did nothing to advance the state of American corrections. The prisoners were housed in long mine shafts, and the administration buildings were placed near the entrances. Underground mine shaft prisons constituted one of several American attempts to provide a special place in which to house and work convicted felons. The establishment of such a special facility was finally accomplished in Pennsylvania in 1790.

The Walnut Street Jail, until the innovation of solitary confinement for felons, was typical of colonial jails. They are described in David J. Rothman's *Discovery of the Asylum* (Boston: Little, Brown, 1971, p. 55). Jails in fact closely resembled the household in structure and routine. They lacked a distinct architecture and special procedures. When the Virginia burgess required that county prisons be "good, strong, and substantial" and explicitly recommended that they follow "after the form of Virginia housing," results were in keeping with these directions. The doors were perhaps somewhat sturdier and the locks slightly more impressive, but the general design of the jail was the same as for an ordinary residence. True to the household model, the keeper and his family resided in the jail, occupying one of its rooms; the prisoners lived several together in the other rooms, with little to differentiate the keeper's quarters from their own. They wore no special clothing or uniforms, and usually neither cuffs nor chains restrained their movements. They walked—not marched—about the jail. The workhouse model was so irrelevant that nowhere were they required to perform the slightest labor.

correctional **practice 1.3**

Newgate Prison

The Newgate Prison (later the Copper Mine) began as a copper mine in 1773 and was first used to house serious offenders. The first prisoner (John Hinson) was committed in 1773. During the Revolutionary War, both Tories and Loyalists were housed there. It was the first state prison in America and the site of the first prison riot. Newgate closed as a prison in 1827 and was then repurposed as a mine.

policy positions 1.1

Correctional Officers Smuggling Marijuana and Cell Phones to Inmates

You are the chief administrator of a correctional facility that has a strong security threat group ("prison gang") that frequently violates the fraternization rules of your institution, including at least 10 officers who are suspected of participating by bringing contraband and cell phones into the facility. Four of your female correctional officers are pregnant and name a certain inmate as the father. That inmate is the leader of the security threat group.

1. As superintendent, what would you do?
2. How would you handle the "pregnant officers" issue?
3. How could you lessen the power of the security threat group?

key term

Penitentiary
Originally a detention center in which inmates could do penance and repent or turn away from crime; now any larger penal institution for detention of inmates.

key term

Walnut Street Jail
First penitentiary created in Philadelphia by the Quakers.

It is hard to imagine a time when there were no long-term penitentiaries for felons, but before 1790 that was the case. Ironically, in that year, the first **penitentiary** in America, the prototype of the modern prison system, was born in the same city that spawned the fledgling United States as a nation. Philadelphia, Pennsylvania, the home of the Declaration of Independence, is also—thanks to the Quakers—the home of the **Walnut Street Jail**, the first true correctional institution in America.

Originally, the penitentiary was a place where offenders reflected on their crimes and repented (or changed). Today the term refers to a major adult facility where felons are incarcerated as punishment.

Despite earlier efforts at prison reform, the Quakers had been thwarted in their humanistic goals by the repeal of Penn's Great Law in 1718. In 1776, the first American Penitentiary Act was passed, but its implementation was delayed because of the War of Independence. In 1790, with the Revolution behind them, the Quakers reasserted their concern with the treatment of convicted criminals.[34] After much prodding, they convinced the Pennsylvania legislature to declare a wing of the Walnut Street Jail a penitentiary house for all convicted felons except those sentenced to death.[35] Thus, although prisons, gaols, dungeons, and workhouses had been in existence for years, this wing was the first to be used exclusively for the correction of convicted felons.

Some of the concepts embodied in the Walnut Street Jail had their antecedents in the charter of William Penn in 1682. Those provisions, repressed by the harsh Anglican Code, were as follows:

1. All prisoners were to be bailable.
2. Those wrongfully imprisoned could recover double damages.
3. Prisons were to be free as to fees, food, and lodging.
4. The lands and goods of felons were to be liable for confiscation and double as restitution to injured parties.
5. All counties were to provide houses to replace the pillory, stocks, and the like.[36]

key term

Pennsylvania system
The system of prison discipline using isolation or solitary confinement with both a work requirement and moral and religious instruction.

Although not all of the idealistic reforms were adopted, the direction of change had been established. The system of prison discipline developed at the Walnut Street Jail became known as the **Pennsylvania system**. The Pennsylvania system was developed through the ideas and efforts of such reformers as Benjamin Franklin (1706–1790) and Benjamin Rush (1745–1813), building on the humanitarian ideals of Howard, Bentham, Beccaria, and Montesquieu. Patriot and war hero William Bradford (1721–1791), who drafted the codes that implemented the system, praised the European reformers in the state legislature.

As originally conceived, the basic element of the Pennsylvania system called for solitary confinement without work. It was assumed that this method would result in quicker reformations. Offenders could reflect on their crimes all day and would soon repent so they might rejoin humanity. The terrible effects of such isolation—physical and psychological—soon became apparent. Some kind of work had to be provided, as well as moral and religious

policy **positions 1.2**

Assassination of the Director of Your State's Department of Corrections

The director is sitting at home just before dinner when the doorbell rings. The director goes to the door, where he is shot to death by a recently released parolee. The killer flees, only to be tracked to another state where he exchanges gunfire with state police. The killer is slain, and ballistic tests show that the gun he used in the firefight is identical to the firearm used to shoot the director. You are selected to be the director's replacement.

1. As director, what personal safety strategies would you adopt to lessen your being killed by other parolees?
2. What would you ask local law enforcement officials to do for you?
3. What changes would you ask the State Parole Agency to make?

policy **positions 1.3**

Court Intervention

Your prisons are so overcrowded that the medical staff cannot handle the overload. A lawsuit initiated by inmates leads state and federal courts to order reducing your number of prisoners as a first step in providing constitutionally guaranteed minimum medical treatment. You have to release 43,000 inmates. Which ones would you release?

instruction, to maintain the prisoners' mental and bodily health. The work schedule thus was from 8 to 10 hours a day, and the prisoner worked in isolation, usually on piecework or handicrafts.

Increasingly more convicts were sent to the new state prison, and overcrowding shattered early hopes for its success. Even the original system of separate areas for women and children broke down with the flood of inmates. But despite the ultimate failure of the Walnut Street Jail program, it represented a major breakthrough for penology. New prisons were soon in demand throughout America, and the Walnut Street Jail was copied extensively in at least 10 states and many foreign countries.[37]

Summary

Corrections refers to those elements of social control that deal with criminal offenders who are arrested, convicted, and processed within the criminal justice system. In more recent years, with the developments of alternatives to imprisonment and decreasing corporal punishment, the role of corrections has been extended to include nonincarcerative punishments. Contemporary corrections, then, has been extended to include diversion, intermediate punishments, and clemency.

Summarize the Definition, Mission, and Role of Corrections

The role of corrections is to both punish and rehabilitate. The objective is to protect society through punishment and offender change. Punishment is a basic objective, but there is room for rehabilitation. Thus, many state departments of corrections are known as the Department of Rehabilitation and Corrections.

Summarize Early Responses to Crime Prior to the Development of Prisons

Original punishments by the state included banishment, corporal and capital punishments, torture, and shaming. Stocks, pillories, branding, maiming, and executions were the primary means of crime control. There were no jails or prisons, and corporal and capital punishment prevailed. In the eighteenth through twenty-first centuries, corrections moved to become more humanitarian and less brutal. It was in this later period that correctional leadership embraced development of correctional facilities (such as gaols, workhouses, and jails.) Until very recently, places in which offenders could do penance and turn their lives around (repent) were rare. Most correctional changes resulted from the contributions of highly religious and usually wealthy humanitarians.

Describe How Secular Law Emerged

The earliest form of corrections was no doubt *banishment*: the expelling of a criminal offender from the group and nation. Left alone, most banished offenders fell victim to predatory animals and perished. In addition, avengers of blood began a form of retribution now known as *vengeance*. Later, when society became more complex and organized, the state and political leaders imposed themselves as the major victims, punishing and controlling crime in the name of the state. This was particularly true as found in the conflict between church law and the state, an argument eventually won by the state. Church punishments were minimized, but the power of the state to regulate behavior increased.

Summarize Sentencing Goals and Primary Punishment Philosophies

In this chapter, you have learned the primary sentencing goals: correct the offender, initiate repentance and contrition, control behavior by reinforcing the difference between right and wrong, reducing crime to provide increased public safety, and eradication of dangerous offenders intent on pursuit of a predatory and punitive life. The questions of this era boiled down to three arguments: (1) offenders are evil and must be extinguished, (2) offenders are out of step with God and need to repent, and (3) offenders are sick and need to be cured. In the coming chapters, we will encounter additional arguments: (1) offenders are poorly prepared to function as constructive and favorable citizens, so the state needs to provide education and training to prevent the offender's return to crime ("recidivism"), and (2) crime is generated by the society that fails to provide the necessary services, so the state needs to change to help all people. All told, these are the evil, religious, curative, educational, and societal reformation thrusts.

Outline the Development of the Prison

The prison developed through local innovations: segregation of inmates by sex, convicted from the unconvicted, and juveniles from adults. The Quakers made major impacts on American corrections, organizing the first penitentiary ("place to do penance") and establishing sufficient societal interest to encourage a place of confinement both before and then after conviction. The great thinkers and actors of the Enlightenment, especially in France and England, provided the intellectual background from which the prison system grew.

Key Words

retaliation, 4
blood feud, 4
vendetta, 4
lex salica, 4
wergeld, 4
friedensgeld, 4
outlaw, 5
lex talionis, 5
civil death, 6
"get right with God," 6
Inquisition, 6
corporal punishment, 7
brank, 7
cat-o'-nine-tails, 8
lex eterna, 9
lex naturalis, 9
lex humana, 9
criminology, 9
Mamertine Prison, 11
sanctuary, 11
Bridewell, 11
jail fever, 12
Age of Enlightenment, 12
Cesare Beccaria, 12
Classical School, 12
Jeremy Bentham, 13
"hedonistic calculus," 14
John Howard, 14
workhouse, 14
gaols, 14
banishment, 16
transportation, 16
hulks, 17
Maison de Force, 17
Hospice of San Michele, 18
William Penn, 18
The Great Law, 18
penitentiary, 20
Walnut Street Jail, 20
Pennsylvania system, 20

Review Questions

1. At what point in a society's development does retaliation begin to become criminal law?
2. What effect did the kings' increasing power have on punishment?
3. What was the first punishment imposed by society?
4. What is meant by civil death?
5. What is meant by free will?
6. What form of punishment has been most widely used?
7. What is meant by "deterrence as a result of punishment"?
8. What were some of the earliest forms of imprisonment?
9. From what does most American law derive?
10. What was Beccaria's main contribution to corrections?
11. What were John Howard's four principles for a penitentiary system?
12. Many reformers tried to improve prison conditions in the eighteenth century. Name at least three and describe their major contributions.
13. Why is it important to study corrections?

Application Case Studies

1. Your summer internship requires you to join other full-time employees in evaluating the conditions of jails within your county. Your team stumbles across a jail extension that you find is unacceptable by local standards. If these conditions are revealed, the county would be in violation of local health standards. Your coworkers want to keep these conditions secret. What would you do?
2. A local juvenile male facility was built in 1890 and now has a large "debtor's graveyard" in which juveniles in custody were buried. Rumors have widely circulated that the dead probably died at the hands of the institutional staff. A former facility guard informs you that three particular juveniles he knew in the facility died suddenly and were buried without autopsy. What would you do?
3. Your father worked for 20 years as the curator of an old but small state prison that was closed about a decade ago. His particular job was to maintain the physical plant and keep intruders away. Since you were age 12, you helped him during the summers. Now that he is going to retire and you are an adult, he recommends you as his replacement, and the Board of Oversight offers you the job. What five things would you try to do in the first year?

Endnotes

1. American Correctional Association (ACA), *2012 Directory of Adult and Juvenile Correctional Departments. Institutions, Agencies, and Probation and Parole Authorities* (Alexandria, VA: ACA, 2012), pp. 28–35.
2. Albert Kocourek and John Wigmore, *Evolution of Law, Vol. 2, Punitive and Ancient Legal Institutions* (Boston: Little, Brown, 1915), p. 124. See also Jeffrie Murphy, "Two Cheers for Vindictiveness," *Punishment and Society* 2:2 (2000): 134–143.
3. Ronald Akers, "Toward a Comparative Definition of Criminal Law," *Journal of Criminal Law, Criminology and Police Science* (1965): 301–306.
4. Kocourek and Wigmore, *Evolution of Law, Vol. 2,* p. 126. See also John Schmidt, Kris Warner, and Sarika Gupta, "The High Budgetary Cost of Incarceration," at http://www.cepr.net/documents/publications/incarceration-2010-06.pdf.
5. Thorsten Sellin, "A Look at Prison History," *Federal Probation* (September 1967): 18.
6. Gustav Radbruch, *Elegantiae Juris Criminalis,* 2nd ed. (Basel, Switzerland: Verlag fur Recht und Gesellschaft A. G., 1950), p. 5.
7. Slaves were also marked by branding on the forehead or by metal collars that could not be easily removed.
8. This religious requirement brought the two issues of sin and crime into the same arena and broadened the scope of the church courts. The offender was obligated to make retribution to both God and the state.
9. V. A. C. Catrell, *The Hanging Tree: Execution and the English People: 1770–1868* (New York: Oxford University Press, 1994).
10. Editors, "Guards Get Jail and Cane for Prisoner's Death," *The Straits Times* (March 21, 1996), p. 2. See also Roger Mellem, "Government Violence in the War

against Drugs," *International Journal of Comparative and Applied Criminal Justice* 18:1 (1994): 39–51.
11. Stephen Schafer, *Theories in Criminology* (New York: Random House, 1969), p. 25.
12. Edwin H. Sutherland, *Criminology* (Philadelphia: Lippincott, 1924), p. 317.
13. Reckless, *The Crime Problem*, p. 504. There is little evidence that increased use of incarceration will lead to lower levels of crime. See Rodney Henningsen, W. Johnson, and T. Wells, "Supermax Prisons: Panacea or Desperation," *Corrections Management Quarterly* 3:2 (1999): 53–59, and Jesenia Pizarro and Vanja Stenius, "Supermax Prisons." *The Prison Journal* 84:2 (2004): 228–247.
14. Norman Johnston, *The Human Cage: A Brief History of Prison Architecture* (Washington, DC: American Foundation, 1973), p. 5. See also John Britton and E. Brayley, *Memoirs of the Tower of London* (Littleton, CO: Fred Rothman, 1994), and Dana Priest, "U.S. Preparing for Lifetime Jailing of Terror Suspects," *Seattle Times* (January 2, 2005), p. 3.
15. Johnston, *The Human Cage*, p. 6.
16. The practice of granting a criminal sanctuary from punishment was generally reserved for holy places. It was abandoned in England in the seventeenth century.
17. For a historical view of the development of Western criminal justice systems up to the eighteenth century, see Herbert Johnson and Nancy Wolfe, *History of Criminal Justice* (Cincinnati, OH: Anderson, 2003), pp. 24–109.
18. The *Persian Letters* was a satirical essay by Montesquieu on the abuses of current criminal law. The essay greatly influenced Beccaria. This, along with Voltaire's activities, led Beccaria to write his *An Essay on Crimes and Punishment.*
19. Barnes and Teeters, *New Horizons in Criminology*, p. 322.
20. Cesare Beccaria, *An Essay on Crimes and Punishment* (Philadelphia: P. H. Nicklin, 1819).
21. Beccaria's contributions to corrections as the father of modern criminology have been called into question in recent years. See Graeme Newman and Pietro Morongu, "Penological Reform and the Myth of Beccaria," *Criminology* 28 (1990): 325–346. Nonetheless, Beccaria remains the central figure in liberal penology.
22. Thorsten Sellin, "A Look at Prison History," *Federal Probation* 31:3 (1967): 20.
23. *Hedonistic calculus* was a term devised by Jeremy Bentham to describe the idea that "to achieve the most pleasure and the least pain is the main objective of an intelligent man."
24. Barnes and Teeters, *New Horizons in Criminology*, p. 335. See also John Freeman, *Prisons Past and Present* (London: Heinemann, 1978), for an excellent set of papers celebrating Howard's contributions to prison reform, and Jacques Petit et al., "The History of Incarceration in Penal Populations," *Criminologie* 28:1 (1995): 3–147 (in French).
25. The John Howard Society is a nonprofit organization supported by contributions. It provides casework service to inmates and their families, and it also works to promote community understanding of prison problems and offers technical assistance to correctional agencies (608 South Dearborn Street, Chicago, IL 60605). A biography of John Howard can be found at http://www.johnhoward.ca/about/biography/.
26. John Howard, *The State of Prisons* (New York: Dutton, 1929). For more background on Bridewells, see Leonard Roberts, "Bridewell: The World's First Attempt at Prisoner Rehabilitation through Education," *Journal of Correctional Education* 35:3 (1984): 83–85. One example of Howard's influence can be found in the Wakefield Prison History, http://freepages.rootsweb.ancestry.com/~wakefield/prison/histpris.html.
27. Robert G. Caldwell, *Criminology* (New York: Ronald Press, 1965), p. 494.
28. Margaret Wilson, *The Crime of Punishment* (New York: Harcourt, Brace and World, 1931), p. 224.
29. Bob Reece, *The Origins of Irish Convict Transportation to New South Wales* (New York: Palgrave, 2001). A British pound (£) meant 10 ounces of purse silver. The typical farmer in the United States at that time might earn three pounds a year.
30. Alexis Durham, "Origins of Interest in the Privatization of Punishment: The Nineteenth and Twentieth Century American Experience," *Criminology* 27 (1989): 107–139. See also the National Archives of Ireland, *Sources in the National Archives for Research into the Transportation of Irish Convicts to Australia (1791–1853): Introduction.*
31. For a discussion of contemporary punishment for profit, see David Shichor, *Punishment for Profit: Private Prisons, Public Concerns* (Thousand Oaks, CA: Sage, 1995), and Colorado Criminal Justice Reform Coalition, "For Profit Incarceration," http://www.ccjrc.org/pdf/forprofit.pdf.

32. Only larceny was exempt from capital punishment. All other major crimes were punishable by death. For a poignant view on contemporary flogging, see Azam Kamguian, *Why Islamic Law Should Be Opposed,* http://www.secularislam.org/articles/opposed.htm.
33. For a short history of this facility, see Charles W. Dean, "The Story of Newgate," *Federal Probation* (June 1977): 8–14. See also Alexis Durham, "Newgate of Connecticut: Origins and Early Days of an Early American Prison," *Justice Quarterly* 6 (1989): 89–116m and Judith Cook, *To Brave Every Danger* (London: Macmillan, 1993).
34. Barnes and Teeters, *New Horizons in Criminology,* p. 336.
35. Negley K. Teeters, *The Cradle of the Penitentiary* (Philadelphia: Pennsylvania Prison Society, 1955).
36. Donald R. Taft, *Criminology,* 3rd ed. (New York: Macmillan, 1956), p. 478.
37. Harry E. Barnes, *The Story of Punishment,* 2nd ed. (Montclair, NJ: Patterson Smith, 1972), p. 136.

Philip Scalia/Alamy

Objectives

- Summarize the definition, mission, and role of corrections.
- Describe prison development from the reformatory era to the modern era.
- Summarize issues related to correctional policy.
- Summarize sentencing goals and primary punishment philosophies.
- Compare and contrast the Pennsylvania and Auburn systems.
- Explain why the Auburn system became the dominant prison design.

chapter 2

Prisons *(1800 to the Present)*

Outline

The Pennsylvania System

The Auburn System

- Discipline at Auburn

Prison Competition

Prison Rules

Change in the Wind

- Maconochie and Crofton: A New Approach
- Maconochie and the Indeterminate Sentence
- Crofton and the Irish System

The Reformatory Era (1870 to 1910)

Post–Civil War Prisons

The Twentieth Century and the Industrial Prison

The Period of Transition (1935 to 1960)

The Modern Era

Internally Sought Reform

- The Prison Population Boom

"To the builders of this nitemare Though you may never get to read these words I pity you; For the cruelty of your minds have designed this Hell; If men's buildings are a reflection of what they are, This one portraits the ugliness of all humanity. IF ONLY YOU HAD SOME COMPASSION"

—On a prison wall

Overview

The first chapter acquainted the student with how corrections has grown from individual to group punishment, then from group punishment to legal codes and punishment applied by the country or state. We saw how the idea of reform by penitence in the Walnut Street Jail grew to be a whole new concept—the penitentiary. In this chapter, we examine how this simple concept grew into the vast network of prisons across America by exploring the first two competing concepts or systems of prison design and construction in the United States.

The student should remember that corrections must always ask the question "Who are offenders, and what are we expected to do with them?" The most common schools of thoughts are the following: Offenders are (1) evil and must be punished, (2) out of touch with God and need to repent, (3) uneducated and ill trained to function in modern society, and (4) sick and in need of being cured. The answers to these questions are commonly known as the punishment, reform, education, and medical models of corrections. In the final part of this chapter, we explore the philosophical foundations on which these models were constructed and explain some of the rationales underlying current correctional developments. It is essential for the student to understand why this nation has entered into an age of massive change in public acceptance of crime and criminal and prison operations, what goals are being sought, and what might be the implications of the adoption of new programs, operations, and facilities. We begin with the two major competing concepts or systems that evolved and fought for prison designs and construction in the United States for the majority of the twentieth century.

THE PENNSYLVANIA SYSTEM

key term

Pennsylvania system
Early prison system requiring inmate silence, individual cells, and inmate labor in those cells.

key term

Outside cells
Prison cells attached to a corridor with the back of the cell extending outward toward a peripheral wall.

key term

Eastern Penitentiary
Prison facility designed on the Pennsylvania system with rows of individual cells attached to corridors and outside cells.

With the advent of the nineteenth century and the social upheaval produced by the Industrial Revolution, the citizens of Pennsylvania led the way in developing the penitentiary system. The Walnut Street Jail had been fairly effective for a decade, and the earlier **Pennsylvania system** was copied extensively in both architectural design and administration. But when the Philadelphia Society for the Alleviation of the Miseries of Public Prisons[1] observed the many emerging problems at the Walnut Street Jail, a radically new kind of prison was proposed for the state. It was suggested by some that solitary confinement without labor continue to be used as the sole reformatory process.

The Western Penitentiary at Pittsburgh, built in 1826, was based on the cellular isolation wing of the Walnut Street Jail. Essentially, the Western Penitentiary amounted to a poor imitation of Jeremy Bentham's proposed prison (Panopticon), an octagonal monstrosity that originally provided for solitary confinement and no labor. The legislature amended the program in 1829, maintaining solitary confinement but adding the provision that inmates perform some labor in their cells. In 1833, the small dark cells were torn down, and larger cells with enclosed exercise yards (**outside cells**)[2] were built. The efforts influenced the development of what became the Eastern Penitentiary, located in Philadelphia.

The **Eastern Penitentiary** became the model and primary exponent of the Pennsylvania, or "separate," system. This prison was built like a square wheel, with the cell blocks arranged like spokes around the hub, or central rotunda. The routine at Eastern was solitary confinement, silence, and labor in outside cells. This arrangement clearly stressed the maximum and continuous amount of separation of each inmate from all the others.

Although the Pennsylvania system aroused great international interest, it was adopted by only two other states. The New Jersey State Penitentiary in Trenton began operations in 1837, along the lines of the separate system. It was soon abandoned, however, in favor of that used at Auburn, New York. Rhode Island followed the same pattern as that of New Jersey. Its first prison, built in 1838 along the lines of the Eastern Penitentiary, had abandoned the separate system by 1852. By contrast, many European countries wholeheartedly adopted the Pennsylvania model.[3]

Photo 2.1
Al Capone's cell in Eastern Penitentiary.

THE AUBURN SYSTEM

The major evils of the jails and other confinement facilities before 1800 were indiscriminate congregate confinement and enforced idleness. The rapid debasement of the prisoners when kept in filthy conditions, with men, women, and children thrown together under a regime of neglect and brutality, appalled the early reformers. The long-term prisons established in the last decade of the eighteenth century were not just a substitute for capital and corporal punishment; they were total administrative and custodial systems intended to remedy the evils of the old methods. In the first quarter of the nineteenth century, administrators experimented with many new systems. The leading contenders for the world's attention were the Eastern Penitentiary and the New York State Prison at Auburn, opened in 1819.

The Auburn prison administrators developed a system that was almost the opposite of that used at the Eastern Penitentiary. The building itself was based on a new **inside cell** design,[4] and the cells were quite small when compared with those at Eastern. The small cells were designed to be used only for sleeping, not as a place for work. In addition, a new style of discipline was inaugurated at Auburn that became known as the **Auburn,** or "congregate," **system**.

key term

Inside cells
Prison cells that do not touch the outside walls of the cell block.

key term

Auburn system
Prison model consisting of small individual cells, a large work area for group labor, and enforced silence.

In the early years of the Auburn prison, administrators tested the efficacy of the Pennsylvania system. They selected 80 of the most hardened convicts, placing them in solitary confinement and enforced idleness for two years, from Christmas 1821 through Christmas 1823. So many of those men succumbed to sickness and insanity that the experiment was discontinued long before the two-year mark. The Auburn administration thus claimed failure for solitary confinement when the method included idleness. Given the small inside cells in Auburn, their claim was no doubt a valid one. However, the Auburn experiment cannot be considered a fair comparison to the Pennsylvania system because the latter system used large outside cells and provided for handicraft and other labor in the cells.[5]

Discipline at Auburn

An unfortunate by-product of the badly planned Auburn experiment was the use of solitary confinement (now usually termed administrative segregation) as a means of punishment within the prison. The discipline regimen at Auburn also included congregate work in the shops during the day, separation of prisoners into small individual cells at night, silence at all times, lockstep marching formations, and a congregate meal at which the prisoners sat face-to-back.[6] There was great emphasis on silence. In the belief that verbal exchange between prisoners was contaminating, conversation was prevented by liberal use of the whip. An excellent description of the Auburn system in its early stages, drawn from a letter by Louis Dwight (1793–1854), who was an early advocate of the Auburn system, as quoted by Harry Elmer Barnes (1889–1968) follows:

> At Auburn we have a more beautiful example still of what may be done by proper discipline, in a prison well constructed. It is not possible to describe the pleasure which we feel in contemplating this noble institution, after wading through the fraud, and the material and moral filth of many prisons. We regard it as a model worthy of the world's imitation. We do not mean that there is nothing in this institution which admits of improvement; for there have been a few cases of unjustifiable severity in punishments; but, upon the whole, the institution is immensely elevated above the old penitentiaries. The whole establishment, from the gate to the sewer, is a specimen of neatness. The unremitted industry, the entire subordination and subdued feelings of the convicts, has probably no parallel among an equal number of criminals. In their solitary cells they spend the night, with no other book but the Bible, and at sunrise they proceed, in military order, under the eye of the turnkeys, in solid columns, with the lock march, to their workshops; thence, in the same order at the hour of breakfast, to the common hall, where they partake of their wholesome and frugal meal in silence. Not even a whisper is heard; though the silence is such that a whisper might be heard

> through the whole apartment. The convicts are seated, in single file, at narrow tables, with their backs towards the center, so that there can be no interchange of signs. If one has more food than he wants, he raises his left hand; and if another has less, he raises his right hand, and the waiter changes it. When they have [finished] eating, at the ringing of a little bell, of the softest sound, they rise from the table, form the solid columns, and return, under the eye of the turnkeys, to the workshops. From one end of the shops to the other, it is the testimony of many witnesses that they have passed more than three hundred convicts, without seeing one leave his work, or turn his head to gaze at them. There is the most perfect attention to business from morning till night, interrupted only by the time necessary to dine, and never by the fact that the whole body of prisoners have done their tasks, and the time is now their own, and they can do as they please. At the close of the day, a little before sunset, the work is all laid aside at once, and the convicts return, in military order, to the solitary cells, where they partake of the frugal meal, which they were permitted to take from the kitchen, where it was furnished for them as they returned from the shops. After supper, they can, if they choose, read Scripture undisturbed and then reflect in silence on the errors of their lives. They must not disturb their fellow prisoners by even a whisper.[7]

The Auburn system became the pattern for more than 30 state prisons in the next half century. Sing Sing Prison in New York followed the Auburn pattern in 1825. Wethersford Prison in Connecticut copied the Auburn system but used a more moderate form of brutal punishments. Later prisons modeled their disciplinary systems after Wethersford.

key term

Cell blocks
Multitier living cells usually stacked one atop the other, built within a hollow building and not touching exterior walls.

Auburn's structural design, with inside cells and wings composed of two to four tiers of cells (**cell blocks**), became the model for most prisons built in the following 150 years. Many variations and innovations on the Auburn concept were developed. The most popular of those types, first constructed in 1898 at Fresnes, France, became known as the "telephone pole" design. Regardless of the cell-block arrangement, the inside cell design became the most common model in America.

One of the more important but less noted aspects of early prison architecture was the grand scale and sheer size of the institutions. "Bigger is better" (and more cost effective) was the watchword of early prison builders. Huge gothic-style structures achieved an effect similar to that of the medieval castles or cathedrals of Europe. They made the people inside seem small and insignificant. This feeling was further enhanced by the stern discipline employed in these huge castles of despair. Size is discussed again in later chapters, but we should note here that the size of the early prisons gave rise to a subtle pressure to keep them filled with society's castoffs.

PRISON COMPETITION

The main theme in both the Pennsylvania and the Auburn prison systems was the belief that a regimen of silence and penitence would prevent cross infection and encourage improved behavior in the prisoner. Supporters of the Pennsylvania system claimed it was easier to control the prisoners, gave more consideration to their individual needs, prevented contamination by the complete separation of prisoners from one another, and provided more opportunity for meditation and penitence. Another advantage they cited was that prisoners could leave the Pennsylvania system with their background known only to a few administrators because they did not come in contact with other prisoners.

key term

Congregate system
Prison modeled on the Auburn system with inmate work and feeding done en masse, in total silence.

On the other hand, supporters of the Auburn or congregate system argued that it was cheaper to construct and get started, offered better vocational training, and produced more money for the state.[8] The persuasive power of economics finally decided the battle, and the **congregate system** was adopted in almost all other American prisons, even in Pennsylvania. The Western Penitentiary was converted in 1869, and finally, in 1913, the Eastern Penitentiary changed its system. The capitulation of the Pennsylvania system followed many long years of fierce controversy between the two systems. "The only gratifying feature of the controversy was that both systems were so greatly superior to the unspeakable . . . system which they displaced that their competition inevitably worked for the betterment of penal conditions."[9]

PRISON RULES

As mentioned in Chapter 1, prisons can be viewed as yet another method to implement social vengeance for wrongs against society. Europeans examining the Auburn and Pennsylvania systems made a keen observation on the American society and its prisons:

> It must be acknowledged that the **penitentiary system** in America is severe. While society in the United States gives the example of the most extended liberty, the prisons of the same country offer the spectacle of the most complete despotism.[10]

In this context, the individual citizen's sense of guilt when he or she inflicts brutal or cruel punishment on another is diffused by the need for revenge on criminal offenders as a class and for the protection of society. The "out of sight, out of mind" principle was especially evident in the early-nineteenth-century prisons. Most of them were located far out in the countryside, free from either interference or inspection by the communities that supplied the prisoners. It is not too hard to understand why rules and procedures emphasized the smooth and undisturbed operation of the prison rather than the modification of the individual prisoner's behavior. Administrators were usually judged by the prison's production record and the number of escapes, not by the number of successful rehabilitations. Because of this, rules were designed to keep prisoners under total control. It is those early and well-established prison practices that have been the most difficult to overcome in the emerging standards of good correctional practices.

Elam Lynds, warden of Auburn and later of Sing Sing (which he built), was one of the most influential persons in the development of early prison discipline in America. He is described as having been an extremely strict **disciplinarian** who believed that all convicts were cowards who could not be reformed until their spirit was broken. To this end, he devised a system of brutal punishments and degrading procedures, many of which remained as accepted practice until very recent times.

The imposition of **silence** was seen as the most important part of the discipline program. The rule of absolute silence and noncommunication was maintained and enforced by the immediate use of the lash for the slightest infraction. Lynds advocated flogging as the most effective way to maintain order. He sometimes used a "cat" made of barbed-wire strands but more often a rawhide whip. The stereotype of the ex-con who is always talking out of the side of his mouth actually developed in the "silent" prisons to get around the silence rules.

Another bizarre form of discipline that was developed at Auburn was the **lockstep formation**. Prisoners were required to line up in close formation with their hands on the shoulders or under the arms of the prisoner in front. The line then moved rapidly toward its destination as the prisoners shuffled their feet in unison, without lifting them from the ground. Because this nonstop shuffle was "encouraged" by the use of the lash, any prisoner who fell out of lockstep risked a broken ankle or other serious injury from the steadily moving formation. Breaking the rule of silence during formation was considered especially objectionable and was punished viciously.

The use of degrading prison garb was also initiated at Auburn and Sing Sing. Early prisoners were allowed to wear the same clothing as the free society did. At Auburn and Sing Sing, different colors were used for the first-time offenders and for repeaters. Bizarre outfits served to reveal the prisoners' classification at a glance, to institutionalize them further, and to facilitate identification of escapees. The famous **prison stripes** came into being in 1815 in New York. The stripes were abandoned in most prisons but they have since been returned

key term

Penitentiary system
Prison designed to enforce penitence and prisoner anonymity, with individual manual labor in inmate cells.

key term

Disciplinarian
Prison administrator usually using harsh punishments to reinforce institutional rules.

key term

Silence
Absence of speech between inmates within early prisons.

key term

Lockstep formation
Lines of inmates marching closely behind their leader, with hands on top of shoulders or under the armpits. Requires shuffling and muteness in march from one area of the prison to another.

key term

Prison stripes
Prison uniforms with horizontal black bands and white stripes, frequently colored to designate inmate classification.

Photo 2.2

A modern chain gang helps with community cleanup.
Mark Peterson/Corbis News/Corbis.

by the Mississippi legislature in 1994 and by many other local jails and prisons. Some jurisdictions have reimposed black and white prison stripes or green and white striped uniforms on men working as roadwork crews; other jurisdictions require sex offenders to wear pink uniforms or pink underwear.

The methods used to prevent conversation or communication during meals were also humiliating. As mentioned, prisoners were required to sit face-to-back. They were given their meager and usually bland and unsavory meal to eat in silence. (Some state prisons still feed inmates on administrative segregation slices of a loaf made with kitchen scraps.) If they wanted more food, they would raise one hand; if they had too much, they raised the other. Any infraction of the rule of silence resulted in a flogging and the loss of a meal. This kind of entrenched procedure, very resistant to modern reforms, has been the source of many prison riots. Earlier prisons also had **treadmills** on which inmates labored, sometimes for exercise but frequently as a form of physical punishment.

key term

Treadmills
A mill worked by inmates treading on the periphery of a wide wheel having a horizontal axis and used in prison as a punishment.

One of the earliest and most well-known forms of prison discipline was the "prison within a prison," or **solitary confinement**, used as punishment for violation of institutional rules. Although the early experiment with total solitary confinement at Auburn showed it could not serve as the basis of a permanent prison system, the administrators saw its possibilities as a punishment for infractions of prison rules. Most of the prisons designed along the Auburn model therefore had a block of cells somewhere inside the walls, often referred to as the "hole." Usually, a sentence to solitary confinement was accompanied by reduced rations as well, consisting often of only bread and water. Solitary confinement is frequently used to discipline prisoners even today, although under much more humane conditions. Some contemporary inmates have been isolated in solitary confinement for decades.

key term

Solitary confinement
A punishment program requiring isolation of an inmate in a cell, also known as a "prison within a prison."

The many new prisons that were constructed in the century after the Eastern Penitentiary and the Auburn Prison made few, if any, contributions to the development of penology or corrections. The two greatest innovations, which persist today, were prison industries and the massive structures that used the interior cell-block design. Enforced silence was finally seen as a failure and abandoned. Cruel and barbaric punishments, though publicly decried, are still sometimes used—largely because most prisons are isolated from society and its controls. The development of corrections between

1800 and 1870, using policies, procedures, and philosophies that were unjust, still produced better results than did the universally accepted capital and corporal punishment that preceded it. And in the following era, the swing toward a more realistic and humanistic correctional approach began.

Photo 2.3

A "sweat box" punishment cell for solitary confinement.
State Archives of Florida, Florida Memory/Duane Perkins.

CHANGE IN THE WIND

Maconochie and Crofton: A New Approach

The reformatory system in America owes a great deal to the work of an Englishman, Captain Alexander Maconochie, and an Irishman, Sir Walter Crofton. Together they laid the foundation for reformative rather than purely punitive programs for the treatment of criminals.

Maconochie and the Indeterminate Sentence

In 1840, Captain Maconochie was put in charge of the British penal colony on Norfolk Island, about 800 miles east of Australia. To this island were sent the criminals who were "twice condemned": They had been shipped to Australia from England and then from Australia to Norfolk. Conditions were so bad at Norfolk that men reprieved from the death penalty wept, and those who were to die thanked God[11]—that was the kind of hell Maconochie inherited.

The first thing Maconochie did was to eliminate the flat sentence,[12] a system that had allowed no hope of release until the full time had been served. Then he developed a "mark system" whereby a convict could earn freedom by hard work and good behavior, thus creating the **indeterminate sentence**. This type of sentencing put the burden of release on the convict. As Maconochie said, "When a man keeps the key of his own prison, he is soon persuaded to fit it into the lock." The system had five principles:

1. Release should be based not on the completion of a sentence for a set period of time but on the completion of a determined and specified quantity of labor. In brief, time sentences should be abolished and task sentences substituted.
2. The quantity of labor a prisoner must perform should be expressed in a number of "marks," which he must earn, by improvement of conduct, frugality of living, and habits of industry, before he can be released.
3. While in prison, he should earn everything he receives. All sustenance and indulgences should be added to his debt of marks.
4. When qualified by discipline to do so, he should work in association with a small number of other prisoners, forming a group of six or seven, and the whole group should be answerable for the conduct and labor of each member.
5. In the final stage, a prisoner, while still obliged to earn his daily tally of marks, should be given a proprietary interest in his own labor and be subject to a less rigorous discipline to prepare him for release into society.[13]

It is a sad fact that Maconochie's visionary efforts toward rehabilitation were not appreciated or supported by the unenlightened bureaucrats above him. His results thus were disclaimed, and the colony fell back into its former brutalized routine almost as soon as he left it.

key term

Indeterminate sentence
A period of confinement with specified minimum and maximum length, allowing a parole board to release the inmate when rehabilitation has been achieved.

correctional **profile 2.1**

Lieutenant Alexander Maconochie ("Ma-kon-o-kêy")

Alexander Maconochie was born in Scotland in 1787 and by 1803 saw active duty under Commodore Nelson, being captured and held as a prisoner from 1811 to 1814. He rose in rank and was the only commanding officer in the British transportation system to have served time incarcerated in a prison. In 1836, he was appointed private secretary of the lieutenant governor of Van Diemen's Land (now Tasmania). To augment his pay, he contracted with several charitable bodies, including the Society for the Improvement of Prison Discipline. The latter was the major English body for penal reform and enjoyed considerable influence within the British government.

Maconochie authored scathing reports on the penal conditions he found in Australia, ones he found brutal, demeaning, ineffective, and repressive. He focused on vicious floggings, imposition of heavy irons and manacles, and disciplinarian punishments that frequently included 100 lashes when the inmate was chained to a metal frame. Those reports were eventually presented to the British home secretary, creating a major political storm and leading eventually to the sack of Maconochie, primarily because of the uproar by the free inhabitants who were hiring prisoners as cheap labor. What had begun as another campaign for prison reform ended as a personal mission to improve the penal colony, a mission enhanced by his perception as a Christian devotee.

His reports to charitable bodies continued; in one, he described what he called a better way of running a prison colony. This also was forwarded to the home secretary, who decided to give Maconochie an opportunity to implement his scheme as governor of Norfolk Island (some 1000 miles from Australia). When Maconochie arrived, he ordered all inmates to be collected to hear his plan. In broad stroke, he said this:

1. Sentences limited to specific years of incarceration did little to reform offenders.
2. Every prisoner could find and then fit the key of freedom into the lock on their cells. It was up to them.
3. Inmates would be evaluated every day for their behavior ("earn marks"), and these could be amassed and spent for desired goals (tea, sugar, tobacco, and freedom).
4. If the inmates were frugal and hardworking, they would earn marks ("points") every day.
5. When an inmate earned enough marks, sentences would be commuted, and the inmates would be free to leave the penal colony (but not the island).
6. If serving a seven-year sentence, the inmate would need 6,000 marks to earn his freedom; for a 10-year sentence, the count was 7,000 marks; and for those serving 14 or more years, the cost would be 8,000 marks.
7. Marks could be deducted for further criminal behavior and extravagances.
8. They should all labor together in the direction of reformation.
9. If a former inmate committed another crime while on release, he had to return to the prison colony to complete the full sentence.

Hope had just arrived on Norfolk Island. Inmate assaults on staff decreased sharply. Inmate-on-inmate assaults also declined markedly.

Originally, Maconochie was to implement his reformation package for first-time convicted offenders who were not to associate with the more hardened second-offense inmates. Practically, he could not overcome the mixture of the two classes and decided to include all inmates in the plan. He failed to notify his superiors of this decision. Resistance set in from his warders and officers, and reports were submitted to the governor. In 1846, Maconochie was recalled. He refused to remain silent, and in a series of letters and pamphlets, he continued to argue for his new system of penal reform. While Norfolk Island returned to its former brutal self, Maconochie's plan reached other concerned citizens and prison administrators in other countries (particularly Sir Walter Crofton of Ireland), and the punitive past slowly eroded. He was indeed the "father of parole" in practice.

key term

Irish system
A prison management scheme with multiple stages of control, allowing the inmate to earn higher stages until released when penitence was achieved; release was on a revocable "ticket-of-leave," or conditional pardon.

Crofton and the Irish System

Fortunately, Maconochie's ideas did reach beyond the shores of Norfolk Island. His successful use of the indeterminate sentence[14] showed that imprisonment could be used to prepare a convict for eventual return to the community. If this were true, then the length of sentence should not be an arbitrary period of time but should be related to the rehabilitation of the offender. Sir Walter Crofton of Ireland used that concept in developing what he called the "indeterminate system," which came to be known as the **Irish system**. He reasoned that if penitentiaries are places where offenders think about their crimes and can decide to stop their criminal misbehavior ("repent"), there must be a mechanism to determine that this decision has in fact been made as well as a mechanism for getting the inmate out when penitence has been done. The indeterminate sentence was believed to be the best mechanism.

The system Crofton devised, like Maconochie's, consisted of a series of stages, each bringing the convict closer to the free society. The first stage was solitary confinement and monotonous work. The second stage was assignment to public works and a progression through various grades, each grade shortening the length of stay. The last stage was assignment to an intermediate prison where the prisoner worked without supervision and moved in and out of the free community. If the prisoner's conduct continued to be good and if he or she were able to find employment, the offender would return to the community on a conditional pardon, or **ticket-of-leave**. This ticket could be revoked at any time within the span of the original fixed sentence if the prisoner's conduct were not up to standards established by those who supervised the conditional pardon. Crofton's plan was the first effort to establish a system of **conditional liberty** in the community, the system we know today as parole.

key term

Ticket-of-leave

Certificate issued by the warden certifying the offender has permission to leave the facility but not representing parole.

key term

Conditional liberty

A prisoner release scheme that allows the penitent inmate to be released to the community under specific conditions that can be revoked; a system commonly known as "parole."

THE REFORMATORY ERA (1870 TO 1910)

Leaders in U.S. penology and prison administration met at the American Prison Congress of 1870[15] in Cincinnati, Ohio, to discuss the direction that corrections practices should take. They were especially concerned about overcrowding, and they discussed what new kinds of prisons should be built to alleviate it. Many urged that Maconochie's and Crofton's plans be adopted in America. The members endorsed that idea, and the reformatory era in American corrections was born.

The first **reformatory** in America was built in 1876 in Elmira New York and became the model for all those that followed. **Zebulon Brockway**, the first superintendent, had introduced some new educational methods at the Detroit House of Corrections, and he expanded on that concept at Elmira. Elmira was originally built for adult felons, but it was used instead for youths from 16 to 30 years of age who were serving their first term in prison. One observer cited the following characteristics as the standards for Elmira, and many such characteristics reappeared in its imitators:

key term

Reformatory

An institution for younger offenders that requires education and training, conditional release, and potential revocation of parole.

profile

Zebulon Brockway

The first superintendent of the Elmira Reformatory, who implemented reduction of recidivism through educational programs.

1. The material structural establishment itself. The general plan and arrangements should be those of the Auburn system, modified and modernized; and 10 percent of the cells might well be constructed like those of the Pennsylvania system. The whole should be supplied with suitable modern sanitary appliances and with abundance of natural and artificial light.
2. Clothing—not degradingly distinctive, but uniform, . . . fitly representing the respective grades or standing of the prisoners. . . . Scrupulous cleanliness should be maintained and the prisoners appropriately groomed.
3. A liberal prison diet designed to promote vigor. Deprivation of food, by a general regulation, is deprecated. . . .
4. All the modern appliances for scientific physical culture; a gymnasium completely equipped with baths and apparatus; and facilities for field athletics.
5. Facilities for manual training sufficient for about one-third of the population. This special manual training covers, in addition to other exercises in other departments, mechanical and freehand drawing; sloyd [manual training] in wood and metals; cardboard constructive form work; clay modeling; cabinet making; clipping and filing; and iron molding.
6. Trade instruction based on the needs and capacities of individual prisoners. (Where a thousand prisoners are involved, thirty-six trades may be usefully taught.)
7. A regimental military organization with a band of music, swords for officers, and dummy guns for the rank and file of prisoners.

8. School of letters with a curriculum that reaches from an adaptation of the kindergarten . . . up to the usual high school course; and, in addition, special classes in college subjects . . .
9. A well-selected library for circulation, consultation, and for occasional semi-social use.
10. The weekly institutional newspaper, in lieu of all outside newspapers, edited and printed by the prisoners under due censorship.
11. Recreating and diverting entertainments for the mass of the population, provided in the great auditorium; not any vaudeville or minstrel shows, but entertainments of such a class as the middle cultured people of a community would enjoy. . . .
12. Religious opportunities . . . adapted to the hereditary [and] habitual . . . denominational predilection of the individual prisoners.
13. Definitely planned, carefully directed, emotional occasions; not summoned, primarily, for either instruction, diversion, nor, specifically, for a common religious impression, but, figuratively, for a kind of irrigation.[16]

The only real differences between the programs at Elmira and those at the adult prisons were the emphasis on reforming youth, increased academic education, and more extensive trade training. Two significant features were adopted for the reformatories, though: the indeterminate sentence and a grading system based on marks that could lead to parole.

Elmira was copied, in one form or another, by 17 states between 1876 and 1913. Brockway's leadership produced the first attempt to offer programs of education and reformation to all inmates, adult or youth. Trade training, academic education, and the military type of discipline utilized at Elmira undoubtedly also influenced the programs of many of the older prisoners. Some aspects of the indeterminate sentence and parole concepts were finally extended to the state prisons. It is not surprising that in an era when public education was considered to be the answer to so many problems in the outside world, it was viewed as the answer to crime as well. But because the same physical environment and the same underpaid and poorly qualified personnel found in prisons were also found in reformatories, those institutions were soon reduced to junior prisons with the usual routine. The same-old "prison discipline" was still the most dominant feature in any penal program.

Although the two main contributions of the reformatory era were the indeterminate sentence and parole, the seeds of education, vocational training, and individual rehabilitation had been sown. Even though such radical ideas could not flourish in the barren and hostile environment of that period, they took root and grew to fruition in later years.

Photo 2.4

The Cincinnati Workhouse as it looked in 1870, when the first international Correctional Congress was held in the city. Prisoners were housed there until the late 1980s.
Public Library of Cincinnati and Hamilton County.

POST–CIVIL WAR PRISONS

The 16 states that built prisons between 1870 and 1900 were almost all in the northern or western part of the country. Their only claim to improvement was the introduction of plumbing and running water. All were of the Auburn type, and the only modifications in the older prison routine were the abandonment of the silent system and the use of the indeterminate sentence and parole.

In the South, devastated by the Civil War, the penitentiary system had been virtually wiped out. Some states attempted to solve their prison problems by leasing out their entire convict population to contractors, which became known as the **lease system.**[17] Convict leasing was a system of penal labor, beginning with the emancipation of slaves at the end of the American Civil War in 1865, peaking around 1880, and ending in the last state, Alabama, in 1928. While the lease system was profitable for leasees and the states, it more resembled slavery. Others took in contract work or devised combinations of both leasing out prisoners and taking in contracts. Yet another group of slaves thus replaced the freed blacks: the convicted felons. The South was unique in that many of its prisons ignored both the Auburn and the reformatory systems. The South's agrarian economy made exploitation of cheap labor both easy and desirable. A large portion of the prison population in the South was composed of plantation blacks who had no influence or resources, and they were treated with no mercy.[18] Leasing was eventually replaced by prison farms in most southern states, but the practice was not completely erased until the mid-1920s. This sordid period in penal history, brought to light again in the 1960s in Arkansas,[19] simply confirms the depths to which even so-called civilized people can sink in the treatment of their castoffs. The correctional experience in the South made only a negative contribution in regard to both procedure and discipline.

key term

Lease system
The hiring of inmates to perform work details managed by private entrepreneurs, either while out of or still incarcerated in prison facilities.

THE TWENTIETH CENTURY AND THE INDUSTRIAL PRISON

The introduction of handicrafts into the solitary Eastern Penitentiary cells represented the origin of prison industries in America. In continental Europe and England, the infamous efforts to provide labor in the workhouses and Bridewells had resulted in such fruitless activities as the treadmill. The modern pressure to provide vocational training or earnings for inmates did not concern early American prison administrators; rather, they wanted to make the prisons self-sustaining. Toward this goal, the prison workshops were merely extensions of the early factory workshops. When the factory production system was introduced into prisons and they began to show actual profits from their output, legislators were quickly convinced that prison industries were a sound operation. The Auburn system held out over the less efficient Pennsylvania system because it paid better returns on taxpayer investment. By the 1860s, the system of absolute silence had begun to fall apart because of the necessity for communication in the industrial shops. Early prison industries, in effect, exploited the available free labor for the sole purpose of perpetuating the institution itself. Some leaders in the field, however, saw that a change in emphasis could make the industries an important factor in prisoner rehabilitation.

From the beginning of the twentieth century until 1940, the number of inmates in U.S. prisons increased by 174 percent.[20] Ten new Auburn-style prisons were built during this period—often referred to as the industrial era for prisons in America, which finally reached its zenith in 1935. The new prisons were considered "as cold and hard and abnormal as the prisoners whom they were intended to persuade toward better things."[21]

The **industrial prison** can credit its origins to the profits turned by the first state prisons. Early in the nineteenth century, however, mechanics and cabinetmakers began to

key term

Industrial prison
Any penal institution whose main objective is the use of inmate labor to produce marketable products for prison profit.

complain about the unfair competition they faced from the virtually free labor force available within prisons. The use of lease and contract systems aggravated the problem and led to a series of investigations that reached national prominence in 1886. The emergence of the labor union movement, coupled with abuses of the contract and lease systems of prison labor, eliminated those systems in the northern prisons by the end of the nineteenth century. They were replaced by piece-price[22] and state-account[23] systems. Opposition to prison industries resulted in enforced idleness among the increasing inmate population. This forced the adult prisons to adopt reformatory methods in some measure but made self-sustaining institutions a thing of the past.

key term

Hawes–Cooper Act
Federal legislation that forbids the manufacture and transportation of prison goods made by convicts and prisoners.

key term

Ashurst–Sumners Act
Federal legislation requiring "truth of manufacturing, transportation and interstate shipment of prison-made goods" by requirement that the packages be plainly and clearly marked.

Because the story of the prison industry's battle with organized labor is a history in itself, it is not covered here. The beginning of the end for large-scale prison industries, which kept inmates employed in some kind of work, was the enactment of two federal laws controlling the character of prison products. The **Hawes–Cooper Act**, passed in 1929, required that prison products be subject to the laws of any state to which they were shipped. The **Ashurst–Sumners Act**, passed in 1935, essentially stopped the interstate transport of prison products by requiring that all prison products shipped out of the state be labeled with the prison name and by prohibiting interstate shipment where state laws forbade it. In 1940, the Ashurst–Sumners Act was amended to prohibit fully the interstate shipment of prison products.

The economic strains of the Great Depression, beginning with the Wall Street stock market crash in 1929 and spanning the period from 1929 to 1940, led 33 states to pass laws that prohibited the sale of prison products on the open market. Those statutes tolled the

correctional **profile 2.2**

Sanford Bates

Sanford Bates (1884–1972) is a correctional giant in the field of state and federal correctional systems. Born in Boston, Massachusetts, he attended The Boston English High School, graduating at age 16. He subsequently attended the Y.M.C.A. evening law school (now Northeastern University) and was a lawyer by trade at age 22. He was admitted to the bar, enabled to practice before the U.S. Supreme Court.

Before he became an attorney, he worked as a clerk in the municipal street department and subsequently became active in the Republican Party. His early career catapulted him into the Boston political scene as a member of both the House of Representatives and the Senate. His corrections career began in 1918, when he was appointed the Boston penal commissioner and then the commissioner of the Massachusetts Department of Corrections (1919–1929). In 1929, Assistant Attorney General Willebrandt hired him as the superintendent of federal prisons. In that position, he proposed the legislation that established the Federal Bureau of Prisons (1930).

President Hoover subsequently appointed Sanford Bates as the Bureau's first director (1930), a position that provided a vast canvas for creation of a coordinated and highly reputed prison system. He believed that the best avenue to increased societal safety demanded the rehabilitation of criminals, that this function required a device for identifying when the offender had changed, and that this device would have to supervise released offenders on parole: a parole board. His goals also included a centralized administration, establishing a consistent set of bureau-wide policies, implementing a program of prison construction to reduce institutional overcrowding, reducing if not eliminating political patronage, improving staff training, and constructing a prison industries program. These objectives are discussed in more detail in Chapter 12. He was successful in attainment of his objectives (1930–1937).

Three additional points: First, beginning in 1934, he served as the chairman of the federal prison industries program until his death in 1972. Second, he later served as president of the American Correctional Association and as the executive director of the Boys Clubs of America. Third, after he left the Bureau of Prisons, he served as parole commissioner for the State of New York and as the New Jersey state commissioner of institutions and industries. His was a long and fruitful career that greatly strengthened the development of a modern correctional system.

SOURCE: Sanford Bates Collection at https://archon.shsu.edu/?p=collections/findingaid&id=2&q=, retrieved August 8, 2013. See also Federal Bureau of Prisons, "Former Bureau of Prisons Directors: Sanford Bates, 1930–1937," at http://www.bop.gov/about/history/past_directors.jsp, retrieved August 8, 2013.

death knell for the industrial prison. With the exception of a few license plate and state furniture shops, most state prisons took a giant step backward to their original purposes: punishment and custody. Fortunately, another model was emerging at the same time: the "new penology" of the 1930s and the U.S. Bureau of Prisons under the leadership of **Sanford Bates.**

Sanford Bates is a legendary figure in American corrections. He served as the president of the American Correctional Association (1925), became the first superintendent of federal prisons (1929), and was selected as the first director of the U.S. Bureau of the Prisons (1930). Later he served as commissioner of the New York State Board of Parole and then commissioner of the New Jersey Department of Institutions and Agencies.

profile

Sanford Bates
First director of the U.S. Bureau of Prisons.

THE PERIOD OF TRANSITION (1935 TO 1960)

The quarter century between 1935 and 1960 was one of great turmoil in the prisons. Administrators, stuck with the huge fortresses of the previous century, were now deprived of the ability to provide meaningful work for inmates. The Depression, influx of new immigrants, and criminal excesses of the 1920s and 1930s hardened the public's attitude toward convict rehabilitation at a time when behavioral scientists were just beginning to propose hopeful reforms in prisoner treatment. J. Edgar Hoover, director of the Federal Bureau of Investigation (FBI), led the battle against "hoity-toity professors" and the "cream-puff school of criminology." His war on crime helped give the world the supermaximum prison, **Alcatraz.** Located on an island in San Francisco Bay, Alcatraz was constructed to house the most hardened criminals confined in the federal prison system. When it was built in 1934, it was seen as the answer to the outrages of such desperate criminals as Al Capone, Robert Stroud ("Birdman of Alcatraz"), and Bonnie and Clyde. Eventually, the U.S. Bureau of Prisons abandoned this prison as too expensive to maintain.

key term

Alcatraz
A supermax island prison for inmates in the San Francisco Bay Area and part of the U.S. Bureau of Prisons until its closing; also known as "the Rock."

Such notables as Bernard Glueck at Sing Sing between 1915 and 1920, Edgar Doll and W. G. Ellis in New Jersey in 1925, and A. W. Stearns in Massachusetts in 1930 pioneered early efforts toward diagnostic classification and casework. Sanford Bates introduced procedures into the U.S. Bureau of Prisons in 1934. Although sometimes "borrowing" principles from states across the nation, the U.S. Bureau of Prisons gradually emerged as the national leader in corrections, introducing many new concepts that have been copied by state systems. Two major contributions were diagnosis and classification and the use of professional personnel, such as psychiatrists and psychologists, to help rehabilitate inmates. The federal system also led the way to more humane treatment and better living conditions (see Chapter 12). But no matter how they were cleaned up, prisons remained monuments to idleness, monotony, frustration, and repression. Despite attempts to tear down the massive walls around some prisons, the forces of **lock psychosis** continued to hold out. Prison inmates were feared as the **convict bogey**, which could be dealt with only by locking and relocking, counting and recounting. Interestingly, the convict bogey is the unreasonable fear by prison administrators that leads them to lock prisoners behind several layers of barred doors and other barricades. Counts are usually conducted several times a day to ensure that all prisoners are locked up. (Some modern correctional administrations use plastic wrist identifier bands for continuous inmate counting and location.)

key term

Lock psychosis
Term denoting overconcentration of prison administrators with security and community protection, to be accomplished through extensive use of locks, head counts, and internal control of inmates.

It is not too surprising that the long hours of idleness, forbidding architecture, growing populations, and unnecessarily repressive controls created unbearable tensions among the inmates. The first riots in this country, as noted earlier, were at the mineshaft prison in Simsbury, Connecticut. (A *riot* is a violent, tumultuous disturbance within the prison or other correctional institutional involving seven or more inmates assembled together and acting as a common cause.) Riots at the Walnut Street Jail were reported in the early 1800s

key term

Convict bogey
Irrational fear of prison inmates who can be managed only through head counts, locking, and recounting.

as well. The mid-nineteenth century, when prison industries provided extensive work for convicts, was a time of few riots. Presumably, either the inmates were too tired to riot or the control was too strict. As the prison industries died out, riots began to take place more regularly, adding evidence to the theory that enforced idleness causes restlessness and discontent among prisoners. There was a wave of riots in the prisons between 1929 and 1932. During World War II, there were few problems, but in 1946 there was even a riot in Alcatraz, the super-prison.

Whether neglect of prisons and lack of meaningful activities finally bore bitter fruit or whether the rising prosperity of the 1950s simply presented too sharp a contrast with the bleak life on the inside, there was an explosion of prison discontent during the early part of that decade. More than 300 prison riots have occurred since 1774, and 90 percent of those have occurred in the last four decades.[24] The American Correctional Association investigated the 1950s riots and reported what appeared to be the main causes:[25]

1. Inadequate financial support and official and public indifference
2. Substandard personnel
3. Enforced idleness
4. Lack of professional leadership and professional programs
5. Excessive size and overcrowding of institutions
6. Political domination and motivation of management
7. Unwise sentencing and parole practices

More recent examples of disturbances within prison walls, especially with the lengthy incarceration sentences for security threat groups ("prison gangs"), are hunger strikes in which tens of thousands inmates refuse to eat institution-served food.

correctional **practice 2.1**

Hunger Strike in Prison

Inmates have a wide range of actions they might take to express excessive dissatisfaction with prison conditions and policies. California had, in midyear 2013, an ongoing inmate hunger strike. On July 8, an estimated 30,000 inmates refused their state-issued meals. Inmate advocates argue that the state's use of solitary confinement and excessive indefinite detention are unconstitutional, cause physical and psychological damage, and violate prisoners' constitutional rights. These policies, practices, and conditions are at the heart of a federal lawsuit over these conditions.

Inmates participating in the hunger strike are demanding limits on the length of solitary confinement designed to control prison gangs and how inmates are reclassified following gang-related violence in prison.

Prison administrators investigating the disturbances note that the number of prisoners on strike has shrunk to 1,475 inmates found in some 15 California prisons and claim that the protest per se is coordinated by the incarcerated prison gang members.

Inmate advocates had in part been coordinating the sharing of information with inmates in other prisons, as the California Department of Corrections and Rehabilitation (CDCR) argues. Major inmate advocates formed a mediation team that was assembled to work as a go-between with state corrections officials and protest leaders. Marilyn McMahon, executive director of California Prison Focus, received a fax from the CDCR informing her that access to inmates participating in the statewide hunger strike had been cut off, pending an investigation into an unspecified threat created by a retired paralegal on McMahon's staff who had last visited Pelican Bay Prison, California, inmates two months before. McMahon described the advocacy actions as efforts to end solitary confinement in California and said the CDCR act was intended to sever lines of communication between striking prisoners and their advocates in the free world. McMahon and another civil rights attorney were also banned during a similar inmate hunger strike in 2011. There were no findings then of wrongdoing.

SOURCE: "California bans inmates' rights lawyer from prisons." Retrieved from http://www.latimes.com/local/political/la-me-pc-ffcalifornia-bans-inmates-rights-lawyer-from-prisons-20130717,0,1057896.story. Retrieved July 22, 2013.

SOURCE: Paige St. Johns, "Four inmates on hunger strike require medical attention." Retrieved from www.latimes.com/local/political/la-me-ff-4-hunger-strike-inmates-require-medical-attention-20130718,0,3233502.story. Retrieved July 22, 2013.

The explosion predicted from the conditions created by overcrowding, idleness, and lack of public concern erupted at Attica in the fall of 1971. The modern era became a period of seeking ways to prevent such events: Community-based corrections became the watchword for reform in corrections, and the "correctional filter" (discussed in Chapter 4) was supplied with more outlets for diverting inmates from seething, overcrowded prisons. Supreme Court decisions created further pressure for reform. The result, at least until the end of the 1970s, was a state of uneasy status quo. The status quo was broken in the beginning of the 1980s by riots at a New Mexico prison that resulted in numerous brutal deaths and public outrage. Prison riots continued; in 1996, there were four prison riots over three days in federal prisons. In 2001, several inmates were injured in a California prison riot; in 2004, there was a riot in a privately run correctional institution in Kentucky.[26] In the first nine months of 2013, there were prison riots in two juvenile correctional facilities (Oregon and Florida), four state prisons, a prison in Mississippi, and four correctional facilities in California. For more information about additional correctional facility riots, search the Internet using search terms "prison riot" with the current year.

It appears now that some of the programs designed to relieve the problems in the overcrowded fortress prisons have in fact contributed to many of the conditions and made them even riper for violence. Prison gangs (institutional threat groups) elevate tension, conflict, and riots (see Chapter 8). The fortress prisons are still here, many even more overcrowded, and their maximum-security clients are now the "bottom of the barrel" regarding behavioral problems. This has caused an abandonment of the medical model and steady movement toward a model emphasizing custody and control over everything else in a futile effort to keep peace in the institutions and "protect society." The problem of selecting a philosophy or ideology that is effective and reflective of society's mood is a problem administrators will have to confront in the next decade (see Chapter 3). To comprehend the current issues in corrections, we must examine the decision process and options available to the prosecution, judiciary, and releasing authorities.

THE MODERN ERA

The "modern era" of corrections is generally considered to have begun about 1960, and it was characterized by a pattern of change that was to highlight the next decade. The 1960s era in the United States was noted for turbulent and violent confrontations at almost every level of activity affecting human rights. The forces for change at work in the overall society were also reflected in great pressures for change in corrections. The dramatic reinterpretations of criminal law, the civil rights movement, violent and nonviolent demonstrations in the streets, street gangs, the assassinations of a popular president and two other important national figures, the continuation of three long and unpopular wars in American history—all of these outside pressures were also felt inside the walls of the nation's prisons. Reaction took the form of periodic violent prison riots and disorders. The U.S. Supreme Court emerged as the primary external agent for the enforced recognition of the basic rights of those swept up in the criminal justice system. This external pressure was generated by a long series of significant judicial interpretations. In addition, leadership and funding by the federal government were given to correctional administrators and planners at the state and local levels, enabling them to create, implement, and evaluate new standards, policies, and practices. Unfortunately, aspiring politicians and the media have collectively generated and nurtured inaccurate stereotypes about offenders, blunting correctional gains and giving rise to more intractable problems.[27] The conservative movement in the political arena continues to cause a steady move to the right in corrections, wreaking havoc with the shrinking efforts at rehabilitation, which works based on evidence of correctional outcomes. The turmoil continues.

INTERNALLY SOUGHT REFORM

Early prisons were less secure than modern ones, and escape was far more common. It was easier to "disappear" into early American society with a new name and a new start. Inmate security and control, improved in recent years, have made escape from prisons difficult, and systems of identification and control, including computer banks of data on each of us, have made escape into society almost impossible.

When the prisons became so secure that relief and escape were cut off, the inmates' frustration and agitation turned inward. Prisoners in this "total institution"[28] used disturbances and riots to express their desire for reforms and changes in rules and conditions. Disturbances also served to resolve power struggles between prison gangs[29] and inmate groups. The early disturbances were characterized by disorganization and rapid dispersion; inmates used those methods to settle old grudges, refusing to fall in line behind any kind of leadership. In the 1960s and 1970s, disturbances were common in most large state systems, reflecting the usual grievances: crowded living conditions, harsh rules, poor food, excessive punishment, and guard brutality.[30] Even the highly respected federal prison system was rocked in 1987 by large-scale hostage taking by Cuban inmates who feared deportation. The growing awareness of individual rights on the outside that began in the 1960s led inmates to seek the same rights inside prisons.

Beginning about 1966, the nature of the demands changed from those involving basic conditions to those concerning basic rights. In that year, the Maryland Penitentiary in Baltimore was the scene of a riot involving over 1,000 inmates. The warden claimed the disturbance was caused by heat waves and overcrowding, but "the riot had to have social overtones," said Joseph Bullock, a member of the state house of delegates. "If they don't stop telling these people [blacks] about their rights," Bullock went on, "things will get worse."[31] Rioting and violence spilled over from the streets into the prisons of America. The "political prisoner" label, particularly for blacks and Chicanos, offered a more acceptable way for minority groups to state their feelings of deprivation. They struck out at a system that they perceived gave them an unequal start in life and then jailed them for failing to live up to the rules of that system.[32] Clearly, outside social behavior and conditions do carry over into prison. Little that is new in society starts in prison.

Photo 2.5

Photo of prison riot.

Change, though often temporary, comes about as a result of prison riots. More often today, new voices can help shape prison policies, through an inmate council, grievance procedures, conflict resolution,[33] or inmates serving on regular prison committees, following a collaborative model. Some systems also use an **ombudsman** as a link between the prisoner and the establishment; this official receives and investigates complaints and sees that corrective action is taken. Correctional administrators have learned that the more diverse the correctional staff, the fewer the inmate assaults on other inmates and staff.[34]

key term

Ombudsman
Correctional overseer who investigates reported complaints (as from inmates, prison personnel, and prison staff), reports findings, and helps to achieve equitable settlements.

The Prison Population Boom

Only recently, probably due more to the financial recession than to a change in correctional policy, has the number of state inmates gone down. Figure 2.1 shows that the prison count dropped in 27 states in, starting in 2009. From 1980 to 2009, the number of state and federal prison inmates in the nation increased more than 500 percent, from 320,000 to 1,611,209 prisoners. This population boom resulted from fear of crime[35] fueled by politicians, a "get-tough approach to crime," the **War on Drugs**, the media, and special interest groups. Yet crime declined significantly during the past two decades and currently sits at the level of crime found in 1972. The level of violence also declined during the past few years, but the level of fear has remained steady. Fear of violence, drive-by shootings, juvenile gangs struggling to control the drug trade, drug use, and racism have combined to support a "get-tough" environment.

key term

War on Drugs
A criminal justice program focusing on reducing the manufacture, use, sale, or trafficking of drugs.

The results, covered in more detail in later chapters, were rapid prison population expansion (see Figure 2.2) and an unprecedented growth in prison construction, increased prison overcrowding, reduction of early-release mechanisms from prison, and massive jail populations and jail construction. The recession of 2008–2013 has also forced states

Offense	Federal	State
Violent	8	53
Drug	48	17
Property	5	18
Public Order	35	10

figure 2.1
Federal and State Prison Populations, by Offense.

SOURCE: Carson, A. and Sabol, W. (2013). Prisoners in 2012. Washington, DC: Bureau of Justice Statistics.

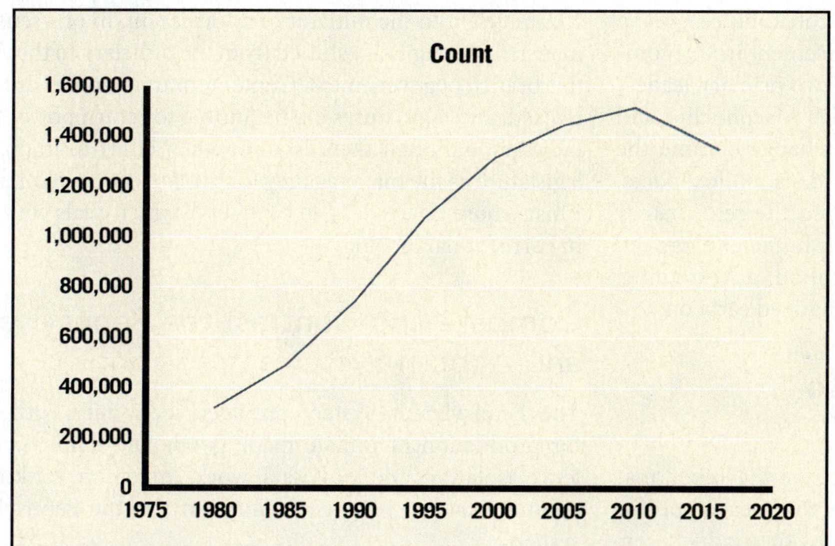

figure 2.2
Growth in Prison Populations: 1980–2016.

SOURCE: From Bureau of Justice Statistics (2010), Correctional Populations in the United States, 2009 (Washington, DC: BJS), and Bureau of Justice Statistics (2013). Prison Population 2012: Advance Count (Washington, DC: BJS). Data for 2016 are extrapolated.

to avoid prison maintenance costs as well as construction costs. (For all tables and figures in which data were extrapolated, a straight-line projection was made using the average of the previous five years in which data were available.) The prison population decreased from 2009 to 2012), more than half of that by court order to California to release the number of inmates to reduce unconstitutional conditions of confinement. See Chapter 11 for more details.

Alternatives to prison—probation, parole, and so-called intermediate punishments—also increased during this time but did not significantly reduce the pressure to build correctional facilities. Alternatives are needed not only to building of jails and prisons but also for policies to buttress and expand corrections in the community. New ideas and programs are badly needed, as the contemporary corrections field appears to be under considerable strain.

Summary

Summarize the Definition, Mission, and Role of Corrections

As mentioned in the summary of Chapter 1, the Quakers had a considerable impact on the development of corrections, both philosophically and in practice. In 1790, they managed to open the first facility devoted primarily to inmate change, the Walnut Street Jail. From that modest beginning, the Pennsylvania system of single-celling, silence, and repentance began, shortly afterward challenged by the new Auburn system and its harsh punishments for rule infractions. Both had flaws but were unbelievably superior to previous alternative punishments.

Describe Prison Development from the Reformatory Era to the Modern Era

Earlier in the eighteenth century, humanitarians interested in reformation of offenders began to experiment with alternative adjuncts to incarceration: parole, probation, extending the limits of confinement to include placement in the community, and indeterminate sentencing. Two primary leaders in this experimentation were Alexander Maconochie and Walter Crofton. Through their efforts, change became the name of the game. In 1870, prison wardens, philosophers, concerned citizens, and others developed the reformatory system, dedicated to the proposition that human beings can be reformed through hard work, education, and training. Parole as a release mechanism was popularized early on.

Summarize Issues Related to Correctional Policy

Competition between advocates of one or the other major systems was eventually decided in the area of profits made through the Auburn system. Rules of conduct were developed for inmates and were reinforced by extensive and frequent punishments, such as flogging, cold plunges, cat-o'-nine tails, straps, starvation, lock-step formation movement, solitary confinement, and required silence.

Summarize Sentencing Goals and Primary Punishment Philosophies

Sentencing goals changed rapidly. In the nineteenth century, prisons developed new sentencing goals. These included the punishment of offenders, getting right with God, the use of education and training to return offenders to the free world as constructive citizens, the focus on rehabilitation, and, finally, the proposition that inmates were sick and needed healing. Punishment as the primary goal of imprisonment began to rapidly change to allow rehabilitation and reform, educational and vocational programming, individual treatment, and religious conversion. In the midst of these mixed goals, the courts shifted from the determiner of the length of punishment and commitment to the initiator of reformation. In one sense, inmate release eligibility shifted from the judiciary to the executive branch of government. Contemporary practices are being revised, and legislatures are beginning to return power to the judiciary, although there is an ongoing effort to impose the legislature as the major agency for the correcting of offenders. This is more clearly seen in Chapter 3, which deals with shifts in correctional ideology.

Compare and Contrast the Pennsylvania and Auburn Systems

The Pennsylvania system provided large cells with room for production of inmate-made goods and emphasized silence, isolation, and individual work. Inmates never knew or communicated with their counterparts in the Pennsylvania system.

The Auburn system consisted of small cells in large cell blocks. Inmates worked in tandem under silence in an assembly-line basis. The intention of the Auburn system was to generate as much income as possible from the prisons, work in silence in designated work areas, and control inmates through corporal punishment and pain. The Auburn system was favored over the Pennsylvania system due primarily to profits generated for states.

Explain Why the Auburn System Became the Dominant Prison Design

The Auburn system won the competition between the Pennsylvania and Auburn models because there was less mental illness, greater profits, and cheaper per-cell construction costs in the Auburn design and operations. It was widely adopted in the nation but seldom copied in European prison design.

Key Words

Pennsylvania system, 28
outside cell, 28
Eastern Penitentiary, 28
inside cell, 29
Auburn system, 29
cell block, 30
congregate system, 30
penitentiary system, 31
disciplinarian, 31
silence, 31
lockstep formation, 31
prison stripes, 31
treadmill, 32
solitary confinement, 32
indeterminate sentence, 33
Irish system, 34
ticket-of-leave, 35
conditional liberty, 35
reformatory, 35
Zebulon Brockway, 35
lease system, 37
industrial prison, 37
Hawes–Cooper Act, 38
Ashurst–Sumners Act, 38
Sanford Bates, 39
Alcatraz, 39
lock psychosis, 39
convict bogey, 39
ombudsman, 43
War on Drugs, 43

Review Questions

1. What effect did the Industrial Revolution have on prisons and prison discipline?
2. Which of the two early nineteenth-century prison systems won out in America? Why?
3. What were the major differences between prisons and reformatories?
4. Why have so many riots occurred in prisons?
5. How were American prison industries reduced in correctional importance?
6. Why have the number of prison inmates jumped so precipitously?
7. Why are Alexander Maconochie and Sanford Bates important in corrections?

Application Case Studies

1. You have been appointed a member of governor's task force on corrections, and your charge is to draft a plan for the governor to reduce prison expenses. What would you want to do?
2. You are a correctional officer in a prison that does not have enough officers to staff all critically necessary posts. You work 10-hour shifts, and the deputy warden asks you to serve another 10 hours as a "holdover" officer. What do you think you would do?
3. You are a student in an introduction to corrections course. The final examination question, delivered in an envelope, asks for you to draft a five-point plan to make prisons safer. What five points would you select? (Alert: Not all students got the same question that you did.)

Endnotes

1. The Philadelphia Society for the Alleviation of the Miseries of Public Prisons was originally formed by a group of concerned citizens in 1787. Because of their continued efforts, the law of 1790 was passed, and the Walnut Street Jail was remodeled to accommodate felons in solitary confinement. The society is now the Pennsylvania Prison Society, 245 N. Broad Street, Suite 300, Philadelphia, PA 19107-1518; 215-564-6005. Retrieved at http://www.prisonsociety.org.
2. Outside cells were each about six feet wide, eight feet deep, and nine feet high, with a central corridor extending the length of the building in between. Some of them had individual yards added on the outside, with high walls between them.
3. That system, in modified form, is used to this day in Belgium, France, and West Germany. Additional international correctional material can be found under "Foreign Coverage" in each issue of *American Jails* and in the *International Journal of Comparative and Applied Criminal Justice.* See also Elmer Johnson, "Rule Violation of Japanese Inmates," *International Journal of Comparative and Applied Criminal Justice* 22:1 (1998): 17–30.
4. Inside cells are built back-to-back in tiers within a hollow building. Doors open onto galleries or runs that are 8 to 10 feet from the outside wall; cells are small and intended only for sleeping. The interior cell block has become characteristic of American prisons.
5. The argument continues. See John Roberts, *Reform and Retribution: An Illustrated History of American Prisons* (Lanham, MD: American Correctional Association, 1997); Norman Johnston, "The World's Most Influential Prison: Success or Failure?," *The Prison Journal* 84:4(S) (2004): 20S–40S; and Deval Patrick (2013). "Criminal Justice Reform,," http://www.mass.gov/bb/h1/fy13h1/exec_13/hbudbrief8.htm.
6. Walter C. Reckless, *The Crime Problem,* 4th ed. (New York: Appleton-Century-Crofts, 1969), p. 548.
7. Harry Elmer Barnes, *The Story of Punishment,* 2nd ed. (Montclair, NJ: Patterson Smith, 1972), p. 136.
8. Robert G. Caldwell, *Criminology,* 2nd ed. (New York: Ronald Press, 1965), p. 506. But see Corrections and Criminal Justice Coalition, "California Prison Industries Worth in Question," http://www.prisontalk.com/forums/archive/index.php/t-96235.html.
9. Barnes, *The Story of Punishment,* p. 140. See also "The Auburn and Pennsylvania Systems of Corrections: A Controversy, " http://2bpositive.expertscolumn.com/article/auburn-pennsylvania-system-corrections-controversy.
10. G. de Beaumont and A. de Tocqueville, *On the Penitentiary System in the United States and Its Application in France* (Philadelphia: Francis Lieber, 1833). See also Marc Mauer, "The Use of Incarceration as a Crime Control Strategy," http://www.sentencingproject.org/doc/publications/OSF-SA_Annual_Report_2006–7%209.pdf (accessed September 3, 2008). See also Ian Urbina (2013), "Officials to Review Immigrants in Solitary Confinement, " http://www.nytimes.com/2013/03/27/us/immigrants-solitary-confinement-to-be-reviewed.html?_r=0.
11. Robert Waite, "From Penitentiary to Reformatory: The Road to Prison Reform," in Louis Knafler (ed.), *Criminal Justice History: An International Annual,* vol. 12 (Westport, CT: Greenwood Press, 1993), pp. 85–106. See also Bob Reece, *The Origins of Irish Convict Transportation to New South Wales* (New York: Palgrave, 2001). A brief biography can be found at ACT Corrective Services, "Biography of Alexander Maconochie," http://www.cs.act.gov.au/amc/home/ambiography.
12. Flat sentence refers to a specific period of time (for example, 5 years or 10 years) in confinement for an offense, with no time off for any reason.
13. Harry Elmer Barnes and Negley K. Teeters, *New Horizons in Criminology,* 3rd ed. (Englewood Cliffs, NJ: Prentice Hall, 1959), p. 419. See also Gilbert Geis, "Negley K. Teeters (1896–1971)," *The Prison Journal* 84:4S (2004): 5S–19S.
14. An indeterminate sentence usually has broad beginning and end figures (three to five years, one to ten years, and so on), instead of a certain fixed period. Prisoners are allowed to earn their freedom by means of good conduct. For the Irish experience, see Burke Carroll, *Colonial Discipline: The Making of the Irish Convict System* (Dublin: Four Courts Press, 2001).
15. Progressive penologists of the era met in Cincinnati, Ohio, on October 12, 1870, to plan the ideal prison system. Two earlier attempts to gather had failed, but this meeting of the American Prison Congress developed into the National Prison Association, later the American Correctional Association, 406 N. Washington Street, Suite 200, Alexandria, VA 22314.
16. Barnes and Teeters, *New Horizons in Criminology,* p. 426.
17. Georgia, Florida, Mississippi, Louisiana, and Arkansas, in particular, followed this procedure. See Matthew Mancini, *One Dies, Get Another: Convict Leasing in the American South, 1866–1928* (Columbia: University of South Carolina Press, 1996).
18. Harry E. Allen and Julie C. Abril, "The New Chain Gang: Corrections in the Next Century," *American Journal of Criminal Justice* 22:1 (1997): 1–12. See also Timothy Dodge, "State Convict Road Gangs in

Alabama," *The Alabama Review* 53:4 (2000): 243–270, and *Encyclopedia of Alabama, Convict-Lease Systems,* http://www.encyclopediaofalabama.org/face/Article.jsp?id=h-1346.

19. Tom Murton and Joe Hyams, *Accomplices to the Crime: The Arkansas Prison Scandal* (New York: Grove Press, 1967).
20. Margaret Calahan, *Historical Corrections Statistics in the United States: 1850–1984* (Washington, DC: U.S. Department of Justice, 1986), p. 36.
21. Wayne Morse, *The Attorney General's Survey of Release Procedures* (Washington, DC: U.S. Government Printing Office, 1940).
22. Under the piece-price system, a variation of the contract system, the contractor supplied the raw material and paid a price for each delivered finished product. Thailand currently uses this system.
23. In the state-account or public-account system, all employment and activity are under the direction of the state, and products are sold on the open market. The prisoner receives a very small wage, and the profit goes to the state. Usually binder twine, rope, and hemp sacks were produced this way; it provided a lot of work for prisoners but little training. See American Correctional Association, *A Study of Prison Industry: History, Components, and Goals* (Washington, DC: U.S. Department of Justice, 1986), and Queensland Criminal Justice Consortium (QCJC), *Queensland Prison Industries 9* (Brisbane: QCJC, 2000).
24. See Mike Rolland, *Descent into Madness: An Inmate's Experience of the New Mexico State Prison Riot* (Cincinnati, OH: Anderson, 1997). See also Alyssa Newcomb (2013), "80 Inmates Moved after Arizona Prison Riot," http://abcnews.go.com/blogs/headlines/2013/03/80-inmates-moved-after-arizona-prison-riot/.
25. As cited in Barnes and Teeters, *New Horizons in Criminology,* p. 385.
26. Jennifer Harry, "Several Injured in California Prison Riot," *Corrections Today* 63:7 (2001): 12; Deborah Yetter and Mark Pitsch, "Prison Riot Followed Increase in Inmates," http://www.prisonpolicy.org/news/courier09172004.html.
27. http://www.nytimes.com/2004/12/27/opinion/27mon3.html (accessed January 12, 2005); James Inciardi, "The Irrational Policy of American Drug Policy," *Ohio State Journal of Criminal Law* 1:1 (2003): 273–288; Joan Petersilia and Jessica Snyder, "Looking Past the Hype: 10 Questions Everyone Should Know about California's Prison Realignment," *California Justice Politics Policy* (2013): 5(2): 266–306.
28. Irving Goffman, "On the Characteristics of Total Institutions: Staff–Inmate Relations," in D. R. Cressey (ed.), *The Prison* (New York: Holt, Rinehart & Winston, 1966), pp. 16–22. This concept refers to the sum of conditions created by a large number of people living around the clock within a close space, with tightly scheduled sequences of activity coordinated by a central authority.
29. Michael Kelley (2013), "America's 11 Most Powerful Prison Gangs," http://www.businessinsider.com/most-dangerous-prison-gangs-in-the-us-2013-4. See also Lauren McGaughy (2013), "Death Row Inmates Sue Angola Prison over 'Extreme Temperatures,'" http://www.nola.com/crime/index.ssf/2013/06/death_row_inmates_sue_angola_p.html.
30. Ibid. See also John Conrad, "From Barbarism toward Decency: Alabama's Long Road to Prison Reform," *Journal of Research in Crime and Delinquency* 26 (1989): 307–328, and Barbara Belot and J. Marquart, "The Political Community Model and Prisoner Litigation," *Prison Journal* 78:3 (1998): 299–329.
31. *New York Times,* July 9, 1966, p. 9. See also John Rudolph (2013), "Georgia Prisons 'Out of Control,' Rights Group Says, as FBI Brutality Probe Deepens," http://www.huffingtonpost.com/2012/08/21/georgia-prisons-guard-brutality-killings_n_1820145.html.
32. Phillip Kassel, "The Gang Crackdown in Massachusetts Prisons," *New England Journal on Criminal and Civil Confinement* 24:1 (1998): 37–63. See also Kalpana Patel and Alex Lord, "Ethnic Minority Sex Offenders' Experiences of Treatment," *Journal of Sexual Aggression* 7:1 (2001): 40–50.
33. Reginald Wilkinson and Tessa Unwin, "Intolerance in Prison," *Corrections Today* 61:3 (1999): 98–100.
34. Ibid.
35. John Hagan and Juleigh Coleman, "Returning Captives of the American War on Drugs," *Crime and Delinquency* 47:3 (2001): 352–367; Ronald Weitzer and Charis Kubrin, "Breaking News," *Justice Quarterly* 21:3 (2004): 497–520.

Bettmann/Corbis

Objectives

- Summarize the definition, mission, and role of corrections.
- Summarize sentencing goals and primary punishment philosophies.
- Explain how public opinion about crime affects crime control policy.
- Summarize issues related to correctional policy.
- Describe and illustrate contemporary corrections in the nation.

chapter 3
Correctional Ideologies: *The Pendulum Swings*

Outline

Conflicting Correctional Ideologies

The Punishment Ideology

- Retribution
- Deterrence
- Incapacitation
- The Effect of Punishment

The Rehabilitation Ideology

The Prevention Ideology

The Pendulum Swings

Restorative Justice

- Balanced and Restorative Justice Philosophy
- The Balanced Approach and Its Application

Contemporary Corrections

"The massive prison construction represents a commitment by our nation to plan for social failure by spending billions of dollars to lock up hundreds of thousands of people while at the same time cutting billions of dollars from programs that would provide opportunity to young Americans."

–Steven Donziger, *The Real War on Crime*

Overview

So far we have looked at the history and early development of corrections, outlining the major construction of prisons and facilities that reflected the thoughts of those years. An underlying policy question explored in the first two chapters of the textbook concerned the role of criminal law and offenders: Who are offenders, and what shall we do with them? The answers identified thus far include the following: They are (1) evil and must be punished, (2) out of touch with God and need to repent, (3) poorly educated and ill trained to function in modern society, and (4) sick and in need of being cured—the punishment, reform, education, and medical models for corrections, respectively. In this chapter, we explore the philosophical underpinnings on which these models were built and explain the rationales that underlie current correctional developments. We need to understand why the nation has entered into an age of massive change in attitudes and prison construction, what goals are being sought, and what the implications of the new programs and facilities might be. We begin with an understanding of what we refer to as ideologies.

CONFLICTING CORRECTIONAL IDEOLOGIES

key term

Ideology
Systematic body of ideas and practices.

key term

Correctional ideology
Systematic body of ideas and practices that pertain to the processing of offenders.

To understand the current state of corrections, its problems and issues, and a possible future, we turn first to a discussion of ideologies. An **ideology**, according to *Webster's*, is "a systematic body of concepts, especially about human life or culture." A **correctional ideology,** then, refers to a body of ideas and practices that pertain to the processing of offenders as determined by the law. Obviously, the actions of various correctional authorities and/or organizational units are shaped in large part by the particular ideologies to which they subscribe or that are the will of the citizens they serve and protect. In the history of treatment and punishment of offenders, the ideologies of different societies have supplied both the basis and the rationalization for the broad range of efforts—draconian to semi-humane—aimed at getting criminals off the streets. When a given effort becomes a clear failure, the ideology eventually will shift to justify a different approach.

In modern times, a strong belief in the efficacy of one correctional ideology or another has sometimes led policymakers to commit vast sums of public treasure to an unproved approach or theory, thus shackling themselves to a possibly worthless plan for an indefinite period. By the same token, if the correctional administrator's ideology happens to conflict with the approach favored by the society he or she serves, the administrator may try to resolve the conflict in one of two ways: by working out a compromise to make it work better or by trying to sabotage the system to ensure its failure. If the superintendent of a juvenile institution believes society is trying to liberalize rules so rapidly that it threatens personal security, he or she may encourage the use of segregation or restraints by the correctional officers. In corrections, the backgrounds and ideologies of the keepers and the kept often diverge sharply, so it becomes difficult to convince both groups they can work toward a mutual goal.

key term

Punishment ideology
Painful sanction applied to the offender, who is seen as an enemy of society.

key term

Rehabilitation ideology
Crime prevention through treatment of offenders and inmates to rehabilitate such offenders.

key term

Prevention ideology
Avoidance or reduction of criminal behavior using methods and programs that contribute to crime prevention.

Most of the ideologies applied to correctional actions over the years fall into one of three categories: **punishment**, **rehabilitation**, or **prevention**. They often overlap, of course—punishment and rehabilitation are usually justified as means to prevention rather than as ends in themselves—but the division is useful for the purpose of this analysis.

THE PUNISHMENT IDEOLOGY

The idea that punishment can result in the offense being "paid" for and that its effect can be expanded from the specific criminal to the general public has been around from the earliest times. Most of the basic reasons for punishment can be placed in three general categories: retribution, deterrence, and incapacitation.

Retribution

key term

Retribution
Getting even with the offender who has violated the rights of others and deserves to be punished.

Since the first system of laws was developed, punishment has been officially sanctioned as a means of regulating criminal behavior. The punishment ideology holds that the criminal is an enemy of society who deserves severe punishment, including banishment or death, for willfully breaking its rules.[1] This philosophy has its roots in a societal need for retribution. As noted in Chapter 1, punishment once was administered in the form of immediate and personal retribution by either the victim or the victim's family. Society's authorization of punishment can be traced to that individual need for retaliation and vengeance. Many theories try to explain the reason for the transfer of the vengeance motive from the individual to the state.

Philosophically, **retribution** generally means getting even with the perpetrator. The term *social revenge* suggests that individuals cannot exact punishment but that the state

correctional **practice 3.1**

Contrasting Ideologies

A major way of understanding ideologies and their effects on handling offenders, prison architecture, roles of correctional officers and inmates, and inmate control is to briefly investigate an alternative prison system: the Swedish prison system.

Sweden operates under a just deserts model. Offenders are evaluated by the perceived gravity of the offense, and that gravity is the major factor in the decision of the ideal sanction to impose for the instant crime. In the United States, serious offenses by bad or evil criminals usually (but not always) lead to the use of time as the punishment unit (sentences of 5 to 10 years, a flat 20 years, incarceration for life and a day, or even the rare death penalty for heinous crimes). This approach heavily contributes to the overcrowding of prisons and the largest number of incarcerated offenders in the world. A brief summary of this approach is "Lock them up and throw away the keys," a punitive ideology.

Such is not the case in Sweden. There they do not have a heavy reliance on incarceration as a sanction for crime. In the past two decades, the Swedish Penal Code has been revamped to reduce prison sentences and to impose sentencing alternatives that do not rely on depriving the offender of liberty. The preferred methods of punishment fall into the categories of use of fines, probation, community service, *civil commitment* (court-defined probation with mandatory treatment), suspended sentences, and other programs we collectively call community corrections. The Swedes do have high-security institutions, especially for murder and high treason, but most prisoners are found in the numerous open facilities close to their homes and families. Swedes argue that the primary purpose of a prison sentence is to promote the offender's adjustment to the community as well as to counteract the negative impacts of incarceration. The Prison Treatment Act of 1974 (PTA) demands that the inmate be treated for his or her human dignity. If services and programs, subsidies and employment, and individual freedoms are available to free citizens, they must be made available to offenders on the same par.

The PTA has four basic principles: (1) use of incarceration as a *last resort* since imprisonment knowingly has observable negative impacts; (2) *normalization*, meaning that any rules governing medical and social care and all forms of public services shall apply to all inmates just as they apply to free citizens; (3) the *rule of vicinity*, or placing the inmate in a facility as close as possible to his or her hometown; and (4) *cooperation*, basically meaning that all parts of the correctional system shall work together in both individual cases and the entire group of offenders. Finally, a humane attitude, good care, and positive influence of offenders characterize the systems operations. The necessary degree of security must be maintained as well as respect for the inmate's integrity and rules of due process.

Prisoner rights reflect correctional ideology differences between the Swedish and American examples. In general, the prison policy of Sweden emphasizes a very progressive approach, particularly regarding visits and furloughs. Regular contact with the outside world is viewed as an important element of prisoner rights. Visits may take place unattended by prison authorities, although both the visitor will be searched on entry to and the inmate on exit from the visiting areas. If there is any question about a security threat, both the police and correctional officers may perform background checks. Security is a required element of all prisons.

There are facilities for conjugal visiting if inmates have a partner, and children may be a part of the visit. Nongovernmental organization representatives are allowed to visit; inmates' lawyers may visit, but no officer may listen to their discussions. Inmates have the right to send and receive letters and other mail; the inmate may be present if incoming mail is opened for possible contraband, drugs, or escape plans. All prisoners are allowed telephone privileges, but for security reasons, a prison officer may listen to any calls after notifying the offender of that fact. Furloughs (short-term leave for about three days) are possible, and those privileges are seldom abused.

Almost every institution has study facilities, including study at a university through distance learning. All inmates are required to participate in program activities: education, specialized treatment programs, day releases for education or work purposes, conventional work, Internet service, and vocational training. Industrial prison work is managed by a special unit.

All prisoners have a right to leisure activities of almost any sort, including darts, table tennis, and billiards; workout opportunities; and outside and intramural games. Libraries are available, and prisoners may have magazines, newspapers, and radio and television access. Medical treatment is routine, but if the inmate requires hospitalization, he or she is transferred to an outside hospital for as long as deemed necessary; medical service is free.

Two more points: First, there is an inmate council elected by other inmates, and the council represents inmate complaints if necessary. Inmates may also appeal to the external ombudsman. Second, many short-term (maximum sentence of six months or less) inmates may request to be transferred to house arrest with electronic monitoring (known in Sweden as "tagging"). Those offenders are thus monitored 24 hours a day but allowed to leave their residence only with prior permission. Inmates are viewed quite differently, and treatment is liberally individualized. Does this sound like a typical American prison?

SOURCES: Peter Lindstrom and Eric Leijonram, "The Swedish Prison System," at http:// www.internationalpenalandpenitentiaryfoundation.org/Site/documents/Stavern/29_ReportSweden. Accessed July 18, 2013. Or if the link is dead, type into your search box: "The Swedish prison system" with "Since the end of the 1980's."

For the Danish prison system, see Dylan Tull, "Danish Prison System Shows Different Understanding of Crime," at http://whitmanpioneer.com/news/2013/03/07/danish-open-prison-system-shows-different-understanding-of-crime/. Accessed July 18, 2013.

The Norwegian prison system can be found at Chih-huei Wendy Wang, "A Liberal Prison System," at http://www.youtube.com/watch?v=Uj3SMiDvjdg. Accessed July 19, 2013.

will do so in their name. Retribution assumes that the offenders willfully chose to commit the evil acts, are responsible for their own behavior, are likely to commit similar acts again, and should receive the punishment they richly deserve. The "just deserts" movement in sentencing reflects the retribution philosophy. For many, it provides a justifiable rationale for support of the death penalty.

Many students of corrections (and penologists) have considerable difficulty with the concept of retribution because it requires the state to make an offender suffer for the sake of suffering. To many, that idea runs counter to the Eighth Amendment's prohibition against cruel and unusual punishment. One respected criminologist has proposed that correctional punishments include electroshock in lieu of incarceration because it can be calibrated, leaves less long-term emotional damage, is cheaper to administer, and would allow the victim the opportunity to witness the retribution. Is it possible that televising the electroshock sessions might act as a deterrent to other potential malefactors?[2]

Philosophers have debated the reasons for this transfer to government of the victim's desire to strike back at the offender. Heinrich Oppenheimer lists several theories in *The Rationale of Punishment* (1913). Three of them are as follows:

1. In the *theological* view, retaliation fulfills a religious mission to punish the criminal.
2. In the *aesthetic* view, punishment resolves the social discord created by the offense and reestablishes a sense of harmony through requital.
3. In the *expiatory* view, guilt must be washed away through suffering. Ledger Wood advances a fourth explanation, a *utilitarian theory.* Punishment is considered to be a means of achieving beneficial and social consequences through application of a specific form and degree of punishment deemed most appropriate to the particular offender after careful individualized study of the offender.[3]

key term

Deterrent effect
The extent of crime control by incapacitation, threat of punishment, or announced potential criminal sanction.

key term

General deterrence
Preventing potential criminal behavior by making examples of offenders openly; the message here would be "See what will happen to you if you commit crime."

key term

Specific deterrence
Punishing individual offenders to prevent their further criminal behavior.

key term

Stigma of conviction
Effect of labeling, interference with ordinary social functioning, and resulting diminishment of offender.

key term

Incapacitation
Depriving offenders of the ability to commit additional crime, usually through imprisonment.

Deterrence

Yet another reason for punishment of criminals is the belief that such actions have a **deterrent effect**, *specifically* on the offender or *generally* on others who might consider a similar act.[4] With **general deterrence**, it is believed that a sanction deters potential offenders by inflicting suffering on actual ones. For example, when we see the "perp" walk on television, it is hoped that potential criminals will not commit a similar crime in fear of being caught and punished. **Specific deterrence** is when a sanction is imposed on an actual offender in the belief that it will stop that individual from committing crimes in the future. It is believed that in order for punishment to serve as a deterrent, it must be swift, visible to others, closely linked to the forbidden action so that it discourages future recurrences of that crime, certain, and categorical (all persons committing a certain crime will receive the same punishment).[5] Furthermore, the state and its representatives must uphold superior values and conforming behavior to serve as irreproachable examples of good citizenship. Finally, after punishment, offenders must be allowed to resume their prior positions in society without stigma or disability.

Unfortunately, as we know, punishment may continue long after a sentence has been served. For example, even after an offender has successfully completed a punishment-oriented correctional process, the **stigma of conviction** and imprisonment is often carried for the rest of the ex-offender's life.[6] Finding it almost impossible to get a job because of a criminal past, the ex-offender may decide, "If I'm going to have the name, I might as well play the game." At that point, neither the punishment nor the stigma is an effective deterrent, and the offender is likely to return to crime.[7]

Incapacitation

A third reason to punish the offender derives from the concept of **incapacitation**. This theory holds that the best way to limit offenders' ability to break the law is to incapacitate

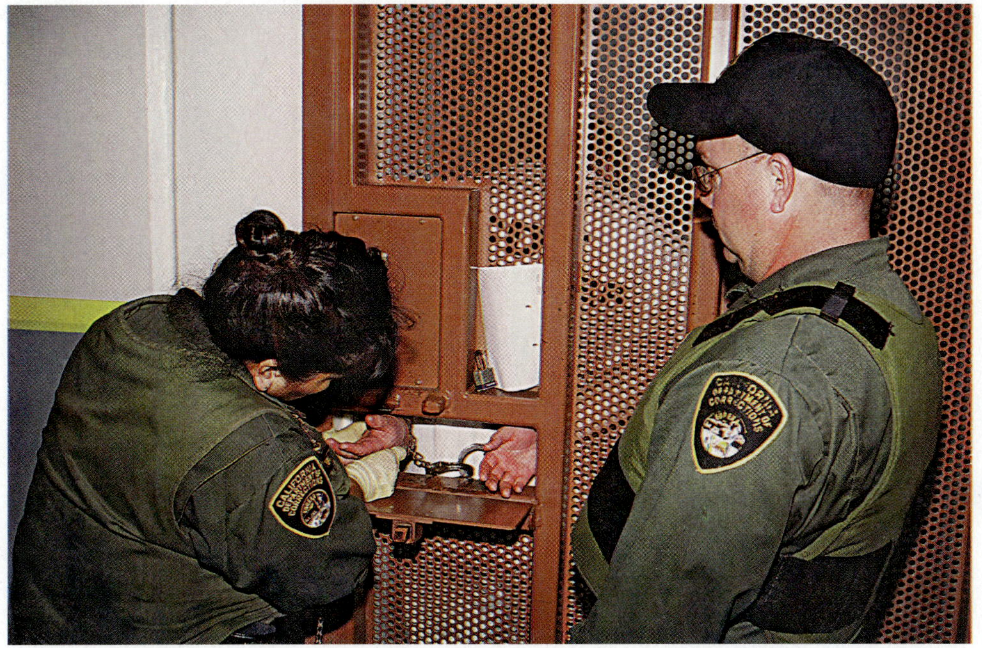

photo 3.1

Guards at the Secure Housing Unit of Pelican Bay State Prison in Crescent City, California, put handcuffs on an inmate through a small hole in the door. Such cells are typically used to house violent gang members who are allowed to leave the cell only for 90 minutes of solo exercise a day.
Photo by Adam Tanner/Corbis.

them, usually by locking them up for long periods of time. The solution, therefore, is to temporarily isolate, remove, or cripple such persons in some way. This approach is sometimes referred to as the **theory of disablement**, a euphemism for death, banishment, or mutilation. Ideally, the disablement should relate to the crime (for example, in some countries castration has been used to punish sex criminals). Incapacitation usually means imprisonment, but it can also include techniques such as house arrest and electronic monitoring. One variation of the isolation rationale of incapacitation is the **selective incapacitation** movement. Greenwood argued that prison overcrowding and the scarcity of beds in prisons require a policy of sending only repetitive or violent offenders to prison; he especially recommended prison for those who commit armed robbery.[8] He believed selective incapacitation[9] would thus result in better uses of correctional resources and more effective crime prevention.[10]

key term

Theory of disablement
Preventing offenders from commission of more crime through isolation, death, banishment, or mutilation.

key term

Selective incapacitation
Incapacitating high-risk offenders believed to pose substantial probability of additional crime, usually through imprisonment.

key term

Recidivism
Continued criminal activity following initial law-violating behavior.

Selective Incapacitation

This doctrine of isolating the offender, or causing "social disablement," proposes adopting a policy of incarcerating those whose criminal behavior is so damaging or probable that nothing short of isolation will prevent **recidivism**. This "nothing-else-works" approach would require correctly identifying those offenders who would be eligible for longer-term imprisonment and diverting others into correctional alternatives. Thus, we would be able to make maximum effective use of prison cells, a scarce resource, to protect society from the depredations of such dangerous and repetitive offenders.

Current correctional technology, however, does not permit us to correctly identify those who require incapacitation. Rather, the evidence is that we would probably incarcerate numerous noneligibles (a "false-positive" problem) and release to lesser confinement many of those eligible (a "false-negative" problem). Whatever benefits might accrue to this sentencing doctrine have thus far eluded corrections. The difficulty is further spotlighted in the *Report to the Nation on Crime and Justice:*

> Career criminals, though few in number, account for most crime. Even though chronic repeat offenders (those with five or more arrests by age 18) make up a relatively small proportion of all offenders, they commit a very high proportion of all crimes. The evidence includes data for juveniles and adults, males and females, and for urban and rural areas.

In Wolfgang's Philadelphia study, chronic offenders accounted for 23 percent of all male offenders in the study, but they had committed 61% of all the crimes. Of all crimes by all members of the group studied, chronic offenders committed:

- *61% of all homicides*
- *76% of all rapes*
- *73% of all robberies*
- *65% of all aggravated assaults.*[11]

The Effect of Punishment

It is recognized that some punishment can be effective when applied in the right amounts and at the right time, and punishment may, in some cases, be a necessary predecessor to rehabilitation. Few serious offenders readily seek or are amenable to rehabilitation without some form of coercion or threat. When the ideology of punishment is applied in a correctional institution, however, the result is often negative for both the punished and the punisher. Correctional personnel tend to watch for minor rule infringements or nonconformism (horseplay, abusive language, skipping classes, etc.) so the punishment can be administered, and they overlook any positive actions by offenders.[12] Often the rules that are prepared for a punishment-oriented environment surround the offender with a wall of "do nots," leaving almost no leeway to "do" anything.

As evidenced by a high crime rate, punishment by the law does not seem to create much respect for the law, even in jurisdictions where punishment may actually be swift, harsh, and certain. Overuse of punishment in a society that claims to be open and free creates a situation in which the punished can characterize their punishers as persecutors of the poor and helpless. The accusation turns attention away from the crimes that put them there and gives rise to the concept of the "political prisoner." Thus, minority-group members are likely to blame their incarcerations on repression by the rich, on political persecution, or on attempted genocide. Punishments are then made more and more severe in a desperate but hopeless effort to compensate for their ineffectiveness. Often such punishments motivate offenders to become more sophisticated criminals (rather than noncriminals) in the belief (no doubt valid) that the more skilled one is at a trade, the less likely one is to be caught. The offenders become hardened to the punishment, and the administrators learn to dole it out automatically as their only means of control.[13] Both parties are degraded in the process.

photo 3.2

A prisoner uses a small mirror to see outside his cell at the Buckingham Correctional Institution, a maximum-security prison.
Shepard Sherbell/Corbis.

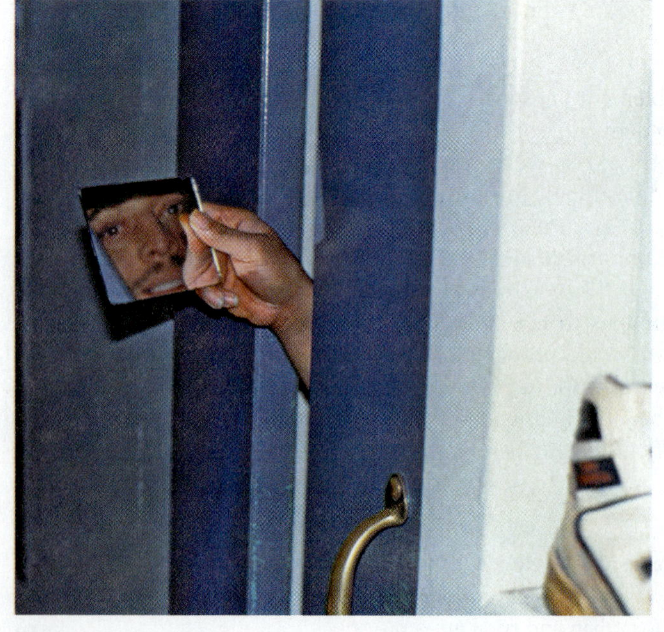

Both history and science refute the argument that the use of punishment can halt crime. For example, those people for whom punishment is least effective are the following:

1. Psychopathic risk takers
2. Those under the influence of drugs or alcohol
3. Those with a history of being punished

Unfortunately, these are the attributes of an offender population. Punishment often does not work with those whom we need it to work most with: criminals.[14]

It must be understood that the significance of punishment as an ideology in correctional practice lies in the viewpoint of the punished offenders. If they see the punishment as an unjust imposition of the will and power of the establishment and are reinforced in that belief by their peers (other offenders), their punishment will only encourage them to maintain negative attitudes and behavior patterns. By contrast, if offenders believe their punishment is both deserved and just and their social group agrees, the punishment may have a startlingly different and more positive result. If a criminal is justly treated, that offender may abandon crime, but excessive punishment may push the offender over the edge and destroy every chance of reform. The punished and stigmatized offenders turn to those who are most like them for support and values. If they are embittered by the punishment they have received, they are likely to reject the very values the punishment was intended to reinforce.[15]

James Austin and Aaron McVey[16] examined the effects of recent political policies designed to increase punishment by increasing the probability of an offender's being arrested, convicted, and imprisoned and serving longer sentences. We extend their predictions by noting that, if current punishment trends continue, the nation will be characterized as follows:

- Have [1.3] million prison inmates by 2016.
- Have 200,000 elderly prisoners ("geriatric inmates") in prison by 2020.
- Remain number one in the world in rate of incarceration per 100,000 residents.
- Have almost 10 million persons under correctional supervision.

Finally, the change in attitude has led to a painful search for alternatives to probation (regarded as too little punishment) and imprisonment (regarded as too expensive a form of punishment). The emerging alternatives—known as intermediate sanctions—promise relief from the pressures of prison overcrowding. In addition, the new wave of punitiveness has contributed to selective incapacitation, an important and effective tool for correctional administrators but only if it is designed to suit an individual offender and an individual situation (see Chapter 6). General and uniform punishment is still the rule rather than the exception, however, and the movement toward a **rehabilitation model** is slow.

key term

Rehabilitation model
Literally means using treatment to restore an offender to levels of social functioning not yet attained; seeks a change in behavior produced by providing treatment and services.

THE REHABILITATION IDEOLOGY

A major trend in corrections is to approach the offender much as one would the mentally ill, the neglected, or the underprivileged. This more humane ideology, reflected in the rehabilitation model, seeks change in behavior of the offender produced by treatment and services. With the rehabilitation ideology, the offender chooses to refrain from new crimes rather than being unable to. Although some refer to the criminal as "sick," the rehabilitation ideology is not analogous to a medical approach. The closest comparison with physical illness lies in the need for offenders to recognize the danger and undesirability of their criminal behavior and then to make significant efforts to rid themselves of that behavior. The rehabilitation model does not "remove" criminal behavior as one might remove an infected limb; rather, the "patient" (inmate) is made to see the rewards of positive behavior and is encouraged and equipped to adopt it as a model.

Treatment, of course, begins with a diagnosis of an offender's needs, the design of a program plan to address that person's needs, the application of the intended program with periodic monitoring, and updating and modification of the plan to maximize effectiveness. Treatment is designed to correct behavior instead of some underlying defect or disease.

The rehabilitation ideology does not encourage inmates to be coddled and allowed to do as they please within the institution. It is a fairly common belief among many elements of the criminal justice system that any program that is not punitive or restrictive is being "soft" or akin to "running a country club." In fact, some form of rehabilitation can be applied in even the most restrictive and security-oriented institutions. The main difference between the rehabilitation and punishment ideologies is that in the former, offenders are assigned to the institution for a correctional program intended to prepare them for readjustment to or reintegration into the community, not just for punishment and confinement. There is room for punishment and security in the rehabilitation approach but little room for rehabilitation in the punitive approach. The more humane treatment methods are intended to be used in conjunction with the employment of authority in a constructive and positive manner, but inmates must be allowed to try, even if they fail. Authoritarian procedures, used alone, only give the offender more ammunition to support a self-image as an oppressed and impotent pawn of the power structure.

The student should recall that the field of corrections, especially in its early history in America, underwent significant change as innovators again sought the answers to the question mentioned earlier: "Who are the offenders, and what should we do with them?" The rehabilitation ideology contains four separate answers to the question, commonly referred to as treatment doctrines.

The Quaker reform movement, arising in 1790, held that offenders were out of touch with God. The corresponding treatment approach was isolation. Prisoners were supplied with a Bible for reading and doing penitence. The doctrine for the Quakers was to help offenders find their way back to God; it was believed that once God was found, crime would cease. The Quakers are a religious group that has a strong pacifist and nonviolent ideology as part of their faith. Probably the best-known Quaker in America was William Penn, after whom Pennsylvania was named.

The belief that criminals have lost their way and need to find "religion" is still strongly believed by many. This movement is still active today through organizations such as Prison Fellowship Ministries and other religious orders that attempt to minister to inmates.

The **reformatory movement** solutions, after 1890, provided somewhat different answers. Offenders were seen as disadvantaged, "unfortunate" persons whose education, training, and discipline had been inadequate. The **educational doctrine** answer was to provide education at a functional level, emphasis on vocational and occupational skills, and a regime of discipline that was aimed at the internalization of controls to prevent recurrence of criminal behavior when the prisoner was released.

The **medical model** that developed in the late 1920s and early 1930s under the leadership of Sanford Bates and the U.S. Bureau of Prisons saw the answers as lying within the individual. It then became necessary to diagnose the individual problem, develop a treatment program that might remedy it, and then apply treatment. When the "patient" was found to be well, he or she would be released to a program of aftercare in the community under the supervision of therapeutic parole officers who would continue casework therapy until the offender was "rehabilitated." The medical model offered hope of rehabilitation. It was the responsibility of corrections to "make the ill well." The "ill" would thus be passive recipients of beneficent therapy like patients in a hospital.

Underlying the medical model is the **indeterminate sentence** and its assumptions of rehabilitation and early release if the offender were treated and reformed. The minimum and maximum periods (such as a one- to five-year sentence) reflect the inability of the sentencing judge to know exactly when the prisoner would be reformed. While the medical model has been largely abandoned in corrections, it is still very much alive in substance abuse treatment.

The indeterminate sentence is thus a sentence to incarceration pronounced by a judge that sets minimum and maximum periods of confinement for the offender (such as "from one to five years"). The minimum term would establish the earliest release date (adjusted for certain time credits for, as an example, jail time during pretrial detention) or the date of the first parole consideration to determine if the inmate should be released. At the maximum term, the inmate would have to be released.

Before 1975, the federal system and all of the state systems had sentencing codes that were indeterminate, and boards of prison terms and parole, commonly called parole boards, were given broad discretion in determining when an inmate was ready for release under parole supervision. Since 1976, almost two-thirds of the states as well as the federal system have limited parole board discretion or abolished discretionary parole completely. In addition, the percentage of inmates released through parole board discretion declined from 72 percent to less than a projected 31 percent at the beginning of 2016. Twenty-three states now use guidelines to structure their release decisions.

key term

Reformatory movement
Offenders are unfortunate persons whose education, training, and discipline are inadequate; offenders should be sent to an educational penal institution for reform.

key term

Educational doctrine
Correctional approach seeking to provide crime prevention by education, emphasizing vocational and educational skills, and teaching inmates to discipline themselves.

key term

Medical model
Model that sees the causes of crime as lying within the individual and that stresses providing treatment and therapy until the offender is well. Leaders in the medical model were Sanford Bates and the Federal Bureau of Prisons.

key term

Indeterminate sentencing
Judge imposes a minimum and maximum period of incarceration time under the assumption that a parole board will identify the maximum benefit from imprisonment and subsequently release the inmate.

The fourth doctrine emerged in the late 1960s. It is acceptable to use either 1965 or 1969 as the date of origin, but whichever date is used, this form of treatment was a significant trend throughout the 1980s. Known as the **reintegration model**, this form of treatment made differing assumptions about the cause and solutions to crime and the criminal. The community was seen as the basic etiological factor, and the offender was considered to be the product of a local community that excluded, failed to provide for, or discriminated against the offender. Because the basic cause is regarded as community related, proponents thought it best to address the problem by using community resources that correctional agencies would be able to marshal or develop. These would include reducing poverty rates, investing in children, urban revitalization, Head Start programs, and job training. The offender's role requires active participation in the effort to resolve the difficulty; correctional agencies then serve as brokers for services. Ideally, a community management approach is used, wherein several officers can specialize to maximize the delivery of opportunities to the offender, who is eager to reintegrate and become part of the community. The four doctrines require treatment and coexist in the correctional ideology called *treatment*, which we discuss in Chapter 9.

key term

Reintegration model
Doctrine that assumes crimes are caused by the community, with the assumption that community resources should be garnered and provided by local agencies to prevent recidivism.

THE PREVENTION IDEOLOGY

As mentioned, the problem of crime cannot be separated from the individual offender. In a sense, the problem can be temporarily removed from the community whenever the offender is sent off to prison. Almost all offenders are eventually released, however, and the problem returns unless it has been effectively treated while the offender was in the prison. Because of the perceived minimal success of present correctional programs (recidivism rates range from 40 to 70 percent),[17] many communities and governmental agencies are turning to crime prevention as a possible solution. Prevention methods have a dual focus: on the individual and on the environment in which he or she lives.[18] Much crime prevention activity is designed to steer potential delinquents away from a life of trouble. Such programs generally begin at the school level, where truancy and dropping out are often the precursors of criminal activity. Those early programs, for the most part, attempt to identify the first signs of criminal behavior.

As Pogo Possum, the 1950s cartoon character of Walt Kelly, said, "Prediction is difficult, 'specially when it's about the future." Prediction is a complex process, even when it is carefully controlled.[19] Prevention programs in schools today aim to treat problem children by providing specialized classes, alternative schools, vocational education, and counseling.[20] The more progressive among them do not aim to force juveniles out of the picture by expulsion from school, but rather seek to keep youth involved in school. The prevention ideology recognizes that problem children must have supportive help, or they are very likely to use crime as an outlet for unhappiness and insecurity.

Those who advocate the prevention ideology are well aware that total prevention of crime is probably impossible. One of the early sociological giants, **Emile Durkheim** (1853–1917), believed that crime in some form was an inevitable accompaniment to human society and that if serious crime were prevented, authorities would focus their attention on minor offenses.[21] Essentially, the prevention ideology holds that crime may at least be reduced through an attack on the social and emotional problems that encourage a person's criminal inclinations.

profile

Emile Durkheim
Early sociologist who believed that crime in some form was an inevitable accompaniment to society.

The individual's environment is recognized as a crucial focus in the prevention of crime; the prevention ideology emphasizes the need to structure the environment so criminal opportunity is minimized. As an example, it has been said that the greatest crime-prevention device ever invented was the streetlight. The movement toward crime prevention through environmental design has great promise for the future. The object of such an approach is not only to provide barriers to crime (such as window bars, fences, locks, airport

correctional practice 3.2

Cincinnati Initiative to Reduce Violence

The Cincinnati Initiative to Reduce Violence is a multiagency and community collaborative effort initiated in 2007 designed to quickly and dramatically reduce gun violence and associated homicides with sustained reductions over time. The initiative is a focused-deterrence strategy that is modeled after the Boston Gun Project from the mid-1990s. A partnership among multiple law enforcement agencies (local, state, and federal), social service providers, and the community has been established to deliver a clear message to violent street groups: The violence must stop. This message is communicated through a number of different mechanisms, including call-in sessions with probationers and parolees; direct contact through street workers (street advocates), police, probation, and parole officers; community outreach; and media outlets. Law enforcement agencies have gathered intelligence on violent street group networks, and consequences are delivered to the street groups that continue to engage in violence. Those offenders seeking a more productive lifestyle are provided streamlined social services, training, education, and employment opportunities. The community and law enforcement are working as partners and as a result, strengthening their relationship.

electronic search, and security checks)[22] but also to enhance the existing features that tend to discourage crime (for example, more lighting around homes and apartment buildings, more windows in dark hallways, and community projects aimed at getting people to know their neighbors). The conditions that produce a high or low crime rate in a given area are not all physical; however, the environment includes the people, activities, pressures, and ideas to which an individual is exposed every day. Recently, crime prevention has begun targeting specific problems, such as violence reduction and gun courts. One such example can be seen in the Cincinnati Initiative to Reduce Violence (see Correctional Practice 3.2), which attempts to target high-risk offenders with a history of violence. This unique program combines the threat of prosecution (deterrence) with an offer of assistance (rehabilitation). The prevention ideology advocates the maximum use of resources in areas that have special problems, such as poverty and overcrowding—funds should be allocated for crime prevention rather than for prison construction.[23]

key term

Community corrections
A model of corrections based on the assumption that the offender should be reintegrated into the community through existing and potential community services.

In **community corrections**, the prevention ideology is combined with treatment. The emphasis is on the identification and treatment of the problems that have caused past criminal behavior to prevent its recurrence. Eventually, the emphasis may lead to a closer, more interdependent relationship between the agencies now involved in crime prevention and

photo 3.3
One example of a crime prevention program is the Cincinnati Initiative to Reduce Violence, which brings together the police, community, and academics, to develop evidence-based approaches to reducing violent crime.
University of Cincinnati.

those that provide community services. As they presently operate, criminal justice agencies actually tend to create more problems for minor offenders instead of treating the problems that got those people into trouble.[24] If schools, churches, service agencies, and similar organizations could become more involved, before persons become entangled in the criminal justice system, many criminal careers could be prevented before they start. **Diversion** and nonjudicial approaches to offenders are seen as potentially valuable alternatives to a more formal punishment-oriented reaction to the problem of crime. A combination of prevention and treatment ideologies would be the most promising and humane organization of correctional beliefs and practices.

key term

Diversion
Minimizing offender processing through the justice system by imposing treatment, supervision, and referral of offenders to service providers outside of the justice system.

THE PENDULUM SWINGS

From the late 1970s to 1990, high crime rates caused the forces of society to turn again to the punishment ideology.[25] As the populations of the country's jails and prisons have grown to almost unmanageable proportions, administrators and legislatures have become more willing to accept the turn backward in order to have at least some way to cope with the growing and more violent criminal populations and prison gangs. The following chapters discuss the problems faced by harried and chronically underfunded correctional administrators trying to deal with institutions that are so overcrowded that they are bursting at the seams. Budgets are stripped of so-called frills such as treatment and must be used to add beds, food, and custody staff to house and feed inmates while trying to protect society. The trend toward determinate sentences and **"get-tough" laws** at all levels exacerbates the situation. At best, treatment is difficult to carry out in a security institution. At worst, treatment is all but impossible to find. That pessimistic situation formed a trend that began in the 1980s. The correctional "nonsystem" entered the first two decades of the new century in a continuing state of indecision as to what to embrace as its core ideology.[26] The results were clear, however, and the hope for treatment that dominated in the 1960s and 1970s seems lost in the cry for "hard time" for offenders. Poor economic conditions in inner-city blighted areas, the Great Recession, and continued overcrowding exist at levels unprecedented in the short history of corrections in America.

key term

"Get-tough" laws
Belief that offenders should be punished to prevent criminal recidivism; such laws would lengthen the term of incarceration and minimize use of community resources. Two important law programs are using the determinate sentence and compelling the inmate to serve a large percentage of the imposed sentence.

Despite the increased reliance on punishment and the backlash that has so negatively impacted corrections during the past three decades, there appears to be growing support for both rehabilitation and prevention among legislators[27] as well as the general public.[28] Indeed, there is some evidence that the pendulum is again swinging toward a less punitive approach. For example, some states are reexamining the age at which juveniles can be bound over to the adult system, and draconian drug laws are being repealed. Recent figures released by the Bureau of Justice Statistics also reveal that the number of offenders under correctional control declined in 2010–2013. It is too early to determine if this is a trend or a short-term response to the financial crisis that began in 2008. Perhaps that is why the best analogy is of the pendulum and its continuous path as it begins to swing from right to left. It will take major changes in the future for the pendulum of justice to begin a swing back toward the center, but there are signs that this may be happening. State and local jurisdictions are finding that current correctional costs must be reduced in light of insufficient tax incomes. The task ahead for today's students will be both important and difficult as they track the path of the pendulum.

RESTORATIVE JUSTICE

The debate over the future of the criminal justice system has historically been between proponents of a retributive, punitive philosophy and advocates of the traditional individual treatment mission. All of these approaches have failed to satisfy basic needs of individual crime victims, the community, and offenders. A new ideology is now being tried, mostly

key term

Restorative justice
Punishment intended to repair the damages done by the offender's crimes against the victim and the community.

in the juvenile justice system, which seems to have some merit for consideration. The balanced and restorative justice (BARJ) model outlines an alternative philosophy, **restorative justice**,[29] and a new mission, "the balanced approach."

The BARJ model requires criminal justice professionals to devote attention to enabling offenders to make amends to their victims and communities, increasing offender competencies, and presumably protecting the public through processes in which individual victims, the community, and offenders are all active participants.

The BARJ model responds to many issues raised by the victims' movement, including concerns that victims have had little opportunity for input into the resolution of their own cases, rarely feel heard, and often receive no restitution or expression of remorse from the offender. The balanced approach is based on an understanding of crime as an act against the victim and the community, which is an ancient idea common to tribal and religious traditions of many cultures. Practitioners have used techniques consistent with this approach for years; however, they have lacked a coherent philosophical framework that supports restorative practice and provides direction to guide all aspects of juvenile justice practice. The BARJ model provides an overarching vision and guidance for daily decisions.

Criminal justice professionals, including probation and parole officers, prosecutors, judges, case managers, and victim advocates, recognize the need for justice system reform. People who work on the front lines of the system are faced daily with the frustration of seeing growing numbers of young people and adults involved in criminal behavior. These offenders often leave the system with little hope for real change, and, unfortunately, countless crime victims and community members are left out of the process. That frustration has inspired many of these professionals to work toward changing organizational culture, values, and programs to reflect a more balanced and restorative approach to juvenile justice.[30]

The BARJ model is a vision for the future of corrections and criminal justice that builds on current innovative practices and is based on core values that have been part of most communities for centuries. It provides a framework for systemic reform and offers hope for preserving and revitalizing the juvenile justice system. Implementation must begin with consensus building among key stakeholders and testing with small pilot projects to develop the model. This evolutionary process can build on existing programs and practices that reflect restorative justice principles, such as victim–offender mediation,[31] victim–offender panels, family group conferencing, community service, restitution, and work experience.

Balanced and Restorative Justice Philosophy

The foundation of restorative justice practice is a coherent set of values and principles, a guiding vision, and an action-oriented mission. The guiding principles of restorative justice are that crime is injury and crime hurts not only individual victims but also communities and offenders and creates an obligation to make things right. All parties should be a part of the response to the crime, including the victim if he or she wishes, the community, and the offender. However, the victim's perspective is central to deciding how to repair (restore) the harm caused by the crime. Accountability for the offender means some acceptance of responsibility to repair the harm done.

The community is ultimately responsible for the well-being of all its members, including both victim and offender, and all human beings have dignity and worth. Restoration means repairing the harm and rebuilding relationships in the community. It is the primary goal of restorative justice. Results are measured by how much repair was done rather than by how much punishment was inflicted. This ideology accepts that crime control cannot be achieved without the active involvement of the community.

The justice process is respectful of age, abilities, sexual orientation, family status, and diverse cultures and backgrounds (for example, racial, ethnic, geographic, religious, and economic backgrounds), and all are given equal protection and due process. The restorative justice vision needs to have support from the community, opportunity to define the harm experienced, and participation in decision making about steps for repair that result in increased victim recovery from the trauma of crime. It accepts that community involvement in preventing and controlling crime, improving neighborhoods, and strengthening the bonds among community members results in community protection.

Through understanding the human impact of their behavior, accepting responsibility, expressing remorse, taking action to repair the damage, and developing their own capacities, offenders become fully integrated and respected members of the community. Justice professionals, as community justice facilitators, organize and support processes in which individual crime victims, other community members, and juvenile offenders are involved in finding constructive resolutions to delinquency.

The Balanced Approach and Its Application

Transforming the current justice system into a more restorative model will and must require that professionals have the power to transform justice into a more balanced and restorative system. By developing new roles, setting new priorities, and redirecting resources, justice professionals can do the following:

1. Make needed services available for victims of crime.
2. Give victims opportunities for involvement and input.
3. Actively involve community members, including individual crime victims and offenders, in making decisions and carrying out plans for resolving issues and restoring the community.
4. Build connections among community members.
5. Give offenders the opportunity and encouragement to take responsibility for their behavior.
6. Actively involve offenders in repairing the harm they caused.

This approach is relatively new and requires additional research and application; it may help turn the tide on the punishment and retribution ideologies that are now so much in favor with politicians and the public.

CONTEMPORARY CORRECTIONS

The need for correctional reforms and structured plans to achieve them was documented by the President's Crime Commission, appointed by President Lyndon Johnson in the 1960s; by the President's Commission on Criminal Justice Standards and Goals; and by task forces in many states. The early 1960s emerged as a period of research that sought alternative methods, programs, treatment procedures, and designs for facilities. The most astonishing and significant findings included the following:

1. Long sentences are self-defeating with regard to rehabilitation, and life sentences for juveniles are violations of the Eighth Amendment to the U.S. Constitution.
2. Most offenders—perhaps as many as 85 percent—do not need to be incarcerated and could function better back in the community under supervision.
3. Most inmates derive maximum benefit from incarceration during their first two years; after that period, it becomes less and less likely that they could function as productive citizens if returned to society.
4. Community-based corrections are more realistic, less expensive, and at least as effective as incarceration.
5. Corrections, as a system, must encompass all aspects of rehabilitative service, including mental health services, employment services, education, and social services.
6. Some offenders, because of their dangerousness, will require extensive incarceration and treatment programs especially designed and implemented in secure institutions. The staff in those institutions must be extensive and of high quality.

7. Most inmates are not mentally ill but suffer from a variety of educational, medical, psychological, maturational, economic, and interpersonal handicaps that are seldom reduced or resolved in contemporary correctional systems.
8. Inmates must be given the opportunity and capability to earn a living wage so as to compensate their victims and support their own families, keeping them off public assistance rolls.
9. The pay for currently incarcerated inmates is too low to be regarded as wages. Thus, the rates of pay must be increased to at least the minimum wage on the outside for similar labor.
10. The private economic sector must be sought out and used to provide both training and work programs that will produce employable workers at the end of the corrections cycle.

key term

Determinate sentencing Judge-imposed fixed term of incarceration with the expectation the inmate will serve that amount of time.

Despite the evidence, five important developments in corrections have occurred since the 1980s: (1) the abandonment of the medical model; (2) the shift to **determinate sentencing** (which places limits on the judge's powers); (3) a search for punishments that would be more effective than court-ordered probation and less severe than long-term incarceration, the so-called intermediate sanctions; (4) renewed emphasis on rehabilitation and effective programming for offenders; and (5) restorative justice (discussed above).

By 2013, the majority of the states embraced determinate sentencing, abolishing discretionary parole release mechanisms in at least 16 states and imposing mandatory add-on time for use of a gun in crimes, sale of narcotics, and some especially brutal crimes. At least 29 states and the District of Columbia have adopted the federal truth-in-sentencing standard that requires Part I violent crime offenders to serve not less than 85 percent of their sentence in prison before becoming eligible for release. The reemergence of retribution in contemporary corrections has led in part to seriously overcrowded prisons, a deluge of lawsuits by prisoners seeking better conditions while incarcerated, and an intense search for new alternatives to imprisonment[32] that would still provide public safety and constitutionally viable conditions for prisoners.[33] As Latessa and Allen noted in 1999, "Ironically, for a movement begun by fiscal conservatives, the new get-tough policy has turned out to be the most costly approach to corrections yet attempted."[34] Recent figures compiled by the PEW Charitable Trusts show that total state expenditures for corrections have risen 315 percent in the past 20 years.[35]

photo 3.4

An inmate who is serving a 40-year sentence for a murder conviction trains Juanita to be a service dog as part of NEADS' Prison Pup program at the John J. Moran medium-security prison. In the NEADS/Dogs for Deaf and Disabled Americans' Prison Pup program, prison inmates train dogs to be placed with deaf and disabled Americans, including disabled combat veterans.

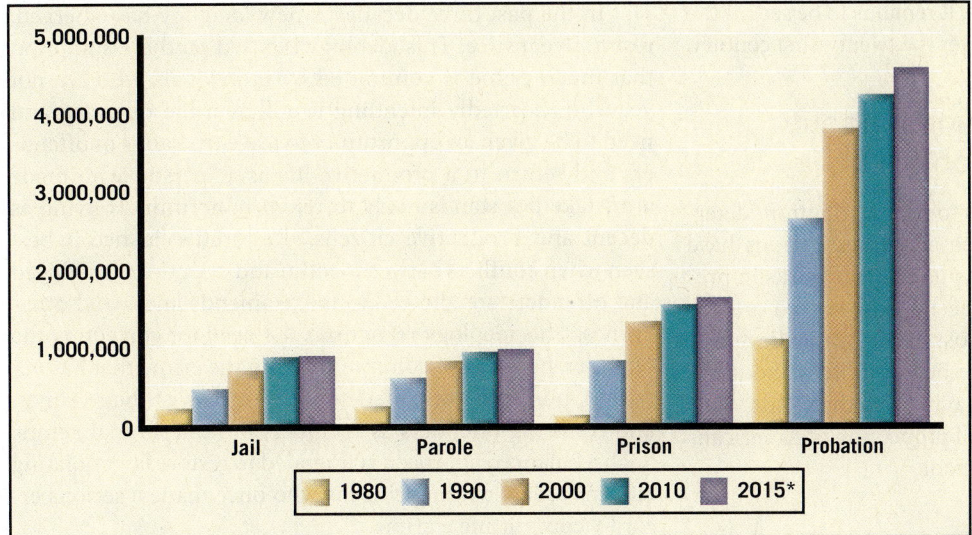

figure 3.1

Adults under Correctional Control: 1980–2015.

Data gathered from: Bureau of Justice Statistics (2011). Correctional Populations, 1980–2010. (http://www.bjs.gov/content/pub/pdf/cpus10.pdf.
*Data for 2015 are estimated.

By the beginning of 2013, 1 in 31 adult Americans was under some form of correctional supervision. Almost two-thirds of federal prison inmates are incarcerated for drug law violations; the national average for state systems is about 20 percent. One in 15 African American men ages 18 or older is incarcerated on any day, and for black men ages 20 to 34, the number is 1 in 9. There are more African American men in prison today that were African American slaves in 1850. Figure 3.1 provides a graphic of the growth curves. Although we are starting to see a reduction in the correctional population, there are now almost 1 in 100 adults behind bars in America. The punishment ideology has contributed heavily to this growth and has fueled the search for intermediate sanctions and more effective programs. These are explored in detail in Chapters 6 and 9.

The War on Drugs has diverted attention from the causes of drug use and social problems, expanded the power of the state in light of the rights of the individual, legitimized intrusion of American politics into Latin and South American governments, and not reduced the volume of drug use. William Weir, an expert on gun control and drugs, argues that cynical politicians have manipulated the public to attain their own agenda and goals and, in so doing, created a "dope fiend" stereotype to generate votes. The "war" has increased violence and enhanced gangster roles for minority inner-city youth.[36]

Summary

Summarize the Definition, Mission, and Role of Corrections

Correctional ideology, a system of beliefs and resultant actions, originated with practices of earliest humankind. Originally, punishment and banishment were the primary missions of corrections, based on the belief that offenders rationally decided to commit crime, were intent on inflicting loss or death, and would not otherwise be deterred from further criminal behavior. They were seen as being evil and deserving of punishment. Thus, retribution and deterrence were intertwined as correctional objectives. When correctional facilities were developed, incapacitation became a major third component of the punishment ideology. Beliefs lead to actions.

Summarize Sentencing Goals and Primary Punishment Philosophies

Corrections has swung into one or another ideological position over the past three decades, bouncing from one type of beliefs and practices to another. During the same period, the rehabilitation ideology has shifted to a more punitive one. In the past decade, with the economic realignment and financial shortfalls that have emerged, the ideology has begun to shift back to the treatment and prevention strategies underlying the rehabilitative and reform positions. It remains to be seen if the shift will continue as we further enter the twenty-first century.

Explain How Public Opinion about Crime Affects Crime Control Policy

While the intent of punishment is to seek retribution, deterrence, and incapacitation, research and investigations have not produced much evidence that punishment works in preventing crime. It is obviously true that those who are executed commit no more crime; most Americans believe that the death penalty is a poor choice between life without parole, especially when linked to repayment to the victim. This may be one reason that only a small proportion of Americans devotedly endorse capital punishment.

Summarize Issues Related to Correctional Policy

In the eighteenth century, with the development of the Age of Enlightenment, a second major ideology emerged: rehabilitation. This ideology is based on the assumption that humans are not perfect but can be made better and that the volume of crime would be lowered if offenders were treated, motivated to cease offending, and given the opportunity to rejoin free society as individuals desiring to merge into mainstream America. To achieve rehabilitation, services and treatments were designed and implemented, however inaccurately, in probation and correctional institutions.

In the late nineteenth and twentieth centuries, a third ideology emerged: prevention. Under this ideologies, offenders were seen as persons ill equipped to cope with demands of contemporary life, being undereducated, having blocked opportunities for individual advancement, and suffering from a variety of adverse social factors that included brutal parenting, living in a drug-impacted environment, local juvenile and adult gangs, crime-infested environments, and so on. A variety of programs focused on prevention emerged and included neighborhood change, increasing resistance to criminal acts, shifting law enforcement strategies, social work, and related efforts. Preventing crime is even more significant in crime reduction than is rehabilitation, the latter being more crime preventive than punishment.

In the past three decades, a new ideology has emerged: restorative justice. This ideology is based on the assumption that much crime is committed by individuals who are not yet wholeheartedly intending to follow a life of crime and need to be given an opportunity to leave the ranks of offenders and return to a productive life as a "person who made a mistake but stands ready to rejoin noncriminals living as decent and productive citizens." Restorative justice is best seen when conflicts between victim and offender are reduced and offenders are allowed to make amends and avoid other crimes. This ideology recognizes the need for correcting the offender, healing the community from the crime that has occurred, punishing offenders for the impacts of their crimes, and restoring offenders as members of noncriminal actors. Such a balanced approach is intended to restore law-violating citizens as law-abiding citizens who once made a serious error by committing a crime.

Describe and Illustrate Contemporary Corrections in the Nation

The nation holds the largest percentage of its population under correctional control than any other nation and has the greatest percentage of its citizenry in prison. This is caused by the effort to handle a large set of societal problems by use of the criminal justice system process. Long sentences defeat the intention of stabilizing and reintegrating social misfits into productive members of society; most inmates make the greatest gains during the first two years of imprisonment. An estimated 85 percent of current inmates are not particularly dangerous and could be habilitated using community corrections options. The latter are more realistic and effective and cost less than imprisonment. Yet there some 15 percent of current imprisoned offenders who are too dangerous to be controlled through community control and should be under correctional supervision in prisons.

It should be stressed that most current inmates are not mentally ill but suffer from a variety of debilitating challenges, particularly in the area of economic needs. Such inmates should be given the opportunity and capability to earn a living, which would involve interfacing and maximizing cooperation with the private economic sector.

Key Words

ideology, 50
correctional ideology, 50
punishment ideology, 50
rehabilitation ideology, 50
prevention ideology, 50
retribution, 50
deterrent effect, 52
general deterrence, 52
specific deterrence, 52
stigma of conviction, 52
incapacitation, 52
theory of disablement, 53
selective incapacitation, 53
recidivism, 53
rehabilitation model, 55
reformatory movement, 56
educational doctrine, 56
medical model, 56

indeterminate sentencing, 56
reintegration model, 57
Emile Durkheim, 57
community corrections, 58
diversion, 59
"get-tough" laws, 59
restorative justice, 60
determinate sentencing, 62

Review Questions

1. What basic ideologies have determined the handling of offenders over the years? Which is the oldest?
2. What criteria must be met if punishment is to act as a deterrent?
3. How does the rehabilitation ideology differ from punishment? Are they necessarily exclusive of each other?
4. What are some of the changes currently taking place in the clientele of the correctional system?
5. What effect has the punishment ideology recently had on corrections?
6. What is restorative justice?
7. Explain the impact of drugs on the race/ethnicity of prisoners.

Application Case Studies

1. Two juveniles have used their car key to scratch the paint along the sides of your car. What do you think would be your desired outcome for those two juveniles?
2. An inmate under a 15-year sentence for burglary "gets right with God," and it appears that he is sincere in his beliefs and repentance. The prison chaplain asks that the offender be released under supervision so he can perform the work he thinks he needs to do. If you were the warden of this institution, what would you do, if anything? If the offender had 12 more years under the current sentence? If the inmate had 18 months remaining on his original sentence?
3. A male being prosecuted for murdering a victim is found guilty by a jury but of manslaughter rather than homicide. In your state, manslaughter is punishable by a sentence ranging from 6 to 20 years' imprisonment. As the sentencing judge, what penalty would you impose, and why?

Endnotes

1. BBC News (2013), "Japan Hangs Three Death Row Inmates," http://www.bbc.co.uk/news/world-asia-21528526. Japan hangs the condemned without telling them their death date, and notifies their families after the fact.
2. Graeme Newman, *Just and Painful: The Case for the Corporal Punishment of Criminals* (New York: Free Press, 1983).
3. As cited by Elmer H. Johnson, *Crime, Correction, and Society* (Homewood, IL: Dorsey Press, 1974), p. 173. See also Roger Hood, "Capital Punishment: A Global Perspective," *Punishment and Society* 3:3 (2001): 331–334, and Kika Young (2013), "The Difference between Positive/Negative Reinforcement and Positive/Negative Punishment," http://bcotb.com/the-difference-between-positivenegative-reinforcement-and-positivenegative-punishment/.
4. Norman Carlson, "A More Balanced Correctional Philosophy," *FBI Law Enforcement Bulletin* 46 (January 1977): 22–25. See also John Cochran and Mitchell Chamblin, "Deterrence and Brutalization," *Justice Quarterly* 17:4 (2000): 685–706.
5. K. Blackman, R. Voas, R. Gullberg, et al., "Enforcement of Zero-Tolerance in the State of Washington," *Forensic Science Review* 13:2 (2001): 77–86.
6. John Irwin and James Austin, *It's About Time* (San Francisco: National Council on Crime and Delinquency, 1987), pp. 12–14. See also and Richard Tewksbury and David Connor, "Incarcerated Sex Offenders' Perceptions of Family Relationships," *Western Criminology Review* 13:2 (2012): 25–35.
7. Bradley Wright, A. Caspi, and T. Moffitt, "Does the Perceived Risk of Punishment Deter Criminally Prone Individuals?," *Journal of Research in Crime and Delinquency* 41:2 (2004): 180–213.
8. Peter B. Greenwood, *Selective Incapacitation* (Santa Monica, CA: Rand Corporation, 1983). But also see Simon Cole, "From the Sexual Psychopath to 'Megan's Law,'" *Journal of the History of Medicine and Allied Science* 55:3 (2000): 292–314.

9. Incapacitation remains a hotly debated topic in corrections. See Daniel Nagin, David Farrington, and Terrie Moffit, "Life Course Trajectories of Different Types of Offenders," *Criminology* 33:1 (1995): 111–139, and Tom O'Connor (2013). "Correctional Ideologies," http://www.drtomoconnor.com/1050/1050lect02.htm.
10. Hennessey Hayes and M. Geerken argue that it is possible to identify low-rate offenders for early release. See H. Hayes and M. Geerken, "The Idea of Selective Release," *Justice Quarterly* 14:2 (1997): 353–370, and Court Services and Offender Rehabilitation Agency for the District of Columbia, "Day Reporting Center," http://www.csosa.gov/supervision/programs/day_reporting_center.aspx.
11. Marianne Zowitz, ed., *Report to the Nation on Crime and Justice* (Washington, DC: Bureau of Justice Statistics, 1983). On the Dutch experience, see Ben Vollard (2011), "Preventing Crime through Selective Incapacitation," http://papers.ssrn.com/sol3/papers.cfm?abstract_id=1738900.
12. More than half of prison inmates will be charged with prison rule violations during their current sentences. See James Stephan, *Prison Rule Violations* (Washington, DC: Bureau of Justice Statistics, 1989). See also Stephen Schoenthaler, Stephen Amos, W. Doraz, et al., "The Effect of Randomized Vitamin-Mineral Supplementation on Violent and Non-Violent Antisocial Behavior among Incarcerated Juveniles," *Journal of Nutritional and Environmental Medicine* 7:1 (1997): 343–352, and National Bureau of Economic Research (2013), "The Impact of Childhood Lead Exposure on Adult Crime," http://www.nber.org/digest/may08/w13097.html.
13. See the comments on the Alabama "dog house" by John Conrad, "From Barbarism toward Decency: Alabama's Long Road to Prison Reform," *Journal of Research in Crime and Delinquency* 26 (November 1989): 307–328; Human Rights Watch, "No Escape: Male Rape in U.S. Prisons," http://www.hrw.org/reports/2001/prison (accessed November 30, 2008); and Women of the World (2013), "Former Inmates Claim Texas Prison Ran 'Rape Camp, " http://www.thedailybeast.com/witw/articles/2013/06/19/former-inmates-claim-texas-prison-ran-rape-camp.html.
14. Johnson, *Crime, Correction and Society,* pp. 361–365. A European view of punishment can be found in Pieter Spirenburg, *Man and Violence: Gender, Honor and Rituals in Modern Europe and America* (Columbus: Ohio State University Press, 1998).
15. There is a current rebirth of the punishment ideology, described in detail by Donald E. J. MacNamara, "The Medical Model in Corrections: *Requiescat in Pace*," *Criminology* 14 (February 1977): 439–448. See also Victor Hassine, *A Life without Parole: Living in Prison Today,* 4th ed. (New York: Oxford University Press, 2008). Victor Hassine committed suicide in 2008.
16. James Austin and Aaron McVey, *The 1989 NCCD Prison Population Forecast: The Impact of the War on Drugs* (San Francisco: National Council on Crime and Delinquency, 1989), p. 13. See also Ann Carson and William Sobel, *Prisoners in 2011* (Washington, DC: Bureau of Justice Statistics, 2012).
17. Patrick Langan and David Levin, *Recidivism of Prisoners Released in 1994* (Washington, DC: Bureau of Justice Statistics, 2002). But see David Hartmann, J. Wolk, J. Johnston, et al., "Recidivism and Substance Abuse Outcomes in a Prison-Based Therapeutic Community," *Federal Probation* 61:4 (1997): 18–25, and Michael Prendergast, Elizabeth Hall, Harry Wexler, et al., "Amity Prison Based Therapeutic Community," *The Prison Journal* 84:1 (2004): 36–60. See also Harry Wexler et al, "The Amity Prison TC Reincarceration Outcomes," http://cjb.sagepub.com/content/26/2/147.abstract.
18. James Unnever, "Two Worlds Far Apart: Black-White Differences in Beliefs about Why African-American Men Are Disproportionately Imprisoned," *Criminology* 46:2 (2008): 301–359. For a list of crime prevention programs, see Bureau of Justice Statistics, *Crime Prevention* (Washington, DC: Bureau of Justice Statistics, 2013).
19. For a discussion of prediction, see Anthony Petrosino and Caroline Petrosino, "The Public Safety Potential of Megan's Law in Massachusetts," *Crime and Delinquency* 45:1 (1999): 140–158; Sonya Goshe (2013), "Malleable Inmates," *Western Criminology Review* 14(1): 38–50; and Richard Tewksbury and David O'Connor, "Inmates Who Receive Visits in Prisons: Exploring Factors That Predict," *Federal Probation Journal* 46:3 (2012), http://www.uscourts.gov/uscourts/FederalCourts/PPS/Fedprob/2012-12/visitation.html.
20. See Linda Dahlberg, "Youth Violence in the United States: Major Trends, Risk Factors and Prevention Approaches," *American Journal of Preventive Medicine* 14:4 (1998): 259–272. See also American Academy of Child and Adolescent Psychiatry, "Children with Oppositional Defiant Disorder," http://www.aacap.org/publications/factsfam/72.htm (accessed January 20, 2005).
21. Emile Durkheim, *Division of Labor in Society*, trans. George Simpson (Glencoe, IL: Free Press, 1947). See also Dario Melossi, *The Sociology of Punishment* (Aldershot: Dartmouth, 1998).
22. Carri Casteel, "Effectiveness of Crime Prevention through Environmental Design in Reducing Robberies," *American Journal of Preventive Medicine* 18:4 (2000): 99–115; City of Mesa, Arizona, "Crime

Prevention through Environmental Design," http://www.cityofmesa.org/police/literature/cpted.asp (accessed January 19, 2005); North Carolina Department of Public Safety (2013), "Crime Prevention through Environmental Design," https://www.ncdps.gov/index2.cfm?a=000003,000011,001443,001576.

23. Eric Fritsch, T. Caeti, and R. Taylor, "Gang Suppression through Saturation Patrol, Aggressive Curfew and Truancy Enforcement," *Crime and Delinquency* 45:1 (1999): 122–139. But see Richard Valdemar (2013), "Failed and Fruitful Tactics for Combatting Gangs," http://www.policemag.com/blog/gangs/story/2009/09/failed-and-fruitful-tactics-for-combating-gangs.aspx.
24. Daniel Nagin and J. Waldfogel, "The Effects of Conviction on Income through Life," *International Review of Law and Economics* 18:1 (1998): 25–40.
25. That trend has stopped. The percentage of U.S. households victimized by violent crime or theft during 2006 remained at the lowest levels since 1994. Since 1994, property crimes have dropped from 320 per 100,000 persons to 150 in 2006. Victimization through violent crime dropped 78 percent in the same time period. Bureau of Justice Statistics, *Criminal Victimization, 2006* (Washington, DC: Bureau of Justice Statistics, 2007). Most likely, property crimes have plateaued and will decrease very slowly in the future.
26. Harry E. Allen, Edward Latessa, and Gennaro Vito, "Corrections in the Year 2000," *Corrections Today* 49:2 (1987): 73–78. See also Wendy Ware, James Austin, and Gillian Thomson (2013), "Nevada Department of Correction Ten Year Prison Population Predictions: 2010–2020," http://www.doc.nv.gov/sites/doc/files/pdf/stats/Population_Forecast_and_CIP/FY_2012_2021/Prison_Population_Forecast_Report_2010_2020.PDF.
27. T. Flanagan, E. McGarrell, and A. Lizotte, "Ideology and Crime Control Policy Positions in a State Legislature," *Journal of Criminal Justice* 17 (1989): 87–101; Marla Sandys and Edmund McGarrell, "Attitudes toward Capital Punishment among Indiana Legislators," *Justice Quarterly* 11:4 (1994): 651–677.
28. Francis Cullen, Bonnie Fisher, and Brandon Applegate, "Public Opinion about Punishment and Corrections," in Michael Tonry, ed., *Crime and Justice* (Chicago: University of Chicago Press, 2000), pp. 1–79. See also Jody Sundt et al. (2012), "Support for Prisoner Rehabilitation," http://www.pdx.edu/cjpri/sites/www.pdx.edu.cjpri/files/CJPRI_ResBrief_Reentry.pdf.
29. See Prison Fellowship International, "Restorative Justice Online," http://www.restorativejustice.org/intro (accessed July 15, 2008). See also Editorial opinion (2013), "It's time for Oklahoma Legislature to Do Something about Overcrowded Prisons," http://enidnews.com/opinion/x738617982/It-s-time-for-Oklahoma-Legislature-to-do-something-about-overcrowded-prisons.
30. Prison Fellowship International, "Lesson 4: Programmes–Restorative Justice Processes," http://www.restorativejustice.org/university-classroom/01introduction/tutorial-introduction-to-restorative-justice/processes. (accessed July 15, 2008). See also Paul Tullis, "Can Forgiveness Play a Role in Criminal Justice?," *New York Times Magazine*, January 20, 2013, p. 1. A brief video on restorative justice can be found at http://www.youtube.com/watch?v=PEO3HeOgQPY.
31. The Restorative-Justice Resource Center, "Victim-Offender Mediation or Dialogues," http://www.cjibc.org/victim_mediation (accessed July 15, 2008). See also David Karp (2013), "Campus Restorative Justice," http://www.skidmore.edu/campusrij.
32. See William Spellman, "What Recent Studies Do (and Don't) Tell Us about Imprisonment and Crime," in Tonry, *Crime and Justice*, pp. 419–494.
33. Craig Hainey, "Mental Health Issues in Long-Term Solitary and 'Supermax' Confinement," *Crime and Delinquency* 49:1 (2003): 124–156; Michael Vaughn Sue Collins, "Medical Malpractice in Correctional Facilities," *The Prison Journal* 84:4 (2004): 505–534; Margaret Severson, "Mental Health Needs and Mental Health Care in Jails," *American Jails* 18:3 (2004): 9–18. But see Susanne Green (2013), "Emergency Transfer for Mentally Ill Colorado Super-Max Concerns Surface," http://www.huffingtonpost.com/2013/10/04/colorado-supermax_n_4045914.html.
34. Edward Latessa and Harry Allen, *Corrections in the Community* (Cincinnati, OH: Anderson Publishing, 2004), p. 43. See also Ryan King, "Disparity by Geography: The War on Drugs in American Cities" (Washington, DC: The Sentencing Project, 2008).
35. PEW Charitable Trusts, "One in 100: Behind Bars in America 2008," http://www.pewtrusts.org/en/research-and-analysis/reports/2008/02/28/one-in-100-behind-bars-in-america-2008. updated.
36. See Daniel Mears et al., "Social Ecology and Recidivism: Implications for Prisoner Reentry," *Criminology* 46:2 (2008): 301–359. See also James Howell and John Moore (2010), "History of Street Gangs in the U.S.," http://www.nationalgangcenter.gov/content/documents/history-of-street-gangs.pdf.

Rich Legg/Getty Images

Objectives

- Explain the role of prosecutorial plea bargaining and how it creates the correctional funnel.
- Summarize the different types of sentences and how sentencing decisions are made.
- Describe alternatives to criminal courts and the criminal trial process.
- Summarize the appeal process.
- Explain how the correctional filter functions to categorize, sort, and divert most offenders into alternatives to incarceration.

chapter 4 The Sentencing and Appeals Process

Outline

The Correctional Filter

- The Prosecutor's Decision

The Sentencing Decision

- Rapid Change in Sentencing Processes
- New Goals
- Reform Options
- Reform Effects
- Predicting Behavior
- The Presentence Investigation
- Judicial versus Administrative Sentencing
- Practical Problems in Sentencing
- Problems in Setting Prison Terms

Felony Sentences in State Court

Deterrence by Sentencing

- Appellate Review

The Issue of Due Process

The Mechanics of an Appeal

- The Courts of Appeal

Appeals from Behind the Walls

Reform by Judicial Decree

Appeals Flood the Courts

- Types of Prisoner Petitions
- Legislative Initiatives to Reduce Prisoner Litigation

"My object all sublime I shall achieve in time—To let the punishment fit the crime, The punishment fit the crime."

—William S. Gilbert
The Mikado

Overview

In this chapter, we examine issues that deal with sentencing criminal offenders and some of the processes used to challenge those sentences. Students will also become acquainted with those processes by which offenders are placed in the major components of corrections and how sentencing practices influence correctional practices, programs, and facilities. We will also briefly look at appellate review of convictions and sentencing.

Perhaps no part of the criminal justice system has had more criticism or controversy than the nation's courts as they struggle to make, as noted above, "the punishment fit the crime." This chapter examines that critical decision and acquaints the student with the impact these decisions have on soaring prison populations and their impact in regard to the "correctional filter," as discussed next. Many criticize the court's efforts to apply "justice" while dealing with public opinion, jail and prison overcrowding, budget shortages, and legislative restrictions on the judge's discretion. Students also need an understanding of the appeals process, which is discussed later in the chapter. The student must keep in mind the incidences of crime and the sheer volume of cases when discussing the sentencing process and decisions made in America's courts. This issue will have a vital relationship to the material already covered and chapters yet to come. It will also prepare the student for understanding the complexities of the appellate process. We begin our examination of sentencing practices and the correctional filter.

THE CORRECTIONAL FILTER

In our examination of the myriad dimensions and trends of corrections in America, we now come to the concept we call the *correctional filter*, representing the various sentencing options that sometimes confuse observers as to what is actually occurring in the criminal justice system. At every point of this filter, certain types of offenders and cases are shunted into alternative dispositions, the great bulk of which involve some type of correctional supervision other than jail or prison. Generally, criminal offenses are divided into one of two types: misdemeanor or felony. A **misdemeanor** is a less serious offense and is usually punishable by up to one year in a local jail or detention facility. A **felony** is a more serious offense, and someone convicted of such a charge can be punished by imprisonment or even death, the latter in the case of a capital crime such as first-degree murder. Those offenders who are finally placed under custody and supervision in prisons are, for the most part, the most serious offenders. We now examine the processes, flows, and rationales of the correctional filter, beginning with the prosecutor.

key term

Misdemeanor
A relatively minor violation of the criminal law, usually punishable by no more than one year in confinement.

key term

Felony
Serious criminal violation, sometimes punished by death or sentence of at least one year in prison.

key term

Plea bargaining
Process by which the defendant agrees to plead guilty for prosecutorial consideration.

A major player in the correctional filter process is the prosecutor's office. It is here that prosecutors implement their broad discretionary power to dismiss charges or reduce them to charges for which the defendant will be more likely to plead guilty.[1] Recent studies indicate that as many as 50 to 90 percent of the felony cases initiated by the police are bargained away by prosecutors; in 2010, this figure was 95 percent in large urban counties. A high percentage of charges not dismissed are reduced through **plea bargaining** to a less serious charge to which the defendant agrees to plead guilty. Plea bargaining refers to the prosecutor's practice of permitting the defendant to plead to a lesser charge than the one he or she was arrested for, usually because the prosecutor does not feel the case is strong enough on the more serious charge or because the prosecutor hopes to persuade the defendant to provide information about other crimes or offenders. Plea bargaining may lead to the prosecutor agreeing to dismiss multiple charges, reducing charges, or recommending a lighter sentence. The most common explanation for this action of the correctional filter stems from high caseloads and limited resources, forcing harried prosecutors to dispense with much of their caseload as quickly as possible to avoid overwhelming their own offices, the courts, and overcrowded jails and prisons. The time factor does not explain, however, why some cases are prosecuted and others dismissed. Here, the wide discretionary power given to prosecutors becomes a crucial issue, and prosecutors consider such factors as the case's strength, even handedness, harm done to the victim, ethnicity, and the attorneys' personal attributes.[2]

correctional practice 4.1

Determinate Sentencing for Crack and Cocaine Use

In 1986, Congress created sentencing disparity for two of the most popular types of cocaine: powdered and crack (crystal). The sale of just five grains of crack cocaine—barely a teaspoonful—results in a minimum of five years in federal prison for the violator. Sale of 100 times that amount for powdered cocaine—the type preferred by whites—is required to result in a comparable sentence. About 90 percent of those convicted of selling crack cocaine are black, and only 30 percent of those convicted of selling powdered cocaine are black. When the U.S. Sentencing Commission recommended changing the sentencing guidelines to equalize sentencing, both the U.S. House of Representatives and the U.S. Senate voted to block any change in the 100:1 ratio. In 2010, Congress enacted the Fair Sentencing Act, permitting retroactive sentence reductions for applying Federal offenders. Just over 7,300 inmates received, on average, a reduction of some 29 months in crack sentences. By 2013, this procedure avoided some 16,000 years of federal imprisonment.

In 2013, the federal attorney general, in seeking to cut mandatory minimum drug sentences, announced it would no longer demand mandatory minimum penalties for certain low-level nonviolent drug offenders. The number of imprisoned federal prisoners has dropped sharply.

SOURCE: Traci Schlesinger, "Racial and Ethnic Disparity in Pretrial Criminal Processing," *Justice Quarterly* 22:2 (2006): 170–192. U.S. Sentencing Commission (2013), "Preliminary Crack Retroactivity Report: Fair Sentencing Act," http://www.ussc.gov/Research_and_Statistics/Federal_Sentencing_Statistics/FSA_Amendment/013-10_USSC_Prelim_Crack_Retro_Data_Report_FSA.pdf.

The important point here is that many justice actors are gatekeepers in terms of processing the accused, creating a winnowing effect that functions to exclude the less serious and less career-committed offenders from incarceration. The decisions made both shuttle the lesser criminals to alternatives to imprisonment and, it is hoped, commit the most hardened and risky offenders to incarceration in jails or prisons. All told, such decisions form the base of the correctional funnel intended to achieve a variety of correctional objectives as listed above and to reserve beds in correctional facilities for those too risky and potentially too dangerous to trust to less controlling correctional alternatives.

THE SENTENCING DECISION

As suggested, defendants who reach the sentencing stage of criminal proceedings are those who have not yet completely evaded the correctional filter. They have either pled guilty to or been found guilty of a crime by either a jury or a bench trial.[3] The court must then decide in what fashion it will dispose of them. Making a sentencing decision is often the most complicated and difficult task for any judge. High rates of violent street crime, along with a large number of drug offenders and lengthier determinate sentences, make the sentencing decision more complex than it has ever been. Of course, deciding the sentence involves a great many factors, such as alternative dispositions allowed by statute, the criminal intent of the offender, the amount of harm or loss to the victim, the remorse expressed by the offender, and other mitigating or aggravating factors.[4]

correctional **practice 4.2**

State Drug Court Programs for DUI Offenders: Sentencing

Offenders driving while intoxicated are increasingly being placed under the jurisdiction of the drug court, commonly described as a "problem-solving court." Such courts are designed to reduce criminal reoffending by chemically dependent adult drivers who are at high risk to recidivate. The targeted group displays a repetitive pattern of driving under the influence (DUI) of drugs or alcohol. Such drivers otherwise cause injuries and deaths on highways and are not deterred by usual DUI sanctions.

While some drug courts will only accept first-time DUI offenders, the typical court focuses on third-time violators who are sent directly to the DUI court for arraignment and sentencing. The basic intentions are to aid such offenders, protect the public by keeping them from reoffending, improve judicial efficiency, and reserve hard bed space for career and dangerous offenders. Georgia's drug court is an accountability court authorized to process drug-using offenders through drug testing, intensive supervision, treatment services, and immediate incentives and sanctions. Drug courts are designed to force the offender to deal with his or her substance abuse problems through a blend of treatment and personal accountability as well as specialized case management. The drug court is a treatment court with a specialized docket managed by a specially trained judge, working with prosecutors, public defenders, probation and law enforcement officers, treatment providers, and other dedicated practitioners to compel the DUI offender to become clean and sober and to cease recidivism.

Tools frequently used in drug courts include both early and long-term treatment intervention; frequent random drug testing; judicial supervision; intensive probation coupled later with follow-up probation; assistance with school, education, and employment, biweekly court appearances; frequent 12-step Alcoholics Anonymous or Narcotics Anonymous meeting attendance; and home visits by compliance officers. Failure to meet requirements will cause the drug court judge to issue immediate sanctions, such as community service, jail time, or both. Interlock devices may be installed that prevent drug court offenders from driving a vehicle. Frequent failure may lead to revocation of probation and imposition of a sentence to incarceration.

The effectiveness of drug courts has not yet been thoroughly investigated, but preliminary results from Georgia reveal that, at 12 months postgraduation, DUI court clients were almost three times less likely to have a new DUI arrest and that, at 24 months postgraduation, drug court participants were 20 percent less likely to be arrested for a new felony. Hennepin County, Minnesota, found that some 89 percent of program participants stayed crime free. Keeping such offenders "off the bottle" results in one-fourth of the cost of sending a person to prison. In most drug courts, participant fees help pay for treatment services.

SOURCE: Eastern Judicial Circuit of Georgia, State Court DUI Court Program, http://www.chathamcourts.org/StateCourt/DUICourtProgram.aspx (accessed October 26, 2012).

key term

Indeterminate sentencing Punishment imposed by a judge that has both a minimum and maximum period (usually of confinement).

key term

Sentencing disparity Difference between both the types and length of sentences imposed for the same crime or seriousness of crimes when there is no legal basis that can be identified to explain this difference.

Rapid Change in Sentencing Processes

In 1930, most states and federal courts were operating under the **indeterminate sentencing** (stet)structure: The judge would impose a prison sentence with both a minimum and a maximum term in years, such as 2 years' minimum to 5 years' maximum or 5 years, minimum to 20 years' maximum. The wide ranges of sentence lengths reflected the dominant rehabilitation goal of the correctional system and its belief that once the offender had been rehabilitated, the parole board would detect the change and then order the inmate's release. Parole boards would actually determine the length of the sentence served, using their authority of discretionary release. Following a long period of relative inactivity (1930–1974), American sentencing laws and practices began to undergo a rapid, fundamental restructuring of the sentencing process. The causes have been identified as follows:[5]

1. Prison uprisings (such as at Attica in New York and others in New Mexico, Oklahoma, California, and Florida) indicated that inmates were particularly discontented with the rhetoric of rehabilitation and the reality of the prison environment.
2. The abuse of discretion caused concerns about individual rights because prosecutors, judges, and parole boards were immune from review and some practiced arbitrary uses of discretion.
3. Court orders and decisions led to a movement that demanded accountability in official decision making and outcomes.
4. The rehabilitation ideal was challenged, both empirically and ideologically, which undermined the rationale of the indeterminate sentence's "parole after rehabilitation" corollary.
5. Experimental and statistical studies of judicial sentencing found substantial disparity and both racial and class discrimination.[6] Such inconsistencies and disparities fostered the conclusion that sentencing practices were unfair. (**Sentencing disparity** means that offenders committing the same crimes under the same circumstances are given different sentences.)
6. Crime control and corrections became a political football,[7] useful for those seeking election to public office.

correctional **practice 4.3**

Presumptive Sentencing

One alternative to limit sentencing disparity is the presumptive sentencing system, in which the state legislature sets minimum, average, and maximum terms, allowing the judge to select a term based on the characteristics of the offender and aggravating circumstances. The sentence imposed will be the time served less any credits against the sentence that the offender earns (such as credit for time served in jail, good behavior in prison, program participation, and so on). California has a presumptive sentencing structure that provides three options to the sentencing judge, as seen here for the crime of burglary:

1. Aggravating circumstances—seven years
2. Presumptive (average) sentence—five years
3. Mitigating circumstances—three years

Ordinarily, the judge would decide if the offender were to be placed on probation or sentenced to prison (the "in–out" decision). Assuming imprisonment to be the answer, the judge would impose the average sentence of five years unless mitigating circumstances were present at the time of the offense (for example, if the offender were under the influence of a controlled substance or had a weak personality and was easily led into committing a crime for peer approval). If mitigating circumstances were proven, the judge would impose the least sentence (three years). However, if aggravating circumstances were proven, the judge must impose the highest sentence (seven years). Some examples of aggravating circumstances are gross bodily harm to victim, prior incarceration in prison, and vulnerability of victim (older than 60 years of age, blind, paraplegic, etc.).

New Goals

Corrections by the 1970s generally functioned under the utilitarian goal of rehabilitation being possible. Dialogue and arguments from "hard-liners" brought other primary goals to the forefront in the 1980s. These included incapacitation of persons likely to commit future crimes and its variant of selective incapacitation, in which the highest-risk offenders would receive much longer sentences to prevent any more criminal activity.[8] From the mid-1990s on, such concepts as "three strikes and you're out" laws[9] have become popular with the public and legislators. A dramatic rash of "headline crimes,"[10] especially heinous, combined with the perception of a growing level of violent crimes, has spurred on such movements since the early 1970s. The specific deterrence of sentenced offenders and the general deterrence of those contemplating committing a crime were legitimized as social policy goals. In addition, the retribution goal became attractive inasmuch as it would impose deserved punishment. (Such a **just deserts** goal looks backward to the offender's personal culpability, focuses on the nature of the act, and considers the harm done.)

In total, 25 states and the federal government have enacted three-strikes legislation, increasing the length of sentences by a multiple of two or setting minimum time to be served at 25, 30, or even 40 years. Despite claims of prosecutors and legislators that such legislation was an essential crime-fighting tool for both deterrence and incapacitation, it has not been applied extensively. There is little creditable evidence from investigations that enacting such laws has reduced crime. Instead, the evidence is that criminals are rarely concerned about being apprehended, that the laws target offenders beyond their peak ages of reoffending, that identifying high-rate offenders early on before they perpetrate a high number of crimes is difficult and fraught with "false-positive" errors, and that other criminals simply replace any who would be incarcerated. Finally, eligible offenders have mostly experienced enhanced penalties prior to the imposition of such laws, and the increased incarceration does not sufficiently increase the severity of punishment. There is some reason to suspect that such ineffective crime control measures serve to increase the geriatric populations in prison, creating a demand for prison nursing homes and other expensive medical treatments.[11] See Table 4.1 for a list of the top 10 states with the highest percentage of inmates over age 55. Costs of incarceration of a prisoner in California can be found in Table 4.2.

key term

Just deserts
Sentencing ideology that stresses that any punishment to be applied must be dependent on the culpability of the offender and the seriousness of the offense.

table **4.1** **Ten States with High Levels of Inmates over the Age of 55**

State	Percentage over Age 55
Kentucky	15.20
New Hampshire	14.00
Kansas	12.40
Missouri	12.40
Idaho	12.19
Nebraska	12.00
Utah	10.80
Alabama	10.75
Massachusetts	9.00
Michigan	8.80

SOURCE: American Correctional Association, *American Correctional Directory* (2012), pp. 38, 39.

table 4.2 Average Cost to House Inmates in Prison per Year: California

1. Security:	$19,663
2. Administration costs:	3,493
3. Health care:	12,442
4. Operations:	7,214
5. Rehabilitation:	1,612
6. Inmate support:	2,562
Total:	$46,986

SOURCE: "The Average Cost to House Inmates in Prison" (2012), http://www.ehow.com/about_5409377_average-cost-house-inmates-prison.html (accessed August 18, 2013).

Reform Options

As a result of the reform movement, sentencing practices were changed in the belief that the new practices would limit disparity and discretion and establish more detailed criteria for sentencing or new sentencing institutions. The resulting contradictory options include the following:

1. Abolishing plea bargaining
2. Establishing plea-bargaining rules and guidelines
3. Setting mandatory minimum sentences
4. Establishing statutory determinate sentencing
5. Setting voluntary or descriptive sentencing guidelines or presumptive or prescriptive sentencing guidelines
6. Creating sentencing councils
7. Requiring judges to provide reasons for their sentences
8. Setting parole guidelines to limit parole board discretion
9. Abolishing parole[12]
10. Adopting or modifying good-time procedures
11. Routinizing appellate review of sentences[13]

These options represent only the principal steps designed to limit unbridled discretion, reduce discrimination, make sentencing fairer, and enhance justice.

Reform Effects

In just a few decades, dramatic changes in sentencing structures and practices became evident. Release by a parole board was abolished in a large number of states, and mandatory sentencing guidelines were established in many others. In 1987, the U.S. Federal Sentencing Guidelines were enacted. More than 20 states were using determinate sentencing (a sentence with a specific release date), and at least 48 states had established mandatory minimum sentences for at least one crime. Several states adopted statewide sentencing councils, and at least 50 jurisdictions drew up local sentencing guidelines. It is against that background of concern and change that we will look at the sentencing decision.

Predicting Behavior

If the sentencing procedure had no purpose but to punish the offender, as was the case until fairly recently, the judge's decision could be easily prescribed by statute. In modern times, however, the sentence is also expected to serve other purposes, such as rehabilitation and reintegration of the offender and restoration of the victim and community. Those broadly divergent objectives create a paradox that may force judges to choose between alternatives based on the offense, the offender, the victim, and the community. The choice is often further complicated by subtle pressures from police, prosecutors, and the general public to incarcerate certain offenders for longer periods of time.[14]

One of the main problems with the sentencing decision is that it requires judges to predict human behavior. As judges ask themselves if specific offenders will respond to prison positively or perhaps benefit more from help while on probation, they have little factual information to guide them. In the final analysis, most judges must rely on a presentence investigation and their own intuition, experience, and imagination to produce the best decision.

The Presentence Investigation

Most of the states make a **presentence report** mandatory for offenses for which imprisonment can be more than one year. It is estimated that more than 85 percent of the states do prepare some kind of presentence report on felony cases, although there may be extreme variation in the report's usefulness and quality. The presentence report, if properly researched and prepared, can be an extremely valuable document for trial judges who are making sentencing decisions.

key term

Presentence report
Document prepared by agent of the court that investigates the offender's background for judicial determination of punishment.

The presentence investigation report is usually prepared by the court's probation officer. The defense attorney usually reviews and may challenge points in the presentence report to help the judge make a sentencing decision based on information from all of the sources. Walter C. Reckless pointed out the essential elements of a workable presentence investigation report. He said that, when written up and presented to the judge, this report should include in summary form the following information:[15]

1. Present offense (including the person's attitude toward it and his or her role in it)
2. Previous criminal record and family situation (including tensions and discord and the factors affecting his or her happiness)
3. Neighborhood environment, school, and educational history
4. Employment history (especially skills and efficiency and stability as a worker)
5. Associates and participation
6. Habits (including alcohol, gambling, promiscuity, and so forth)
7. Physical and mental health (as reported by various sources and by special examinations)
8. Summary and recommendations

Most presentence investigations will emphasize such objective facts in a case as number of prior offenses, employment status, age, grade reached in school, number of children, and so on. It is also important that the investigating officer capture additional information, such as the defendants' attitudes toward the charges, acceptance of responsibility, and willingness to change their behavior.

The presentence investigation report gives the judge a comprehensive and factual overview of the offender, the actual crime, and the offender's nature, history, habits, personality, problems, needs, and risks. It also usually contains a recommendation to the court of an appropriate disposition for the case. Judges tend to accept the presentence recommendation at a rate of about 83 percent for probation and 87 percent for imprisonment.

The presentence report serves many functions. Not only is it of immediate use in determining an appropriate sentence, but it is also used by correctional agencies or institutions for classification and program activities assignments. It will aid the probation officer in handling the case should probation be the sentence imposed. It will also follow the offender to parole, at which time the parole officer will use it in planning and supervising the case. Appellate review courts use the document when considering an **appeal** of sentence, and the presentence investigation reports also offer a database from which to conduct research on convicted offenders, case flows, and court management.[16]

key term

Appeal
Petition to higher courts to reverse procedures and protect offenders based on due process issues.

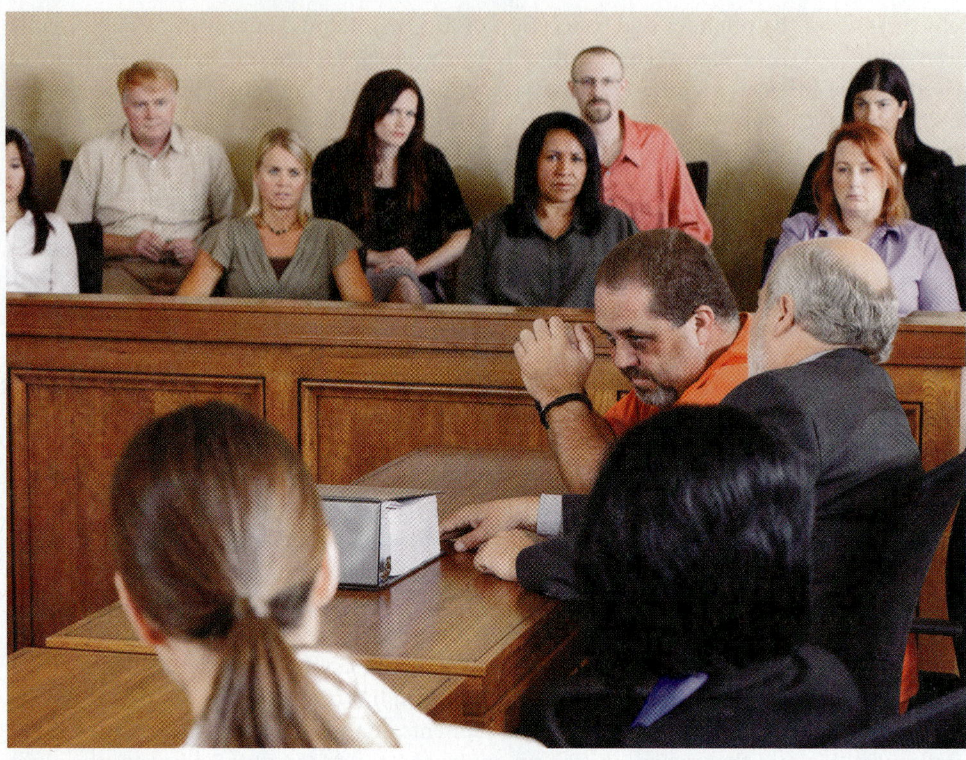

Photo 4.1

A court-appointed attorney argues for his client.
Rich Legg/Getty Images.

Judicial versus Administrative Sentencing

Traditionally, the sentencing process has involved a judicial determination of the appropriate punishment for a specific crime. There have been extensive changes in judicial power in the past century, however, particularly during the past few decades. In the early days, when a judge sentenced an offender to 10 years in prison, it was almost a certainty that the offender would serve 10 years to the day. As administrative forms of sentence shortening (involving such matters as good time, pardon, parole, and clemency) became more common, the correlation between the judge's sentence and the time the offender served largely disappeared. In practice, courts using indeterminate sentencing can establish minimum and maximum sentences within the sentencing statutes, but the actual length of the sentence is often left up to the administrators of the correctional system, that is, to the executive rather than to the judicial branch of government. Therefore, those involved in **administrative sentencing** ultimately decide an offender's fate.

key term

Administrative sentencing Process by which the actual length of the sentence is left up to the administrators of the correctional system, as seen in such processes as good-time credit, probation, parole, and program participation; the actual sentence served is set by the executive branch rather than the judicial.

A comparison of the judicial and administrative styles of decision making in sentencing reveals some similar criteria:

1. A determination of how much time is right for the kind of crime at issue, with the decision maker's own sense of values and expectations usually (but not always) heavily influenced by the pressures of the local environment and perceived norms of colleagues.[17]
2. Classification within that crime category of the offender's particular acts as mitigated, average, or aggravated.
3. Offender's past criminal record (slight, average, or aggravated).
4. Offender's extent of repentance, attitude toward available treatment, and official prognosis of reform ability.
5. Anticipated public (usually meaning law enforcement) reaction to a proposed disposition. Not all of these criteria are used or even relevant in every case, and many other variables may be raised because of the existence of particular facts (such as strong middle-class background and allegiance) or the peculiarities or hang-ups of an individual decision maker. Something approximating the given basic list, however, appears to comprise the critical factors in most sentence fixing.[18]

Practical Problems in Sentencing

As we have seen previously, the correctional filter of the criminal justice process reveals at every step an imbalance of input to output (number of arrests versus number of incarcerations). Many cases are winnowed out in the early stages, and it is a highly select group of prisoners who end up in prisons like Attica, Pelican Bay, and San Quentin. In a statistical sense, the negative selection process that admits the offender to prison may be considered more discriminating than the positive one that admits students to Ivy League colleges. But for the practical need to spread limited resources over an overwhelming number of cases, scores of additional offenders would join each of the relatively small proportion of offenders that ends up in prison. The state and federal correctional systems are finite in size. The sentencing decision may be impacted by the decisions at the other end of the funnel process, which determine release rates. The system can become blocked if sentences do not approximately balance releases, resulting in dangerous overcrowding. At worst, prison overcrowding can contribute to judicial overuse of probation for offenders whose risk level is too high. This can result in overworked probation officers and unacceptably high probation failure rates by offenders who continue to commit serious crimes and whose probation is then revoked, requiring resentencing to imprisonment in state institutions. Sentencing, therefore, sometimes takes into account both the numbers of prisoners in the institutions and the limited resources for handling them.[19] Another source of pressure on the already overloaded correctional and court systems is the seemingly endless number of drug arrests that enter the juvenile and adult courts.

Problems in Setting Prison Terms

In the past, the determination of prison terms has been left largely to the courts. Decisions were made within the broad parameters of plea bargaining and statutory limitations. In the past two decades, however, control over the sentencing process has become more of a concern to state legislatures. Concerns about disparate sentences and other abuses or perceived abuses of the system have resulted in six basic strategies to formalize legislative control over the sentencing process:

1. **Determinate sentencing**—sentencing systems under which parole boards no longer may release prisoners before their sentences (minus good time) have expired
2. **Mandatory prison terms**—statutes through which legislatures require a prison term always to be imposed for convictions for certain offenses or offenders
3. **Sentencing guidelines**—procedures designed to structure sentencing decisions based on measures of offense severity and criminal history
4. **Parole guidelines**—procedures designed to structure parole release decisions based on measurable offender criteria
5. **Good-time policies**—statutes that allow for reducing a prison term based on an offender's behavior in prison
6. **Emergency crowding provisions**—policies that relieve prison crowding by systematically making inmates eligible for release sooner

Prison populations are increasing in many states. Policies for setting prison terms influence the size of prison populations by both the number of people who are sentenced and the length of time that they stay in prison. As a result, many states have attempted to find ways to **modify** prison terms and reduce population pressures. Those methods include sentencing guidelines, such as those in Minnesota, that use available prison capacity as a consideration in setting the length of terms. Mechanisms also exist for accelerating good time and direct release of certain prisoners, usually those already close to their release date, under administrative provisions (such as emergency crowding laws, the use of commutation, sentence revisions, and early release programs).

The determinate sentencing states of California, Colorado, Connecticut, Illinois, Indiana, Maine, Minnesota, New Mexico, North Carolina, and Washington tend to give

key term

Determinate sentencing
A flat sentence of punishment imposed by the sentencing court.

key term

Sentencing guidelines
System of sentencing that imposes a predefined sentence length based on prior criminal history and crime severity, which allows judges to depart from the guidelines if warranted by the circumstances.

key term

Good-time policies
Administrative mechanism reducing sentence length by crediting inmates for good behavior, extra work, or other statutory policies.

key term

Modify
Appeal court order requiring change in the trial court's legal decision on guilt or other rights.

sentencing judges the least amount of discretion. Offenders usually receive fixed sentences, and they are served in full, minus good-time credits. Generally in those states, parole boards continue to handle revocations and good-time decisions.

key term

Presumptive sentencing A sentencing mechanism fixed by a sentencing commission or legislature that identifies maximum and minimum sentences for punishment to be imposed by the judge but that permits adjustment for special circumstances.

Such a sentencing structure limits "judicial imperialism" in sentencing because the legislature heavily influences the sentence length. Whether there are unforeseen problems in **presumptive sentencing** remains to be proven, but California's prison population problems may well be due to a corollary of presumptive sentencing: abolition of parole board early-release authority that had been used in the past to control prison overcrowding. Mandatory prison-term statutes exist in some form, for some crimes, in 48 states. Those statutes apply to certain crimes of violence and to habitual criminals, and the court's discretion in such cases (regarding, for example, probation, fines, and suspended sentences) has been eliminated by statute. There were 159,000 inmates serving life sentences in 2012, a number that has quadrupled since 1984. About 50,000 of those were serving life without parole, an increase of 22 percent since just 2008.

correctional **practice 4.4**

History of the Sentencing Guidelines

More than 20 years ago, Congress dramatically changed the federal sentencing system. The changes followed widespread discontent with the old sentencing system, and they ultimately led to the passage of the Federal Sentencing Guidelines in 1987. In the old system, judges determined criminal sentences. They considered the facts of each particular case—including the circumstances of the offense and the life history of the offender—and chose a sentence they considered fair. The only requirement was that the sentence be within a statutory range, and the ranges were often extremely broad. Statutes typically authorized sentences like "not more than five years," "not more than 20 years," or, in some cases, "any term of years or life." Judges had authority to impose any sentence within the statutory range.

The imposition of the sentence was only the beginning. Once the person was in prison, the parole board determined the actual date of release. The parole board considered circumstances such as the person's conduct in prison and efforts toward rehabilitation, and it released people to parole supervision when it thought they were ready—often after just half the sentence. If the person misbehaved after release, parole could be revoked, and the person could be incarcerated for the remainder of the sentence.

In the 1970s, this practice fell into disfavor because it permitted too much disparity between cases. Different judges sentenced similar offenders differently, and parole boards became too powerful. If two identical offenders were each convicted of a crime carrying a sentence of "not more than 20 years," one might spend three years in custody and the other might spend 15. Evidence accumulated that the system led to arbitrary decision making and sometimes discrimination against poor people and minorities.

In 1984, Congress addressed these concerns by creating the U.S. Sentencing Commission and ordering the promulgation of the Federal Sentencing Guidelines. The new system sharply curtailed parole and confined judicially imposed sentences into narrow ranges. Congress enacted the guidelines into law in 1987, and in 1989 the Supreme Court held that the effort was constitutional. (See *Mistretta* v. *U.S.* [1989], 317–320.)

Guidelines use standardized worksheets to calculate the sentence. In principle, the process is a lot like calculating income taxes with a federal 1040 form. The worksheet is complex and intricate, but in theory it guides everybody to the same conclusions. Guidelines operate by assigning an offense level to every crime—low offense levels for minor crimes and high levels for major crimes. At the same time, the guidelines direct the calculation of the criminal history of each defendant. A person with a clean record starts with zero criminal history points, and points are added for every subsequent offense.

The task of the judge is to look up on a grid the spot where the offense level intersects the criminal history. The grid assigns light sentences to people with low criminal histories who commit lesser crimes and stiff sentences to people with long criminal histories who commit severe crimes. The judge then imposes a sentence in accordance with the sentencing guidelines grid unless there is a reason to depart.

The concept of the guidelines has been well received because it can lead to less sentencing disparity between judges and a more rational system overall. The federal system and roughly one-third of the states now use guideline sentencing systems. Different jurisdictions use different guidelines and have had different experiences with them. The general experience has been that guidelines represent an improvement over unfettered judicial discretion but that they must be well structured and carefully conceived in order to succeed.

SOURCE: "Part A—Introduction and Authority," http://www.ussc.gov/guidelines-manual/2010/2010-1a1 (retrieved August 17, 2014). See also David Keene (2013), "Prison-Sentence Reform," http://www.nationalreview.com/article/349118/prison-sentence-reform-david-keene.

Perhaps the best example of sentencing guidelines can be seen in the federal system. The Federal Sentencing Guidelines matrix is shown in Figure 4.1. The matrix system factors in the severity of the offense and the criminal history of the offender to arrive at a sentence range. Among the most vocal critics of the Federal Sentencing Guidelines are federal judges, who believe that this system has taken away too much discretion. In 2005, the U.S. Supreme Court ruled that the federal guidelines violated a defendant's Sixth Amendment right to a jury trial because the guidelines required judges to make decisions that affect prison time by considering factors that had not come before the jury during trial. Later that month, the Supreme Court ordered lower courts to review hundreds of sentences of defendants then appealing their tainted enhanced sentence.

Good-time policies are another way to control behavior in correctional institutions and to control population pressures as well. The threat of losing up to one-third of their credits toward their sentences earned by good conduct serves as a control over some inmates' behavior.[20] Our review of the changes in sentencing practices and their consequences in the past decade clearly shows the shifts that have taken place. Although discretion in determining sentence length has been somewhat removed from the sentencing judge and parole board, it was reduced by legislatures through their enactment of new sentencing structures, for reasons discussed earlier. In turn, in many jurisdictions, the prosecutor's discretion was increased. The prison populations will continue to climb as more and more offenders are committed and serve longer and longer sentences.[21]

FELONY SENTENCES IN FEDERAL COURT

The U.S. district courts are the trial courts in the federal system. District courts hear nearly all categories of federal cases (including both criminal and civil cases). Cases heard are for violations of federal statutes. Each of the 94 federal judicial districts has at least one district court and courthouse, in which trials are held for persons committing federal crimes. The type of prisoner petitions filed in the U.S. district court (Northern District of Ohio) for 2006–2012 can be found in Table 4.3. Here we are concerned with sentences imposed by federal district courts. The last national data available as we go to press are for fiscal year 2010.

All told, some 102,430 trials resulted in a sentence disposition. The vast majority of sentencing outcomes were sentences to imprisonment, although one in nine cases received probation as the sentence (see Table 4.4). A small percentage were sentenced to a fine only, 183 were sentenced to life imprisonment, and four resulted in the pronouncement of the death penalty. See Figure 4.2 for a detailed display of crimes for which offenders were sentenced. The figure displays the types of offenses for which these criminals were convicted: 31 percent for immigration violations, 30 percent for drug offenses, and about 17 percent for property offenses. The average sentence length for offenders receiving probation was 35 months, and for those incarcerated, the term averaged 54 months. We will return to the federal district courts when we examine the federal prison system.[22]

DETERRENCE BY SENTENCING

A discussion of sentencing would be incomplete without mentioning the policy implications of the increasing demand for deterrence.[23] Some writers now argue that those states that imprison more of the offender population (rather than use community corrections) would have lower crime rates if the proportion of persons sentenced to prison were to increase even more. Though **deterrence by sentencing** may appeal to conservatives who believe that the criminal justice system can affect the rates of crime and serve as a deterrent, the data on the effects of higher imprisonment rates do not bear out the presumed effects.

key term

Deterrence by sentencing
Discouraging the individual's and the public's propensity to commit additional crimes by imposition of harsh punishment; the goal is crime reduction.

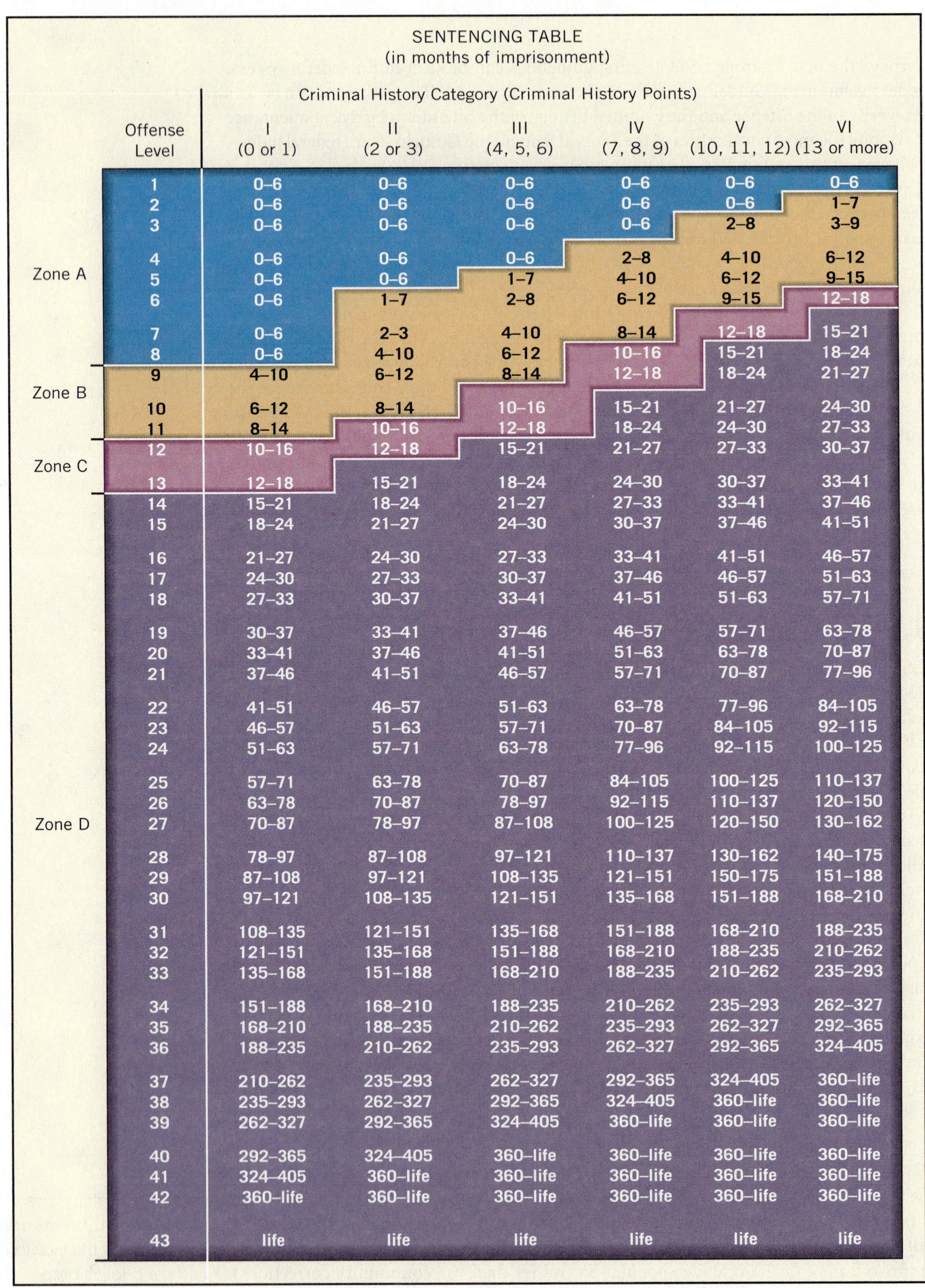

SENTENCING TABLE
(in months of imprisonment)

	Offense Level	Criminal History Category (Criminal History Points) I (0 or 1)	II (2 or 3)	III (4, 5, 6)	IV (7, 8, 9)	V (10, 11, 12)	VI (13 or more)
	1	0–6	0–6	0–6	0–6	0–6	0–6
	2	0–6	0–6	0–6	0–6	0–6	1–7
	3	0–6	0–6	0–6	0–6	2–8	3–9
	4	0–6	0–6	0–6	2–8	4–10	6–12
Zone A	5	0–6	0–6	1–7	4–10	6–12	9–15
	6	0–6	1–7	2–8	6–12	9–15	12–18
	7	0–6	2–3	4–10	8–14	12–18	15–21
	8	0–6	4–10	6–12	10–16	15–21	18–24
	9	4–10	6–12	8–14	12–18	18–24	21–27
Zone B	10	6–12	8–14	10–16	15–21	21–27	24–30
	11	8–14	10–16	12–18	18–24	24–30	27–33
	12	10–16	12–18	15–21	21–27	27–33	30–37
Zone C	13	12–18	15–21	18–24	24–30	30–37	33–41
	14	15–21	18–24	21–27	27–33	33–41	37–46
	15	18–24	21–27	24–30	30–37	37–46	41–51
	16	21–27	24–30	27–33	33–41	41–51	46–57
	17	24–30	27–33	30–37	37–46	46–57	51–63
	18	27–33	30–37	33–41	41–51	51–63	57–71
	19	30–37	33–41	37–46	46–57	57–71	63–78
	20	33–41	37–46	41–51	51–63	63–78	70–87
	21	37–46	41–51	46–57	57–71	70–87	77–96
	22	41–51	46–57	51–63	63–78	77–96	84–105
	23	46–57	51–63	57–71	70–87	84–105	92–115
	24	51–63	57–71	63–78	77–96	92–115	100–125
	25	57–71	63–78	70–87	84–105	100–125	110–137
	26	63–78	70–87	78–97	92–115	110–137	120–150
Zone D	27	70–87	78–97	87–108	100–125	120–150	130–162
	28	78–97	87–108	97–121	110–137	130–162	140–175
	29	87–108	97–121	108–135	121–151	150–175	151–188
	30	97–121	108–135	121–151	135–168	151–188	168–210
	31	108–135	121–151	135–168	151–188	168–210	188–235
	32	121–151	135–168	151–188	168–210	188–235	210–262
	33	135–168	151–188	168–210	188–235	210–262	235–293
	34	151–188	168–210	188–235	210–262	235–293	262–327
	35	168–210	188–235	210–262	235–293	262–327	292–365
	36	188–235	210–262	235–293	262–327	292–365	324–405
	37	210–262	235–293	262–327	292–365	324–405	360–life
	38	235–293	262–327	292–365	324–405	360–life	360–life
	39	262–327	292–365	324–405	360–life	360–life	360–life
	40	292–365	324–405	360–life	360–life	360–life	360–life
	41	324–405	360–life	360–life	360–life	360–life	360–life
	42	360–life	360–life	360–life	360–life	360–life	360–life
	43	life	life	life	life	life	life

figure 4.1

Sentencing Table.

SOURCE: U.S. Sentencing Commission, http://www.ussc.gov/Guidelines/2013_Guidelines/Manual_HTML/index.cfm (accessed November 27, 2013).

table 4.3 **Sentences Imposed in U.S. District Courts, Fiscal 2010**

	Disposition	Average Sentence Length (months)
Fine only	2,345	N/A
Probation	10,157	35
Incarceration	89,741	54
Life	183	N/A
Death	4	N/A
Total	102,430	N/A

SOURCE: Sourcebook of Criminal Justice Statistics online, "Criminal Defendants Sentenced in U.S. District Courts," http://www.albany.edu/sourcebook/pdf/t5222010.pdf.

table 4.4 **Prisoner Petitions Filed in U.S. District Court, Northern District of Ohio**

Description	2006	2007	2008	2009	2010	2011	2012
Habeas-alien detainee	0	0	6	8	5	8	3
Motion to vacate	77	75	80	79	64	56	73
Habeas-death penalty	7	5	3	5	3	3	6
Habeas corpus	297	268	367	329	319	283	273
Mandamus and other	28	24	24	16	10	15	11
Prisoner civil rights	95	103	122	113	167	143	162
Prison conditions	9	6	9	8	9	2	5
Total	513	481	611	556	577	508	533

SOURCE: U.S. District Court-Northern District of Ohio, *Annual Assessment of the Civil and Criminal Dockets* (2012), 6.

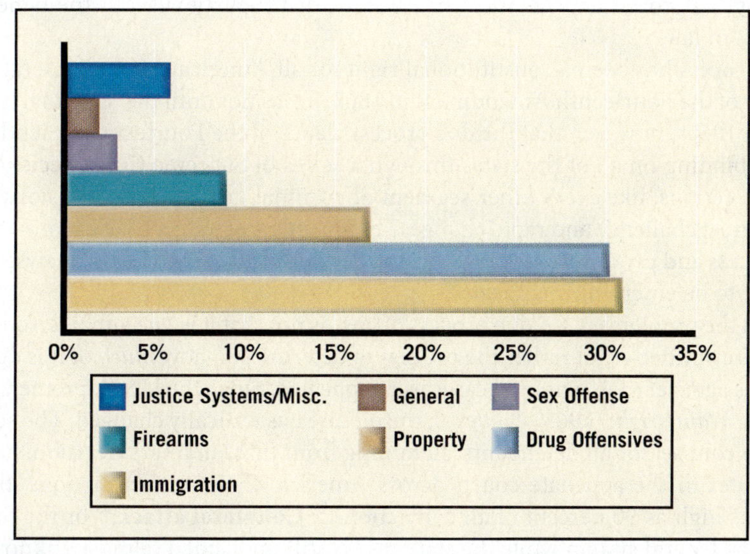

figure 4.2

Criminal Defendants Sentenced to Imprisonment in U.S. District Courts in Fiscal Year 2010.

SOURCE: *Sourcebook of Criminal Justice Stats Online (Fiscal 2010)*, http://www.albany.edu/sourcebook/pdf/t5252010.pdf (accessed August 21, 2013).

In both the United States and Canada, the rates of crime do not go down with increased imprisonment.[24] Instead, the rates of crime go up when the proportion of offenders per 100,000 who are sentenced to prison is raised. Therefore, we may need to reevaluate our thinking about the continued use of imprisonment to deter others from committing crime when studies show that it has just the opposite effect.[25]

Appellate Review

Our examination of sentencing and legal issues surrounding corrections for offenders and law violators would not be complete without a discussion of the path of appeals from convictions, penalties imposed, conditions of imprisonment, and questions about civil rights violations. The prison walls can no more be a "concrete curtain" between offenders and prisoners under correctional control and those living in the free society. In the twenty-first century, offenders are still granted many of the same rights guaranteed by the U.S. Constitution. Prisoner rights are discussed in detail in Chapter 16. This chapter examines such items as motions to vacate sentences, habeas corpus, and civil rights. We begin with some of the basic tenets that apply to the justice system in America. The many types of legal cases involved with corrections are presented here in their most basic forms. Serious students of corrections, whether future academicians or practitioners, should become familiar with those key cases.

THE ISSUE OF DUE PROCESS

A basic tenet of the criminal justice process in America is that every defendant is presumed to be innocent until proven guilty. Our system not only demands proof of guilt but also requires that the proof be obtained fairly and legally. The process of appellate review helps ensure that these conditions will be met. In effect, the appellate review acts as a shield for the defendant caught up in the processes of criminal trial, incarceration, or supervision in the community. The state has considerable resources to prosecute those it considers offenders, and the Constitution protects us from the kind of government **railroading** that could deprive us of life, liberty, or property without the benefit of the due process of law.

key term

Railroading
The formal or even informal violation of the civil rights of the accused that leads to incapacitation or other unjustified punishment.

key term

Due process
Legal requirement that constitutional rights of the accused and correctional clients will conform to guaranteed constitutional protection minimums.

key term

Collateral attack
The process of raising additional legal questions in other courts but before case disposition.

Due process has been a constitutional right for all Americans under federal law since the passage of the Fourteenth Amendment in 1868. It was not until the "criminal law revolution" of the 1960s, however, that the due process clause of the Fourteenth Amendment was also made binding on all of the states through a series of Supreme Court decisions. In the field of corrections, like every other segment of criminal justice, those decisions created a climate of great challenge and rapid change. This chapter includes a brief examination of the appeal process and procedure, a glance at several significant cases, and an analysis of trends that appear to be emerging in appeals.[26]

One of the problems with "due process of law" is not that it is *due*—that is, something to which we are entitled—but rather the process of determining how *much* of it is due. Only a few decades ago, very few criminal cases were appealed. Since the U.S. Supreme Court case of *Gideon* v. *Wainwright* (1963), however, the picture has radically changed. The securing of the right to counsel for all defendants, stemming from that landmark decision, has opened the floodgates in the appellate courts across America. In some jurisdictions, the rate of appeals is as high as 90 percent of all convictions.[27] **Collateral attack**,[28] or the filing of an appeal in the federal system while the state case is still undecided (almost unknown before the 1960s), is now routine in most state courts. The result of this massive overload in the appellate system was a monumental increase in the workload for state and federal judges. It has also created extended periods of litigation, often stretched out over several years, which have eroded any lingering belief that a conviction for a criminal offense must be considered

Photo 4.2
The U.S. Supreme Court.
exacto superstock/SuperStock.

final. The review procedure has as many as 11 steps in some state systems, and it is not unusual for a defendant to explore at least four or five. The 11 steps are as follows:

1. New trial motion filed in court where conviction was imposed
2. Appeal to state intermediate appellate court (in states where there is no intermediate appellate court, this step would not be available)
3. Appeal to state supreme court
4. Petition to U.S. Supreme Court to review state court decision in appeal
5. Postconviction proceeding in state trial court
6. Appeal of postconviction proceeding to state intermediate appellate court
7. Appeal to state supreme court
8. Petition to U.S. Supreme Court to review state court decision on appeal from postconviction proceeding
9. Habeas corpus petition in federal district court
10. Appeal to U.S. Court of Appeals
11. Petition to U.S. Supreme Court to review court of appeals decision on habeas corpus petition[29]

It is easy to see why the review process can take so long, especially when some steps may be used several times in a single appeal, with reviews of the same case taking place simultaneously in different court systems. Thus, due process may be a long and complicated procedure, and when appeal is part of the scheme, it can become a seemingly endless cycle.

THE MECHANICS OF AN APPEAL

Throughout the legal proceedings, there are points at which appealable errors can occur. Following the effects of some of the major cases and the potential of future appeals, it is important to know how one makes an appeal following a criminal conviction. The process is highly fragmented and cumbersome, but a basic scheme applies to most jurisdictions. Although there are many alternatives to this basic model, it covers most of the avenues for appeals.

correctional practice 4.5

The "Landmark Cases" of the 1960s and 1970s

Mapp v. Ohio The case of *Mapp* v. *Ohio* (exclusionary rule), 367 U.S. 643 (1960), opened a Pandora's box of Fourteenth Amendment rulings. A crack in the armor of state proceedings, it paved the way for the flood of cases heard by the Court during the next decade in reference not only to illegally obtained evidence but also to all areas of individual rights.

Robinson v. California In the California case of *Robinson* v. *California* (cruel and unusual punishment), 370 U.S. 660 (1961), the Eighth Amendment's clause forbidding cruel and unusual punishment was made binding on state proceedings.

Gideon v. Wainwright In the crucial decision of *Gideon* v. *Wainwright* (right to counsel), 372 U.S. 335 (1963), the Court held that defendants in noncapital cases are entitled to assistance of counsel at trial as a matter of right. This right was extended to state proceedings, again under the provisions of the Fourteenth Amendment.

Miranda v. Arizona The application of the Fifth Amendment protections against self-incrimination was influenced by *Gideon* v. *Wainwright*, 372 U.S. 335 (1963). For the first time, in the 1966 decision of *Miranda* v. *Arizona*, 384 U.S. 436, a set of specific and detailed police warnings to the arrested person (and now the prison inmate) was required, through the due process clause, at specific and distinct points in the criminal process.

Johnson v. Avery A significant 1969 decision provided prisoners in state penal institutions with legal assistance in preparing habeas corpus proceedings. In *Johnson* v. *Avery*, 393 U.S. 483, the Court held that states not providing adequate legal assistance would have to put up with "jailhouse lawyers," prisoners determined to research and conduct their own and others' appeals.

Furman v. Georgia In *Furman* v. *Georgia*, 408 U.S. 238 (1972), the issue of cruel and unusual punishment as applied to the death penalty was raised in a petition by several states for clarification of that long-standing dilemma. In June 1972, the U.S. Supreme Court held that any statute that permits a jury to demand the death penalty is unconstitutional.

The entire process stems, of course, from a conviction of guilt by some court system at the municipal, county, state, or federal level. In each case, the procedure for appeal is determined by the court of record for that case. Those appeals, known as postconviction remedies, are usually made by the defendant. The state is less likely to appeal a decision regardless of the outcome. If the accused is convicted, that is the result the state was after, and if the accused is declared innocent, the state cannot appeal because the Constitution guarantees that someone who is found innocent cannot be placed in **double jeopardy**[30] (which is being subjected to a second trial, by the same jurisdiction, on the same facts). The effect of an appropriately introduced appeal is to grant a stay (delay) in the execution of the original sentence until the appeal has been decided. As soon as possible, if not immediately after the sentence is pronounced, the defendant's counsel must either move for a new trial or make an appeal on some reasonable grounds because appellate courts usually dislike and make short work of "frivolous" appeals. But as long ago as 1933, the significance of the appeal process was firmly established:

key term

Double jeopardy
The second trying of a suspected offender for the same crime as originally charged.

> Appellate courts do not reverse decisions simply because they disagree with them. Reversal must proceed from error of law and such error must be substantial. But if this account is to be veracious I must call attention to a fact familiar to every experienced lawyer, yet not apparent in the classical literature of the law, and probably not consciously admitted even to themselves by most appellate judges. Practically every decision of a lower court can be reversed. By that I mean practically every record contains some erroneous rulings [and] they can nearly always find some error if they want grounds for reversal.[31]

key term

Court of last resort
The highest appeal court having jurisdiction within that particular geographical area.

Each state has an appellate tribunal that serves as the **court of last resort**. The titles vary, but no matter what the title, a pathway for appeal is open to all in the American judicial system.

The Courts of Appeal

The court level immediately above the trial court is usually called the **court of appeals**. In some states, and in the federal system, there is more than one level of appeal. In those cases, the highest level of appellate court is generally called the Supreme Court. The Supreme Court of the United States is the court of last resort; cases decided there are considered final. The U.S. Supreme Court will usually hear cases from the state systems only after the defendant has exhausted all state remedies and the case has been finally adjudicated.[32]

key term

Court of appeals
Any higher court with post-conviction authority; any court authorized to treat with contempt decisions made by the lower court.

In most state systems, the court of appeals reviews the trial court's decisions for judicial error. The facts in the case are not in question, and the trial court's decisions on that aspect of the case are generally binding on the appellate court. Because of that aspect of appellate review, evidence on the facts of the case is not presented to the court of appeals. Rather, the review is based only on the trial record. An appellate court cannot **reverse** the factual findings of the trial court unless they are totally erroneous. In states that have a second level of review, the trial record and the intermediary court's decision are examined. Usually, the refusal to hear an appeal over a lower appellate court's ruling is the same as upholding the decision, and the case stops there, unless an appeal is filed separately in a federal court of appeals on some constitutional issue.

key term

Reverse
Appeal court's order to cease acting, operating, or arranging in a manner contrary to the usual.

As above, the federal court system currently includes 94 trial courts (federal district courts) and 13 intermediary review courts (courts of appeal) between the federal trial courts and the U.S. Supreme Court. The federal courts of appeal are spread across the country in "circuits" to facilitate servicing the 94 trial courts. Federal courts are restricted in their powers to cases arising under the Constitution, federal laws, or treaties; all cases affecting ambassadors, public ministers, and consuls; admiralty and maritime cases; and controversies where the United States is a party; controversies between states, between a state and a citizen of another state, or between citizens of the same state claiming lands under grants from different states; and in cases between a state or citizens of a state and foreign states, citizens, or subjects.[33]

The federal courts of appeal are similar to the state courts of appeal in that they review for error the cases tried by the federal district courts. In some instances, the appeal court may **remand** a case, which is where they send the case back to the original court for consideration. The Supreme Court is the ultimate interpreter of the Constitution and federal statutes. It reviews the decisions of the courts of appeal, and some direct appeals from district courts. The Supreme Court also reviews the decisions of state courts involving matters of federal constitutional rights where the case has been finally adjudicated in the state court system. Besides its appellate function, the Court has original jurisdiction in suits where a state is a party and in controversies involving ambassadors, ministers, and consuls.[34]

key term

Remand
To send a case back to the trier of fact for considerations not contrary to the appeal court's order.

APPEALS FROM BEHIND THE WALLS

In the early twentieth century, most appeals were based on the specific issues in the trial. In the 1960s, appeals began to move toward issues related to individual rights as stated and interpreted under the U.S. Constitution. Using the Fourteenth Amendment as a lever, the Supreme Court **affirmed** those rights to individuals in the separate states on a piecemeal basis. Under the "hands-off" doctrine established by chief justice Felix Frankfurter, the court had restricted its early decisions to the actions of judges. Later, abandoning the Frankfurter policy, the court began to impose procedural guidelines on law enforcement, corrections, and every other element of the criminal justice system. Constitutional rights of prisoners (discussed in Part 4) were more sharply defined by the appellate courts' decisions. Many of these appeals came from desperate people behind prison walls,[35] and those appeals continue.

key term

Affirm
Appeal court's decision that due processes have not been violated by the government.

Photo 4.3

A "jailhouse lawyer" goes through the law library trying to find an appeal route.
Anne Chadwick Williams/Newscom.

REFORM BY JUDICIAL DECREE

Corrections, as a social system, is above all a political unit established by an authorizing mandate, supported by tax revenues, and subject to political influences. It reflects both the system of justice and the overall sociocultural environment. The latter is the source of externally induced reform. In externally induced reform, individuals or groups outside the correctional system effect changes.[36]

At the state and local levels, correctional reform is usually accomplished through legislative or executive action. Examples of reform by legislation range from the complete revision of a state's criminal code to passage of simple amendments to bills, allowing such benefits as educational and home furloughs. The executive branch of government can also exert a direct effect on correctional reform through executive orders. Those orders can accomplish small but important changes, such as the abolition of mail censorship, the appointment of a task force of involved citizens to seek correctional reform, and the withholding of support for clearly unsound correctional programs.[37]

Between 1960 and 1972, American criminal law passed from a state of *evolution* to a state of *revolution*.[38] The step-by-step extension to the states of the various federal constitutional guarantees of individual rights was clearly the goal of the courts' quiet but effective revolution. The decisions of the much maligned—or revered—Warren Court are more readily understood when viewed from that perspective. During the 1960s, nearly all of the guarantees of the Fourth, Fifth, Sixth, and Eighth Amendments to the Constitution were made binding on the states, although the Rehnquist Court attempted to undo some of these advances. As previously mentioned, the Fourteenth Amendment (due process clause) provided the primary leverage in the landmark decisions that impacted corrections. The extension of constitutional guarantees to all persons accused in state proceedings has produced dramatic and significant changes in criminal law and criminal procedures and important effects on corrections through appeals related to major landmark decisions.

It should be pointed out that in addition to these cases, from the 1960s and 1970s the Supreme Court also entertained cases concerning the civil rights of inmates through interpretation of the Civil Rights Act of 1871. In the first two decades of the twenty-first century, many prisons were placed under court orders or faced constitutional challenges under

Chapter 42, U.S. Code Section 1983.[39] Many states are being sued, and federal masters have been appointed to oversee the conditions in state prisons.

Two major results of inmate litigation were the development of new mind-sets by correctional administrators and the development of nationwide standards to demonstrate to the courts that the level of practice in the institutions being sued was the best the industry could provide.[40] Although litigation is always a trying situation, it may well be the best way to effect change in correctional settings. The threat of federal court suits has brought about significant changes in practices, policies, and procedures.

One example of the effects of litigation can be seen in the overcrowding of the California Department of Corrections and Rehabilitation. Major changes in state sentencing statutes, lengthened prison sentences, enhanced sentencing (through three-strikes statutes), and drug enforcement sharply increased the number of offenders in California's prisons. Both correctional budgets and overtime payments to correctional officers have had deleterious effects on the amount and quality of medical services. Inmates sued under the Eighth Amendment cruel and unusual clause, and federal district and appellate courts agreed that the department violated those requirements. California appealed to the U.S. Supreme Court, and the justices upheld the lower-court decisions. The court monitor recommended that the presiding federal judge order inmate release so as to increase the per-inmate medical care and services. California then appealed that requirement, basically on public safety issues. The appeal went again to the U.S. Supreme Court, which remanded the case for an action not inconsistent with the district court's decision. California appealed a third time to the U.S. Supreme Court and lost. California will probably have to release about another 10,000 prisoners by 2015 to meet the Court's order.

APPEALS FLOOD THE COURTS

A flood of appeals made with the help of court-appointed lawyers and jailhouse lawyers filled the dockets of the appeals courts beginning in the 1960s and accelerating through 2013. As rights were established in the obvious areas outside prison walls (arrest, search and seizure, privacy and intrusion, cruel and unusual punishment), they were eventually tested with regard to events inside the walls as well. The autonomous and discretionary control over inmates was finally lifted as the right to counsel moved into the prison as well as the courtroom. A milestone case was decided in the 1967–1968 Supreme Court term, when *Mempa* v. *Rhay* extended the right to counsel to state probation revocation hearings, previously considered an essentially administrative action. The Court held that the application of a deferred sentence was a "critical point" in the proceeding.

Types of Prisoner Petitions

The three types of suits filed by prison inmates in federal district court are habeas corpus, civil rights, and mandamus. In brief, habeas corpus suits by prisoners challenge the constitutionality of their imprisonment, civil rights suits seek redress of civil rights violations by government officials, and mandamus suits seek to compel a government official to perform a duty owed.[41]

The basic principle of the **writ of habeas corpus** is that the government is accountable to the courts for a person's imprisonment. If the government cannot show that the person's imprisonment conforms to the fundamental principles of law, that person is entitled to immediate release. The most frequently cited reason for habeas corpus petitions by state inmates is "ineffective assistance of counsel" (25 percent). Other commonly cited reasons include errors by the trial court (15 percent), due process violations (14 percent), and self-incrimination (12 percent). For federal inmates, habeas corpus petitions generally challenge the constitutionality of imprisonment or constitute motions to vacate a sentence.

key term

Writ of habeas corpus
A writ of habeas corpus is used to bring a prisoner or other detainee (e.g. institutionalized mental patient) before the court to determine if the person's imprisonment or detention is lawful.

key term

Civil rights
Those rights defined in the U.S. Constitution or accorded through judicial decisions.

key term

Writ of mandamus
A judicial order requiring the recipient to conform to the court's decision.

The foundation for **civil rights** petitions originates in the Fourteenth Amendment of the U.S. Constitution. It prohibits the states from "depriving any person of life, liberty, or property without due process of law." Petitions by state prisoners most frequently challenge physical security (21 percent), inadequate medical treatment (17 percent), and due process (13 percent).

The **writ of mandamus** ("we command") is an extraordinary remedy based on common law that is used when the plaintiff has no other adequate means to attain the desired relief. The mandamus petition is filed when the inmate seeks to compel a government official to perform a duty owed to the inmate (ministerial or nondiscretionary duties). The petitions are infrequent, varied in nature, and more typically specific to individual circumstances.

Legislative Initiatives to Reduce Prisoner Litigation

In 1980, the Civil Rights of Institutionalized Persons Act was enacted by Congress to reduce the number of civil rights petitions filed in the federal courts. This act requires inmates to exhaust state-level administrative remedies before filing their petitions in the federal courts. Congress obviously intended to reserve the federal courts for more serious civil rights violations or other significant constitutional issues.

Despite the intent of Congress, the number of civil rights cases filed in federal court increased more than threefold since the 1990s. This increase was caused primarily by the huge increase in the number of state prisoners. The rate of petitions per 1,000 inmates remained stable.

During 1996, two additional legislative enactments sought to further limit prisoners' ability to file petitions in the federal courts. One was the Prison Litigation Reform Act (PLRA), seeking to reduce the number of petitions filed by inmates claiming civil rights violations. The three major changes were requiring inmates to exhaust all administrative remedies before filing in federal court, requiring inmates to pay applicable filing fees and court costs even if filing *in forma pauperis* ("I am a pauper"), and forbidding inmates from filing in *forma pauperis* if they have had prior petitions dismissed as being frivolous or malicious.

The second act (Antiterrorism and Effective Death Penalty Act [AEDPA]) requires inmates to exhaust direct appeals at the state level before filing a petition in federal court, establishes a one-year statute of limitations from the time their conviction becomes final (after all direct appeals of the conviction and/or the sentence have been exhausted), and requires that a panel of the appeals court approve successive petitions being filed in district court.

After the PLRA was enacted, both the rate and the number of civil rights petitions decreased dramatically, as was the intent of Congress. After AEDPA, both the filing rate and the number of habeas corpus petitions by state inmates increased, primarily as a consequence of the increasing size of the prison population.

By either measure (the rate per 1,000 prisoners or volume of petitions filed), prisoner petitions filed in U.S. district courts decreased after the law was changed.

Some state appellate courts have responded to caseload growth in a variety of other ways. Those coping strategies include adding judgeships, creating new or expanding existing appellate courts, deciding cases without published opinions or writing memo opinions, temporarily assigning judges from the retired ranks or from lower courts, and reducing panel sizes. Expediting hearings, limiting oral arguments, and setting time limits on arguments and briefs are other mechanisms. The reduction of protections of cherished constitutional rights in the name of expediency to meet a crisis or facilitate vague political goals in the name of the War on Drugs (regardless of the nobility of the espoused goals) poses some serious and unacceptable threats to every citizen, convicted criminal or not.

Summary

Explain the Role of Prosecutorial Plea Bargaining and How It Creates the Correctional Funnel

Chapter 4 speaks to both sentencing of criminals and appeals. We started with a discussion of the power and authority of the prosecutor in criminal matters. Incumbents in that role have unfettered authority to exercise a range of decisions, many of which affect the correctional funnel. They can *nolle pros* a case, seek the death penalty, charge the defendant guilty of a lesser but included offense, initiate diversion, compel probation without adjudication, challenge presentence investigation details, and act in violation of both ethics and law. Such an example would be to introduce a detail into a trial that has never been legally proved or mentioned by witnesses. The prosecutor's decision is key.

Summarize the Different Types of Sentences and How Sentencing Decisions Are Made

In general, the judge is the sentencing figure in criminal trial. The sentencing judge is asked to make a presentence estimation of the dangerousness of the offender, the likelihood that offender will benefit from available treatment, what services the offender apparently needs, risk, and other behavior that might be possible, both favorable and unfavorable in content. The sentencing judge has little knowledge about the offender and depends in large part on the fact-finding and investigation by the presentence investigator. The degree of concordance between the investigator's recommendation and the judge's sentence is remarkably high, almost 90 percent agreement at the time.

The sentencing judge faces other problems in sentencing an offender. In some jurisdictions, judges are required to impose incarceration of a specific term, even when they might know that the period of time incarcerated is too long to achieve correctional goals. After all, the favorable impacts of incarceration tend to abate after two years of imprisonment. In other cases, the judge may sentence for the *deterrent* goal: The offender is too dangerous to receive any supervision under the level of maximum security imprisonment, or the defendant is believed to be a major officer in a *security threat group*. Perhaps the crime committed is so brutal and monstrous that few would be safe if released. And sometimes that can be seen in the sentencing patterns of the judiciary. As an example, one *heinous offender* kidnapped and raped a young girl, killing her and dismembering her body, in part for consumption of her flesh. In this case, the sentencing judge imposed life without parole, to be followed by a consecutive sentence of 68 years of imprisonment.

It should be noted that the judiciary usually seeks to find a community-based sanction for most first-time and youthful offenders, those not hardened as criminals. It is this search for rational sanctions that effects change with minimal risk to public safety. Probation, for example, is at least 60 percent effective. We examine probation and intermediate sanctions in Chapters 5 and 6.

Describe Alternatives to Criminal Courts and the Criminal Trial Process

Sentences are frequently appealed to a higher court by the guilty offender. Only a small percentage of the sentence appealers are successful. But appeals can continue during incarceration, some with valid legal grounds and others with whom the personal goal is continue to be a major thorn in the side of correctional administrators.

Summarize the Appeal Process

In addition to appeals on the question of guilt, inmates can appeal almost every condition in the confinement facility. Most such appeals are not successful, but a successful appeal on a major issue can considerably change correctional practice both in community supervision and in confinement facilities. It is the judiciary that sentences, handles appeal issues, decides on due process items, and, on occasion, imposes the will of the court by appointment of a court monitors empowered to test correctional administrators and enforce judicial oversight.

Explain How the Correctional Filter Functions to Categorize, Sort, and Divert Most Offenders into Alternatives to Incarceration

The correctional filter functions to categorize, sort, and divert most offenders into alternatives to incarceration. If the prosecutor did not use discretion in handling cases referred to the office, the entire criminal justice system would collapse. There are too many cases; some represent quite petty offenses, and others are evidently not convictable due to issues such as evidence, qualities of witnesses, and victim instigation of the crime. Because of such complications, decisions must be made to divert the accused into appropriate community corrections or other diversion programs, decide the exact charge to be imposed, estimate the dangerousness posed by some offenders, and ascertain how the processing of certain cases would fit into the ends of justice. In this function, the prosecutor serves as a gatekeeper; if the caseload is too great, some cases must not be tried. Diversion is the alternative to "trying a turkey," losing cases, and not having the resources to ensure that the truly dangerous are incapacitated.

Key Words

misdemeanor, 70
felony, 70
plea bargaining, 70
indeterminate sentencing, 72
sentencing disparity, 72
just deserts, 73
presentence report, 75
appeal, 75
administrative sentencing, 76
determinate sentencing, 77
sentencing guidelines, 77
good-time policies, 77
modify, 77
presumptive sentencing, 78
deterrence by sentencing, 79
railroading, 82
due process, 82
collateral attack, 82
double jeopardy, 84
court of last resort, 84
court of appeals, 85
reverse, 85
remand, 85
affirm, 85
writ of habeas corpus, 87
civil rights, 88
writ of mandamus, 88

Review Questions

1. What is the principal reason for the judge's diminished sentencing power?
2. What aids are available to help the judge decide what sentence to impose?
3. What factors have led to the rapid changes in the sentencing structures in the United States?
4. Identify the basic policy goals of sentencing and define each.
5. What roles can the presentence investigation report play in corrections?
6. Explain sentencing disparity.
7. In what ways can a prosecutor influence sentence length?
8. Why are prison populations increasing?
9. Cite the advantages and disadvantages of the indeterminate sentence. Explain the difference between a court of appeals and a supreme court.
10. Why is there such a logjam in the appellate system? What are some suggestions for easing the pressure?
11. What rights does an inmate have? What rights does an inmate not have?
12. Explain why the rights of inmates began to be extensively defined in the 1960s.
13. What are appeals, and what options are available to appeal courts when a decision is made?
14. What might be done to cut down on frivolous appeals?
15. How can appeal courts manage caseloads more efficiently?
16. What steps has Congress taken to reduce the number of appeals in federal courts?
17. What innovations have states taken to reduce the backlog of appeals in state courts?
18. What are the areas of civil rights violations state prisoners are raising in federal courts?

Application Case Studies

1. Inmates incarcerated in your state's prisons accurately believe that their being locked up in prison prevents their seeking appropriate medical care outside the prison walls and argue that your state must release inmates from incarceration if they cannot provide enough medical care at least equal to that of civilians in your local jurisdiction. What could your state inmates do to force adequate medical care?
2. An inmate with some knowledge of legal proceedings takes up the role of "jailhouse lawyer" but charges other inmates for his expertise. If you were the warden, what if anything would you do?
3. The federal district court receives a petition for release from prison based on the prison facility's unwillingness to install air conditioning that would bring the inside prison temperature down from

130 degrees to a more comfortable level. In the suit, it is noted that the building to house pigs is air conditioned but that the cell block is not. Much to your surprise, the correctional officer union files a supportive lawsuit with the same complaint. If you were the institutional warden, what would you recommend to your supervisors?

Endnotes

1. Alaska abolished plea bargaining in 1975. In 1986, approximately 56 percent of all felony arrests were not prosecuted, and 7 percent of the felony arrests were reduced to misdemeanors. Alan Barnes, *Disparities between Felony Charges at Time of Arrest and Those at Time of Prosecution* (Anchorage: Alaska Statistical Analysis Unit, 1988). California abolished plea bargaining at the superior (trial) court level in 1988, but numerous strategies were devised to avoid this restriction. See *New York Times* (2013), "Plea Bargaining," http://www.nytimes.com/2003/09/24/us/new-plea-bargain-limits-could-swamp-courts-experts-say.html.
2. John Wooldredge, "The Impact of Jurisdiction Size on Guilty Pleas in 569 State Courts," *Sociology and Social Research* 74:1(1989): 26–33. On prosecutorial power, see Sherod Thaxton, "Leveraging Death," *Journal of Criminal Law and Criminology* 103:2 (2013): 475–552. See also David Ball (2013), "Defunding State Prisons," http://www.law.umich.edu/workshopsandsymposia/Documents/defunding%20state%20prisons%20for%20michigan%20jan%202013.pdf (accessed August 17, 2013), and John Howser (2013), "Bench Trial Ends in Conviction for Sex Offenders," http://www.disclosurenewsonline.com/2013/08/16/bench-trial-ends-in-conviction-for-sex-offender/#sthash.XiQm2XTR.dpbs.
3. Matthew Durose and Patrick Langan, *Felony Sentencing in State Courts, 2004* (Washington, DC: U.S. Department of Justice, 2007), http://www.bjs.gov/content/pub/pdf/fssc04.pdf. See also Tracey Kyckelhahn and Thomas Cohen, *Felony Defendants in Large Urban Courts, 2004* (Washington, DC: Bureau of Justice Statistics, 2008), and Nicole Porter (2013), "The State of Sentencing 2012," http://sentencingproject.org/doc/publications/sen_State%20of%20Sentencing%202012.pdf.
4. Although highly contentious, ethnicity has also been found as a factor in the sentencing of felony defendants. Latinos and African Americans are more likely to receive pretrial detention than are Anglos, and pretrial detention is more likely to lead to harsher sentences. Guilty pleas will lessen sentence severity. Latinos benefit more than Anglos and African Americans by entering a guilty plea. See John Sutton, "Structural Bias in the Sentencing of Felony Defendants," *Social Science Research* 42:5 (2013): 1207–1221.
5. David Kopel, *Prison Blues: How America's Foolish Sentencing Policies Endanger Public Safety* (Washington, DC: Cato Institute, 1994); Michael Tonry, "Parochialism in United States Sentencing Policy," *Crime and Delinquency* 45:1 (1999): 48–65; The Sentencing Project, "The Sentencing Project Submits Letter to the U.S. Sentencing Commission Recommending Future Priorities," http://www.sentencingproject.org/doc/publications/dp_CommissionLetterFSARetroactivity.pdf (accessed September 12, 2008).
6. Nelson James, *Disparities in Processing Felony Arrests in New York State* (Albany: New York State Division of Criminal Justice, 1995). See also Jean Chung (2013), "Felony Disenfranchisement," http://www.sentencingproject.org/doc/publications/fd_Felony%20Disenfranchisement%20Primer.pdf, and *The Economist* (2013), "Prison Reform: An Unlikely Alliance of Left and Right," http://www.economist.com/news/united-states/21583701-america-waking-up-cost-mass-incarceration-unlikely-alliance-left-and.
7. Steven Donziger, *The Real War on Crime* (New York: HarperCollins, 1996). See also Ted Gest, *Crime and Politics* (Oxford: University of Oxford Press, 2001).
8. Franklin Zimring and Gordon Hawkins, *Incapacitation: Penal Confinement and the Restraint of Crime* (Oxford: Oxford University Press, Studies in Crime and Public Policy, 1995).
9. Ben Vollard, "Preventing Crime through Selective Incapacitation," *The Economic Journal* 123:567 (2013): 262–284.
10. The cost of prison health care increased about 52 percent from 2001 through 2008. This increase is attributable to aging inmate populations, prevalence of diseases, substance abuse, and mental illness. See the PEW Charitable Trust report on prison health care spending at http://www.pewstates.org/research/reports/managing-prison-health-care-spending-85899515729.
11. Tomislav Kovandzic, John Sloan, and Lynne Vieraitis, "'Striking Out' as Crime Reduction Policy," *Justice Quarterly* 21:1 (2004): 207–239. See also New York Daily News editorial (2013), "Save Lives—Abolish Parole," http://www.nydailynews.com/opinion/save-lives-abolish-parole-article-1.235481.

12. P. Martinez, B. Bryan, E. Benson, W. L. Cawthon, S. Dhir, and R. Fuessel, *Abolishing Parole for Offenders Sentenced to Prison for Violent Offenses* (Austin: Texas Criminal Justice Policy Council, 1998).
13. Sandra Shane-Dubow, Alice Brown, and Erik Olsen, *Sentencing Reform in the United States: History, Content, and Effect* (Washington, DC: U.S. Department of Justice, 1985). See also Barry Krisberg, A. Breed, M. Wolfgang, et al., "Special Issue: NCCD 90th Anniversary," *Crime and Delinquency* 44:1 (1998): 5–177.
14. The Sentencing Project (2013), "Attorney General Holder Proposes Drug Sentencing," http://www.sentencingproject.org/detail/news.cfm?news_id=1600.
15. Walter C. Reckless, *The Crime Problem*, 4th ed. (New York: Appleton-Century-Crofts, 1967), pp. 673–674. See also Jeanne Stinchcomb and Daryl Hippensteel, "Presentence Investigation Reports," *Criminal Justice Policy Review* 12:2 (2001): 164–177.
16. Paul Wice, "Leadership," *Justice System Journal* 17:2 (1995): 271–372. See also Michael Cavadino, "Pre-Sentence Reports: The Effects of Legislation and National Standards," *British Journal of Criminology* 37:4 (1997): 529–548, and Lauren Glaze and Thomas Bonczar, *Probation and Parole in the United States, 2006* (Washington, DC: Bureau of Justice Statistics, 2007).
17. Peter Brimelow, "Judicial Imperialism," *Forbes*, June 1, 1987, 109–112. See in particular Gordon Bazemore and L. Feder, "Rehabilitation in the New Juvenile Court," *American Journal of Criminal Justice* 21:2 (1997): 181–212. See also Department of Justice Canada, "The Changing Face of Conditional Sentencing," http://www.justice.gc.ca/eng/rp-pr/csj-sjc/jsp-sjp/op00_3-po00_3/op00_3.pdf (accessed September 12, 2008).
18. Mike McCorville and Chester Mirday, "Guilty Plea Courts: A Social Disciplinary Model of Criminal Justice," *Social Problems* 42:2 (1995): 216–234. But see Jon'a Meyer and Tara Gray, "Drunk Drivers in the Courts: Legal and Extra-Legal Factors Affecting Pleas and Sentences," *Journal of Criminal Justice* 25:2 (1997): 155–163.
19. Lisa Stolzenberg and S. D'Alessio, "The Impact of Prison Crowding on Male and Female Imprisonment Rates in Minnesota," *Justice Quarterly* 14:4 (1997): 793–809. See also Sean Nicholson-Crotty, "The Impact of Sentencing Guidelines on State-Level Sanctions," *Crime and Delinquency* 50:3 (2004): 395–411; The Sentencing Project (2013), "Life Goes On: The Historic Rise in Life Sentences in America, http://sentencingproject.org/doc/publications/inc_Life%20Goes%20On%202013.pdf; and Craig Lerner (2013), "Life without Parole as a Conflicted Punishment," *Wake Forest Law Review* 48: 1011–1171 (September 20, 2013).
20. Controversy concerning whether the Federal Sentencing Guidelines are only guidelines from which sentencing judges might deviate or are mandatory continue. See, for example, the 2013 U.S. Supreme Court decision of *Peugh v. US*, in which the court ruled the Federal Sentencing Guidelines change after the commission of crime to be *ex post facto* violation. The case is SCOTUS 675 F. 3rd 736, 2013.
21. Steve Rempe (2013), "Increasing 'Good Time' for Federal Prisoners," http://www.prisonfellowship.org/2013/02/increasing-good-time-for-federal-prisoners/.
22. National data can be found at the home page of the administrative unit of the federal courts at http://www.uscourts.gov/FederalCourts/UnderstandingtheFederalCourts/FederalCourtsInAmericanGovernment.aspx.
23. Deterrence is not an adequate objective, as few offenders consider the consequences of their behavior before acting.
24. Conservatives are likely to argue that the decline in crime volume and rates that began in 1990 is a direct result of harsher punishment. Yet crime, as measured by the National Crime Victimization Survey, began to drop in 1971 and dropped about 27 percent since that time. The cause of a phenomenon has to precede the effect. The crime rates began to drop long before increases in sentence length and harsher laws began.
25. Charles Murray, Malcolm Davies, Andrew Rutherford, et al., *Does Prison Work?* (London: Institute of Economic Affairs, Health and Welfare, 1997).
26. Editors, "Supreme Court Review," *Journal of Criminal Law and Criminology* 83:4 (1993): 693–717. But see John Capone, "Facilitating Fairness: The Judge's Role in the Sixth Amendment Right to Effective Counsel," *Journal of Criminal Law and Criminology* 93:4 (2004): 881–912.
27. Because plea bargaining reduces the offender's ability to appeal, it is not surprising that most appeals arise from trials. Trials typically involve crimes against the person and sentences of five years or less. Defendants are not particularly successful; offenders win about 20 percent of the time and have their convictions overturned in only about 10 percent of their appeals. See Jimmy Williams, "Role of Appellants, Sentencing Guidelines, Decision Making in Criminal Appeals," *Journal of Criminal Justice* 23:1 (1995): 83–91. Some 16 percent of offenders convicted in federal courts appealed in 1999. Bureau of Justice Statistics, *Federal Criminal Case Processing, 2004* (Washington, DC: Bureau of Justice Statistics, 2008).
28. For an excellent review of legal trends and issues in corrections, see Rolando del Carmen, S. Ritter, and B. Witt, *Briefs of Leading Cases in Corrections* (Cincinnati, OH: Anderson Publishing, 2005).

29. National Advisory Commission on Criminal Justice Standards and Goals, *Corrections* (Washington, DC: U.S. Government Printing Office, 1973), p. 113.
30. David Chu, "The Substitution of Words for Analysis and Other Judicial Pitfalls: Why David Sattazahn Should Have Received Double Jeopardy Protection," *Journal of Criminal Law and Criminology* 94:3 (2004): 587–623. See also the Colorado Court of Appeals case of an offender charged with two counts of leaving the scene of an accident based on the fact that two people were killed in the single accident. The court ruled that the second charge was an example of double jeopardy. The case is *People v. Medrano-Bustamante*, decided November 31, 2013.
31. Joseph N. Ulman, *The Judge Takes the Stand* (New York: Knopf, 1933), pp. 265–266.
32. Appeals in federal courts have been reduced in number by congressional initiatives to reduce prisoner litigation.
33. U.S. Constitution, Article III, Section 2. See Singer Hausser, *The State of Corrections: Tennessee's Prisons before and after Court Intervention* (Nashville, TN: The Comptroller of the Treasury, 1998).
34. John Palmer, *Constitutional Rights of Prisoners* (Cincinnati, OH: Anderson, 1999), p. 12.
35. Prison jailhouse lawyers can resist controls and conditions placed on them by correctional institutions by assisting in filing lawsuits and have been described as "primitive rebels." See Hawkeye Gross, *Tales from the Joint* (Boulder, CO: Palladin Press, 1995), and Dragan Milovanovic, "Jailhouse Lawyers and Jailhouse Lawyering," *International Journal of the Sociology of the Law* 16:4 (1998): 455–475.
36. John Conrad, "The Rights of Wrongdoers," *Criminal Justice Research Bulletin* 3:1 (1987): 18–24. See also Christopher Smith, "The Prison Reform Litigation Era," *The Prison Journal* 83:3 (2003): 337–358, and Roibin O' hEochaidh."Fault Lines: California Prisons in Crisis," *Correctional News* 14:3 (2008): 20–22.
37. Such as prison farming.
38. Editors of *Criminal Law Reporter, The Criminal Law Revolution and Its Aftermath, 1960–71* (Washington, DC: BNA Books, 1972).
39. Richard Ball, "Prison Conditions at the Extreme," *Journal of Contemporary Criminal Justice* 13:1 (1997): 55–72.
40. Malcolm Feeley and E. Rubin, *Judicial Policy Making and the Modern State* (New York: Cambridge University Press, 1998); John Fliter, *Prisoners' Rights: The Supreme Court and Evolving Standards of Decency* (Westport, CT: Greenwood Press, 2001).
41. This section was drawn primarily from the Bureau of Justice Statistics, *Prisoner Petitions Filed in U.S. District Courts, 2000, with Trends 1980–2000* (Washington, DC: Bureau of Justice Statistics, 2002). See also Bureau of Justice Statistics, *Federal Criminal Cases Processing 2004, with Trends 1982–2002* (Washington, DC: Bureau of Justice Statistics, 2005).

Suggested Readings: Part 1

Austin, James. *It's about Time: America's Imprisonment Binge*. 4th ed. Belmont, CA: Thomson Learning, 2009.

Barnes, Harry Elmer. *The Story of Punishment*. 3rd ed. Independence, KY: Cengage, 2012.

Barnes, Harry Elmer, and Negley K. Teeters. *New Horizons in Criminology*. 2nd ed. Englewood Cliffs, NJ: Prentice Hall, 1959.

Brockway, Zebulon Reed. *Fifty Years of Prison Service*. Montclair, NJ: Patterson Smith, 1969.

Bureau of Justice Statistics. *Felony Sentences in State Courts, 2004*. Washington, DC: Bureau of Justice Statistics, 2005.

Bureau of Justice Statistics. *Prisoners in 2012-Advanced Counts*. Washington, DC: Bureau of Justice Statistics, 2013.

Chung, Jean. *Felony Disenfranchisement: A Primer*. Washington, DC: The Sentencing Project, 2013.

Currie, Elliott. *Crime and Punishment in America; Why the Solutions to America's Most Stubborn Social Crises Have Not Worked—And What Will*. New York: Metropolitan Books, 1998.

Donziger, Steven. *The Real War on Crime*. New York: HarperCollins, 1996.

Edwards, Todd. *The Aging Inmate Population*. Atlanta: Council on State Governments, 1998.

Gest, Ted. *Crime and Politics*. Oxford: Oxford University Press, 2001.

Hassine, Victor. *Life without Parole: Living in Prison Today*. New York: Oxford University Press, 2008.

Irwin, John, and James Austin. *It's about Time*. Independence, KY: Cengage, 2001.

King, Ryan. *Disparity by Geography: The War on Drugs in American Cities*. Washington, DC: The Sentencing Project, 2008.

Latessa, Edward, and Paula Smith. *Corrections in the Community*. 5th ed. Cincinnati, OH: Anderson, 2011.

Mauer, Marc, and Ryan King. *Schools and Prisons: Fifty Years after Brown v. Board of Education*. Washington, DC: The Sentencing Project, 2005.

Nagel, William. *The New Red Barn*. New York: Walker, 1973.

PEW Charitable Trusts. "One in 100: Behind Bars in America 2008." http://www.pewcenteronthestates.org/report_detail.aspx?id?35904.

PEW Charitable Trusts. "U.S. Prison Population Drops for Third Year as States Adopt New Policy Strategies." http://www.pewstates.org/news-room/press-releases/us-prison-population-drops-for-third-year-as-states-adopt-new-policy-strategies-85899496150.

Roberts, John. *Reform and Retribution: An Illustrated History of American Prisons*. Lanham, MD: American Correctional Association, 1997.

Ross, Jeffrey. "Supermax Prisons." *Society* 44:3 (2007): 60–64.

Ross, Jeffrey. *The Globalization of Supermax Prisons*. New Brunswick, NJ: Rutgers University Press, 2013.

Rothman, David J. *The Discovery of the Asylum*. Boston: Little, Brown, 1971.

part 2

Alternatives to Imprisonment

chapter 5 

Probation

chapter 6 

Diversion and Intermediate Sanctions

Overview

Part 2 is concerned with those processes and programs that deal with clients on the "front end" of the corrections system, before offenders are committed to jail or prison for their law-violating behavior. We examine probation and other court sanctions for controlling offenders that fall short of imprisonment: intermediate sanctions. Corrections handles more offenders on the front end than can be found at any other portion of the system, and the next chapter identifies the strengths, challenges, and outcomes of alternatives to imprisonment.

Eddie Moore/Albuquerque Journal/ZUMA Press, Inc./Alamy.

Objectives

- Outline the history of probation.
- Summarize modern probation operations, including the conditions of probation.
- Explain how probation can be revoked.
- Summarize the characteristics of probationers.
- Summarize the risk assessment process.
- Understand how probation targets criminogenic risk factors.
- Summarize the use of economic sanctions.
- Identify and explain successful approaches underlying contemporary probation practices.

chapter 5 Probation

Outline

Suspended Sentence and Sanctuary

The History of Probation

The Spread of Probation

Organization and Administration of Probation

- The Role of the Probation Agency
- The Decision to Grant Probation
- The Presentence Investigation Report
- The Sentencing Hearing
- Risk Assessment

Targeting Risk Factors: Challenge for Probation

- Improving Probation Supervision

Conditions of Probation

Probation Revocation

Felony Probation

The Broken Windows Approach

Probation and Its Role in Corrections

"I can forgive, but I cannot forget, is only another way of saying, I will not forgive. Forgiveness ought to be like a cancelled note torn in two, and burned up, so that it never can be shown against me."

—Henry Ward Beecher

Overview

Our examination of the correctional process now turns to probation and probation supervision, the major alternative to incarceration as used by sentencing judges across America. Although it is the most commonly used correctional sentence, probation is also one of the most maligned and underappreciated aspects of the correctional system. Often seen as a "letting off" of the offender, probation has struggled to gain respect and support from the media, the public, and, perhaps most important, those officials who make funding decisions.

Probation is a sentence that does not include confinement and imposes conditions governing the release of the offender into the community based on good behavior. The sentencing court retains authority to supervise, modify conditions, and cancel the status and resentence if the probation client violates the terms of probation. Increasingly, across the nation, courts are using recent developments in technology to better monitor the behavior of the probationer. This chapter presents a brief history of probation and its developments into the twenty-first century.

key term

Probation
A court sentence to release the offender to the community under supervision, with possible revocation of sentence if conditions warrant.

SUSPENDED SENTENCE AND SANCTUARY

key term

Suspended sentence
Court determination to stop some formal processing of an offender, primarily stopping prosecution, not pronouncing a determination of guilt, or court not requiring a sentence.

key term

Right of sanctuary
Privilege to avoid punishment by the offender's relocation to a sacred city or location.

key term

Benefit of clergy
The exclusion of offenders from the death penalty if able to read particular segments of ancient texts.

key term

Stigma
A mark of shame and disgrace attached to the offender by virtue of his or her having committed an offense.

key term

Sursis
A suspended sentence in European countries requiring no future punishment provided the offender remains crime free during a specified time period.

profile

John Augustus
The "father of probation" who motivated the creation of probation in Boston, working with alcoholics and appearing before the court to request no further or minimal punishment.

Probation is a derivative of the suspended sentence, handed down to us somewhat indirectly by way of past judicial procedures. Both the **suspended sentence** and probation mitigate the punishment for an offender through a judicial procedure, and their earliest antecedent is found in the right of sanctuary,[1] frequently cited in the Bible. In many cultures, holy places and certain cities were traditionally set aside as places for sanctuary.

The **right of sanctuary** was written into Mosaic law.[2] To escape the blood vengeance of a victim's family, a killer could go to certain specified cities and find refuge. During the Middle Ages, many churches offered sanctuary for those hiding from harsh secular law. The practice of sanctuary disappeared in England in the seventeenth century and was replaced with **benefit of clergy**. This practice, originally reserved for clerics, was eventually extended to those who could pass the Psalm 51 test—a test of the offender's ability to read the verse that begins "Have mercy upon me." Since anyone who could read (such as the clergy) was eligible to be tried under Church law and thus escape the death penalty, this became known as the "neck verse," meaning they could not be hung by the neck until dead. The result was a form of suspended sentence that allowed the offender to move about in society.

The suspended sentence differs from probation, though the terms are sometimes used interchangeably. The suspended sentence does not require supervision and usually does not prescribe a specified set of goals for the offender to work toward. It is merely a form of quasi freedom that can be revoked, with a prison sentence imposed at the instruction of the court. Sentence can be suspended in two ways:

1. The sentence is imposed, but its execution is suspended.
2. Both the imposition and execution of the sentence are suspended.

Of the two, the second is the more desirable because of the reduced **stigma**; however, the practice of suspending sentences, like sanctuary, has generally been replaced in America with supervised probation. Sentences may be vacated by the sentencing judge, and the offender may be placed at liberty in the community, but that is a relatively infrequent occurrence.

Under the European model of suspended sentence, or **sursis** (surcease), the offender has satisfactorily fulfilled the conditions if no further offense is committed during the established period. Little control or supervision is provided, with the result that most offenders with suspended sentences are denied the specialized or therapeutic services needed to prevent further criminal involvement.[3]

THE HISTORY OF PROBATION

Probation has undergone a number of changes since its informal beginnings in the nineteenth century. Let us take a brief look at how the concept was born. **John Augustus** (1785–1859),[4] a Boston shoemaker, is credited with being the "father of probation." As a member of the Washington Total Abstinence Society, he worked at getting men to give up alcohol. He liked to spend his spare moments observing what took place in the courts, and he was disturbed that minor offenders and common drunks were often forced to remain in jail because they had no money to pay their fines. He convinced the authorities to allow him to pay their fines and offered them friendly supervision. Between 1841 and 1858, Augustus bailed out almost 2,000 men, women, and children.

His method was to bail the offender after conviction, to utilize this favor as an entering wedge into the convict's confidence and friendship, and, through such evidence of friendliness as helping the offender to obtain a job and aiding his or her family in various ways,

correctional profile 5.1

John Augustus

John Augustus is considered the "father of probation" and is considered the first true probation officer.

Born in 1785, Augustus was a boot maker in Boston and a member of the Washington Total Abstinence Society who believed that abusers of alcohol could be rehabilitated. In 1841, John Augustus attended court and bailed out a "common drunkard"—the first probationer. Over the next 18 years, Augustus provided bail for over 1,946 men and women. He is also credited with founding the investigation process as well as intake and supervision and was the first to apply the term "probation" to his method of treating offenders.

to drive the wedge home. When the defendant was later brought into court for sentencing, Augustus would report on his progress toward reformation, and the judge would usually fine the convict one cent and costs instead of committing him or her to an institution.[5]

Augustus's efforts encouraged his home state of Massachusetts to pass the first probation statute in 1878. Four more states had followed suit by 1900.[6] Probation was thus established as a legitimate alternative to incarceration, and a strong impetus to employ it—the need to supervise young offenders and keep them out of adult prisons—came with the creation of the first juvenile court[7] in Cook County, Illinois, in 1899.

THE SPREAD OF PROBATION

Juvenile probation service developed with the growing movement for creation of juvenile courts. By 1910, 37 states and the District of Columbia had passed a children's court act, and 40 had established some kind of probation service for juveniles. Every state had enacted juvenile probation service in some measure by 1927 as the practice became firmly entrenched.

Photo 5.1
A juvenile defendant in front of a juvenile court judge.
Mike Brown/Alamy Images.

table 5.1 Imposition of Probation by Crime of Conviction

Crime of Conviction	Percentage of Convicted Felons Receiving Probation Sentences
All offenses	27
Violent offenses	20
Property offenses	29
Drug offenses	30
Weapons offenses	25
Other offenses	27

SOURCE: Sean Rosenmerkel, Matthew Durose, and Donald Farole, *Felony Sentences in State Courts, 2006* (Washington, DC: Bureau of Justice Statistics, 2009), p. 4.

Not until 1956, however, was probation available for adult offenders in every state. The variations in the organization and operation of probation services make it difficult to compare them by state, but the growth in the number of registered probation officers attests to the rapid acceptance of this area of corrections. In 1907, the first directory of probation officers identified 795 volunteers, welfare workers, court personnel, and part-time personnel serving as officers. Most of them were in the juvenile system. By 1937, the figure had grown to more than 3,800, of which 80 percent were in full-time service. By 2010, it was estimated that probation officers numbered over 103,000, and it is expected to reach over 123,000 by 2018.[8]

The enabling legislation eventually passed at state and federal levels not only enacted statutes that permitted probation but eventually defined specific categories of offenses for which probation could not be granted. The latter could include crimes of violence, assaultive behavior that inflicted gross bodily harm on the victim, rape or other sex offenses, capital offenses, train robbing, livestock rustling, certain habitual offenders, and related offenses. Despite these restrictions imposed by legislatures, granting probation is a highly personalized process that focuses not only on the offender but also on the victim. Restorative justice, which will be discussed in more detail later in the book, is an example of a contemporary thrust that maximizes focus on the offender, victim, and community.[9]

It is clear that the legislators enacting probation statutes intended juvenile offenders and misdemeanants to be its beneficiaries, not hard-core criminal offenders. This was in keeping with the child-saving and progressive agenda that intended to reclaim offenders before they became antisocial and professional offenders committed to criminal careers. As we shall see later, probation is also a sentencing option for adult felons and, depending on the criminal circumstances, an occasional violent offender. Table 5.1 provides an overview of the frequency with which probation is imposed by crime category of conviction. As these figures illustrate, probation is used for a wide range of offenses, but property crimes and drug offenses are the most dominant.

The American Probation and Parole Association policy statement given in the accompanying Policy Positions 5.1 identifies the purpose and mission of probation. Judges and corrections and justice advocates have identified the advantages of probation, which can be summarized as follows:

- Uses existing community resources to assist offenders to address their personal and individual problems.
- Saves fiscal resources over the cost of imprisonment.
- Avoids prisonization, a process that tends to exacerbate the underlying causes of criminal behavior in an artificial setting that lessens the ability of the prisoner to function when released to society.
- Keeps offenders' families and dependents off local welfare rolls.

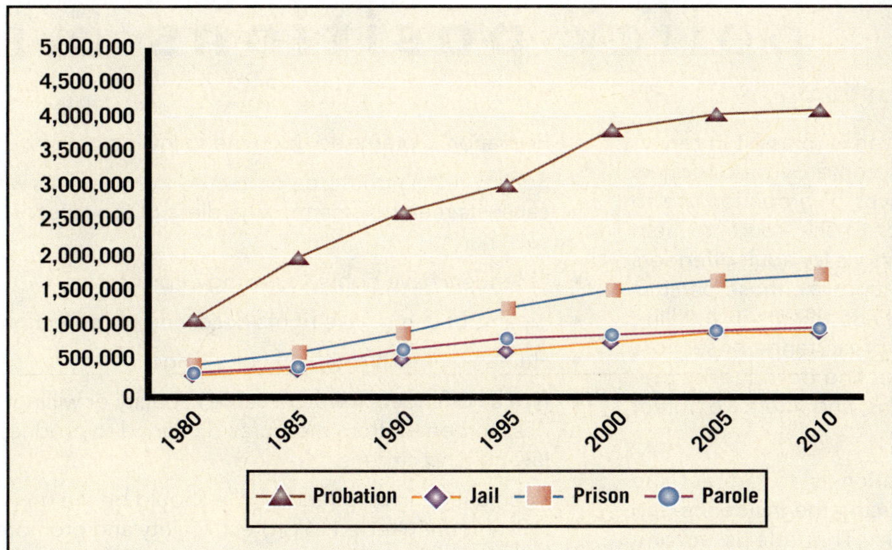

figure 5.1

Adult Correctional Populations.

SOURCE: Bureau of Justice Statistics, *Correctional Populations in the United States* (December 2010).

- Provides restitution for and reconciliation with victims.
- Allows selective incapacitation, permitting the use of scarce prison cells to isolate and control aggressive and assaultive offenders.[10]

Thus, it should be of little surprise that the majority of offenders are under sentence to probation (see Figure 5.1), with 1 in 60 U.S. adult residents on probation. The good news is that the number of persons on probation fell below 4 million in 2011. This was the third consecutive year the number has declined. The last time this level was observed was 2002.[11]

ORGANIZATION AND ADMINISTRATION OF PROBATION

The problems associated with a lack of organization in the criminal justice system are exemplified in probation services. Under the original concept, the judges themselves were to administer the probation services. For many jurisdictions, this is still the way in which probation is managed, whereas in other states probation is administered through state or district offices. Unfortunately, the various organizational and operational systems found in probation are often unresponsive to one another's goals or efforts. The most common plan offers probation service at the state level. Even in those states that have attempted to form a state-administered probation system, county participation has sometimes been maintained at the discretion of local officials. This concept of local autonomy is an American tradition, but it has hampered efforts to develop integrated probation services on a statewide basis.

The means of administering probation programs also vary. In some states, such as Florida, private service contractors, such as the Salvation Army, provide presentence investigation services as well as probation case supervision for select offenders. It is not uncommon to have misdemeanant probationers supervised by contracted providers.

The Role of the Probation Agency

The role of the probation department has traditionally been viewed as a dichotomy. The supervision role involves maintaining surveillance (societal protection) as well as helping and treating the offender (counseling and rehabilitation). Supervising officers are often left to their

policy positions 5.1

Position Statement on Probation

Purpose The purpose of probation is to assist in reducing the incidence and impact of crime by probationers in the community. The core services of probation are to provide investigation and reports to the court, to help develop appropriate court dispositions for adult offenders and juvenile delinquents, and to supervise those persons placed on probation. Probation departments in fulfilling their purpose may also provide a broad range of services including, but not limited to, crime and delinquency prevention, victim restitution programs, and intern/volunteer programs.

Position The mission of probation is to protect the public interest and safety by reducing the incidence and impact of crime by probationers. This role is accomplished by:

- Assisting the courts in decision making through the probation report and in the enforcement of court orders;
- Providing services and programs that afford opportunities for offenders to become more law abiding;
- Providing and cooperating in programs and activities for the prevention of crime and delinquency; and furthering the administration of fair and individualized justice.

Probation is premised upon the following beliefs:

- Society has a right to be protected from persons who cause its members harm, regardless of the reasons for such harm.
- Offenders have rights deserving of protection.
- Victims of crime have rights deserving of protection.
- Human beings are capable of change.
- Not all offenders have the same capacity or willingness to benefit from measures designed to produce law-abiding citizens.
- Intervention in an offender's life should be the minimal amount needed to protect society and promote law-abiding behavior.
- Probation does not recognize the concept of retributive justice.
- Incarceration may be destructive and should be imposed only when necessary.
- When public safety is not compromised, society and offenders are best served through community correctional programs.

Source: American Probation and Parole Association, "APPA Position Statement on Probation," APPA website, http://www.appa-net.org/ (accessed September 14, 2008).

own devices with regard to which role would be most appropriate in supervising their caseloads. This dilemma is likely to remain with us even though calls from several quarters of the criminal justice system point toward coming changes in the role of the supervising officer.[12]

To begin, it is necessary to examine the duties and responsibilities of probation agencies. First and foremost, they provide supervision of offenders in the community. The basic question remains: What is the purpose of supervision? To some, the function of supervision, drawn from the social work field, is based on the casework model. Supervision is the basis of a treatment program. The officer uses all information available about the offender to diagnose that person's needs and to design a treatment plan. Yet providing treatment is only one aspect of supervision. In addition, the probation officer is expected to maintain surveillance of those offenders who make up the caseload. Surveillance can take many forms, ranging from office and field contacts to drug testing to electronic monitoring. Although some believe that the treatment and surveillance responsibilities of the probation department are almost diametrically opposed, the reality is that probation has two missions: to rehabilitate the offenders who are amenable to treatment while simultaneously protecting society from those who have broken the law. The agency that can adequately balance these goals can best meet the challenges of probation in the twenty-first century.

The Decision to Grant Probation

The decision to grant probation is a complicated process, one further impacted by the plea-bargaining process. Recall that plea bargaining is usually undertaken by the prosecutor and defense counsel and can include a reduction in the severity of the charge,

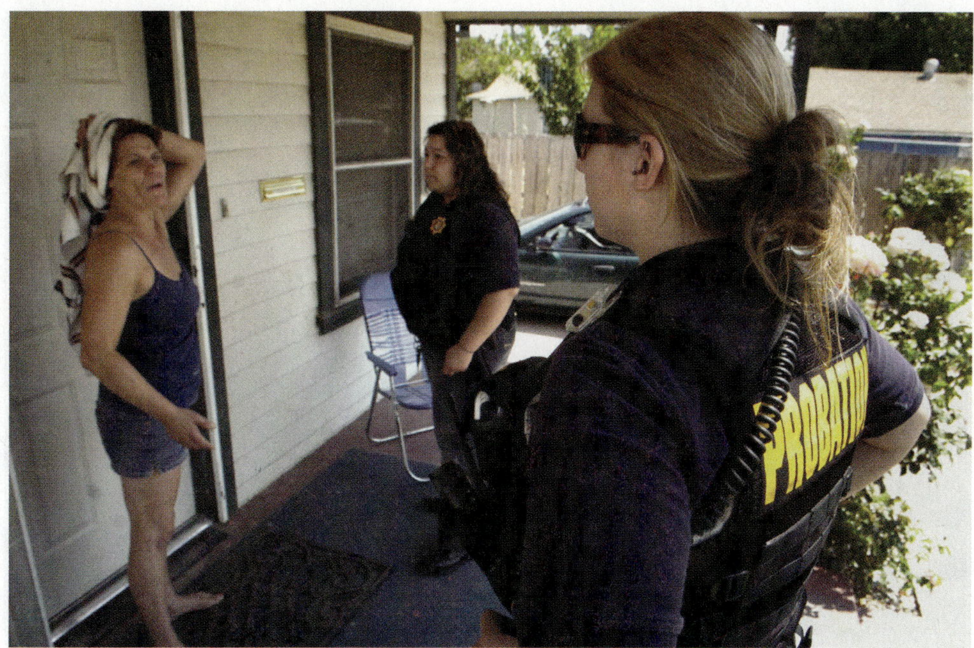

Photo 5.2

Probation officers conduct a surprise home visit of a female probationer.
Bart Ah You/Newscom.

the number of counts to which the offender would plead guilty, probation versus incarceration, the length of sentence to be imposed, and whether sentences are to be served concurrently or consecutively. More recently, with the passage of sentence enhancement, habitual offender, and third-strike statutes, defendants might also negotiate on pleading to a misdemeanor versus a felony charge to avoid the first strike necessary for the imposition of sentence enhancement, particularly third-strike sentences. In California, for example, an offender with two previous felony convictions who was facing conviction for a third felony could receive a sentence of 25 years to life and must serve a minimum of 25 years.[13] In November 2012, California voters overwhelmingly voted to reform the state's infamously harsh three-strikes law. Proposition 36, the ballot measure that passed with an amazing 69 percent of the vote, changed the state's three-strikes law so that offenders who have committed no serious and violent crime will no longer go to prison for life. Often a judge will combine some jail time with probation. This is called a split sentence. Other variations include combining probation with weekend confinement, boot camps, and residential programming.

The judiciary tends to acquiesce to the negotiated plea outcomes but, in many cases, can decide the sentencing outcome or refuse to accept the proposed agreement ("bust the deal"). This is a crucial point, inasmuch as some 90 percent of felony arrestees may have pled guilty for preferential consideration. Such a plea usually means that the offender cannot appeal, sharply reducing the legal bases for initiating appellate court review.

When the crime for which someone is convicted falls within the legally permissible range of offenses for which probation may be imposed or where mandated by state law, a presentence investigation will be ordered, although some states permit the offender to waive the presentence investigation. The basic function of the presentence report is to provide information permitting the most appropriate sentence to be imposed. It can also serve as a background document for the supervising probation officer and the prison classification committee as well as any later parole supervision officer should the offender be imprisoned. The presentence report also provides a wealth of information permitting process and outcome evaluations as well as developing sentencing guidelines, probation supervision strategies, and specific programs designed to meet emerging challenges for probation agencies (such as identifying offenders with high drug relapse potential and instituting drug treatment programs particularly designed for higher-risk cases).

Photo 5.3
A public defender works with a jail inmate on getting him probation.
ZUMA Press, Inc./Alamy.

The Presentence Investigation Report

One of the primary responsibilities of the probation agency is investigation. Other responsibilities include supervision, program advocacy, restitution management, victim–offender reconciliation, brokerage, enforcement of probation conditions, and community safety. Investigation includes gathering facts and information about the offense and arrest, offender background, technical violations, and, more immediately, preparing the presentence investigation report.

The **presentence investigation (PSI) report** is the document that results from an investigation undertaken by a court-authorized officer or agency. Under the direction of the criminal court, it evaluates the background, past criminal behavior, offense situation, personal and family circumstances, personality, need, and level of risk of the offender convicted of the crime in order to assist the court in making an informed disposition decision and, hence, determining the most appropriate sentence.

key term

Presentence investigation (PSI) report
Document that results from an investigation undertaken by a court-authorized officer or agency, designed to provide information on the defendant so the judge can make an informed sentencing decision.

In addition to such facts about the offender as educational and employment histories, residential stability, financial circumstances, marital and parental responsibilities, and military history, the report also must provide certain subjective data that are useful to the court. These data would include an assessment of the offender's personality and character, needs and risks, and attitude of remorse and contrition. Most reports conclude with a sound recommendation for sentence disposition and relevant conditions to be imposed if the disposition were to be probation. Both reliability and accuracy are essential because the court tends to closely follow the recommendation of the investigator. The latter needs are so crucial that the PSI report (minus any specific details that might permit identification of sources who might fear retribution) is generally shared with defense counsel and can be challenged or refuted in a sentencing hearing.

A final note about the PSI report: No report is complete without a plan of supervision developed by the investigator and presented to the court. Not only would the report include such traditional supervision options as fines, restitution, community service orders, day reporting, and probation, but increasingly it also gives attention to the victim by allowing a victim impact statement and, on occasion, the victim's recommendation for sentence outcome. Surprisingly, some victims are willing to propose constructive responses and solutions in addition to the self-serving request for restitution and compensation.[14]

The Sentencing Hearing

Most criminal courts conduct sentencing hearings independent of the determination of guilt. At such a hearing, the court would consider the PSI report's contents and recommendations, statements by prosecution and defense counsel, statements from victims, and other evidence that might be germane and relevant to the deliberations.

There are no clear-cut factors that heavily influence the outcome of the sentencing hearing, although it is clear that the presentence investigation report plays a central role. If the offender has prior convictions, has inflicted bodily harm, used a weapon in the commission of the crime, is unknown to the victim or has committed a stranger-to-stranger crime, has previously been imprisoned in a correctional institution, has indicators of mental illness, or appears to be engaged in a career of crime, the more likely recommendation would be incarceration in an institution for adult offenders (prison). Judges tend to concur with such recommendations about 85 percent of the time.[15]

If the bulk of the evidence before the court is that the offender displays most of the following, then the sentencing judge is more likely to impose probation:

- Basically a prosocial offender who has committed a first crime
- Good education and work histories
- Married with dependents
- Underlying need to address a personal problem, such as drug or alcohol abuse
- Low-risk assessment score
- Committed a nonviolent offense

Offenders, of course, seldom fall into the two extreme examples. For this reason, probation departments have adopted **risk and needs assessment** instruments that provide good to excellent prediction of future offender behavior. Such instruments tend to classify clients into risk level (high, medium, and low) and need level (high, medium, and low).

key term

Risk and needs assessments Instruments used to determine the probability of recidivism or future criminal behavior.

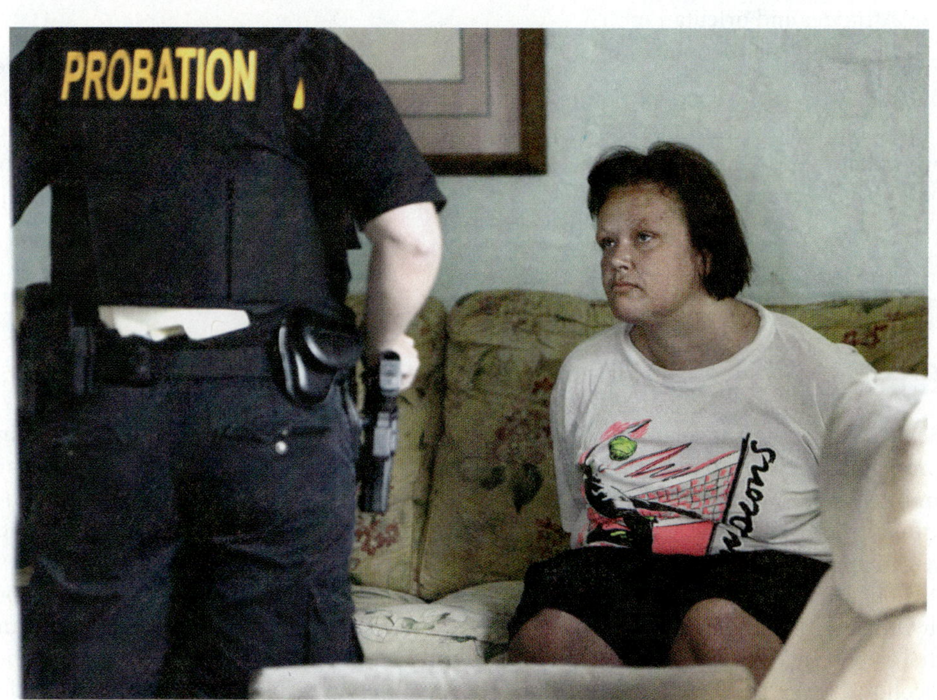

Photo 5.4

A probation officer makes an arrest of a probationer in her home.

Hayne Palmour IV/Zuma/Newscom.

figure 5.2

The Level of Services—Revised and Recidivism.

SOURCE: Data from: Don Andrews and James Bonta, *"LSI-R": The Level of Service Inventory–Revised* (Toronto: Multi-Health Systems, Inc., 1995).

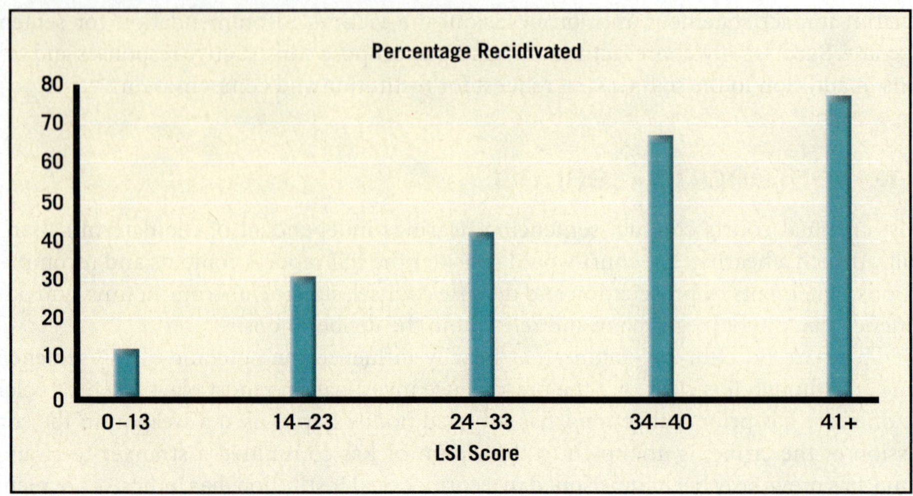

Risk Assessment

The latest generation of classification instruments has successfully combined risk and needs and is relatively easy to use. For example, the Level of Service Inventory—Revised (LSI-R)[16] assesses offender risk by examining 10 domains:

- Criminal history
- Financial situation
- Companions
- Accommodations
- Alcohol and drug problems
- Education and employment
- Leisure and recreation activities
- Family/marital status
- Emotional problems
- Attitudes and orientation

Figure 5.2 shows recidivism rates as they correspond to LSI-R scores; in general, the higher the LSI-R score, the more likely the offender group to reoffend. Assessments such as the LSI-R help judges and probation departments make better decisions about whom to place on probation, whether to increase conditions and supervision levels, and what range and type of services are needed.

TARGETING RISK FACTORS: CHALLENGE FOR PROBATION

Before addressing the conditions of probation that could be imposed by the sentencing court, it is necessary to explore some of the dimensions and problems that probationers face and that cause offenders many additional problems and contribute to the commission of crime. These figures will help you understand the serious and complicated issues with which sentencing courts and supervising probation officers must deal in the corrections process. Although recent national figures are not available, a 2005 study of community corrections in Ohio examined more than 17,000 offenders under community control. This study found that 84 percent of offenders in the community had a history of drug use, 69 percent had prior alcohol abuse, 70 percent had not completed high school, 62 percent were unemployed at the time of arrest, and the vast majority had a prior criminal record.[17] There is no reason to believe that these rates are not similar across the country. In addition to substance abuse problems and a lack of employment and education, probationers also have a number of other problems and risk factors that must be addressed. These include a lack of self-control, bad companions, antisocial attitudes, emotional problems, family conflict, and mental illness.

Fortunately, studies have demonstrated that recidivism can be significantly diminished if offenders on probation or in detention receive treatment and services specific to their risk and need factors and if they complete the treatment program.[18] Posttreatment reductions of criminal activities are especially pronounced when certain principles are adhered to. Known as the principles of effective correctional intervention, they form the basis of what has become referred to as the "what works" research.[19]

It should be evident that probationers as a group tend to have a wide range of risk and need factors and that treatment and services should play a large part in supervision. It also requires the sentencing court to impose specific treatment conditions and for supervising officers to direct the implementation of that treatment.

Improving Probation Supervision

Given the large caseload and varied responsibilities of probation and parole agencies, the question remains: Can probation officers influence change in their offenders? Preliminary evidence from training initiatives in Canada as well as Australia has produced some promising results.[20]

First developed by the Canadians and called Strategic Training Initiative in Community Supervision (STICS), initial research indicates that trained officers have higher caseload retention rates, fewer technical violations, and fewer new arrests than untrained officers. A modified model is currently being tested in the United States by researchers at the University of Cincinnati who call their approach "Effective Practices in Community Supervision" (EPICS). As with the Canadian approach, the purpose of the **EPICS model** is to teach probation officers how to more effectively target criminogenic risk factors. Both STICS and EPICS are designed as training tools to increase the effectiveness of probation as administered by probation officers by upgrading officer skills, training, and management of offenders and achieving correctional objectives. EPICS, in particular, provides a series of skill-honing approaches that lessen client resistance and hostility and focus on client understanding of the role of the probation officer and interpretation of situations clients commonly encounter.

key term

EPICS model
Training tool used to sensitize probation officers to major possible management crises and provide understanding and management strategies directed to helping probationers overcome treatment resistance.

With EPICS, probation officers follow a structured approach to their interactions with their offenders. Specifically, each session includes four components: (1) Check-In, in which the officer determines if the offender has any crises or acute needs, builds rapport, and discusses compliance issues; (2) Review, which focuses on the skills discussed in the prior session, the application of those skills, and troubleshooting continued problems in the use of those skills; (3) Intervention, where the probation officer identifies continued areas of need, trends in problems the offender experiences, teaches relevant skills, and targets problematic thinking; and finally (4) Homework and Rehearsal, when the offender is given an opportunity to see the model the probation officer is talking about, provided opportunities to role play, assigned homework, and given instructions to follow before the next visit. In addition to restructuring their sessions with offenders, the EPICS model focuses on teaching probation officer how to apply some core correctional practices to their interactions with offenders.[21] These practices include the following:

Anticriminal modeling Probation officers serve as an anticriminal model for offenders by engaging in prosocial behaviors and reinforcing them when they do the same.

Effective reinforcement Probation officers use effective reinforcement to reinforce a specific behavior that includes immediate statements of approval and support and the reasons why this behavior is desirable followed by consideration of the short- and long-term benefits associated with continued use of the behavior.

Effective disapproval Probation officers use effective disapproval to communicate disapproval for a specific behavior that includes immediate statements of disapproval and the reasons why this behavior is undesirable followed by consideration of the short- and long-term costs associated with continued use of the behavior and a clear demonstration of an alternate, prosocial behavior.

Effective use of authority Probation officers make effective use of their authority by guiding offenders toward compliance, which includes focusing their message on the behavior exhibited, being direct and specific concerning their demands, and specifying the offender's choices and attendant consequences.

Problem solving Problem solving is a specific social skill that is taught to offenders to address a variety of high-risk situations.

Relationship skills Effective probation officers possess several critical relationship skills, including being warm, open, nonjudgmental, empathetic, flexible, engaging, solution focused, and directive, to name a few.

Cognitive restructuring Probation officers need to help offenders understand the link between their thoughts and their behavior. What they think (e.g., attitudes, thoughts, and beliefs) affects how someone emotionally and behaviorally responds to a given situation as opposed to situations directly dictating a person's response.

Skill building In order for an offender to learn ways to behave, probation officers need to teach and practice new skills with offenders. There are cognitive skills (e.g., how well people solve problems, experience empathy toward others, and rationally assess situations) that affect how a person behaves.

Motivational enhancement Effective probation officers help motivate offenders to change by increasing intrinsic motivation (getting them to want to change). Techniques include motivational interviewing, weighing the pros and cons, goal setting, and so forth.

The EPICS model is designed to use a combination of monitoring, referrals, and face-to-face interactions to provide the offender with a sufficient "dosage" of treatment interventions and make the best possible use of time to develop a collaborative working relationship. Preliminary research has shown that officers that use the EPICS model are more effective in reducing recidivism than those who do not.[22]

CONDITIONS OF PROBATION

Offenders call being on probation being on "paper." Being on "wet paper" means that they are not allowed to drink while under supervision. As we will learn, courts may impose any reasonable condition on the offender as long as the condition is related to some identifiable correctional objective. The probation officer is expected to monitor the probationer's adherence to these conditions. General conditions imposed on all offenders would include reporting regularly to the supervising officer, obeying laws, submitting to searches, not being in possession of firearms or using drugs, avoiding excessive use of alcohol, not associating with known criminals, not leaving the jurisdiction of the court without prior approval, notifying the officer of any change of job or residence, paying probation fees, and so on.

Specific conditions, not capriciously imposed, can be required of the probationer, such as participating in methadone maintenance, taking Antibuse, attending Alcoholics Anonymous meetings, urine testing, obtaining psychological or psychiatric treatment, attending a day attendance center or halfway house, restitution or victim compensation, house arrest, electronic monitoring, weekend confinement in jail or a residential center, vocational training, or other court-ordered requirements. Such specific conditions are individually designed to assist the probationer in successful completion of court requirements and expectations as well as reintegration. The proportion of probationers who successfully complete probation ranges from about 60 percent to some 85 percent. Specific conditions are frequently imposed as part of the original court order for probation but could also be imposed by the

table 5.2 **Special Conditions Imposed of Probationers**

Condition of Sentence	Percentage of Probationers
Supervision fees	61
Fines	56
Court costs	55
Employment	35
Mandatory drug testing	33
Restitution to victim	30
Alcohol abuse treatment	29
Community service	26
Drug abuse treatment	23
At least one condition	99

SOURCE: Thomas Bonczar, *Characteristics of Adults on Probation* (Washington, DC: Bureau of Justice Statistics, 1997), p. 7.

court later if the probation client is not abiding by the conditions of probation or poses a danger for failure of probation (see Table 5.2). Probation officers sometimes ask the court to impose more than one special condition after probation begins, especially if the client ignores the orders or deliberately refuses to participate in a program. Urine tests that reveal continued drug abuse or excessive use of alcohol or irregular employment attendance may result in tourniquet sentencing, which happens when the court increases the conditions of supervision to enforce participation in programs until the client agrees to conform his or her behavior to expectations.

The most frequently imposed **special conditions of probation** include intermediate sanctions, which are discussed in more detail in Chapter 6. Some of these are house arrest, day attendance centers, electronic monitoring, intensive supervision, halfway house residency, boot camp programs, and split sentences (jail time followed by probation or by weekend jail time). The point here is that probation supervision can be strengthened by a variety of alternative sanctions that can be imposed to maximize the benefits of probation, avoid criminal reoffending, protect the local community, and assist clients to address their basic and underlying crime-causative needs. The alternative programs are explored in more detail in the following chapter.

key term

Special conditions of probation
Additional punishments ordered by the courts to probationers, such as fines, electronic monitoring, and house arrest.

PROBATION REVOCATION

Once placed on probation, clients are supervised and assisted by probation officers who increasingly use community resources and programs to assist in the reintegration effort to meet the individual's needs. If the probationer addresses these, secures assistance from community resources, and resolves underlying problems, the probation officer may request the court to dismiss the offender from supervision by closing the case. Some jurisdictions permit the issuance of "certificates of rehabilitation" for offenders who have been successful on probation. Other offenders do not pursue official recognition and are never seen in the criminal justice system again (see Table 5.2).

Offenders vary in their ability to conform their behavior to expectations. Some are indifferent or hostile, being unwilling or unable to cooperate with their supervising officer or the court. Some are too immature emotionally to comply with directions. A few face unrealistic conditions with which compliance is not possible, such as extensive victim restitution or employment in an economically depressed period or area. Still others drift toward further criminal behavior by violating the conditions of their probation (particularly the alcohol and drug abuse requirements) that might not be illegal per se but are interpreted as indicators of future illegal behavior. In these circumstances, the supervising probation officer must deal with **technical probation violations.**

key term

Technical probation violation
Probation sentence change due to charges that the offender violated the rules imposed by the court but not by committing a new crime.

In such circumstances, supervising officers must act to issue stern warnings or arrest their clients. Probationers are taken back to court with requests that court-ordered conditions be tightened (or relaxed, if they are inappropriate). The judge typically warns the probationer and may increase conditions or frequency of supervision. The conditions often imposed on probationers can be found in Table 5.2. Frequently, these warnings and official actions are sufficient to coerce client conformity, but if not, or if the client repetitively violates conditions of probation or is arrested by law enforcement officers for an alleged new crime, a hearing may be held to determine if probation should be revoked (a process called **probation revocation**) and a different sentencing alternative imposed (such as a jail sentence or imprisonment). If the probationer is not in jail, a warrant may be issued for the arrest of the probationer.

key term

Probation revocation
Change of sentence from probation to another correctional control status due to violation of the conditions of probation.

The probation hearing is a serious event because it poses a potential for "grievous loss of liberty" for the offender. The hearing is governed by the U.S. Supreme Court decision known as ***Gagnon* v. *Scarpelli*.** In brief, this case held that probation is a privilege, not a right, but that, once granted, the probationer has an interest in remaining on probation (an "entitlement"). The Court ruled that probation cannot be withdrawn or be revoked without observing the following elements of due process:

key term

Gagnon* v. *Scarpelli
U.S. Supreme Court decision that held that probation is a privilege, not a right, but that, once granted, the probationer has an interest in remaining on probation.

- The probationer must be informed in writing of the charge against him or her.
- The written notice must be given to the probationer in advance of the revocation hearing.
- The probationer has the right to attend the hearing and to present evidence on his or her own behalf.
- The probationer has the right to challenge those testifying against him or her.
- The probationer has the right to confront and cross-examine witnesses.

correctional **practice 5.1**

Probation Violations and Deterrence: Project HOPE

In 2004, a First Circuit judge in Hawaii brought criminal justice stakeholders together to design and initiate a probation program known as HOPE. The judge believed that linking probation violations with swift, certain, and proportionately graded punishment (such as jail time) would reduce probation violation behaviors, reoffending by probationers, and revocations of probation. Proportionate punishment imposed quickly after probation violations (such as failure to appear at a probation hearing, testing positive for drugs, and not going to see their probation officer) was intended to deter further criminal behavior. Linking behavior that is criminogenic with certain punishment and consequences would force the offender to learn from it. The underlying theory is a deterrence philosophy: Certain punishment for a probation violation will lead to desistance in future criminal behavior.

An evaluation of this program compared HOPE probationers with a control group, and the major findings were very promising, revealing that HOPE probationers were

1. 72 percent less likely to use drugs,
2. 61 percent less likely to skip appointments with their probation officer,
3. 55 percent less likely to be arrested for a repeat crime, and
4. 53 percent less likely to have their probation status revoked.

Investigations are ongoing to determine if such programs linking certainty with swift and increasingly proportionate punishment will deter other probationers in different locations of the nation and different populations.

For more information, see: Kevin McEvoy (2012), "HOPE: A Swift and Certain Process for Probationers," *National Institute of Justice Journal* 269 (http://www/nij.gov/nij/journal/269/hope.htm (accessed July 30, 2012).

correctional practice 5.2

Federal Offenders on Probation

The number of federal offenders on probation increased since 2008 and at the beginning of fiscal year 2013 included 132,340 offenders (United States Courts, 2012a). The increase resulted from the number of drug law violations since 2008. Offenders required to comply with at least one special condition of supervision totaled almost 94 percent. The success rates (offenders terminating supervision successfully) were high (United States Courts, 2012b):

- 85 percent of those on probation were successes.
- 76 percent of supervised releases were successes.

SOURCE: United States Courts (2012a), "Federal Court Conviction Supervision Fiscal Years 2008–2012," http://www.uscourts.gov/Statistics/JudicialBusiness/2012/post-convictionsupervision.aspx; United States Courts (2012b), "Most Offenders under Federal Supervision Remain Arrest Free," http://www.uscourts.gov/news/NewsView/10-12-29/Most_Offenders_Under_Federal_Supervision_Remain_Arrest-Free.aspx.

- The probationer has the right to have legal counsel present if the charges are sufficiently complicated or the case is so complex that an ordinary person would not be able to comprehend the legal issues.

States may provide more rights than those just listed, but cannot provide less.

The revocation hearing can lead to several outcomes:

- The supervision level of the case may be increased.
- The offender is warned and admonished, then returned to probation supervision.
- The court can impose additional conditions, then return the offender to community supervision.
- The court can revoke probation and resentence the offender to an incarceration setting, such as jail or prison.
- The court can consider the legal competence of the offender and order a mental health examination, the outcome of which could be commitment to a mental health service or transfer of the case to a probate court for proceedings under the jurisdiction's health and welfare code or commitment to a state mental facility.
- A bench warrant can be issued for offenders who cannot be found or who have left the jurisdiction of the court.

Of those probationers who experienced a disciplinary hearing, the most frequent reason for the hearing was absconding or failure to contact a probation officer. This was followed by arrest or conviction on a new offense (38 percent). Among persons under probation supervision who had experienced one or more disciplinary hearings, 42 percent were permitted to continue their sentence but only with the imposition of additional conditions. Almost 30 percent were incarcerated in jail or prison; and 29 percent had their supervision reinstated without any new conditions.

FELONY PROBATION

The rapid growth of serious and violent crime in America during the 1980s contributed to prison overcrowding and spurred a movement toward the increase in the use of **felony probation**. Probation, as we have seen, had traditionally been for misdemeanors and low-level nonviolent crime. But prison overcrowding and bulging jails forced the correctional administrators to take a close look at some other categories of felons for relief of an

key term

Felony probation
The offender is placed on probation for committing a felony.

table 5.3 **The Daily Cost of Correctional Programs per Client in a Federal Bureau of Prisons Facility**

Program	Cost
Probation	$10.79
Incarceration	$77.49
Pretrial detention	$70.56
Pretrial supervision	$6.62

SOURCE: "Costs of Incarceration and Supervision," http://www.uscourts.gov/news/newsView/11-06-23/Newly_Available_Costs_of_Incarceration_and_Supervision_in_FY_2010.aspx (accessed August 23, 2014).

Photo 5.5

Most probationers are required to work.
Photofusion/Getty Images.

overtaxed system. Because incarceration costs (see Table 5.3) and building costs have become so high and the institutions so crowded, felony probation has become quite common. We need only look at the dismal results from incarceration to agree that it may be possible to increase this option when combined with a thorough and complete presentencing investigation report and consideration of risk. Programs combined with probation services to protect the community are explored in more detail in the next chapter.

THE BROKEN WINDOWS APPROACH

Recently, some leaders of the probation and parole approaches have called for a dramatic change in the way in which community supervision achieves public safety.[23] This new model is called the "broken windows" approach. Borrowing heavily from community policing, the application of **broken windows probation** in probation and parole calls for a new partnership with the community. With this approach, the probation officer is asked to collaborate with the community and victim, hold the offender accountable, and improve and expand the leadership of probation. The key strategies outlined with this model include the following:[24]

- Placing public safety first
- Working in the community
- Developing partners in the community
- Rationally allocating scarce resources
- Enforcing conditions and penalizing violations
- Emphasizing performance-based initiatives
- Encouraging strong and steady leadership

Although the goals of the broken windows approach are lofty, the model is not without its critics. Taxman and Bryne[25] argue that the model is filled with rhetoric, is unrealistic, and is based on a flawed approach. Furthermore, they contend that it ignores the significant body of research indicating that the most effective way to achieve public safety is through well-designed and implemented treatment. Table 5.4 illustrates the differences between what Taxman and Bryne call the **proactive supervision** model and the broken windows model.[26] The Maryland Department of Public Safety and Correctional Services recently initiated the proactive approach to community supervision. Moving away from traditional supervision, this approach advocates a much more prescriptive strategy that includes more fieldwork combined with evidenced-based practices. The accompanying Correctional Brief describes this strategy. The debate about how to make probation more effective will continue, and it remains to be seen if the broken windows model can live up to its promises.

key term

Broken windows probation
Concept that the probation officer is asked to communicate with victim(s) and the community, hold the offender accountable, and improve the leadership of probation.

key term

Proactive supervision
Treatment strategy serving to prepare for, intervene in, or control an expected occurrence or situation by offenders on probation, especially a negative or difficult one.

table 5.4 Fixing Broken Windows Probation: A Comparison of Two Strategies

	The Broken Windows Model	The Proactive Supervision Model
Definition of the public Safety Problem	Probation should be held responsible for the level of public safety in each community, including crime rates, fear of crime, school safety, and quality of life.	Probation should be held responsible for the supervision and control of all offenders under their direct supervision.
The duties of probation officers	Probation officers should be involved not only in offender surveillance and control but also in crime prevention efforts and various forms of advocacy and community change.	Probation officers should focus their efforts on the direct supervision of offenders, while the responsibility for resource development and coordination should be completed by creating a new "resource specialist" position within probation.
The location of probation officers	Probation officers should supervise offenders exclusively in the community rather than in the office. Supervision should be place based rather than offender based.	Probation officers should utilize a combination of office and field visits, but the purpose of the contact is always the supervision of the offender, not the place.
The role of the probation officers	The probation officer should be a "generalist" with the ability to supervise a wide range of offenders (e.g., drug offenders, alcohol offenders, nonviolent offenders, sex offenders, mentally ill offenders), utilizing a classic brokerage model.	Probation officers should be hired and trained with the skills to handle a specialized caseload (e.g., drug offenders, alcohol offenders, nonviolent offenders, sex offenders, mentally ill offenders), including assessment procedures, counseling techniques, and a comprehensive knowledge of the treatment network (inpatient and outpatient).
The acquisition and allocation of probation resources	Probation departments need to develop improved strategies for the rational allocation of existing resources, focusing on two primary agency needs: (1) better assessment offender "risk" to public safety (e.g., sex offenders, gang members, drug dealers) and (2) the assignment of field staff to areas with the greatest public safety needs.	Probation departments need to "make the case" for increased resources for offender treatment and supervision by proposing legislation that mandates minimum levels of probation (e.g., caseload size services) and allows agents to use sanctions as a tool to improve public safety.
Enforcement of probation conditions	Probation officers utilize a range of surveillance techniques to identify offender noncompliance and technical violations. A structured hierarchy of sanctions will be used for initial violations and (return to) prison/jail for repeat "offenders."	Probation departments develop strategies (in conjunction with local judiciary) to reduce the number of conditions established and to enforce the conditions set, using a structured hierarchy of nonincarcerative sanctions.
Location of absconders	Probation departments establish separate probationer absconder and apprehension units to better protect the community..	Probation departments develop a task force to better understand the nature (and impact) of the absconder problem. Utilizing a problem-oriented probation strategy, probation officers will be required to focus directly on addressing the cause(s) of the problem rather than the consequences.
Partnerships in the community	A wide range of probation–community partnerships will be developed, including both crime-prevention and community-betterment activities.	Probation departments will focus on improving the treatment networks in their community and on those related activities that will enhance the supervision function.

SOURCE: Data from: Faye Taxman and James Bryne, "Fixing Broken Windows Probation," *Perspectives* 25:2 (2001): 23–29.

PROBATION AND ITS ROLE IN CORRECTIONS

Because of the prison population crisis across the nation, states are exploring many strategies to reduce the overcrowding. The basic strategies can be described as front-end solutions and back-end solutions. Probation (a front-end solution) is the mostly widely used alternative (see Table 5.4).

key term

Front-end solutions
Options for controlling the number of inmates being sent to prison.

key term

Back-end solutions
Strategies for reducing prison population overcrowding by early release programs, such as parole, shock parole, and expanded good-time credits.

Front-end solutions are alternative sentences such as probation and intermediate punishments that include house arrest, deferred prosecution, electronic monitoring, shock probation, intensive supervised probation, intermittent jail incarceration, and other programs (see Chapter 6).

Back-end solutions refer to ways used to reduce prison populations after the offender arrives in prison. They can be viewed as "early-out" or "extended limits" options: parole, shock parole, emergency release (usually court ordered), expanded good-time credits to count against the minimum sentence, work and educational furlough, prerelease at halfway houses (used extensively by the U.S. Bureau of Prisons, the federal prison system), and other programs. These are explained in Chapter 12.

Probation has established itself as a major component of corrections. It appears that the emphasis on probation as the preferred disposition will keep it in the forefront of correctional reform. If the costs of probation and prison are compared, as shown earlier in Table 5.3, daily costs of $10.79 per day as opposed to an average of $77.49 per day in prison, the taxpayer will rule in favor of probation. As the population grows, the number of offenders and variations on probation strategies will surely increase as well. Students of probation concur that the practice is approximately 60 percent effective on a national basis. An alternative to imprisonment that is about one-eighth as costly (and at least as effective) has great appeal and clearly answers the need for a sound and economical approach to corrections.

correctional **practice 5.2**

Being Proactive with Offenders in the Community

Proactive community supervision (PCS) improves community supervision by improving offenders' lives and fully restoring them as productive participants to the community. To accomplish this task, agents are active in the communities in which they serve. The PCS model emphasizes offender management tools such as motivational interviewing, risk and needs assessment, quality contact standards, and implementation of "what works" principles that improve an offender's ability to succeed in the community. By using these tools, the role of the agent is changed: Agents become role models of helpful and prosocial behavior for the offenders and the community.

By working with the community, supervision can accomplish the following:

- Protect public safety,
- Hold offenders accountable to victims and the community, and
- Help offenders become responsible and productive.

Under the PCS model:

- Agents' caseloads are reduced to appropriate levels so that agents can spend more time in neighborhoods working one-on-one with offenders;
- Agents and supervisors receive training on how to motivate offenders, identify critical risk factors, and create practical supervision plans; and
- Agents and supervisors receive suitable technological tools such as laptop computers to help them perform their jobs while working outside the office in the community.

The community can expect agents to:

- Spend their days near where parolees and probationers call home;
- Work with parolees and probationers to help them beat the drug and alcohol addictions that can lead them back to crime and violence;
- Help parolees and probationers get basic education and job skills so they can become contributing citizens;
- Build relationships with offenders' families, friends, and neighbors—people who can alert agents before trouble arises;
- Intervene before an offender commits a new crime; and
- Respond quickly when an offender's behavior necessitates removal from the community.

SOURCE: Maryland Department of Public Safety and Correctional Services, http://www.dpscs.state.md.us/rehabservs/ (accessed March 8, 2005).

Summary

Outline the History of Probation

Probation antecedents can be found in both the practice of sanctuary and the judicial suspension of sentence. In the United States, the "Youth Saving Movement" included a solution that would identify problems youth faced and search for services that would addresses solutions to those problems. Since youth were seen as less committed to a life of crime and more amenable to such care, treatment, and guidance efforts, probation quickly became the major disposition alternative for the higher-need and lower-risk juveniles. By 1923, all states extended statutory authority for probation to juvenile courts. The adult concept was slower to be endorsed; the last state to authorize adult probation did so in 1956.

Summarize Modern Probation Operations, Including the Conditions of Probation

On the defendant's conviction through plea bargaining or trial, the offender must be sentenced. The sentencing judge typically knows little about the newly convicted criminal and relies on the presentence report to marshal information related not only to the legal case but also to the offender. That judge might also have input from victims or their next of kin if the victim has died. Assisted in most states by a sentencing matrix requiring certain lengths of imprisonment (or alternative sanctions) and a large set of other factors the presentencing officer thinks should be called to the attention of the judge, the sentencing judge makes a determination as to which sentence should be imposed. This is far from an exact science since forecasting future behavior is a large part of the judge's armentarium. Sometimes the sentence is too brief; at other times the imposed sentence is too punitive. Most probation officers, in a brief period of time, can observe the offender and determine if the sentence is appropriate. Bear in mind that some judicial errors are possible and judges are fallible.

Explain How Probation Can Be Revoked

Probation can be revoked by the sentencing judge and the offender can be resentenced to a period of incarceration. The courts have the power to enforce their reformation and personal improvement strategies. Defiance, lying to the probation officer, or repeatedly violating conditions imposed by the judge ("do not drink" or "you are on wet paper") can have serious consequences. Repeatedly violating officer expectations can result in another appearance before the judge, a tightening of the tourniquet in terms of supervision requirements, and other related behavior that can be a ticket to jail or prison.

Summarize the Characteristics of Probationers

Felons on probation tend to successfully complete their period of supervision and conform to expectations. Depending on the state, social services support, employment, and selectivity in sentencing decisions, more than 60 percent of probationers cease their criminal activities during the probation period. Those who do not adequately satisfy conditions of release might commit another crime or fail to conform their behavior to expectations. Those who fail in conformity but do not commit another felony can be returned to court for a resentencing. Probationers committing other felonies are quite likely to be incarcerated or returned to prison. The key factor is abiding by appropriate rules and limited backsliding. Remember, the court can impose any reasonable probation condition, including imprisonment, banishment, or return to incarceration (jail or prison). In some jurisdictions, the appropriate punishment might be a life sentence. In other jurisdictions, the sentence for failing on supervised probation could well be life plus 68 years. Such a sentence clearly indicates that the judge intended that the offender never leave prison.

Summarize the Risk Assessment Process

Probation officers are trained on how to work effectively with probationers and how to model appropriate behavior. They are adept at cognitive restructuring to determine the probationer's whereabouts, reinforce positive behavior, solve problems, and use authority effectively. It is crucial to target risk factors that might lead to probation failure, and a variety of assessment tools are used to identify those factors. Such skills are required under the EPICS model. This improves the quality and effectiveness of probation officers. Remember that many characteristics of the probation population function to interfere with their daily living, and new skills, behavior rehearsals, and rewards for good behavior are necessary.

Understand How Probation Targets Criminogenic Risk Factors

Contemporary correctional practices have shifted to evidence-based treatment, meaning that programs and practices must show evidence of effectiveness in treatment. Those that reduce delinquent and adult criminal behavior should be used in probation to reduce recidivism. This evidence-based movement targets factors that contribute to legal offending rather than "feel-good" practices that either make no change or result in higher rates of reoffending (such as boot camps or Project Dare).

Summarize the Use of Economic Sanctions

The most frequently imposed sanction in the probation area is the economic fine, restitution, and victim compensation, all programs that attempt to encourage fiscal responsibility by criminal violators. If the offender has caused social harm and negatively impacted others, such inmates can be ordered to participate in victim compensation, restorative judgment, and making the community whole. Surprisingly, most offenders pay fines and participate in making the victim whole.

Identify and Explain Successful Approaches Underlying Contemporary Probation Practices

The best practices of probation service require an extensive presentence investigation that identifies, inter alia, those factors and goals that a probationer should address. When probation is granted, the sentencing judge may impose required behavior to avoid those risks, and the probation officer is expected to manage this case according to the judge's orders and use evidence-based programs that directly target potential probation outcomes. Examples of these include securing employment, budgeting, the officers' appropriate contact with clients, enforcing the "wet paper" rule, referring clients to available public service providers training in caging the client's rage, parenting training, avoidance of domestic violence, and related programs. Some jurisdictions have begun to demand that appropriate fund allocations be made to implementing effective and evidence-based probation services. When the goals and objectives of improving probation service are achieved, client failure and recidivism decrease, and the public is made safer.

Key Words

probation, 97
suspended sentence, 98
right of sanctuary, 98
benefit of clergy, 98
stigma, 98
sursis, 98
John Augustus, 98
presentence investigation (PSI) report, 104
risk and needs assessment, 105
EPICS model, 107
special conditions of probation, 109
technical probation violations, 110
probation revocation, 110
Gagnon v. *Scarpelli*, 110
felony probation, 111
broken windows probation, 112
proactive supervision, 112
front-end solutions, 114
back-end solutions, 114

Review Questions

1. Explain the purpose of probation and describe the methods by which it is usually administered.
2. How do probation officers enforce the conditions ordered by the court?
3. What are some of the restrictions often applied to probation? What kinds of offenders are usually denied probation?
4. Do you think a conflict exists between surveillance and treatment? How might you reconcile this conflict?
5. Identify and define five front-end solutions to prison overcrowding. Why do you think that front-end solutions are usually more politically acceptable than backdoor options?
6. What are the national trends in probation?
7. Why should probation be the sentence of choice?
8. What are special conditions of probation? Give three examples and explain why they might be imposed.
9. Who is credited as the "father of probation," and why was his work so important?
10. Does drug abuse treatment work? Under what circumstances?
11. Explain the general process of probation revocation.
12. The EPICS model attempts to teach the probation officers how to be a change agent by teaching the offender new skills. Why do you think this is important?

13. Why would an LSI-R be useful in probation supervision?
14. A defense lawyer authorizes an informed citizen to undertake a private presentence investigation of the accused in order to submit the result of the investigation to a sentencing judge prior to possible incarceration. This presentence report usually emphasizes a treatment plan designed to address the offender's needs. What are your thoughts about this practice?

Application Case Studies

1. If you were a probation officer and one of your probationers tested positive for drugs, what are some of the ways you might respond to this violation?
2. A defense lawyer authorizes an informed citizen to undertake a private presentence investigation of the accused in order to submit the result of the interview to a sentencing judge prior to possible incarceration. This presentence report usually emphasizes a treatment plan designed to address the offender's needs. What are your thoughts about this practice?
3. The family of a victim who was assaulted and almost killed was asked what they thought should happen to the perpetrator. Much to the investigator's surprise, the family unanimously agreed that the perpetrator be fined and released. You know that two of the males in this family have a history of violent assaults. What would you recommend to the judge?
4. You are a probation officer with a client who repeatedly consumes large amounts of alcohol, even though the judge make probation dependent on remaining sober. The client, when drunk, drives in his inebriated state. What would you do?
5. Another of your probation clients is a hard drinker but takes his 12-year-old son with him to bars so that the son can drive his father home when the latter is too inebriated to drive. The judge had imposed a "no drinking" demand as a condition of probation and suspended the client's driver's license for the period of probation. What would you do with your probation client?

Endnotes

1. Norman Johnston, *Forms of Constraints: A History of Prison Architecture* (Urbana: University of Illinois Press, 2007). See also Herman Bianchi, *Justice as Sanctuary* (Bloomington: Indiana University Press, 1994).
2. See Numbers 35:6 and Joshua 20:2–6.
3. David Fogel, "Nordic Approaches to Crime and Justice," *CJ International* 3:1 (1987): 8–21. See also D. Farabee, M. Prendergast, and D. Anglin, "The Effectiveness of Coerced Treatment for Drug-Abusing Offenders," *Federal Probation* 62:1 (1998): 3–10, and James Clare, "Methamphetamine Use and Health Implications in Corrections," *American Jails* 21:3 (2007): 40–44.
4. Alexander Smith and Louis Berlin, *Introduction to Probation and Parole* (St. Paul, MN: West, 1976), pp. 76–78. See also Edward Latessa and Paula Smith, *Corrections in the Community* (Cincinnati, OH: Anderson Publishing, 2007), pp. 48–50.
5. Harry Elmer Barnes and Negley K. Teeters, *New Horizons in Criminology*, 3rd ed. (Englewood Cliffs, NJ: Prentice Hall, 1959), p. 554.
6. Missouri (1897), Rhode Island (1899), New Jersey (1900), and Vermont (1900).
7. Cook County (Chicago), Illinois.
8. Bureau of Labor Statistics, *Occupational Outlook Handbook 2010–2011 Edition* (Washington, DC: Bureau of labor Statistics, 2012). For an examination of probationer work groups, see G. Bayens, M. Manske, and J. Smykla, "The Attitudes of Criminal Justice Workgroups toward Intensive Supervised Probation," *American Journal of Criminal Justice* 22:2 (1998): 189–206, and Bill Conlon et al., "Education: Don't Do Prisons without It," *Corrections Today* 70:1 (2008): 48–52.
9. Dennis Sullivan, L. Tifft, and P. Cordella, eds., "Special Issue: The Phenomenon of Restorative Justice," *Contemporary Justice Review* 1:1 (1998): 1–166. See also Restorative Justice Online, "Introduction to Restorative Justice," http://www.restorativejustice.org/university-classroom/01introduction/tutorial-introduction-to-restorative-justice/tutorial-introduction-to-restorative-justice (accessed August 24, 2014).
10. Latessa and Smith, *Corrections in the Community,* p. 57.

11. Laura Maruschak and Erika Parks, *Probation and Parole in the United States, 2001* (Washington, DC: U.S. Department of Justice, 2012).
12. See F. Taxman and J. Bryne, "Fixing Broken Windows Probation," *Perspectives* 25:2 (2001): 23–29.
13. Harry E. Allen and Julie C. Abril, "Fanning the Flames of Fear Revisited: Three Strikes in California, paper presented at the annual meeting of the American Society of Criminology, Washington, D.C., November 11, 1998. See also Eric Lotke, Jason Coburn, and Vincent Schiraldi, "Three Strikes and You're Out," http://www.justicepolicy.org/images/upload/04-03_REP_CAStillStrikingOut_AC.pdf (accessed August 24, 2014). For a sobering discussion, see Michael Tonry, "Crime and Human Rights—How Political Paranoia, Protestant Fundamentalism, and Constitutional Obsolescence Combined to Devastate Black America," *Criminology* 46:1 (2008): 1–33.
14. See also Mark Umbreit and W. Bradshaw, "Victim Experience of Meeting Adult and Juvenile Offenders," *Federal Probation* 61:4 (1998): 33–39, and David Karp, Gordon Bazemore, and J. D. Chesire, "The Role and Attitudes of Restorative Board Members," *Crime and Delinquency* 50:4 (2004): 487–515.
15. E. Latessa, *An Analysis of Pre-Sentencing Investigation Recommendations and Judicial Outcome in Cuyahoga County Adult Probation Department* (Cincinnati, OH: University of Cincinnati, Department of Criminal Justice, 1993).
16. D. Andrews and J. Bonta, *LSI-R, The Level of Service Inventory—Revised* (Toronto: MultiHealth Systems, Inc., 1995).
17. Lia Gormsen, "Judge Uses His Legal Knowledge to Empower Reentering Offenders," *Correctional Today* 70:3 (2008): 3.
18. Christopher Lowenkamp and Edward J. Latessa, *Evaluation of Ohio's CCA Funded Programs* (Cincinnati, OH: Division of Criminal Justice, University of Cincinnati, 2005).
19. See Edward Latessa, "What Works in Correctional Intervention," *Southern Illinois University Law Review* 23 (1999). See also Paul Gendreau, "The Principles of Effective Interventions with Offenders," in *Choosing Correctional Options That Work: Defining Demand and Evaluating the Supply*, ed. A. T. Harland (Thousand Oaks, CA: Sage, 1996), pp. 117–130.
20. See J. Bonta, T. Rugge, T. L. Scott, G. Bourgon, and A. K. Yessine, "Exploring the 'Black Box' of Supervision," *Journal of Offender Rehabilitation* 47:3 (2008): 248–270; G. Bourgon, J. Bonta, T. Rugge, T. L. Scott, and A. K. Yessine, "Program Design, Implementation, and Evaluation in 'Real World' Community Supervision," *Federal Probation* 74:1 (2010): 1–10; and C. Trotter, "The Impact of Different Supervision Practices in Community Corrections: Cause for Optimism," *Australian and New Zealand Journal of Criminology* 29 (1996): 1–18.
21. In 1980, Andrews and Kiessling first introduced five core correctional practices (effective use of authority, anticriminal modeling and reinforcement, problem solving, use of community resources, and interpersonal relationships) that were later expanded into a training curriculum by Andrews and Carvell in 1998. In 1989, Gendreau and Andrews added to this list of practices with the development of the Correctional Program Assessment Inventory (CPAI). See D. A. Andrews and C. Carvell, *Core Correctional Training-Core Correctional Supervision and Counseling: Theory, Research, Assessment and Practice,* unpublished training manual (Ottawa: Carleton University, 1998); D. A. Andrews and J. J. Kiessling, "Program Structure and Effective Correctional Practices: A Summary of the CaVic Research, in *Effective Correctional Treatment*, ed. R. R. Ross and P. Gendreau, pp. 441–463. (Toronto: Butterworths, 1980); and P. Gendreau and D. A. Andrews, *Correctional Program Assessment Inventory* (St. John: University of New Brunswick, 1989).
22. P. Smith, M. Schweitzer, R. M. Labreque, and E. J. Latessa, "Improving Probation Officer's Skills: An Evaluation of the EPICS Model," *Journal of Crime and Justice 35* (2012): 189–199.
23. T. Arola and R. Lawrence, "Broken Windows Probation," *Perspectives* 24:1 (2000): 27–33.
24. The Reinventing Probation Council that drafted the initial report on broken windows and probation included Ronald Corbett, Dan Beto, John DiIulio, J. Richard Faulkner, Bernard Fitzgerald, Irwin Gregg, Norman Helber, Gerald Hinzman, Robert Malvestuto, Mario Paparozzi, Rocco Pozzi, and Edward Rhine. See Reinventing Probation Council, *Transforming Probation through Leadership: the Broken Windows Model,* http://www.manhattaninstitute.org/html/broken_windows.htm (accessed September 14, 2008).
25. Faye Taxman and James Bryne, "The Truth about 'Broken Windows' Probation: Moving towards a Proactive Community Supervision Model," *Perspectives,* Spring 2001.
26. Taxman and Bryne, "The Truth about 'Broken Windows' Probation."

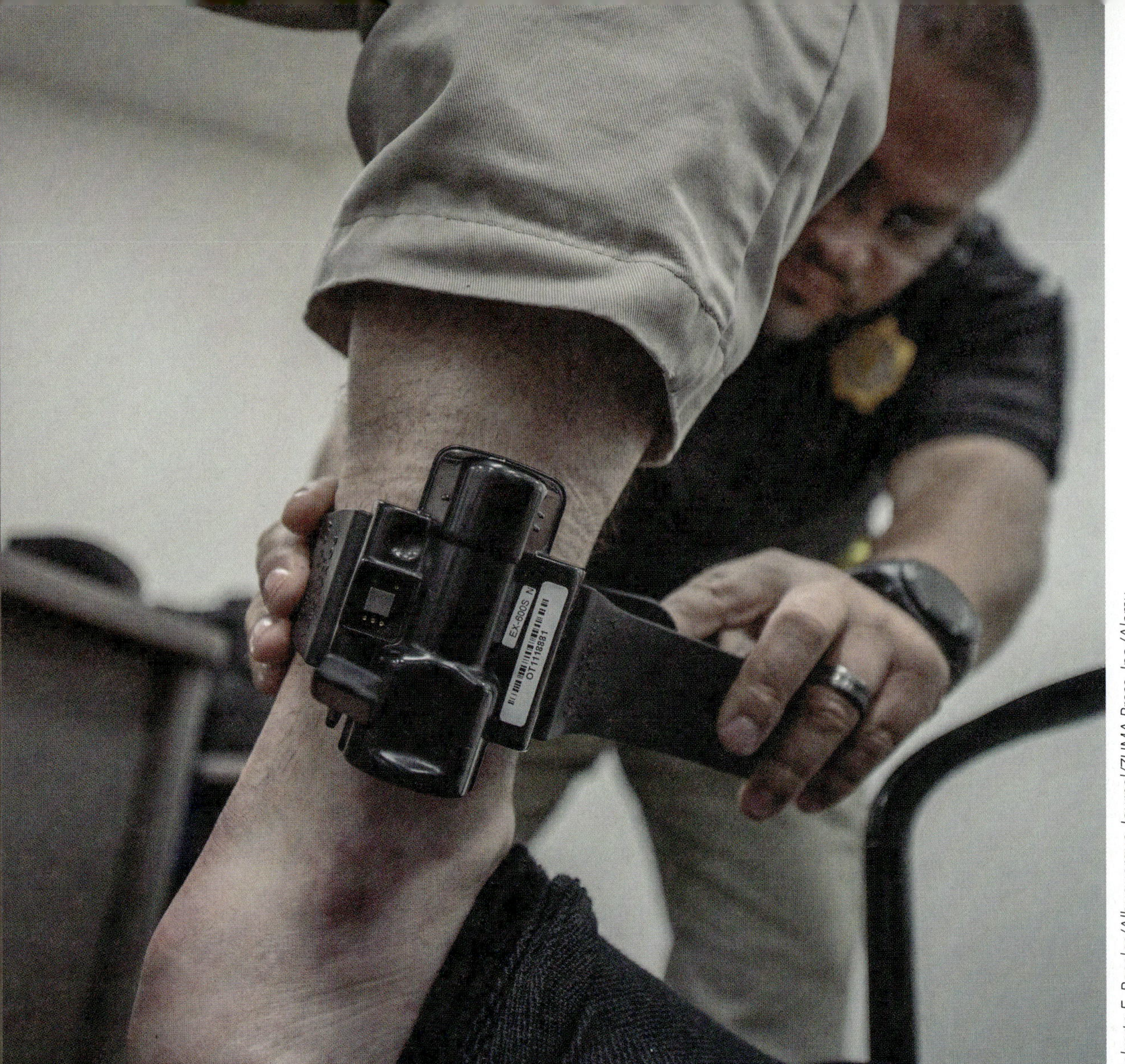

Roberto E. Rosales/Albuquerque Journal/ZUMA Press, Inc./Alamy.

Objectives

- Explain how diversion is used to keep offenders out of the corrections system.
- Summarize the goals of intermediate sanctions.
- Explain restitution programs.
- Explain the goals and operations of boot camps as well as issues associated with them.
- Explain the goals and operations of community correction facilities as well as issues associated with them.

chapter 6

Diversion and Intermediate Sanctions

- Describe drug, mental health, and other problem-solving courts.
- Explain how electronic monitoring and global positioning systems are used and issues associated with their use.
- Summarize the advantages and disadvantages of home confinement.
- Explain the goals of intensive supervision probation.
- Summarize the development of day reporting centers as well as issues associated with them.
- Explain the goals and operations of community service programs.
- Explain the goals and operations of shock probation.

"In every year between 1990 and 2000, State prisoners released by a paroleboard had higher success rates (54%) than those released through mandatoryparole (35%)."

—Bureau of Justice Statistics, Reentry Trends in the United States.

Outline

Diversion: Keeping the Offender Out of the System

- Police-Based Diversion Programs
- Community-Based Diversion Programs
- Court-Based Diversion Programs

Between Probation and Prison

Overcrowding

Intermediate Sanctions

- Restitution Programs
- Intensive Supervised Probation
- Drug, Mental Health, and Other Problem-Solving Courts
- Community Service Programs
- Home Detention
- Electronic Monitoring
- Community Residential Treatment Centers (Halfway Houses)
- Day Reporting Centers
- Shock Incarceration
- Shock Probation
- Boot Camp Programs

Overview

Our investigation of the alternatives to imprisonment has focused on probation as the major nonincarceration sanction arrow in the quiver of the sentencing judges. Although probation is by far the most widely used correctional sanction, it is but one aspect of community corrections. In this chapter, we explore some diversion options along with the growing use of intermediate sanctions, which are the various new correctional options used as adjuncts to and part of probation. Note, however, that some jurisdictions use these sanctions not as part of probation but as stand-alone programs.

policy positions 6.1

Intermediate Sanctions

Intermediate sanctions are those correctional options that fall somewhere between probation and incarceration and can range from fines to placement in a residential facility. As more and more jurisdictions wrestle with the increasing costs of jails and prisons, many have turned to less restrictive and less costly alternatives. While the concept has been around for many years, recent developments have focused on finding both cheaper *and* more effective options. These include drug and mental health courts, day reporting centers, residential treatment facilities, and more traditional options, such as electronic monitoring, community service, and restitution programs. While research has shown that not all intermediate sanctions are effective in reducing recidivism, today there is a renewed effort to divert offenders into programs that hold offenders accountable and that provide the interventions and services that they need to stay out of trouble and pay their debt to society without the stigma of incarceration.

DIVERSION: KEEPING THE OFFENDER OUT OF THE SYSTEM

key term

Diversion
Minimizing penetration into the criminal justice system through police, community, or court programs.

Some jurisdictions have established policies to minimize assignment of certain nondangerous or problematic offenders to the justice system, particularly the mentally disordered,[1] drug abusers,[2] and alcohol abusers.[3] **Diversion** from the criminal justice system has taken place in one form or another since social controls were first established. In most cases, informal diversions merely indicate an official's exercise of discretion at some point in the criminal process.

More formal diversions include suspension of the criminal process in favor of some noncriminal disposition. Fewer than 25 percent of reported offenses in America result in an arrest, and only about one-third of those arrests result in a criminal conviction. This is the correctional funnel at work and an indication that preconviction diversion is not uncommon.

Diversion may occur at a number of points in the criminal justice system. The primary points are prior to police contact, prior to official police processing, and prior to official court processing. Three basic models emerge to determine which agency might be responsible for diversion: police-based diversion programs, community-based diversion programs, and court-based diversion programs. Although each of the models usually involves more than one agency or group, programs will generally be grouped according to who initiates the action and what agency will have primary responsibility for its implementation.

Most diversion programs now in effect constitute informal responses to the ambiguities of existing legislation. The value of such programs is difficult if not impossible to estimate. Again, one must try to measure an event that was prevented: What did not happen as a result of diversion? Their goals and procedures must be clearly articulated and integrated into the rest of the criminal justice system.

Police-Based Diversion Programs

Police agencies have practiced diversion, informally, by using their power of discretion at the time of an offender's arrest. Several programs have been established to encourage more diversions on a formal basis. Police have been reluctant in the past to formalize their practice of discretion because of public opinion criticizing their actions as being too soft. Most formalized programs are aimed at youthful offenders in an effort to keep them from beginning a career of crime.

Another example of diversionary tactics at the police level is the family crisis intervention approach. This approach, which has been used in several large cities, is especially important as domestic violence laws across the country become tougher and are enforced more often.[4] Laws often now result in the arrest of both parties until the question as to who initiated the violence is resolved. There are indications that the police, by identifying conflict situations at an early stage of development, can prevent the escalation of violence. A general model involves the use of officers specially trained for effective family crisis intervention to respond to family disturbances. The officers attempt to resolve the conflict on the scene. If they cannot, the antagonists are arrested and, in some jurisdictions, referred to a community agency instead of jail.

Community-Based Diversion Programs

Diversion projects are most effective when integrated into a community-based correctional system with many levels of supervision and custody. The currently informal options on an accountable basis must be formalized without making the process too rigid. If community-based programs are too restricted, they will become mere institutions without walls. Diversion is seen as the first threshold of the community corrections system, designed to remove as many offenders as possible from the process before their conviction and labeling as a criminal.

Although programs that aim toward a total or partial alternative to incarceration are improvements, they do not always eliminate the stigma of a criminal record. Diversion programs tied to treatment and services in the community, however, both avoid the problems of incarceration and remove the criminal label. Those programs are seen not as a substitute for probation services but as a method of filling the gap between offenders eligible for probation and cases in which the charges can be dropped. Diversion should be accompanied by a formalized agreement with offenders as to what they are to do in return for the elimination of their arrest records. A set of alternative treatment services and residential reinforcements may be needed to help diverted individuals handle their problems. The diverted individuals should have the advantages available to all other categories of offenders who are being treated in the local network.

Court-Based Diversion Programs

The courts are involved with diversion in several ways. One method is to use civil commitment for individuals who presumably can be treated more efficiently in a hospital situation. A more common and reasonable use of diversion by the courts is found in **pretrial intervention programs**, which have been funded extensively by the U.S. Department of Labor. The general pattern of such actions, at the end of the prescribed period of the continuance, is to allow the following:

1. Dismissal of pending charges based on satisfactory project participation and demonstrated self-improvement
2. Extension of the continuance to allow the program staff more time to work with the person (usually for an additional 30 to 90 days)
3. Return of the defendant to normal court processing, without prejudice, because of unsatisfactory performance in the program

key term

Pretrial intervention programs
Requiring defendants awaiting trial to report to a supervision officer.

Diversion is especially appropriate for the public drunk, low-level misdemeanant offenders, and the first-time drug abuser, a major thrust behind the drug court movement. The current alternative to incarceration for public drunks is to send them to a detoxification center. Voluntary attendance at detoxification centers demonstrates the willingness of many problem drinkers to accept treatment, if only for free room and board.

The severity of criminal sanctions and public reaction to most drug offenses makes the diversion of drug abuse cases a sensitive area. With the country awash in illegal drugs and drug use by the general population quite high, the wave of enforcement activity has made it difficult to divert all but the least violent of users, leaving the hard cases to sweat

key term

Treatment in lieu of conviction
Diversion offered to offenders in which successful completion of probation allows the prosecutor or judge to cease prosecution if treatment program results in no conviction.

key term

Community corrections acts (CCAs)
Legislation that funds local community correctional programs designed to divert offenders from prison.

it out in institutions that seldom provide meaningful programs. One example of a diversion program is found in Ohio and is called **treatment in lieu of conviction**; it is designed for first-time substance abusers. Successful completion of treatment and no new charges can result in a clean record for these offenders. Most diversion programs for drug users are concentrated on juveniles and first-time adult arrestees, although drug courts address all age-groups and often deal with persons who have serious drug and alcohol problems. Students interested in reading more about this program should consult http://codes.ohio.gov/orc/2951.041+.

The spectrum of diversionary programs is geared toward the same goal: provision of a reasonable alternative to incarceration in large, overcrowded, and punitive prisons.[5] Again, as in the development of many other aspects of correctional services, such programs often begin as independent actions by concerned professionals and community groups. As a result of earlier efforts, **community corrections acts (CCAs)** have been authorized as a statutory medium for including citizens and bringing funding to local governments and county agencies to plan, develop, and deliver correctional services and sanctions at the local level.[6] At least 22 states have passed such enabling legislation, encouraging intermediate sanctions, advocacy for juveniles, local community organization involvement, victim–offender reconciliation, victim restitution, employment services, and county residential facilities, among many others. Some states contract with private agencies for county programs, whereas others fund local programs run by local officials. Either way, the goal is to offer community correctional programs with control at the local level. The best-implemented CCAs are in Minnesota, Iowa, Colorado, Ohio, and Indiana and offer model programs that could be copied by other jurisdictions.

BETWEEN PROBATION AND PRISON

The dominant characteristic of intermediate sanctions is the use of increased surveillance and tighter controls over nonincarcerated offenders. In this context, intermediate sanctions are often referred to as "punishing smarter" since the sanction is thought to be tough enough to impress on the offender the seriousness of the act, without the costs associated with longer-term incarceration. Advocates for the offender object on the basis that these efforts use increased punishment as a rationale and that tighter controls are not needed. Others argue that prison construction is too expensive for most jurisdictions and that intermediate sanctions save the costs of constructing, staffing, and maintaining incarceration facilities. Still other proponents see intermediate sanctions as a way to push for more treatment and services, which are thought to be more readily available (and more effective) in the community. These advocates note the reintegrative aspects of intermediate sanctions and point to reduced recidivism among offenders assigned to such programs. Some intermediate sanctions are less expensive and more effective than incarceration, while others are clearly intended to "get tough" with offenders. Although not yet fully integrated into the coordinated system of community corrections, these intermediate sanctions have been adopted across the nation into a wide system of local, county, state, and federal correctional systems. We first review the use of intermediate sanctions as an adjunct to probation.

As we saw in the previous chapter, probation has become the backbone of contemporary corrections and is used to treat offenders and provide protection to the community through supervising probationers. In the past two decades, prompted by crowding of jails and prisons as well as a shift in the philosophical assumptions about controlling offenders,[7] a broad range of different treatments and innovative technologies has been developed. These innovative programs and control schemes are generally called **intermediate sanctions**.[8] A study of intermediate sanctions must start with a look at the overcrowding issue.

key term

Intermediate sanctions
Correctional programs that fall somewhere between probation and prison.

OVERCROWDING

A major impetus for the development and expansion of community corrections and intermediate sanctions has been the overcrowding of our jails and prisons. Most repeat offenders receive increasingly severe punishments,[9] including sentences to jail and prison. In the United States, the lag between onset of offending and eventual confinement as an adult is approximately 10 years. In other words, *persistent* offenders are more likely to have been subject to other correctional control (fines, probation, **day reporting centers**, community service, **restitution orders**, **house arrest**, and even **electronic monitoring**) while in the community prior to their first incarceration.

The processing of offenders in the justice system has become a **risk management** strategy, and persistent offenders are usually given increasingly restrictive alternatives while corrections tries to stop their criminal behavior (that is, encourage **desistance**). Many offenders are given a number of such opportunities and assistance before a sentencing judge resorts to incarceration, the most punitive weapon in the armory of corrections.

Before the 1970s, many if not most offenders were placed on probation to achieve the ideal of rehabilitation.[10] Individualized treatment during that relatively progressive era became subject to strong attack by conservatives, researchers, and liberals of many stripes. The arguments were that prison and parole officials were abusing their discretion, rehabilitation did not work, strict law and order should be used to recapture the streets, and offenders richly deserved punishment. This was seen as the only way to protect law-abiding citizens as well as to retain the social fabric. This philosophy was particularly evident in the nation's War on Drugs program, a war that has clearly not been won.[11]

Coupled with the demise of the medical model, politicians at both local and national levels used the issue of crime as a vehicle to demonstrate how getting tough would solve the problem.[12] Seeking reelection on the hard-line bandwagon may have served narrow political ends. However, it also led to the enactment of a series of stringent policies ranging from a shift to determinate punishment to mandatory minimum sentences to prison to the building of more supermax prisons.[13]

key term

Day reporting center
Facility to which offenders are sent for scheduling and monitoring of their activities.

key term

Restitution order
Requirement that offender repay the victim.

key term

House arrest
Being confined to one's home except when permission is granted to leave.

key term

Electronic monitoring
Tracking of offender whereabouts electronically.

key term

Risk management
Strategies designed to provide increased supervision and surveillance for higher-risk offenders and less restrictive options for those of lower risk.

key term

Desistance
Ceasing of criminal behavior by the offender. Can also imply lessening of the severity of criminal offenses.

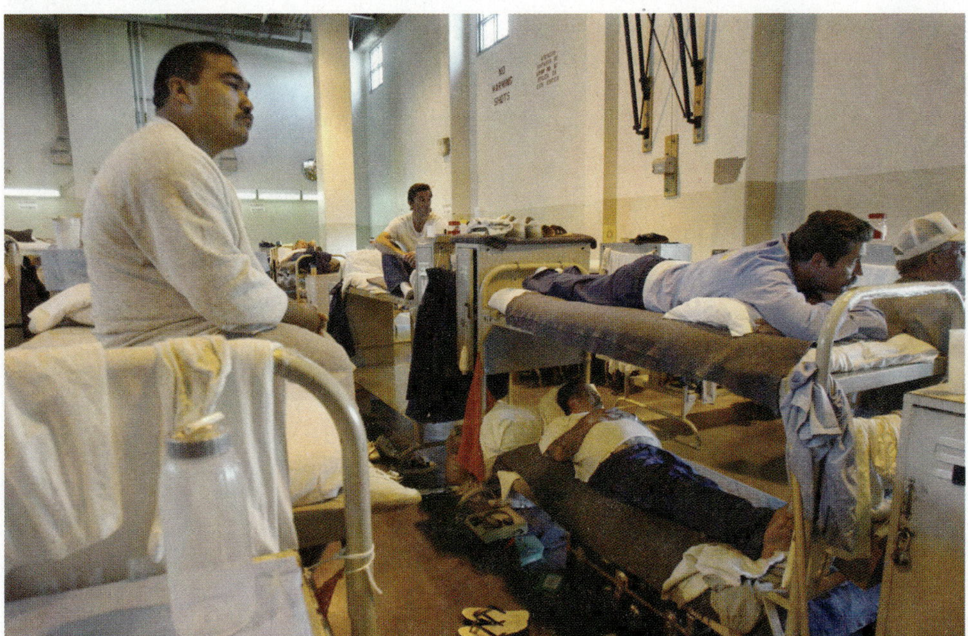

photo 6.1

Prisoners in overcrowded dormitory located in prison's gym.
ZUMA Press, Inc./Alamy.

figure 6.1

Incarceration Rates in Selected Countries per 100,000 Residents.

SOURCE: Data from: International Centre of Prison Studies, University of London, http://www.idcr.org.uk/wp-content/uploads/2010/09/WPPL-9-22.pdf.

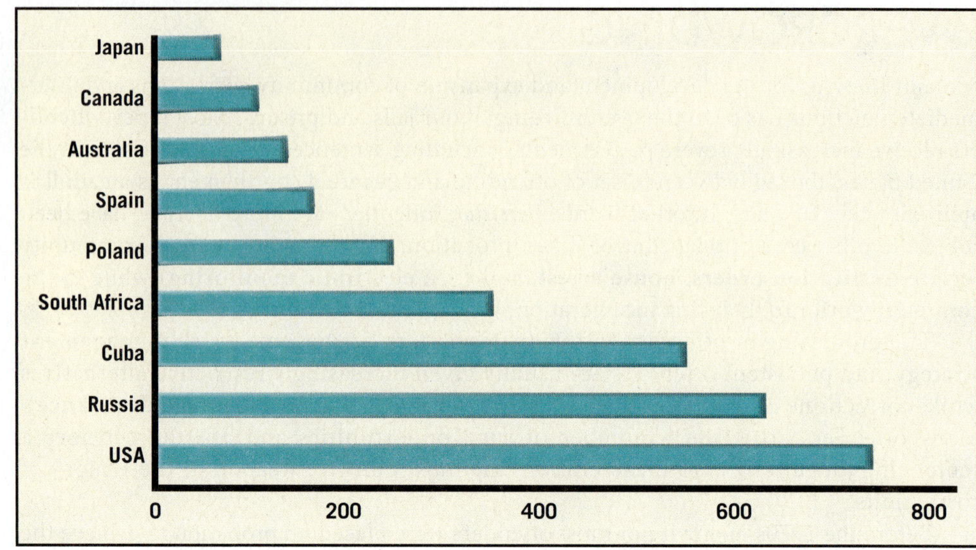

These events coincided with the 1945 to 1976 "baby-boom" population bulge, whose members entered the "high-commitment" years of ages 29 to 39 between 1975 and 1985. These four major forces—a larger number of persons at risk to commit crime and be incarcerated, the shift to conservative beliefs about how to deal with offenders and crime, the War on Drugs,[14] and enactment of more stringent punishments—contributed to an ever-increasing stream of offenders committed to prison (up from 448,264 in 1975 to over 2,315,537 in 2012).[15] By 1998, the combined number of prisoners in the nation and in jails exceeded any previous total. "America the Free" has become the free world's leader in rate of incarceration, exceeding even the Russian Republic of the former Soviet Union. Prisons bulged, and the nation began its building binge, trying to construct sufficient numbers of jail and prison cells to accommodate the massive increase of incarcerated offenders. When it earlier became evident that the bricks-and-mortar approach could not be met, correctional innovators turned to developing alternative punishment programs, variously known as intermediate sanctions or intermediate punishments. Recent figures show comparisons of rates of incarceration among the United States, Cuba, the Russian Republic, and other nations[16] (see Figure 6.1). What is interesting in these data is the comparison with the rest of the world and the fact that we are far ahead of all other countries.

policy **positions 6.2**

Federal Pretrial Services

While federal pretrial services officers are charged with supervising each defendant released to their custody, not every offender is actively supervised. Some defendants—primarily those the court has determined pose no flight risk or danger to the community—are released only under the condition that they do not commit any offense. Other defendants are released under more restrictive release conditions. These defendants are typically required to report to a pretrial services officer on a predetermined reporting schedule or to reside in a community treatment facility or halfway house. During the release period, the pretrial services officer monitors the defendant's compliance with the release conditions and reports any violations to the court and to the U.S. attorney. Additionally, pretrial services officers might assist released individuals with securing employment and medical, legal, or social services.

SOURCE: John Scalia, *Federal Pretrial Release and Detention, 1996* (Washington, DC: U.S. Department of Justice, 1999), p. 8. See also the American Bar Association (2013), "Pretrial Release," http://www.americanbar.org/publications/criminal_justice_archive/crimjust_standards_pretrialrelease_blk.html.

INTERMEDIATE SANCTIONS

Intermediate sanctions provide midrange dispositions that better reflect the severity of the offense than do probation or imprisonment. While many if not most offenders can best be served by reintegration programming, some are thought to be too dangerous to be released to traditional probation supervision with infrequent face-to-face contacts. Thus, a continuum of sanctions ranging from probation to imprisonment has been developed: restitution, fines, community service, intensive supervised probation, house arrest, electronic monitoring, residential placement, and shock incarceration. The latter includes shock probation and shock parole as well as boot camps. Figure 6.2 depicts the range of sentencing options. James Byrne has identified the major sanction options that sentencing might impose and ranked them by levels of punishment inherent in each. Restitution, for example, is seen as less punitive than community service; house arrest is a lower level of punishment than jail incarceration.[17] You should remember that judges can and frequently do impose several sanctions simultaneously and retain authority to initiate tourniquet sentencing, a process that increases and tightens the numbers and conditions of punishments until the probationer is brought under the most effective control.

Intermediate sanctions are attractive for the following five reasons:

1. Channeling offenders into community-based corrections is believed to be able to reduce or delay prison overcrowding.
2. Intermediate punishments are designed for offenders believed to pose too much risk for probation services but not enough risk to be sent to prison.
3. They are generally less expensive than incarceration in either jail or prison.
4. They are believed to offer more rehabilitation and reintegration potential than does incarceration.
5. It is believed that expansion and fine-tuning of alternative sanctions will eventually lead to a valid continuum of sentencing alternatives.[18]

We begin our more detailed examination of these programs with restitution.

Restitution Programs

A common condition for probation is the requirement that victims be compensated for their losses or injury as a form of **restitution**. The emphasis given to the study of victimology in the past few years has resulted in some state compensation of crime victims by payment of

key term

Restitution

A court-ordered sanction requiring the offender to make the victim whole or to compensate the community for the offender's illegal behavior.

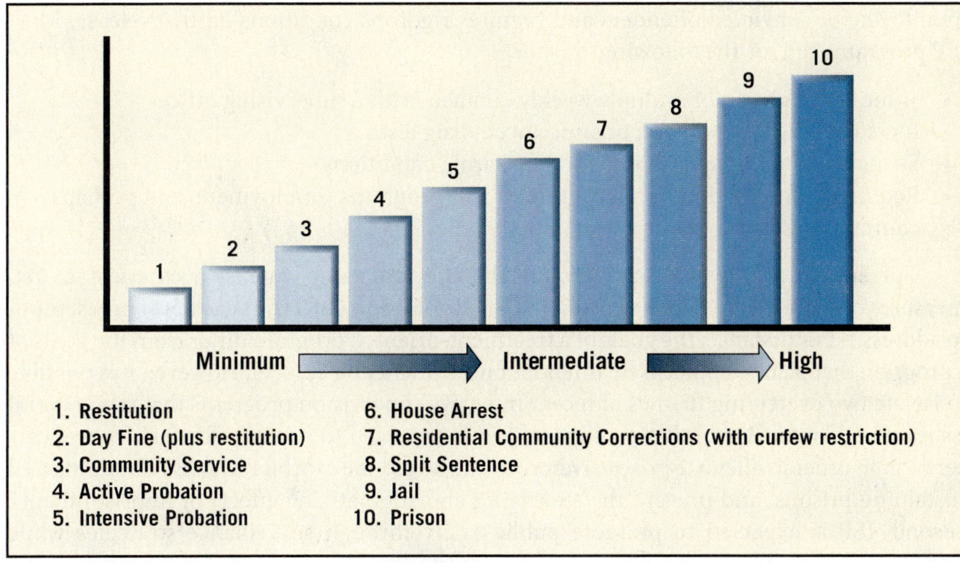

figure 6.2

A Range of Sentencing Options, Ranked by the Level of Punishment.

SOURCE: Data from: James Byrne, "The Future of Intensive Probation Supervision," *Crime and Delinquency* 36:1 (1990): 3–34.

medical costs and other financial reimbursement, such as loss of work. Through the system of probation, however, the offender often repays the victim. It is important that probation authorities link the amount of payment to the offender's ability to pay. Paying through installments is usually the most realistic approach. In some cases, a partial restitution may be all that is reasonably possible (for example, in the case of an arsonist who burns down a multi-million-dollar building).

Many reasons are offered to support restitution programs. Obviously, restitution offsets the victim's loss when property is stolen; restitution can even be ordered for the deductible amount an insurance company might require an insured victim to pay before the insurance coverage would become effective. Time lost from work while being a witness in court and being hospitalized is subject to offender restitution. It appears that restitution may be ordered for any injury caused by the offense for which the offender was convicted. Other rationales are that restitution forces the offender to accept personal responsibility for the crime, restitution can lead to reconciliation of offender and victim,[19] and, finally, it provides one way the victim can overcome the otherwise impersonal processing of victims within the justice system. Although it is estimated that more than 30 percent of all adults on probation and 12 percent of offenders on felony probation are ordered to make restitution,[20] it appears that restitution programs are more numerous in the juvenile justice systems than they are in the adult system.[21] Although almost every state has restitution programs in operation, Georgia, Texas, Florida, Minnesota, and Michigan appear to be leaders in program development. (Restitution programs also have been extensively implemented and evaluated in Great Britain, Austria, Germany, and Australia.) In Minnesota, parolees may also be required to reside in a residential restitution center and pay part of their wages to victims. Other jurisdictions require victim–offender conferences to establish the amount of financial compensation due to the victim.

Intensive Supervised Probation

key term

Intensive supervised probation (ISP)
Intermediate sanction requiring increased supervision for probationers.

key term

Tourniquet sentencing
When a judge increases the sanctions and conditions imposed on an offender.

Another alternative sanction program is **intensive supervised probation (ISP)**, which is designed to provide increased surveillance of offenders deemed to be too serious for "routine" probation. The program is a management strategy for probation services that need to increase the level of surveillance for individuals who do not adjust to regular probation requirements. ISP is a program frequently found in **tourniquet sentencing**.

Georgia is believed to have been the first jurisdiction to impose a statewide system of ISP (starting in 1974), and by 1990, every state had at least one jurisdiction city, county, or state with the program. There is no generic ISP. It is a form of release that emphasizes close monitoring of convicted offenders and requires rigorous conditions on that release. Most ISP programs call for the following:[22]

- Some combination of multiple weekly contacts with a supervising officer
- Increased and random and unannounced drug testing
- Stringent enforcement of probation or parole conditions
- Required participation in relevant treatment programs, employment, and perhaps community service

Current issues largely revolve around the effectiveness of intensive supervision. Yet, measures of success vary depending on the stated goals and objectives each program sets out to address.[23] For instance, the goals of a treatment-oriented program differ from the goals of a program that places emphasis on offender punishment and control. However, it is possible to isolate two overriding themes of recent intensive supervision programs that raise several issues. First, "intensive probation supervision is expected to divert offenders from incarceration in order to alleviate prison overcrowding, avoid the exorbitant costs of building and sustaining prisons, and prevent the stultifying and stigmatizing effects of imprisonment." Second, ISP is expected to promote public safety through surveillance strategies while promoting a sense of responsibility and accountability through probation fees, restitution, and community service activities.[24] These goals generate issues regarding the ability of ISP programs to reduce recidivism, divert offenders from prison, and ensure public safety.

In a study summarizing the state of ISP, Fulton, Latessa, Stichman, and Travis[25] summarize the findings concerning ISP:

- ISPs have failed to alleviate prison crowding.
- Most ISP studies have found no significant differences between recidivism rates of ISP offenders and offenders of comparison groups.
- There appears to be a relationship between greater participation in treatment and employment programs and lower recidivism rates.
- ISPs appear to be more effective than regular supervision or prison in meeting offenders' needs.
- ISPs that reflect certain principles of effective intervention are associated with lower rates of recidivism.
- ISP does provide an intermediate punishment.
- Although ISPs are less expensive than prison, they are more expensive than originally thought.

The debate over control versus treatment has raged for many years. Recently, there has been a new movement, initiated by the American Probation and Parole Association, to develop a more balanced approach to ISP supervision.[26] This approach continues to support strict conditions and supervision practices but within the context of more services and higher-quality treatment.

Drug, Mental Health, and Other Problem-Solving Courts

In recent years, many judges have become disillusioned with the revolving door of jail and prison for offenders who suffer from addictions and mental disorders. As a result, there has been an explosion of so-called therapeutic courts, ranging from mental health to domestic violence. Figure 6.3 shows the number of drug problem-solving courts throughout the United States. **Drug courts** divert drug-abusing offenders to intensively monitored treatment instead of incarceration. The main purpose of drug court programs is to use the authority of the court to reduce crime by changing defendants' drug-using behavior. Under this concept, in exchange for the possibility of dismissed charges or reduced sentences, defendants are diverted to drug court programs in various ways and at various stages of the

key term

Drug court
Problem-solving court that requires drug offenders to participate in court-mandated treatment programs.

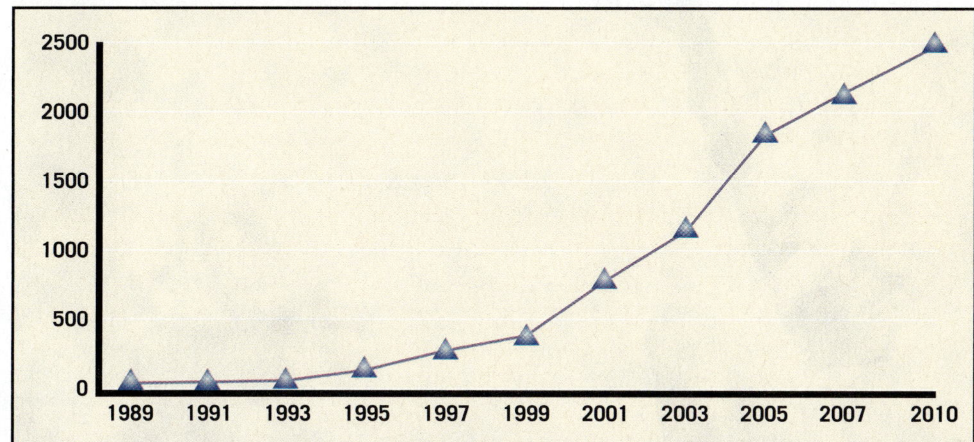

figure 6.3

Operational Drug Court Programs in the United States (Number of Courts).

SOURCE: National Drug Court Institute, http://www.ndci.org/research.

judicial process, depending on the circumstances. Judges preside over drug court proceedings, monitor the progress of defendants through frequent status hearings, and prescribe sanctions and rewards as appropriate in collaboration with prosecutors, defense attorneys, treatment providers, and others. Basic elements of a drug court include the following:[27]

- A single drug court judge and staff who provide both focus and leadership
- Expedited adjudication through early identification and referral of appropriate program participants, initiating treatment as soon as possible after arrest
- Both intensive treatment and aftercare for drug-abusing defendants
- Comprehensive, in-depth, and coordinated supervision of drug defendants in regular (sometimes daily) status hearings that monitor both treatment progress and offender compliance
- Enhanced and increasing defendant accountability under a graduated series of rewards and punishments appropriate to conforming or volative behavior
- Mandatory and frequent drug (and alcohol) testing
- Supervised and individual case monitoring

Drug court programs are highly diverse in approach, characteristics, and completion and retention rates, as discussed later. Some programs report that they deferred prosecuting offenders who would enter the program, others allowed offenders to enter the program after their cases had been adjudicated, and still others allowed offenders to enter their programs on a trial basis after entering a plea. Yet all programs have a treatment component as part of their overall approach, although there is wide variation in the type and extent of treatment provided to offenders. Both adults and juvenile offenders are served by drug courts, as are nonviolent and violent offenders and first-time or repeat offenders. Overall, most courts treat offenders with a substance addiction.

The growth in drug court programs has been nothing short of phenomenal. Starting with one program in Miami in 1989, there were 2,734 programs in operation in the beginning of 2013, with over 70,000 clients processed or in treatment at any given time. Of these,

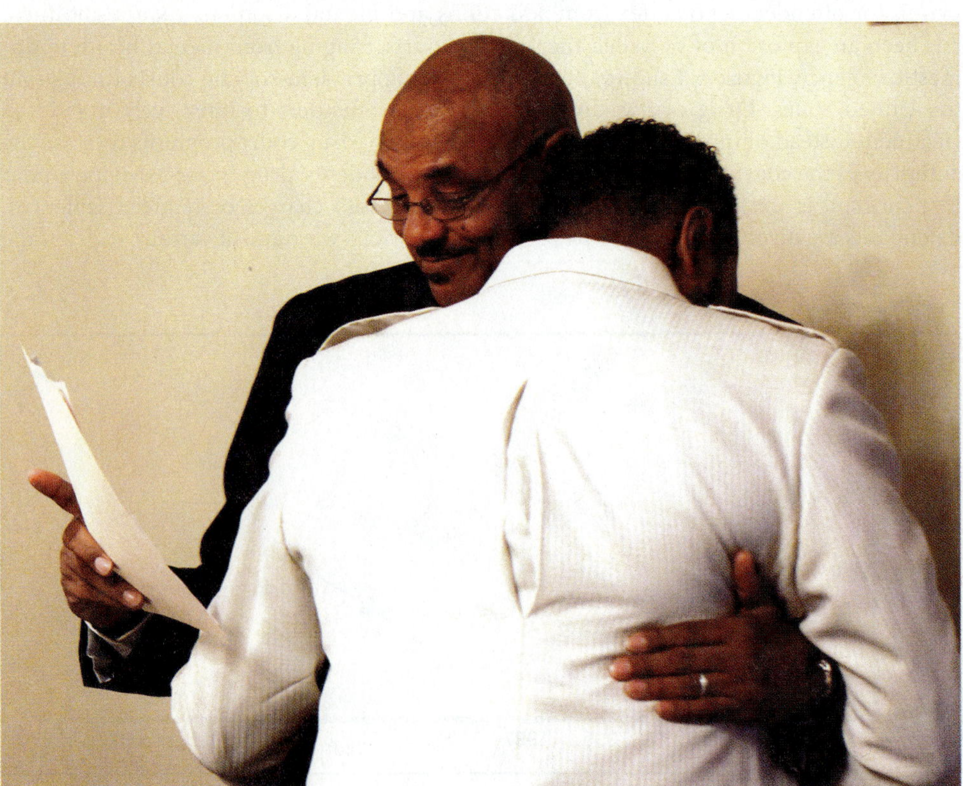

photo 6.2
Drug court judge reading Certificate of Completion to emotionally overcome successful graduate.
Rainier Ehrhardt/Newscom.

about 800 juvenile and family drug courts were operating with more in the planning stage, and more than 9,000 juveniles were in treatment.[28] The threat of immediate sanctions (jail time, return for prosecution, probation revocation, commitment to prison) is a powerful tool to ensure client compliance and retention in the treatment program.

While findings from drug court studies have generally been favorable, most have been limited to local drug court programs. The largest statewide study on drug courts to date was recently conducted in New York. The study found that, on average, the reconviction rate was 29 percent lower for drug court participants than for nonparticipants.[29] In another statewide study of drug courts in Ohio, Latessa, Shaffer, and Lowenkamp examined outcome data from both adult (felony and misdemeanants) and juvenile drug court programs.[30] The results from this study are illustrated in the previous Correctional Brief. The data show some variation in the results across drug courts, but, overall, participants in drug courts reported 15 percent lower rearrest rates than those drug offenders who did not participate in a drug court program (see Figure 6.4). While the research has generally shown adult drug courts to be effective, studies of juvenile drug courts have not been as favorable. In a recent study of 10 juvenile drug courts from across the country, researchers at the University of Cincinnati found that youth in juvenile drug courts did worse than comparison cases. The researchers speculated that, in general, most youth may not be particularly well suited to the treatment and monitoring process of a juvenile drug court.[31] Finally, a national meta-analysis of drug court programs conducted by Shaffer found that across all types of drugs courts, the average reduction in recidivism was 9 percent.[32]

In addition to reducing recidivism, adult drug courts have been found to be cost effective. A study done by the Washington State Institute for Public Policy estimated that the average drug court participant produces $6,779 in benefits.[33] In New York, researchers estimate that $254 million in incarceration costs were saved by diverting 18,000 offenders to drug court. Finally, California researchers concluded that drug courts in that state save $18 million per year.[34]

Compared to jail and prison, drug courts appear to be cost effective and to reduce criminal conduct. The success of drug courts has led to the development of other problem-solving courts, including reentry (designed to assist those released from prison ["returning citizens"]), DUI, mentally ill, gun, veterans, and gambling courts. While similar data are not yet available on mental health courts and other problem-solving court programs, drug courts are galvanizing if not revolutionizing the criminal justice system response to drug abuse.[35]

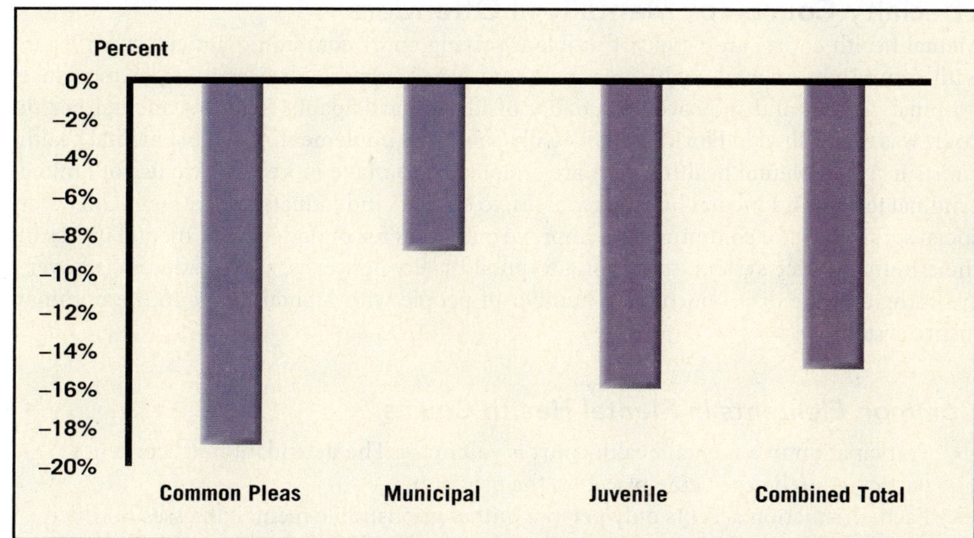

figure 6.4

Reductions in Rearrest Rates between Drug Courts and Comparison Groups across All Drug Court Groups.

SOURCE: Data from: Edward Latessa, D. Shaffer, and C. Lowenkamp, *Outcome Evaluation of Ohio's Drug Court Efforts* (Cincinnati, OH: Center for Criminal Justice Research, University of Cincinnati, 2002), p. 7.

Specialty Courts for DUI Offenders

Offenders driving while intoxicated are increasingly being placed under the jurisdiction of the drug court, commonly described as a "problem-solving court." Such courts are designed to reduce criminal reoffending by chemically dependent adult drivers who are at high risk to recidivate. The targeted group displays a repetitive pattern of driving under the influence of drug or alcohol. Such drivers otherwise cause injuries and deaths on highways and are not deterred by usual DUI sanctions.

While DUI drug courts will accept only first-time DUI offenders, the typical court focuses on multiple violators who are sent directly to the DUI court for arraignment and adjudication The basic intentions are to aid such offenders, protect the public by keeping them from reoffending, improve judicial efficiency, and reserve hard bed space for career and dangerous offenders. Georgia's DUI court is an accountability court authorized to process drug-using offenders through drug testing, intensive supervision, treatment services, and immediate incentives and sanctions. DUI courts are designed to force the offender to deal with his or her substance abuse problems through a blend of treatment and personal accountability as well as specialized case management. The DUI court is a treatment court with a specialized docket managed by a specially trained judge, working with prosecutors, public defenders, probation and law enforcement officers, treatment providers, and other dedicated practitioners to compel the DUI offender to become clean and sober.

Tools frequently used in DUI courts include both early and long-term treatment intervention, frequent random drug testing, judicial supervision, intensive probation coupled later with follow-up probation, assistance with school, education and employment, biweekly court appearances, frequent 12-step Alcoholics Anonymous or Narcotics Anonymous meeting attendance, and home visits by compliance officers. Failure to meet requirements will cause the DUI court judge to issue immediate sanctions, such as community service, jail time, or both. Interlock devices may be installed that prevent drug court offenders from driving a vehicle. Frequent failure may lead to revocation of probation and imposition of a sentence to incarceration.

The effectiveness of DUI courts has not yet been thoroughly investigated, but preliminary results from Georgia reveal that, 12 months postgraduation, DUI court clients are almost three times less likely to have a new DUI arrest and that, 24 months postgraduation, drug court participants are 20 percent less likely to be arrested for a new felony. Hennepin County, Minnesota, found that some 89 percent of program participants stayed crime free. Keeping such offenders "off the bottle" results in one-fourth the cost of sending a person to prison. In most drug courts, participant fees pay for treatment services.[36]

Specialty Courts for Mentally Ill Offenders

Mental health courts are a type of problem-solving court combining judicial supervision with community mental health treatment and other support services in order to reduce criminal activity and improve the quality of life of participants. The first mental health court was established in Florida in 1997 with California implementing its first mental health courts in 1999. Mental health courts are established to make more effective use of limited criminal justice and mental health resources, to connect individuals to treatment and other social services in the community, to improve outcomes for offenders with mental illness in the criminal justice system, to respond to public safety concerns, and to address jail overcrowding and the disproportionate number of people with mental illness in the criminal justice system.

Common Elements in Mental Health Courts

- Participation in a mental health court is voluntary. The defendant must consent to participation before being placed in the program.
- Each jurisdiction accepts only persons with demonstrable mental illnesses to which their involvement in the criminal justice system can be attributed.

- The key objective of a mental health court is either to prevent the jailing of offenders with mental illness by diverting them to appropriate community services or to significantly reduce time spent incarcerated.
- Public safety is a high priority, and offenders with mental illness are carefully screened for appropriate inclusion in the program.
- Early intervention is essential, with screening and referral occurring as soon as possible after arrest.
- A multidisciplinary team approach is used, with the involvement of justice system representatives, mental health providers, and other support systems.
- Intensive case management includes supervision of participants, with a focus on accountability and monitoring of each participant's performance.
- The judge oversees the treatment and supervision process and facilitates collaboration among mental health court team members.[37]

Recent studies have found that mental health courts are having a positive effect on the quality of life for participants and a small to moderate effect on recidivism.[38]

Specialty Courts for Veterans

With the recent wars in Afghanistan and Iraq, there has been increased attention given to veterans. As a result, there are now veteran treatment courts popping up all over the country. The veteran treatment court is a problem-solving court providing military veterans with extensive services and are frequently designed to deliver confinement avoidance alternatives in lieu of prosecution (or conviction for lesser and included offenses). These are collaborative justice courts involving the public prosecutor, judge, public defender, Veteran Administration representatives, and volunteer mentors. The latter are typically veterans and serve to counsel veterans in contact with the criminal justice system. Because veterans are eligible for a wide range of government services, these courts often help the offender access programs and services that they might otherwise not be aware of.

There is a wide variety of such courts. Some are single-docket courts with a judge who devotes full time to managing the docket and individual cases (dedicated criminal calendar). Some will accept only first-time offenders; others restrict eligibility for service to persons charged with misdemeanors or who have outstanding bench warrant problems. There are even some homelessness courts functioning to resolve outstanding misdemeanor warrants by providing housing or subsidies to stabilize housing needs of homeless veterans. Finally, some veterans' courts require the accused to have served in combat; others require only military service. Because of the variety of such courts, it is difficult at this time to offer broad generalizations on the benefits to program participants and their families and benefits for the public.

Three threads can be found in most courts. First, they serve to minimize future involvement with the justice system through provision of services for identified issues. Second, the benefits for program participants include increased mental stability, recovery from addiction, and reintegration into society. Intended benefits for the public include increased public safety, reduction in use of jail and prison beds, and reduction in recidivism. Third, the U.S. Department of Veterans Affairs typically provides personnel, resources, referrals, subsidies, and treatment to eligible veterans.

Since the recent implementation of the first veterans court (2008), few studies of court effectiveness have been conducted. The National Association of Drug Court Professionals report that the best argument for veterans courts is that they seem to work: 70 percent of defendants finish the programs, and 75 percent are not arrested for at least two years after.[39]

Community Service Programs

Community service or work-order programs represent court-ordered unpaid work for a specific number of hours that offenders must perform, usually in the form of free labor to some charitable organization or in public service, such as serving as a volunteer hospital

correctional practice 6.1

Philadelphia Veterans Court

One example of veterans courts can be seen in the Philadelphia Veterans Court, which focuses on problem solving and services for veterans to overcome the challenges they face:

Veterans are directed to representatives of the Veterans Administration, who are on site in one of our courtrooms. The VA staff schedules eligible Veterans for an assessment to determine appropriate needs and levels of care, and directs them to benefits to which they may be entitled. The assessment determines the Veteran's suitability for an array of VA programs, including any required medical treatment (alcohol, drug, mental health, or medical) as well as housing, job training and job referrals. After consultation with a defense attorney, if an eligible veteran chooses to accept the terms of the offer from the Philadelphia District Attorney to participate in this voluntary program, we pair the veteran with a *mentor*. The mentor will assist the Veteran in working toward the successful resolution of the criminal charges, including a change in life choices, so that future contacts with the criminal justice system can be avoided (Veterans Court @ The Philadelphia Court).

SOURCE: "Special Courts for Veterans Expanding across US," http://www.foxnews.com/us/2013/09/02/special-courts-for-veterans-expanding-across-us/ (accessed August 26, 2014); California Department of Veterans Affairs, "Homeless Veterans," http://www.calvet.ca.gov/vetservices/HomelessVeterans.aspx (accessed October 25, 2013).

orderly, doing street cleaning, performing maintenance or repair of public housing, or providing service to indigent groups. Some examples of the latter would be sentencing a dentist to perform 100 hours of free dental service for welfare recipients or a physician to provide 50 hours of free medical attention to jail inmates on Saturdays.

key term

Community work order
Requiring offenders to provide service to the community to help repair the harm they have committed.

Both **community work orders** and restitution programs have their critics.[40] Some argue that offenders committing crimes of violence should not be allowed a penalty less than incarceration for their offenses and that the physical and psychological costs to victims of crimes of violence are almost impossible to calculate. There also seems to be some uncertainty over whether an offender sentenced to perform community work or restitution ought to be resentenced to incarceration for noncompliance. Despite the criticism, there appears to be consensus that offenders should repay their victims for losses, even if the repayment is as symbolic as community work. A study of a community service program designed as an alternative to incarceration for adult misdemeanor offenders found a 66 percent completion rate.[41]

Home Detention

key term

Home detention
Sentence whereby offenders serve at least some of their sentence in their own domicile.

In the United States, house arrest usually conjures up images of political control and fascist repression,[42] but it is actually court-ordered **home detention**, the confining of offenders to their households for the duration of their sentence. Introduced in 1984 in Florida, home detention rapidly spread throughout a nation searching for punitive, safe, and secure alternatives to incarceration.[43] The sentence is usually imposed in conjunction with probation but may be imposed by the court as a separate punishment (as it is in Florida). Florida's Community Control Program (FCCP) was designed to provide a safe diversion alternative and to help address the problem of prison population escalation and associated high costs.[44]

Participants may be required to make victim compensation, perform community work service, pay probation fees, undergo drug and alcohol testing, and, in some instances, wear electronic monitoring equipment to verify their presence in the residence. (In some jurisdictions, house arrest is used on a pretrial basis, as an isolated sentence, in conjunction with probation or parole, or with a prerelease status, such as education or work furlough.) House arrest allows the offender to leave his or her residence only for specific purposes and hours approved by the court or supervising officer. Being absent without leave is a technical violation of conditions that may result in resentencing to jail or prison.[45] Home detention is a punitive sentence and was designed in most cases to relieve institutional overcrowding. For many offenders, it is their last chance to escape from being committed to prison. In addition

photo 6.3

Community work orders can include painting of fences for the elderly.
Jacky Chapman/Janine Wiedel Photolibrary/Alamy.

to surveillance of the offender, home detention is viewed as a cost-avoidance program, a front-end solution to prison overcrowding, and a flexible alternative for certain offenders (such as a pregnant offender until time of delivery). The use of telemonitoring devices, discussed later, can significantly increase the correctional surveillance of offenders.

The most significant critical argument against home detention is that, by making a nonincarcerative control mechanism available to corrections, many petty offenders who would best be handled by diversion, fines, or mental health services are brought under correctional control. In general, such inclusive actions are viewed as "net widening," which occurs when offenders who might otherwise have received a lesser or even no sentence are sentenced to community control.[46]

The National Council on Crime and Delinquency conducted an evaluation of the FCCP and concluded that the impact on prison crowding, offender behavior, and state correctional costs has been positive. With an estimated prison diversion rate of 54 percent, community control is cost effective despite the combined effect of net widening and the punishments imposed on almost 10 percent of FCCP participants for technical violations. Furthermore, the new offense rate for community control offenders is lower than that for similar offenders sentenced to prison and released without supervision. For every 100 cases diverted from prison, Florida saved more than $250,000.[47] Home detention is expected to receive increased endorsement in the coming years and may become the sentence of choice for many nonviolent offenders in lieu of jail, prison, or even formal probation.[48]

Electronic Monitoring

Home detention has a long history as a criminal penalty, but its new popularity with correctional authorities is due to the advent of electronic monitoring, a technological link that is thought to make the sanction both practical and affordable. The concept of electronic monitoring is not new and was proposed in 1964 by Schwitzgebel as **electronic parole**. It was initially used to monitor the location of mental patients.[49] One of the first studies of home detention enforced by electronic monitoring began in 1986, and by 2013, it was estimated that there were more than 1,500 electronic programs and nearly 200,000 monitoring units in use.[50]

key term

Electronic parole
Community supervision technique that uses electronic devices to maintain surveillance on parolees. Can also include Global Positioning System (GPS) surveillance.

correctional practice 6.2

Sex Offenders Tracked by the Global Positioning System (GPS)

Although it sounds like something out of a science fiction movie, the reality of GPS tracking is much more down to earth. Recently, a number of states have enacted legislation to require convicted sex offenders to wear an electronic tracking device for the rest of their lives that monitors their whereabouts.

As of 2012, 23 states had laws requiring or allowing GPS tracking. For example, Wisconsin has proposed increasing funding by $10 million for expanded use of GPS tracking from 639 currently to 783 offenders in fiscal year 2014 and to 939 offenders in fiscal year 2015. Michigan has begun tracking over 1,000 sex offenders. In 2009, California allocated funds to follow 2,500 offenders and by 2013 had placed all 290 registered sex offenders on parole onto GPS monitoring for the duration of their parole.

The increase in GPS is attributed to dramatic advancements in the technology. Not only have the devices become smaller and less expensive, but accuracy has increased, allowing systems to pinpoint a person's location to within 30 feet.

Despite these advancements, GPS tracking is not without its critics. "It is not an effective way to prevent sexual assaults," says Richard Wright, professor of criminal justice at Bridgewater State College. He believes that many serious sex offenders evade police by failing to register and that others may reoffend regardless of tracking systems. Others believe that GPS tracking is best used as an augmentation of good supervision, not a replacement for it. There are also numerous complaints about false alarms.

Critics of use of the GPS system have also denounced those GPS monitoring units that are equipped with a telephone feature that, without warning, allows overhearing and tape-recording of conversations of defendants without a court warrant. These are capable of covertly tape-recording any meeting of the defendant with his or her defense counsel. As such, this maneuver would be a violation of the Fourth Amendment and of the constitutions of those states forbidding this intrusion. Despite these concerns, it appears that GPS tracking is here to stay. In a 2013 study sponsored by the National Institute of Justice, researchers found that high-risk sex offenders placed on parole with GPS tracking had lower recidivism rates than those who received traditional supervision. While GPS was about $8.50 a day more expensive than traditional parole supervision, it led to a 12 percent decrease in the number of arrests.[51]

SOURCE: Adapted from: Wendy Koch, "More Sex Offenders Tracked by Satellite," *USA Today*, June 6, 2006; "Sex Offenders Monitored by GPS Found to Commit Fewer Crimes," *NIJ Journal* 271 (February 2013), http://nij.gov/nij/journals/271/gps-monitoring.htm; and Waldo Covas Quevedo (2013), "Caution: Your GPS Bracelet Is Listening," http://www.thecrimereport.org/news/inside-criminal-justice/2013-10-caution-your-gps-ankle-bracelet-is-listening.

Most electronic monitoring systems use a transmitter attached to the offender's wrist or ankle that sends signals to the supervising office during the hours the offender is required to be at home. The goals and objectives of electronic monitoring include the following:

- Provide a cost-effective community supervision tool for offenders selected according to specific program criteria.
- Administer sanctions appropriate to the seriousness of the offense.
- Promote public safety by providing surveillance and risk control strategies indicated by the risk and needs of the offenders.
- Increase the confidence of legislative, judicial, and releasing authorities that electronic monitoring is a viable sentencing option.[52]

National surveys indicate that electronic monitoring was initially used for property offenders on probation, but a much broader range of offenders is being monitored now than in the past. Monitoring has been expanded to include probationers but also to follow up on persons after incarceration, to control those sentenced to community corrections, and to monitor persons before trial or sentencing. Studies of telemonitoring of offenders noted certain findings:

- Most jurisdictions using electronic monitoring tested some offenders for drug use, and many routinely tested all. Some sites charged for the testing; more than 66 percent charged offenders for at least part of the cost of leasing the monitoring equipment.

- The average monitoring term is about 80 days. The longer the period of monitoring, the higher the odds of success. The chances of termination do not vary by type of offense, except that those committing major traffic violations committed fewer technical violations and new offenses.
- There were no significant differences in successful terminations among probationers, offenders on parole, or those in community corrections. All had successful termination rates ranging between 74 and 86 percent.
- Rule violations often result in reincarceration, brief confinement at a residential facility, intensified office reporting requirements, stricter curfews, or additional community service.[53]
- The experience of other countries using electronic monitoring indicates an uneven value as a reintegration program.[54]

The latest trend in electronic monitoring is the Global Positioning System (GPS), which is increasingly being used with high-risk sex offenders. A number of states have passed legislation that requires selected offenders to wear a device that tracks their whereabouts 24/7 (see Correctional Practice 6.2).

A recent evaluation in Florida of offenders placed on electronic monitoring or GPS found significantly reduced likelihood of technical violations, reoffending, and absconding.[55] Other studies in Los Angeles; Lake County, Illinois; Oklahoma; Florida; Texas; England; and Wales[56] have shown mixed results. While the technology no doubt will be improved and expanded in the coming decades, many unanswered questions remain about the effectiveness of electronic monitoring.

Community Residential Treatment Centers (Halfway Houses)

Formerly known as halfway houses, **community residential treatment centers** are a valuable adjunct to community control and treatment services. Originally designed as residences for homeless men, they are now seen as the possible nuclei of community-based correctional networks of residential centers, drug-free and alcohol-free living spaces, prerelease guidance centers, and private-sector involvement with multiple-problem offenders in need of intensive services. They also serve as noninstitutional residence facilities for a number of different classes of offenders, most of whom are high-need offenders and pose a medium to high risk to community corrections.

key term

Community residential treatment center
Also known as a halfway house, a residential facility that provides room and board as well as rehabilitation programming.

University of Cincinnati investigators headed by Edward Latessa have conducted much of the contemporary evaluative work in the area of community residential centers. A synopsis of a program evaluation will suffice to suggest how community residential centers fit into intermediate sanctions. In evaluating a treatment program for adult offenders sentenced to probation, Latessa and Travis found that, in comparison with other similarly situated offenders, members of their study group had less formal education and were far less likely to have married. They exhibited more prior involvement in alcohol and drug treatment and suffered from more psychiatric problems. Hence, the study group was higher need, higher risk, and more likely to recidivate. The center's clients received more services and treatment in almost every area examined. Even though prior criminal histories would have predicted higher failure rates, the center's clients did as well as the comparison group in terms of reoffending. Employment services and enrolling in an educational program reduced recidivism.[57]

In 2002, one of the largest studies of residential correctional programs ever conducted was completed. University of Cincinnati researchers examined nearly 14,000 offenders served by over 45 residential programs in Ohio. Overall figures indicated that the residential programs resulted in slightly reduced recidivism rates. However, when the risk level of the offenders was factored in, the results showed that most of the programs had a significant

correctional **practice 6.3**

Effectiveness of Community Corrections

"What works" is not a program or an intervention but a body of knowledge based on more than 30 years of research that has been conducted by numerous scholars in North America and Europe. Also referred to as evidence-based practice, the "what works" movement demonstrates empirically that theoretically sound, well-designed programs that meet certain conditions can appreciably reduce recidivism rates for offenders. Through the review and analysis of hundreds of studies, researchers have identified a set of principles that should guide correctional programs. The first is the risk principle, or the "who" to target—those offenders who pose the higher risk of continued criminal conduct. This principle states that our most intensive correctional treatment and intervention programs should be reserved for higher-risk offenders. *Risk* in this context refers to those offenders with a higher probability of recidivating. Why waste our programs on offenders who do not need them? This is a waste of resources, and, more importantly, research has clearly demonstrated that when we place lower-risk offenders in our more structured programs, we often increase their failure rates (and thus reduce the overall effectiveness of the program). This occurs for several reasons.

First, placing low-risk offenders in with higher-risk offenders only serves to increase the chances of failure for the low-risk offender. For example, let's say that your teenage son or daughter did not use drugs but got into some trouble with the law. Would you want them in a program or group with heavy drug users? Of course you wouldn't since it is more likely that the higher-risk youth would influence your child more than the other way around.

Second, placing low-risk offenders in these programs also tends to disrupt their prosocial networks; in other words, the very attributes that make them low risk become interrupted, such as school, employment, family, and so forth. Remember, if they do not have these attributes, it is unlikely they are low risk to begin with. The risk principle can best be seen from a recent study of offenders in Ohio who were placed in a halfway house or community-based correctional facility (CBCF). The study found that the recidivism rate for higher-risk offenders who were placed in a halfway house or CBCF was reduced, while the recidivism rates for the low-risk offenders who were placed in the programs actually increased.

The second principle is referred to as the need principle, or the "what" to target—criminogenic factors that are highly correlated with criminal conduct. The need principle states that programs should target crime-producing needs, such as antisocial attitudes, values, and beliefs; antisocial peer associations; substance abuse; lack of problem-solving and self-control skills; and other factors that are highly correlated with criminal conduct. Furthermore, programs need to ensure that the vast majority of their interventions are focused on these factors. Noncriminogenic factors such as self-esteem, physical conditioning, understanding one's culture or history, and creative abilities will not have much effect on recidivism rates. An example of a program that tends to target noncriminogenic factors can be seen in offender-based military-style boot camps. These programs tend to focus on noncriminogenic factors, such as drill and ceremony, physical conditioning, discipline, self-esteem, and bonding offenders together. Because they tend to focus on non-crime-producing needs, most studies show that boot camps have little impact on future criminal behavior.

The third principle is the treatment principle, or the "how"—the ways in which correctional programs should target risk and need factors. This principle states that the most effective programs are behavioral in nature. Behavioral programs have several attributes. First, they are centered on the *present* circumstances and risk factors that are responsible for the offender's behavior. Second, they are *action* oriented rather than talk oriented. In other words, offenders do something about their difficulties rather than just talk about them. Third, they teach offenders new, prosocial skills to replace the antisocial ones (e.g., stealing, cheating, lying) through modeling, practice, and reinforcement. Examples of behavioral programs would include structured social learning programs where new skills are taught and behaviors and attitudes are consistently reinforced; cognitive behavioral programs that target attitudes, values, peers, substance abuse, anger, and so on; and family-based interventions that train family on appropriate behavioral techniques. Interventions based on these approaches are very structured and emphasize the importance of modeling and behavioral rehearsal techniques that engender self-efficacy, challenge cognitive distortions, and assist offenders in developing good problem-solving and self-control skills. These strategies have been demonstrated to be effective in reducing recidivism. Nonbehavioral interventions that are often used in programs would include drug and alcohol education, fear tactics and other emotional appeals, talk therapy, nondirective client-centered approaches, having them read books, lectures, milieu therapy, and self-help. There is little empirical evidence that these approaches will lead to long-term reductions in recidivism.

Finally, a host of other considerations will increase correctional program effectiveness. These include targeting responsivity factors, such as a lack of motivation or other barriers that can influence someone's participation in a program, making sure that you have well-trained and interpersonally sensitive staff, providing close monitoring of offenders' whereabouts and associates, assisting with other needs that offenders might have, ensuring the program is delivered as designed through quality assurance processes, and providing structured aftercare. These program attributes all enhance correctional program effectiveness.

If we put it all together, we have the "who, what, and how" of correctional intervention, also known as "what works."

SOURCE: Edward J. Latessa, "From Theory to Practice: What Works in Reducing Recidivism?," in *State of Crime and Justice in Ohio* (Columbus: Ohio Office of Criminal Justice Services, 2004). See also M. Miller, M. Drake, and M. Natziger, "What Works to Reduce Recidivism by Domestic Violence Offenders?" (Olympia: Washington State Institute for Public Policy, 2013).

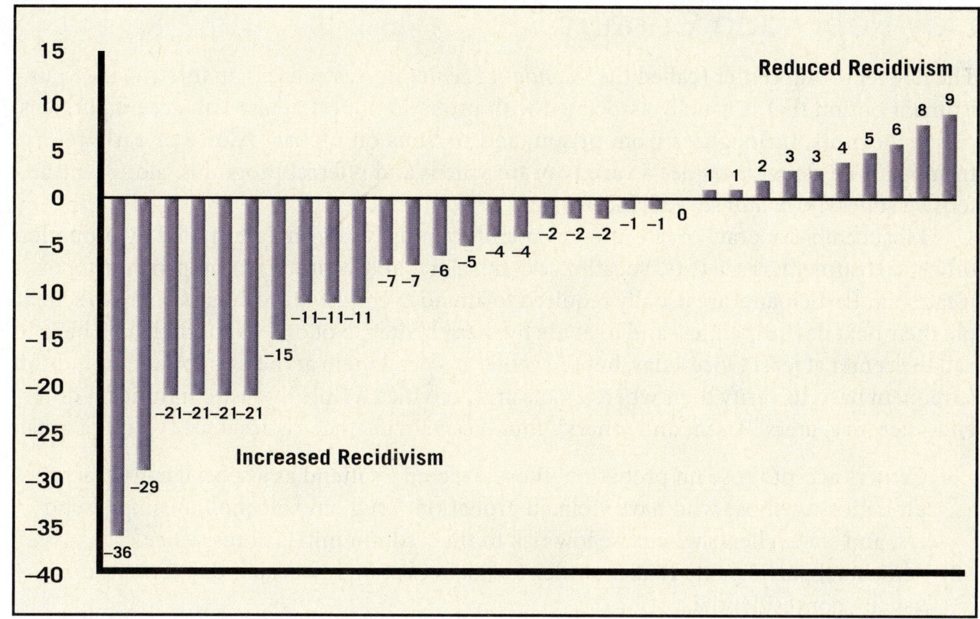

figure 6.5

Treatment Effects for Low-Risk Offenders.

- Numbers represent difference in predicted recidivism rates between the comparison and treatment groups.
- Negative numbers indicate a difference favoring the comparison group.
- Each column represents a different program in the study.

SOURCE: Data from: C. Lowenkamp and E. Latessa, *Evaluation of Ohio's Halfway House and Community Based Correctional Facilities* (Cincinnati, OH: University of Cincinnati, 2002).

impact with high-risk offenders but actually increased the failure rates for lower-risk offenders.[58] This finding was not unexpected since other studies have also shown detrimental effects with low-risk offenders.[59] Figures 6.5 and 6.6 show the results from this study. In 2010, this study was replicated by University of Cincinnati researchers and involved nearly 20,000 offenders and 64 residential programs. Findings were similar to those found in the first study. Overall, recidivism was reduced by 14 percent for high-risk offenders and 6 percent for moderate-risk offenders, and increased by 3 percent for low-risk offenders.[60]

Clearly, for high-risk offenders, residential centers that provide specific client-needed services can be valuable assets in offender control and outcome,[61] particularly for community control clients whose technical violations are a result of high needs otherwise unaddressed within the community.

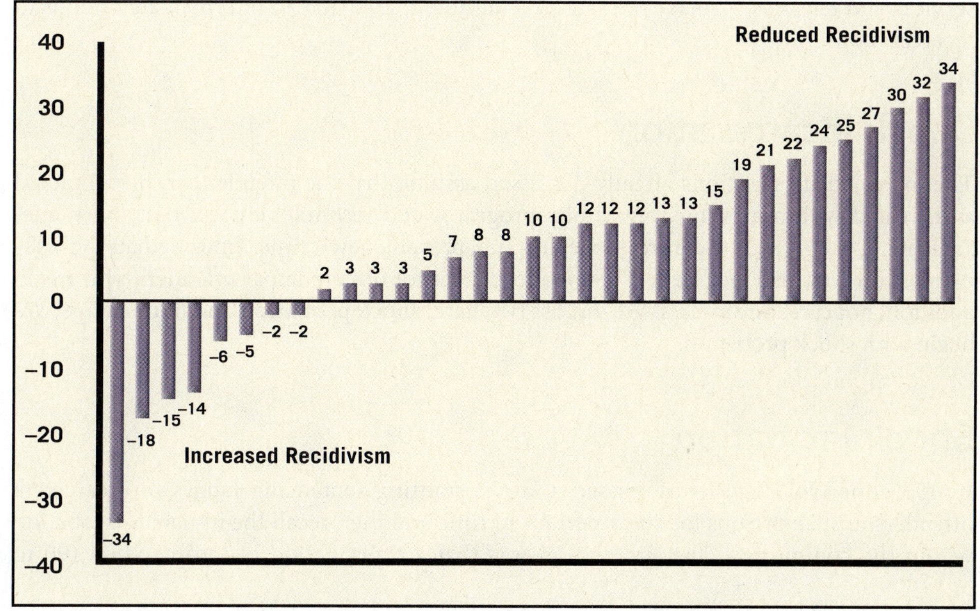

figure 6.6

Treatment Effects for High-Risk Offenders

- Numbers represent difference in predicted recidivism rates between the comparison and treatment groups.
- Negative numbers indicate a difference favoring the comparison group.
- Each column represents a different program in the study.

SOURCE: Data from: C. Lowenkamp and E. Latessa, *Evaluation of Ohio's Halfway House and Community-Based Correctional Facilities* (Cincinnati, OH: University of Cincinnati, 2002).

Day Reporting Centers

The day reporting center (called the *attendance center* in Australia) is an intermediate punishment option that is usually associated with probation but that also can accept parolees, parole violators, furloughees from prison, and persons on pretrial release or early release from jail. The center provides a variety of treatment and referral programs, along with extensive supervision and surveillance.

Most centers operate in late afternoon and evening hours and are staffed by probation officers, treatment specialists, vocational counselors, and volunteers; the primary focus is treatment. Participants are usually required to attend every day the center is open, to schedule their next day's activities, and to abide by the schedule. Not only do participants have to call the center at least twice a day, but the center may call them at their appointed rounds on a frequent basis to verify their whereabouts and activities. While there are significant differences across centers, Parent and others[62] found certain characteristics to be typical of most:

1. Centers accept those on probation, those ordered to attend as a special condition of probation, or those who have violated probation; drug- and alcohol-abusing offenders; and some clients who pose low risk to their communities of residence.
2. Almost all participants return to their residences at night because day centers are usually nonresidential.
3. The primary focus is on treatment and reduction of institution crowding.
4. Most are open five days a week and frequently 50 or more hours within the week.
5. Centers maintain a strict regimen of surveillance and demand more contact with clients than would be available even through intensive, supervised probation.
6. Centers direct clients through several phases of control, tapering off in the latter phase by providing about 70 hours per week of surveillance.
7. Centers test clients for drug use at least once a week during the initial and most intensive phases.
8. Centers offer several services on-site that can address clients' unemployment, counseling, education, and life-skill needs while also referring offenders to off-site drug-abuse treatment, attendance at which is required.
9. Centers demand that clients fulfill community service orders.
10. Centers collect program fees from each client.

This nonresidential alternative is designed to ensure a high level of community safety and offender participation. Offenders are forced to accept responsibility for their own behavior and change. Service provision audits indicate that centers are providing the required services and referrals.[63] Such centers have a definite role to play in intermediate options to incarceration.

Shock Incarceration

The intermediate sanctions already discussed assume that the offender can be contained and treated within existing community programs and technologies and that tourniquet sentencing will serve to control behavior and prevent new crime. Intermediate punishments, however, also include two major alternatives for nonpredatory offenders who are, in addition, not career criminals. We discuss two here: **shock probation** and **boot camps**. We begin with shock probation.

key term

Shock probation
Designed to give offenders a short "taste of the bars," followed by a period of supervised probation.

key term

Boot camp
Modeled after military boot camps, offenders are required to engage in strict discipline and a physical regimen.

Shock Probation

In 1965, the Ohio legislature passed a law permitting sentencing judges to incarcerate offenders in state prisons for short periods of time and then recall the inmate to probation within the community. The assumption was that a short period of incarceration (90 to

correctional practice 6.4

Community Correctional Programs

In a study of nonresidential community correctional programs in Ohio involving over 13,000 offenders, Lowenkamp and Latessa found four factors significantly related to outcome. Programs with the following characteristics were more effective:

- Those programs having a greater proportion of higher-risk offenders (at least 75 percent) were more effective.
- The level of supervision for higher-risk offenders averaged longer periods of supervision than the level for low-risk offenders.
- Higher-risk offenders spent at least 50 percent more time in treatment than lower-risk offenders.
- Higher-risk offenders received at least three referrals for every referral received by low-risk offenders.

The following chart shows the difference in impact between programs that met these conditions and those that did not.

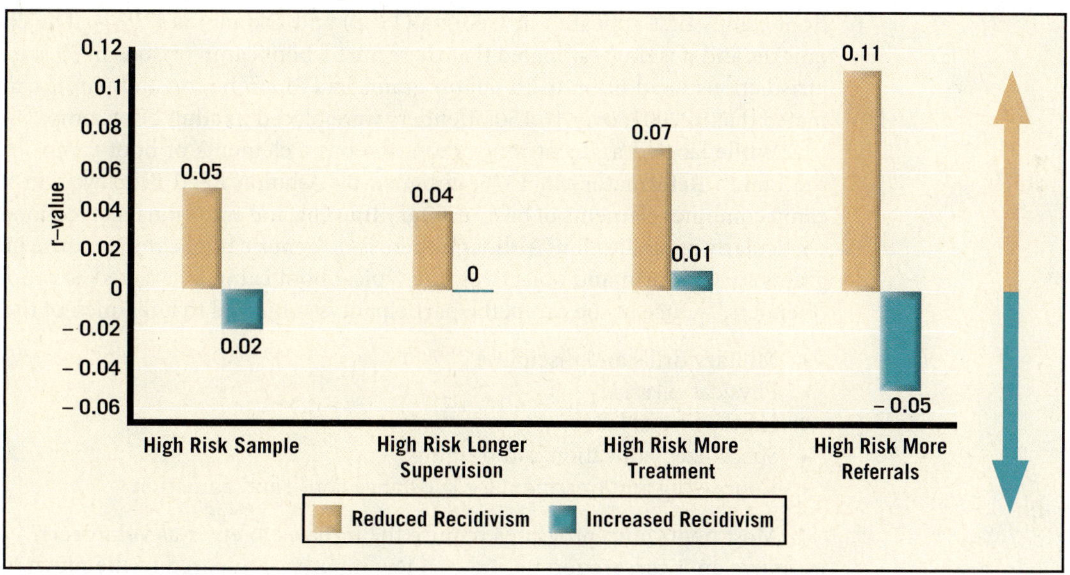

Changes in Recidivism by Program Factors for Community Correctional Programs.
SOURCE: Christopher T. Lowenkamp, Jennifer Pealer, Paula Smith, and Edward Latessa, "Adhering to the Risk and Need Principles: Does It Matter for Supervision-Based Programs?," *Federal Probation* 70:3 (2006): 3–8.

130 days), followed by a period of probation, would "shock" the offender into abandoning criminal activity and into pursuit of law-abiding behavior. Clearly, this program was based on a specific deterrence model and was designed for a segment of the offender population for whom probation was insufficient punishment but long-term imprisonment was not necessary. The method would not be used for first-time offenders but rather for persons not yet committed to giving up predatory behavior.

This option, rapidly adopted by at least 14 states,[64] puts decision making squarely in the hands of the judiciary. The sentencing judge is allowed to reconsider the original sentence to prison and, on motion, to recall the inmate and place him or her on probation, under conditions deemed appropriate.

Evaluations of the effectiveness of shock probation in preventing recidivism and cost avoidance have focused on Ohio, Texas, and Kentucky. Vito has conducted the most sophisticated evaluations and concluded the following:[65]

1. The shock experience should not be limited to first-time offenders; eligibility should properly include those with prior records, as deemed eligible by the judge.

2. The length of incarceration necessary to secure the deterrent effect could be much shorter, probably 30 days or less.
3. Reincarceration rates have never exceeded 26 percent and, in Ohio, have been as low as 10 percent. The level of these rates clearly indicates that the program has potential for reintegration.
4. Shock probation has considerable potential to reduce the institutional overcrowding characteristic of contemporary corrections.[66]

Shock probation can be seen as an alternative disposition for sentencing judges who wish to control probationer behavior through deterrence and tourniquet sentencing. It is one of the last-ditch programs of prison avoidance available to judges faced with the difficult decision of how best to protect the public while maximizing offender reintegration.

Boot Camp Programs

Boot camps first appeared in Georgia (1983) and Oklahoma (1984). The concept spread quickly, and it is now estimated that there are 52 boot camp prisons in 39 state correctional jurisdictions in addition to 15 jail programs and 32 probation and parole camps. It is estimated that in 2001, over 16,150 offenders were placed in adult boot camps.[67]

While labeled a recent innovation, the basic elements of boot camp were present in the Elmira Reformatory in 1876, designed by Zebulon Reed Brockway. In its form, boot camp combines elements of basic military training and traditional correctional philosophy, particularly rehabilitation. Although there is no generic boot camp because individual programs vary in form and objectives, the typical boot camp is targeted at young, nonviolent offenders.[68] Once in the camp, the participant is subjected to a regimen of the following:

- Military drills and discipline
- Physical exercise
- Hard physical labor
- Specialized education and training
- Counseling and treatment for substance abuse and addiction

Most boot camp programs require the inmates to enter as volunteers,[69] offering as an incentive an incarceration period of a few months, compared to the much longer periods they would have spent in prison or on probation. Generally, a state boot camp graduate is released to parole, intensive supervision, home confinement, or some type of community corrections. The philosophy behind the prison boot camps is simple. Offenders who can be turned around before they commit a major crime should be able to improve their

correctional **practice 6.5**

Probationers in Programs

At some time since entering probation supervision, more than 60 percent of all 4.2 million probationers had participated in some type of special supervision or other program. The most common was alcohol or drug treatment/counseling: 33 percent of felons and 42 percent of misdemeanants had received such treatment while under their current sentence of probation.

Nearly one-third had been tested for drugs at least once since entering probation. Some 1 percent of felony probationers had participated in intensive probation supervision, and another 10 percent received psychiatric or psychological counseling.

Participation in Other Programs

Day reporting program	5.3% (132,500 probationers)
Residential program	4.9%
Electronic monitoring	3.5%
Sex offender program	2.7%

SOURCE: Thomas Bonczar, *Characteristics of Adults on Probation, 1995* (Washington, DC: U.S. Department of Justice, 1997), p. 9.

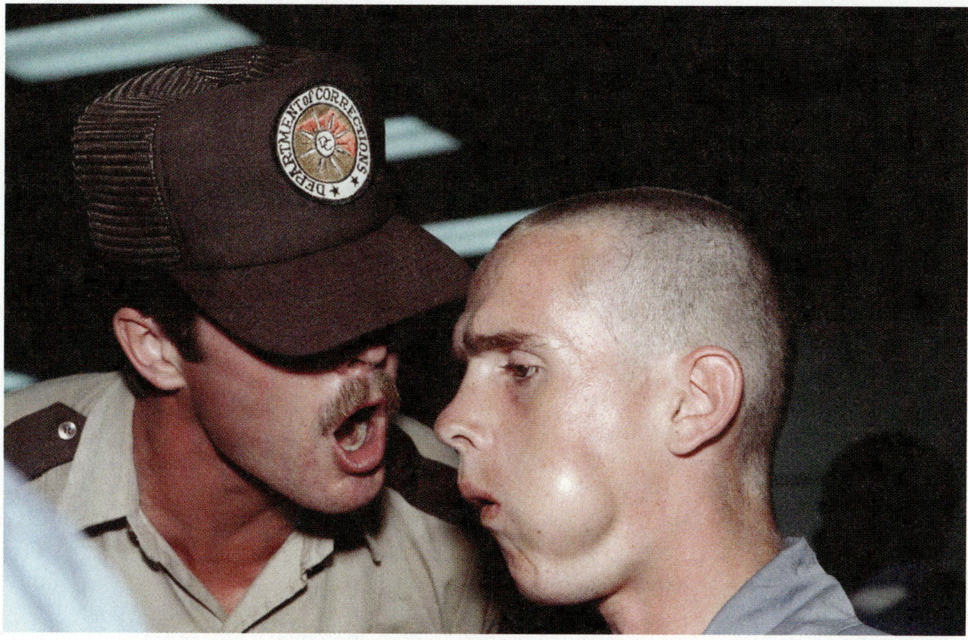

photo 6.4

Correctional officer admonishing boot camp prisoners over rule violations.
© Bettmann/Corbis.

opportunities for living a successful life free of incarceration. Traditional prisons generally have not been viewed as successful in rehabilitating offenders. According to boot camp advocates, the populations at greatest risk of entering prison are the poorly educated, young adult offenders. They come from a low-income background, have not had proper role models or discipline, have few or no work skills, and are subjected to an environment where drug use, violence, and trafficking are common. Because many misdirected young persons have become productive citizens after exposure to military training, the boot camp endeavors to provide this same discipline and direction to persons who still have a chance of being diverted from a life of crime and incarceration (see Figure 6.7).

Although boot camps were popular with judges, the public, and politicians, results from studies of the effectiveness of boot camp programs in reducing recidivism have not been positive. An outcome study conducted in Texas[70] compared the rearrest rates of four different types of community facilities for adult offenders: boot camps, treatment centers, intermediate sanction facilities (used for probation violators), and substance abuse treatment facilities. The boot camp reported rearrest rates nearly double those of the other programs. Note also that when risk and need scores from a standardized assessment tool were compared for offenders in all four programs, the only difference was in the need scores, with the boot camp residents reporting fewer higher-need offenders than the other options. Finally, a study conducted by researchers in Washington State found that, on average,

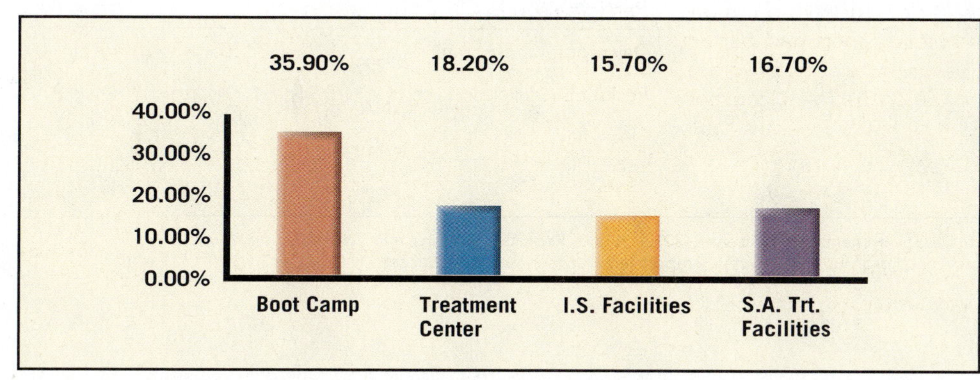

figure 6.7

Rearrest Rates for Residents Discharged from Community Correctional Facilities in Texas: Two-Year Follow-Up (in percent).

SOURCE: Texas Department of Criminal Justice, *Community Corrections Facilities Outcome Study,* January 1999.

correctional practice 6.6

States Report Reductions in Recidivism

Many jurisdictions, both state and local governments, have intensified ongoing efforts to reduce recidivism. Policymakers face tremendous pressure to cut spending (on almost every level) wherever such cuts might be possible. There has developed a consensus that enhanced efforts to reduce recidivism (reoffense) rates among offenders exiting jail and prison confinement would enhance public safety and also save money. This argument is buttressed by an extensive, compelling and increasing body of research that documents the impact that programs, policies, and practices have in reducing the likelihood that offenders released from confinement (both jails and prisons) will recidivate.

A significant 2010 report identified and defined four basic principles that research demonstrates are crucial to every effort to reduce recidivism among such targeted groups:

1. Expend resources on individuals who are most likely to reoffend (not those with the least likelihood).
2. Support and enhance research-driven and evidence-based programs.
3. Invest in effective community supervision practices and policies.
4. Invest in place-based approaches.

See Marshall Clement et al., "The National Summit on Justice Reinvestment and Public Safety on Justice Reinvestment and Public Safety: Addressing Recidivism, Crime and Corrections Spending," http://www.nationalreentryresourcecenter.org/publications/states-report-reductions-in-recidivism (accessed October 2, 2012).

Many jurisdictions have amassed data that demonstrate declines in statewide reoffending rates for adults after imprisonment. In Table 6.1, we highlight the more successful states and strategies identified by that state that contributed significantly to a decline in recidivism rates.

These data in Table 6.1 confirm the reduction in recidivism rates for Michigan (−28 percent, 2000–2007), Kansas (−15 percent, 2005–2008), Ohio (−21 percent, 2000–2008), Texas (−22 percent, 2000–2008), Mississippi (−9 percent, 2005–2008), Oregon (−8 percent, 2000–2007), and Vermont (−22 percent, 2000–2007). In brief, these states have reduced recidivism and the number of individuals returned to prison.

The strategies used by these states differ, as would be expected across differences in political structures found in these states. In sum, however, they represent creation of new approaches, coordinated planning, investing in programs and practices, and intensive training and supervision.

For example, in Kansas, the legislature developed a comprehensive strategy for reducing recidivism and implemented pilot programs targeting parolees at high risk of offending. Community supervision officials provided intensive training to parole officers and strengthened strategies connecting individuals in need of services and treatment to community-based providers and resources. State officials provided funding for reentry initiatives at county levels, specifically linking released individuals to development sources in the area of housing and the

table **6.1** Reductions in Statewide Recidivism Rates (for 2005 and 2007 Releases)

State	Decline in Recidivism Rate (2005 and 2007 Releases)	Decline in Recidivism Rate (2000/3 and 2007 Releases)
Michigan	−18%	−28%
Kansas	−15%	NA
Ohio	−11%	−21%
Texas	−11%	−22%
Mississippi	−9%	NA
Oregon	−8%	−11%
Vermont	−6%	−22%

SOURCE: Council of State Governments Justice Center (2012), "States Report Reductions in Recidivism," http://www.nationalreentryresourcecenter.org/publications/states-report-reductions-in-recidivism (accessed October 2, 2012). Table constructed by authors.

workforce. Finally, legislation created a 60-day earned-time credit for successful completion of educational, treatment, and vocational programs.

Mississippi increased the use of supervision options for people at low risk, thereby conserving crucial resources for high-risk and violent offenders. Ohio implemented evidence-based practices and developed training programs for probation and parole officers in areas such as conducting effective assessments and implementing effective interventions. Ohio also invested resources to improve felony probation supervision and provide incentive funding for community corrections agencies that demonstrably reduce recidivism. And Oregon developed in-prison treatment programs targeted primarily to medium- and high-risk individuals likely to recidivate and developed individualized reentry plans that are based on crime-causing factors.

This list does not exhaust all the strategies, programs, funding, resource allocation, training, community coordination, and intramural programs designed to lessen the rate of recidivism for adults on probation or released from confinement. It does, however, reflect the most recent developments in corrections that increase the effectiveness in preventing crime across states.

SOURCE: Council of State Governments Justice Center (2012), "States Report Reductions in Recidivism," http://www.nationalreentryresourcecenter.org/publications/states-report-reductions-in-recidivism (accessed October 2, 2012). Written entirely by authors.

juvenile boot camps increased recidivism rates about 11 percent.[71] Findings from boot camp evaluations make the following conclusions:

- Low- or moderate-risk juvenile and adult offenders who are subjected to a high level of supervision (boot camps) actually do worse than those left on traditional probation.[72]
- High percentages of minority youth are served by boot camps. The conclusion is that the boot camp model fails to connect with this population.
- Some evidence shows that the rate of recidivism declined in boot camp programs for adults where offenders spent three hours or more per day in therapeutic activity and had some type of aftercare.[73] In general, studies have found similar recidivism rates for those who completed boot camps and comparable offenders who spent long periods of time in prison. There are several reasons why boot camps are not producing the desired reductions in recidivism.[74]

Boot camps tend to do the following:

- Bond delinquent and criminal groups together.
- Target non-crime-producing needs, such as physical conditioning, drill and ceremony, and self-esteem.
- Mix low-, medium-, and high-risk offenders together.
- Model aggressive behavior.

Despite these findings, the boot camp concept still appeals to diverse elements of the justice system. Offenders generally will be returned to the community in a much shorter period without the stigma of having been in prison. For the judge, it is a sentencing option that provides sanctions more restrictive than probation but less restrictive than a conventional prison. For the correctional system, it allows the placement of individuals outside the traditional prison environment and reduces costs and crowding by moving the persons through the system in less time.

As a result of the research, some boot camp programs have abandoned the military-style training and incorporated education, substance abuse treatment, aftercare, job corps, and industrial components. Only future research will tell if these efforts have been successful.

Summary

Explain How Diversion is Used to Keep Offenders out of the Corrections System

Persons suspected or convicted of committing crime face the possibility of incarceration or imprisonment in a jail or prison. Some are dangerous and committed to a career as a criminal, and incarceration probably is the necessary control strategy for protecting society from the deprivations of such offenders. Others, on the other hand, are youthful, first-time or nondangerous offenders; committing those to incarcerative settings may well not serve the correctional goals of public safety. Unnecessary incarceration is expensive, detrimental to social ties that bind others to successful change, dangerous, and destructive to high- need but low-risk offenders. Due to these issues, a variety of diversion and intermediate sanctions have been developed for managing such offenders. They fall between probation and incarceration as mechanisms for social control and safety.

Summarize the Goals of Intermediate Sanctions

The goals of intermediate sanctions are providing effective social control, enhancing public safety, minimizing the costs of correctional programming, and lessening the negative impacts of incarceration.

Intermediate sanctions fall between probation and imprisonment and are designed to provide care, custody and sanction in the goals of successful integration, lowered recidivism, increased public safety, and lowered expenses. This is akin to sentencing smarter. Parenthetically, intermediate sanctions include deferred probation, intensive supervised probation, probation without adjudication, drug treatment programs, home confinement, boot camp, home confinement, therapeutic communities, day reporting centers, community service programs, shock probation, and restitution. At the top of the potential intermediate sanctions are shock probation, shock parole, and split sentencing.

Identifying offender needs and management strategies are, on a daily basis, the duty of officers undertaking presentence investigations and offering suggestions to the sentencing court on which intervention and sentencing length might be effective. The tools for determining offender needs and risk level continue to improve, and sentencing smarter while imposing evidence-based programs is continuing to emerge. Intermediate sanctions are increasingly used as treatment and management strategies and services, yet the search for evidence-based programming is not yet complete. Correctional effectiveness will increase when offender needs and risks are matched with the best practices suggested through evidence-based treatments.

Explain Restitution Programs

Restitution seeks to offset the victim's loss and forces the offender to accept personal responsibility for the crime. It can lead to reconciliation of offender and victim and "personalize" the justice system for the victim. Not all losses might be covered in restitution, but there is usually better understanding of them by both the victim and the perpetrator.

Explain the Goals and Operations of Boot Camps as Well as Issues Associated with Them

Boot camp programs seek to lower crime recidivism by instilling a sense of worth, accomplishments, physical training, and obedience to command and culture. They are widely popular with judges, lawmakers, police and victims who believe that the offenders would benefit from the military training they experienced or know.

Among their shortcomings are bonding between more risky and less risky cases, usually increasing rather then decreasing subsequent illegal behavior. Aggressiveness is modeled, and little is usally done to address the criminogenic underpinnings with which offenders are struggling. Evaluations of boot camp programs do not generally support the alleged positive benefits of boot camps, and there is considerable evidence that boot camps are not effective in crime prevention. Boot camps have not been effective in reducing recidivism by juveniles, and the evidence of effectiveness is mixed for boot camps for adults.

Explain the Goals and Operations of Community Correction Facilities as Well as Issues Associated with Them

Community correction centers range from state-funded to private-sector providers working with offenders sentenced by the local judiciary, probationers in danger of failing on probation, and parolees needing additional services to prevent recidivism. Some centers are known as private-sector halfway houses; others are community correctional centers supported by units of government.

Correctional practice has usually provided access to available community services that would address offender needs. With the emerging emphasis on "what works," there has become a general realization that assignment to such facilities should be detailed to provide services to high-risk offenders rather than a mix of levels of risk. There is considerable evidence that low-risk offenders should not be assigned to correctional facilities since such combination of low- and high-risk offenders can unwittingly increase recidivism by lower-risk cases. There is an emerging body of evidence indicating the effectiveness of such facilities with high-risk offenders, supporting the argument that scarce correctional resources should be addressed to those most likely to fail.

Describe Drug, Mental Health, and Other Problem-Solving Courts

Many eligible offenders suffer from drug, mental health, and weak problem-solving strengths. A range of specialized treatment courts have been developed, including drug courts, veteran courts, domestic violence courts, gun courts, and teen courts. All are specialized courts that offer and require treatment specific to the needs of the offender. Emerging evidence of effectiveness is favorable.

Explain How Electronic Monitoring and GPS Are Used and Issues Associated with Their Use

Most electronic monitoring systems use a transmitter attached to the offender's wrist or ankle that sends signals to the supervising office during the hours the offender is required to be at home. Although some studies have shown electronic monitoring to be effective, others have produced mixed results. GPS can identify the exact location of the offender (and some systems transmit the conversations in which the offender participates). As such, this monitoring is particularly useful in managing sex offenders once released,

Summarize the Advantages and Disadvantages of Home Confinement

Home confinement, while more cost effective than incarceration, nonetheless can be subverted by clients determined to avoid the consequences of their behavior. Home confinement is substantially less expensive than jail confinement, allowing the offender to retain or obtain employment, enforce curfews, and lessen the opportunity of further criminal violations. Disadvantages include the ability of some offenders to remove any tracking device that might be used to verify offender compliance, the commission of additional crimes (such as drug violations) in the home, and the inability of supervising officers to control those residing in the offender's domicile. Effectiveness and crime prevention studies are positive.

Explain the Goals of Intensive Supervision Probation

Some probation clients face more numerous challenges and have higher potential for failure to conform to routine probation supervision. To increase public safety and control over the actions and to lower recidivism of the latter clients, the judge may impose a sentence calling for intensive probation supervision. Usually such probationers are assigned to a probation officer more skilled than others in ensuring conformity to conditions as ordered by the court, requiring several face-to-face contacts on a weekly basis between the officer and client as well as the clients' reporting their whereabouts to the officer. Routine drug tests may be ordered. This allows increased surveillance, supervision, lower recidivistic crime, and greater public safety. Some agencies also impose GPS and electronic tagging to assist the supervising probation officer in the quest for conformity.

Summarize the Development of Day-Reporting Centers as Well as Issues Associated with Them

Day reporting centers are locations where offenders congregate at least five days per week, being required to identify and schedule daily actions. Clients list their activities by time of the day and receive assistance and surveillance of offenders by probation and police officers, volunteers, treatment specialists, and referral officers. Frequent checks, usually by telephone, verify if the offenders are following their proposed schedules. Some centers use this strategy to teach time management, help offenders focus on positive activities, establish priorities, and lessen the potential for recidivism. Not all evaluations of some types of day reporting centers indicate significant reductions in recidivism.

Explain the Goals and Operations of Community Service Programs

Community service programs involve offenders performing court-ordered unpaid work for a specific number of hours, usually in the form of free labor or public service, such as sanitation, maintenance and repair, and helping older citizens with daily activities (such as driving them to grocery stores, banks, and shopping) and volunteer work. This program also avoids incarceration of those minor offenders who are unable to pay fines.

Explain the Goals and Operations of Shock Probation

Some clients pose greater risk for recidivism but are not hardened career criminals. They need an exposure to the incarceration system but do not require long-term imprisonment to effect cessation of criminal behavior ("desistance"). Shock probation combines a relatively brief period of imprisonment followed by probation or even intensive supervised probation. It is believed that an intense but short experience of the rigors and demands of imprisonment will motivate these offenders to conform to societal demands and desist from crime. Jurisdictions with shock probation options allow the sentencing judge to recall the prisoner and usually vacate the imprisonment sentence, imposing some condition of probation on the former inmate. Evaluations of the effectiveness of this program are generally favorable.

Key Words

diversion, 122
pretrial intervention programs, 123
treatment in lieu of conviction, 124
community corrections acts (CCAs), 124
intermediate sanctions, 124
day reporting center, 125
restitution order, 125
house arrest, 125
electronic monitoring, 125
risk management, 125
desistance, 125
intensive supervised probation (ISP), 128
tourniquet sentencing, 128
drug court, 129
community work order, 134
home detention, 134
electronic parole, 135
community residential treatment center, 137
shock probation, 140
boot camps, 140

Review Questions

1. Explain several ways in which offenders can be diverted from the correctional system.
2. Differentiate between shock probation and boot camp shock incarceration.
3. What roles do community residential treatment centers play in corrections? How have these types of programs changed over the years?
4. Did Florida's Community Control Program achieve its objectives?
5. Describe a boot camp program. Why haven't boot camps been effective in reducing recidivism?
6. Describe the day reporting center and its purposes.
7. Define a drug court and describe its operations. Why is this a good alternative for drug abusers?
8. Explain the effectiveness of drug courts and of day reporting centers.
9. What are some other types of specialty courts that are emerging in the United States?
10. Juvenile drug courts have not been found to be as effective as adult drug courts. Why do you believe this is the case, and what are some ways to improve their effectiveness?
11. What types of offenders should be placed in residential correctional facilities?

Application Case Studies

1. If you were a judge and wanted to develop a drug court, list some of the reasons you might give to justify the expenditure.
2. If you are the director of your state's department of corrections and the state governor told you to develop a plan to reduce your correctional budget by 25 percent over the next decade, what would you do? (Resignation is not one of your options!)
3. The director of court services wants to consider the possibility of instituting a specialty court for military veterans who might come before your county judiciary. You're tasked with preparing a white paper on the advantages and disadvantages of undertaking such a court devoted singularly to veterans having criminal charges. What five basic steps should you undertake to complete this effort?
4. Your prison permits cigarette smoking but three inmates sue you to reduce the dangerousness of this health hazard. An amicus brief petition was filed on behalf of the correctional officer union seeking relief from the dangers of secondhand cigarette smoke. What five things would you do?

Endnotes

1. Maryland Governor's Office, *Administration Report to the State/Local Criminal Justice/Mental Health Task Force* (Baltimore: Maryland Governor's Office, 1995); James Byrne and F. Taxman, "Crime Control Policy and Community Corrections Practice," *Evaluation and Program Planning* 17:2 (1994): 221–233; Richard Lamb and L. Weinberger, "Persons with Severe Mental Illnesses in Jails and Prisons," *Psychiatric Services* 49:4 (1998): 483–492; Huffington Post Chicago (2013), "Patrick Kennedy Visits Mentally Ill Inmates of Cook County Jail, Largest Illinois Mental Health Facility," http://www.huffingtonpost.com/2013/09/20/patrick-kennedy-cook-county-jail_n_3964699.html.
2. A. Barthwell, P. Bokos, and J. Bailey, "Interventions/Wilmer: A Continuum of Care for Substance Abusers in the Criminal Justice System," *Journal of Psychoactive Drugs* 27:1 (1995): 39–47. Note that stereotypes of drug users are generally erroneous, particularly the ideas that most drug users are burned out and disconnected from mainstream society. Some 7 in 10 drug users work full-time and are not poor. Laura Meckler, "7 in 10 Drug Users Work Full-Time," America Online, September 8, 1999.
3. Robert Langworthy and E. Latessa, "Treatment of Chronic Drunk Drivers," *Journal of Criminal Justice* 24:3 (1996): 273–281. See also K. Blackman, R. Voas, R. Gulberg, et al., "Enforcement of Zero Tolerance in the State of Washington," *Forensic Science Review* 13:2 (2001): 77–86, and Ted Greggry (2013), "The DUI Treatment Court in Illinois Mixes Intense Alcohol Monitoring with Treatment," http://articles.chicagotribune.com/2013-08-06/news/ct-met-hardcore-dui-court-20130807_1_dui-treatment-court-drunk-driving-outside-court.
4. Richard Tolman and A. Weisz, "Coordinated Community Incarceration for Domestic Violence: The Effects of Arrests and Prosecutions on Recidivism of Women Abuser Perspectives," *Crime and Delinquency* 41:4 (1995): 401–495; Christopher Calson and F. Nidey, "Mandatory Penalties, Victim Compensation, and the Judicial Processing of Domestic Abuse Assault Cases," *Crime and Delinquency* 41:1 (1995): 132–149; Carole Chancy and G. Saltzstein, "Democratic Control and Bureaucratic Responsiveness: The Police and Domestic Violence," *American Journal of Political Science* 42:3 (1998): 745–768.
5. Harry E. Allen, R. Seiter, E. Carlson, et al., *Halfway House: Program Models* (Washington, DC: U.S. Department of Justice, 1979). See also Bobbie Huskey, "Community Residential Centers," *Corrections Today* 54:8 (1992): 70–73, and Rhonda Reeves, "Future Forecast: Examining Community Corrections' Role in the Justice System," *Corrections Today* 54: 8 (1992): 74–79.
6. Edward Latessa, L. Travis, and A. Holsinger, *Evaluation of Ohio's Community Corrections Acts Programs in Community-Based Correctional Facilities* (Cincinnati, OH: Division of Criminal Justice, University of Cincinnati, 1997).
7. Malcolm M. Feeley and Jonathan Simon, "The New Penology: Notes on the Emerging Strategy of Corrections and Its Implications," *Criminology* 30:4 (1992): 449–474. See also Steven Donziger, *The Real War on Crime* (New York: HarperCollins, 1996), pp. 55–62, and Michael Tonry, "Parochialism in U.S. Sentencing Policy," *Crime and Delinquency* 45:1 (1999): 48–65.
8. Voncile Gowdy, *Intermediate Sanctions* (Washington, DC: U.S. Department of Justice, 1993). See also the theme issue of *Corrections Today* 57:1 (1995) and Jeffrey Ulmer, "Intermediate Sanctions," *Sociological Inquiry* 71:2 (2001): 164–193.
9. Daniel Nagin and David Farrington, "The Onset and Persistence of Offending," *Criminology* 30:4 (1992): 501–524; Mark Cohen, "The Monetary Value of Saving a High-Risk Youth," *Journal of Quantitative Criminology* 14:1 (1998): 5–33; Shadd Maruna, *Making Good: How Ex-Convicts Reform and Rebuild Their Lives* (Washington, DC: American Psychological Association, 2001).
10. Francis Cullen, Edward Latessa, Velmer Burton, and Lucien Lombardo, "The Correctional Orientation of Prison Wardens: Is the Rehabilitative Ideal Supported?," *Criminology* 31:1 (1993): 69–92; Jody Sundt and F. Cullen, "The Role of the Contemporary Prison Chaplain," *Prison Journal* 78:3 (1998): 271–298.
11. John Hagan and Juleigh Coleman, "Returning Captives of the American War on Drugs," *Crime and Delinquency* 47:3 (2001): 352–367.
12. Editors, "Alternatives to Prison: Cheaper Is Better," *The Economist*, November 19, 1994, p. 33; Steven Barkan and S. Cohn, "Racial Prejudice and Support by Whites for Police Use of Force," *Justice Quarterly* 15:4 (1998): 743–753.
13. Michael Tonry, "Racial Politics, Racial Disparities, and the War on Crime," *Crime and Delinquency* 40:4 (1994): 475–494. See also Christiana DeLong and K. Jackson, "Putting Race into Context: Race, Juvenile Justice Processing, and Urbanization," *Justice Quarterly* 15:3 (1998): 448–504.
14. Bruce Benson, D. Rasmussen, and I. Kim, "Deterrence and Public Policy," *International Review of Law and Economics* 18:1 (1998): 77–100.

15. Ann Carson and Daniela Gotinelli, *Prisoners in 2012: Advance Count* (Washington, DC: Bureau of Justice Statistics), p. 1.
16. "ICPS World Prison Brief" (2013), http://www.prisonstudies.org/highest-to-lowest/prison-population-total.
17. James Bryne, "The Future of Intensive Probation Supervision," *Crime and Delinquency* 36:1 (1990): 3–34. See also Pennsylvania Department of Corrections (2013), "State Intermediate Punishment Program," http://www.cor.state.pa.us/portal/server.pt/community/major_initiatives/21262/state_intermediate_punishment/1354887.
18. Peter Wood and H. Grasmick, "Toward the Development of Punishment Equivalencies," *Justice Quarterly* 16:1 (1999):19–50. On restitution, see the National Center for Victims of Crime (2013), http://www.victimsofcrime.org/training/national-conference/2013-national-conference.
19. William Bradshaw and M. Umbreit, "Crime Victims Meet Juvenile Offenders," *Juvenile and Family Court Journal* 49:3 (1998): 17–25; Audrey Evje and Robert Cushman, *A Summary of the Reconciliation Programs* (Sacramento: Judicial Council of California, 2000).
20. Thomas Bonczar, *Characteristics of Adults on Probation, 1995* (Washington, DC: U.S. Department of Justice, 1997), p. 7; Matthew DuRose and Patrick Langan, *Felony Sentences in State Courts, 2004* (Washington, DC: Bureau of Justice Statistics, 2007), p. 10.
21. Roy Sudipto, "Juvenile Restitution and Recidivism in a Midwestern County," *Federal Probation* 59:1 (1995): 55–62. See also Karen Suter, *Delinquency Prevention in Texas* (Austin: Texas Juvenile Probation Commission, 1997).
22. Joan Petersilia and Susan Turner, *Evaluating Intensive Supervised Probation/Parole: Results of a Nationwide Experiment* (Washington, DC: U.S. Department of Justice, 1993). See also Angela Robertson, P. Grimes, and K. Rogers, "A Short-Run Cost Benefit Analysis of Community-Based Interventions for Juvenile Offenders," *Crime and Delinquency* 47:2 (2001): 265–284.
23. B. Fulton, S. Stone, and P. Gendreau, *Restructuring Intensive Supervision Programs: Applying "What Works"* (Lexington, KY: American Probation and Parole Association, 1994). See also F. Cullen and P. Gendreau, "From Nothing Works to What Works," *The Prison Journal* 81:3 (2000): 313–338.
24. J. Byrne, A. Lurigio, and C. Baird, "The Effectiveness of the New Intensive Supervision Programs," *Research in Corrections* 2:1 (1989): 1–48. See also Chris Trotter, "Reducing Recidivism through Probation Supervision," *Federal Probation* 77:2 (2013), http://www.uscourts.gov/uscourts/FederalCourts/PPS/Fedprob/2013-09/reducing-recidivism.html.
25. B. Fulton, E. Latessa, A. Stichman, and L. F. Travis, "The State of ISP: Research and Policy Implications," *Federal Probation* 61:4 (1997): 65–75.
26. B. Fulton, P. Gendreau, and M. Paparozzi, "APPA's Prototypical Intensive Supervision Program: ISP as It Was Meant to Be," *Perspectives* 19:2 (1996): 25–41. See also B. Fulton et al., *Restructuring Intensive Supervision Programs.*
27. C. West Huddleston, "Drug Court and Jail-Based Treatment," *Corrections Today* 60:6 (1998): 98. See also Paul Stageberg, B. Wilson, and R. Moore, *Final Report of the Polk County Adult Drug Court* (Des Moines: Iowa Division of Criminal Justice Policy, 2001).
28. C. West Huddleston, Douglas Marlowe, and Rachel Casebolt, *Painting the Current Picture: A National Report Card on Drug Courts and Other Problem-Solving Court Programs in the United States* (Washington, DC: Bureau of Justice Assistance, U.S. Department of Justice, 2008).
29. M. Rempel, D. Fox-Kralstein, A. Cissner, et al., *The New York State Adult Drug Court Evaluation: Policies, Participants and Impacts* (New York: Center for Court Innovation, 2003).
30. Deborah Shaffer, Shelley Listwan, Edward Latessa, and Christopher Lowenkamp, "Examining the Differential Impact of Drug Court Services by Court Type: Findings from Ohio," *Drug Court Institute* 6:1(2007): 33–66.
31. This study examined 10 juvenile drug courts from across the United State and was funded by OJJDP. See Edward Latessa, Carrie Sullivan, Lesli Blair, Christopher J. Sullivan, and Paula Smith, *Outcome and Process Evaluation of Juvenile Drug Courts* (Cincinnati, OH: Center for Criminal Justice Research, University of Cincinnati, 2013).
32. Shaffer-Koetzle, D. (2011) Looking Inside of Drug Courts: A Meta-Analytic Review. *Justice Quarterly* 28 (2011): 493–521.
33. Washington State Institute for Public Policy, *Drug Courts for Adult Defendants: Outcome Evaluation and Cost Benefit Analysis* (Olympia: Washington State Institute for Public Policy, 2003).
34. NPC Research, Inc., and Administrative Office of the Courts, Judicial Council of California, *California Drug Courts: A Methodology for Determining Costs and Avoided Costs: Phase I: Building the Methodology: Final Report* (Portland, OR: Authors, October 2002). See also Partnership at Drugfree.org (2013), "Federal Government Embraces Drug Courts, but Critics Remain," http://www.drugfree.org/join-together/drugs/federal-government-embraces-drug-courts-but-critics-remain.

35. James Brown, "Drug Courts: Are They Needed and Will They Succeed in Breaking the Cycle of Drug-Related Crime?," *New England Journal on Civil and Criminal Confinement* 23:1 (1997): 63–99.
36. Eastern Judicial Circuit of Georgia, "State Court DUI Court Program," http://www.chathamcourts.org/StateCourt/DUICourtProgram.aspx (accessed October 26, 2012).
37. California Courts, Judicial Branch of California.
38. See Christine Sarteschi, "Assessing the Effectiveness of Mental Health Courts: A Meta Analysis of Clinical and Recidivism Outcomes" (doctoral diss., University of Pittsburgh, 2009), and Brittany Cross "Mental Health Courts Effectiveness in Reducing Recidivism and Improving Clinical Outcomes" (master's thesis, University of South Florida, 2011).
39. National Association of Drug Court Professionals, http://www.nadcp.org/.
40. Julie Martin, "Community Services: Are the Goals of This Alternative Sentencing Tool Being Met?," *Court Review* 28:4 (1991): 5–11. But see Wade Myers, P. Burton, Paula Sanders, et al., "Project 'Back-on-Track' at One Year," *Journal of the American Academy of Clinical and Adolescent Psychiatry* 39:9 (2000): 1127–1134.
41. Gail Caputo, D. Young, and R. Porter, *Community Services for Repeat Misdemeanants in New York City* (New York: Vera Institute, 1998).
42. Michael Maxfield and Terry Baumer, "Home Detention with Electronic Monitoring: Comparing Pretrial and Postconviction Programs," *Crime and Delinquency* 36:4 (1990): 521–536; Ann Farrell, "Mothers Offending against Their Role: An Australian Experience," *Women and Criminal Justice* 9:4 (1998): 47–67.
43. Leonard Flynn, "House Arrest," *Corrections Today* 48:5 (1986): 64–68.
44. K. Courtright, B. Berg, and R. Mutchnick, "The Cost Effectiveness of Using House Arrest with Electronic Monitoring for Drunk Drivers," *Federal Probation* 61:3 (1997): 19–22.
45. Government Accounting Office, *Intermediate Sanctions* (Washington, DC: Government Accounting Office, 1990). Evaluations of the home detention program in Great Britain found a 5 percent "recall to prison" rate for prison inmates released to home detention. Kath Dodgson, P. Goodwin, H. Philip, et al., *Electronic Monitoring of Released Prisoners* (London: Home Office, 2001).
46. James Kammer, K. Minor, and J. Wells, "An Outcome Study of the Diversion Plus Program for Juvenile Offenders," *Federal Probation* 61:2 (1997): 51–56; M. Cusson, "Intermediate Punishments, Electronic Monitoring and Abolitionism," *Revue Internationale de Criminologie et de Police Technique Scientifique* 51:1 (1998): 34–45.
47. Dennis Wagner and Christopher Baird, *Evaluation of the Florida Community Control Program* (Washington, DC: U.S. Department of Justice, 1993), p. 5. It is possible to have cost savings and similar outcomes. See Elizabeth Deschenes and P. Greenwood, "Alternative Placements for Juvenile Offenders," *Journal of Research in Crime and Delinquency* 35:3 (1998): 267–294.
48. See Alison Church and S. Dunston, *Home Detention: The Evaluation of the Home Detention Pilot Programme, 1995–1997* (Wellington: New Zealand Ministry of Justice, 1997).
49. R. K. Schwitzgebel, R. L. Schwitzgebel, W. N. Pahnke, and W. S. Hurd, "A Program of Research in Behavioral Electronics," *Behavioral Scientist* 9:3 (1964): 233–238. See also Michael Vitello, "Three Strikes: Can We Return to Rationality?," *Journal of Criminal Law and Criminology* 87:2 (1997): 395–481.
50. Scott Vollum and Chris Hale, "Electronic Monitoring: Research Review," *Corrections Compendium*, July 2002, p. 1. See also "Electronic Monitoring of Offenders in the Community," http://www.michigan.gov/corrections/0,4551,7-119-1435_1498-5032--,00.html (accessed August 26, 2014).
51. See P. Bulman, "Sex Offenders Monitored by GPS Found to Commit Fewer Crimes," *NIJ Journal* 271 (February 2013).
52. Bureau of Justice Assistance, *Electronic Monitoring in Intensive Probation and Parole Programs* (Washington, DC: U.S. Department of Justice, 1989).
53. Joan Petersilia, *Expanding Options for Criminal Sentencing* (Santa Monica, CA: Rand, 1987), p. 37; C. Camp and G. Camp, *The Corrections Yearbook 1998* (Middletown, CT: Criminal Justice Institute, 1998), p. 124. See also Editors, "Florida to Mandate GP [Global Positioning] Devices for Sex Offenders," *Correctional News* 11:3 (2005): 1.
54. See Government Accounting Office, *Intermediate Sanctions*, pp. 6–7.
55. William Bales, Karen Mann, Thomas Blomberg, Gerry Gaes, Kelle Barrick, Karla Dhungana, and Brian McManus, *A Quantitative and Qualitative Assessment of Electronic Monitoring*. (Washington, DC: National Institute of Justice, January 2010).
56. See Church and Dunston, *Home Detention;* Mike Nellis, "The Electronic Monitoring of Offenders in England and Wales," *British Journal of Criminology* 31:2 (1991): 165–185; R. Lilly, "Tagging Revisited," *The Howard Journal* 29:4 (1990): 229–245; National Association for the Care of Offenders and the Prevention of Crime, *The Electronic Monitoring of*

Offenders (London: National Association for the Care of Offenders and the Prevention of Crime, 1989); and Michael Brown and Preston Elrod, "Electronic House Arrest: An Examination of Citizen Attitudes," *Crime and Delinquency* 41:3 (1995): 332–346.

57. Edward J. Latessa and Lawrence F. Travis, "Halfway Houses or Probation: A Comparison of Alternative Dispositions," *Journal of Crime and Justice* 14:1 (1991): 53–75; Edward Latessa, L. Travis, and A. Holsinger, *Evaluation of Ohio's Community-Based Correctional Facilities: Final Report* (Cincinnati, OH: Division of Criminal Justice, University of Cincinnati, 1997).
58. Christopher Lowenkamp and Edward J. Latessa, *Evaluation of Ohio's Residential Correctional Programs* (Cincinnati, OH: Center for Criminal Justice Research, University of Cincinnati, 2002). See also Christopher Lowenkamp and Edward Latessa, "Increasing the Effectiveness of Correctional Programming through the Risk Principle: Identifying Offenders for Residential Placement," *Criminology and Public Policy* 4:2 (2005): 501–528.
59. J. Stephen Wormith and Mark E. Oliver, "Offender Treatment Attrition and Its Relationship with Risk, Responsivity, and Recidivism," *Criminal Justice and Behavior* 29:4 (2002): 447–471.
60. Edward Latessa, Lori Brusman-Lovins, and Paula Smith, "Follow-Up Evaluation of Ohio's Community Based Correctional Facility and Halfway House Programs—Outcome Study," Center for Criminal Justice Research, University of Cincinnati, 2010.
61. Edward J. Latessa and Lawrence F. Travis, "Halfway Houses or Probation"; Joseph Callahan and K. Koenning, "The Comprehensive Sanctions Center in the Northern District of Ohio," *Federal Probation* 59:3 (1995): 52–57.
62. Dale Parent, J. Byrne, V. Tsarfaty, et al., *Day Reporting Center* (Washington, DC: U.S. Department of Justice, 1995). See also Michelle Boots (2013), "New Prisoner Re-entry Center Takes Aim at Criminal Rehabilitation," http://www.adn.com/2013/10/02/3106779/new-prisoner-re-entry-center-takes.html.
63. Stan Orchowsky, L. Jodie, and T. Bogle, *Evaluation of the Richmond Day Reporting Center* (Richmond: Virginia Criminal Justice Research Center, 1995); Jack McDevitt, M. Domino, and K. Baum, *Metropolitan Day Reporting Center: An Evaluation* (Boston: Center for Criminal Justice Policy Research, Northeastern University, 1997).
64. Gennaro Vito and Harry Allen, "Shock Probation in Ohio: A Comparison of Outcomes," *International Journal of Offender Therapy and Comparative Criminology* 25:1 (1981): 7.
65. Gennaro Vito, "Developments in Shock Probation: A Review of Research Findings and Policy Implications," *Federal Probation* 50:1 (1985): 22–27.
66. See also Michael Vaughn, "Listening to the Experts: A National Study of Correctional Administrators' Responses to Prison Overcrowding," *Criminal Justice Review* 18:1 (1993): 12–25.
67. Ibid., pp. 23–25. But also see Bruce Mendelsohn, *The Challenge of Prison Crowding* (Frederick, MD: Aspen, 1996). See also C. Camp and G. Camp, *The Corrections Yearbook Adult Corrections 2002* (Middletown, CT: Criminal Justice Institute, 1998).
68. See also Blair Bourque et al., *Boot Camps for Juvenile Offenders* (Washington, DC: U.S. Department of Justice, 1996).
69. The bulk of the following section is drawn from the U.S. Government Accounting Office, *Prison Boot Camps* (Washington, DC: U.S. Department of Justice, 1993).
70. Texas Department of Criminal Justice, *Community Corrections Facilities Outcome Study* (Austin: Texas Department of Criminal Justice, 1999).
71. Steve Aos, P. Phipps, R. Barnoski, and R. Lieb, *The Comparative Costs and Benefits of Programs to Reduce Crime: A Review of the National Research Findings with Implications for Washington State* (Olympia: Washington State Institute for Public Policy, 1999). See also Justice Center, Council of State Governments (2013), "Lessons from the States: Reducing Recidivism and Curbing Corrections Costs through Justice Reinvestment," https://www.bja.gov/Publications/CSG_State-Lessons-Learned-Recidivism.pdf.
72. David Altschuler and Troy Armstrong, *Intensive Aftercare for High-Risk Juveniles: A Community Care Model: Program Summary* (Washington, DC: Office of Juvenile Justice and Delinquency Prevention, Office of Justice Programs, U.S. Department of Justice, 1994).
73. Doris MacKenzie and Sam Souryal, *Multisite Evaluation of Shock Incarceration* (Washington, DC: National Institute of Justice, Office of Justice Programs, U.S. Department of Justice, 1994).
74. Dale Colledge and J. Gerber, "Rethinking the Assumption about Boot Camps," *Journal of Offender Rehabilitation* 28:1 (1998): 71–87. See also Kay Harris, "Key Differences among Community Corrections Acts in the United States: An Overview," *Prison Journal* 76:2 (1996): 192–238.

Suggested Readings: Part 2

Bonta, James, S. Wallace-Capretta, and J. Rooney. "Can Electronic Monitoring Make a Difference?" *Crime and Delinquency* 46:1 (2000): 61–75.

Gendreau, Paul, Shelia A. French, and Angela Taylor. *What Works (What Doesn't Work)—Revised 2002: The Principles of Effective Correctional Treatment.* Monograph Series. La Crosse, WI: International Community Corrections Association, 2002.

Latessa, Edward, Francis T. Cullen, and Paul Gendreau. "Beyond Correctional Quackery: Professionalism and the Possibility of Effective Treatment." *Federal Probation* 66:1 (2002): 43–44.

Latessa, Edward, and Paula Smith. *Corrections in the Community.* 4th ed. Cincinnati, OH: Anderson Publishing, 2007.

Lowenkamp, Christopher, and Edward Latessa. "Increasing the Effectiveness of Correctional Programming through the Risk Principle: Identifying Offenders for Residential Placement." *Criminology and Public Policy* 4:2 (2005): 501–528.

Lowenkamp, Christopher T., Edward J. Latessa, and Alex Holsinger. "The Risk Principle in Action: What We Have Learned from 13,676 Offenders and 97 Correctional Programs." *Crime and Delinquency* 52:1 (2006): 1–17.

Lutze, Faith, and D. Brody. "Mental Abuse as Cruel and Unusual Punishment: Do Boot Camp Prisons Violate the Eighth Amendment?" *Crime and Delinquency* 45:2 (1999): 242–255.

Marciniak, Liz. "The Use of Day Reporting as an Intermediate Sanction." *The Prison Journal* 79:2 (1999): 205–225.

Taxman, Faye, D. Soule, and A. Gelb. "Graduated Sanctions." *The Prison Journal* 79:2 (1999): 182–204.

Tonry, Michael. "Crime and Human Rights." *Criminology* 46:1 (2008): 1–33.

part 3

Institutional Corrections

Overview

Every correctional facility for adults, whether called a jail, prison, reformatory facility, institution, or correctional hospital, has basic minimal functions that must be performed. These fall into two broad categories: custody and treatment. Both functions are defined as correctional organization components and will be explained in this part: identifying the major problems, challenges, pitfalls, and current solutions as well as the routine of the institution. We also explore correctional institutions, such as jails, the federal system of corrections, and private-sector corrections, focusing particularly on prison gangs, parole and reentry, and the death penalty.

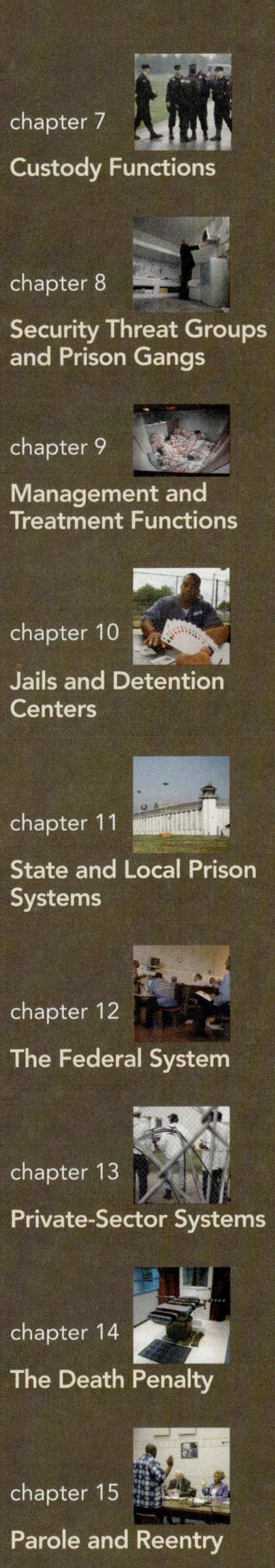

Regina H. Boone/MCT/Newscom.

Objectives

- Outline the organizational structure of prisons.
- Describe the various jobs and functions of prison staff.
- Outline the recruiting, hiring, and retention of prison staff.
- Describe the general challenges and issues corrections officers face.
- Summarize prison culture for staff.
- Describe the unique challenges and issues faced by female and minority correctional officers.
- Summarize how a prison unit is managed.
- Describe methods for controlling inmate behavior.
- Describe methods for preventing escape.
- Explain the unit team and other methods designed to avoid compartmentalization.
- Describe ways in which correctional staff can be upgraded.

chapter 7 Custody Functions

Outline

"Our endeavors to control violence, in whatever setting, should be shared similarly by what we know about treating violent behavior. . . . Criminal behavior is learned behavior and ignoring its origin is wrong."

—Joseph D. Lehman

Overview

The primary mission for any confinement facility, prison, or jail is to "protect the public." That prime directive sometimes has been and still is carried to the extreme. Whether from fear, ignorance, apathy, or poor training, custody staffs are defensive of their role and tactics. Emotions in a high-security cell block can run high, with tensions spawning inappropriate behaviors on both sides of the bars. The custody staffs are the front lines of corrections and deserve utmost respect and appreciation for what they do. If the entire staff of an institution cannot work together, they will fail separately.

Custody over another person came into being when the first tribal member was asked to guard a thief until punishment was meted out. The long history of custody far outstrips the short time that "treatment" has been on the correctional scene. Treatment has been on the agenda of correctional management only since the early 1930s in any seriously organized fashion. The long-standing battles between custody and treatment started at the beginning and have continued, sometimes subdued, since that time. Outwardly, although the basic arguments seem to be over one or the other philosophy of corrections, the differences are more often seen in conflict over budgets, manpower, and turf. Chapters 7, 8, and 9 examine and compare the various organizational components of corrections to see what they do and how they might do it better. Because custody comprises the largest part of that organizational system, we start with it.

INSTITUTIONS: BUREAUCRATIC CONTROL

key term

Bureaucratic control
Predominant public administration format for prison operations.

Despite technological and educational advances, the prevailing management climate for correctional institutions seems to be one of **bureaucratic control**, especially in long-term adult felony institutions. In most major correctional facilities, the inmate population is usually controlled by a combination of coercive rules that are intended to prohibit certain kinds of behavior and punishments that are imposed when the rules are broken. Bureaucratic organizations are insulated by all kinds of documented rules, regulations, and procedures, and violations are quickly punished in the name of equity and control.

In institutions that house thousands of prisoners, each with his or her own personal problems, the bureaucratic style seems to be the only functional way to maintain order and control; the processes take precedence over the individual, and prisoners become faceless commodities to be housed, moved, worked, fed, secured, and released. This nineteenth-century model stressed warehousing and subjugation of offenders. Any rehabilitation was incidental, a welcome but low-priority by-product, because the bureaucratic style clearly conflicted with any emphasis on rehabilitation. The separate functions of the rigid and formalized organizations create an impoverished climate for behavioral change.[1]

Administration's Problem: Punish, Control, or Rehabilitate?

The lack of coordination articulated for both within the correctional system and outside of it, outlined in the previous chapters, suggests some of the reasons correctional administrators are often harried and hampered in their efforts to secure, control, and rehabilitate inmates. Although the public is willing to espouse reformatory goals for corrections, it is seldom willing to provide the support and funding that would make such reform a legislative priority. That inconsistency places dedicated correctional administrators in an awkward position: They can implement only the most meager of programs, and even then they must maintain an overall emphasis on control and punishment. Regardless of the approach to the problem, some aspect of operations will suffer.[2] If improvement requires an increase in the number of security guards, the administrator must obtain the necessary funds by decreasing the support for a treatment or other type of program; and if the administrator tries to amplify the treatment programs, it must usually be done at the expense of the custody staff.

CUSTODY: A 24-HOUR IMPACT

Institutional behavior and the attitudes of incarcerated persons are usually learned by observing and responding to those staff who have direct and continuous contact with them. Administrative and treatment staffs have limited interaction with inmates on a daily basis. Custody staffs, however, are with them 24 hours a day. It has been found that, if the whole institutional staff is not working as a team, months of discipline can fall by the wayside as a result of one serious event. Conversely, months of professional counseling can be destroyed by a single custody officer's words or actions. The term **custody** refers to the level of immediate control exercised over offenders within correctional institutions. The levels can range from supermax to maximum (or close) to medium and minimum.

key term

Custody
Term referring to the level of immediate control exercised over offenders within correctional institutions.

The Federal Bureau of Prisons classifies inmates into security levels. The contrasts of characteristics between the medium- and high-security inmates can be found in Table 7.1 and indicate some of the parameters on which classification depends.

Supermax, maximum, or close custody usually means the inmate is seen as a security risk and cannot be trusted to move from one area to another, in the general prison or in the cell blocks, without being escorted by a correctional officer. It also implies that inmates will not be allowed to have contact visits or to associate with other prisoners freely without

table 7.1 **Characteristics of Federal Medium- and High-Security Inmates, 2013**

Medium-Security Inmates	High-Security Inmates
67% are drug or weapon offenders	70% are drug or weapons offenders or robbers
75% have a history of violence	10% have been convicted of murder, aggravated assault, or kidnapping
40% have been sanctioned for violating prison rules	50% have sentences in excess of 10 years
50% have sentences in excess of 8 years	70% have been sanctioned for violating prison rules

SOURCE: U.S. Department of Justice (2013), "FY 2013 Performance Budget," http://www.justice.gov/jmd/2013summary/pdf/fy13-bud-summary-request-performance.pdf#plan.

supervision. They are also limited in their contacts with other persons in general. The ratio of correctional officers to inmates in most facilities designated as supermax, maximum, or close is usually quite high, as many as one for every three or four inmates. (Death row inmates are usually considered to be in close custody and therefore are expensive to house, especially with their time from conviction to execution running sometimes to 20 years and 12 years on the average. See Chapter 14.)

Medium- and minimum-custody levels generally accommodate less risky or dangerous offenders or those closer to the end of their sentences. Generally speaking, the difference between medium and minimum custody is the presence of a high wall or fence and armed guard towers surrounding the former, with reasonably free movement within the facility for both categories. The inmates classified as medium security in an enclosed institution are allowed in what is referred to as **general population** (all prisoners not under special custody control). Staff-to-inmate ratios generally decrease at this level, with 1 custody staff to every 8 or 12 inmates being a common range.

Inmates classified as minimum in a fenced or walled prison are often used on institutional jobs with very little supervision or observation (i.e., grounds keeping, sweeping, and cleanup). Minimum-custody offenders are often placed in honor camps or farms, with low levels of supervision for a period of time prior to release, usually three to six months. This is a system that can reimpose a higher level of security, which often serves as both a carrot and a stick: a reward for good behavior and a loss of privileges for misbehavior. Most custody staff see this as a control mechanism and a pathway to **graduated release**. Generally speaking, custody administrators will err on the "side of the angels" and assign a higher level of custody when there is any level of doubt, especially until the inmate becomes established in the institution.

Even though much better trained and educated **correctional officers** have now replaced the old-time prison guards in almost all prisons, many institutions still follow the same oppressive custodial procedures, especially in times of unrest. Until the cause-and-effect relationship between autocratic organizational styles and institutional disturbance is openly acknowledged, the advocates of rigid custodial control will retain their influential role.

Correctional officers serve in a variety of prison conditions across the nation. Little attention has been directed to them as actors in a correctional facility, yet they are a major part of the prison situation. When they enter into correctional academies prior to employment, a training program designed to introduce them to their functions and duties as a correctional officer, they learn that inmates are not to be trusted, are dangerous, and might be less than human beings ("scumbags, vermin, filth of the earth," etc.) They are instructed to be cautious, not to trust any inmate, and to follow the rules.

key term

General population Prisoners not restricted to tighter controls than other inmates.

key term

Graduated release Programs bridging inmate status from imprisonment to community control.

key term

Correctional officers Line prison officers working directly with the inmate population.

photo 7.1

ADX Supermax Prison in Colorado.
Lizzie Himmel/Sygma/Corbis.

In the nation currently, there are more inmates incarcerated than any other country; about 1 in 100 adult citizens are incarcerated. Even worse, about 1 in 10 adult Black males is currently incarcerated, and about one in three African American males born in 2013 will be imprisoned in their lifetime.[3] Prison overcrowding, "get tough on criminals," and restricted services and recreation flow from all these factors. As a result, the conditions in the nation's prisons are widely varied.

Many allow or even pursue prison conditions that exacerbate the impact of incarceration on inmates. They also negatively impact correctional officers. Such conditions include excessive cold and heat, constant noise, loud screams, little privacy or cell space, little attention to both dilapidated and physical conditions, dirty space, and increased individual duress and distress among not only the inmates but also the correctional staff. Physical and mental health problems relate to the impact of the environment. Many of these conditions could be easily remedied by correctional administrators.

Two particular examples of ways to increase the negative impact on correctional officers include the following. First, refuse to air-condition facilities in which the internal temperature hits 130 degrees. Second, limit inmate access to recreational activities, television, weight training, hot meals, and medical treatment. Inmates frequently complain about food. They may be even more distressed when their everyday lunch is a bologna sandwich. Some administrators may see inmates as not deserving to demand better and believe that a tougher prison reduces crime.

These harsh prison conditions also have pronounced impacts on staff, including high blood pressure, stress, impaired hearing, obesity, mental health issues, and cardiovascular disease. Correctional staff members in harsher conditions of a prison have increased drinking and smoking levels and increased sick leave among officers. Addressing these conditions by administrative improvement will also yield benefits by ameliorating deleterious conditions. It would lessen sick leave, improve workplace efficiency, and resolve related stress issues. Correctional staff deserve better.

WARDENS AND SUPERINTENDENTS

Wardens (sometimes called superintendents) are the chief executive officers of prisons and have management responsibility for attaining mission goals. The warden's primary responsibility is to manage the operations, supervisory staff, support staff, and inmates. To do this, the warden is usually assisted by several deputy wardens, typically one each for management, custody, industry, and treatment programs. Most wardens are male, although the number of female administrators has grown dramatically over the years and will be an estimated 44 percent in 2015 (see Figure 7.1). We also see a higher percentage of

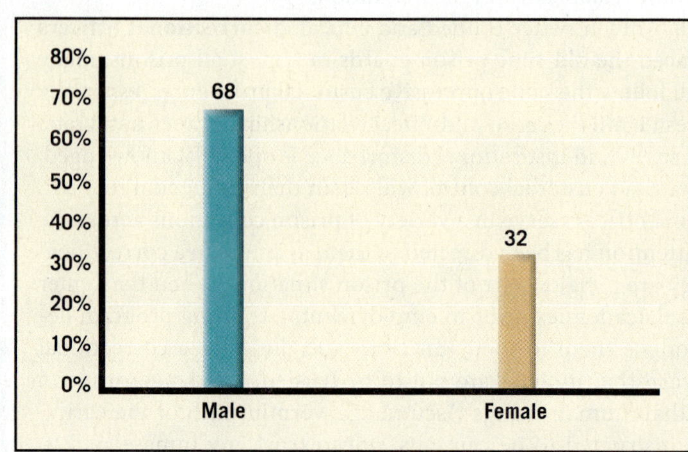

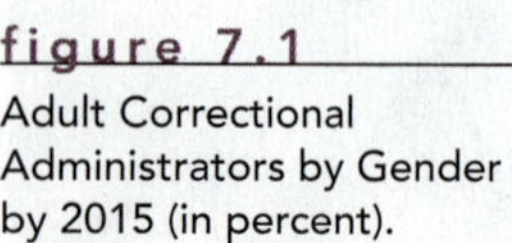

figure 7.1

Adult Correctional Administrators by Gender by 2015 (in percent).

SOURCE: Based on data from American Correctional Association, *2012 Directory* (Alexandria, VA: American Correctional Association, 2012), pp. 56–57.

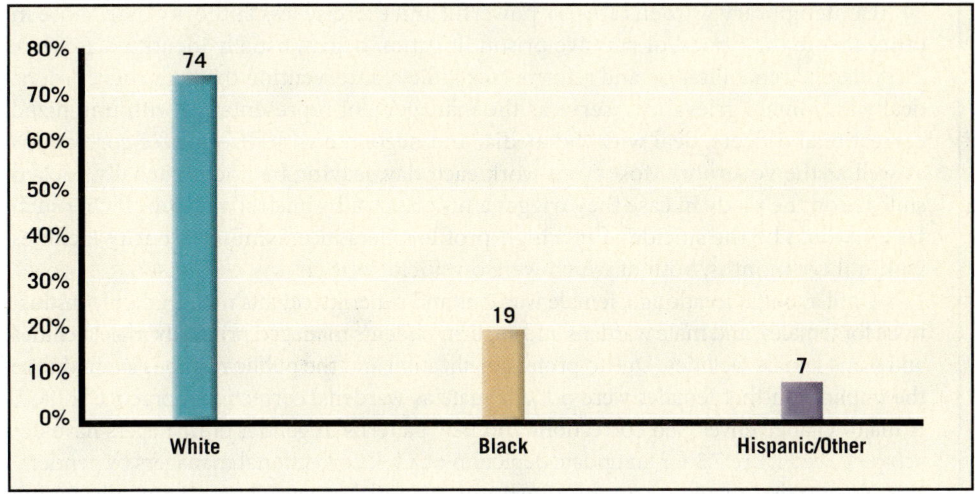

figure 7.2
Adult Correctional Administrators by Race by 2015 (in percent).

SOURCE: Based on data from American Correctional Association, *2012 Directory* (Alexandria, VA: American Correctional Association, 2012), pp. 56–57.

minorities in these positions (see Figure 7.2). Most wardens are believed to "earn their way up" by serving in subordinate positions in the chain of command within a prison, assuming higher ranks and authority with experience and proven abilities. For many correctional workers, the post of warden is the capstone of a lengthy career, occasionally served within only one institution.

Wardens tend to "face outward" in their daily duties, dealing with politicians, administrators in the central office of corrections, the media, and interest groups. Running the daily affairs of the prison facility is usually delegated to a deputy warden, usually the custody deputy. As former Warden Benjamin Cooper said, "The warden's job is made much easier if he follows the MBWA ('management by walking around') principle. You have to tour the facility every day."

correctional **profile 7.1**

Prison Warden

The prison warden, also known in some states as a prison superintendent or correctional manager, is the top administrative person who supervises and controls the day-to-day affairs of a correctional facility. Wardens administer and manage funds and resources in the facility, coordinate policy planning and upgrading of technology, and direct staff leadership and facility upkeep. The warden is also responsible for directing, managing, and developing work and entertainment for inmates.

Wardens recruit, train and monitor correctional and medical staff, meet daily with some inmates, provide training and programs for inmates, control interactions with media and criminal justice stakeholders (law enforcement, state attorneys general, parole boards, and so on), and manage security threat groups. Wardens are also responsible for developing both working conditions and staff morale to minimize facility crisis and secure protection of staff and inmates. Wardens frequently engage in MBWA (management by walking around) within the facility and, in that role, are vulnerable to inmate attack. Salaries *frequently* exceed $125,000 a year. Being warden is a full-time job, the responsibilities for which demands constant attention. Due to the complexities of the warden's job, most wardens interact with unit leadership within the correctional complex and are assisted by deputy wardens responsible for security, treatment, and medical services.

Most wardens begin their careers as correctional officers and undertake systematic growth and increased skills. Minimal requirements are at least a high school/college education (preferably in criminal justice), accounting, business, or law enforcement, among others. Most have at least a year's experience in facility management before serving as a warden. Candidates must pass background checks, drug tests, and polygraph tests. In some states, wardens are political appointees; in others, they are selected within the prison system or through a civil service search.

In particular, candidates for warden more likely have a degree in criminal justice, criminology, or psychology from an accredited university or college. They will have a background in administration or management in other jobs, particularly in law enforcement, as a probation officer or investigator.[4]

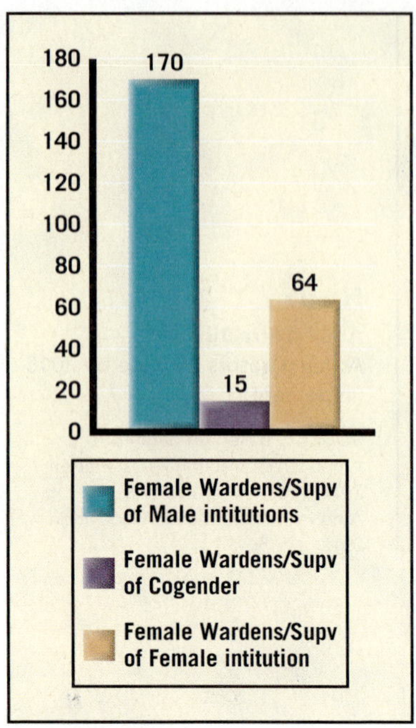

figure 7.3
Adult Correctional Administrators by Gender.

SOURCE: American Correctional Association, *2012 Directory* (Alexandria, VA: American Correctional Association, 2012), p. 65.

Contemporary wardens are less powerful and exercise less authority than those in office before the period of massive prison litigation began, usually identified as 1970. They defend rehabilitation and reform, face judicial intervention through court orders, deal with inmate grievances, serve as the management representative with unionized correctional officers, deal with the media, and negotiate with directors of corrections as well as the governor. Most go to work each day, leaving behind a partially packed suitcase on the ready in case they trigger a notorious administrative failure.[5] One such failure would be the suicide of two high-profile killers in maximum-security facilities within three months, both of which were on suicide watch.[6]

Until about a decade ago, female wardens and superintendents managed only institutions for females, and male wardens and superintendents managed primarily male facilities and some female facilities. Due to professionalization and the public relations snafu due to the implication that females were not adequate as wardens, correctional practice shifted. A major change enveloped corrections and new patterns in gender of managers have developed. See Figure 7.3 for an update depiction of adult correctional managers by gender.

No discussion of prison administrators would be complete without discussing some basic facts about wardens. Adult correctional agency directors and institutional managers have not been extensively researched in corrections.

In 2013, the average length of time an agency director had been in office was about eight years, and a director's average salary was over $100,000 a year. Both the average length of time in office and salary varied by region of the country. In the Northeast, salaries for wardens and superintendents from high-paying states were from $150,000 to $181,000. Most wardens express moderate to strong support for the rehabilitation model and also strong support for treatment. Most would approve of conjugal visits. While wardens vary in background and orientation, there is evidence that such correctional managers have similar attitudes and values, particularly on the death penalty and sexual assault in prisons.

CORRECTIONAL OFFICERS AND JAILERS: ON THE FRONT LINES

key term
"Screws"
Inmate term for correctional officers.

Although custody staff members have been called guards, jailers, prison guards, turnkeys, **"screws,"** hacks, detention officers, correctional officers, or security staff, for purposes of this text we choose to use the term *correctional officer.* Regardless of the title used, it refers to those women and men charged with control, movement management, and observation of the inmates in the jails and prisons of America. In late 2012, more than 265,310 uniformed security staff members were working in state, federal, and local adult prisons in America.[7] Also, more than 118,000 line officers worked in jails and local detention facilities. The proportion of female officers in the prison systems is about 34 percent, and 40 percent are nonwhite (see Figure 7.3).

Among the general duties that corrections officers in prison fulfill are the following:

- Enforce rules and keep order within prisons
- Supervise and control activities of inmates
- Aid in counseling and rehabilitation of offenders
- Inspect facility conditions to ensure that they meet established institutional standards
- Search inmates for contraband items, particularly drugs and knives
- Report on inmate conduct, including written descriptions of inmate defiance

Correctional Officer Attitudes

The past century saw the "get-tough-on-crime" advocates place new and greater demands on correctional officers to do more with less, with little or no recognition. Moreover, prisons can be antagonistic and stressful working environments, as evidenced by the increasing number of assaults on correctional officers by inmates and by the number of disciplinary actions taken by administrators against correctional officers.

Diminished Control

Correctional officer degradation is a recent phenomenon that has emerged largely as a result of court rulings and an increase in violence and gang (institutional threat group) membership among inmates. Specifically, some administrators are seen to have adopted a "hands-off" doctrine concerning inmate behavior. Some researchers argue that this doctrine has exposed prison regimes to outside accountability, limited an institution's recourse to coercive sanctions, and provided inmates with a legitimate means of expression with which to challenge the system of social control.

The impact of recent court decisions has been to establish a perceived link between the administrative and inmate control systems. The prison system's typical response to court decisions has been to develop administrative structures to maintain order consistent with the procedural and substantive rights of inmates. However, it appears that the rights of correctional officers might have been neglected while correctional administrators conformed to litigation. For instance, a latent result of court compliance by prison administrators is increased bureaucratic regulations and obligations for corrections personnel. This can be accomplished in a variety of ways, including a drastic increase in the direction and length of a correctional officer's training program. Also, when custody personnel arrive at basic or in-service training classes, correctional instructors should explain the mission of the training, which is to protect the state from further inmate litigation, and they should inform their students that future responsibility for courtroom resolutions rests with corrections personnel.

New legal standards have emerged, burying correctional officers in bureaucratic responsibilities. For instance, when correctional officers use force, they now must complete an official report, with videotapes and other corroborating evidence. This new "bureaucratic-legal order" also forces officers to conform to the letter of the law in the application of force. Some researchers suggest that several prison riots, including the Attica riot of 1971, can be traced to excessive inmate freedoms and the responses of prison systems to court decisions. Thus, inmate rights have produced a variety of bureaucratic regulations that have taken the authority and structure of custody away from the corrections professional.

photo 7.2
Ohio State Reformatory Museum, site of filming of *The Shawshank Redemption*.
Walter Bibikow/Corbis.

An increase of violence, due in part to a rise in prison gangs, puts many officers in the trenches of our nation's prisons. Prison violence, crime, and drug trafficking are ways of life for most inmates in high-custody prisons. In fact, some experts say that as gangs and violence increase in high-custody penitentiaries, the less likely an officer is to want to deal directly with inmates; instead, he or she will want to transfer into administrative work.

If the primary concern is to render humane and quality custody service, it appears highly unlikely that alienated officers are motivated toward those ends. A second concern is the need to enhance in-service training at a professional level conducted outside the prison facility. Other recommendations from this study included the idea that administrations should manage through encouraging positive values instead of regulations and that raises and promotions should be linked to merit, education, and experience.[8]

Unionization and the Correctional Officer

key term

Unionization
Organization of correctional officers for purposes of improved work conditions or salaries.

key term

"Blue flu"
Ploy used by correctional officers to strengthen their hands in negotiations with command officers.

Unionization, found in almost every sector of business and industry, has in recent decades spread to the ranks of state and federal employees. The union movement has extended to the "sworn" officers charged with the police, fire, and correctional protection of the public. Police officers and firefighters have established collective bargaining agencies in most urban departments, with improved working conditions and better pay as a result.

Because many jurisdictions forbid government employees from striking, other tactics are employed to create power negotiation in collective bargaining. Correctional officers have resorted to **"blue flu,"** the practice by uniformed personnel of taking sick leave en masse to back up their demands for improved working conditions, salary increments, and other items on their agenda. This method permits negotiating leverage without forcing the employees to strike, an illegal act.

As agents of public protection became more successful in their demands, their counterparts in the correctional institutions took notice. The great move in the late 1960s toward more professionalism and the sharp increases in prisoner populations, community corrections, and other programs pointed up some of the needs of the long-neglected correctional officer. Initial efforts to organize met with disapproval from administrators, often because of limited budgets and already overtaxed custody forces in the crowded prisons. Most administrators wanted the few available funds to be used for new personnel, not pay raises for the officers they already had. In some cases, the correctional officers did go on strike, and their duties were assumed by internal administrative and office personnel and by state troopers.[9]

INMATE ORGANIZATION: THE SOCIAL SYSTEM

key term

Total institution
Term describing institutional control over inmates and prison operations.

key term

Prisonization
The process of adopting the culture of the prison.

Prisons are **total institutions**[10] in which the residents' every moment, activity, movement, and option are carefully regulated by the correctional administrators. Inmates are given little individual responsibility and autonomy, important characteristics of everyday life in a modern achievement-oriented society. The tight regime compounds their personal inadequacies rather than correcting them. Cut off from ordinary social intercourse and their families and friends, then isolated in bastion-like prisons, inmates are quickly taught by the other residents how to exist in that environment. As we described earlier, the process of learning how to exist in prison—the appropriate attitudes and behaviors, the norms of prison life—is called **prisonization**. This process leads to the adoption of the folkways, mores, customs, and general culture of the prison.[11]

Former inmates can import prisonization into prisons if they are reincarcerated. It also occurs spontaneously even in newly opened institutions. The process is handed down from prisoner to prisoner, remaining a strong force that is later transmitted between prisons, working against the rehabilitation goals of even the most enlightened administrator. It impedes rather than facilitates treatment efforts, preventing inmates from acquiring the skills, talents, attitudes, and behavior necessary for successful adjustment in free society. Indeed, the opposite tends to occur: Inmates become more like infants[12] than mature adults.

As part of the process of prisonization, inmates learn codes and roles, and they are subjected to a reward and punishment system that encourages them to act like "good cons." Prison codes emphasize a number of specific behaviors: loyalty to other inmates ("never rat on a con"), maintenance of calm ("keep cool," "don't start feuds"), avoidance of trickery or fraud ("always share with your cellmates," "sell hoarded goods at the going rate"), manliness ("don't complain," "never cry"), and quick-wittedness in prison dealings ("don't be a sucker," "guards are screws, never to be confided in or trusted").

Inmates who conform to those expectations become "right guys," "home boys," or "stand-up guys" who can be trusted and are looked up to by other inmates. They share in the privileges available in prisons, and they can count on support if another inmate attacks them physically. Those who violate the normative structure become outcasts and are referred to by various descriptive and unpleasant names, such as rat, snitch, fag, merchant, fink, and punk.

Two recent developments in America's jails and prisons have exacerbated those problems. The first is the rise of gangs in prisons. Most of these gangs have street-gang origins and are racial or ethnic in nature, grouping together for power and protection. Conflicts

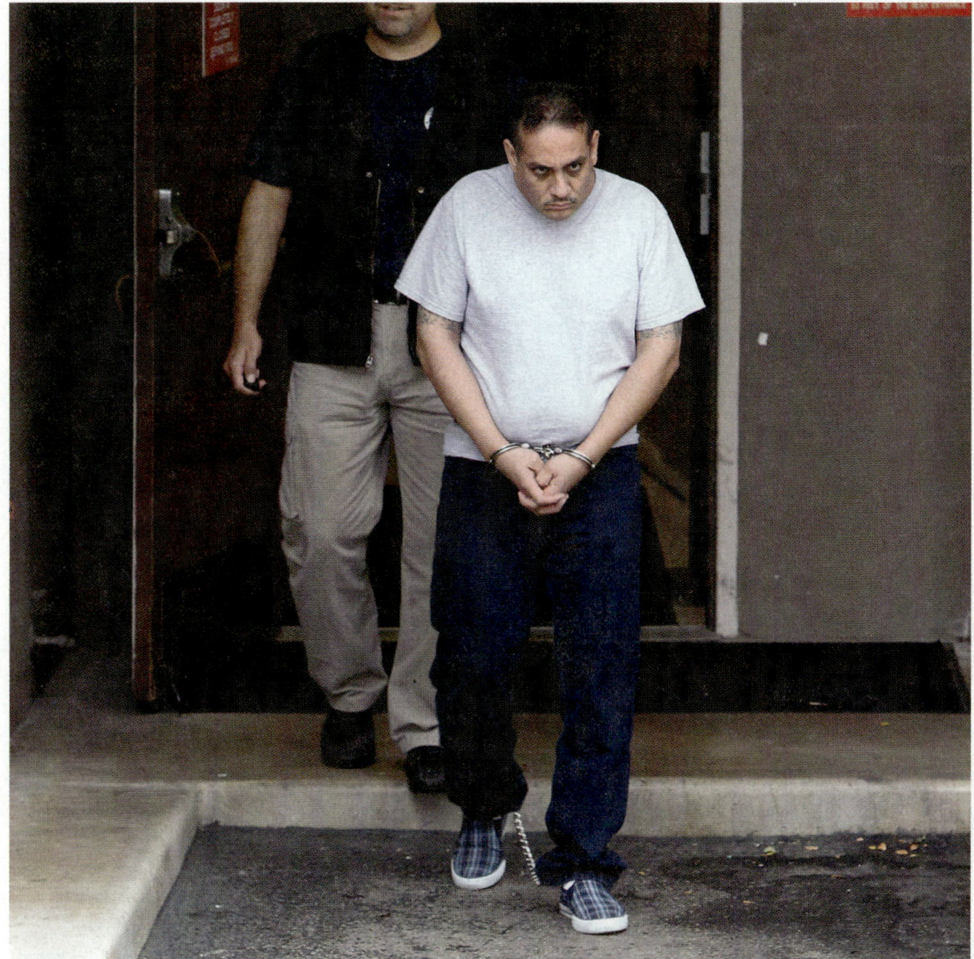

photo 7.3

Leg irons are used in prison.
ZUMA Press, Inc./Alamy.

key term

Lockdowns

Control of prison and inmates by not permitting inmates to leave their cells or rooms.

between the gangs have led to stabbings, murder outside prison, rape, blackmail, and exploitation of nonaligned prisoners. All prison gangs are organized strictly to take part in antisocial and criminal behavior. Many administrators have ordered **lockdowns** that confine prisoners to their cells to avoid bloodshed and violence. Such lockdowns have been criticized by legislators and other staff.[13] Jail and prison overcrowding has made matters worse, and many an administrator has resigned because of a sense of hopelessness. Due in large part to institutional threat groups, correctional managers have developed secure housing units to isolate and control violent and aggressive gang members and operations. See Chapter 8 for more detailed information.

We stress again that the importance of prisonization lies in its negative impact on attempts to provide rehabilitative programs that encourage inmates to engage in legitimate noncriminal activities.

CUSTODY AS A WAY OF LIFE

key term

Count

Method used to verify that all inmates are present in prison.

The *assistant superintendent for custody* or *security programs*, also known as the *deputy warden for custody* or the *captain of custody* in jails, is one of the most important figures in any correctional facility. His or her main responsibility is to develop ways of accounting for the whereabouts of all prisoners at all times. Techniques have become more humane and permissive in recent years, but in most institutions the **count** is still the principal method of determining the prisoners' whereabouts, and counts are sometimes conducted as often as every two hours. Preoccupation with counting and recounting prisoners makes it difficult to conduct meaningful programs or permit individualized operations. To some extent, however, outside work details and opportunities for educational and vocational training and furloughs have been included in more streamlined counting methods. Today, counts are often called in to a central office in the prison's control room and tabulated against the daily tally of inmates, in some cases using bar-coded wristbands, access cards with magnetic data stripes, and computers.[14] Although the count is more sensibly administered nowadays, it still remains the most important task for which the custody staff is responsible.

Another function of the custody staff is to establish and maintain security procedures. Security procedures, at a minimum, include the inspection of persons and vehicles passing

photo 7.4

A prison command center where all units of the institution are constantly monitored.
© David R. Frazier Photolibrary, Inc./Alamy.

in and out of the institution, usually at a **sally port** at entry and exit points. The sally port is an area enclosed by a double gate. A vehicle or individual enters through the first gate, which is then closed. Before the second gate is opened, the search for forbidden articles (contraband) is made. After the search is completed, the second gate is opened, and the individual or vehicle passes through that gate. At no time may both gates be open, and many gate systems are mechanically adjusted so it is impossible to open both at the same time. Sometimes a visitor feels it is as hard to get into the institution as it is to get out. The fear that inmates and visitors will try to smuggle in contraband or other items to assist escape pervades the maximum-security prison. Searches of vehicles and the requiring of visitors to pass through electronic metal detectors have become standard practices and procedures at major institutions.

key term

Sally port
Double-gated entry or exit point that restricts movement between the free world and prison.

Unfortunately, under the assumption that all inmates are alike, medium- and minimum-security prisons have also adopted similar security practices. It took over a century before America was prepared to build a prison without massive walls; it may take even longer to convince old-guard custody personnel that higher technology and less stringent security measures may serve as well to ensure control.[15]

Discipline and Inmate Traffic Control

Rules and regulations for inmates are usually aimed at strict traffic control. Prisoners' movements are carefully planned and controlled in every detail. In the past, all prisoners were awakened, moved to work, and fed at the same time, always under the eye of custody personnel. That degree of planning has slackened in many institutions; the trend is toward more reasonable controls over inmate traffic within the walls.

The suggestion that when inmates are treated as if they are dangerous they will become dangerous is generally considered valid. One way to avoid that problem is for staff and inmates to maintain meaningful communications. If the custody staff loses contact with inmates, the latter responds only to the inmate subculture. All too often, such limited interaction results in violence among the inmates. The most effective controls over inmate traffic and movement may well be those that guide our behavior in the free community.

The most recently available report on prison rule violators analyzed the characteristics of state prison inmates charged with infractions of institutional rules. Despite an increase of 64 percent in state prison populations from the previous study conducted 10 years earlier,

correctional **practice 7.1**

Nonlethal Weapons in Prison

As correctional facilities become more crowded, administrators are searching for nonlethal weaponry to run smarter and safer jails and prisons. One approach uses computerized inmate tracking and alarm systems to update the location of every inmate every two seconds. Inmates wear wristwatch-size devices that emit wireless signals that are collected by receivers and fed back along a cable system to display on a control-room computer the exact location of inmates. Lurking inmates are easily detected. Other facilities provide officers with pager-size wireless systems worn on their belts that automatically sound an alarm if the officer falls or is forced into a horizontal position. Assistance can immediately be dispatched.

In addition, various pepper spray devices can be carried on belts, sprayed from fire extinguishers, deployed from water pistols, or used with hoses to douse inmates up to 150 feet away. Pepper spray canisters in inmate dining rooms can be used to quell uprisings, riots, and gang disturbances. Some of these devices are marketed as nonlethal weapons filled with "food-grade pepper with water."

Guns that fire rubber bullets, hard rubber rounds, hard sponge devices, and bean bags are also being adopted as nonlethal armature for prisoner control in close environments, although lawsuits have been filed and are pending that allege excessive force, cruel and unusual punishment, and wanton infliction of unnecessary pain. Does the U.S. Constitution reach behind prison walls? The two major U.S. Supreme Court cases broadly spell out what is permissible in correctional personnel use of force against convicted prisoners: *Whitley v. Albers,* #84-1077, 475 U.S. 312 (1986), and *Hudson v. McMillan,* 390-6531, 503 U.S. 1 (1992).

some 54 percent of prisoners had infractions charged to them in both studies. Other important aspects of this study are as follows:

key term

Prison rules
Written documents designed to control inmate behaviors.

- Younger inmates and those with more extensive criminal careers or drug histories were the most likely to have violated **prison rules.**[16]
- Inmates housed in larger prisons or maximum-security prisons had higher percentages of rule violations than prisoners in other types of facilities.
- More than 90 percent of the inmates charged with violating prison rules were found guilty in prison administrative proceedings.
- The 90-percent-and-above rate of guilty decisions occurred for different racial/ethnic, age, and sex categories and did not vary by size or security level of the prison.
- Inmates serving their first sentence in prison had a lower average annual rate of infraction than did recidivists (1.6), regardless of how long they had served on their current sentence. A higher percentage of male inmates (53 percent) than female inmates (47 percent) was charged with rule breaking. On an average annual basis, however, women had a higher prison infraction rate than men (2.0 average violations per year versus 1.4 for men).
- Inmates who used drugs prior to admission were more likely to violate prison rules than were nonusers of drugs, 57 percent compared to 37 percent.
- Whites and blacks committed infractions at the same rate—approximately 1.5 violations per inmate per year. White and black rule violators reported nearly identical distributions of punishments received for rule violations. The most common penalties were solitary confinement or segregation and loss of good-time credit.

More recent studies of rule violation behaviors found that the pattern and types of misconduct were the same for males and females in a state prison, although levels of infractions were lower for women. Younger prisoners began their "misconduct careers" sooner.

A second study focused on major and minor ("serious" and "regular") infractions in a medium-security prison and found the ratio to be about 1:3, respectively. Minor infractions include theft of food, horseplay, lying, and use of abusive language to a correctional officer. More serious offenses include homicide, assault, possession of a weapon, and threatening to set a fire. The average processing cost of an infraction is estimated to be about $70 for each infraction charged that results in a finding of guilty. The figures tend to show that

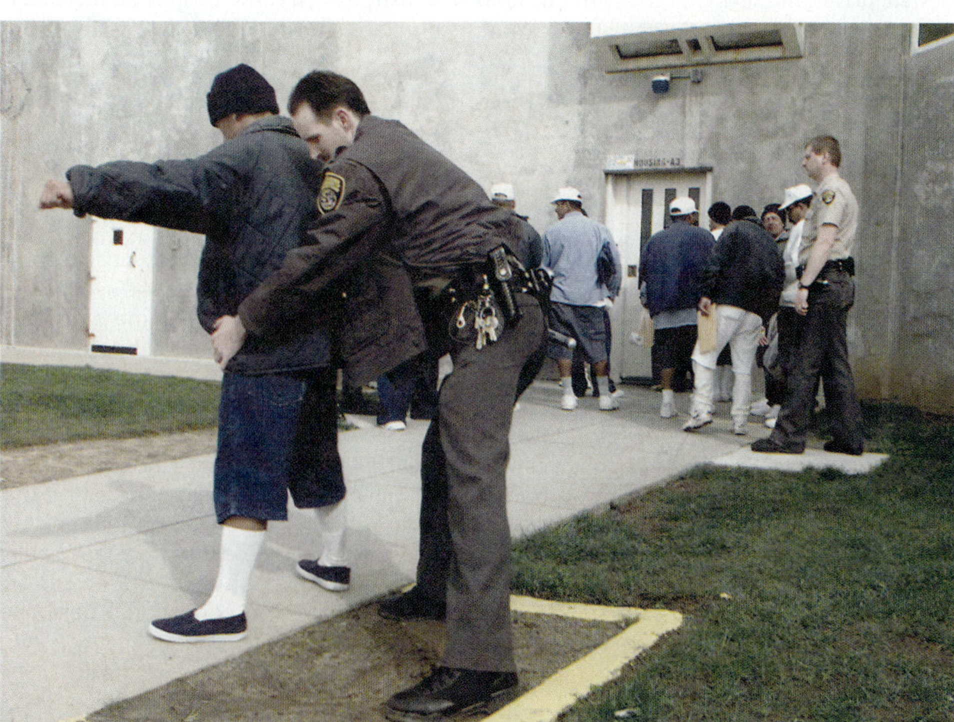

photo 7.5
A correctional officer searches an inmate at California State Prison, Sacramento, in Folsom, California. Guards throughout state prisons are being ordered to limit use of deadly force in breaking up inmate fistfights.
Photo by AP Wide World Photos.

the problems with inmate infractions do not seem to have increased any faster than the growing population and that disciplinary actions may deter many other rule infractions. Institutional rules were designed to regulate inmate behavior.

Note, however, that most correctional officers are dedicated and humane persons, and maximizing their potential is an important challenge to concerned administrators. The situation with regard to educating those officers is improving. Prison guards were once hired off the street and trained on the job. Most states now offer extensive preservice training to ensure a minimal level of competence in the officers before they are placed on the job; all states require at least minimal preservice training. The basic course ranges from 40 to 640 hours of preservice training. In-service training is generally 56 hours annually, but many states provide 80 hours.[17] As this trend continues, salaries, the quality of personnel, and working conditions will improve. The tendency to use outdated and counterproductive forms of discipline should decrease accordingly, and the correctional officer, long recognized as the single most important agent for change in institutions, will be able to realize his or her[18] potential contribution to the rehabilitation approach.

Contraband and Shakedowns

key term

Contraband
Any object forbidden in prison.

In early years of corrections in America's jails and prisons, **contraband** was officially defined as any item that could be used to break an institution's rule or to assist in escape. In practice, the term usually ended up referring to anything the custody staff designated as undesirable for possession by the inmates. Such banning power is unrestricted. It can start with a particular object, such as a knife, and extend to anything that might conceivably be made into a knife—a policy that has placed some relatively innocuous items on contraband lists.

Any item that is not issued or not authorized in the institution is contraband. Control of contraband is necessary for several reasons, including the following:

- To control the introduction of articles that can be used for trading and gambling
- To control the collecting of junk and the accumulation of items that make housekeeping difficult
- To identify medications and drugs and items that can be used as weapons and escape implements

Controlling contraband requires a clear understanding of what contraband is, of regulations that are designed to limit its entry into the institution, and of effective search procedures. The definition of contraband just given is simple and clear. However, this definition can become useless if the facility attempts to supplement it with a long list of approved items. If the institution permits prisoners to have packages, the problem of contraband control will be made difficult since the list of authorized items may grow long.

Long lists of approved and forbidden items often complicate what appears to be a relatively simple definition. A broad and clear definition, followed by the use of common sense by trained correctional officers, will usually result in better control and less conflict over what is or is not contraband. Prison administrators often see an excessively long contraband list as a challenge to the inmate and an indication of suppression. Such items as guns, however, are clearly dangerous contraband, and prison administrators must continually check packages, visitors, and correctional officers to detect such material. This is usually accomplished using modern metal detecting and X-ray equipment.

The generally accepted way of defining contraband was to use the affirmative approach. For example, "contraband is any item, or quantity of an item, that is not specifically authorized by the institution rules." This clearly defines what is not contraband and leaves the decision as to what is contraband to the inmate. Contraband is more often found to be the acquisition of excess items that are authorized (e.g., extra blankets, extra books, hoarded food) rather than those items that are dangerous per se. Amassing contraband in this sense is seen as an expression of an inmate's power and a way to beat the system and show fellow inmates that the forbidden can be done. That power is used to trade favors or show

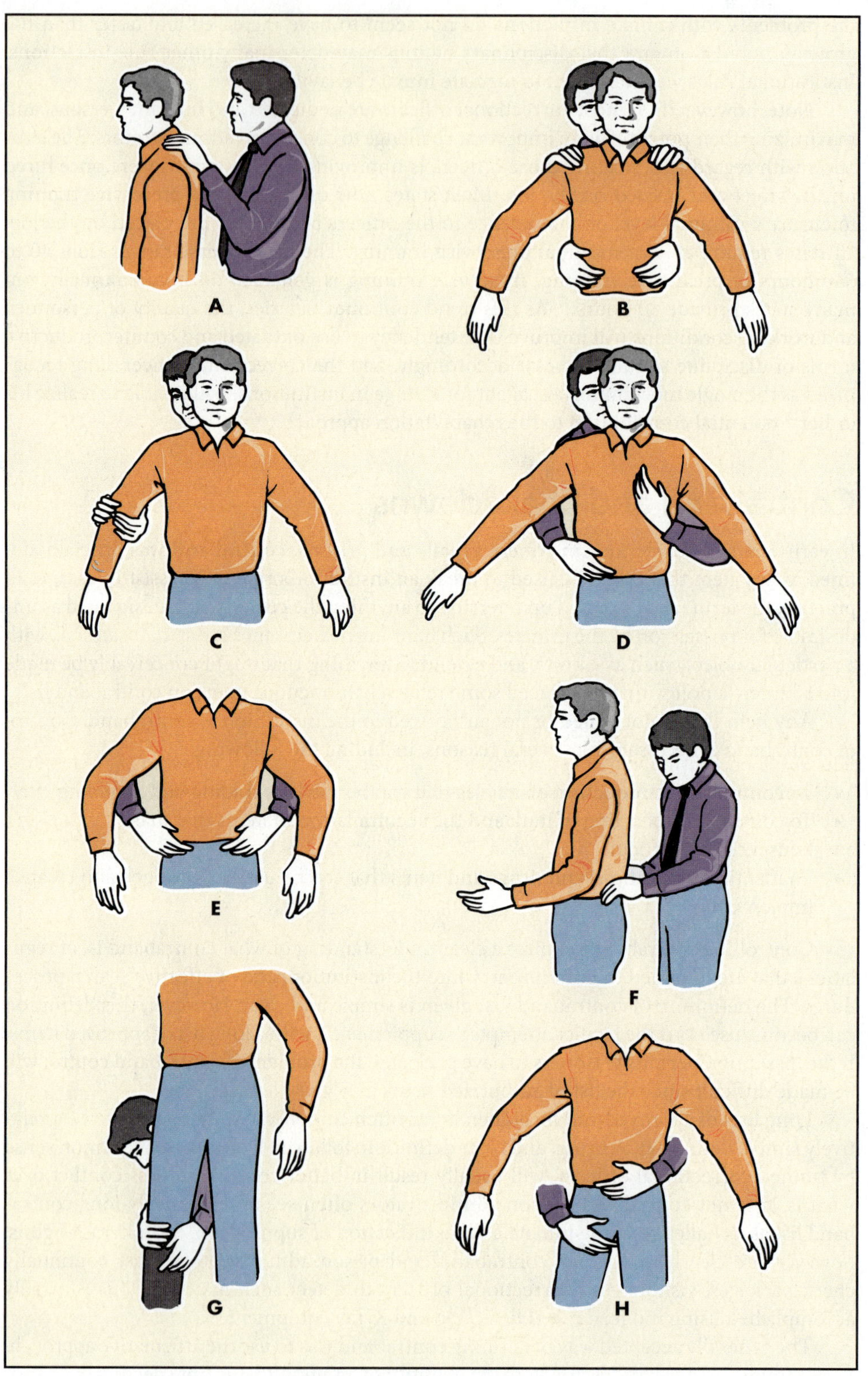

figure 7.4

The Frisk Search.

SOURCE: Nick Pappas, *The Jail: Its Operation and Management* (Lompoc, CA: Federal Prison Industries, 1971), p. 23.

favoritism to more powerful inmates. Contraband is often used in bartering and as currency (cigarettes and matches, for example) just as we use barter on the outside.

Because the loss of contraband is the loss of power, searches and shakedowns are another source of potential conflict with inmates in security institutions. The most common type of search to prevent contraband entry into and movement within institutions is the

frisk search. This type of search is used when prisoners enter or leave the institution and when institutional personnel suspect a prisoner may be hiding contraband on his or her person. Figure 7.4 shows the proper procedures for a frisk.

When a prisoner is suspected of having access to drugs, weapons, or other items that can be secreted on the body or in a body cavity and a frisk reveals nothing, a **strip search** may be conducted. The strip search is ordinarily made in a location where the prisoner will not be observed by other inmates and subjected to ridicule. The basic strip search requires only the visual observation of the entire body and orifices. If a more extensive body cavity search is merited, it must be conducted with the knowledge and permission of the chief administrator of the facility (superintendent, sheriff, etc.). Qualified medical personnel must conduct a body cavity search. Failure to follow those procedures can result in serious lawsuits against the institution.

Plastic capsules or vials inserted in the inmate's rectum are one way to hide (**"keester"** or "keestering") drugs and other small items of contraband, so when there is probable cause, body cavities may need to be examined. The strip search frequently follows visits, usually for every inmate or on a random sample basis. In the past, frequent strips were used to debase and abuse prisoners, a practice that greatly increased prison tension and resulted in many legal actions against offending staff. Frisks are a necessary part of institutional security, but if strip searches become part of an everyday routine, the procedure soon degrades not only the searched but also the searcher.

As rules prohibiting contraband grow more detailed, inmates seek ways to secret those items in the living area and throughout the institution. There is virtually no limitation to the ingenuity employed in hiding contraband in prisons. Ironically, the older—and presumably more "secure"—institutions and plants lend themselves best to secret hiding places. The process can almost be seen as a game, with correctional officers periodically searching the same old spots. The need for **shakedowns** (searching of an entire cell or cell block) is reduced when contraband rules are made realistic and humane; prohibiting such items as family pictures and toothpicks creates a needless irritant. The shakedown also has greater effect if used only to locate items that represent a clear and present danger to the institution, not just for the sake of what inmates call "Mickey Mouse" harassment.

key term

Frisk search
Process of detecting inmate contraband by manual search of the bodies of inmates.

key term

Strip search
Process of detecting inmate contraband by visual inspection of the bodies of inmates.

key term

"Keester"
To hide contraband objects within the rectum or vagina of prison inmates.

key term

Shakedown
Cell search to detect and control contraband.

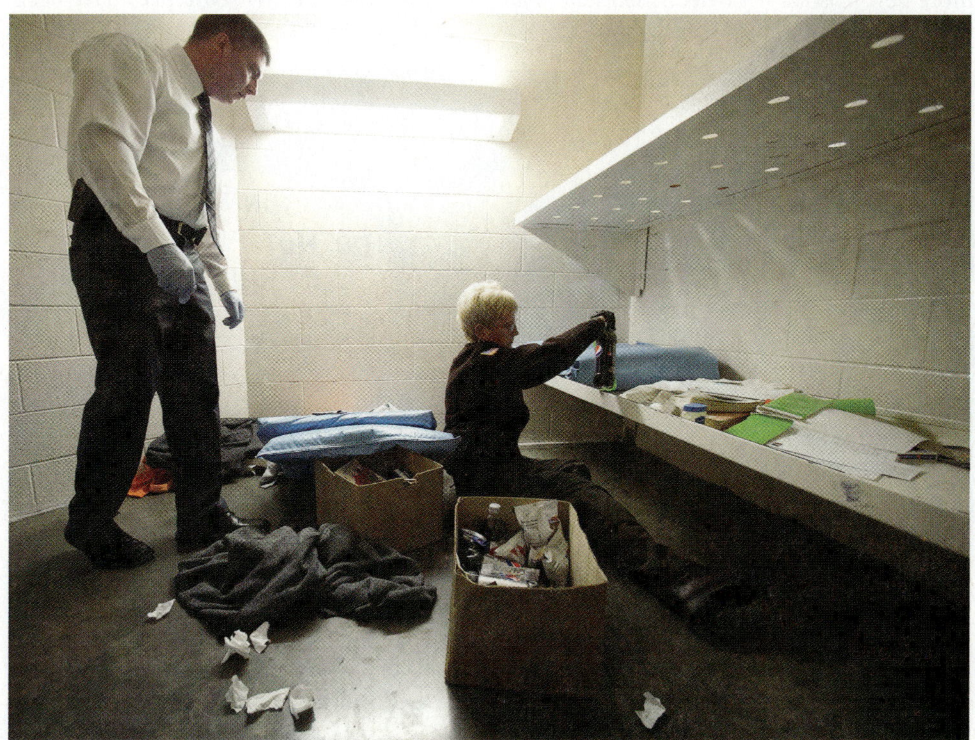

photo 7.6

Correctional officers search a cell for contraband, including weapons.
Scott Anger/AP Images.
Swikar Patel/AP Images.

PREVENTION OF ESCAPE

key term

Escape
Flight from prison facilities and illegal absences from institutions.

Maximum-security jails and adult prisons were built as though they had to contain the most dangerous creature imaginable. "A jail or prison is designed to be as strong as the strongest inmate" is an old correctional chestnut.[19] The high walls, corner towers, and armed guards are external signs of preoccupation with escape. The nature of most jail and prison populations, although changing to harder types, does not seem to justify that model. **Escape**[20] (flight of a confined person from an institution) and riots are serious concerns for administrators, however, and although in 2011 there were about 2,050 escapes and 3,417 returned escapees, most escapees were recaptured quickly.[21] They were mostly walkaways from minimum-security or community programs and represented only a miniscule percentage of the average daily population. When we consider the increasingly dangerous nature of some of the incarcerated inmates, this is actually a very good record (but bad news when they commit serious crimes while on escape status).

The conception of inmates as highly dangerous, when coupled with the extreme overcrowding of institutions, increases the concern of many correctional officers about the possibility of escape.[22] The issue is complex but revolves around two problems. The first is the philosophy of mass treatment, firmly established since the time when lockstep and silence were required for all prisoner movements. The second reason is political. Seasoned superintendents know that frequent escapes will be extremely damaging to their records, so their extreme measures to prevent them are directed toward all prisoners rather than toward the few who might actually try to escape. In a few prisons, however, administrators have begun to realize that a tax evader and an ax murderer do not have the same potential for escape attempts.

Technology to Prevent Escapes: Electrified Fences

key term

Electrified fence
Barrier to prevent inmate escape through electronic punishment or death.

The move to replace continuously staffed guard towers with lethal electrified perimeter fences could very well become a national trend because of state governments' urgent need to reduce operating costs. In November 1993, the California Department of Corrections and Rehabilitation (DOC) activated an electrified fence model at Calipatria State Prison in Imperial County. Since then, another 23 have been installed, one is under construction, and more new prisons with electrified fences are being planned. **Electrified fences** have been

photo 7.7
A roadside sign warns motorists not to pick up hitchhikers near North Kern State Prison vicinity, Delano, California.
Rich Pedroncelli/AP Images. Henryk Sadura/Alamy.

photo 7.8

The State of California uses electric fences in high-security facilities.
Lacy Atkins/Corbis.

installed at adult facilities for men and women throughout California's agricultural areas, foothills, deserts, and coastal and urban areas and a few at higher elevations.

At most of the facilities included in the California Statewide Electrified Fence Project, traditional perimeter guard towers are spaced at distances that allow correctional officers to use deadly force to prevent escapes. At newer facilities, as many as 10 towers (or 48.3 staff positions over three watches) can be deactivated. Using lethal fences greatly reduces the need for armed tower staff, for the fences can stop escapes by stunning or killing the inmates.[23]

Project Costs and Operational Savings

The construction cost of electrified fences varies depending on the perimeter length and site-specific conditions at each prison. The construction cost typically is within the range of $1 million to $2 million for an individual electrified fence of approximately 8,000 linear feet. The average cost is approximately $1.5 million. The operational cost savings of the electrified fence project result from the reduced staffing of the prison's guard towers and berm positions, minus the operations and maintenance costs of the fence and the additional roving patrol vehicle. Generally, the cost savings range between $400,000 and $2.1 million per year per prison, with an average operational cost savings of $1.38 million per year each. Therefore, the cost of each fence is recouped within the first or second year. For example, in California, the DOC estimates a systemwide reduction of more than 750 positions for a savings of approximately $40 million per year.

The Military Model

The need for an organized and effective custody and control force in jails and prisons has instilled a paramilitary flavor in most security staffs. The adoption of militaristic organizational structures and procedures early in corrections history made it easier to train a force with limited background to do a specific job. The **paramilitary model** is seen in the uniforms, titles, and procedures of custody personnel. Training is directed to the mission of security, and there is little emphasis on interaction with inmates. The model of the aloof but efficient guard has emerged, and the hiring of custody personnel until very recently was rarely based on the applicant's ability to work with people. The shift to unit management and new-generation prisons (see following discussion) has shifted prehire qualifications,

key term

Paramilitary model
Organization of custody staff into ranks of armed forces.

photo 7.9

A SWAT team stands watch outside the cafeteria where inmates were holding prison guards hostage at the Broad River Correctional Institution near Columbia, South Carolina. The inmates released the hostages and then surrendered.
AP Wide World Photos.

and potential officers are increasingly being hired for their "human-skills" qualifications. To a great extent, correctional hiring practices have inhibited those people who can best fulfill the newer mission of rehabilitation. The seniority system and the growing power of correctional officer unions still often discourage the infusion of custody personnel with higher education in the behavioral sciences.[24]

To provide the best entry-level personnel and to maintain a level of quality and growth in their staff, many jurisdictions have established rigid training standards along the lines recommended by the American Correctional Association. Such requirements will ensure that all staff are eventually exposed to methods that are not simply "more of the same." To reflect the population in institutions, personnel should actively recruit from minority groups, women, young persons, and prospective indigenous workers and see that employment announcements reach those groups and the general public.[25]

It is useful to conduct a task analysis of each correctional position (to be updated periodically) to determine the tasks, skills, and qualities needed. Hands-on testing based solely on relevant features, to ensure that proper qualifications are considered for each position, helps the administrator determine what is needed and can be provided by training. Those procedures will lead to an open system of selection in which any testing device is related to a specific job and is a practical test of a person's ability to perform, at an acceptable standard, the tasks identified for that job. Professionalization of corrections will continue well into this century, in part because it lowers the potential for a successful lawsuit.

These are a few of the steps that might help span the currently large communication gap between keepers and the kept. Correctional officers and custody staff spend more time with

correctional **practice 7.2**

Glass-Topped Cells for Violent Inmates

Surveillance of violent inmates in jails and prisons can be both dangerous and dirty. Even local jails using direct supervision experience frequent officer assault by violent inmates. When confined to their cells, these inmates routinely throw feces, urine, and other bodily fluids at officers. Some incarceration facilities are considering glass ceilings over special management unit cells for violent offenders, allowing the officers to walk on the glass ceiling, where they can observe and check on every movement of violent inmates yet not come into direct contact with them.

the inmate population than does anyone else in the institution. They should relate well to others because they can be the most positive agents of change in that corrections subsystem. They can also destroy any efforts toward change attempted by a treatment staff that tries to bypass them. A further move away from the military/police image to the correctional image is critical to effective change in the institutional setting.

UNIT TEAM AND OTHER METHODS TO AVOID COMPARTMENTALIZATION

With regard to ongoing conflicts between custody and security, a few final comments seem appropriate to show the student the situation is not hopeless. Many institutions already adhere to these concepts, and only the overcrowding, prison gangs, and violence are keeping progress in the slow lane.

First, policies should be developed jointly to define the relationships between critical custody and security functions. All staff must be involved in meeting rehabilitative program goals and custody needs for their institutions. The obvious dichotomy between custody and treatment must be erased and greater recognition given to the fact that each is supportive of the other. This kind of activity has been instituted in many institutions as **unit team management**, in which all members of the team of a given cell block, tank, pod, or wing work as a team to provide custody, support, and rehabilitative services in a single coordinated package.[26]

key term

Unit team management
Control scheme uniting all staff into a coherent and unified force to attain prison objectives.

Second, policies and guidelines for institutional rules and regulations should be developed and all present rules and regulations revised to ensure that the demands of security do not negate the objectives of treatment. In policy formation and in specific rules, the principle of clear and present danger should apply; if the regulation is required for the safety of the institutional community, it should be kept. If not, it should be abolished.

Third, in cases where force has been used on an inmate, videotaping of the extraction or other safety procedures should be conducted. When possible, a command officer should be present and a medical examination of the inmate undertaken. In addition, an investigation by the institution and/or an outside agency, resulting in a written report, should routinely be conducted, and that report should include information from the prison physician and by the inmate. Finally, the correctional authority should respond to requests from families that they be permitted to visit and see inmates if they believe excessive force has been used against them. If they desire an outside physician to examine prisoners, their request should be granted without delay, in accordance with rules to be promulgated by the correctional authority. Copies of all "Use of Force" reports should be filed with the correctional authority and be made available for inspection by the inmate's family, attorney, and, with the inmate's written permission, other appropriate people.

UPGRADING CORRECTIONAL PERSONNEL

The most important rehabilitative tool is the impact of one person on another. Thus, a primary goal for the correctional system is the recruitment, training, and retention of employees who are able—physically, emotionally, educationally, and motivationally—to work as a team. In the correctional system, including the nation's prisons and jails, it is hard to hire or keep qualified personnel. There are few reasons for the correctional officer and jailer to complain about salaries in the field. The national average pay of about $42,000 is not bad when one considers that the current minimum qualifications for applicants is usually only a high school diploma or equivalent (GED) and no criminal record.

But even now, still emerging from a nationwide recession, some jail and prison jobs go begging. With an average turnover rate of 14.6 percent, there are an estimated

28,448 vacant positions.[27] Because of the persistent problem of unfilled slots on most shifts, supervisors ask officers on duty to work another shift (work "doubles"). That situation leads to overtired staff and high overtime budgets, but legislators are seldom willing to increase expenditures for staff. They fear that correctional officers are just padding the rolls or perhaps are trying to avoid the costs of providing fringe benefits to more employees. Yet the fact is that prisons need a certain number of officers on duty at all times: "minimum critical staffing." Many administrators have tried to implement this concept, but budget needs still seem to override attempts at rationalizing staffing patterns.[28]

Perhaps more important than salary is the custody employees' sense of public rejection, reinforced in some institutions by the belief (whether true or false) that the administrators and professional staff do not consult them, treat them fairly, or care what they think.[29] New channels of communication must be opened between administrators and employees as well as between employees and inmates. Administrators should meet with staff to discuss employee problems; custodial and treatment staff should also meet together. Those meetings should be regularly scheduled and formally integrated into institutional procedures.

Summary

Outline the Organizational Structure of Prisons

As prison facilities developed, their administrators opted for bureaucratic control, accepting a military model for future development of the prison. This model features accepting and expanding the use of military ranks and scope of responsibilities. It is intended to maximize control of inmates, lessen the dangerousness to correctional personnel, prevent escape, and minimize potential for mass disturbances, including riots and security threat groups. Custody became even more important over the past 50 years, and inmate controls were refined and expanded.

Describe the Various Jobs and Functions of Prison Staff

The prison is managed by a warden, also known as a superintendent. The warden is the chief executive officer of the prison and manages all staff, recruitment, training, and discipline. The warden is assisted by deputy wardens for the areas of security, treatment, industry, and services. The military model is widespread in the prison industry, and lower-ranking officers assist in the custody and security of the facilities and services. The correctional officer, in a line position, conducts the daily functions of the institution and provides immediate supervision of both staff and inmates.

Outline the Recruiting, Hiring, and Retention of Prison Staff

Correctional staff are increasingly being recruited by expanding the search for possible employees from the general population and targeting female and minority communities. The goal is to have the correctional staff match the inmate population on demographic parameters. Background checks are conducted, and, in most jurisdictions, a list of possible hires is developed. One of the main dimensions of prehire eligibility is the applicants' managerial skills. Training programs are offered to new hires, and in-service training is stressed, A career track is used to encourage new hires who receive specialized in-house training and professional training offered by reputable providers. Staff recruitment and retention remain a hurdle for correctional systems, and the turnover rate remains high across the nation.

Describe the General Challenges and Issues Corrections Officers Face

Inmate control operations have, in the past two decades, been subject to court review and intervention. Certain procedures (such as the Alabama "hitching posts" and the Texas "deliberate indifference" to medical need) have been determined to violate portions of the U.S. Constitution that accords protections to all citizens, even imprisoned offenders. A pronounced rift has developed between institutional managers and correctional staff; in some facilities, officer attitudes toward employment, conditions of employment, and institutional legal assistance have become festering sores. Diminished control over inmates, coupled with new interactions between staff and administrators, has contributed to the unionization of correctional officers. The increased use of technology (electric fences, "officer down" alarms, and electronic inmate locators, for example) has served to counterbalance the dangerousness of life inside confinement facilities and create operational cost savings.

Summarize Prison Culture for Staff

The inmate social systems have undergone marked change since the 1950s. The population control exerted by "senior inmates" has diminished, and institution security threat groups have emerged. The latter pose major challenges to custody and institutional safety as well as between gang leaders and prison officers. Correctional officers have been corrupted in some prisons, and officer smuggling of contraband (drugs, alcohol, tobacco, and the occasional knife) has increased. Prison administrators have responded by formation of intelligence staff, frequent shakedowns of inmate cells, required security screening of correctional staff on entry to a facility, and lie detector use in questioned officer staff. The assassination of correctional administrators, judges, and correctional officers has led to increased pressure on justice personnel to "underperform" security duties.

Describe the Unique Challenges and Issues Faced by Female and Minority Corrections Officers

Historical stereotypes of females and minorities as being too weak or having inadequate motivation to serve as correctional officers have plagued both the recruitment and the retention of female and minority staff. Old-line correctional managers fear that the backup potential is inadequate if "weaker, dumber, or slacker officers" are hired. As such, hiring and retention issues have been impacted; recent new hires have exhibited desired qualities, the stereotypes are being undermined, and managing correctional staff has improved.

Summarize How a Prison Unit Is Managed

In the more traditional prison, the military model of ranks, chain of command, responsibility, and performance influence how the facility is run. There is a strong emphasis on following orders and security. Innovation is not emphasized; conformity is. The prison architecture stresses large congregations of inmates, and prison facilities are generally ranked by and inmates assigned on the basis of perceived custody needs. Treatment is usually not a major thrust in these facilities.

Recent developments in management theory and architectural design are focused on the unit team management system, stressing an effort to blur the custody–treatment division and forming a unit team. This is discussed more thoroughly below.

Describe Methods for Controlling Inmate Behavior

It has long been known that custody and treatment staffs do not trust each other and that the conflict can bifurcate inmate control. Many of the better-operated prison systems have adopted a new style (and required a changed architecture) in the development of unit team management. This dual-responsibility effort lessens compartmentalization and contributes to inmate control. Upgrading of prison staff will abet the need for additional inmate control. The unit management team strategy as described below is one method of developing a new style. Prison architecture is being changed to stress the increased number of specialized pods and wings and decrease the traditional housing and separation models.

Describe Methods for Preventing Escape

The basic tactic for prevention of escape remains the count of inmates, which occurs frequently in prison facilities. Electrified fences (often with lethal voltage levels), perimeter and gun-tower guards, information signs by prisons warning vehicle drivers of the presence of the prison and admonition not to pick up hitchhikers, and extensive video surveillance help to reduce escapes.

Explain the Unit Team and Other Methods Designed to Avoid Compartmentalization

In the past two decades, leading correctional administrators have initiated a different program and adapted correctional architecture that increases inmate deterrence, lessens social distances between the keeper and the kept, humanizes the environment within prisons, and enhances safety for staff and inmates. By creating prison pods and assigning teams of workers responsible for the activities of inmates therein, the perceptions of correctional officers by other workers have been blurred. All workers assigned to the team are responsible for the management of the assigned inmates, and treatment staff have more authority and responsibility than before. Yet all staff are collectively responsible for the activities of the prisoners with whom they interact. More innovations are anticipated.

Describe Ways in Which Correctional Staff Can Be Upgraded

Recent developments in hiring, training, and retention of correctional staff bode well for correctional practice. Prehire qualifications have been increased, training academies have flourished, in-service training has expanded, and staff monitoring has contributed to upgraded correctional practices. Providing correctional staff with a career ladder, offering specialized training for correctional officers, and rewarding competent workers increasingly leads to better-staffed and better-trained workers and, subsequently, safer working conditions.

Key Words

bureaucratic control, 158
custody, 158
general population, 159
graduated release, 159
correctional officers, 159
"screws," 162
unionization, 164
"Blue flu," 164
total institution, 164
prisonization, 164
lockdowns, 166
count, 166
sally port, 167
prison rules, 168
contraband, 169
frisk search, 171
strip search, 171
"keester," 171
shakedown, 171
escape, 172
electrified fence, 172
paramilitary model, 173
unit team management, 175

Review Questions

1. What is the primary focus of the bureaucratic style of prison management?
2. Where have prison guards been obtained from in the past? How does this situation create problems?
3. Why has the military model been so popular in the prisons?
4. Why do disciplinary and security considerations so greatly affect treatment programs? How can those issues be resolved?
5. What are the effects of imprisonment on inmates? Staff?
6. In what ways have the roles and positions of correctional officers improved during the past two decades?
7. Give a description of unit team management. How does it work?
8. Discuss the effects of a prison escape.
9. How can management and staff work toward making prison work more rewarding?
10. Does the use of the electric fence around the prison perimeter equate to the death penalty for attempting to escape from prison?

Application Case Studies

1. As deputy warden for custody, you hear from the inmate grapevine that a few officers are smuggling drugs into your prison. This has to stop. What would you do?
2. You are serving on the institution's classification committee and thus conduct an in-depth analysis of the behavior, characteristics, and affiliations of an incoming inmate. Law enforcement officers from the jurisdiction from which the inmate was committed and the sentencing judge report that the incoming inmate is a gang member. What actions would you recommend that the classification committee undertake?
3. A leader of one of your prison gangs threatens a female officer, telling her that she will beg for mercy when she is killed outside of the prison. What should the prison administrators do? (Do not insist that the gang leader be segregated in a single cell and that the keys be thrown away.)

Endnotes

1. Clifford English, "The Impact of the Indeterminate Sentence on an Institutional Social System," *Journal of Offender Counseling, Services and Rehabilitation* 8:1/2 (1983): 69–82; Victor Hassine, *Life without Parole: Living and Dying in Prison Today* (New York: Oxford University Press, 2010).
2. Michael Vaughn and C. Morrissey, "Violence in Confinement," *Journal of Offender Rehabilitation* 25:1/2 (1997): 21–42; Elizabeth Gudrais, "The Prison Problem," *Harvard Magazine*, September–October 2013.
3. David Bierie, "The Impact of Prison Conditions on Staff Well-Being," *International Journal of Offender Therapy and Comparative Criminology* 56:1 (2012): 81–96.
4. American Correctional Association (2013), "Warden, Division of Adult Institutions," http://cjca.net/index.php/cjca-news-2/334-california-department-of-corrections-and-rehabilitation-employment-opportunity (accessed September 2, 2013). See also Warden Career Profile (2013), "Prison Wardens: Combining Dedication and Protection," http://www.myonlinecriminaljusticedegree.com/criminal-justice-career/warden.asp (accessed September 2, 2013).
5. Research on prison wardens and superintendents is minimal. The major professional organization is the North American Association of Wardens and Superintendents, c/o Gloria Hultz, P.O. Box 11037, Albany, NY 12211-0037.

6. Alan Johnson (2013), "Director Views Inmate Suicide as Failure; New Steps Being Taken," *Columbus Dispatch,* http://www.dispatch.com/content/stories/local/2013/09/28/director-views-inmate-suicides-as-failures-new-steps-being-taken.html.
7. Donald Clemmer, *The Prison Community* (New York: Rinehart, 1940); Anthony Scacco, *Rape in Prison* (Springfield, IL: Charles C Thomas, 1975).
8. See Missouri Office of Administration (2013), "Corrections Officer III," http://content.oa.mo.gov/personnel/classification-specifications/5003.
9. Capitolfax.com (2013), "Legit Sickness or Blue Flu?," http://capitolfax.com/2013/01/06/legit-sickness-or-blue-flu/.
10. Carlene Firmin (2013), "We Must Identify Girls at Risk from Gangs," http://www.theguardian.com/society/2013/may/21/identify-girls-risk-gangs.
11. Venancio Tesoro (2013), "Prisonization and Its Effects," http://philippineprisons.com/2013/07/08/prisonization-and-its-effects/.
12. David Shichor and Harry Allen, "Correctional Efforts in the Educated Society: The Case of Study Release," *Lambda Alpha Epsilon* 39 (June 1976): 18–24. See also Judith Clark, "The Impact of Prison Environment on Mothers," *Prison Journal* 75:3 (1995): 306–329.
13. Jamey Dunn (2013). "Prison Assault Is Product of Overcrowding," http://illinoisissuesblog.blogspot.com/2013/05/afscme-prison-assault-is-product-of.html.
14. Peter Nacci, Kevin Jackson, and Karry Cothorn, eds., "The Future of Automation and Technology," *Corrections Today* 57:4 (1995): 66–120 (theme issue); Kevin Jackson, F. Roesel, T. Roy, et al., "Technology and Society," *Corrections Today* 60:4 (1998): 58–96 (theme issue).
15. Michael Reisig, "Rates of Disorder in Higher-Custody State Prisons," *Crime and Delinquency* 44:2 (1998): 229–244. See also Daniela Anasseril, "Care of the Mentally Ill in Prisons: Challenges and Solutions," *Journal of the Americana Academy of Psychiatry and the Law Online* 35:4 (2013): 406–410.
16. Lorenza Benton (2013), "Pelican Bay Prison Hunger-strikers' Stories," http://truth-out.org/news/item/18023-pelican-bay-prison-hunger-strikers-stories-lorenzo-benton.
17. Fox News (2013), "Texas Prison Guards to Join Inmate Lawsuit over Sweltering Jails," http://www.foxnews.com/us/2013/09/02/texas-prison-guards-union-to-reportedly-join-inmate-litigation-over-hot-state/.
18. Stephen Walters, "Changing the Guard," *Journal of Rehabilitation* 20:1/2 (1993): 46–60; Mark Pogrebin and E. Poole, "Sex, Gender and Work," in *Sociology of Crime, Law and Society,* ed. Jeffrey Ulmer (Stamford, CT: JAI Press, 1998), pp. 105–126; Ohio Department of Rehabilitation and Corrections (2013), "Corrections Training Academy," http://www.drc.ohio.gov/web/cta.htm.
19. See coverage of Eastern State Penitentiary (2013), http://www.easternstate.org/visit/regular-season/history-artist-installations/towercam.
20. Laura Sullivan (2013), "50 Years Later, Mystery of Alcatraz Escape Endures," http://www.npr.org/2012/06/12/154766199/50-years-later-mystery-of-alcatraz-escape-endures.
21. American Correctional Association, *2012 Directory of Adult and Juvenile Correctional Departments, Institutions, Agencies, and Probation and Parole Authorities* (Alexandria, VA: American Correctional Association, 2012), pp. 38–40 and also pp. 44–45.
22. USAJOBS (2013), "Bureau of Prisons/Federal Prison System," http://www.bop.gov/jobs/; James Lyons, *Inmate Escape Incidents 1992–1996* (Albany, NY: Department of Correctional Services, 1997); Centre for Research Evaluation and Social Assessment, *Escape Prisoners: Inside Views of the Reasons for Prison Escapes* (Wellington: New Zealand Ministry of Justice, 1996); Matt Clarke, *Prison Legal News* (2013), "Allegations of Contraband Smuggling: Sex and Corruption at Texas Prison," https://www.prisonlegalnews.org/news/2009/jan/15/allegations-of-contraband-smuggling-8232sex-and-corruption-at-texas-prison/.
23. Brian Hoffman, Gary Straughn, Jack Richardson, and Allen Randall, "California Electrified Fences: A New Concept in Prison Security," *Corrections Today* 58:4 (1996): 66–68. See also Florida Department of Corrections (2013), "Inmate Escape Report," http://www.dc.state.fl.us/pub/escape/quarter/.
24. Joshua Page, "Prison Officer Unions and the Perpetuation of the Penal Status Quo," *Criminology and Public Policy* 10:3 (2011): 735–770.
25. New Jersey Civil Service Commission (2013), "State Corrections Officer Recruit Examination Administration Guide," http://www.state.nj.us/csc/seekers/jobs/safety/2013%20State%20Correction%20Officer%20Recruit%20Examination%20administration%20guide.pdf.
26. U.S. Bureau of Prisons (2013), "Admission and Orientation Handbook," http://www.bop.gov/locations/institutions/mon/MON_aohandbook.pdf.
27. American Correctional Association, *2012 Directory.*
28. John Shuiteman, "Playing the Numbers Game: Analysis Can Help Determine Manpower Requirements," *Corrections Today* 49:1 (1987): 40–42. See also Henry Steadman, S. Steadman, and D. Dennis, "A National Survey of Jail Diversion Programs for Mentally Ill Inmates," *Hospital and Community Psychiatry* 45:11 (1994): 1109–1113, and Marcus Nieto, *Health Care for California State Prisoners* (Sacramento: California Research Bureau, California State Library, 1998).
29. Carl ToersBijins (2013), "Stress: The Silent Correction Officers Silent Killer," http://www.corrections.com/articles/31896.

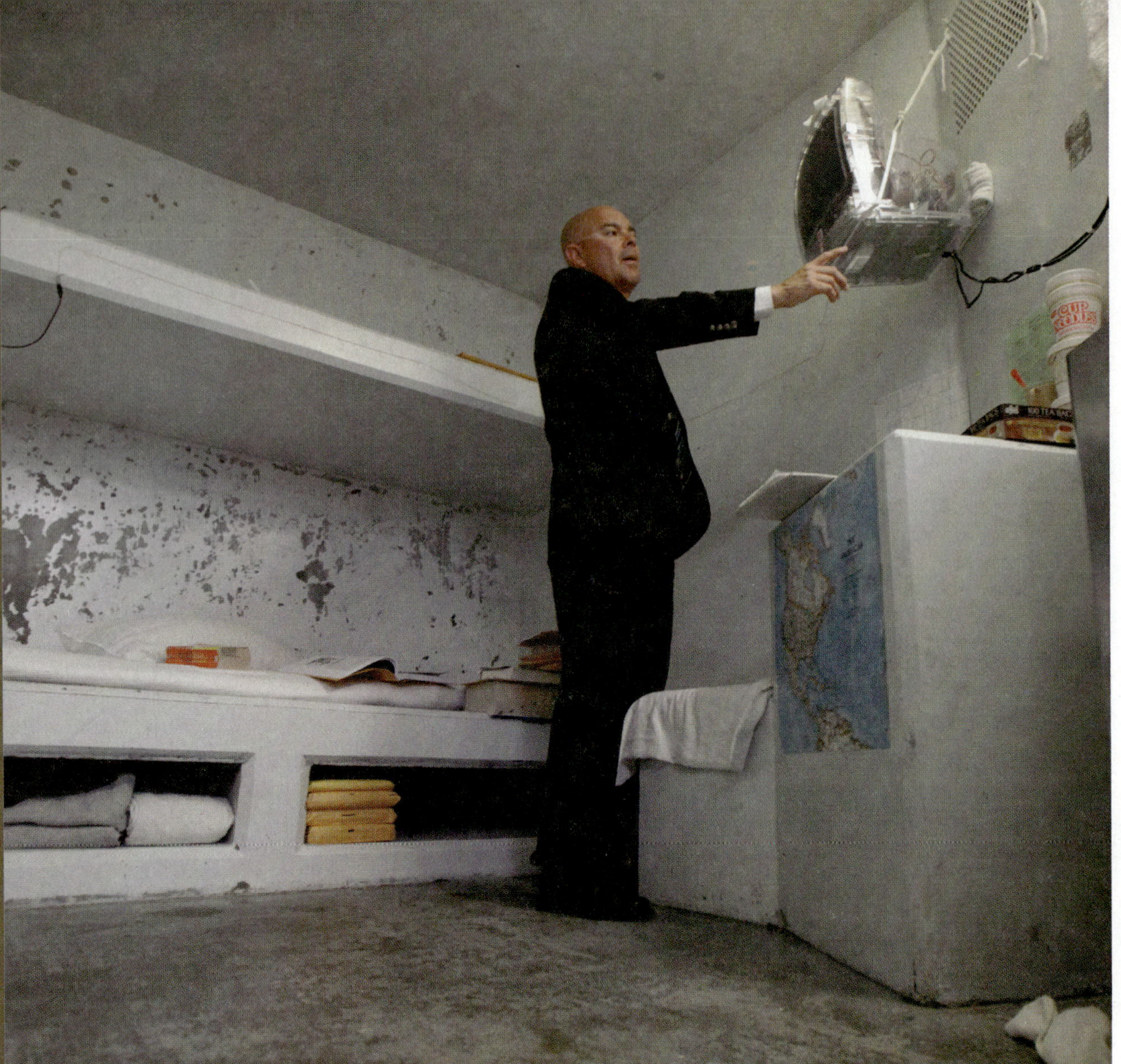

Rich Pedroncelli/AP Images.

Objectives

- Summarize the threat of prison gangs within prison and after release from confinement.
- Explain the basic history of gang development and gang differences.
- Identify the scope of criminal activities perpetrated by prison gangs.
- Explain the role of intelligence in coping with prison gangs.
- Outline basic interdiction and control programs for security threat groups.
- Describe the influence security threat groups exert on correctional staff.

chapter 8 Security Threat Groups and Prison Gangs

Outline

Security threat groups are one form of domestic terrorism.

"Homeland Security and Intelligence: How We Know." Public lecture given to the Seven Lakes Country Club, Palm Springs, CA, April 6, 2013.

—Bruce S. Ponder

Overview

You will recall that, in Chapter 7, the emergence and challenges of security threat groups (also known as "prison gangs") were introduced but not widely discussed. Originally known as "prison gangs," contemporary correctional practice is to use the broader term "security threat groups," although on occasion the term "prisons gangs" is used (as per the published source). In this chapter, we deal with a number of criminal gangs, their activities, threats, and management issues. We focus on the creation of prisons gangs, now collectively known as prison security threat groups. In addition, we focus on the extent of cooperation and collective actions perpetrated by these groups, with a brief historical discussion of their formation.

SECURITY THREAT GROUPS

First, we deal with the definition of a **security threat group (STG)**. Many students and law enforcement officials struggle with a concise but accurate definition. An initial definition to be used in this chapter is this: STGs are criminal organizations that originated within the penal system and operate within correctional facilities throughout the United States, although released members may be operating on the street. The gangs are also self-perpetuating criminal entities that can continue their criminal operations outside the confines of the penal system.

In broad stroke, criminal gangs, regardless of their location, fall into five categories of offenders:[1] street gangs, prison STGs, outlaw motorcycle gangs (OMGs), one percenter OMGs, and neighborhood/local street gangs. Most STGs have their own membership symbols. Working definitions of these groups, another point in which not all investigators agree, are the following:[2]

Street gangs are criminal organizations formed on the street operating throughout the United States.

Prison gangs (now known as STGs) are, as above, criminal organizations that originated within the penal system and operate within correctional facilities in the United States, although released members are frequently operating on the street. Prison gangs are also self-perpetuating criminal entities and entities that can continue their criminal operations outsides the confines of the penal system.

OMGs are organizations whose members use their motorcycle clubs as conduits for criminal enterprises.

One percenter OMGs are any group of motorcyclists who have voluntarily made a commitment to band together to abide by their organization's rules, enforced by

key term

Security threat group (STG)
Any organization or group of three or more persons having as one of its primary activities the commission of one or more criminal acts within the prison setting.

key term

Street gang
Criminal street gang means any ongoing organization, association, or group of three or more persons, whether formal or informal, having as one of its primary activities the commission of one or more of the criminal acts, having a common name or common identifying sign or symbol, and whose members individually or collectively engage in or have engaged in a pattern of criminal gang activity.

key term

Prison gang
A correctional term used earlier in the gang development process but now coterminous with STG.

key term

Outlaw motorcycle gang (OMG)
OMGs are organizations whose members use their motorcycle clubs as conduits for criminal enterprises.

Photo 8.1
Gang members shooting gang signs in Florida.
Estevan Oriol/PYMCA/Alamy.

violence, and who engage in activities that bring them and their club into repeated and serious conflict with society and the law. To fit this definition, the group must be an ongoing organization, associations of three or more persons who have a common interest and/or activity characterized by the commission of or involvement in a pattern of criminal or delinquent conduct. The Bureau of Alcohol, Tobacco, Firearms, and Explosives estimates that there are approximately 300 one percenter OMGs in the nation.

Neighborhood/local street gangs are confined to specific neighborhoods and jurisdictions and often imitate larger, more powerful national gangs. The primary purpose for many neighborhood gangs is drug distribution and sales.

key term

One percenter OMG

Any group of motorcyclists who have voluntarily made a commitment to band together to abide by their organization's rules enforced by violence and who engage in activities that bring them and their club into repeated and serious conflict with society and the law.

key term

Neighborhood/local street gang

Neighborhood or local street gangs are confined to specific neighborhoods and jurisdictions and often imitate larger, more powerful national gangs.

It has been argued that there are 1.4 million active street, prison, and OMG gang members found in the more than 33,000 gangs in the United States. Collectively, "gangs are responsible for an average of 48 percent of violent crimes in most jurisdictions, and up to 90 percent in others."[3] The NGIC reports that gangs are increasingly committing nontraditional gang-related crime (prostitution, assaults, kidnapping, murder, smuggling, and human trafficking) and engaging more in such white-collar crime as mortgage fraud, identity theft, and counterfeiting.

Even while incarcerated, gang members continue to direct and coordinate gang activity.[4] Gang members use family members to assist or facilitate gang activities during the gang members' imprisonment. Messages are also written in tiny script on small pieces of paper, to be smuggled out and distributed to gang leaders in the free world. Gangs also encourage relatives and others to work in law enforcement, judiciary, and other legal occupations so as to gather information on what law enforcement activities might reveal on the operations of other gangs as well as home addresses of justice employees. Gang member operations have also been identified in the nation's military, where, in their role as military personnel, they learn the operation of a variety of high-powered firearms, equipment, and combat techniques as well as communication devices (cell phones, cyber-crime, e-mail messaging, communication through the Internet, and recruitment of members as well as infiltration of computer systems).

HISTORY OF GANG DEVELOPMENT AND GANG DIFFERENCES

Since the 1960s, small groups of disruptive inmates could be found in most institutions. Some members united behind ethnic, racial, or ideological divisions. Correctional administrators quickly noticed their presence and potential disruptiveness. At that time, prison investigators focused on identifying gang members who had created a formal structure, such as by-laws, or mission statement or even constitutions. But less visible or smaller groups could be disruptive, and the term "prison gangs" was changed to "security threat groups" to reflect the presence of a mix of gangs.

During the period of the 1960s and 1970s, prison gangs tried primarily to unite inmates both for self-protection and for monopolization of illegal prison operations, all for monetary gain. Gang rivalry developed, and gang members bonded to protect their gang members from predatory and violent members of other gangs. Violence escalated. In the 1980s, inmates described themselves as **political prisoners** and assumed the role of liberators of the oppressed. Alliances of gang members in the community spread, and they were interested primarily in profiting from illegal prison crimes, avoiding gang conflicts, and increasing income from drug traffic. As an example, if a prison contains a large number of drug addicts and a gang supplies those illegal drugs (as well as tobacco

key term

Political prisoner

A political prisoner is someone who is imprisoned for his or her participation in political activity.

key term

Secure housing unit (SHU)
"Control units" within prisons, including single-cell and cell-confinement practices, to lessen directives by inmates to outside criminal organizations.

key term

Correctional officer corruption
A form of misconduct by correctional officers in which officers seek personal gain, such as money or protection from inmate violence, through the abuse of power, such as accepting bribes in exchange for not pursuing an investigation or not writing up an inmate for proscribed behavior. Includes criminal acts forbidden by the prison, such as smuggling drugs or alcohol or excessive use of force for vengeance.

key term

"Bad news list"
A list of persons the group defines as troublesome, unwelcome, or dangerous and are to be harmed, sanctioned, or killed.

key term

Racially or ethnicity-oriented prison gang
Prison gang comprised almost exclusively of offenders from the same racial background, place of birth, or residence.

key term

Graffiti
Unauthorized writing or drawing on a public surface, such as a wall, building, fence, and so on, defacing it.

and alcohol) within the prison compound, the gang stands to profit both financially as well as by influence. Such influence and power frequently compel drug users to obey the STG's orders.

The War on Drugs swept up both small-time addicts supporting their habits by selling drugs to others and higher-level operatives. Former inmates were apprehended and returned to confinement, as were higher-level drug suppliers. Gang leaders among the returned offenders began to exert directions to free-world organized-crime members and to control and coordinate criminal activities on the outside as well as the inside of the prison. Correctional administrators decided to lessen that activity by isolating gang leaders through segregation and developing highest-security **secure housing units (SHUs)**. These single-celled and cell confinement practices have lessened the directives to outside criminal organizations but have not completely controlled inmates and organizations. In California, most institutional threat group leaders are housed in the strongest controlled prison units, known as "special housing units" (such as the prison at Pelican Bay, California), where they are single-celled almost 24 hours a day. The objective is to provide long-term, segregated housing for inmates classified as the highest security risks or as STGs or prison gangs. The leadership's control over free-world crime has been lessened but not been extinguished.

Finally, on a contemporary note, released gang members and their associates are required to increase the gang's activities when released or face the threat of violence if they do not. Correctional officers are pressured to smuggle drugs and other illegal substances as a means to protect themselves from the powerful institutional threat groups, a form of self-defense and **correctional officer corruption**. One example will suggest the range of criminal involvement of the institutional threat groups. To maximize profits from drug sales and distributions, some mothers, wives, girlfriends, and others are required to meet a "sales goal" set by the organization and to deposit some 25 percent of those sales in bank accounts controlled by gang members. Those who fail to conform and even correctional staff may find themselves on the **"bad news list,"** from which free-world associates are to enforce gang discipline.

IDENTIFYING PRISON GANG MEMBERS

There are too many institutional threat groups to make meaningful conclusions and generalizations across the entire country in the state, federal, and territorial jurisdictions. Complicating this effort is the fact that prison gang names may be the same as another prison gang in another jurisdiction but bear no similar organizational, criminal enterprise, membership, or level of threat. We mention here only a few of the major STGs and, where relevant, their "enemy gangs." Students looking for more detail are encouraged to use the Internet to search for more information, using such search terms as "security threat group" with the name of the organization or jurisdiction you might want to examine (Chicago, Texas, Florida, Illinois, and so on).

Many (but not all) gangs are **racially or ethnicity oriented**. They are frequently seen in prisons, and members are identified by individuals' use of hand signs, tattoos, aggregation in the prison exercise yard, and colors. They engage in criminal activity, share a common prison gang name, associate together on an almost continuous basis, use explicit **graffiti**, bear gang tattoos, and stake out claims on prison areas. One such group is the Aryan Brotherhood.

Identifying a gang member is relatively easy but requires gathering of intelligence to be accurate. Many of these approaches are addressed in the American Correctional Association's Professional Certification course, which that leads to the officer's certification as "Corrections Supervisor/STG." Correctional investigators focusing on identifying gang members look for the following:

1. The inmate under classification admits to being a member of a particular STG.
2. Other inmates (and law enforcement officers) identify a given individual as being a member of a STG. This usually requires a reliable informant.
3. Even informants with as yet unproven reliability might identify the individual and STG to which he belongs, with another source making the same identification.
4. The inmate may have been arrested in the company of other known gang members, committing crime reflecting gang activity (execution, drug trafficking, human trafficking, extortion, and other criminal acts).
5. An incoming prison inmate lived in or frequented a gang crime zone known to evidence gang activity.

The correctional investigator usually makes the gang affiliation identification based on an inmate's possession of at least two of these factors.

Some of the major **Hispanic STGs** are the following:

1. La Eme, or the **Mexican Mafia**, a gang populated mainly by Hispanics but with some Caucasian members. They are allied with the Aryan Brotherhood. Their major enemy is the *Nuestra Familia* (in Spanish, "our family").
2. The **Texas Syndicate** is another primarily Hispanic group that occasionally accepts Caucasian members. The main STG with which they associate is the "Border Brothers," comprised largely of Mexican immigrant prisoners.
3. The final Hispanic group listed here are the *Nñtas,* comprised of Hispanics from Puerto Rico and found along the eastern coast of the nation. Their major enemy is the United Blood Nation.

Photo 8.2

Incarcerated white supremacists pose a direct threat to members of other gangs and "hang out" together for self-defense.
A. Ramey/PhotoEdit.

Photo 8.3

Barry Mills, cofounder of the Aryan Brotherhood.
Orange County Register/AP Images.

key term

Hispanic STG
Groups of inmates of Latino origin who have formed STGs within prison for intramural and community criminal activities.

key term

Mexican Mafia
A large and disruptive STG composed of Hispanic prison inmates drawn primarily from Mexico, and the largest STG in Texas. The Mexican Mafia is structured under paramilitary lines with a president, vice president, and generals that members are expected to follow strictly.

key term

Texas Syndicate
The Texas Syndicate (Spanish: *Syndicato Tejano*) is a (mostly Texas-based) prison gang that includes about 20,000 Hispanic members. The Texas Syndicate has been more associated or allied with Mexican immigrant prisoners ("border brothers") and is based on a paramilitary model.

key term

The 211 Crew
The 211 Crew was founded in 1995 by Benjamin Davis at Colorado's Denver County Jail. 211 Crew operates under a loose or semiorganized structure, common in newer prison gangs with younger members. The prison gang focuses on generating illegal funds and committing crimes such as robbery, theft, and drug dealing.

key term

Shot caller
A group leader with authority to order events or changes, such as assault on a member of another prison gang.

Photo 8.4

Gang member tattoos affirm inmate identity and serve as warnings to correctional officers and other prison inmates.
Andrew Lichtenstein/Corbis.

Other non-Hispanic STGs include the following:

1. Most *African American* STGs retain their original street names. This includes both the Crips and the Blood groups. The Black Guerilla Family, an originally politically based gang, has a leading presence in prisons.
2. The "Folk Nation," found in both southern and midwestern states, is allied with the Bloods and intense rivals of the People Nation.
3. Finally, the "D.C. Blacks," located in the nation's capital, were founded by African American inmates. Their enemies are the Aryan Brotherhood and the Mexican Mafia.
4. *Caucasian* STGs include the Aryan Brotherhood, a group frequently found in "supermax" prisons. Many gang members are incarcerated or under indictment.
5. The Nazi Low Riders are a relatively new white STG whose members are frequently found in the supermax housing units in California or have been transferred to federal prisons.

CRIMINAL ACTS OF STGS

Before we speak about managing STGs in corrections, it would be helpful to know more about some of the criminal activities of members of prison and outside-world gang members. These crimes are only suggestive of the range of activities and syndicated coordination across gangs. First, it should be remembered that STGs's criminal activities are intended to generate cash and assets. They might be seen as splintered "corporate" businesses, preying on the wealthy, the addicted, and marginal criminals, such as local corner-drug sellers and prostitutes. They practice blackmailing, kidnapping, extortion, and violence, the latter to cement their control over a criminal activity. The violence can frequently be ordered by key gang members incarcerated in correctional facilities and includes assassination of the state directors of corrections, judges, law enforcement, district attorneys, and other justice personnel, including correctional staff. Violence is also used to achieve monetary goals and corporate power. As an aside, some investigators describe STGs as **domestic terrorist groups**.

It is not unusual for imprisoned gang members to threaten and intimidate correctional officers, minimizing correctional order and control.[5] Such threats also maximize the comfort enjoyed by STG members, protect gang members, gain power over non-aligned inmates, and extend their criminal reach beyond prison walls.[6] See Correctional Profile 8.2, for an example of gang activities in both the prison and the free world.

key term

White supremacist soldier
A low-ranking member of a white prison gang who acts on the orders of a higher gang officer. In this example, the prison gang claims that white people are superior to other ethnic groups.

key term

Domestic terrorist group
Terrorist group that operates within the nation or commits crime in the local law enforcement jurisdiction.

key term

Evidence-based classification system
A practical criminological procedure intended to identify the behavioral characteristics of certain offenders and use of those attributes to classify inmates as gang members or not.

MANAGING STGS IN CORRECTIONAL FACILITIES

Managing STGs within a correctional facility is a complex process, primarily due to the need for exact information and the need for an **evidence-based classification system**. Neither of these is readily available and must be developed. We start here with a complex approach.

First, those who manage prison gangs need to know what behaviors, membership, and traits indicate gang membership. The intent of identifying such illegal behavior and classification is to detect a suspect's or gang's membership and take effective steps to isolate any suspected gang member from the ability to operate within the prison. **Interdiction** will lead to gang suppression and inmate segregation. Another intent is to weaken gang ties and

correctional **profile 8.1**

Profiles of Texas: Seven Major Gangs

Texas prisons contend with seven major gangs. Each insists on a lifetime commitment: Once committed to one of these organizations, death is the only way out. Each prison gang is highly structured and operates under a specific "constitution" or set of rules. What follows is a brief description of these gangs and their histories.

- **Texas Syndicate** The Texas Syndicate began in the California Department of Corrections in the mid-1970s. It is made up mostly of Hispanic inmates who migrated to California from Texas, although a few white inmates have been accepted. Through violent acts, the gang made a reputation for itself as a group to be feared and respected among general-population inmates.

  On release from the California Department of Corrections, gang members returned to Texas and continued their illegal activities. Many were subsequently incarcerated in Texas. Since their arrival in Texas, gangs have been involved in more than 48 inmate and many correctional officer and other prison staff homicides as well as numerous other nonfatal assaults on staff and inmates.

  The Texas Syndicate is structured along paramilitary lines and has a set of strictly enforced rules; violations may result in death. The group's members are known to have been incarcerated in California, New Mexico, Arizona, Florida, Illinois, and the Federal Bureau of Prisons.

- **Mexikanemi** Mexikanemi, or MM, is the largest and fastest-growing prison gang in the Texas Department of Criminal Justice (TDCJ). Mexikanemi is an Aztec term meaning "free or liberated Mexican." The group originated in Texas prisons in the early 1980s. It initially started as a group of inmates interested in their cultural background, but it rapidly transformed into a prison gang involved in extortion, narcotics trafficking, and assaults on inmates and staff.

  The gang is structured along hierarchical lines, with a president (its founder), a vice president, and three generals, each of whom is responsible for a specific region in the state. Generals can appoint members under them to run activities in specific facilities.

  The gang's constitution states that "in being a criminal organization, we will function in any aspects or criminal interest for the benefit or advancement of the gang. We will traffic in drugs, contracts of assassinations, prostitution, robbery of high magnitude, and anything we can imagine."

- **Aryan Brotherhood of Texas** This group, made up of white racist inmates, originated in the TDCJ in the early 1980s and should not be mistaken with other groups with similar names found across the country.

  The Aryan Brotherhood of Texas has been involved in assaults and murders of inmates in Texas and also conspired to have a state judge assassinated. Operating under a structure resembling a steering committee or a commission, this group has extended its illegal activities to the outside.

- **Texas Mafia** The Texas Mafia is made up of mostly white inmates, but a few Hispanics have been accepted. The gang has an extensive background in narcotics; many of its members are involved in producing crystal methamphetamine and have ties with motorcycle gangs. The group is very violent and has been involved in inmate homicides and staff assaults. It has a close working relationship with the Texas Syndicate.

- **Nuestro Carnales** This group has fewer than 100 members. However, they have established a reputation for violence by being involved in several inmate assaults, including one homicide. Formed along a hierarchy structure with one recognized leader, this group is attempting to gain a foothold in the community as well as maintaining its status inside the prison walls. This gang appears to have strong ties with the Texas Syndicate.

- **Hermanos de Pistoleros Latinos** Composed of 174 members within TDCJ, this group has posed security problems for the agency by being involved in numerous illegal activities, including inmate assaults and inmate homicides. An additional 104 members have been released to the community and will have an impact for outside law enforcement agencies. This group appears to have ties with the Texas Syndicate and has been known to discuss joint illegal activities with that group.

- **Raza Unida** This group is the most recent to be identified as a disruptive group within the TDCJ. With a membership of only 64 members, this group has yet to achieve the status and respect afforded the other prison gangs by the inmate population. However, they are rapidly gaining notoriety due to their recent assaults on inmates at various facilities within the agency. Classification of inmates from one specific region has assisted the group in forming and evolving into a prison gang.

SOURCE: Salvador Buentello, "Texas Turnaround: New Strategies Combat State's Prison Gangs," *Corrections Today* 54:5 (May 1992): 59. See also Gary Klivans, "Gang Codes: Gang Identity Theft," *American Jails* 22:4 (2008): 70–77, and Gary Klivans, "Gang Codes: Not Hiding in Plain Sight," *American Jails* 22:3 (2008): 57–59. The direct quote for the Mexikanemi is from Sheriff Sigifredo Gonzalez, "Southwest Border Gang Reconition," http://www.senate.state .tx.us/75r/senate/commit/c640/wtpdf/1108-SigifredoGonzalez-2.pdf (accessed September 5, 2014).

key term

Interdiction
Any law enforcement practice designed to confront and halt the activities, advance, or entry of members of an STG or their contraband.

key term

Intelligence
Secret information that a government agency collects about a suspect, inmate, or group.

key term

Institutional gang investigator
An institutional gang investigator is a trained individual whose primary or sole function is to gather information on institutional STGs and individuals and propose isolation or control of such so as to neutralize potential disruptive behavior.

key term

Step-down program
A prison practice designed to encourage inmates to earn release from an SHU, earn more privileges, and get out of isolation units faster if they stop engaging in gang activities and participate in anger management and drug rehabilitation programs.

key term

Programming
Implementation of a specific set of activities carried out according to guidelines to achieve a defined purpose, such as encouragement of inmates to earn a GED certificate as one activity that would reduce offender recidivism.

influence and prevent acts that would endanger others and the institution's order, staff, and other inmates. All such activities are **intelligence** functions.

The early identification of suspected gang members would require detailed information overseen by an **institutional gang investigator**, a highly skilled and articulate correctional officer to whom relevant information flows from correctional and justice personnel. Through this officer, information allows correctional personnel to make informed assessments of the inmate's behavior, including the following:

1. Information from other state departments of corrections, jail or prison facilities, and law enforcement agencies as to the potential disruptive nature of the group under consideration
2. History of gang behavior in the community, history of threatening staff or offender safety, riots, possession or manufacturing of weapons, assaults/battery, trafficking in narcotics, extortion, and/or coercion of others
3. Tattoo and graffiti documentation, group association documentation, and related information

Once the initial classification is undertaken, individual gang members are rated by the evidence that was secured. We use here the basic system of the State of California as an example of the factors that would make up the classification scheme. We also chose California because it arguably has the largest number and longest history of prison gangs of other states.[9] In broad stroke, inmates are scored on the following information (inter alia):

a. Symbols (2 points)
b. Documentation from informants (3 points)
c. Debriefing reports (3 points)
d. Written materials (4 points)
e. Photographs (4 points)
f. Staff information (4 points)
g. Other agency's information (4 points)
h. Association with STG affiliates (4 points)
i. Visitors known to be gang affiliated (4 points)
j. Self-admission (5 points)
k. Tattoos (6 points)

Any inmate scoring 10 points is classified as a gang member and most likely will be placed into single-cell isolation in a maximum-security unit in the prison SHU for an indeterminate period of time (typically six years). Depending on his behavior and absence of continuing involvement with an STG, he will be allowed to participate in a **step-down program** in which he earns increasingly more privileges by avoiding gang activities. At the end of the last of the five-step program, he will be returned to the general prison population.

Programming to prevent future criminal behavior and lessen inmate involvement in prison gangs exists. Inmates received at the institution are given "Advisement of Expectations" at their entry, shown a Gang Diversion Video, and participate in a variety of gang diversion programs, including such programs as "Alternatives to Violence," "Thinking for a Change," "7 Habits on the Inside," "Cage Your Rage," "Gangs Anonymous," and "Breaking Barriers." The effectiveness of these modalities alone or in combination is still unclear.

Despite specific programming and prison policies designed to discourage prison gang activities, violence, and assaults, "hard-core" gang leaders continue to exert influence and encourage attacks on inmate and staff. The isolation policies are strongly resisted by prison gangs. More recently, gang leadership has forced non–gang members to unite behind hunger strikes, trying to lower the levels of isolation and cement gang power anew.[10] The power struggle and outcome of such actions are not yet evident.

correctional **profile 8.2**

Evan Ebel

Evan Ebel was a member of **The 211 Crew**, formed in 1995 in the Denver County Jail by Benjamin Davis, now serving the remainder of his 108-year sentence for the crimes of racketeering, conspiracy, and solicitation to commit assault. Davis is the major leader ("**shot caller**") of The 211 Crew, a security threat group (STG) of between 200 and 1,000 members and now headquartered in Buena Vista Correctional Facility in Colorado.

Ebel was sentenced to eight years for carjacking and armed robbery and further sentenced to another four years for hitting a correctional officer. Ebel could be called a **white supremacist soldier**.[7]

When Ebel was in the Sterling Correctional Facility, he was targeted for violence by another STG; Benjamin Davis protected Ebel from the targeting STG, and thus Ebel incurred a debt to The 211 Crew. By the time he left prison on parole, he was an active member of The 211 Crew, which carries out fatal retributions in prison and allegedly earns money running guns and methamphetamines outside prison. Earnings are distributed to incarcerated 211 Crew members.

Prison records indicate that, while incarcerated, Ebel was a source of much trouble. He was ticketed a minimum of 28 times on disciplinary charges for a wide range of behavior, including robbery, menacing, and threatening a female correctional officer. He promised to kill the officer if he recognized her on the street and stated that the officer would beg for her life before he killed her.[8] Ebel was put into lockdown for 59 days and stripped of visitor privileges. He threatened to kill another two correctional officers as well as an inmate. In addition to threatening correction staff, he disobeyed guard orders and fought with other inmates. Ebel can be characterized as both a violent and a dangerous inmate who was to serve his entire prison sentence. A clerical error caused Ebel to be released early, and he went onto electronic monitoring parole. Ebel is reported to have removed his monitor. The parole agency failed to quickly revoke his parole.

He was in immediate contact with fellow members of The 211 Crew as his cell phone records indicate. It is alleged that other gang members gave him money to buy a car, secured mismatching license plates, and helped arrange a murder of a pizza delivery driver. This murder was to secure the driver's jacket for yet another murder, described below. In addition, gang members reportedly guided him to the target's home in preparation for the murder of Tom Clements. After the murder, The 211 Crew allegedly sequestered him in a "safe house."

Wearing the pizza delivery jacket, Ebel knocked on the front door of prison chief Tom Clements and shot him dead. Evan Ebel fled to northern Texas and died during a gunfight with law enforcement officers. The weapon he was firing when he died was, ballistic tests revealed, the same gun that was used to kill Tom Clements. Bomb-making materials were found in Ebel's car, along with handwritten instructions on how to make explosive devices. El Paso County, Colorado, Judge Jonathan Walker who has, along the way, signed some 20 search warrants that empowered investigators to track members of The 211 Crew, was also notified that he was a person to be killed. Judge Walker went into hiding when he heard about the warnings.

Photo 8.5

Tom Clements, head of the Colorado Department of Corrections, allegedly assassinated by Evan Ebel.
SOURCE: *Harry Allen.*

Investigators argue that major gang members in Colorado Springs are being directed to violate parole or commit more crime so that they could return to prison and strengthen the ranks of The 211 Crew inside the correctional facility.

SOURCE: Kirk Mitchell, "Evan Ebel May Have Killed Prisons Chief to Repay 911 Crew Favor," *Denver Post,* March 25, 2013, http://www.denverpost.com/breakingnews/ci_23947814/evan-ebel-may-have-killed-clements-repay-favor (accessed June 27, 2013).

CNN U.S., "Texas Authorities: Bomb-Making Materials Found in Colorado Suspect's Car," http://www.cnn.com/2013/03/26/us/texas-suspect-car-search/index.html (accessed August 27, 2013).

Jim Spellman and Chelsea Carter, "Records: Evan Ebel Told Prison Guard She Would 'Beg for Her Life,'" http://www.cnn.com/2013/03/28/justice/colorado-prison-chief-killed (accessed August 27, 2013).

Summary

Summarize the Threat of Prison Gangs within Prison and after Release from Confinement

Prison STGs ("prison gangs") are criminal syndicates composed of three or more offenders engaging in criminal conduct. They pose a clear and present danger to correctional officers, other gangs, unaligned inmates, and potential victims in the general society as well as the order, security, and safety of the institution. Their power and influence extend well beyond the prison per se, as leaders of these STGs coordinate ongoing crime against potential citizens in the free society.

Explain the Basic History of Gang Development and Gang Differences

Prison gangs emerged from the major cultural challenges that stoked reform during the last half of the twentieth century. The Black Muslims emerged first, but it was soon evident that STGs could arise in many forms and for a variety of criminal intentions. The term "prison gangs" reflects this complexity. Many criminal gangs are organized along racial, ethnic, and territorial bases. Most exclude "outsiders" and other gang members and threaten free-world non criminals. Gangs obviously differ in size and level of violence as well as type of organization and leadership. Some developed in local jails; others are a response to the threat current incarceration gangs pose (offensive and defensive purposes). The largest STGs are drawn from the ranks of Hispanic criminals and have a paramilitary organization. Whatever their size and degree of complexity, each poses certain challenges to the security of prisoners, correctional officer staff, order within the institution, and free-world citizens whose frailities and culture make them higher in potential vulnerability.

Identify the Scope of Criminal Activities Perpetrated by Prison Gangs

STGs commit a wide range of coordinated criminal activities, including murder, assassination, blackmail, drug law violations, corruption, intimidation, extortion, robbery, and aggravated assault. Gang leaders serve as syndicate directors, ordering crime to be committed both inside the prison and in the free society. Another major impact can be seen in the corruption of power of institutional officers and the personal dangers such criminal syndicates pose to all officers and other correctional personnel, including judges, state directors of corrections, and community control officers.

Gangs communicate in foreign languages (including Arabic), on scraps of paper smuggled out from the institution, through coded letters, and face-to-face through use of languages that few correctional officers might understand. Visitors communicate direct messages that are memorized and that prison workers cannot understand. Often tape recordings can be translated, but much time in attempting to do so may be lost, and criminal actions can be completed before interdiction.

Explain the Role of Intelligence in Coping with Prison Gangs

Controlling these prison criminal syndicates often requires massive gathering of intelligence as well as coordination of intelligence services between prisons and other justice agencies. Some prisons have full-time intelligence officers working diligently to interdict contraband and identify high-level leaders. Once identified, inmates may be reassigned to SHUs where they are isolated, tightly controlled, and exposed to a variety of programs deemed relevant to their leaving their gang and reduced recidivism.

Outline Basic Interdiction and Control Programs for Prison Gangs

When a prison gang association membership is established, gang leaders frequently are transferred to SHUs, where they are single-celled and communication with lower level associates is restricted if not prevented. Gang members wishing to leave the gang or the tight restrictions of the SHUs in which they live can decide to leave the gang and "step down" from tightest security housing into the general prison population. Most states with large prison populations have developed identification, isolation, and step-down programs. STGs may never be extinguished but can be managed.

Describe the Influence That STGs Exert on Correctional Staff

STGs exert considerable threat to individual inmates, correctional officers, female and minority officers, and members of opposing gangs. Under threats, many correctional offices yield to corruption to preserve their lives and the lives of their families. Interdiction efforts can reduce the level of threat and danger to officers as well as reduce tensions and assaults within prison.

The ability of STG members to intimidate, neutralize, and corrupt correctional staff can contribute to rules not being enforced, special and favorable concessions to STG leaders, and high levels of emotional distress that plague current and potential staff.

Key Words

security threat group (STG), 182
street gang, 182
prison gang, 182
outlaw motorcycle gang (OMG), 182
one percenter OMG, 183
local/neighborhood street gang, 183
political prisoner, 183
secure housing unit (SHU), 184
correctional officer corruption, 184
"bad news list," 184
racially or ethnicity-oriented prison gang, 184
graffiti, 184
Hispanic STGs, 185
Mexican Mafia, 185
Texas Syndicate, 185
domestic terrorist group, 186
evidence-based classification system, 186
interdiction, 186
intelligence, 188
institutional gang investigator, 188
step-down program, 188
programming, 188
The 211 Crew, 189
shot caller, 189
white supremacist soldier, 189

Review Questions

1. What are security threat groups (STGs), and how did they arise?
2. What are the national trends among prison gangs?
3. How do STGs pose a threat?
4. What are some approaches to managing STGs? Are they effective?
5. Describe the role and importance of the institutional gang investigator.
6. How can gang members be classified?
7. What is the future of STGs?
8. If STGs continue to grow in the prison setting, what can correctional administrators do to control their influence?
9. Should low risk inmates be released from confinement to free up cell assignments to increase controls over STGs?
10. What are the national trends in STGs?

Application Case Studies

1. An prison informant reveals that an attack on a certain inmate is pending. What would you do to protect that inmate?
2. The "officer-prone" alarm of one of your correctional officers has indicated an ongoing assault against that officer is in progress. What would you do?
3. Leaders of two prison gangs have declared open season against each other. A major clash is pending. What would you do to contain such a conflict?

Endnotes

1. National Gang Intelligence Center, *2011 National Gang Threat Assessment: Emerging Trends* (Washington, DC: U.S. Department of Justice, 2012).
2. Ibid.
3. Ibid., p. 7.
4. Federal Bureau of Investigation (2012), "Gangs," http://www.fbi.gov/about-us/investigate/vc_majorthefts/gangs (accessed September 6, 2014).
5. Michael Montgomery (2015), "Gangs Reach Out of Prison to Commit Crimes," http://www.npr.org/templates/story/story.php?storyid=4525733&sourceCode=RSS (accessed July 22, 2013). See also Gary Klivans (2013), "The Art of Deciphering a Gang Code," http://www.correctionsone.com/gang-and-terrorist-recruitment/articles/5885211-The-art-of-deciphering-a-gang-code/; "How Prison Gangs Communicate," http://prisonoffenders.com/gangs_in_prisons.html.
6. Scott Barber, "District Attorney's Murder Could Mark Deadly New Chapter for White Supremacist Group," http://news.nationalpost.com/2013/04/06/district-attorneys-murder-could-mark-deadly-new-chapter-for-white-supremacist-gang/ (accessed August 27, 2013) "Prison Offenders: Extortion in Prison," http://prisonoffenders.com/prison_extortion.html.
7. Barber, "District Attorney's Murder Could Mark Deadly New Chapter for White Supremacist Group."
8. Jim Spellman and Chelsea Carter (2013), "Records: Evan Ebel Told Prison Guard She Would 'Beg for Her Life,'" http://www.cnn.com/2013/03/08/justice/colorado-prison-chief-killed (accessed September 6, 2014).
9. State of California Department of Correction and Rehabilitation, "Security Threat Group Identification and Management," http://www.cdcr.ca.gov/Regulations/Adult_Operations/docs/NCDR/2014 NCR/14-02/Supplemental_Documents_Assorted_1.pdf (accessed September 6, 2014).
10. Maggie Caldwell and Josh Harkinson, "50 Days without Food: The California Prison Hunger Strike Explained," http://www.motherjones.com/politics/2013/08/50-days-california-prisons-hunger-strike-explainer (accessed September 5, 2014).

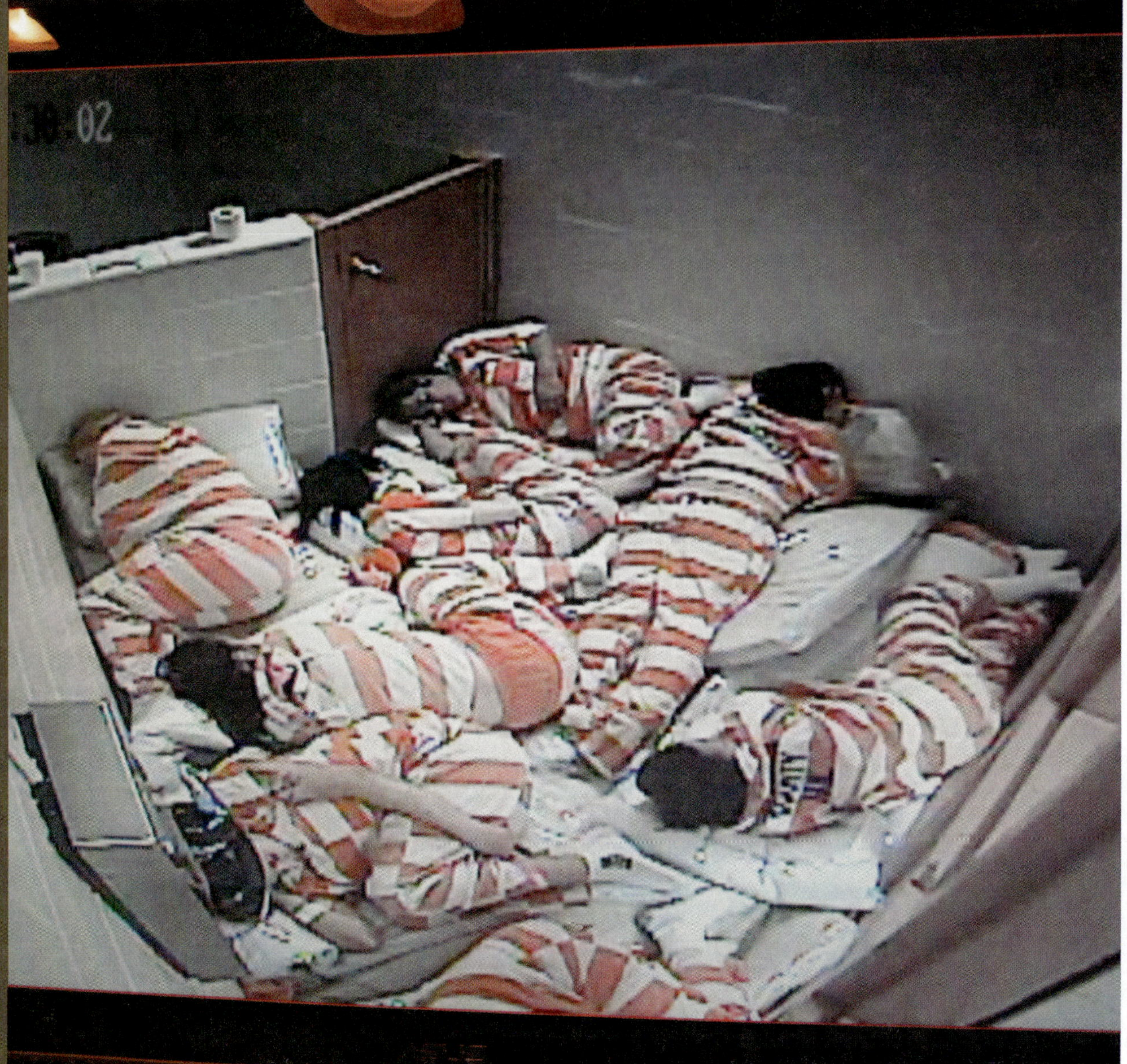

Livingston County Daily Press/AP Images.

Objectives

- Summarize the security and custody functions within a correctional facility.
- Summarize various treatment programs within a prison, including prison labor.
- Summarize treatment issues associated with inmate health care.
- Explain the three pervasive themes that have run through correctional management.
- Differentiate between classification for security versus classification for treatment.
- Explain how inmate needs are identified.
- Explain how prison programs can lessen recidivism.

chapter 9

Management and Treatment Functions

Outline

"Recently published evaluative studies [of prison-based therapeutic communities involving drug-abusing inmates] show remarkably consistent reductions in recidivism for offenders who complete the programs."

—Douglas S. Lipton *"The Effectiveness of Treatments for Drug Abusers Under Criminal Justice Supervision," National Institute of Justice, November 12, 1995.*

Overview

In Chapter 7, we focused attention on such custody issues as contraband, security, personnel, custody, and discipline. These issues are, understandably, the dominant concerns of correctional administrators and their management staff, and they consume great amounts of administrative time as well as large fiscal allocations by state or local correctional institutions. That led us to explore the development of management styles in corrections and the application of those styles to the major strategic processes of corrections—custody and treatment. Custody was seen as having a long history of a bureaucratic style of management.

Above all, corrections and correctional institutions are a product of the people's will and legislative action to resolve a perceived problem in society. The early prisons and penitentiaries had no problem with the "lock 'em up" wishes of society. In the twentieth century, however, we have been struggling to determine just what we really want to do with, to, or for our offenders. As noted in Chapter 3, this "model muddle" continues to be a problem for the correctional administrator. As a manager, the correctional leader must contend with staff members who are typically bifurcated into those who are mainly concerned with security and custody and those who are concerned with programs and treatment. As we progress through the second decade of the twenty-first century, we need to understand the problems faced by administrators who are required to accomplish both goals while dealing with crowding, budget cuts, a changing clientele, and various other issues. As discussed in Chapter 7, custody's primary role is to protect society. Treatment efforts attempt to return inmates to society prepared to serve it in a humane fashion. Treatment leads to lowered recidivism and thus enhanced public safety.

Living within the prisons but seldom part of the management and administrative components are the inmates, who are involuntarily sentenced to prison facilities and, for the most part, eager to be released. In the better prison systems, inmates receive humane treatment and handling designed to prepare them for their eventual return to society. For most inmates, however, the demands of custody and the philosophical orientations of administrators and staff will mean restriction or denial of treatment opportunities. This chapter deals with the current status of treatment programs and policies designed to reduce criminal inclinations and tendencies while strengthening motivations to adopt law-abiding behavior.

THE TREATMENT MODEL

Treatment services generally include those areas in which inmates often have deficits, including but not limited to vocational training, education, substance abuse, sex offender behavior, violence reduction interventions, mental health services, counseling, religious activities, therapeutic communities, and other clinical activities, and are believed to play a significant role in offender rehabilitation.[1] In the past, especially in the larger institutions, the allocation of resources and personnel for treatment bore little, if any, relation to that assumed significance. As a national average, the resources allocated for **treatment services** amounted to only about 10 percent of the expenditures for the institutional staffs.

key term

Treatment services
Any in-prison program designed to meet an inmate's needs and lower recidivism.

Part of the disproportionate allocation of resources results from a basic difference in nature between treatment and custody operations. Staff on the custody side must work 24 hours a day, 7 days a week, 365 days a year. Prisons do not close in observation of national or religious holidays. Furthermore, some inmates are mobile within the correctional facility at all hours of the day or night, inmate-to-inmate violence occurs hourly, and there is never silence in the general population, regardless of the hour.

Treatment staff members, on the other hand, usually work only eight hours a day, five days a week, and have holidays, vacations, and weekends off. When a custody officer is sick or takes vacation, he or she must be replaced (the common term is **backfilled**) by another correctional officer. This often requires someone working overtime but will be done because minimum critical staffing must be maintained to protect the public. That protection is still the primary mission of corrections. When treatment staff members are sick or take vacation, their position usually goes unfilled until they return to work. Because each 24-hour post requires 5.4 to 5.6 full-time staff, the ratio will always seem heavily weighted toward custody staff.

key term

Backfilled
Management strategy to meet minimum critical staffing by asking corrections officers to work the next tour of duty.

In the entire corrections system, a very small percentage of institutional personnel are employed in social work or psychological services, and the number of psychiatrists in corrections is infinitesimal. Diagnostic work-ups, crisis intervention, and testing processes tend to consume the workday of those involved in these services. Also, some treatment personnel must often spend long hours sitting on disciplinary hearing courts, classification and reclassification committees, and honor placement committees, leaving little time to spend

correctional **profile 9.1**

Prison Psychiatrists

Psychiatrists in service to the correctional system are not always underpaid or earn less than in private practice. For example, California has been under federal court order for years to reduce understaffing in the mental health services, a situation found to allow excessive and preventable prisoner deaths. The then current salary for psychiatrists ranged from $13,300 per month for a prison psychiatrist up to $24,200 for chief psychiatrists. Due to the court order, California increased the wages by 82 percent. Psychiatrists working in state mental hospitals migrated to the Department of Corrections and Rehabilitation, a move that significantly increased the ratio of physician to mental health patient to 100 patients per psychiatrist and a 70 percent vacancy rate for mental health psychiatric staff. The same federal court then ordered California to boost the then median annual pay to $251,000 for state mental health hospital psychiatrists, effectively ending the migration of psychiatrists to corrections.

Payments in California to psychiatrists are salaries, averaging approximately $123 per hour. There is the option of remaining on duty for extended hours for extra pay, including being on call nights and weekends and serving as the "medical officer of the day." The highest-paid state prison psychiatrist in 2011 received $822,300. A California labor leader argued in favor of such incomes, arguing that "extra duty" costs were much less than hiring outside contractors, that California is an expensive state in which to live, and that there is a national shortage of psychiatrists.

SOURCE: *Coleman v. Schwarzenegger,* U.S.D.C. (E.D. Cal, Case No. CIV S-90-0520 LKK J FM P), 2009, http://harvardlawreview.org/2010/01/eastern-district-of-california-holds-that-prisoner-release-is-necessary-to-remedy-unconstitutional-california-prison-conditions-ae-coleman-v-schwarzenegger-no-civ-s-90-0520-lkk-jfm-p-2009/.

on ongoing treatment with inmates. For example, group psychotherapists in the nation's prisons for men spend about one-third of their time providing individual psychotherapy and less than one-third of their time providing group therapy.[2] In addition, correctional administrators and the treatment staff frequently have to contend with the deeply ingrained antagonism of the staff members who are oriented primarily toward custody, security, and maintenance of calm.[3]

Due to the inherent nature of conflict between the major thrusts of the institutional mission and the rehabilitative treatment staff, many progressive incarceration systems (Federal Bureau of Prisons, some jails, Kansas, etc.) have embraced what is frequently known as unit team management. Inmates and appropriate security and treatment staff are responsible for both security and rehabilitative treatment, based on a housing plan known as a "pod." The intent of the "pod management" is to integrate the basic functions of security and programming. No programming can be safe or effective without a basis for security and safety, and the uniformed staff is trained to maximize both.

Inmates are evaluated on risk and need levels at intake. Close attention to inmates' needs is designed to ensure effective programming and provide rehabilitative treatment to assist prisoners in their reentry to society. This means that all members of the team (see below) are collectively responsible for making communities safer by offering a variety of programs intended to aid inmates in preparing themselves for an ultimate return to society. These services are tailored to an individualized treatment program, implemented, delivered, and maintained for each individual in the housing unit. It is the unit team treatment plan, coupled with the provision of accurate programming and delivery of services, that would make communities safer when the inmate begins reentry.

In addition to the uniformed staff, the unit team includes corrections counselors, job assignment staff, and educators who coordinate academic and vocational education and self-help groups; provide or facilitate mental health services; and specialize in enhancing cognitive skills. Additional focuses are on programs that would enhance work ethics, goal setting, and relapse prevention. Typically, a unit team manager is responsible for the day-to-day operations of the housing unit. The purposes of the unit team are to decentralize provision of services and programs, provide increased attention to individual needs, address the particular needs of individual inmates, and coordinate medical, mental health, and education programs.

The unit teams also provide inmate work assignments designed to inculcate inmate work skills and attitudes, review progress and inform inmates of evaluations of their personal growth, provide individual attitudinal and adjustment counseling, and focus on release counseling and planning. Inmate disturbances on functioning unit teams are believed to be minimal.

Only in recent times has the associate superintendent or deputy warden for treatment been selected from candidates with training in the social sciences rather than through the promotion of a faithful custody supervisor. This is important because the typical rank-and-file custody person was usually someone who had earned the job not through training and education but through experience and staying out of trouble. Thus, a person with a high school education (or less) was often placed over psychiatrists, psychologists, medical doctors and nurses, social workers, and educators who possessed far more academic credentials. Understandably, those roles created many problems as treatment became more important.

PERCEPTIONS AND CORRECTIONAL MANAGEMENT

Three pervasive themes have run through correctional management. First, the goals of restraint and reformation have helped reinforce correctional administrators' perceptions of offenders as morally, psychologically, physically, and educationally inferior human beings who must be upgraded and, in the meantime, controlled. As a result of that perception, correctional administrators focused the resources at their command primarily on the individual offender. Because the offender was the principal target of organizational activity, little effort was made to mobilize and co-opt community resources, a function that is the very essence of the reintegration model of correctional intervention. That management posture has many consequences, such as the division of offenders into caseloads for purposes of treatment and supervision, recruitment of varied specialists (therapists) whose efforts are seldom coordinated, and, as we mentioned earlier, the scarcity of well-conceived efforts to work cooperatively with such community institutions as the schools, employment services, and neighborhood centers.

key term

Gradualism approach
A "go-slow" approach to design and implementation of new programs.

A second persistent attribute of correctional management has been a **gradualism approach** to program development and change. This approach has been characterized by a somewhat frivolous subscription to "new" ideas (such as boot camps) and generally nonrigorous, nonscientific rules of thumb for determining what to delete from the old system and what to add to it. The predominant conservatism of system managers has militated against deviations from familiar ways, has encouraged the avoidance of risk, and has led to tokenism in the launching of new measures.

Correctional administrators are not so much responsible for that condition as they are victims of two realities: society's uncertainty about the causes of and solutions to the crime problem and, until recently, the inability of social science and research to provide a solid frame of reference for considering alternative courses of action and estimating their consequences.[4] Nevertheless, in any effort to understand how correctional executives might be effective innovators, it is necessary to confront the difficulties and frustration that currently surround the process of change.

key term

Meta-analysis
A quantitative statistical analysis that is applied to separate but similar experiments of different and usually independent researchers and that involves pooling the data and using the pooled data to test the effectiveness of the results, such as the effectiveness of education in reducing recidivism.

It is important to note the numerous examples of change in correctional organization and programming that run counter to the general pattern we have described.[5] Some experimental programs have been firmly supported by theoretical premises and have been evaluated objectively. The use of **meta-analysis**, a recent development in detecting the effectiveness of programs in reducing recidivism, has provided substantial evidence that demonstrates how certain programs (such as education, anger management, vocational training, and cognitive behavioral therapies) reduce criminal reoffending after parole. It is that growing edge of innovation, of improved dissemination of knowledge, and of close connection between discovery and implementation of technique that offers hope for more treatment gains in the near future. Indeed, as resources become more scarce, many correctional systems are taking a closer look at the effectiveness of the programs they offer and are moving toward more evidence-based practices. One state, Oregon, actually passed legislation that requires that 75 percent of dollars spent on correctional programs have to go to proven, evidence-based programs.

key term

Isolationism and withdrawal
Implementing programs without a systematic, rational scheme.

The third and final theme, which has its roots in the prison culture of the past and still runs through correctional management today, is the syndrome of **isolationism and withdrawal**. That condition has helped conceal from the public the realities of life in institutions and probation and parole agencies and has thus acted to perpetuate stereotypes and myths. Prisons, after all, were designed and located to keep criminals out of the sight and mind of the larger populace. Prison administrators found it expedient to honor that mandate. When community-based correctional programs gingerly sought to gain a foothold, their managers seemed intuitively to avoid exposure to public scrutiny and judgment. Whereas the police tend to publicize aggressively their views of crime and punishment, the leaders of corrections tend to avoid public debate, particularly debate centering on controversial issues,[6] although former (and even current) prisoners have been more active in this area.

That tendency has had serious consequences. The correctional field has had little success in developing public understanding and support for needed changes. Simplistic or erroneous conceptions of the nature of crime and its treatment have flourished, partly because of the lack of effective spokespersons for more sophisticated interpretations, especially at times of "opportunity" when conflict or crisis has awakened the interest of an otherwise apathetic public.[7]

Photo 9.1
Return of mentally ill inmate to his single cell following treatment.
Corbis.

CLASSIFICATION FOR SECURITY AND TREATMENT

Classification is the process of dividing an inmate population into manageable groups for custody and treatment purposes. One major goal is to aggregate persons roughly similar on such characteristics as danger, escape potential, need for treatments, gang affiliation, and so on. The similar groups can then be assigned to custody level and treatment programs. Dividing inmates into groups to be assigned to various prison facilities is known as **external classification**. Inmates can then be assigned to various housing or cell units, work assignments, and programming based on an inmate's perceived level of risk (aggressiveness, violence, escape potential), treatment needs, and time to be served. This latter process is called **internal classification**. Both classification processes typically occur at the receiving institution, such as a reception and classification center, or prison intake unit. Over the passage of time and based on the inmate's record, inmate assignments may be (and most routinely are) reviewed and **reclassification** may be undertaken. Most state prisoner reclassification occurs at regularly scheduled intervals, such as every 12 months during the inmate's annual review.

Classification is a relatively recent management innovation in corrections and can be found more often in probation and parole supervision situations than in jail and prison facilities. The classification process can frequently intensify the conflict between treatment and custody staff if it is not carefully handled. In most correctional classification processes (either at the individual institution or at a central classification facility), concern lies more with the danger the new inmates might present to the institution than with the possibility that they might respond to treatment. As a result, new inmates are often assigned to higher custody grades than their backgrounds warrant, until they can prove themselves. This security-oriented concept of classification often excludes inmates from participation in programs that could lead to their rehabilitation. Their early treatment, in fact, may be restricted to health care, an essential program because most offenders are in poor physical condition when they enter the institution.

There are advantages to classification. First, classification will assign dangerous or aggressive inmates to a high-security institution, thus increasing prison security by lessening

key term
Classification
The process of dividing and assigning incoming inmates into meaningful categories for assignment to institutions and programs.

key term
External classification
Process leading managers to assign inmates to an institution.

key term
Internal classification
Process of assigning inmates to types of programs and work and cell locations.

key term
Reclassification
The process by which inmate control and programming are changed.

tensions in prison. It will also avoid misclassification of most inmates, as correctional staff members have a tendency to classify inmates into higher-custody facilities than might be necessary, ineffectively expending valuable resources and creating inmate resentment. Finally, a good classification system (such as the Adult Internal Management System and behavior-based systems) more likely correctly places inmates and contributes significantly to the effective deployment of staff.

TREATMENT IN PRISON

The treatment model for corrections is seen in the three basic services first offered to prisoners: religious, medical, and educational. We now examine the development of those services, along with an analysis of some more recent treatment innovations. Much of the public still views any "special programs" for inmates as a form of coddling, and many politicians have responded to this view by rejecting new and promising rehabilitation techniques created by behavioral scientists. Instead, they chose to favor "wars"—against crime, criminals, drugs, ad infinitum—as the easiest way to garner votes from the uninformed and often uncaring public. In fact, the protection of society, not the pampering of offenders, is also the basic reason for treatment and specialized programs in corrections. If at least some of the sources of an individual's criminality can be dealt with before he or she is referred back to the community or released from aftercare back to the community, corrections should achieve that.

The basic services provided by the treatment side of corrections can be combined as health and medical services, religious services, and educational and training programs for inmates. Descriptions of these services and programs follow.

Health and Medical Services

key term

Sick call
Opportunity for inmates to seek medical treatment.

key term

Goldbrickers
Inmates seeking sick calls for other than medical needs.

key term

Medical services
Any treatment programs designed to treat physical or psychological maladies of inmates.

key term

Hepatitis A and B
Viral infections resistant to medical treatments.

Even in the earliest days of American prisons, certain times were set aside for **sick call**. Of course, the treatment provided was less than one would expect to receive at a clinic in the community. Prisoners often use sick call merely to obtain a brief respite from prison labor or from the dull routine. Time wasted on **goldbrickers** is time the medical staff cannot give to those who really need care. Because the correctional funnel selects out all but the most serious and manipulative offenders, the cream of society does not often end up in prisons; therefore, those who are imprisoned usually have numerous medical and dental needs.

Medical services are often a source of inmates' complaints and frequently become a real headache for administrators. In many areas throughout the country, qualified medical personnel are generally in short supply, and that shortage is felt even more acutely in correctional institutions. To supply the total medical care for which an institution is responsible, it is often necessary to combine the services of full-time medical employees, contractual consultants, and available community resources. Even with all those efforts, inmates and the public often tend to look down on any medically trained person who is willing to become involved with a correctional institution. Any doctor who accepts the prison physician's relatively low income and standard of living, it is thought, must have been a failure in the community. Proper medical care is important to the overall rehabilitation effort. Poor diet, drug abuse, a history of inadequate medical attention, and other debilitating conditions are not uncommon among inmates. Once they have been restored to reasonable health, it is often easier to work on the causes behind their problems.[8]

Major medical problems now commonly faced by jail and prison inmates are **hepatitis A and B**, HIV infection, mental illness, geriatric issues, prenatal care, rubella (measles), and drug-resistant tuberculosis. Drug-dependent inmates,[9] frequent transfers of inmates among facilities, and overcrowded living conditions are conducive to rapid transmission

correctional practice 9.1

Health Care Services

Within a state's department of corrections, health care staff provide access to dental, medical, mental, and pharmaceutical health services for both female and male inmates within the department. Such services include health education, chronic illness, and preventive career (and usually hospice care) clinics. Services are required to meet the minimum community standard of health care. The scope of services includes critical care, maternal care, primary care, emergency care, specialty care, and inpatient hospitalization. Most states have a medical facility that deals exclusively with provision of medical care to inmates.

Most states have a chief physician and surgeon of correctional facilities who supervise other physicians and medical professionals administering both medical and psychiatric care to inmate patients. The chief advises staff on appropriate treatment techniques for specific medical issues, including diagnostic, clinical, and ward techniques. This physician might also examine and treat unusual and difficult presenting medical issues and would recommend approval on such matters as hospital policy and the need for specific equipment, facilities, personnel, and budgeting. The chief of medical care maintains and supervises the treatment of inmates committed to that state's incarcerative facilities and does other, related work, including supervising other physicians, family nurse practitioners, and physician's assistants, among others.

Medical correction care is a difficult job and presents many challenges to corrections. Nurses provide the bulk of immediate health care, working long hours in a wide range of treatment issues and problems. Nurses treat inmates who are diabetic, hypertensive, or hepatitis positive. In a given tour of duty, nurses could treat cardiac arrest, stab wounds, and emergency events. Most nurses have multiple specialties and engage in in-service training to improve levels of skills and certifications. The nursing staff would include registered nurses, licensed practical nurses, neurology specialists, orthopedic nurses, and psychiatric nurses. The departments of corrections offers competitive salaries commensurate with education and experience.

Meeting the community standards of health care is potentially difficult if the prison is located close to a city providing high-quality medical care to free-world citizens. That community standard would require a department of corrections to meet the minimal standard of outstanding medical facilities with nationally recognized and superior physicians.

of diseases that could result in epidemics, especially multidrug-resistant tuberculosis. Tuberculosis is easily airborne transmitted, and even dormant carriers can transmit the bacillus. Tuberculosis transmission from inmates to staff has already been documented. And staff could spread the infection to family and friends (tertiary infection), bringing this serious disease into the outside community. Inmates and staff should have tuberculin skin tests on a routine basis[10] because the incidence of the disease has increased dramatically.[11]

Type of Expenditure	Amount
Security:	$19,663
Inmate health care:	12,442
Operations:	7,214
Administration:	3,493
Inmate support:	2,562
Rehabilitation programs:	1,612
(Academic education: $944)	
(Vocational training: $354)	
(Substance abuse programs: $313)	
Miscellaneous:	116
Total:	$ 47,102

figure 9.1

California's Annual Costs to Incarcerate an Inmate in Prison (2008–2009).

SOURCE: Legislative Analyst's Office, California State Legislature, *"How Much Does It Cost to Incarcerate an Inmate?,"* http://www.lao.ca.gov/handouts/crimjust/2009/Overview_of_Corrections_Spending_3_11_09.pdf.

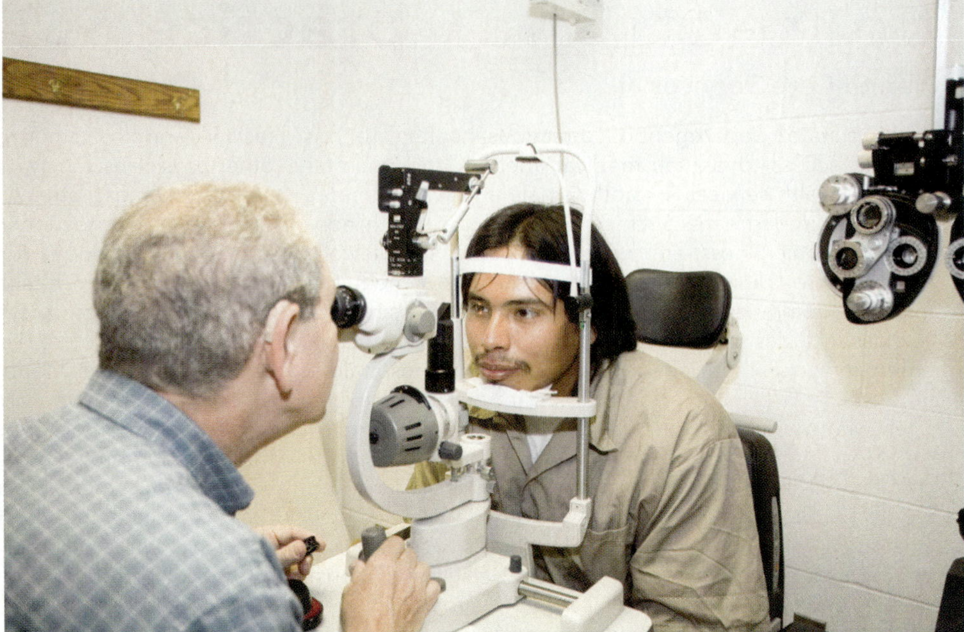

Photo 9.2
Inmate undergoing eye examination by optometrist.
Mikael Karlsson/Alamy.

Treatment of prisoner health problems is expensive; almost $1 of every $2 spent on adult prisoners in California is for medical care, a major increase due to court-ordered improvement of all medical services (see Figure 9.1).

As early as 1988, it was recognized that about 80 percent of all state prison inmates had been serious alcohol and drug abusers. More than three in four state inmates and almost 70 percent of federal prisoners and jail inmates had used drugs regularly in the month preceding arrest. Furthermore, substance-abusing inmates were more likely to be repeatedly reimprisoned. From 1980 until 2006, drug law violators accounted for at least 30 percent of the growth in the number of imprisoned felons, two-thirds of the increase in federal prisoners, and more than 40 percent of the jail populations.

Photo 9.3
Drug dependent inmates engaged in music therapy.
St Petersburg Times/Newscom.

correctional practice 9.2

Inmates Providing Hospice Care for Other Inmates

Nearly one in five of Maine's prison inmates are at least 50 years old. Maine State Prison administrators, at the prodding of its inmates, allow other inmates to care for terminally ill and other inmates who suffer from chronic disease. A dozen inmates trained as hospice volunteers render end-of-life care and train other inmates to serve as hospice volunteers. Services range from bathing and dressing the sick, assistance in mobility, music therapy, and outings for inmates who want to meet and talk with their friends.

Fiercely protective of their program, the volunteers have kicked out two other inmates who did not live up to the code of ethics the volunteers developed. Inmates are not paid for their work, and time is not deducted from their sentences for pursuit of their new career. Inmates claim that giving back to others helps them to feel human again and that the hospice patients are like family. Hospice patients do not die alone.

In addition to drug and alcohol problems, inmates also have a number of other problems and risk factors that must be addressed. These include lack of employment, bad companions, antisocial attitudes, emotional problems, mental illness, and lack of education.

Drug use has been found to predict subsequent violent behavior among both females and males. When substance abuse occurs among persons with psychopathological problems (**comorbidity**), there is a stronger correlation with subsequent violent behavior among females. One study of probationers undergoing mandatory substance abuse treatment in a residential facility found that 80 percent of the sample had psychopathological problems, more than 70 percent had drug abuse problems, and almost 60 percent had concurrent drug abuse and psychopathological problems (comorbidity). Furthermore, prison inmates with both drug abuse and psychopathological problems engaged in more frequent preadmission illegal behaviors, had more extensive social impairments, and were found to have *higher* motivation for treatment. Female inmates are even more impacted by co-occurring conditions and higher needs (see Chapter 17).

key term

Comorbidity
Two or more occurring medical treatment needs for one inmate.

In 2007, an estimated one-third of state and federal prison inmates reported having a physical impairment or mental condition. More than 3 in 10 state inmates and one in four federal inmates reported having a learning or speech disability, a hearing or vision problem, or a mental or physical condition. About one in five of all inmates said they had been injured in an accident since admission. The longer the period of incarceration, the more likely the inmate was to report an injury.

About one in five inmates reported a medical condition that limits their ability to work. On the federal level, the medical conditions of record were high blood pressure (8 percent), poor mental health (5 percent), asthma and diabetes (4 percent each), heart problems (3 percent), and HIV/AIDS (1 percent). Medical problems were more common among inmates who had used a needle to inject drugs (one in three inmates) and those who were alcohol dependent (38 percent of inmates). Much time and resources are needed to meet the minimal health needs and mandatory medical care.[12] Information on participation in educational programs can be found in Figure 9.2.

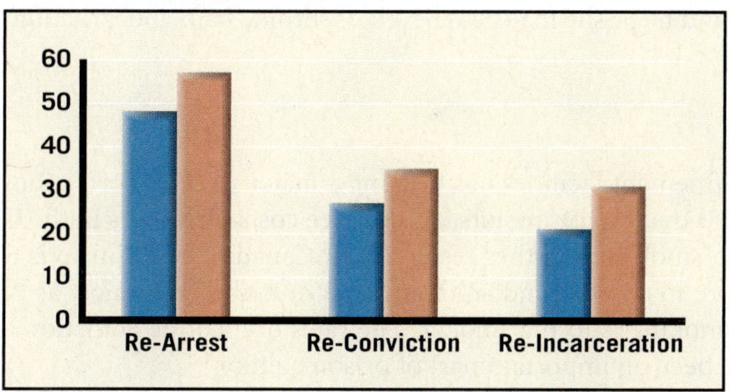

figure 9.2

Recidivism Rates for Education Program Inmates (in blue) and Nonparticipants (in red).

SOURCE: Stephen Steurer and Linda Smith, *Education Reduces Crime* (Alexandria, VA: Correctional Education Association, 2003), p. 12. Similar results were found by Lois Davis et al., *Evaluating the Effectiveness of Correctional Education* (Washington, DC: Bureau of Justice Statistics, 2013).

correctional practice 9.3

Challenges Geriatric Inmates Face in Prisons

Most prison systems in the nation have not yet adapted to the needs of inmates over age 50. Age 50 (or age 55 in some jurisdictions) is commonly used as the defining point at which inmates are known as "geriatric inmates" (or "Gerries"). Prisons were not designed for and are unusual challenges to geriatric inmates.

To maintain independence, inmates must be able to perform unique physical behaviors, some of which (bathing, dressing, and using bathroom facilities) are shared across all geriatric persons, whether in prison or in the free world. There are unique additional intramural (in prison) activities that must be performed in the incarcerative setting. These include the following:

1. Jumping off the bed to the floor when an alarm is sounded, as all inmates must drop to the floor immediately so staff can count and control inmates
2. Climbing into and out of the top bunk in dormitory settings
3. Hearing and responding to orders from correctional personnel
4. Standing in line for long periods of time (as in waiting to be served food and inmate counts)
5. Walking to the dining room

In some prisons, wheelchair-bound inmates are expected to drop to the floor and stand for the count or get out of their wheelchairs when the alarm sounds. Others with brittle bones or having trouble walking may find a drop to the "boots to the floor" order hazardous. In addition, falls are hazardous and can be a quick entry to being wheelchair or bed bound.

Medical challenges that geriatric inmates face revolve around the absence of health care services available when they were in the free world. These act to compound medical problems in prison, including arthritis, hypertension, renal insufficiencies, asthma, inability to sleep, and fear of termination (death). Our prison systems were never designed for a geriatric population, and it has been estimated that by 2030, some one in three prisoners will be geriatric inmates.

What are some basic prison changes needed for geriatric inmates in the short haul? (Changes in the long haul are explored in Chapter 21.) In no particular order, these are as follows:

- All geriatric inmates should be assigned to the lower bunks unless the inmate requests another "home," such as top bunk or single cell.
- Such cells should have grab bars in reach of toilet facilities.
- Geriatric inmates should be celled near dining facilities.
- More time should be allocated for geriatrics for dropping to the floor during alarms.
- Showers should be retrofitted with grab bars in and immediately beside the entry to a shower.
- Nonskid rubber mats should be on shower and other wet floors.

In this era of post–financial collapse world and with most states facing demands for services that cannot be provided, we wonder what to do with a geriatric inmate so demented that he or she cannot even remember his or her name (much less the day and month of the year or who is president of the nation)? Or a near-end inmate who has suffered one or more strokes or is totally paralyzed? Should prisons be geriatric hospitals?

Another major service for the offender is found in the dental clinic because most prisoners have very bad teeth. Even in an institution fortunate enough to have good dental care facilities, dental service can take many months because prisoners' teeth have often suffered from long neglect and need extensive work. The effects of dental treatment are similar to those of plastic surgery: Improved appearance enhances the offender's feelings of confidence and well-being, and he or she may be relieved of chronic pain and irritation as well.

Smoking

Smoking in confinement facilities has become a major issue in corrections, primarily due to related medical treatment, lawsuits, and service costs. Prisoners in the United States are twice as likely to smoke than other residents. In Canada, the estimate is 50 percent more (three times more likely). Secondhand smoke is described as almost as dangerous to the nonsmoker as smoking is to the smoker. The rates of nicotine addiction are high, yet tobacco is and has been an important part of prison culture.[13]

Correctional systems also face significant danger of class-action and constitutional-issue lawsuits. Inmates have been suing over the degree of risk they face when others smoke. Prison staff members are also vulnerable to secondhand smoke, and both lawsuits and union pressures for better working conditions are frequent. Prisoners, inmates, and visitors must be protected from the dangers of secondhand smoke.

Across the nation, most states have restricted smoking to designated open-air spaces or have implemented total institutional bans. Twenty-five states and Canada have banned smoking outright. Canada forbids both tobacco within the institution and staff smoking anywhere on the prison grounds while at work. The Federal Bureau of Prisons has been smoke free since 2004. Nicotine withdrawal leads to significant psychological and physical symptoms. Administrators have implemented a wide variety of strategies to enforce a smoking ban while not letting inmates withdraw "cold turkey." Both inmates and staff have been given large lead times so they can prepare for the ban, mostly through reducing cigarettes over a year.[14] Also provided across the nation are the following:

- Gradually increasing the number of the facility's areas with smoking bans
- Smoking cessation classes
- Reprimanding or sanctioning staff for smuggling tobacco into a facility
- Offering counseling therapies
- Providing nonsmoking tools, such as nicotine patches and gum[15]
- Transferring repeat inmates to higher-custody facilities

Smuggling of tobacco into facilities (by some visitors and staff) is highly lucrative. One pencil-lead-thin self-rolled cigarette can sell for $12 to $15, perhaps ever higher in certain institutions. Inmates receiving a six-ounce bag of tobacco can easily earn $3,000 per bag. Staff in many institutions can sell cigarettes to inmates at comparable profit margins.

Perhaps the clearest policy can be found in Canadian prisons, where inmate smoking is banned at all institutions. Staff may not smoke while on duty, cannot bring cigarettes into prisons, cannot smoke on campus, and must keep all personal tobacco products in a locked container (such as a glove compartment) in their vehicles while at work.[16]

Religious Assistance and Services

From 1790 until today, one service that has traditionally been available to the incarcerated felon is religious assistance and guidance. Solitary meditation in the Walnut Street Jail was intended to make offenders realize the error of their sinful ways and make them penitent. Penitence was often encouraged by visits from local ministers and priests. Later, the large institutions of the early 1800s created the need for a full-time chaplain on the premises.

The **correctional chaplaincy** has been and is currently the least-sought-after position among ministers, who evidently prefer to serve more conventional congregations. Part of the problem, too, is the remote location of most prisons and a widespread public belief (shared by many administrators) that religion in prisons should be confined to the chaplain's traditional duties. Not well known by the public is the range of services, types of counseling, guidance, and innovation offered by chaplains within prisons.[17] A movement has sprung up to establish a core of clinically oriented clerics, but the correctional field is less attractive to them than are other kinds of institutions. There is a definite need to upgrade the role of the correctional chaplain to attract the best into the institutions. The role of the chief chaplain can be enhanced if it becomes accredited by the Association for Clinical Pastoral Education. With that background, the chaplain can develop programs, recruit and train chaplaincy candidates, and even use seminary students to augment his or her resources.

key term

Correctional chaplaincy
A program of recruiting clergy who minister to the religious needs of inmates.

The new and growing special interest groups inside prisons—those whose religious orientation is toward a particular ethnic group, culture, or subculture—do not accord with the traditional religious outlets. As noted in Chapter 1, their right to pursue their faiths while confined has been firmly established. The traditional correctional institution has

correctional profile 9.2

The Contemporary Prison Chaplain

There are almost 1,500 prison chaplains in the United States, whose duties are very similar to a priest or minister serving in a church, hospital, or military unit. They are mostly male, middle-aged, Protestant, and white. They are also highly educated. Most have the degree of master of divinity, earned from a seminary. In some states, they are also required to have served at least two years in a pastoral role prior to being hired.

The prison chaplain fulfills a wide range of roles, such as providing education and spiritual growth programs for inmates, recruiting and training volunteers, counseling prisoners in their prerelease status, and coordinating programs (seminars and family programs in particular). The chaplain spends time circulating throughout the prison, counseling inmates and, sometimes, staff. The duties also include clearing inmates to make emergency telephone calls to family and friends, reporting deaths of family members, providing grief counseling to prisoners, and attending funerals as needed.

Chaplains must be sensitive to the needs and sacraments of religious denominations other than their own and must sometimes conduct religious services within the other denomination. Sometimes the chaplain recruits other priests, ministers, or rabbis or recruits volunteers to conduct those services. Finally, chaplain duties include developing and supervising special religious diets.

As a group, they spend considerable time managing massive paperwork duties, such as ordering supplies, amassing and managing a religion library, and recording inmate participation in services and programs. Most chaplains are very satisfied with their jobs.

provided Protestant, Roman Catholic, and sometimes Jewish chaplains as representatives of the three major religious groups in the United States because it was not feasible to have a cleric for every religion observed by different inmates. The chaplains attempt to offer ecumenical services and try to provide worship for all prisoners; however, the more vocal members of the smaller sects have protested that arrangement. Sometimes it is difficult to secure a qualified spiritual leader to conduct ceremonies in prison.[18] The number of prisoners of the Islamic faith who are incarcerated has grown considerably. As the need to provide religious services to these Muslims increases, local imams are beginning to be more active in that ministry.

It is possible, if the chaplain's salary and image can be sufficiently upgraded, that ministers trained in the behavioral sciences will become part of the contemporary prison scene, a far cry from the Walnut Street missionaries whose sole function was to provide Bible reading and prayer. The new chaplains might well play different roles as an integral part of the treatment team in future rehabilitation programs, including unit team management.

Educational and Training Programs for Inmates

In most state correctional systems, education of incarcerated inmates is a legislative mandate. The largest group of treatment personnel is the teachers, who usually far outnumber those in counseling services. Although most institutions have some kind of educational program, there are marked differences in kind and extent. Early efforts were aimed simply at teaching prisoners to read. With 12 million adults in the United States considered to be **functionally illiterate** (cannot read, write, or compute above the third-grade level), it is not too surprising that those considered to be at the bottom of the barrel have literacy problems in even greater measure.

key term

Functionally illiterate
Unable to read, write, or spell above the third-grade level.

key term

GED
General equivalency diploma certifying inmate's achievement of the equivalent of a high school diploma.

Today, most inmates are able to achieve at least a high school education (or the **GED**, the high school equivalency certificate or general equivalency diploma) through institutional programs, and the more progressive institutions are offering courses at the two-year and four-year college level.[19] It is acknowledged that lack of education is a serious handicap when inmates return to the free world: Former offenders who cannot get jobs because of insufficient education are likely to return to crime. For that reason, education has long been regarded as a primary rehabilitative tool in the correctional field. The gap between the need for educational services and the provision of adequate educational and vocational training is wide, however.[20] Yet the fact remains: Inmates earning the GED while in prison and completing a vocational training program are *significantly less likely to recidivate.*

One of the first barriers to effective educational programs is, once again, the problem of administrative considerations: operational requirements, security needs, shortage of teachers, shortage of educational materials, tight budgets, and a lack of inmate motivation.[21] Inmates and staff are often handicapped by unsuitable or out-of-date textbooks, often below the level of the street sophistication of the average adult prisoner. Inmates who are prevented from attending classes for disciplinary reasons may miss enough to be required to forgo the rest of the term. Denying education as part of disciplinary action devalues its effectiveness as a treatment component and doubles the punishment factor.

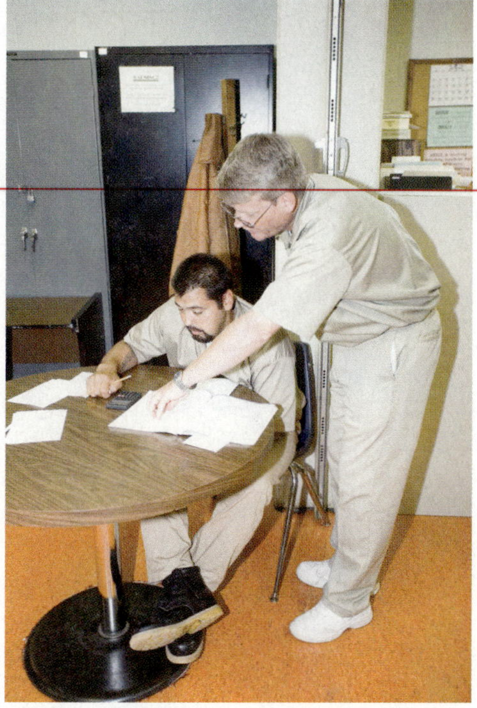

Photo 9.4

Teacher tutoring inmate in mathematics.
Mikael Karlsson/Alamy.

The classes held in some institutions are conventional and relatively old fashioned, in contrast with those that use the new learning technologies and innovations available to students at all levels on the outside. Yet educators are making considerable headway with computer technology, and rapid change is under way. Most prisoners have had little formal education and probably resisted whatever teaching they were exposed to. Material that bored them as children or truant teenagers is not likely to hold them enthralled as adults. What mature felons neither want nor need are "Dick and Jane" readers or other textbooks designed for children. Inmates may be actually or functionally illiterate, but they are adults in the main and are in possession of a lot of street smarts. To be given such materials is embarrassing and difficult for them. But because of the low priority and minimal funds assigned to education in most institutions, useless texts are often provided to prisoners, usually by public schools that no longer use them—small wonder that most prison programs are neither accredited nor enthusiastically supported by inmates. Inmates prefer listening and reading modes for learning.[22] Those with learning disabilities (from 7 to 25 percent of institutional populations) may respond best to tape recorders, television, and computers.[23]

The surprising fact is that some educational services thrive and contribute to the inmates' rehabilitation.[24] Texas has an education district that covers the entire prison system.

key term

Project Newgate
Prison treatment program stressing full-time college work, group counseling, and aftercare following parole.

Photo 9.5

Islamic inmates pray during a religious service at Hutchins State Jail.
Jerry Hoefer/AP Images.

Photo 9.6

Teacher assisting female inmates in mastery of keyboarding.
Marmaduke St. John/Alamy.

In Ohio, the Department of Rehabilitation and Correction also established a complete school district composed entirely of the educational programs within the state prison system. In the states of New York and Washington, education programs are contracted with local community colleges and provide excellent programs, from adult basic education[25] to degree programs in the institutions. **Project Newgate**, a program bringing the first years of college into the prisons, along with instructors and a complete curriculum, was the model for such programs in the 1970s.

Two other education-related programs that have been attempted, with varying results, are work/training release and educational release (sometimes called **furlough**). Furloughs are release from custody for a discrete and prescribed amount of time for specific reasons, with prior formal authorization by prison authorities. Of the 8,964 furloughs granted in 1999, only 44 inmates failed to return or committed another crime, a 0.005 percent failure rate.[26] In educational release, inmates are allowed to leave the institution to attend college, high school, or vocational-technical schools during the day, though they must return to the institution or an approved site when not at school or at night. The use of educational release became quite widespread in the United States before 1990, but the programs have been somewhat curtailed due to highly visible failures or budget cuts. In the work/training release program, an inmate may be allowed to leave the limits of confinement to secure education and a job; this enables offenders to develop a work history, learn a trade, support dependents, or even make restitution to the victim of their crimes. Forty-two of the 50 states and both the Federal Bureau of Prisons and the District of Columbia have work and education release programs. Of the 44,000 participating prisoners in 1999, few were arrested and reconvicted, although a small number were recalled to prison. This high success rate is partially a function of the process by which eligible inmates are selected and in part a result of the legal status of the participant who remains an inmate, easily returned to prison for noncomformity to rules and regulations.

key term

Furlough
Program of temporary leave from a prison for educational, work, or emergency purposes.

correctional **practice 9.4**

Inmate Program Involvement

One of the fears of correctional experts when states began to shift to determinate sentences was that, since the best motivator for inmate program participation appeared to be the need to convince releasing authorities of prisoners' reform through completion of prison treatment programs, determinate sentences would render treatment programs underenrolled if not superfluous. After all, if inmates were "playing the reform game" to convince a parole board of their readiness for release and the parole board's discretion to release were abolished, inmates might very well stop participating in any treatment programs.

This fear has been proven unfounded. The rates of program participation in Illinois, Minnesota, and Connecticut, for example, remained about the same or increased somewhat. How much of the noted participation was voluntary, however, remains in question. Prison administrators need concrete criteria for making decisions about transfers to less secure institutions, institutional job and housing assignments, furlough eligibility, and awarding of meritorious good-time credits based on program participation. The incentives for inmate involvement may have changed, but participation rates and levels appear to be unaffected by the determinate sentence. There is substantial evidence that meaningful job participation can significantly reduce recidivism, particularly for male offenders. The conclusion of the Federal Bureau of Prisons is as follows: "Research has conclusively demonstrated that participation in a variety of programs that teach marketable skills helps to reduce recidivism."

SOURCE: Stephen Anderson, *Evaluation of the Impact of Participation in Ohio Penal Industries on Recidivism* (Columbus: Ohio Department of Rehabilitation and Correction, 1995); Larry Motiuk and B. Belcourt, "CORCAN Participation and Post-Release Recidivism," *Forum* 8:1 (1996): 15–17; Federal Bureau of Prisons, "Inmate Matters," http://www.bop.gov/inmate_programs/index.jsp (accessed November 2, 2008).

Education, medical care, and religious practice have served as the basic treatment programs in America's prisons since the days of the Walnut Street Jail. In recent years, this limited three-sided approach to treatment has expanded to include a wide variety of programs aimed at the rehabilitation of incarcerated offenders.

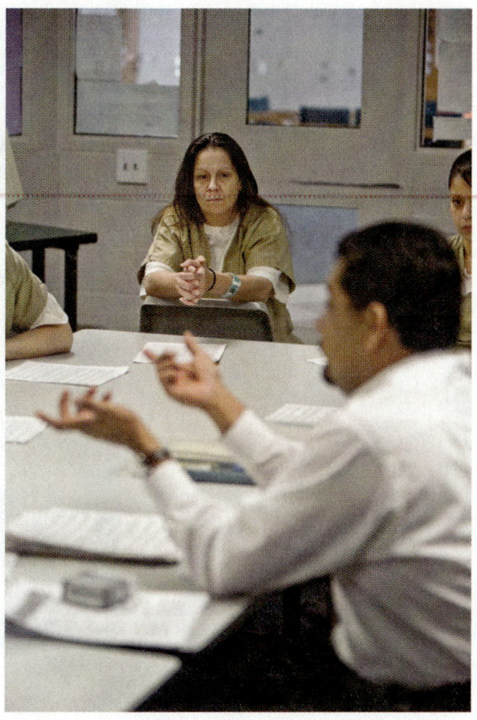

Photo 9.7

Vocational educator preps inmates on work skills prior to beginning training.
Spencer Grant/Art Directors & TRIP/Alamy.

THE VOCATIONAL-REHABILITATION MODEL

Vocational and technical training in prisons has been available to prisoners ever since the industrial prison was established in the early 1800s. That early training, however, was aimed not at prisoner rehabilitation but at institutional profit. Later, at the Elmira Reformatory, the concept of training for the purpose of teaching a trade to ex-offenders was introduced, and it has slowly taken root over the years. A major setback to adequate **vocational training** came with the passage of restrictive federal laws on the interstate transport of prison industry goods. Those laws, passed during the Depression era, sounded the death knell for many work programs in state prisons. Only in the past 30 years have institutions begun to reemphasize vocational training programs.

Prison industry has continued on a somewhat smaller scope since the restrictive laws were enacted. Prison industry went through several phases, starting at the contract labor level through increasingly more restricted systems. In contract labor, part, if not the whole, of the prison population was rented to private contractors who used their labor for private gain. Next came the piece-price scheme, in which private contractors provided raw materials and paid a set price to the prison for produced items (such as soccer balls). The next phase was the public account system, in which the prison became the manufacturer of a product to be sold on the open market, such as twine, bailing wire, bags ("croaker sacks"), and airplane chocks. These efforts failed for a variety of reasons, including prison corruption, union resistance, excessive cruelty, padded budgets, and inordinate up-front costs. The current prison industry system is the state-use system in which prison labor produces items that do not enter the open market and are instead sold to state-run institutions, facilities, and agencies. This includes the ubiquitous license plate manufacture, tables and chairs used in educational institutions, clothing for inmates and mental patients, soap and eggs, and so on. Critics have raised the question of the usefulness of the limited skills learned in prison industry and have labeled the work by inmates as exploitation of prisoners.

key term

Vocational training
Any training program designed to increase job readiness and skills for inmates.

A common problem with prison industries is their multiple goals, for they sometimes shift and are always ambiguous. The prison administrator may believe the goal of prison industries to be generation of profits, shop managers are convinced it is to train inmates, and inmates believe that it is "make-work" and that they will receive some wage unrelated to productivity.[27] Leadership in resolving those conflicting goals was exerted by Congress in 1979, when it passed the Prison-Industries Enhancement Act, selectively repealing portions of the federal laws limiting prison industries. Since then, more than 20 states (such as Arizona, Minnesota, Washington, and Kansas) have authorized some form of private-sector involvement with state penal industries, such as in the areas of data processing, hotel chain reservations, and manufacturing. Many of those private-industry efforts must deal with insurance, initial plant investment costs, and quality control problems. It remains to be seen how effective private industry will be in collaborating with prisons,[28] but such efforts are welcome signs in times of prison overcrowding.

Exciting programs working with companies in South Carolina, California, and Connecticut have formed successful projects with state and local correctional agencies. Some positive features of these collaborations include the following:[29]

Photo 9.8

Inmates receiving training in the mastery of PowerPoint presentations.
John Zich/Corbis News/Corbis.

1. A cost-competitive, motivated workforce that can continue to work after release from prison
2. The proximity of a prison-based feeder plant to the company's regular facility
3. Financial incentives, including low-cost industrial space and an equipment purchase subsidy, that are offered by correctional officials

correctional **practice 9.5**

Literacy and Its Impact on Reoffending

The federal prison system established a mandatory literacy program in 1982, requiring sixth-grade reading as the minimum literacy standard. This was changed to eighth-grade reading in 1986 and to a GED certificate in 1991. The adult basic education program has been very successful when completion rates are compared from 1981 to 1990, which saw an encouraging 724 percent increase in the number of inmates achieving basic literacy.

Twelve studies on the effects of education on reoffending are also encouraging. One investigator reported on three studies by David Fairchild. On the first, there was only a 15 percent reoffending rate for New Mexico inmates who had completed at least one year of college compared to 68 percent for the general population. Fairchild found zero recidivism for college graduates versus a reoffending rate of 55 percent for the general prison population studied at a California prison. Finally, Fairchild reported that none of the first 200 Indiana reformatory inmates earning a college degree offered by a university extension program returned to the reformatory. (We discuss the issues of self-selectivity and motivation later in this textbook.)

Consistently favorable outcomes have been linked to education in Canada, where three of four prisoner-students remained free of subsequent incarceration for at least three years. Significantly lower relapse and recidivism rates have been found for education and work release in Delaware and college education in North Carolina and Georgia.

Adult basic education programs show promise for decreasing recidivismz even for inmates with learning disabilities. Technology education (particularly computers) provides inmates with marketable skills. Studies have concluded that the recidivism rate can be as low as 11 percent for inmates who successfully complete training and as high as 70 percent for those who do not. The National Literacy Trust of the United Kingdom reported a statistically significant connection between repeated offending and poor literacy.

SOURCE: Robert Hall and Mark Bannatyne, "Technology Education and the Convicted Felon," *Journal of Correctional Education* 51:4 (2000): 320–323; National Literacy Trust, "Literacy Changes Lives: The Role of Literacy in Offending Behaviour,"http://www.literacytrust.org.uk/assets/0000/0422/Literacy_changes_lives__prisons.pdf (accessed November 2, 2008).

4. Safe work environment due to the presence of security personnel and a metal detector that keeps weapons out of the shop area
5. The partial return to society of inmate earnings to pay state and federal taxes, offset incarceration costs, contribute to the support of the inmate's families, and compensate victims

THE REINTEGRATION MODEL

The movement toward treatment and corrections in the community has highlighted the need to make programs inside the walls relate to circumstances in the outside world. Crime cannot be controlled by the reformation of prisoners alone. Efforts at reformation and reintegration into the community must continue.

Toward that end, many of the barriers shutting off prisons from their communities have come down in the past decade. The treatment concept has been expanded to include a variety of inmate treatment programs and models usually discussed in correctional treatment courses. We mention several major offender-based institutional models to illustrate the entry and increase of treatment professionals into the prison system.

Perhaps the most effective of therapies is **cognitive behavioral intervention**, an approach that focuses on the ways in which offenders think. Thinking includes a wide array of skills and processes, such as problem-solving skills, the ability to empathize with others and victims, the ability to formulate and then achieve plans for the future, and the ability to foresee the consequences of one's own behavior. For example, hitting a correctional officer on the head with a battery wrapped in a sock ("sucker punch") would be perceived by some inmates as away to deal with a difficult officer but would certainly have consequences, such as isolation in a punitive segregation cell. **Cognitive** also refers to the beliefs, values, attitudes, and stability we impose on our conception of the world around us (see Chapter 7). Flowing from this approach are techniques that attempt to influence and change the cognitions of offenders. This is done through role playing, appropriate reinforcement, modeling, and changing of irrational beliefs.

One example of program application to prisoners is **anger management**. Anger management focuses on preventing the negative behavior that arises from impulsive hostile aggression by teaching self-awareness, self-control, and alternate thinking and behavior. The facilitator may intend to reduce aggressive behavior through teaching self-control and management skills. The key is to teach the inmate how to lower arousal levels, increase self-control, change thinking, communicate feelings, recognize anger, and use coping mechanisms (to "cage the rage").

Another popular interventional program in prisons is the **therapeutic community**. Several years ago due to the influx of federal support, many states created in-prison substance abuse programs, many in the form of therapeutic communities. Although first developed after World War I to treat "shell-shocked" soldiers, the concept was expanded to address other behavioral problems, including addiction and criminal behavior. The primary focus is on helping the offender change those thoughts, beliefs, attitudes, and actions that create the potential for and actual criminal behavior. These are almost always preparatory to release back into the community.

Prison treatment also encompasses the efforts of community-based professionals, and community volunteers have begun to give offenders the support and guidance needed to ensure successful reintegration.[30] The main objective of the **reintegration model** (or now often called "reentry") is to return the offender to the community as a responsible and productive citizen rather than as a feared and shunned "ex-con" with little hope for success. Institutions dedicated to that objective have learned to overcome deficits in funding and personnel by using the ingenuity of prison staff and the resources available in the community. Teachers and graduate students are encouraged to offer courses on topics that will help reintegrate the inmate, including such subjects as social problems, mental health, and the use of community resources.[31]

key term

Cognitive behavioral intervention
A structured process that attempts to change how an offender thinks and sees the world through cognitive restructuring (what they think) and behavioral rehearsal (how they think).

key term

Cognitive
Mental processes that generally hinder change in prisoners but can be corrected by various thinking, speaking, and conceptual treatments.

key term

Anger management
Treatment programs within a correctional system designed to help offenders rein in their anger and aggression by understanding how and why anger arises and rehearsing alternative nonviolent expressions.

key term

Therapeutic community
A term applied to a participative, group-based approach to treating criminal behavior and drug addiction.

key term

Reintegration model
A treatment approach to prevent relapse and recidivism by use of existing community services, often bundled into a reentry plan to lower recidivism.

correctional practice 9.6

Prison Release Programs

Work, occupational training, and education are three major objectives for which inmates are allowed to leave the prison. In most states, the legal mechanism for allowing an inmate to leave prison is the furlough program: The legislature extends the limits of confinement to include placement in the community while the prisoner pursues some common and identifiable correctional goal.

Furlough candidates are usually screened carefully and supervised by an agency. Although the extent of recidivism among furlough users is unknown, it is generally believed to be low. One reason for the low recidivism probably is that furloughees in most jurisdictions remain inmates and can be returned to prison easily if they show overt signs of being unable to conform their behavior to community expectations.

Oklahoma has used home furlough (house arrest of inmates) as a mechanism to reduce prison overcrowding, and the recidivism rate is markedly low. In Massachusetts, furlough participation had a pronounced and consistently positive impact on recidivism. More states are exploring the opportunities of increasing furlough programs to extend the limits of confinement for low-risk and near-death inmates and plan to couple house arrest with electronic monitoring, unscheduled drug and alcohol testing, and supervision fees. This approach may become a major prison-release mechanism in the next decade, and California is currently releasing near-sentence-end inmates, the terminally ill, and candidates for "old age" homes.

In many institutions, the barriers are coming down for traffic in both directions ("the door swings both ways"). Outside activity by inmates and prison personnel ranges from touring lecture programs to work and educational furloughs. The latter programs serve as a method of graduated release back to the community.[32] The rationale for graduated release has its roots in the problems faced by the newly released inmate. Release is a very stressful time for inmates, especially when they emerge directly from an institution. Inmates know they have failed in the past and fear they will fail again. Without a chance to ease back into society in stages, as is possible with graduated release, the inmate feels vulnerable if he or she has been inside the walls for a long time. The released prisoner needs new social skills and a chance to catch up with a rapidly moving society.

correctional practice 9.7

The Effects of Prison Visitation on Offender Recidivism

Visitation of offenders who are in prison has a socially positive impact on recidivism in terms of both reducing recidivism and shrinking the size of the prison populations. Newly released prisoners are unprepared for life outside the walls and face a number of challenges to successful reentry. The latter include family conflict, search for employment, offender debt, substance abuse challenges (especially comorbidity with mental illness), and homelessness. The factors contribute to the high arrest rate (almost two-thirds) of prisoners within three years of their release. Successful reintegration and reentry are critical to decreasing recidivism as well as managing prison populations.

Recent investigations of the impacts of prison visitation have concluded that it is a crucial social support that can lead offenders to desist from reoffending and technical violations. Prison visitation programs, such as visits from family and friends, support establishing, nurturing, and increasing social support networks. For example, many parolees depend on friends and family for financial help, job opportunities, and housing. The evidence is that both the frequency and the existence of prison visits in the past 12 months leading up to prison release are strongly associated with crime desistence and lowered recidivism. Unfortunately, many prison visits tend to be brief and limited, and conducted in sterile and uninviting environments.

Yet the evidence remains that visits from siblings, fathers, inlaws, and clergy are particularly crime suppressive and permit more effective reintegration and reduced recidivism. (Visits from ex-spouses, however, increase the probability of recidivism.) The best policy to prevent offender recidivism after release from confinement appears to be marshaling and allocating greater sources of social support for prerelease inmates by increasing visitation from family and friends of inmates with little (or no) social support as well as use of volunteer parole mentors.

SOURCE: Minnesota Department of Corrections (2012), "The Effects of Prison Visitation on Offender Recidivism," http://www.doc.state.mn.us/pages/files/large-files/Publications/11-11MNPrisonVisitationStudy.pdf (accessed September 7, 2014).

Prisons and Recidivism

Despite the tremendous amount of money spent on prisons and prison programs, recidivism remains stubbornly high. Recently, the Pew Center for the States released a new report comparing state-by-state recidivism rates for inmates released between 1999 and 2002 and those released between 2005 and 2007. These rates remain high and in many cases have actually increased over this span of time.[33]

In the Pew study, data revealed that more than 45 percent of the cohort released onto parole in 1999 was reincarcerated by 2002. About 43 percent of the cohort released onto parole had also returned to incarceration. The states of South Dakota, Washington, and Minnesota had large increases in recidivism: 35, 31, and 11 percent, respectively.

Minnesota had the highest return-to prison rate: 61 percent. It is clear that recidivism rates are unlikely to fall anytime soon without major changes in the way the justice system handles and treats offenders. Clearly, correctional officials still have a lot of work to do in the areas of rehabilitation and reentry.

Summary

Summarize the Security and Custody Functions within a Correctional Facility

Our review of the findings and conclusions evident in this chapter indicate that security functions within a correctional facility frequently prevent effective treatment and management functions. Prisons are expected to provide control and rehabilitation; control and custody are the main but not only functions of incarceration.

Summarize Various Treatment Programs within a Prison, Including Prison Labor

Since the early beginnings of prisons in America, religious, educational, and vocational programs existed. Prison labor programs initially generated profits from the prison, although Congress enabled states to banish prison-made goods from their jurisdictions. In the past several decades, that list has been expanded to include substance abuse, sex offender behavior, violence reduction interventions, mental health services, counseling, religious activities, therapeutic communities, and other clinical activities. With the extension of the limits of confinement to include education, training, and vocational programs, prisons have added many major programs. Evidence-based programs have been introduced, including cognitive behavioral intervention and such clinical programs as "cage the rage." Treatment programs are expanding, and their effectiveness in reducing recidivism is being validated.

Summarize the Issues Associated with Inmate Health Care

Incoming offenders have multiple medical and dental health care issues, particularly since most have not been able to afford adequate care. Many have chemical substance abuse dependencies (drugs and alcohol), mental health disturbances and inadequacies, psychological and psychiatric issues, and infections with viruses resistant to even excellent health care. By law, prisoners must receive treatment similar to that in their local community.

There are frequently inadequate numbers of medical staff to address inmate needs, and sometimes available staff have limited qualifications to provide medical care. More and better medical staff and care are required. The failure to provide adequate medical care can result in major court cases and federal court intervention.

Explain the Three Pervasive Themes That Have Run through Correctional Management over the past 100 Years

Since at least since 1870, correctional managers, wardens, and superintendents have adopted a gradualist approach, making no major changes in their operations or programming. Change has been implemented gradually; prison managers welcomed the distance between major urban settings and their facilities, preferring isolationism and withdrawal from public sight and oversight. This has resulted in only a few innovations and experiments and constrained the development of the prison. Other themes are restraint and reformation and isolation and withdrawal to conceal prison actions.

Differentiate between Classification for Security versus Classification for Treatment

After new inmates are received in a prison, the institution undertakes a variety of needs and risk assessments designed to determine inmate needs and the risks that inmates might pose. In practice, the risk that inmates are believed to have outweigh their individual needs, leading to assigning new inmates to higher-security institutions that would, parenthetically, be less able to provide the type of treatments that would address their needs. Since there are frequently inadequate reclassification efforts, such inmates tend to be retained in their initial institutions; the lack of treatment options and services contributes to the recidivism later seen amongst high-needs inmates.

Explain How Inmate Needs Are Identified

Most states do a thorough job in assessing needs of the individual offenders as well as the risks each poses. The outstanding assessments are behavioral: What crimes did the inmate commit? What has been the pattern of the offender's life? Has an alias been used? Does the inmate regret the criminal action and the victim's pain? Is there an effort to improve behavior and desist in crime? What are the inmate's objectives and plans? Once readings on these and other behavioral criminogenic factors have been determined, the better systems can initiate an adequate treatment plan to return the offender to the free society as a functioning and constructive member. In an ideal world, treatment functions within the confinement facility would be linked to a continuation of community-based services, including location of housing, employment, food services, and other individual needs that must be addressed. To the uninitiated, expending resources on bad/evil people is a waste of time and money. But since the underlying mission is to lessen crime, lessen recidivism, and prevent victimization, such programming is vital.

Explain How Prison Programs Can Lessen Recidivism

Currently, there is a rehabilitation thrust that focuses on evidence-based treatments. Did the program being used actually reduce inmate recidivism? If the evidence indicates that the intervention was effective, correctional managers could pursue the same program with other inmates. If there is no evidence that the intervention worked, that program could be defunded and alternative programs implemented. Basically, this means that if a program did not achieve its goals, it would be foolhardy to try that program again. Effective prison programs address criminogenic needs and lessen the probability of recidivism, preparing the inmate for reintegration and a less criminal future.

Key Words

treatment services, 194
backfilled, 194
gradualism approach, 196
meta-analysis, 196
isolationism and withdrawal, 196
classification, 197
external classification, 197
internal classification, 197
reclassification, 197
sick call, 198
goldbrickers, 198
medical services, 198
hepatitis A and B, 198
comorbidity, 201
correctional chaplaincy, 203
functionally illiterate, 204
GED, 204
Project Newgate, 206
furlough, 206
vocational training, 207
cognitive behavioral intervention, 209
cognitive, 209
anger management, 209
therapeutic community, 209
reintegration model, 209

Review Questions

1. Why are there more correctional officers than treatment staff?
2. Is classification more properly a security or a treatment function? Why?
3. Define classification, internal classification, external classification, and reclassification.
4. Explain why corrections in general has so few spokespersons.
5. Describe the roles of the chaplain in prison.
6. What motivates inmates to participate in prison treatment programs?
7. What are five common health problems found in prisons?
8. How are religious services delivered inside prisons?
9. Does education lower recidivism when inmates are paroled?
10. What kinds of inmates are given furloughs?
11. What jobs are available in prisons for staff? Inmates?
12. What can be done to prepare inmates for community reintegration?

Application Case Studies

1. You have just been promoted to director of the Institutional Planning unit in your state department of corrections (DOC). On the first day of your new job, the governor asks the director of the DOC to develop a plan to reduce recidivism among inmates when released. In turn, the director instructs you to develop a plan to lower recidivism by 20 percent within four years. What would you propose?
2. Your next task is to offer a recommendation to the DOC on whether the educational programming of your prisons should be contracted out to a "for-profit" company that has proposed to manage all educational programming in your prisons. What five points would you consider in your initial report?
3. Your state parole board decides that no one will be released from prison early or on their authority unless she or he can read and write at the eighth-grade level. This is clearly a signal by the parole board to inmates to start working on some educational goal. What programs should be offered, and how would you document their educational achievements?
4. Your prison chaplain has received a letter from a Wiccan priest, volunteering to provide religious services to inmates. The chaplain is irritated and not supportive of the offer. As the warden of the prison, what (if anything) would you do? Hint: Go online and read two sources, one that regales the Wiccans and one that disparages them. (Learn what you are dealing with.) What would you do?

Endnotes

1. See Don Gibbons, "Review Essay—Changing Lawbreakers: What Have We Learned since the 1950s?," *Crime and Delinquency* 45:2 (1999): 272–293, and Elizabeth Gudrais, "The Prison Problem," *Harvard Magazine*, November–December 2013, http://harvardmagazine.com/2013/03/the-prison-problem.
2. Robert Morgan, C. Winterowd, and S. Ferrell, "A National Survey of Group Psychotherapy Services in Correctional Facilities," *Professional Psychology Research and Practice* 30:6 (1999): 600–606.
3. See Rob Wilson, "Who Will Care for the 'Mad' and the 'Bad'?," *Corrections Magazine* 6:1 (1980): 5–17. See also Joan Petersilia, "Justice for All? Offenders with Mental Retardation and the California Corrections System," *Prison Journal* 77:4 (1998): 358–380, and Julio Arboleda and David Weisstub, *Forensic Research with the Mentally Disordered Offender* 55:1 (2013): 103–122, http://link.springer.com/book/10.1007%2F978-94-007-0086-4.
4. But see the excellent evaluation of Joan Petersilia, *The Influence of Criminal Justice Research* (Santa Monica, CA: Rand Corporation, 1987), and Jeffrey Fagan and M. Forst, "Risk Fixers and Zeal: Implementing Experimental Treatment for Violent Juvenile Offenders," *Prison Journal* 76:1 (1996): 22–59.
5. Francis Cullen and B. Applegate, eds., *Offender Rehabilitation: Effective Treatment Intervention* (Aldershot: Ashgate, 1997); U.S. Office of Justice Programs Drug Courts Program Office, *Looking at a Decade of Drug Courts* (Washington, DC: U.S. Department of Justice, 1997); Substance Abuse and Mental Health Youth Substances Administration (2013), "Drug Treatment Courts Offer Hope for Youth," http://www.samhsa.gov/samhsanewsletter/Volume_21_Number_1/drug_treatment.aspx.
6. Francis Cullen and Karen E. Gilbert, *Reaffirming Rehabilitation. Thirty-Year Anniversary Edition* (Waltham, MA: Anderson/Elsevier, 2013).

7. See Steve Donziger, *The Real War on Crime* (New York: HarperCollins, 1996), pp. 194–219: John Irwin and J. Austin, *It's about Time: America's Imprisonment Binge,* 3rd ed. (Belmont, CA: Wadsworth, 2011); and Charles Terry, "Managing Prisoners as Problem Populations: The Evolving Nature of Imprisonment: A Convict's Perspective," *Critical Criminology* 12:1 (2003): 43–66.
8. The relationship between ingestion of drugs and crime appears quite strong. See in particular Christopher Mumola, *Substance Abuse and Treatment: State and Federal Prisoners, 1997* (Washington, DC: U.S. Department of Justice, 1999), and Henry J. Kaiser Family Foundation (2013), "HIV Testing in the United States," http://kff.org/hivaids/fact-sheet/hiv-testing-in-the-United-States/.
9. Drug abuse is widespread among prison inmates, but treatment programs are in short supply. See Donald Dowd, S. Dalzell, and M. Spencer, eds., "The Sentencing Controversy: Punishment and Policy in the War against Drugs," *Villanova Law Review* 40:2 (1995): 301–427; and Federal Bureau of Prisons, "The Federal Bureau of Prisons Annual Report on Substance Abuse and Treatment," http://www.bop.gov/inmates/custody_and_care/docs/annual_report_fy_2012.pdf.
10. Theodore Hammett, *Public Health and Corrections Collaboration: Prevention and Treatment of HIV/AIDS, STDs, and TB* (Washington, DC: Office of Justice Programs, 1998).
11. U.S. Department of Health and Human Services, *Control of Tuberculosis in Correctional Facilities: A Guide for Health Care Workers* (Washington, DC: U.S. Department of Health and Human Services, 1992); Centers for Disease Control (2013), "Tuberculosis in Correctional Facilities Is a Public Health Concern," http://www.cdc.gov/features/dstbcorrections/.
12. Bureau of Justice Statistics, *Medical Problems of Inmates, 1997* (Washington, DC: Bureau of Justice Statistics, 2001), pp. 1, 12; Sophie Davidson and P. Taylor, "Psychological Distress and Severity of Personality Disorder Symptomatology in Prisoners Convicted of Violent and Sexual Offenses," *Psychology, Crime and the Law* 7:3 (2001): 263–272; Kristen Rasmussen, R. Almvik, and S. Levander, "Attention Deficit Hyperactivity Disorder, Reading Disability, and Personality Disorders in a Prison Population," *Journal of the American Academy of Psychology and the Law* 29:2 (2001): 186–193; Jack Baillergeon, Sandra Black, Charles Leach, et al., "The Infectious Disease Profile of Texas Prison Inmates," *Preventive Medicine* 38:5 (2004): 607–612.
13. Mannix Porterfield, "Smoking Has Its Problems in W. VA. Prisons," *The Register-Herald,* June 16, 2008, http://www.register-herald.com/archivesearch/local_story_168222359.html (accessed November 1, 2008).
14. William Petroski, "Despite Exemption, Prisons to Ban Smoking," http://m.desmoinesregister.com/news.jsp?key=252368&rc=In&p=2 (accessed November 1, 2008). See also Crime Beast (2013), "With Cigarettes Banned in Most Prisons, Gangs Shift from Drugs to Smokes," http://www.thedailybeast.com/articles/2013/06/02/with-cigarettes-banned-in-most-prisons-gangs-shift-from-drugs-to-smokes.html# (accessed September 7, 2014).
15. Editors, "Michigan Prisons Prepare for Total Smoking Ban," *Correctional News* 14:3 (2008): 18.
16. *CBC News*, "'Tempers Will Flare' as Prison Smoking Ban Takes Effect, Inmate Says," http://www.cbc.ca/news/canada/tempers-will-flare-as-prison-smoking-ban-takes-effect-inmate-says-1.721325 (accessed September 7, 2014).
17. But see Jody Spertzel, "Rev. Henry Bouma: Chaplain's Ministry Links Facility with Community," *Corrections Today* 55:3 (1993): 91, and Jody Sundt and F. Cullen, "The Contemporary Prison Chaplain," *The Prison Journal* 78:3 (1998): 271–298.
18. Robert Marsh and V. Cox, "The Practice of Native-American Spirituality in Prison: A Survey," *Justice Professional* 8:2 (1994): 79–95.
19. Dennis Stephens and C. Ward, "College Education and Recidivism: Educating Criminals Is Meritorious," *Journal of Correctional Education* 48:3 (1997): 106–111. See also Grace Merritt, *Connecticut Times,* "CT's Multi-Pronged Approach to Reducing Recidivism Is Working," http://www.ctmirror.org/story/2013/09/18/cts-multi-pronged-approach-reducing-recidivism-working.
20. Richard Lawrence, "Classroom v. Prison Cells: Funding Priorities for Education and Corrections," *Journal of Crime and Justice* 18:2 (1995): 113–126; Elliott Currie, *Crime and Punishment in America (Revised)* (New York: Picador/Macmillan, 2013).
21. James Anderson, J. Burns, and L. Dyson, "Could an Increase in AIDS Cases among Incarcerated Populations Mean More Legal Liabilities for Correctional Administrators?," *Journal of Criminal Justice* 21:1 (1998): 41–52.
22. T. L. Felton, "The Learning Modes of the Incarcerated Population," *Journal of Correctional Education* 4:3 (1994): 118–121; Theodore Hammett, P. Harmon, and L. Maruschak, *1996–1997 Update: HIV/AIDS, STDs, and TB in Correctional Facilities* (Washington, DC: U.S. Department of Justice, 1999), pp. 25–45.

23. Eva Fisher-Bloom, "The Import of Learning Disabilities in Correctional Treatment," *Forum* 7:3 (1995): 20–26; Barbara Belot and J. Marquart, "The Political Community Model and Prisoner Litigation," *Prison Journal* 78:3 (1998): 299–329.
24. Arnie Nielsen, F. Scarpitti, and J. Inciardi, "Integrating the Therapeutic Community and Work Release for Drug-Abusing Offenders," *Journal of Substance Abuse and Treatment* 13:4 (1996): 349–358. On reentry after prison drug treatment, see also Illinois Criminal Information Authority (2012), http://www.icjia.state.il.us/public/pdf/researchreports/reentry_sheridan_report_012012.pdf.
25. See Rick Linden and L. Perry, "The Effectiveness of Prison Educational Programs," *Journal of Offender Counseling, Services and Rehabilitation* 6:1 (1982): 43–57, and Lois Davis et al., *Evaluating the Effectiveness of Correctional Education* (Santa Monica, CA: Rand Corporation, 2013).
26. C. Camp and G. Camp, *The Corrections Yearbook 2000: Adult Corrections* (Middletown, CT: Criminal Justice Institute, 2000), pp. 126–129.
27. Neil Singer, *The Value of Inmate Manpower* (Washington, DC: American Bar Association Commission on Correctional Facilities and Manpower, 1973). See also David Scharf, "Are Day Reporting and Reentry Programs the Future of Corrections in Our Country?," *American Jails* 12:3 (2008): 25–27. But see D. Burton-Rose, D. Pens, P. Wright, et al., *The Celling of America: An Inside Look at the U.S. Prison Industry* (Monroe, ME: Common Courage Press, 1998).
28. Betty Fortuin, "Maine's Female Offenders Are Reentering—and Succeeding," *Corrections Today* 69:2 (2007): 34–37; Bonnie Johnson, "First Book and Hope House: Bridging the Gap for Families from Behind Bars," *Corrections Today* 22:3 (2008): 88–90.
29. Larry Mays and T. Gray, eds., *Privatization and the Provision of Correctional Services* (Cincinnati, OH: Anderson Publishing, 1996). See also Cody Mason, (2013), "International Growth Trends in Prison Privatization," http://sentencingproject.org/doc/publications/inc_International%20Growth%20Trends%20in%20Prison%20Privatization.pdf.
30. George Sexton, *Work in American Prisons: Joint Ventures with the Private Sector* (Washington, DC: U.S. Department of Justice, 1995), p. 2.
31. Edward Latessa, L. Travis, and H. Allen, "Volunteers and Paraprofessionals in Parole: Current Practices," *Journal of Offender Counseling, Services and Rehabilitation* 8:1/2 (1983): 91–106; American Probation and Parole Association, *Restoring Hope through Community Partnerships* (Lexington, KY: American Probation and Parole Association, 1996).
32. David Onek, *Pairing College Students with Delinquents: The Minnesota Intensive Case Monitoring Program* (San Francisco: National Council on Crime and Delinquency, 1994); Pamela Hewitt, E. Moore, and B. Gaulier, "Winning the Battles and the War," *Juvenile and Family Court Journal* 49:1 (1998): 39–49.
33. Pew Center for the States, "State of Recidivism: The Revolving Door of America's Prisons," April 2011. See also Bureau of Justice Statistics (2013), "U.S. Prison Population Declines for Third Consecutive Year during 2012," http://www.bjs.gov/content/pub/press/p12acpr.cfm.

Alex Quesada/Sipa PressSipa/Newscom.

Objectives

- Outline the history of jails.
- Describe the purpose, function, and operations of today's jails.
- Describe the various types of pretrial release.
- Describe the characteristics of jail inmates.
- Summarize the design and supervisory options in jails.
- Summarize issues in jails.
- Summarize pretrial services and other alternatives to jail incarceration.

chapter 10
Jails and Detention Facilities

Outline

"[T]he number of persons confined in county and city jails increased by 1.2% between midyear 2011 and midyear 2012. The majority of the increase occurred in California jails."

—Bureau of Justice Statistics, 2013

Overview

Now that we have explored the custody, management, and treatment functions of institutions, it is time to examine the major forms of imprisonment, starting with jails. The vast majority of offenders begin their journey through the correctional system in a **jail** or detention facility. For some, this is the last stop, whereas for others, it is only the beginning.

This chapter provides an overview of one of the most used sanctions in the correctional system: the local jail. Clearly our nation has developed many different processes and institutions to meet the primary mission of corrections, that is, to protect society. This chapter takes an in-depth look at local jails and detention centers as the very first step in an often long and winding road taken in the name of justice. That path will eventually result in most of the offenders returning to society, having paid a debt for crimes committed, large or small. The "scales of justice" attempt to balance the crime and the appropriate punishment, and this process starts with apprehension by the police and booking at a local facility.

As the student will discover, of all the institutions through which offenders pass on their way through the correctional funnel, none has a more diverse population (or a more sordid past) than the jails. Jails are confinement facilities, usually operated by a local law enforcement agency, for holding detained persons pending a hearing or trial and/or persons committed after conviction for less than one year (although there are some exceptions to this practice, most notably in Texas). The jail is the first institutional contact within the criminal justice system that most accused adult males and females (and many juveniles) experience. Most jails are small, although some are huge. For example, Los Angeles County operates the largest jail system in the free world with about 171,000 offenders per year going through its doors. Whether large or small, however, jails are predominantly city, county, or regional facilities, funding for which can be erratic and unpredictable. And, as we will discover, jails serve as the primary mental health system in our nation.

key term

Jail
A local secure facility designed to house offenders, usually for one year or less.

JAILS: A GRIM HISTORY

The housing of offenders and suspected criminals in local detention facilities is a practice as old as the definition of crime. The processes and practices at the local gaol, lockup, workhouse, stockade, hulk,[1] or detention center changed little over the centuries, until about the mid-1900s. Only recently has any serious attempt been made to provide programs or treatment for jail inmates, and even those efforts must be carefully monitored, or officials are likely to abandon them.[2] Originally devised as a place to lock up and restrain all classes of misfits, the jail has a long and sordid history. As discussed in Chapter 1, John Howard was made keenly aware of the appalling gaol conditions in eighteenth-century England when he found himself the proprietor of one of its worst. His effort to reform the practices and improve the conditions in the gaols and prisons of England and the rest of Europe parallels the periodic attempts by American reformers to clean up our jails. As recently as the early 1970s, little had changed with regard to the jails of America, some of which were almost a century old.

The early jails in America were similar to those in Europe. Most were composed of small rooms in which as many as 20 to 30 prisoners were jammed together. The purpose of jails, as originally conceived by Henry II of England when he ordered the construction of the first official English jail at the Assize of Clarendon in 1166, was to detain suspected or accused offenders until they could be brought before a court. Seldom were the jails adequately heated or ventilated, and food was either sold by the jailer or brought in by family or friends. Conditions within the early jails defy description, and the problems of overcrowding and poor sanitation continue to plague some jails today. Many are exemplary, but at best a few are warehouses for the misdemeanant, vagrant, petty offender, and common drunk. At worst, they are overcrowded, understaffed, underfunded "festering sores," as described by a former director of the Law Enforcement Assistance Administration. The jail, perhaps more than any other segment of the correctional system, has been difficult to change and tends to deteriorate more quickly than it can be improved. Undoubtedly, some of this is because most jails are funded through local taxes. Traditionally, jails have not been high on the priority list for support from local politicians. Thus, jails have been called the "cloacal region of corrections."[3]

key term

Jail inmates
Offenders housed in a local facility, including those waiting for trial, those awaiting transport to a state or federal prison, and those convicted of a crime, usually punishable by less than one year.

Felons, misdemeanants, and those awaiting trial make up the major population of jails. However, additional categories of **jail inmates** include persons with mental illnesses for whom there are no other facilities, parolees and probationers awaiting hearings, federal

Photo 10.1
Jail intake officer fingerprinting a newly arrested suspect.
David R. Frazier Photolibrary, Inc./Alamy.

prisoners awaiting pickup by marshals, and offenders sentenced to departments of corrections for whom there is not yet space but who cannot be released. In some states, felons serving relatively short sentences can also be housed in local jails to complete their sentences (for example, in Texas, offenders serving two-year sentences or less can be housed in jail).

The jail has been at the end of the line for receiving public and governmental support since the days when John Howard inherited the abomination of a gaol at Bedfordshire, England, in 1773. Though public attention turns to jails from time to time when politicians or the media expose a particularly appalling situation, the jails seem to revert quickly back to their original deplorable state. In the past few years, a number of new facilities based on new management concepts have been constructed to provide better conditions and programs for the misdemeanant prisoners and felony detainees, but these new facilities are still too few, and many jurisdictions still operate antiquated facilities from another era. While community programs and facilities are sometimes used to provide work and educational programs for short-term sentenced prisoners, there are too few of these programs to alleviate the boredom and poor conditions of many jails.

Of all the problems that plague the criminal justice system, none is more confused and irrational than the question of what should be done with the offender in the period before trial. In the United States, the concept of "innocent until proven guilty" creates many problems for the local jail. Pretrial detention and procedures for pretrial liberty have been the subject of hot debate among personnel in the criminal justice system for many decades.[4] The **presumption of innocence** is difficult to maintain once the defendant has been arrested and detained in jail. The police find that presumption difficult to accept if they have acted on probable cause (high probability of guilt) in first making the arrest or have caught the individual in the act. Several projects studying the effects of pretrial decisions on sentencing offer evidence that this period is critical to later correctional efforts.[5] It is even more difficult for the public to realize that "not guilty" does not necessarily mean that the offender is "innocent." Not guilty simply means that it was not possible to establish guilt "beyond a reasonable doubt" for the offense for which the defendant was charged and tried.

key term

Presumption of innocence
Under the U.S. Constitution, those charged with a crime are presumed innocent until convicted in a court of law.

The problem of pretrial release is clear when we consider that the Sixth Amendment to the Constitution guarantees a "speedy and public trial." This presents a problem for the innocent person being held because he or she looks guiltier with each passing day in confinement. A 2002 study found that the median time from arrest to adjudication for felony defendants was about six months. In 2004, 72 percent of all convicted offenders received sentences to incarceration.[6]

Photo 10.2
Inmates from Calhoun County Jail who have been dumped at a state prison door due to overcrowding at that jail.
Jamie Martin/AP Images.

JAILS TODAY

Urban dwellers in America have responded to the need for local lockups and correctional facilities in a number of ways. The most common confinement facility is the lockup, but the size and quality of those facilities vary greatly. There is quite a difference between the one-cell lockup of a small town and the gigantic facilities of New York City and Los Angeles, which have capacity ratings of 19,636 and 22,477, respectively. The counterpart of the city lockup is the county jail, but jails, lockups, detention facilities, workhouses, and a number of other units are all commonly referred to as jails. (We refer to all of these facilities as city or county jails, except when it is more relevant to refer to them by another designation.) Policies and programs vary greatly among cities and counties, but some general descriptions and suggestions can be made for small, medium, and large systems. Over 86 percent of U.S. jails hold fewer than 250 inmates, yet the 159 largest jail systems hold about half of all jail inmates.

JAIL POPULATIONS AND CHARACTERISTICS

key term

Mental health issues
A range of diagnosed mental illnesses that often afflict jail inmates.

The felon and the misdemeanant, the first-time and the repeat offender, the adult (male and female), the juvenile, and the accused and the convicted, not to mention the guilty and the innocent, are housed in America's jails. Jails house individuals pending arraignment as well as those awaiting trial, conviction, and sentencing; probation, parole, and bail-bond violators and absconders; persons with mental illnesses awaiting transfer to appropriate

policy **positions 10.1**

The Mentally Ill in Jails

Jails process at least 2.1 million mentally ill inmates per year; state and federal prisons hold hundreds of thousands more. Most are not equipped to handle such a large number of problem inmates, but there are few functional alternatives than jail incarceration. Most mentally ill offenders do not want to be in such facilities.

At one time, the mentally ill were housed or warehoused mainly in huge state mental hospitals, but the federal courts ruled that if the mentally ill are held under state control to receive treatment, treatment must be provided. The sheer number of mentally ill inmates has come to mean that states cannot provide sufficient treatment. Such liability contributed significantly to the demise of state-managed mental health hospitals, so now there are more mentally ill citizens in jails than in mental health hospitals. The decline began in the 1970s and has accelerated since. The hospital within the prison opened about 1977.

The largest de facto mental institution in the nation is the Los Angeles County jail system, but there are not enough beds for all eligible offenders. What has developed is a "revolving door" process initiated through acting-out **mental health issues**, followed by jail incarceration and then release back onto the streets. On release, such inmates walk a few blocks to an open drug market and quickly fall back into the same behavior and patterns for which they were initially incarcerated. Linkage with community mental health services seldom occurs, although this population requires comprehensive and coordinated treatment.

It should be remembered that jails do not choose to take such people in, although a few of the better jails provided diagnosis, classification, treatment, and stabilizing. When released, the mentally ill jail inmates seldom follow through with medication, and many evince bizarre behavior.

There are glimmers of hope. Many local police departments have provided in-service and ongoing training for officers. Some jurisdictions have developed mental health courts designed to divert the mentally ill offender to comprehensive and usually coordinated services. Yet money is in short supply, and clinics, day centers, and community centers constantly battle to raise sufficient funds to improve both acceptance of the mentally ill and effective services.

SOURCE: National Public Radio, (2013), "What Is the Role of Jails in Treating the Mentally Ill?," http://www.npr.org/2013/09/15/222822452/what-is-the-role-of-jails-in-treating-the-mentally-ill (accessed November 17, 2013); Stephanie McCrummen (2013), Prince George's Mental Health Court Aims to Treat, Rather Than Jail, Defendants," http://articles.washingtonpost.com/2013-08-17/national/41419806_1_Mental-Health-Court-Mental-Illness-Drug-Addiction (accessed August 17, 2013).

table 10.1 Average Daily Population and Jail Incarceration Rates, 2002–2015

Year	Total	Number	Percent Change from Previous Year	Jail Incarceration Rate/100,000
2002	652,082	26,116	4.2%	231
2004	706,242	25,482	3.7%	243
2006	755,320	21,878	3.9%	256
2008	776,573	3,435	0.4%	258
2010	748,553	−19,582	−2.5%	242
2012	735,983	418	0.1%	237
2015*	722,293	−13,855	−0.3%	232

SOURCE: Todd D. Minton, "Jail Inmates at Midyear 2012—Statistical Tables" (Washington, DC: Bureau of Justice Statistics 2012), p. 5. *2015 data extrapolated from 2008–2012 data.

facilities in the mental health system[7]; chronic alcoholics; and drug abusers.[8] Individuals in jail also include persons being held for the military or in protective custody; material witnesses; persons found in contempt of court; persons awaiting transfer to state, federal, or other local authorities; and temporarily detained persons. Six in 10 of the persons jailed are there pretrial, about 10 percent have been found guilty but are as yet not sentenced, and the remainder are actually serving sentences. (This latter category is rising as local jurisdictions crack down on those who drive while intoxicated[9] and on domestic disturbance[10] crimes.) Each of these categories represents a challenge to jail administrators and managers.

Because jails are so scattered and varied in operations and record keeping, it is always difficult to develop accurate data regarding jails and jail populations. However, the most recent study of jail inmates available from the U.S. Department of Justice provides reasonably current and reliable information.[11]

For the first time in three decades, the average daily jail population in large jurisdictions declined since 2010—down 2.3 percent from the previous year (see Table 10.1). It is too soon to tell whether this short dip is the start of a new trend, but given the fiscal climate, many jurisdictions seem intent on reversing the population growth of prior years. From 1999 to 2008, jail populations climbed by 30 percent nationally. Table 10.2 shows the change in

table 10.2 Jail Capacity in Use

Jurisdiction	Number of Inmates, 2010	Percent of Capacity Occupied
Harris County, TX	10,264	109.3%
San Diego County, CA	4,863	103.6%
Jacksonville City, FL	3,837	122.3%
Riverside County, CA	3,342	106.7%
Clark County, NV	3,311	111.0%
Bernalillo County, NM	2,688	120.2%
Suffolk County	2,934	111.0%
Polk County, FL	2,214	122.5%
Salt Lake County, UT	2,238	106.7%

SOURCE: Todd D. Minton, "Jail Inmates at Midyear 2010—Statistical Tables Revised 6-28-2011" (Washington, DC: U.S Department of Justice), p. 10.

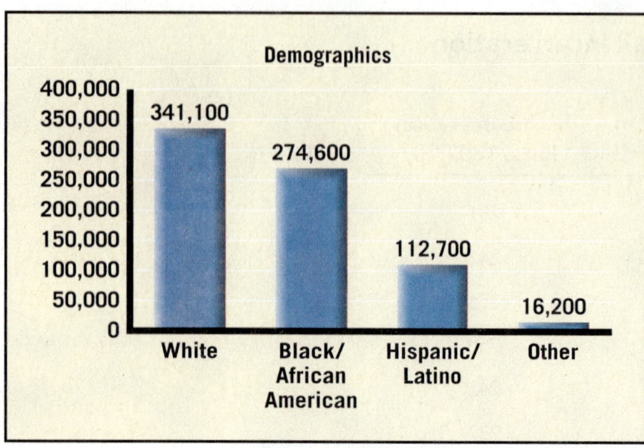

figure 10.1

Demographics of the U.S. Jail Population: 2012.

SOURCE: Todd D. Minton, "Jail Inmates at Midyear 2012—Statistical Tables (Washington, DC: U.S. Department of Justice, Bureau of Justice Statistics, May 2013), p. 5.

jail populations for some of the largest systems in the United States. It is estimated that about 12.8 million persons were admitted to jail during 2010, a figure that dropped to 12.6 in 2012. The latest profile of jail inmates reflected the traditional twofold function of a jail: a place for the temporary detention of pretrial defendants and a confinement facility where many convicted persons, predominantly misdemeanants, serve out their sentences, usually for less than one year. To further complicate the situation, many pretrial inmates may be kept in a jail for several months or longer before they can get a trial date. Slightly more than 60 percent of all jail inmates have not been convicted of a crime. To reduce the number of inmates and control some jail costs, many persons accused of first-time, nonviolent offenses are released onto pretrial house arrest, their location determined through the use of Global Positioning Systems.[12]

In 2012, 61 percent of the jail inmates were pretrial, accused but not convicted of a crime. Court-appointed lawyers, public defenders, or legal aid attorneys were representing most of those who had counsel. A large percentage of all pretrial inmates remained in jail, even though the authorities had set bail for them.

For those persons held in the nation's jails in midyear 2012, there were 9 percent more whites than blacks, but blacks were still disproportionately represented. Relative to the number of black U.S. residents, blacks were some five times more likely than whites to have been held in a local jail in midyear 2012. Hispanics were the fastest-growing segment of the jail population, which is consistent with their rising number in the U.S. population (see Figure 10.1).[13]

The 2012 adult jail population consisted predominantly of males, at 87 percent, and the number of women was just over 98,600, down from about 100,000 in 2008. Most jail inmates were young men in their twenties. The overall number of jails declined between 1999 and 2010, but this was due to the closing of small jails, many of which were consolidated with other facilities to form larger jails. In 2012, there were 2,799 jail facilities of every size and description.[14]

In addition to the pretrial and convicted offenders who are serving short sentences (usually less than a year) that typify city and county jails, some states (such as Texas) operate state jails. Texas has 16 adult detention facilities (jails) housing nonviolent third-degree felony offenders or Class A misdemeanants. Punishment for this group of offenders could be up to two years of incarceration in a state jail facility and a fine not to exceed $10,000, with possible community supervision following release from the state jail. In 2008, the state jail facilities in Texas housed more than 70,000 offenders.[15]

The most effective way to deal with nondangerous persons or to protect the innocent is either to keep them out of jail or to release them as soon as possible. Pretrial diversion, electronic monitoring, weekend confinement, community work orders, increased use of bail and personal recognizance, more extensive use of fines (including day fines and time payments), and various forms of work and study release all are viable alternatives to the destructive and expensive enforced idleness of most jails.[16] In many jurisdictions, jail crowding has forced many public officials to seek creative ways to handle offenders. Table 10.3 illustrates programs that jails are using to supervise offenders outside of the jail facility.

key term

New-generation jail
Developed in the 1970s, a new-generation jail is a facility designed for maximum interaction between the staff and inmates.

THE NEW-GENERATION JAIL

Jail design was essentially unchanged until the 1970s, when we began to see a new type of jail facility now referred to as the **new-generation jail**. This jail is a radical departure from the traditional jail in its architecture, interior design, and design philosophy.

table **10.3** **Number of Jail Inmates Supervised Outside of Jail Facilities in 2012**

Total Held in Jail	744,524
Weekend programs	10,351
Electronic monitoring	13,779
Home detention	2,129
Day reporting	3,890
Community service	14,761
Other pretrial supervision	7,738
Other work programs	7,137
Treatment programs	2,164
Other	2,149

SOURCE: Todd D. Minton, "Jail inmates at Midyear 2012—Statistical Tables" (Washington, DC: U.S. Department of Justice, (Bureau of Justice Statistics, May 2013), p. 9.

The new-generation jail is a facility designed for maximum interaction between the staff and inmates. In traditional jails, inmates were only occasionally observed by correctional officers ("intermittent supervision"). In the new-generation jails, inmates are under continuous and direct supervision.

In the third-generation new jails, cells continue to be laid out in a line, but inmates can spend most of their waking hours in a communal dayroom area (instead of in their cells). The fourth-generation jail contains a podular cell block, a central control and observation room, and a dayroom with corridors for circulation to and from services. The **new podular/direct supervision** created a common area within a ward of the jail (pod) with a jail officer intermingling with inmates within a cell block, within a common room and connecting corridors. The jail officer has direct supervision of inmates, interacts with them on a daily basis, and assists them with programs and jail issues. This fourth-generation jail included commercial-level furniture, carpet, soft surfaces that effectively reduced the sound level in the pod, and vitreous china toilets and washstands. When this generation was created, there were general expectations that jail inmates would destroy such a jail in short order, attack jail officers, and burn the pod down. Such expectations proved to be unfounded.[17]

key term

Podular/direct supervision
With podular/direct-supervision housing units, inmates have interaction with staff and other inmates through dayrooms or common areas. Jail officers directly interact with and supervise inmates daily.

Local jails were slow to emulate this new approach, whereby a correctional officer stayed inside the pod with the inmates for the entire shift. It was not until 1981 that the first local facility opened as a direct supervision jail in Contra Costa County, California. Still, many people who worked in jails could not believe that this new approach would work. Some assumed erroneously that federal inmates were not as tough as local inmates. These local inmates, they believed, would tear up the jail and assault the single officer controlling a pod that held up to 50 inmates. Of course, some resented the idea of commercial-grade furnishings that produced a more humanized environment and made it more livable. These inconsiderate individuals conveniently forget that the staff who manage and supervise the inmates spend their working days in the jail environment. Pleasant surroundings and reduced noise levels can help inhibit stress. Despite the initial reluctance at the local-government level, there was a substantial increase in the number of new jails adopting the direct supervision model. By the time the American Jail Association had published its second edition of *Who's Who in Jail Management 1994,* it listed 114 jails that had switched to direct supervision (pp. 401–405). The following year, the National Institute of Corrections Jails Division published *Podular Direct Supervision 1995,* which showed a considerable increase in direct supervision jails.

The direct supervision/strategy is believed to reduce inmate violation of and formal processing for contraband possession, destruction of property, escapes, insolence, suicides, and violence problems.

THE JAIL IN CONTEXT

The Problem with Overcrowding

Mandatory sentences, get-tough policies, and increased pressure from state correctional systems to reduce institutional populations is rapidly changing the makeup of America's jails, with serious offenders being housed together with local drunks and misdemeanants. Already overcrowded and difficult to control, many jails have become dumping grounds where little is accomplished other than locking up and feeding the population.

Although there have been improvements, in many physical facilities these have been set back by overcrowding and by the more violent populations.[18] Many of our largest jails are under court order to limit population and to improve specific conditions of confinement (food service, medical services, fire hazards, inmate classification, segregation policies, etc.).

Who are the "rabble" that the jail accepts at entry to the justice system and will probably discharge after a brief stay? Are they dangerous predators? Or are they just marginal people who pose some threat to the community and must be controlled? The answer may be both. We turn first to an examination of the makeup of these residents of the nation's jails. About one in every eight jail inmates is being held for other correctional authorities, about 12 percent of the total inmates, a consistent pattern for the past several years. They are being held back for state and federal prison systems as well as other local correctional agencies. Almost all of the **"holdback" jail inmates** were being delayed due to overcrowding in adult prisons for felony offenders. A small percentage was federal prisoners being held for transfer to U.S. Bureau of Prisons institutions. The Bureau of Prisons has recently developed jail facilities in its own system and therefore reduced its population of holdbacks drastically. Holdbacks are found at about half of all jails. Most jails charge fees for holding inmates for other jurisdictions. Those holdbacks, while helpful to the jail's budget, can contribute to jail overcrowding in many local jail jurisdictions.

key term

"Holdback" jail inmates Inmates held in jail awaiting transportation to a federal or state prison or mental hospital.

A large percentage of jail inmates has used alcohol and drugs sometime in their lives, and more than 4 of 10 had been drinking just before their offense, almost half being drunk or very drunk at the time of their offense. This pattern of substance abuse is even more pronounced among convicted jail inmates. More than half were under the influence of drugs or alcohol (or both) at the time of their current offense. About a quarter of the jail inmates had participated in a drug treatment program and nearly a sixth in an alcohol abuse treatment program.

As noted earlier, the 25 largest jails in the United States house 48 percent of the nation's total jail inmates, with 36 percent exceeding their capacity. Most jail administrators acknowledge that all flexibility in a jail, with regard to classification and housing, is lost when the jail is at 90 percent of capacity. The local jails in 2012 were at 84 percent of capacity.[19] A major cause of overcrowding in facilities is the pressure to close other facilities that do not meet acceptable standards.[20] Between 2008 and 2012, the number of jails available to house adult prisoners dropped from 2,999 to 2,829. That number of jail facilities will most likely continue to decline. Rated capacities (total beds) for jails have dropped to 722,293, indicating that while there were fewer jails, the size was increasing. The explanation for this trend is due largely to the fact that most new jails that replace the older, smaller facilities are built to hold many more beds. Although most of the old, decrepit jails probably deserved to be closed, the expanding jail populations and related problems have created management and control problems within the system. Overcrowding and idleness have thus become typical

Photo 10.3

Growing populations have made vast and varied jails—including tents.
Scott Houston/Alamy.

of those jails that have not expanded programs along with the "brick-and-mortar" approach to jail crowding.

Some efforts to find solutions to reduce overcrowding include conversion of an abandoned motel to a jail annex, purchase of manufactured housing units (modular units that can be interconnected), construction of a canvas tent—based housing community, leasing bed space from other jurisdictions, house arrest for work-release prisoners, electronic monitoring of defendants not otherwise eligible for pretrial release, double-bunking at an existing facility, and contracting with community residential programs for alcohol- and drug-dependent inmates in need of such services.[21]

Photo 10.4

Jail overcrowding can lead to using corridors as dormitories in jails.
Mark Richards/PhotoEdit.

correctional practice 10.1

Rape in a County Lockup

This story began on February 14, 2003 (Valentine's Day). An unidentified 18-year-old boy was caught and arrested after trying to flee from a state trooper. The teen was clocked doing 35 miles per hour over the speed limit on a narrow, two-lane road. He was taken to the local detention center to be booked on traffic violations.

While being processed at the jail, a number of guards began to tease the teen about his appearance. He was about five feet nine inches and weighed 125 pounds. They said he would make a "good girlfriend" for inmates locked up in cell 101, part of a 300-bed facility housing some very dangerous inmates, located in a far-flung corner of the jail. Jail protocol called for the teen to be locked up in a holding cell just off the booking room. However, the shift supervisor decided that the teen needed to be scared and taught a lesson, so he ordered two of the guards to tell the group of 14 inmates in cell 101 to expect some fresh meat.

As the teen was being escorted to the cell in the 300-bed jail, inmates screamed, "He's such a cutie" and "Bring him to me." As the guards pushed the scared teen youth into the cell, yet another inmate yelled, "Happy Valentine's Day."

In civil litigation, the teen says he was carried overhead by a mob of inmates and led to the showers. The teen was stripped naked, beaten with jail slippers, forced to perform sexual acts, and raped. The brutal attack was carried out right through the night with multiple inmates participating in raping the youth. "This is a case of a tenth grader's worst nightmare," said the Federal Civil Rights prosecutor.

After the victim told his father he was raped, the supervisor began organizing a cover up, according to court papers. He lied to investigators when he said the victim was locked up with felons because the floor drain was clogged in the drunk tank. He also fabricated shift logs to make it appear that guards under his watch were checking on the victim's welfare, but the victim was not let out of the cell until the first shift came on duty the next morning. He also threatened a female guard who was considering telling the truth.

Two prison guards pleaded guilty in the case, and two other guards stood trial and were found guilty of conspiring to violate the teen's civil rights by allowing other inmates to sexually assault him. They were also found guilty of obstruction of justice because the jury also found there was aggravated sexual abuse.

The teen survived the ordeal and reached a $1.4 million settlement with the county in 2005. The traffic violations against the teen were ultimately dropped. A total of three inmates were also convicted in the sexual assault.

The victim, who is now 23, leads a very nonsocial life, said his lawyer, who sued the jail on behalf of the teen. "It is a day-by-day thing for him," he said. "He stays to himself. He doesn't go out in public."

SOURCE: Edward Latessa.

Problems with Personnel

The structures used to house our jails reflect the multitude of problems connected with those facilities. Certainly, the lack of adequate personnel is a crucial factor. Most jails are operated by the law enforcement agency that has jurisdiction in the particular area, although in at least one state, Kentucky, "jailers" are elected by the public. Many sheriff's deputies begin their service with a mandatory two-year tour of duty as a jailer, which many feel is not the role for which they were hired and trained. Because many of the full-time jail personnel are county police officers, dedicated to putting offenders into jail, the primary emphasis is on custodial convenience rather than correctional services. The philosophy behind that includes an almost fanatical concern with security, leaving the responsibility for the jails' internal operation to the inmates themselves. It is that situation that has produced the most reprehensible conditions in many of the large municipal jails. When jail personnel are not sworn officers but lower-paid custodial individuals, the conditions can become still worse. The need for preservice and in-service training of jailers and other jail personnel has been clearly perceived by jail inspectors. The immediate requirement is not an influx of professional staff but extensive training aimed at breaking the habitual work patterns of uninterested, politically appointed, and unqualified jail personnel. Low pay, high turnover, and poor working conditions contribute significantly to the personnel problems faced by many jail facilities.

key term

Fee system
Fees charged to state and federal prison systems to house inmates in local jails.

One problem with upgrading personnel and facilities has its roots in the long history of the jail's separate **fee system**, which stems from a practice in early England. The office of

Photo 10.5

Jail inmates exercising and relaxing in their day room—dining area.
Scott Houston/Alamy.

sheriff in those days was an important political position of pomp and prestige (the sheriff was the king's executive officer at the local government level), but the sheriff did very little work in the jail. The distasteful duty of caring for the jail and its inmates was usually sold as a concession to a keeper, or gaoler. Fees for maintaining the inmates were extracted from their families, friends, or estates. Under that system, the greater the number of inmates and the longer they were kept, the more income would accrue to the jailer. To increase his profit, the jailer cut his expenses to a minimum and operated the jail as cheaply as possible.

The fee system was used in America for many years until it was largely replaced by a variation. The inmates themselves are no longer required to pay the fees for their upkeep (although in some jurisdictions, inmates housed in jail are now being required to pay for their keep or, at a minimum, an "intake fee" or are charged a fee for medical attention, prescriptions, and telephone use). In many states, a per diem fee for each prisoner's upkeep is paid by the state or by federal agencies with which the jail has a contract. Leasing bed space from other jurisdictions is a more current example. Some states (such as California) pay their counties to incarcerate state-sentenced offenders with short sentences. Not surprisingly, sheriffs will often exploit a system that pays the sheriff to arrest and jail as many persons as possible. In other states, it is the local county that pays for the keep of offenders housed in jail. In rural counties, it is not unheard of for a judge to send someone to prison to save the county the cost of housing the offender.

Jail Standards

The standards for jails have been a matter of concern for many years. Many argue that given the diversity of size and function, not to mention funding disparity, it is difficult to implement standard criteria. However, at least 21 states report having some jail standards, with all but four being mandatory. Maine was the first to report the establishment of some standards in 1951, followed by Michigan in 1953 and California with full standards in 1963.[22] In addition, professional organizations, such as the American Jail Association and the American Correctional Association, have developed standards and accreditation processes, and the National Institute of Corrections has provided technical assistance to numerous jails across the country. Despite the challenges, there has been an increasing movement to upgrade and improve the jails operating in America. Making jails more humane is a worthy goal;

however, for many public officials, the most persuasive reason for adopting jail standards is to avoid costly litigation and lawsuits. It is clear that upgrading jails is as critical a need as any other in the criminal justice system.[23]

Health Care in Jails

No discussion of jail conditions would be adequate without addressing health conditions. During the past two decades, the health care of jail inmates has been the subject of endless litigation,[24] included in civil rights mandates, addressed through court orders, and mandated through state regulation. It is clear that provision of adequate inmate health and mental health care[25] is no longer an option but compulsory. Across the nation, jail managers are taking steps to meet these mandates, including the following:

1. Determining the real costs of and identifying existing community medical service providers; adopting health maintenance organization models
2. Resolving security issues for transporting inmates to hospitals and medical care appointments
3. Innovating scheduling for medical staff
4. Providing special housing (for geriatrics, tuberculosis patients, early-stage HIV inmates, pregnant inmates, etc.)
5. Seeking accreditation (sometimes as a defense against litigation and claims of deliberate indifference)
6. Planning for future problems[26]

Demands of this nature will require jail managers to find ways to creatively adopt proven techniques and implement innovations that would permit continued quality health care while curtailing costs of services[27]

It is estimated that about 44 percent of jail inmates have a mental health problem, which is defined as a recent history of symptoms within the past 12 months, including a clinical diagnosis or treatment by a mental health professional. Findings from this recent study included the following:[28]

- Female inmates in jails had higher rates of mental health problems than males (75 percent versus 63 percent).
- About 76 percent of local jail inmates who had a mental health problem met criteria for substance.
- Dependency or abuse.
- Jail inmates who had a mental health problem (24 percent) were three times as likely as jail inmates without (8 percent) to report being physically or sexually abused in the past.
- One in six jail inmates with a mental health problem had received treatment since admission.

These findings help illustrate some of the difficulties local officials face in managing the jail population. Some believe that jails have become a dumping ground for the mentally ill, especially since many states have closed mental health hospitals. Clearly, many of these inmates require treatment that often becomes difficult to provide in a jail setting.

ALTERNATIVES TO JAIL

Extended confinement of presumed innocent persons, as with pretrial detention of the nonadjudicated felon later found not guilty, is a serious problem. The defendant who is truly innocent but is exposed through long pretrial confinement to the conditions of even the finest jail will soon build up considerable resentment and animosity toward the

Photo 10.6

Jail officer removing chains from feet of female chain gang crew.
Scott Houston/Alamy.

criminal justice system and to corrections in particular. The convicted offender eventually sent to a correctional institution also will have negative feelings about the inequities of a system that appears to choose arbitrarily to confine some defendants before trial while releasing others.

Fines

The confusion in defining and enforcing misdemeanor statutes is reflected in the absence of uniform techniques and systems for dealing with misdemeanants. Although different states vary greatly in their approaches and jurisdictions within states may also be inconsistent, some patterns are fairly constant. As mentioned, the bulk of the misdemeanor cases are disposed of through confinement or probation, but alternatives for disposition exist, the most prevalent being the use of fines.

Cynical inmates often refer to fines as **price-tag justice**. In the case of misdemeanor offenses, the fine is in many cases offered as an alternative to a period of confinement, meaning the offender who cannot pay is confined, in effect, for being "poor" rather than for being "guilty." The sheer number of misdemeanor cases the lower courts must hear forces the judges to be able to provide only the most cursory kind of justice. Some lower courts may hear more than 100 misdemeanor cases in a single morning. It is difficult, under such circumstances, to conduct any kind of in-depth diagnosis of the offender, the offense, or the offender's ability to pay a fine. The amount of fine for a particular crime is virtually standardized, and paying it is like paying forfeited bail or a parking ticket. For the individual unable to pay, a term in the lockup is often seen as the only alternative. In some cases, however, fines can be paid on the installment plan. That procedure gives offenders a chance to keep their jobs or seek work to pay the fine. Combined with weekend confinement and community work orders, the installment plan has greatly improved misdemeanor justice.

key term

Price-tag justice
A term used by inmates to refer to fines imposed as a result of a criminal conviction.

As part of the increased enthusiasm for intermediate punishments and search for a graduated progression of intermediate sanctions (see Chapter 6), courts have increasingly begun to use community service and fines and, in some jurisdictions, day fines (a sliding dollar amount determined by the offender's daily wages). While less frequently used than other alternatives, day fines have shown some success. For example, in the 1990s, the Vera

Institute of Justice implemented a project to demonstrate and then evaluate the efficacy of using day fines in Staten Island, New York. The project demonstrated the following:

1. The day-fine concept could be implemented in a typical American court of limited jurisdiction.
2. Day fines could substitute for fixed fines ("the same or similar amount to be imposed on all defendants convicted of similar offenses").
3. Fine amounts were higher for more affluent offenders under the day-fine system.
4. Overall revenues increased.
5. High rates of collection could be sustained despite the higher average day-fine amounts.
6. The deep skepticism among criminal justice professionals about the court's ability to enforce and collect such fines was unfounded.[29]

Both fines and other alternatives are likely to be used more extensively by courts to achieve a graduated progression of penalties for less serious crimes as well as to enhance the programs and efforts aimed at reducing jail overcrowding.

Weekend Confinement

key term

Weekender
A jail inmate who is allowed to live at home during the week (usually to work) and who must report to jail to serve his or her sentence on weekends.

To lessen the negative impacts of short-term incarceration and allow offenders to retain current employment, some jurisdictions permit sentences to be served during nonworking weekends. Many refer to it as "doing time on the installment plan." Such weekend confinement generally requires a guilty misdemeanant to check into the jail on Friday after work and leave Sunday (sometimes early enough to permit church attendance). A **weekender** serving his or her sentence over a number of months would generally be credited with three days of confinement per weekend. Minimum-security facilities (not the maximum-security jails) are appropriate for such of-fenders.

Community Work Orders

Sentencing judges sometimes order misdemeanants to perform a period of service to the community as a substitute for or in partial satisfaction of a fine. This disposition is generally a condition of a suspended (or partially suspended) sentence or of probation. It can be used in a variety of ways: a sentence in itself, work in lieu of cash fine, a condition of suspended sentence, or a condition of probation.[30]

The offender "volunteers" his or her services to a community agency for a certain number of hours per week over a specified period of time. The total number of hours, often assessed as the legal minimum wage, is often determined by the amount of the fine that would have been imposed or by the portion of the fine that is suspended.

Other alternatives for the misdemeanant are probation without adjudication and the suspended sentence. Both are variations on the same theme: holding formal disposition over the head of the offender for a period of time, often under specified conditions, and then nullifying the conviction. In probation without adjudication (also known as deferred prosecution), offenders can forgo prosecution as long as they meet certain established conditions, usually for a specific period of time. The suspended sentence is used whenever offenders obviously do not require supervision to ensure their good behavior. This alternative is used primarily for first offenders considered to be so impressed with their arrest and conviction that further sanctions against them would be of little positive value.

The extent to which these alternatives are employed is not really known because little research has been conducted in this area; at midyear 2012, at least 6 percent of jail inmates were outside the facility on confinement alternatives.[31] It is apparent that the misdemeanants, like adult felons, often fall out of the correctional funnel before it narrows. If they did not, the jails of the country simply could not hold them.

ALTERNATIVES TO JAIL AT THE PRETRIAL STAGE

Incarceration is one of the most severe punishments meted out by the American criminal justice system. Yet more than one-half of all persons in local jails are awaiting trial. In effect, we are using our most severe sanction against many individuals who have not yet been convicted of a crime. If detention were necessary and if there were no reasonable alternatives to the jailing of suspects, that situation would be understandable, but experience with alternatives to jail has indicated that many (but not all) people now incarcerated could probably be released safely and economically, pending disposition of the charges against them. Most of them would appear in court as required without being held in jail.

Some tentative conclusions can be drawn from the experience of existing programs:

1. Pretrial alternatives generally cost much less than jail incarceration.
2. Persons released before trial seem to fare better in court than do those who are incarcerated.
3. Pretrial release alternatives appear to be as effective as jail in preventing recidivism and can reduce the size of criminal justice agency workloads.
4. Alternative programs can reduce jail populations and eliminate the need for expansion or new construction.

Pretrial Release

Most Americans who are arrested are given the opportunity to make bail. In larger jurisdictions, pretrial diversion programs (see Chapter 6) afford the defendant the opportunity to be released on their **"own recognizance,"** eligibility for which is usually based on two factors: risk to the community and failure to appear. Over the years, a number of studies have been conducted to help courts decide who to release and who to detain. The results of this research have led to the development of pretrial assessment tools. Figure 10.2 is an example of one such tool that researchers at the University of Cincinnati developed.[32]

key term

Own recognizance
When an arrestee is released from jail under promise that he or she will return for their court hearing.

Pretrial alternatives to detention run along a continuum of increasing controls or sanctions. Any community wishing to maximize the use of alternatives will provide a series of options that offer varying levels of supervision and services. Such a process will permit the release of more persons with less waste of expensive resources. The least interventionary and least costly options are used for low-risk cases. More expensive options and options involving greater interference in the life of the individual, such as house arrest and electronic monitoring, are reserved for cases in which those are the only alternatives to the even more costly option of jail incarceration.

key term

Pretrial alternatives
Programs and sanctions designed to release those jail inmates who are awaiting trial; alternatives can include electronic monitoring, supervision, treatment programs, house arrest, and other creative options designed to reduce jail populations.

Although jails keep alleged offenders off the streets, they also keep those same individuals away from their work, family, friends, and business (even if crime might be their business). Already tenuous ties to the community may be further strained by the jail experience. Moreover, other disreputable members of society (derelicts, drug abusers, hustlers, drunks, etc.) may vandalize and/or burglarize their residence, which may have been left unattended and unguarded for even the brief time of jail detention. The average length of stay in jails nationwide (both pretrial and sentenced) is a combined average of almost 90 days. Finally, jails are important because of what happens to the inmates there. The shock of incarceration, loss of control over their environment, danger from violent inmates, absence of meaningful activity, and dead time weigh heavily on the minds of new inmates. Psychological problems already affecting behavior may be exacerbated; self-mutilation[33] and suicide[34] occasionally occur. Sometimes it is difficult to rebut those who argue that the purpose of **pretrial jail incarceration** is punishment.

key term

Pretrial jail incarceration
Holding someone accused of a crime who cannot make bail.

figure 10.2
Ohio Risk Assessment System: Pretrial Assessment Tool.

SOURCE: Christopher T. Lowenkamp, Richard Lemke, and Edward Latessa, "The Development and Validation of a Pretrial Screening Tool," *Federal Probation* 72:3 (2008).

OHIO RISK ASSESSMENT SYSTEM: PRETRIAL ASSESSMENT TOOL (ORAS-PAT)

Name: ____________ Date of Assessment: ____________

Case #: ____________ Name of Assessor: ____________

Pretrial Items		Verified
1. Age at First Arrest 0=33 or older 1=Under 33	☐	☐
2. Number of Failure-to-Appear Warrants Past 24 Months 0=None 1=One Warrant for FTA 2=Two or More FTA Warrants	☐	☐
3. Three or More Prior Jail Incarcerations 0=No 1=Yes	☐	☐
4. Employed at the Time of Arrest 0=Yes, Full-time 1=Yes, Part-time 2=Not Employed	☐	☐
5. Residential Stability 0=Lived at Current Residence Past Six Months 1=Not Lived at Same Residence	☐	☐
6. Illegal Drug Use During Past Six Months 0=No 1=Yes	☐	☐
7. Severe Drug Use Problem 0=No 1=Yes	☐	☐
Total Score:	☐	

Scores	Rating	% of Failures	% of Failure to Appear	% of New Arrest
0–2	Low	5%	5%	0%
3–5	Moderate	18%	12%	7%
6+	High	29%	15%	17%

Fewer than one-half of all jail inmates grew up in a household with both parents present; almost 4 in 10 have lived in a single-parent household. More than one-third have family members (usually a brother or sister) who have also been incarcerated. More than one-fourth have a parent or guardian who abused alcohol while the inmate was growing up. One in six male inmates reported sexual or physical abuse (or both) by an adult before the current incarceration, and one in eight had taken medication prescribed by a psychiatrist or other doctor for an emotional or mental problem.

Characteristics of female jail inmates are explored in greater detail in Chapter 18, and the patterns just described are generally more egregious for female than male jail inmates. Self-reports on drug abuse by jail inmates, sometimes known for their self-serving and deceptive purposes, are in part verified through urinalysis testing conducted at jail sites

correctional practice 10.2

The Purpose of Correctional Sanctions

Two important issues have been given a great deal of attention in the media: the need for new jails and the reentry of offenders back in the community. These issues are obviously related and lead us to the question "What is the purpose of correctional sanctions?" While most would agree that public protection is the primary goal of corrections, disagreements arise as to the best methods to achieve this goal. On one side are advocates for more punitive policies, such as increased use of incarceration or simply increasing control and monitoring if the offender is supervised in the community. Those advocating such strategies of crime control do so on the basis of the often-interrelated goals of punishment: retribution, deterrence, and incapacitation. On the other side are those who argue that we must address the underlying causes of crime and criminal behavior and provide programs and services to address the needs of the offender, especially for those returning to the community. So can we achieve the goal of public protection and meet the dual needs for punishment *and* rehabilitation? I believe that we have to consider both sides if we want to reduce the revolving door that has become our penal system.

Punishment is an inherent part of the correctional system and is often justified simply because a person has broken the law. Society demands that certain offenders be punished and expects our elected officials to see that offenders be held accountable. The problem is the belief that somehow punishment alone will deter offenders from continuing to break the law in the future. The underlying assumptions of deterrence is that the offenders are aware of the sanction, they perceive it as unpleasant, they weigh the cost and benefits of their criminal conduct, and they assess the risk and, in turn, make a rational choice to break the law (or not). The problem is that most street-level criminals act impulsively; have a short-term perspective; are often disorganized and have failed in school, jobs, and relationships; have distorted thinking; hang around with others like themselves; use drugs and alcohol; and are not rational actors. In short, deterrence theory collapses. Incapacitation, which attempts to limit offenders' ability to commit another crime (usually by locking them up), can have some effect, but, as many have found out, simply locking up offenders and "throwing away the key" has proven to be a very expensive approach to crime control. This strategy is also limited since the vast majority of offenders return to society. Without treatment, many will return unchanged at best and, at worst, with many more problems and intensified needs for services. Even if one supports incapacitation, one must ask, "What should be done with offenders while incarcerated?" This leads us to rehabilitation. With this approach, the offender chooses to refrain from new crimes rather than being unable to. So what works in changing offender behavior?

Most researchers who study correctional interventions have concluded that without some form of human intervention or services, there is unlikely to be much effect on recidivism from punishment alone. If you do not believe that, just look at the number of offenders who have been incarcerated in our jails over and over again. As Einstein once said, "The sign of insanity is doing something over and over again and expecting a different outcome." Unfortunately, not all correctional treatment programs are equally effective; however, considerable research has demonstrated that well-designed programs that meet certain conditions can appreciably reduce recidivism rates for offenders. Effective programs have many characteristics, and space does not allow me to elaborate; however, two are particularly noteworthy. First, it is important to target crime-producing needs that are highly correlated with criminal conduct. The most effective programs are centered on the *present* circumstances and risk factors that are contributing to the offender's behavior. Antisocial attitudes, values, beliefs, and peer associations; substance abuse; lack of problem-solving skills; and poor self-control are some of the more important targets for change for offenders. Second, effective programs are *action* oriented rather than talk oriented. In other words, offenders do something about their difficulties rather than just talk about them. These types of programs teach offenders new prosocial skills to replace the antisocial ones (e.g., stealing, cheating, lying, etc.). Interventions based on these approaches are very structured and emphasize the importance of modeling and behavioral rehearsal techniques that engender self-efficacy, challenge cognitive distortions, and assist offenders in developing new prosocial skills. So should we hold offenders accountable for their behavior? Absolutely. But punishment and treatment need not be incompatible, and doing one without the other is not likely to achieve long-term public safety.

SOURCE: Edward Latessa.

across the nation. Results for arrestees and across different charges at arrest indicate even more extensive drug use than previously self-reported, particularly by robbery and burglary arrestees.

As for their criminal activities, usually almost one in four has been arrested at least once for a crime of violence and another three of four have been arrested for crimes against property. A large percentage of criminals are charged with drug violations. A bit less than one-half have been previously sentenced to incarceration or probation prior to their current offense. As you have already learned, the proportion of inmates with mental health illness is high.

key term

Criminal history data Information related to an offender's prior arrests and convictions.

Those sociodemographic and **criminal history data** suggest a marginal group of mostly male offenders who have had a lengthy but not necessarily serious involvement in criminal activity. They could best be seen as a group of high-need disadvantaged urban dwellers whose needs have not been adequately addressed by the social service agencies in their local communities. The number of inmates of the largest jails who died further describes their needs. Of the 919 inmates who died in jails at the beginning of 2000, more than one in three died at their own hands (suicide). Almost 42 percent died of natural causes (excluding AIDS). The fact that 1 of 11 inmate deaths in jails was attributed to causes related to AIDS suggests that compassionate release of the fatally ill is a concept that still has to be fully embraced by local correctional facilities.

Summary

Outline the History of Jails

We began by noting the grim history of early jails. Pioneers in jail reform and innovation began in the eighteenth century to propose innovative and humanitarian practices, seeking to develop what eventually became the contemporary American jail system. Systems of classification were eventually developed that allowed jail management leaders to implement a variety of programs and alternatives to pretrial and postconviction options, although incarceration in the contemporary jail remains the major option for correcting misdemeanor and less dangerous low-level and first-time felony offenders.

Describe the Purpose, Function, and Operations of Today's Jails

The jail is the one correctional facility through which almost all offenders will pass as they are processed through the criminal justice system. This includes defendants, the guilty, others detained for other justice agencies, juveniles and adults, material witnesses, males and females, the mentally ill awaiting transport to mental health facilities, military members awaiting transfer to military custody, drunk drivers undergoing sobering up, weekenders, and illegal immigrants, among others. It is a diverse amalgamation of Americans.

Describe the Various Types of Pretrial Release

In larger jurisdictions, pretrial diversion programs allow the defendant the opportunity to be released on his or her own recognizance. Eligibility is determined through pretrial assessment tools and is usually based on risk to the community and failure to appear.

Describe the Characteristics of Jail Inmates

Jail inmates can be characterized as mainly ill-equipped, marginal urban dwellers who have a number of personal problems and are drawn mostly from minority or undereducated groups, sometimes incorrectly called the "rabble." Broken homes, single-parent households, and impoverished backgrounds typify the majority of jail inmates. Others have mental health issues, acting-out and impulsive behavior, alcohol and drug addictions, and inability to anticipate the consequences of their behavior. They tend to act on the spur of the moment. They are not irredeemable, but most are challenged.

Summarize the Design and Supervisory Options in Jails

All jails are not alike. Most are institutions managed and staffed to contain, control, and correct offenders. Many are exemplary institutions; some are miserably organized and incorrectly staffed by a mediocre management ill equipped to achieve correctional and public safety goals. Fortunately, that latter category is not the largest group.

The largest jails in the country house almost half the total number of jail inmates, and most are understaffed and overcrowded. Some jail staff have not been adequately trained and lack interpersonal skills that create barriers between the keepers and the kept. Some of the larger jails do not meet acceptable professional standards of organization, safety, medical service, and reentry programs, among others. The largest area of challenge is in the broader medical services area, including mental health. Some but not all jails have managed to construct a coordinated ladder of intramural and community services. Yet there are many jail professionals whose driving goals revolve around community safety and lessened recidivism.

Summarize Issues in Jails

Due to the combined nature of the inmate population, their employment circumstances, insecurity, poor education, family parenting, and economic straits, recent jail developments have begun to stress alternatives to jail incarceration, punishment, community services, staff training, and alternatives to detention as well as new jail architecture and organization. The latter include such programs as fines, community service orders, house arrest, weekend confinement, pretrial service, and release, among others. Fortunately, the drive to increase professionalism, add effective alternatives to jail incarceration, and meet the increasing costs of jails and the lack of adequate resources to imprison every misdemeanant and eligible felon have led to the developing of standards of jail management that are making meaningful and positive impacts on improved jail organization and operations. Jails need interested, motivated, better-trained, and enlightened leadership to further overcome current challenges.

Summarize Pretrial Services and Other Alternatives to Jail Incarceration

Pretrial alternatives to detention include various levels of supervision and services. Such a process will permit the release of more persons with less waste of expensive resources. The least interventionary and least costly options are used for low-risk cases. More expensive options and options involving greater interference in the life of the individual, such as house arrest and electronic monitoring, are reserved for cases in which those are the only alternatives to the even more costly option of jail incarceration.

Key Words

jail, 217
jail inmates, 218
presumption of innocence, 219
mental health issues, 220
new-generation jail, 222
podular/direct supervision, 223
"holdback" jail inmates, 224
fee system, 226
price-tag justice, 229
weekender, 230
own recognizance, 231
pretrial alternatives, 231
pretrial jail incarceration, 231
criminal history data, 234

Review Questions

1. Why has the fee system been such a detriment to jail progress?
2. Do you think offenders housed in jail should be made to pay for their upkeep? Their medical care?
3. What is the area of greatest weakness in the jails? Would more personnel be the answer? Why or why not?
4. What are the major alternatives to pretrial confinement?
5. Describe the operation of a new-generation jail.
6. What medical problems must jails address?
7. Draft a plan for reducing jail overcrowding.
8. Why is the jail so important to the correctional system?
9. What is meant when we describe the jail population as "rabble"?
10. Identify five major problems that jail inmates bring to the institution.
11. Why are so many prison-bound inmates held back in jails?
12. Describe the diversity of the jail inmate population.
13. What special problems do inmates bring to the jail setting?
14. Identify three trends in jail facilities.

Application Case Studies

1. You are the sheriff in a county in which the elected county supervisors decide to cut your jail budget by 10 percent, effective in 12 months. What would you do to meet these demands?
2. The night-watch commander in your jail, contrary to written policy, houses a 16-year old male overnight in the same holding cell in which 10 sentenced inmates are housed. During the night, the youth is repeatedly raped. You discover this only when the youth's father reports to you that his son was raped. What would you do?
3. The department's internal affairs officer reports that two of your jail officers have been accused of smuggling a controlled substance (in this case, methamphetamines) into your jail. Assuming that your written standard operating procedures identify this behavior as illegal, what would you do?

Endnotes

1. Norval Morris and David Rothman, eds., *The Oxford Dictionary of the Prison: The Practice of Punishment in Western Society* (Oxford: Oxford University Press, 1995).
2. For an excellent overview of involving the community in jail administration, see William Wood, "A Practical Guide to Community Relations," *American Jails* 6:5 (1992): 14–17, and Taylor Dueker, "Visitation Boom in Omaha," *American Jails* 18:5 (2004): 65–67. See also National Institute of Corrections, "Training Action Center," http://nicic.gov/training/ (accessed November 19, 2013).
3. Hans Mattick and Alexander Aidman, "The Cloacal Region of Corrections," *The Annals* 381:1 (January 1969): 109–118. See also Karol Lucken, "The Dynamics of Penal Reform," *Crime, Law and Social Change* 26:4 (1997): 367–384. Yet jails are deluged with mentally ill people. See Sandy Fitzgerald, (2013), "Nation's Prisons Becoming Modern-Day Asylums for Mentally Ill," http://www.newsmax.com/US/prison-mental-health-inmantes/2013/09/26/id/527895.
4. Thomas Bak, *Defendants Who Avoid Detention: A Good Risk?* (Washington, DC: Administrative Office of the U.S. Courts, 1994).
5. Marian Williams, "The Effect of Pretrial Detention on Imprisonment Decisions," *Criminal Justice Review* 28:2 (2003): 299–316; Richard Aborn and Ashley Cannon, (2013), "Prisons: In Jail but Not Sentenced," http://www.americasquarterly.org/aborn-prisons.
6. Matthew Durose and Patrick Langan, *State Court Sentencing of Convicted Felons, 2002* (Washington, DC: Bureau of Justice Statistics, 2004), p. 1, and *State Court Sentencing of Convicted Felons, 2004* (Washington, DC: Bureau of Justice Statistics, 2007), p. 1, Bureau of Justice Statistics, *Felony Defendants in Large Urban Counties, 2004,* http://www.ojp.usdoj.gov/bjs/pub/html/fdluc/2004/tables/fdluc04st25.htm (accessed October 4, 2008).
7. Paul McEnroe and Glenn Howatt, "Left in Limbo, Hundreds of Minnesotans with Mental illness Languish in Jail," http://www.startribune.com/lifestyle/health/222828641.html (accessed November 17, 2013).
8. Todd Minton, *Jail Inmates at Midyear 2009* (Washington, DC: U.S. Department of Justice, Bureau of Justice Statistics, 2010).
9. David DeYoung, "An Evaluation of the Effectiveness of Alcohol Treatment Driver License Actions and Jail Terms in Reducing Drunk Driving in California," *Addiction* 92:8 (1997): 989–997; Robert Langworthy and Edward Latessa, "Treatment of Chronic Drunk Drivers: The Turning Point Project Five Years Later," *Journal of Criminal Justice* 24:3 (1996): 273–281; The Partnership of Drugfree.org (2013), "Choosing Substance Abuse Treatment over Prison Could Save Billions, Study," "http://www.drugfree.org/join-together/drugs/choosing-substance-abuse-treatment-over-prison-could-save-billions-study (accessed November 19, 2013).
10. Amy Thistlewaite, J. Wooldredge, and D. Gibbs, "Severity of Dispositions and Domestic Violence Recidivism," *Crime and Delinquency* 44:3 (1998): 388–398; Edward Gondolf, *The Impact of Mandatory Court Review on Batterer Program Compliance* (Harrisburg: Pennsylvania Commission on Crime and Delinquency, 1997); Eric Smith, Matthew Durose and Patrick Langan, *State Court Processing of Domestic Violence Cases* (Washington, DC: Bureau of Justice Statistics, 2008).
11. Minton, *Jail Inmates at Midyear 2009.*
12. Kimball Perry. "GPS Units to Save Taxpayer Money, Space in Jail," *Cincinnati Inquirer,* July 18, 2013, http://news.cincinnati.com/article/20130718/NEWS0107/307180016/?nclick_check=1.
13. Although blacks are disproportionately involved in the criminal justice system, a long-standing criminological taboo exists against discussing the relationship between crime and race. There is no "black criminology" to tease out the data or theoretically interpret the observed overinvolvement. The three basic arguments are that there are more black offenders per 100,000 population, that certain black offenders tend to commit very large numbers of crime, or that criminal justice system personnel decision makers are biased against blacks in decision making. See the excellent critique by Kathleen Russell, "Development of a Black Criminology and the Role of the Black Criminologist," *Justice Quarterly* 9:4 (1992): 667–683; Shawn Gabiddon, Helen Greene, and Kideste Wilder, "Still Excluded?," *Journal of Research in Crime and Delinquency* 41:4 (2004): 384–406; and Editors, "Racial Inequality and Drug Arrests," *New York Times*, May 10, 2008, p. 18. For an examination of the juvenile justice system issues, see Christina DeJong and K. Jackson, "Putting Race into Context: Race, Juvenile Justice Processing, and Urbanization," *Justice Quarterly* 15:3 (1998): 487–504. The number of jail inmates by race/ethnicity can be found in Todd Minton, *Jail Inmates at Midyear 2012* (Washington, DC: U.S. Department of Justice, Bureau of Justice Statistics, 2013), p. 5.
14. Minton, *Jail Inmates at Midyear 2012.*
15. Doris J. James and Lauren E. Glaze, *Mental Health Problems of Prison and Jail Inmates* (Washington, DC: Bureau of Justice Statistics, 2006).
16. John Clark and H. Alan, *The Pretrial Release Decision Making Process* (Washington, DC: Pretrial Services Resource Center, 1996); Brian Paine and Randy Gainey, "The Electronic Monitoring of Offenders Released from Jail or Prison," *The Prison Journal* 84:4 (2004): 413–435.

17. See Ken Kerle, *American Jails* (New York: Butterworth-Heinemann, 1998), pp. 190–191. See also Jeffrey Senese, Joe Wilson, Arthur Evans, et al., "Evaluating Jail Reform: Inmate Infraction and Disciplinary Response in a Traditional and a Podular/Direct Supervision Jail," *American Jails* 6:4 (1992): 14–24, and James Skidmore, "Tarrant County Sheriff's Metropolitan Confinement Bureau," *American Jails* 13:5 (1998): 80–81.
18. Virginia Hutchinson, K. Teller, and T. Reid, "Inmate Behavior Management," *American Jails* 19:2 (2005): 9–14. In 2012, Oklahoma transferred all inmates in one prison under age 40 to higher-security prison facilities, retaining the older inmates and allowing older inmates to transfer in from other institutions. Violence dropped significantly in the older inmate population, although the per-inmate medical costs increased significantly.
19. Todd Minton, *Jail Inmates at Midyear 2010* (Washington, DC: U.S. Department of Justice, Bureau of Justice Statistics, 2011); Wayne Welsh, *Counties in Court: Jail Overcrowding and Court-Ordered Reform* (Philadelphia: Temple University Press, 1995). See also Ernest Cowles, R. Schmitz, and B. Bass, *An Implementation Evaluation of the Pretrial and Drug Intervention Programs in Illinois' Macon and Peoria Counties* (Chicago: Illinois Criminal Justice Information Agency, 1998).
20. Ken Kerle, "Jail Crowding and Increasing Jail Populations," *American Jails* 23:5 (2008): 5, 95.
21. National Center of Addiction and Substance Abuse at Columbia University, *Behind Bars: Substance Abuse and American Prison Population* (New York: National Center of Addiction and Substance Abuse at Columbia University, 1998). See also Michael Havens, "ACLU Sues Nevada DOC over Inmate Care," *Correctional News* 14:3 (2008): 28.
22. Mike Howerton, "Jail Standards in 2001: Results of a 21-State Survey," *American Jails* 15:5 (2001): 9–11.
23. A review of the first two decades of new-generation jails can be found in Raymond Harris and David Russell, "Podular Direct Supervision: The First Twenty Years," *American Jails* 9:3 (1995): 11–12. See "Florida Model Jail Standards," http://www.flsheriffs.org/our_program/florida-model-jail-standards/ (accessed September 8, 2014). In 2013, Los Angeles Sheriff Lee Baca was found personally liable in a case involving physical abuse of a jail inmate and ordered to pay $100,000 personally for a deputy use-of-force attack on an inmate. See Abby Sewell and Robert Faturechi, "L.A. Sheriff Baca Held Liable for $100,000 in Inmate Abuse Case," *Los Angeles Times*, October 18, 2013, http://articles.latimes.com/2013/oct/17/local/la-me-ln-baca-inmate-abuse-damages-20131017 (accessed September 8, 2014).
24. Frederick Bennett, "After the Litigation: Part I," *American Jails* 6:3 (1992): 81–84, and "After the Litigation: Part II," *American Jails* 6:4 (1992): 30–36; Matthew Lopes, "The Role of the Masters in Correctional Litigation," *American Jails* 6:4 (1993): 27–29; David Heinzman and Juan Peres Jr. (2013), "Woman Sues LaSalle County over Strip Search," http://articles.chicagotribune.com/2013-10-01/news/ct-met-jail-strip-search-lawsuit-20131001_1_lasalle-county-jail-video-deputies (accessed November 19, 2013).
25. Patrick Kinkade, M. Leone, and S. Semond, "The Consequences of Jail Crowding," *Crime and Delinquency* 41:1 (1995): 150–161. See also the special issue "Mental Health Issues in Corrections," *Corrections Today* 67:1 (2005): 22–53, and Editors, "Cal Prison Health Czar Heads to Court," *Correctional News* 14:6 (2008): 8.
26. James Tesoriero and Malcom McCullough, "Correctional Health Care Now and into the Twenty-First Century," in *Vision for Change* (New York: Prentice Hall, 1996), pp. 215–236.
27. Patricia Satterfield, "Creating Strategies for Controlling Health Care Costs," *Corrections Today* 54:2 (1992): 190–194. See also Frank Cousins, "The Business Side of Health Care in the Corrections Industry," *American Jails* 18:3 (2004): 56–60.
28. For information about Texas jails, see http://www.tcjs.state.tx.us/index.php?linkID5320.
29. Linda Winterfield and Sally Hillsman, *The Staten Island Day-Fine Project* (Washington, DC: U.S. Department of Justice, 1993). See also the policy statement of the National Council on Crime and Delinquency, *Criminal Justice Policy Statement* (San Francisco: National Council on Crime and Delinquency, 1992); Judith Greene, *The Maricopa County FARE Probation Experiment* (New York: Vera Institute of Justice, 1996); and the fine system for the State of Wyoming, http://www.dmv.org/wy-wyoming/point-system.php (accessed September 8, 2014).
30. Paul Hudson, *The State Jail System Today* (Austin: Texas Criminal Justice Policy Council, 1998). See also Robert Wood, (2013), "Tax Excuses to Avoid Penalties, or Even Jail," http://www.forbes.com/sites/robertwood/2013/11/17/tax-excuses-to-avoid-penalties-or-even-jail/.
31. Todd Minton, *Jail Inmates at Midyear 2012—Statistical Tables*. (Washington, DC: Bureau of Justice Statistics, 2013), p. 9.
32. For more information, see Christopher T. Lowenkamp, Richard Lemke, and Edward Latessa, "The Development and Validation of a Pretrial Screening Tool," *Federal Probation* 72:3 (2008).
33. Janet Haines et al., "The Psycho-Physiology of Self-Mutilation," *Journal of Abnormal Psychology* 104:3 (1995): 471–489, and Human Rights Watch, "Suicide and Self-Mutilation," http://www.hrw.org/reports/2003/usa1003/22.htm (accessed October 4, 2008).
34. Lindsay Haines and Eric Blauw, eds., "Prison Suicide," *Crises* 18:4 (1997): 146–189; Alexander Smith (2013), "Suicide Kills More Inmates Than Homicide, Overdoses, Accidents Combined," http://usnews.nbcnews.com/_news/2013/09/04/20321084-suicides-kill-more-inmates-than-homicide-overdoses-accidents-combined.

Philip Scalia/Alamy.

Objectives

- Explain the organization and basic functions of state prisons.
- Outline the development of the state prison system.
- Explain the classification and assignment process in state prisons.
- Summarize the characteristics, trends, and issues of the adult prison population.
- Explain the impact that politics and government policy have on corrections.
- Explain the impact that budgets have on correctional policy.

chapter 11

State and Local Prison Systems

Outline

"Federal courts ordered California to reduce its prison population to 137.5 percent of rated capacity."

—Harry E. Allen

Overview

In past chapters, we have examined the philosophies, the clients, and the functions and tasks of the operators of jails, probation services, and America's prisons. We have seen the male–female and racial allocations to the facilities that make up systems that cost the taxpayers almost $73 billion to operate each year. (See Figure 11.1 for the costs of these systems.) This chapter takes you into the basic functions and characteristics of the state prisons, using male adult offenders, who constitute 93 percent of the population, as our vehicle.[1] Female inmates are discussed separately in Chapter 18 because they are not an insignificant part of daily state and local adult prison activity. The male inmate and institution are used here as a demonstration of how most of the systems operate.

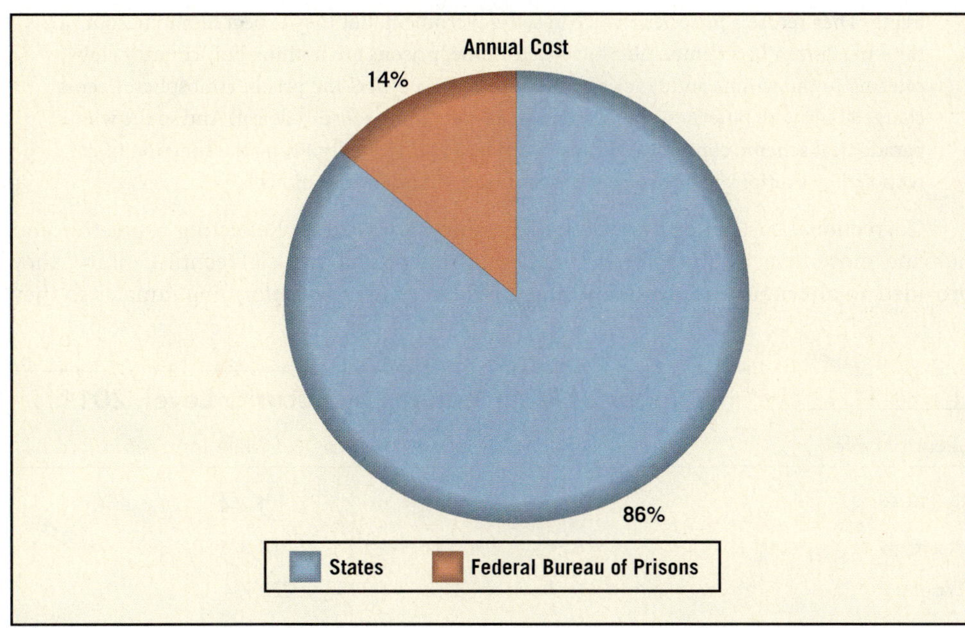

figure 11.1

Annual Cost to Operate Our Correctional Systems—More Than $73 Billion per Year.

SOURCE: American Correctional Association, *2012 Directory* (Alexandria, VA: American Correctional Association, 2012), p. 28; Bureau of Justice Statistics, *Local Government Corrections Expenditures FY 2005* (Washington, DC: Bureau of Justice Statistics, 2011), p. 2.

STATE CORRECTIONAL INSTITUTIONS: THE CORE OF THE SYSTEM

This chapter explores the state systems for housing over 1,466,933 adult sentenced male and female offenders in more than 1,600 adult state and local prisons in America[2] as of 2016. Juvenile institutions, detention centers, jails, workhouses, and other facilities for misdemeanants and minor offenders are not included. The major correctional institutions contained in the state systems are super-maximum (supermax) prisons, maximum/close prisons, medium-security prisons, and minimum-security prisons (see Table 11.1), many of which are modeled after the concepts of the nineteenth-century Auburn penitentiary.

Those institutions form the core of most state correctional programs charged with the simultaneous and often conflicting functions of punishment and reform. Most are short on money and personnel, but they are still expected to prevent their graduates from returning to crime. Security and custody are the primary emphases in these prisons, and their environments are isolated both physically and philosophically from the mainstream of life. James V. Bennett, a former director of the Federal Bureau of Prisons, described the ironic situation over 50 years ago:

> Even our modern prison system is proceeding on a rather uncertain course because its administration is necessarily a series of compromises. On the one hand, prisons are expected to punish; on the other, they are supposed to reform. They are expected to discipline rigorously at the same time that they teach self-reliance. They are built to be operated like vast impersonal machines, yet they are expected to fit men to live normal community lives. They operate in accordance with a fixed autocratic routine, yet they are expected to develop individual initiative. All too frequently restrictive laws force prisoners into idleness despite the fact that one of their primary objectives is to teach men how to earn an honest living. They refuse a prisoner a voice in self-government, but they expect him to become a thinking citizen in a democratic society. To some, prisons are nothing but "country clubs" catering to the whims and fancies of the inmates. To others the prison atmosphere seems charged only with bitterness, rancor, and an all-pervading sense of defeat. And so the whole paradoxical scheme continues, because our ideas and views regarding the function of correctional institutions in our society are confused, fuzzy, and nebulous.[3]

key term

Alternative to death and flogging
Any correctional punishment less than the death penalty, such as imprisonment, probation, diversion, and so on.

Correctional institutions are both a blessing and a curse. Reflecting a positive and humane movement away from the cruel punishments of the eighteenth century, they provided an **alternative to death and flogging**; but in terms of reforming inmates so they

table **11.1** **Number of Male Inmates by Security Level, 2011**

Security Level	Number of Male Inmates
Supermax	1,254
Maximum	101,377
Close/high	223,934
Medium	440,750
Minimum/low	263,924
Unclassified	48,753
Other	28,908
Administrative segregation/protective custody	40,831

SOURCE: American Correctional Association, *2012 Directory of Adult and Juvenile Correctional Departments, Institutions, Agencies, and Probation and Parole Authorities* (Alexandria, VA: American Correctional Association, 2012), pp. 40–41.

table 11.2 **Prisoners in America (Extrapolated for 2013–2016)—Prisoners under the Jurisdiction of State and Federal Correctional Authorities**

Year	Total
2002	1,440,144
2004	1,497,100
2006	1,568,674
2010	1,613,803
2012	1,576,013
2013	1,537,493
2014	1,513,973
2016	1,466,933

SOURCE: Bureau of Justice Statistics, *Prisoners in 2012—Advance Counts* (Washington, DC: Bureau of Justice Statistics, 2013).

can lead a noncriminal life in the free world, prisons have mostly failed. Still, the public's perceived need to feel safe and secure and the prison's effectiveness in isolating offenders from society have unfortunately made this system the primary response to criminal behavior. The 1,466,933 male and female inmates confined in state correctional institutions for adults were distributed among maximum-security, close-medium-security, and minimum-security institutions, along with institutions of other security levels.[4] The good news is that there appears to be some abatement in the growth of the state prison populations due in part to the budget shortfalls that are afflicting most states. Still, we project that by 2016, the prison population (state, federal, and local city systems) will have grown to approximately 1.466 million Americans (see Table 11.2 and Figure 11.2).

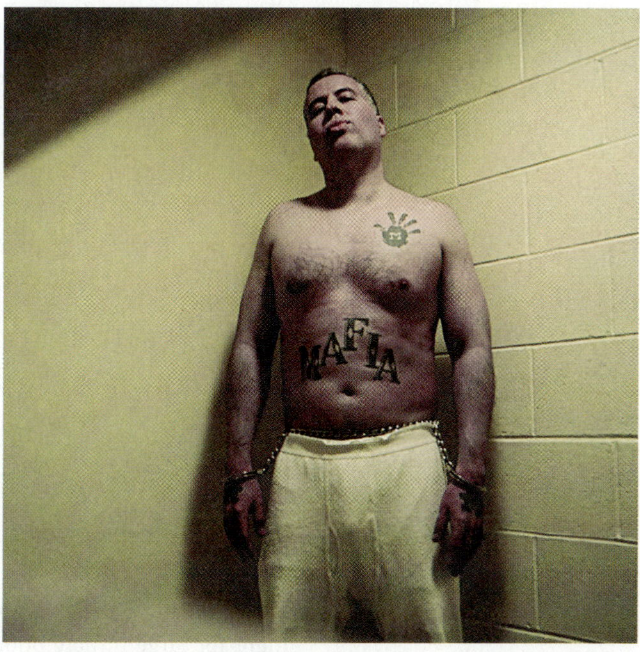

Photo 11.1
Raol Leon, who is serving a life sentence for an execution-style murder, as photographed in a holding cell through a slot in the cell door at Pelican Bay Prison in California.
Adam Tanner/Corbis.

Organization of State Systems

Of all the various types of correctional facilities in America—public and private, adult and juvenile, community and city, and others—only 16 percent of them are under the control of state agencies. It is not surprising that the correctional "system" in most states is not really systematized at all. Organizational rigidity and huge investments in "bricks-and-mortar" responses have sometimes limited meaningful revision and modernization of corrections. Rehabilitation and reintegration require that organizational structures be concerned with more than just institutional programs. In at least six states, that organizational need has been met by exercising control over all correctional activities at the state level. Hawaii, for example, has a unified jail and prison system. In Canada, all offenders sentenced to two years or less of imprisonment are incarcerated at a provincial ("state-level") prison, whereas those serving longer sentences are committed to the federal prison system.

Corrections at the state level generally is organized into a separate department of corrections (with a cabinet-level secretary or director appointed by the governor) or a division within a larger state department. Most correctional administrators consider the separate department to be more effective, and having the director at the cabinet level adds great

figure 11.2

Population Growth: 1990–2014.

Note: *Data for 2014 are extrapolated.

SOURCE: Ann Carson and Daniela Golinelli, *Prisoners in 2012: Trends in Admissions and Releases, 1991–2012.* (Washington, DC: Bureau of Justice Statistics, December 2013), pp. 1–2.

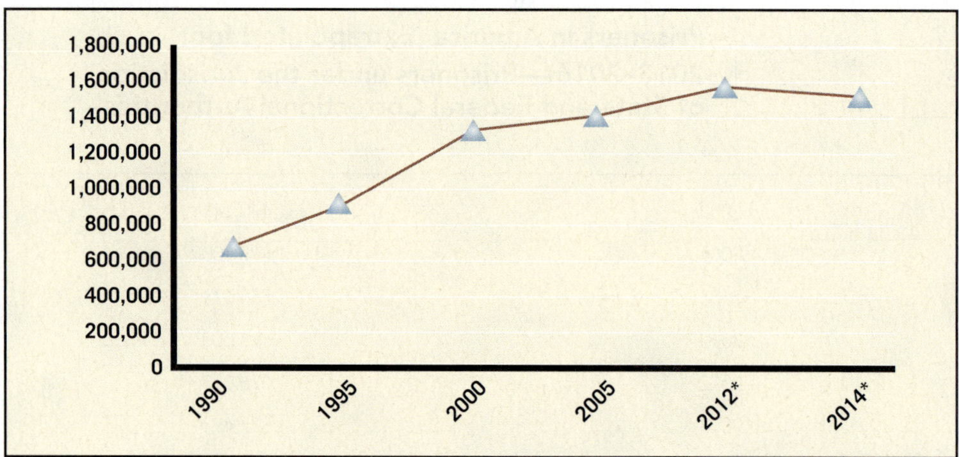

flexibility and prestige to the correctional operation. Without an intermediate level of organization, the director of a separate department has the ability to move more freely at the policymaking level. An autonomous department is able to control the allocation of personnel and fiscal resources, using economy-of-scale purchasing and operating with minimum competition from other divisions within the same department. Centralized control also has the advantage of providing effective administrative functions that are unique to correctional problems.

The corrections process must include a system of multilevel programs and facilities to provide the spectrum of services required to make a statewide program work. Most state correctional systems are concerned only with the principal institutions and parole services, leaving the majority of correctional problems in the state to units of local government.

Development of State Systems

Each type of state correctional system has developed as a matter of historical accident as much as in response to a state's particular needs. As might be expected, the large industrial prisons of the northeastern United States are more in evidence in the major industrial states, generally in the area between Illinois and New York. Most of those institutions were built early in the prison movement and were designed to take advantage of the cheap labor force inmates represented. They were the hardest hit by the restrictions the government later placed on prison industries in the 1930s.

At present, the industry allowed in the giant institutions does not provide full employment for large inmate populations.[5] In an effort to spread the few jobs among the many inmates, supervisors try to slow production and make the work last as long as possible. Those procedures are not likely to provide the inmate with a very good model for job success on the outside. The general picture of activity in the one-time industrial prisons is one of idleness and boredom. Despite even the most dedicated attempts by the staff inside and outside the institutions, there are just not enough meaningful jobs or other programs to help the thousands crowded into the likes of the Raifords (Florida), Atticas (New York), and San Quentins (California) of the country, although some exceptional programs exist.

key term

Agricultural prison
Any prison whose main products are agricultural and whose institutional value is the foodstuffs and produce grown.

The **agricultural prison** was begun in the southern states. Prison farms became very profitable ventures for those states and thus have been slow to change. Prisoners who served on public works and state farms replaced the pre–Civil War slave labor in many states, not only in the South.[6] Here again, authorities may have rationalized that the training received from farmwork and mines[7] helped prepare offenders for return to a basically agrarian southern economy, but the real intent was to use free labor to produce farm products. Cheap prison labor was often leased out to farm owners at a great profit to both the farmer and the

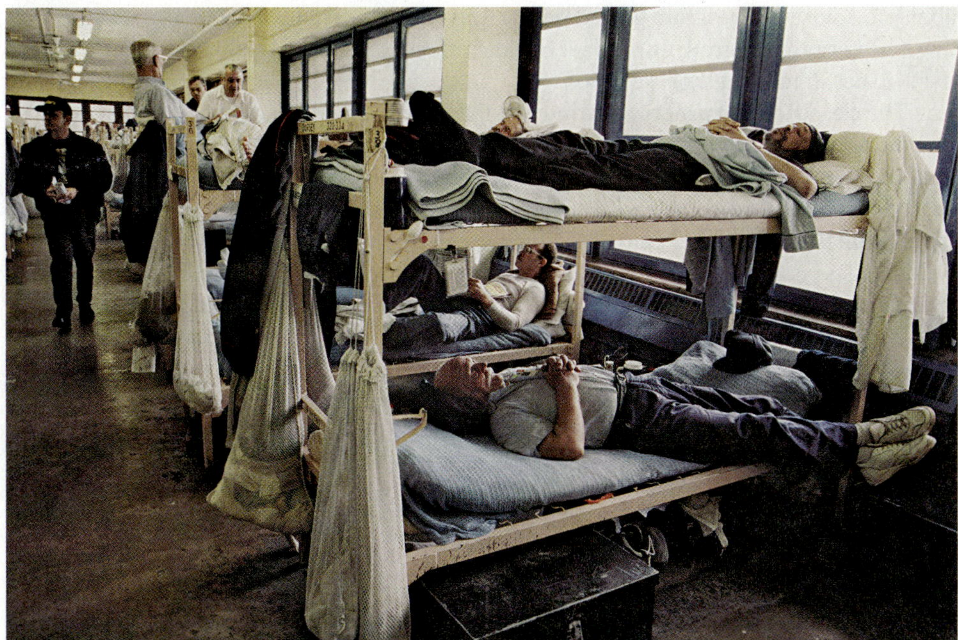

Photo 11.2
Geriatric inmates are seldom engaged in educational, vocational, and institutional work details and serve much "dead time" in most prisons. Here they are relaxing and bored.
Shepard Sherbell/Corbis.

state that collected the fee. The use of prison farms has become less profitable, however, with the advent of highly mechanized farming methods in most agricultural states.

Other regions of the country have designated certain institutions as farm oriented. The food produced in those institutions has been used to feed inmates in the rest of the institutions in the state. Many states have now abandoned that practice, as the realization has hit that farming experience is of little value to the primarily urban inmate found to be a large majority in most contemporary prisons. Another problem with prison farms has been the negative reaction from farm organizations, whose members argue that competition from the state is unfair, much the same argument that union workers used when protesting about prison manufacturing industries in the early part of the twentieth century.[8]

Many states have chosen to set up **work camps** and other forms of prisoner activity appropriate to their particular needs. Lumber camps have been used, as have road prisons or camps to construct and maintain roads. Recent versions of the work camp have been geared to provide a combination of hard work in the outdoors and programmed treatment aimed at preparing the offender for release. One example would be the use of inmates to fight wildfires in western states. It is considered more beneficial for offenders to do time in the relatively healthful atmosphere of a small work camp than to languish in the idleness and boredom of the large prisons.

key term
Work camp
A low-security facility organized around work on the exterior of the prison facility.

Classification and Assignment in State Prisons

Most state codes provide for the separation or classification of prisoners,[9] their division into different grades with promotion or demotion according to merit or demerit. In other words, inmates can be reclassified (maximum to medium or vice versa) based on behavior, escape attempts, harm to self or others, their employment and instruction in industrial pursuits, and participation in education or other programs.

In most systems, the **initial classification** determines the institution to which an inmate will be assigned. The receiving institution then determines whether the individual shall remain in maximum security or be transferred to a medium- or minimum-security penitentiary. (Each state in the United States has at least one maximum-security institution.) Most states base their reclassification decisions on a perception of the individual's ability to handle the next-lowest level of security. Also important is an evaluation of the individual's

key term
Initial classification
The initial process by which offenders are assigned to level of custody, work assignment, and treatments.

key term

Classification process
The process by which offenders are assigned to types of custody and treatment programs based on such factors as offense category, escape potential, substance-abuse patterns, previous experience with the criminal justice system, and so on.

key term

Institutional needs
Basic and mandatory functions for assigning prisoners to support institutional objectives.

ability to adjust to a program geared primarily to work, to academic or vocational training, or to the needs of the growing number of older offenders. A classification committee usually participates in making those decisions.

The **classification process** continues at the institutional level. Although each receiving institution emphasizes different programs, each has some version of education, counseling, and the other ingredients of rehabilitation programs. Theoretically, individuals are assigned according to their needs, but, realistically, assignments are too often made to conform to **institutional needs**. For example, an inmate may genuinely want to learn welding. If the welding class is filled but there is a vacancy in the furniture shop, the inmate may be assigned to the furniture shop, and no effort would be made to offer additional welding instruction. Also, inmates will often be assigned to a maintenance operation, such as food service or janitorial work, which is unlikely to conform to their own vocational plans or ambitions. An essential element of effective classification is a periodic review of the inmate's progress through the recommended program. All institutions allow for this reevaluation, usually called *reclassification*. The purpose is to adjust the program in accordance with the inmate's progress and needs. Realistically, however, decisions are all too frequently made on the basis of the available vacancies and institutional needs.

In 2005, the U.S. Supreme Court determined that new or recently transferred inmates may not be segregated by race in the classification process. Prison administrators would argue that such segregation serves institutional interests and has legitimate correctional functions, lowering the volume of conflicts between security threat groups ("gangs") and staff and inmates who bear grudges against other inmates or groups.[10]

Institution personnel may genuinely wish to provide the recommended program for an inmate. However, the need to keep the institution going smoothly inevitably shapes these decisions. Personnel may rationalize maintenance assignments on the basis that many, if not most, inmates need the experience of accepting supervision, developing regular work habits, learning to relate to coworkers, and other such skills. All of that may be true, but the treatment staff members are no less frustrated than the inmates when their recommended and prescribed programs are ignored. The classification and assignment process just described is only a composite of what the more effective programs provide.

INMATES IN STATE PRISONS

In 1983, the U.S. Department of Justice conducted a national survey of inmates in state correctional facilities in the United States and found an estimated 381,955 offenders under the jurisdiction of state government.[11] Since that study was conducted, the population of state prisons has skyrocketed to just over 1.6 million, an increase of over 450 percent. The average daily costs of inmates in the 10 most expensive states can be found in Table 11.3.

An overwhelming majority of the inmates (93 percent) are males, and relative to the numbers of men and women in the U.S. resident population, their incarceration rate is about 10 times higher (1,406 males to 136 females) per 100,000 population. The number of white male and black male inmates has been increasing at the state level and is now 35 percent and 41 percent, respectively.[12] All other minority males (Hispanics and others) now total 24 percent of the state prison populations. Hispanics are the fastest-growing group in state prisons.[13] The average inmate age is about 32 years, and about 10 percent of the total inmate population was at least age 50, reflecting the graying of America's general population as well as populations of inmates. Imprisonment rates for adult males by race, age, and ethnicity can be found in Figure 11.3. Minorities, particularly African American males, are incarcerated at a much higher rate than are white males in every age category (see Table 11.4).[14]

The offenses for which the state prisoners were currently incarcerated are shown in Figure 11.4. In sum, two in three inmates in state prisons were convicted of crimes of

table 11.3 **Ten States with the Highest Average Daily Costs per Inmate in 2011**

State	Daily Cost per Inmate
Rhode Island	$165.26
New York	$154.27
California	$129.00
Hawaii	$127.00
Massachusetts	$124.66
Maine	$112.00
New Jersey	$107.43
Delaware	$106.85
New Mexico	$95.67
North Dakota	$95.32

SOURCE: American Correctional Association, *2012 Directory of Adult and Juvenile Correctional Departments, Institutions, Agencies, and Probation and Parole Authorities* (Alexandria, VA: American Correctional Association, 2012), p. 25.

violence, including murder, manslaughter, rape, sexual assault, robbery, and assault. About one in six was incarcerated for a drug offense, usually drug trafficking. Fewer than one in four were in prison for property and all other crimes (see Figure 11.4).

Correctional Practice 11.1 provides an overview of characteristics of the adult prison population, and Correctional Practice 11.2 provides details of the issues faced by this population. As a group, state prison inmates were much less educated than their counterparts in the civilian population. At least 70 percent of the inmates had not received a high school diploma or general equivalency diploma, in contrast with 36 percent of the general population 18 years of age or older who had not.

In terms of their criminal offenses, almost 60 percent were classified as violent in 2012. The average sentence length imposed was more than eight years,[15] although 9 percent of the prisoners were incarcerated under life sentences. One in three had incurred at least one other sentence, in addition to the instant offense, and one in four had previously served time as a juvenile offender.

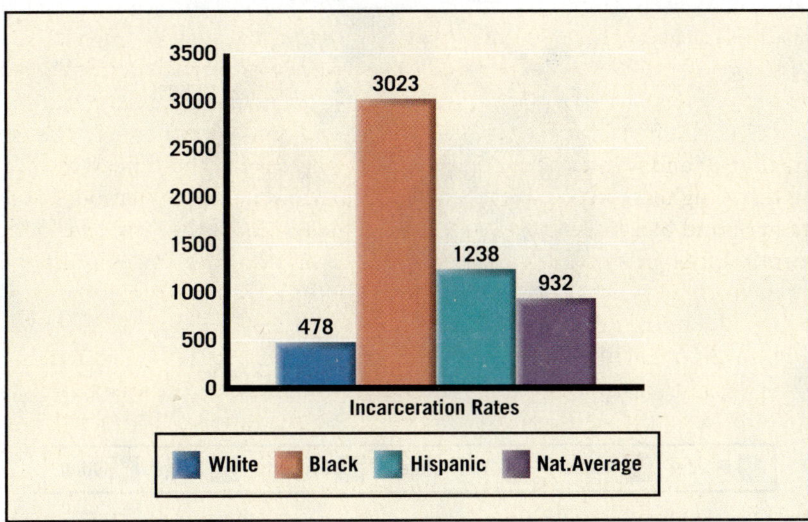

figure 11.3

Incarceration Rates of Male Prisoners by Demographic Group per 100,000.

SOURCE: Ann Carson and Daniela Gollnelll, *Prisoners in 2012* (Washington, DC: Bureau of Justice Statistics, 2012), p. 8.

table 11.4 **Estimated Imprisonment Rate of Sentenced Prisoners under State and Federal Jurisdiction, by Race, Hispanic Origin, and Age, December 31, 2011 (per 100,000)**

Age-Group	White	Black	Hispanic
18–19	166	1,544	574
20–24	712	4,702	1,898
25–29	1,074	6,883	2,666
30–34	1,115	7,517	2,762
35–39	1,049	6,603	2,460
40–44	949	5,450	2,084
45–49	834	4,604	1,830
50–54	565	3,257	1,402
55–59	345	1,999	990
60–64	230	1,125	685
65 or older	95	409	286

SOURCE: Ann Carson and William Sobel, *Prisoners in 2011* (Washington, DC: Bureau of Justice Statistics, 2012), p. 8.

In 2016, the 1,460,000 adult male inmates will be in state facilities with an average capacity over 100 percent (full). Twenty-two states (and the federal prison system) will be operating at or above their highest capacity. Texas will have the largest number of inmates (156,300), but Louisiana is estimated to have more inmates per 100,000 residents than any other state (about 881 inmates).

To keep abreast of the crush of new commitments, states over the past 30 years have been forced to resort to a bricks-and-mortar construction binge. The number of prison beds constructed during this period was astounding. Prison beds are expensive to build, averaging $74,000 per bed in 2000 (excluding interest to be paid on any construction bonds).[16]

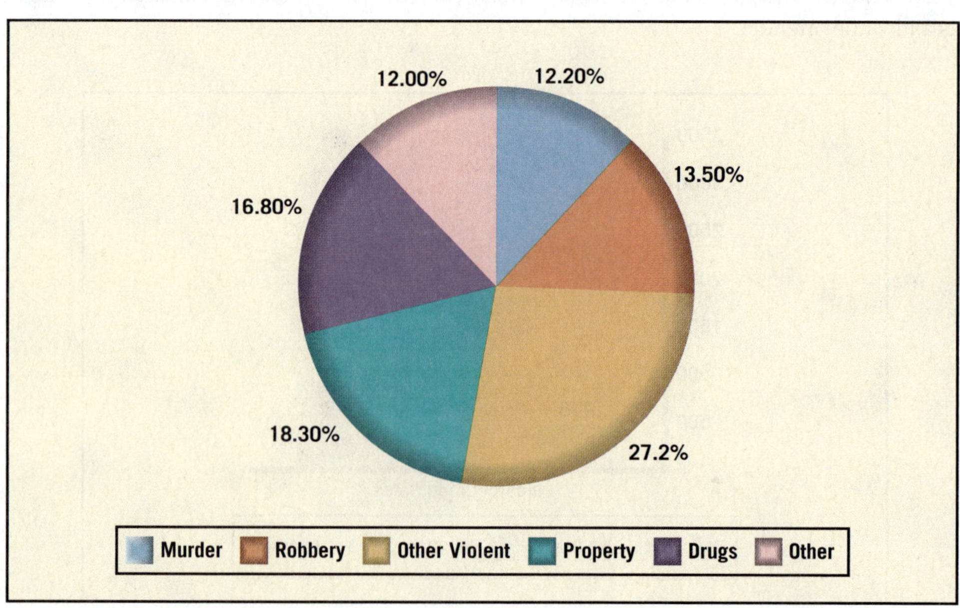

figure 11.4
Estimated Percentage of Sentenced Prisoners under State Jurisdiction by Offense.

SOURCE: E. Ann Carson and Daniela Galinelli, *Prisoners in 2012—Advance Counts* (Washington, DC: Bureau of Justice Statistics, July 2013), p. 10.

correctional **practice 11.1**

Characteristics of the Adult Prison Population

As noted in Chapter 3, the state prison population rapidly expanded from 1980 through 2010, caused in part by the War on Drugs, the War on Crime, and lengthening terms of imprisonment, as federal legislation was enacted requiring federal offenders to serve 85 percent of their original sentence. Other factors include increasing parole revocation rates and lack of adequate prison programs designed to address inmate needs and lower recidivism. Since 2010, some states have reduced their prison populations, occasioned primarily by the Great Recession of 2007 through 2012. States had insufficient tax resources to support the massive numbers of state inmates, and some state legislatures moved to reduce commitments to and hasten exit from prison. Most of the drop in the state prison population in California was due to a lawsuit by California inmates to secure adequate medical and mental health care. In ruling on the case, federal courts ordered California to reduce its prison population to 137.5 percent of rated capacity, leading to the ensuing reduction of state prisoners by almost 39,000 inmates. These trends in decreases of state prison populations continue.

SOURCE: Joan Petersilia (2014), "Voices from the Field: How California Stakeholders View Public Safety Realignment," https://www.law.stanford.edu/sites/default/files/publication/443439/doc/slspublic/Petersilia%20VOICES%20no%20es%20Final%20022814.pdf; The Sentencing Project (2014), "Trends in Corrections," http://sentencingproject.org/doc/publications/inc_Trends_in_Corrections_Fact_sheet.pdf.

Prison cells are expensive because almost everything is "heavy duty." For example, toilets are metal not ceramic; walls and ceilings are cement, not drywall; and so forth. In addition, locks, fire suppression systems, video security, and other features are costly. Prisons are used 24/7 every day of the year and need to be built to withstand the best efforts of the inmates to destroy and damage the facility. If the state borrows funds ("floats a bond") to construct a prison and pays the loan off over 30 years at 4 percent interest, the cost of a maximum-security bed could be as much as $200,000.

In general, the lower the security level, the less the cost per bed; minimum-security beds cost an average of $29,311 versus $80,000 or even more for maximum-security beds. The prison-bed construction costs for 2003 alone were over $6.7 billion. The per diem cost of incarceration for adults averages $79.64 per inmate, or over $88 million a day to house, feed, control, and care for the nation's adult male state inmates. At least one state, Ohio, has just announced that it will begin charging inmates $1 per month for electricity for the use of appliances such as radios. Despite the construction, remodeling, redesigning, and renovations, American prisons generally remain overcrowded. The U.S. Supreme Court may have

Photo 11.3

Several states still hold inmate rodeos, including Louisiana and Oklahoma. Here, inmates try their luck at bull riding.
Gerrit de Heus/Alamy.

correctional **practice 11.2**

Characteristics and Issues of State Prison Populations

Imprisoned inmates differ in many important respects from free U.S. residents. Common characteristics, without belaboring the numbers, are found across many offenders. Many face risk factors for future offending occasioned by low family income when a child, delinquency and crime of parents and siblings, witnessing violence, poor relationships with parents, parental mental illnesses, low academic achievement, and single-parent households. Circumstances of childhood have a strong impact on individuals and their life careers.

In terms of living arrangements while young, it should be noted that about 60 percent of state inmates have young children who are being cared for by relatives, foster care, juvenile institutions, and children's homes. Possibly as many as one in four adult inmates was cared for by the state, other relatives, or foster care sometime before adulthood. Many families suffer from inadequate income and lack of prenatal care.

Violence and abuse are frequent childhood experiences for inmates. About one in four experienced emotional, physical, and/or sexual abuse while a child. This figure includes physical abuse by both fathers and mothers. At least two-thirds of the male inmates witnessed domestic abuse in their childhood. Female inmates report more sexual abuse in their past than do male inmates. Some one in three inmates had parents who abused alcohol or took illegal drugs. Family criminality (referred to as "intergenerational transmission of criminal careers") is not uncommon. More than half of the male inmates noted brother/stepbrother and father/stepfather family members with previous or current incarceration. In general, male inmates have significant medical and dental challenges on entry to imprisonment as well as mental health problems and chronic physical ailments. In particular, they are more likely than the general population to be sicker, with higher rates of type 2 diabetes, depression, alcohol and drug addiction, mood disorders, and hypertension than those in the non-imprisoned population. Prisons must stabilize the health of their inmates, and this is expensive. For example, the pharmacy in the Santa Rita Jail in Alameda County, California, dispenses more than 350,000 prescription drugs every *month*. In general, the older the prison inmate, the more likely that inmate is to need treatment for multiple difficulties. For prisoners, their "medical age" (in terms of state of health) is frequently older than their chronological age.

Many male inmates were unemployed or underemployed at the time of the current offense, and had low levels of education and few prospects for employment improvement. The fact of imprisonment weighs heavily on future prospects. Many inmates are paroled to the streets and have issues finding suitable living arrangement. Such impediments lessen the opportunity for a successful reintegration. Inmate needs are frequently not addressed in prison or parole systems. More rehabilitation and reintegration could significantly impact future recidivism, increase public safety, and lower the number of prison inmates.

SOURCE: Editors of the *Crime Report* with Criminal Justice Journalists, "How Medicaid for Ex-Offenders Affects California County," http://www.rand.org/pubs/periodicals/rand-review/issues/2011/winter/prisoner.html (accessed September 11, 2014); Georgia Department of Community Affairs, "Re-Entry Partnership Housing, 2014, https://pap.georgia.gov/transitional-housing-offender-reentry.

to examine again the realities of imprisonment in the first decades of the 2000s and their relationship to the Eighth Amendment, thus forcing change in corrections. Clearly, the escalating problems for harried correctional administrators are only beginning. Fortunately, some of those problems are being addressed by the U.S. Supreme Court.

Correctional Practice 11.3 details California's attempt to decrease its prison population in response to a court-mandated order.

LOCAL ADULT CITY-OPERATED PRISONS

In calculating the numbers of inmates in adult prisons, one must not forget the "Big Four," a group of local institutions that are even larger than most states' prison systems:

1. Cook County Department of Corrections
2. New York City Department of Corrections
3. Washington, D.C., Department of Corrections
4. Philadelphia Prison System

correctional **practice 11.3**

California Prison Population Decline and Realignment

As noted in Correctional Practice 11.1, federal judges and courts in California required the California Department of Corrections and Rehabilitation (CDCR) to reduce the prison population and to increase the level of medical treatment for inmates. In 2009, it was ordered that the CDCR reduce its prison population to 137.5 percent of design capacity, or a reduction of approximately 39,000 inmates, within two years. The State of California appealed this order to the U.S. Supreme Court, which upheld the lower court's order in 2011.

The legislature quickly enacted a "realignment" program, designed to redirect nonviolent, nonsex, and nonserious offenders from incarceration in state prisons to supervision by local jurisdictions (counties). That legislation also made returning parolees to prison for nonfelonious parole violations more difficult and restricted sanctions for nonfelonious parole supervision to imposition of jail time. If the releasees commit other felony crimes, they must be ordered to a new trial. It was decided that most prison offenders would return to their home counties following parole, and thus the county had a strong vested interest in developing strategies that would reduce recidivism. Counties also provide alternative, evidence-based approaches to preventing recidivism, including drug and alcohol abuse treatment, job training, mental health treatment, and housing. In 2012, the CDCR was ordered to provide counties with funds diverted from its budget to reimburse counties for their expenses.

The crime rate in California has been falling for about 20 years and now stands at the levels previously found in 1972. Commitments to prison for crimes contributed to the population growth, but the main factor was the unusually high number of parolees returned to prison basically for technical parole violations. Other factors include three-strikes legislation, a sentencing enhancement sanction that requires the court, when finding three convictions of an offender for crimes, to impose a sentence of 25 years to life, with no possibility of parole.

California is beginning to meet its mandated obligations. As noted, the state prison population declined by almost 39,000 inmates to meet the court-ordered stipulation. The primary reason for the shrinkage is that technical parole violations can no longer be punished by imprisonment time in state prison. Another factor was shifting the responsibility for incarcerating new low-level felony offenders to the county level: jail time, house arrest, electronic monitoring, tourniquet sentencing, fines, and other graduated sanctions combined to assure offender compliance. Counties are investing in community-based alternatives, hiring more probation officers, and implementing effective programs proven to promote criminal desistance and increase reentry chances for released offenders. Such programs include family reunification, job assistance, housing subsidies and stability, and drug treatment, among others.

Whether California can meet the mandated prison population level remains am open question, but evidence to date suggests that the state is close to this goal and has accomplished this by redirecting offenders who have committed low-level and nonviolent crimes away from state imprisonment to county programs and supervision. The intended goals of realignment are to (1) save money, (2) encourage all counties to develop and maintain best practices in alternatives to imprisonment, (3) conform to court orders to reduce prison populations to constitutional levels (*Brown v. Plata*, 2011, No. 19-1233), and (4) reserve scarce prison cells for offenders who have committed serious offenses.

A recent study of disparities across counties in using imprisonment to transfer county costs of handling offenders to state coffers found that, overall, new prison admissions have been reduced by 34 percent, primarily in the area of such nonviolent crimes as property and drug offenses. Seventeen counties sentenced more offenders to prison than the state average—as a result, those counties cost taxpayers more than $170 million in 2012. Taxpayers in more self-reliant (i.e., following realignment principles) counties are being forced to subsidize those counties that avoid realignment and still rely on prisons to handle their offenders. The average annual cost in 2012 to incarcerate one prisoner in state prison was almost $52,000. Perhaps California needs a state sentencing commission that would establish guidelines for ranges of types and length of sentences for each committable offense.

SOURCE: Magnus Lofstrom, Joan Petersilia, and Steven Raphael (2012), "Evaluating the Effects of California's Corrections Realignment on Public Safety," http://www.ppic.org/content/pubs/report/R_812MLR.pdf (accessed October 24, 2012). See also Mike Males and Lizzie Buchen, *Beyond Realignment: Counties' Large Disparities in Imprisonment Underlie Ongoing Prison Crisis* (San Francisco: Center on Juvenile and Criminal Justice Research, March 2013).

These four large systems consist of 110 adult prisons and a large number of other institutions and programs and could hold over 30,000 adult offenders by 2016. One seldom thinks of cities as needing their own correctional systems, but these four cities have chosen to do so. Their operations are similar to the state prisons, but they allow inmates to be housed nearer to home. It may be that some of the other large U.S. cities may get into their own corrections game as well, but most have shown little interest. Many local jail systems are already so overcrowded that most do not have the time to plan that far ahead. The trends of the Big Four should be followed carefully.

ARE PRISONS "CRUEL AND UNUSUAL PUNISHMENT"?

Whether prisons are state or local or house males or females, the problems of institutionalization are ever present in our prisons. Understaffing, underbudgeting, and lack of citizen interest or involvement often become excuses for allowing conditions to deteriorate and sink to the lowest levels. Beginning in the 1970s, both state and federal courts were asked to examine the operations and policies of correctional facilities and personnel to ensure compliance with the Eighth Amendment's prohibition against cruel and unusual punishment. By February 1983, the courts had declared unconstitutional the entire prison systems of Alabama, Florida, Louisiana, Mississippi, Oklahoma, Rhode Island, Tennessee, and Texas and all the male penal institutions of Michigan. In addition, at least one or more facilities in another 21 states were operating under either a court order or a consent decree (permission to continue to operate until a fix has been completed within a specific timeframe) as a result of inmate crowding and/or the conditions of confinement. Yet another seven states were involved in ongoing litigation relating to overcrowding and/or the conditions of release from prison. Finally, in eight states, the courts had appointed receivers or masters to operate the state prison system or facility, had ordered the emergency release of inmates because of crowding, or had designated specific prisons to be closed.[17] The courts took those actions only as a last resort and when it was clear the impacted states had relinquished their responsibility to protect the constitutional rights of the inmates under their custody and care. Correctional construction began in earnest as a response to prison overcrowding. Between 1987 and 2012, more than 800 new prisons were built and added to correctional systems.[18]

The states, understandably, have reacted with great indignation over the Supreme Court's intrusion into the domain of the executive branch at the state level. Politicians in California are currently objecting strongly to court intervention and its ordering of inmate release until medical services are adequate for the number of offenders remaining. Where does the Court get the right to intervene in such matters? The Civil Rights Law of 1871 provides for the principal method of allowing such inmate complaints into the federal courts. That statute provides that citizens denied constitutional rights by the state may sue in the federal court. Originally designed to protect the newly freed slaves in the post–Civil War era, the statute was generally forgotten until a landmark case in 1964 (*Cooper* v. *Pate*). In that case, the Court finally ruled in favor of a prisoner's seeking relief in federal court by way of the 1871 act.

Photo 11.4

Inmate chain gang at work cleaning trash from roadside.
Rob Schoenbaum/Newscom.

Over the years, the procedures used have been tentative and careful, each step breaking new ground for prisoners' rights. The legal groundwork for these condition suits was laid by these decisions, and all came during the era of the Earl Warren court. In some cases, the Supreme Court has extended prisoner rights, but in others, the Court has been reluctant to do so. The Court has been clear, however, that inmates have the right to take their complaints to the federal courts. The balancing act is between the constitutional rights of the inmates versus the prison officials' concerns about security and order.

Increased activism by attorneys and legal aid programs as well as the extension of the class-action suit also led to more challenges of prison conditions.[19] The states are not giving up easily, however, and have appealed these decisions. Each case is different, of course, but they have all been slowed in their immediate impact by the issuance of a decision of the Fifth Circuit Court of Appeals, written in regard to an Alabama order. A three-judge appeals panel upheld the finding of unconstitutionality but reduced the scope of the order by ordering a new hearing on the requirement of 60 square feet of space per inmate in new construction, dissolving the Human Rights Committee, and limiting the role of the court-appointed monitor. The appeals court also overturned the order forbidding the state to require women visitors to prisons to stand over a mirror and drop their underwear as part of a routine search for contraband. The most significant part of the order, that dealing with idleness, was also cut back. The appeals court ruled that rehabilitation programs could not be required. However, the appeals court did agree that each inmate should be assigned to a job because it "should not impose any real burden" on prison officials. The decision stated, "If the state furnishes its prisoners with reasonably adequate food, clothing, shelter, sanitation, medical care, and personal safety, so as to avoid the imposition of cruel and unusual punishment, that ends its obligations under Amendment Eight."[20] Eighth Amendment lawsuits over prison conditions continue (*Madrid* v. *Gomez*, for example).[21]

Photo 11.5

Jail inmates stand in the doorway of their dorm in the Los Angeles County Jail, some of the 20,000 inmates in a system built for half that number.

Damian Dovarganes/AP Images.

Realistically, it is important to remember that a prison system has little control over who will be committed. Nor does it exercise much control over sentence length, parole eligibility, minimal sentence proportion to be served, or legislative allocations. The current prison situation is in part due to mandatory sentences that were a result of the more conservative response to crime, the public's fear of crime and criminals, increased sentence lengths, and the higher failure rates of parolees who must then be returned to prison. Yet the cruel and unusual punishment conditions continue.

Prior to the mid-1970s, the inmate social system was controlled internally by "old-hand" inmates whose exemplary behavior had won them the grudging respect of the inmate body. Challenges to their status and the prison routine desired by the old hands would be met with the necessary force to remove the challenger through murder or, where necessary, institutional riot. When the War on Drugs began, members of street gangs and "crazies" were committed to prison, where they challenged the former social system. The old hands lost control of the institutions, and prison gangs emerged as a segment of the social structure in these institutions, in part as a defense mechanism against the increasingly violent and aggressive acts of the crazies and other gangs.[22] Correctional administrators, faced with violent acts and correctional officer casualties, began to create supermax prisons (see Correctional Practice 11.4) to isolate the most dangerous and violent as well as gang members (**security threat groups**). Supermax prisons were greeted with an explosion of lawsuits that continue today.[23] Corrections administrators thus face many emerging challenges.

key term

Security threat group
A prison gang; a criminal enterprise having an organizational structure and internal leadership, acting as an ongoing criminal conspiracy that uses violence and other criminal activity to continue.

key term

Supermax
A freestanding prison or designated area within a prison that functions to control and contain dangerous, violent, disruptive, and other serious behavior in a prison facility.

One other response by corrections was to add more correctional personnel. More than 450,000 persons will be employed in state correctional facilities in 2015, an increase of over 160 percent of the number in 1985.[24] Correctional opportunities will continue to increase, and recruits will be sought who have the skills and willingness to work in the prisons of tomorrow. There is clearly a need for active citizen support for corrections, especially at the state level, and for active monitoring of our prison conditions.

correctional practice 11.4

The Supermax Prison

Violent, seriously disruptive, assaultive, and escape-prone inmates, including active gang members, pose immense challenges to prison security and custody. Challenges include threats to the safety of staff and other inmates, danger to the security of the institution, and inmates who require protective custody. The super-maximum prison (**supermax**) is a response to the need to manage and securely control inmates exhibiting violent or seriously disruptive behavior while incarcerated. A supermax prison is a freestanding facility (or distinct unit within a facility) that provides for the management and secure control of inmates who have been officially designated as exhibiting violent or seriously disruptive behavior while incarcerated.

The first supermax prison was Alcatraz; the earliest supermax housing opened in 1954 in Mississippi. At present, there are at least 57 supermax facilities or units nationwide, providing about 20,000 beds, or about 2 percent of those serving sentences of at least a year.

Within the supermax can usually be found a special housing unit (SHU) for the most difficult-to-handle offenders, sometimes called the "worst of the worst." The SHU enforces the strictest discipline and isolation, reinforced by physical means. There, inmates are typically held in their cells 23 hours a day and eat in their cells. There are few interactions between staff and inmates and almost none between inmates.

When an SHU inmate leaves the cell, that prisoner is typically cuffed and leg-shackled; two or three officers escort each SHU inmate. Recreation is solitary, typically for 30 minutes, perhaps three times a week, in a bare cell with no equipment.

Controversy abounds over the operations of an SHU. First is the question of how inmates are selected for SHU isolation; one sufficient criterion is gang membership. How does a gang member earn release from the SHU? By renouncing the gang and providing intelligence to correctional officers? What are the implications of this snitch behavior for a "blood-in, blood-out" prison gang, and would this lead to shortened life expectancy?

Second is the cost penalty because SHUs are labor intensive; multiple escorts are required for each inmate leaving the cell. Third is the surge of litigation over sensory deprivation, classification, access to law libraries and attorneys, quality of mental health services, and excessive use of force (*Madrid* v. *Gomez*, 889 F. Supp. 1146, 1995). The Pelican Bay, California, lawsuit of *Madrid* v. *Gomez* determined that holding mentally ill inmates in an SHU where there was extremely limited mental health services and in isolation (which can accelerate mental health deterioration) was cruel and unusual punishment, a violation of the Eighth Amendment. In California, the average annual cost of housing an inmate in an SHU is $74,600.

On the other hand, using the supermax prison can dramatically cut down on prison violence, assaults, and murders of prison officers and other inmates. What would you do if you were man-aging an institution operating at 83 percent over its maximum capacity, with several gangs and a high concentration of severely violent and aggressive inmates present?

SOURCE: LIS, Inc., *Supermax Housing: A Survey of Current Practice* (Longmont, CO: National Institute of Corrections, 1997), pp. 1–6.

Summary

Explain the Organization and Basic Functions of State Prisons

Corrections at the state level generally is organized into a separate department of corrections or a division within a larger state department. Most correctional administrators consider the separate department to be more effective, and having the director at the cabinet level adds great flexibility and prestige to the correctional operation. An autonomous department is able to control the allocation of personnel and fiscal resources, using economy-of-scale purchasing and operating with minimum competition from other divisions within the same department. Centralized control also has the advantage of providing effective administrative functions that are unique to correctional problems.

The corrections process must include a system of multilevel programs and facilities to provide the spectrum of services required to make a statewide program work. Most state correctional systems are concerned only with the principal institutions and parole services, leaving the majority of correctional problems in the state to units of local government.

The major correctional institutions contained in the state systems are super-maximum (supermax) prisons, maximum/close prisons, medium-security prisons, and minimum-security prisons These institutions are charged with the simultaneous and often conflicting functions of punishment and reform. Most are short on money and personnel, but they are still expected to prevent their graduates from returning to crime. Security and custody are the primary emphases in these prisons, and their environments are isolated both physically and philosophically from the mainstream of life.

State and local prison systems serve to house male and female offenders and provide such care, custody, and treatment as needed for public safety, lessened recidivism, and reintegration of clients. Many state correctional systems provide institutional treatment programs and services that address the needs of most prisoners, although other states fall far short of the minimum services needed. Prisoners need to address their sometimes numerous needs, and state prisons are expected to make such treatments available. In some states, there are insufficient funds and other resources provided to correctional administrators who sincerely desire to provide meaningful services.

Outline the Development of the State Prison System

Each type of state correctional system has developed as a matter of historical accident as much as in response to a state's particular needs. The large industrial prisons of the northeastern United States were built early in the prison movement and were designed to take advantage of the cheap labor force that inmates represented; they were the hardest hit by the restrictions the government later placed on prison industries in the 1930s. Currently, despite even the most dedicated attempts by the staff inside and outside the institutions, there are just not enough meaningful jobs or other programs available to maintain the work production focus, resulting in prisoner idleness and boredom in these institutions.

Agricultural prisons began in the southern states. Prisoners who served on public works and state farms replaced the pre–Civil War slave labor in many states, where the intent was to use free labor to produce farm products. Cheap prison labor was often leased out to farm owners at a great profit to both the farmer and the state that collected the fee. The use of prison farms has become less profitable, however, with the advent of highly mechanized farming methods in most agricultural states.

Many states have chosen to set up work camps and other forms of prisoner activity appropriate to their particular needs, such as lumber camps, road prisons or camps, and recent versions geared to provide a combination of hard work in the outdoors and programmed treatment aimed at preparing the offender for release, such as the use of inmates to fight wildfires in western states. It is considered more beneficial for offenders to do time in the relatively healthful atmosphere of a small work camp than to languish in the idleness and boredom of the large prisons.

Summarize the Characteristics, Trends, and Issues of the Adult Prison Population

State prisoners have high needs posed by many possible criminogenic factors. They are more physically and mentally ill, have medical treatment and dental needs, and seldom have insurance to cover service provider costs when they were free citizens. On arrival in prison, they require individualized treatment, which, if not provided, contributes to return to prison after release and less public safety.

Both male and female prison inmates face a variety of medical, mental health, and physical ailments and are sicker, more stressed, and more emotionally challenged than the general population. In sum, they need extensive medical and mental health services, stabilizing, and, when failing on parole, restabilizing again on return to incarceration. This is an expensive cycle.

Explain the Impact That Politics and Government Policy Have on Corrections

Politics and governmental policies impact the composition and complexities of prison systems. The War on Drugs coupled with an increase in street and gang crime, contributed to public alarm and a determination to isolate such criminals in prison as a public safety response. In the past three decades, prison populations tripled, and changes in sentencing practices slowed the process of exiting from prison. More offenders were detected, sentenced, and committed for longer periods of time. Release programs, such as shock probation, shock parole, parole, and good-time credits, were reduced. Offenders remained in prison for increasingly longer periods of time. State funding of imprisonment facilities was insufficient to control and manage dangerous offenders; incarceration of mostly petty drug offenders increased the resource shortfall.

In the past decade, state governments have come to the realization that continued construction of additional facilities is inappropriate when low-risk but high-need offenders are incarcerated and that recidivism can be reduced without overdue reliance on mass incarceration. Legislatures have begun to reexamine and subsequently reduce overcommitment of low-level offenders to prisons, largely by increasing dependence on intermediate sanctions, reducing sentence lengths, and forcing counties to accept responsibility for reductions in recidivism. A drop in the number of prison inmates has resulted, a decrease that will probably accelerate further within the next decade.

Explain the Impact That Budgets Have on Correctional Policy

Despite the increase in new and different facilities across both state and federal jurisdictions, prison overcrowding continued to plague the prison system. In the 1930s, federal legislation led to the downgrading of industrial prisons, further increasing the negative impacts of prison overcrowding. This circumstance eviscerated correctional programming and led to a major increase in prison overcrowding (and prison riots). This problem in turn was further enhanced by a marked increase in the number of imprisoned felons. A subtle but catastrophic hardening of attitudes toward "evildoers" contributed to enhanced sentences, mandatory sentencing, and truth-in-sentencing laws that required inmates to serve 85 percent of the sentence the judge had pronounced. Only in the past two decades have the voices embracing sentencing smarter, enhancing community corrections, and using evidence-based programs led to a decline in the number of offenders sentenced to prison.

Incarcerating offenders is an expensive process. Most state correctional systems are chronically underfunded. Even more problematic is the fact that most prisons have posts and positions that *must* be staffed: the critical custodial positions. Whatever transpires in the higher-security prisons and whatever new ideas are generated cannot escape the realities of lack of resources. Budgets must sometimes be distributed almost totally to custody functions, with scant funds for increasing treatment staff or initiating effective programs. Running a prison system that stresses the custody functions and shortchanges inmate reentry will continue to deliver high and unacceptable recidivism rates, doing little to protect citizens from inmates who have grown even harder through the furnace of danger, gangs, and prison custody efforts.

Four cities have their own prison systems, but most prison inmates are housed within state prisons. There they receive a variety of rehabilitative and reintegrative programs, although these are limited in number in the supermax facilities. The supermax prison developed as a response to a significant intake of street and syndicate gangs and the systems' need to establish appropriate controls due to the dangerousness security threat groups posed.

Three major changes have resulted from prison overcrowding. First, it has been recognized that a revolving-door policy does not protect the general public. Second, institutional threat groups ("prison gangs") have been increased and solidified in number and strength, posing additional challenges to the institution's intelligence system. Third, the court system has increasingly found that prison overcrowding creates violations of constitutionally guaranteed inmate rights and has forced change in the use of programming in and an increase of inmate treatment services. Because each of these three has major implications for future correctional practices, an emphasis has arisen to maximize community correctional programs and enhance reentry services. Other major changes will be forthcoming. Budgetary restrictions are having significant impacts on correctional policy.

Key Words

alternative to death and flogging, 240
agricultural prison, 242
work camps, 243
initial classification, 243
classification process, 244
institutional needs, 244
security threat group, 251
supermax prison, 251

Review Questions

1. Characterize the current state inmate population in the nation.
2. How much time does a state inmate generally spend in prison?
3. How would you decide whether the conditions of a prison constitute "cruel and unusual" punishment?
4. Why are alternatives to incarceration becoming a necessary focus for correctional administrators?
5. What impact does overcrowding have on the reform of institutional programs in state systems?
6. How are inmates classified?
7. Has the institutional inmate-to-staff ratio gone up or down? Why?
8. What are three likely trends in state correctional facilities over the next 10 years?
9. Why did the supermax prison arise?
10. What can be done to reduce the challenge of prison gangs?

Application Case Studies

1. You are the director of your state's corrections department, and your state legislature cuts your department's budget allocation by 5 percent. What five actions would you take to cope with this budgetary shortfall?
2. Inmates filed and won a lawsuit about your correctional practice of single-celling mentally ill inmates. The federal court with jurisdiction gives you six months to draft a plan of action to cease such isolation. What would you, as the state director of corrections, do?
3. The director of prison services for your institutions was tasked with the development of a new classification system for the initial classification of inmates. The director conducted a preliminary evaluation study of the impacts of the new system in accelerating inmate departure from confinement and found a reduction in the level of recidivism for such early releases. What five things would you, as director of the state's department of corrections, do to implement the new classification system throughout your institutions?

Endnotes

1. American Correctional Association, *2010 Directory* (Alexandria, VA: American Correctional Association, 2010).
2. Ibid.
3. Quoted in Harry Elmer Barnes and Negley J. Teeters, *New Horizons in Criminology*, 3rd ed. (Englewood Cliffs, NJ: Prentice Hall, 1959), pp. 461–462.
4. Heather West, *Prison Inmates at Midyear 2009* (Washington, DC: Bureau of Justice Statistics, 2009).
5. Steven Garvey, "Freeing Prisoners' Labor," *Stanford Law Review* 50:2 (1998): 339–398. Camp and Camp report that 64 percent of adults in prison were employed in a prison industry, on a prison farm, or in other prison work in 2000. Camille Camp and George Camp, *The Corrections Yearbook 2000: Adult Corrections* (Middletown, CT: Criminal Justice Institute, 2000), pp. 96–97.
6. Harry E. Allen and Julie C. Abril, "The New Chain Gang: Corrections in the Next Century," *American Journal of Criminal Justice* 22:1 (1997): 1–12. See also David Oshinsky, *Worse Than Slavery: Parchman Farms and the Ordeal of Jim Crow Justice* (New York: Free Press, 1996), and Rebukah Chu, Craig Rivera, and Colin Loftin, "Herding and Homicide," *Social Forces* 78:3 (2000): 971–978.
7. Karen Shapiro, *The New South Rebellion: Tennessee Coalfields, 1971–1986* (Chapel Hill: University of North Carolina Press, 1998); Mary Curtin, *Black Prisoners and Their World* (Charlottesville: University Press of Virginia, 2000).
8. James Vardalis and Fred Becker, "Legislative Opinions concerning the Private Operations of State Prisons," *Criminal Justice Policy Review* 11:2 (2000): 136–148.
9. Editors, "California Prisons End Housing Segregation," *Correctional News* 14:5 (2008):18.
10. Bureau of Justice Statistics, *Prisoners in 2003* (Washington, DC: Bureau of Justice Statistics, 1985).
11. Bureau of Justice Statistics, *Prisoners in 1983* (Washington, DC: Bureau of Justice Statistics, 1984).
12. West, *Prison Inmates at Midyear 2009*. See also Katti Gray (2013), "Growing Old (and Sick) in Prison," http://www/thecrimereport.org/news/inside-criminal-justice/2013-11-growing-old-and-sick-in-prison (accessed November 13, 2013).
13. West, *Prison Inmates at Midyear 2009*, p. 9. See also Karen Garrison, "Home for the Holidays," *Crack the Disparities Newsletter* 1:2 (2008).
14. Disproportionate minority confinement is a heated controversy in corrections, particularly in secure juvenile facilities. See Patricia Devine, K. Coolbaugh, and S. Jenkins, *Disproportionate Minority Confinement: Lessons Learned from Five States* (Washington, DC: Office of Justice Programs, 1998). See also Leadership Conference on Civil Rights, *Justice on Trial: Racial Disparities in the American Criminal Justice System* (Washington, DC: Leadership Council on Civil Rights, 2000), and Cheryl Corley (2013), "Wisconsin Prisons Incarcerate Most Black Men in the U.S.," http://www.nprorg/blogs/codeswitch/2013/10/03/228733846/wisconsin-prisons-incarcerate-most-black-men-in-us (accessed October 3, 2013).
15. Bureau of Justice Statistics, *Trends in State Parole, 1990–2000* (Washington, DC: Bureau of Justice Statistics, 2001), p. 6; Bureau of Justice Statistics, "Criminal Sentencing Findings," http://www.ojp.usdoj.gov/bjs/sent.htm (accessed September 24, 2008).
16. Extrapolated from Camp and Camp, *The 2000 Corrections Yearbook*, p. 73. See the annual costs for individual prison facilities published in American Correctional Association, *2012 Directory* (Alexandria, VA: American Correctional Association, 2012). See also Bureau of Justice Statistics (2013), "The Justice Reinvestment Initiative," http:///www.urban.org/UploadedPDF/412879-the-justice-reinvestment-initiative.pdf (accessed August 9, 2013), and Christian Hendrickson and Ruth Delaney, Vera Institute of Justice, *The Price of Prisons: What Incarceration Costs Taxpayers* (Washington, DC: Vera Institute of Justice, 2013).
17. Bureau of Justice Statistics, *Report to the Nation on Crime and Justice* (Washington, DC: U.S. Department of Justice, 1983), p. 80.
18. American Correctional Association, *2010 Directory*.
19. S. Gettinger, "Cruel and Unusual Prisons," *Corrections Magazine* 3 (December 1977): 3–16.
20. Ibid., p. 10.
21. 889 F. Supp. 1146 (1995). See also Nadine Curran, "Blue Hair in the Bighouse," *New England Journal on Criminal and Civil Confinement* 26:2 (2000): 225–264, and John Rudolph (2012), "Georgia Prison 'Out of Control,' Rights Group Says, as FBI Brutality Probe Deepens," http:www.huffingtonpost.com/2012/08/21/Georgia-prisons-guard-brutality-killings_n_1820145.html?view=print&comm_ref=false.
22. Victor Hassine, *Life without Parole: Living in Prison Today* (Los Angeles: Roxbury, 2002).
23. To learn more about supermax prisons, see also David Ward, "A Corrections Dilemma: How to Evaluate Super-Max Regimes," *Corrections Today* 57:5 (1997): 108; Rodney Henningsen, W. Johnson, and T. Wells, "Supermax Prisons: Panacea or Desperation?," *Corrections Management Quarterly* 3:2 (1999): 53–59; Jeffrey Ross, "Supermax Prisons," *Society* 44:3 (2007): 60–64; and Paige St. John (2013), "Brown Seeks 3-Year Delay on Easing Prison Crowding," http://articles.latimes.com/2013/sep/16/local/la-me-ff-prisons-20130917.
24. American Correctional Association, *2010 Directory*.

Kristopher Skinner/Contra Costa Times/ZUMA/Newscom.

Objectives

- Outline the development of the federal prison system.
- Explain the development of federal prison facilities.
- Describe and illustrate the use of contract facilities by the federal prison system.
- Identify and contrast the federal prison security levels.
- Explain the operations of UNICOR.
- Compare and contrast the education and training of federal inmates and staff.
- Summarize the characteristics of female federal inmates.
- Summarize the organization of the federal prison system.

chapter 12
The Federal System

Outline

"That there is hereby established in the Department of Justice a Bureau of Prisons responsible for the safekeeping, care, protection, instruction, and discipline of all persons charged with or convicted of offenses against the United States."

—Public Law No. 218, approved by President Herbert Hoover, May 14, 1930

Overview

With this proclamation, the federal government went into the business of corrections in a big way. The history of incarcerating offenders for violations of federal law is long and interesting. With the power of the federal government (and the federal purse) behind it, the Federal Bureau of Prisons has become an innovator and leader in correctional management and operations. The Bureau of Prisons is a system entirely separate from state and local correctional agencies. It is designed and intended to deal primarily with adults and juveniles who have violated federal laws. Based on a 1997 federal law, the Bureau of Prisons is also responsible for incarcerating the District of Columbia's sentenced felon inmate population. Because the federal system, like the juvenile system discussed in Chapter 18, slowly developed as an independent entity, a review of its background and history is necessary and useful for understanding how this system originated, what it is doing, and where it might be going.[1]

THE USE OF STATE FACILITIES

In the late 1700s and for most of the 1800s, federal prisoners were sent to state and local institutions to serve their sentences. One of the first acts of Congress was to pass a bill (An Act to Establish the Judicial Courts of the United States) encouraging the states to pass laws providing for the incarceration of federal law violators in state institutions. Most of the states did pass such laws, and all federal offenders sentenced to one year or more served their sentences in state facilities. Offenders who were sentenced to terms of less than one year or those being held in detention awaiting trial were usually confined in local jails, a practice that continues today on a limited scale.

key term

Justice Department
The unit of the federal government in which the Federal Bureau of Prisons is located.

In 1870, Congress established the **Justice Department**. A general agent was established in the Department of Justice and was placed in charge of all federal prisoners in state and local institutions. Later, the "general agent" became the superintendent of prisons, responsible to an assistant attorney general for the care and custody of all federal prisoners.

State prisons became seriously overcrowded in the period that followed the Civil War. With increased numbers of both state and federal prisoners, many states became reluctant to take federal prisoners when they could not even care properly for their own. Consequently, in some states only federal prisoners from that specific state were accepted. In states where neither suitable nor adequate facilities were available, transporting federal inmates to appropriate facilities involved lengthy travel and high costs. In 1885, there were 1,027 federal prisoners in state prisons and approximately 10,000 in county jails. By 1895, those numbers had risen to 2,516 federal prisoners in state prisons and approximately 15,000 in county jails.

On March 3, 1891, the U.S. Congress passed a bill (An Act for the Erection of United States Prisons and for the Imprisonment of United States Prisoners, and for Other Purposes) authorizing the construction of three penitentiaries, although their funding was not approved until later. The establishment of federal prison facilities was considered necessary because of the rapidly increasing number of federal inmates, the states' growing reluctance to house federal prisoners, and the exclusion of federal prisoners from contract labor.

Photo 12.1

An aerial view of Fort Jefferson in the Dry Tortugas National Park. It served as a federal prison during and after the American Civil War; surrounded by a wide, shark-infested moat, the prison was popularly known as Shark Island.
Tony Arruza/Corbis.

EARLY FEDERAL PRISON FACILITIES

Until 1895, all military prisoners not in state prisons were confined at Fort Leavenworth in eastern Kansas. But the War Department then decided to house its prisoners in several different military installations. Consequently, the Department of Justice acquired the surplus military prison at Fort Leavenworth. For the first time, federal prisoners, including those transferred from state institutions as well as new commitments, were confined in a federal facility. In short order, the Department of Justice realized the prison, adapted from former quartermaster warehouses, was inadequate. Therefore, on July 10, 1896, Congress appropriated funds for the construction of one of the previously authorized penitentiaries. It would be capable of holding 1,200 inmates and was to be built on the Fort Leavenworth military reservation three miles from the existing prison. Because the penitentiary was built by convict labor, construction took many years. The Leavenworth Penitentiary opened in 1906 but was not finally completed until 1928.

A second penitentiary at McNeil Island, Washington, was constructed between 1872 and 1875. The federal government designated it as a **U.S. penitentiary** in 1909.[2] Construction on a third penitentiary at Atlanta, Georgia, began in 1899 and opened in 1902. The Auburn style of architecture, characterized by multitiered cell blocks and a fortress-like appearance, was adopted for all three penitentiaries.

key term

U.S. penitentiary

A correctional facility in which offenders are incarcerated to keep them from society and from each other so they can reflect on their crimes, repent, and be rehabilitated.

Between 1900 and 1935, American prisons, including federal institutions, were primarily custodial, punitive, and industrial. Overcrowding at the federal prisons during this period left few resources for anything but custodial care. Nevertheless, significant developments during the early 1900s affected the operation of federal institutions, including passage of the following acts:

- White Slave Act in 1910 (interstate commerce of prostitution)
- Harrison Narcotic Act in 1914 (records must be kept and taxes paid on controlled substances)
- Volsteadt Act in 1918 (prohibited the sale and consumption of alcohol)
- Dyer Act of 1919 (interstate transportation of stolen vehicles)

Together, these acts brought a large number of people under federal criminal jurisdiction. The number of offenders incarcerated under those statutes swelled the federal prison population beyond the available physical capacity. Largely because of the population increase in federal prisons, Congress authorized in 1925 a reformatory for "male persons between the ages of seventeen and thirty," which was constructed in Chillicothe, Ohio.[3]

By the 1920s, growth in the number of female prisoners being housed in state facilities warranted the building of special federal facilities for women. In 1927, a new 500-bed female institution opened at **Alderson**, West Virginia. In 1929, when overcrowding reached a critical stage in the New York City area, the state and local authorities ordered all federal prisoners removed from the Tombs and the Raymond Street Jail. Responding to this crisis, a federal detention center was built in a newly constructed three-story garage and called the Federal Detention Headquarters (also known as the West Street Jail).

key term

Alderson

The first federal institution for female offenders.

THE BUREAU OF PRISONS IS BORN

In 1929, Congress created the House Special Committee on Federal Penal and Reformatory Institutions. After extensive deliberations, it offered the following recommendations:

- Establishment of a centralized administration of federal prisons at the bureau level
- Increased expenditure for federal probation officers, to be appointed by federal judges and exempt from civil service regulations
- Establishment of a full-time parole board
- Provision of facilities by the District of Columbia for its prisoners

Photo 12.2
Sanford Bates.
Federal Bureau of Prisons.

- Transfer of all military prisoners held in civil prisons to Fort Leavenworth military barracks
- Removal of the minimum age of prisoners at the U.S. Industrial Reformatory at Chillicothe, Ohio
- Expeditious establishment of the two narcotic treatment farms previously authorized
- Passage of House Resolution 11285 authorizing road camps for federal offenders
- Provision of additional employment opportunities for federal offenders
- Employment of an adequate number of nonfederal jail inspectors and linking payments for those facilities to conditions and programs found in them
- Construction of institutions to include two additional penitentiaries, a hospital for the care of the criminally insane, and a system of federal jails and workhouses in the more congested parts of the country

key term
Federal Bureau of Prisons
The federal correctional system located within the Department of Justice.

Legislation was drafted, passed, and signed into law by President Herbert Hoover on May 14, 1930, creating the **Federal Bureau of Prisons** within the Department of Justice. **Sanford Bates**, an experienced warden, was appointed by President Hoover to be the first director of the Bureau of Prisons (see Chapter 2). The selection of Bates signified that the attitude toward penal administration in the federal government had shifted from political patronage to professional qualifications.

profile
Sanford Bates
The first director of the Federal Bureau of Justice.

Early Growth of the Federal Bureau of Prisons

It was soon obvious that three penitentiaries, a reformatory for young men and one for women, a jail, and eight camps did not meet the growing needs of the federal prison system. Federal prisoners with sentences of a year or less could not be legally confined in the penitentiaries, and many were unsuitable for open camps. The Department of Justice decided to build new structures or remodel existing structures to serve as regional jails.

In the early 1930s, the old New Orleans Mint was modified for use as a jail. A new regional jail was opened in La Tuna, Texas, primarily to house the influx of immigration violators.

Photo 12.3

A view of Alcatraz Island today.
Universal Images Group/DeAgostini/Alamy.

A similar institution was opened in Milan, Michigan (near Detroit). Another penitentiary was added in Lewisburg, Pennsylvania, and a men's reformatory was constructed west of the Mississippi River in El Reno, Oklahoma. A hospital for mentally ill prisoners (and for those with chronic medical ailments) was opened in Springfield, Missouri. The crime wave of the 1930s, combined with the expanding role of the federal government in crime control, brought the old military prison on Alcatraz Island in California under the control of the Department of Justice in 1934.

Recent Developments

Public attitudes toward criminals and the appropriate societal response to them were influenced by many factors during the 1980s. Chief among those were increasing crime rates and the growing problems in administering prisons. Inmate disruptions at Attica and other institutions provided opportunities for the public to reexamine the goals of prisons.[4]

In the early 1970s, the courts began to intervene more often in prison issues. Then-director Norman A. Carlson realized the direction the court system was taking. He saw to it that some significant changes were made in inmate management in the Bureau of Prisons, including (1) enhancements to due process in disciplinary procedures, (2) an administrative remedy process (allowing inmates to express concerns and gain relief from prison administrators before burdening the courts), and (3) an enhanced equal employment opportunity program that increased recruitment of minorities for staff positions.

Director Carlson (who served from 1970 to 1987) believed that the bureau should cooperate with and assist state and local correctional systems. In 1972, the National Institute of Corrections was established within the Bureau of Prisons as an entity to provide assistance and training to state and local correctional and detention facilities. In 1974, the bureau was divided into five regions, with each region being managed by a regional director. Also that year, Carlson formed an executive staff of the agency's assistant directors and regional directors. In the mid-1970s, Bureau of Prisons institutions began to seek accreditation from the American Correctional Association, the country's premier professional organization for corrections.

Carlson's insistence on the importance of staff training resulted in the establishment of several small staff training facilities and later the consolidation of training at the Federal Law Enforcement Training Center in Glynco, Georgia, in 1982. The mainstay of the bureau's

Photo 12.4
A low-security facility torched by rioting inmates.
Patrick Tehan/Newscom.

Staff Training Academy at the Federal Law Enforcement Training Center is a three-week introduction to basic correctional techniques course for all new employees.

A significant development during the 1970s and 1980s was the assignment of responsibility for the planning and management of inmate programs to treatment teams under the concept of unit management. Although the staff makeup of the teams varied among institutions, they usually included a caseworker and a correctional counselor. Unit management gives inmates direct daily contact with the staff members who make most of the decisions about their daily lives. Most of these staff members have offices in inmate living units. This results in improved inmate access to staff and greater staff access to inmates, providing staff with an awareness of significant inmate concerns and potential problems. The unit staff is directly responsible for the program involvement of inmates in the unit. Unit staff receive input from other employees involved in an inmate's progress (such as work supervisors, teachers, and psychologists) and meet with the inmate on a regular basis to develop, review, and discuss the work assignment and programs in which the inmate should be involved as well as any other needs or concerns. These regularly scheduled meetings do not preclude inmates from approaching a member of the unit team or any other appropriate staff member at any time to discuss their particular issues. The Bureau of Prisons considers its staff to be the most important part of inmate management. Constructive interaction and frequent communication between staff and inmates help to ensure accountability, security, and positive inmate behavior. The Bureau of Prisons encourages staff to talk with and be available to inmates and to be receptive to inmate concerns.

The Bureau of Prisons's rehabilitation programs and their increasing sophistication were challenged in the mid-1970s by academicians, researchers, and practitioners who pointed out that little documentation supported the existing traditional rehabilitation programming.[5] The bureau had relied on the medical model, which viewed crime as a "sickness" and inmates as "treatable." In 1976, the bureau formally deemphasized the medical model and adopted a more balanced approach, recognizing that rehabilitation, retribution, incapacitation, and deterrence were legitimate objectives of corrections. Within the balanced model, the bureau continued to provide a variety of work and literacy programs as well as educational, vocational training, counseling, and self-improvement programs.

The 1970s found the Bureau of Prisons with more new facilities than it had at any time since the 1930s. A steady increase in inmate population during the first five years of the decade dictated the acquisition of additional and modernized facilities to reduce overcrowding, create more humane and safe living conditions, and possibly close the first three old penitentiaries at McNeil Island, Washington; Atlanta, Georgia; and Leavenworth, Kansas.[6] Later, the Bureau of Prisons began to contract with private-sector correctional organizations as one strategy to manage inmate over-population.

The Bureau of Prisons experienced as much change in the 1970s as it did at any other time in its history, yet many of its fundamental activities remained unchanged. This apparent contradiction can be explained as the result of contradictory input from Congress, public professional corrections personnel, and others who, on the one hand, wish prisons to be secure and protective of the public and, on the other, wish in some way to reform or change the individual.

ORGANIZATION AND ADMINISTRATION

The Federal Bureau of Prisons provides administration at the central office in Washington, D.C., and from six **regional offices**. The central office consists of the director's office and eight divisions that are responsible for establishing national policy, developing and reviewing programs, providing training and technical assistance to the field, and coordinating agency operations in the various disciplines. The Bureau of Prisons has divided responsibility for overseeing day-to-day operations of federal prisons into six regions. An assistant director heads each division; an Office of General Counsel and an Office of Inspections report to the director. The six regions are headed by regional directors and are located in Atlanta, Dallas, Philadelphia, Kansas City, Dublin (near San Francisco), and Annapolis Junction (in Maryland).

key term

Regional offices
Second-tier management level of the Federal Bureau of Prisons.

The regional offices and the central office provide administrative oversight and support to federal prisons and community corrections offices. Institution wardens are responsible for managing the prisons and report to a regional director. Community corrections offices oversee community-based programs such as halfway houses and home confinement.

Photo 12.5
Bernard Madoff perpetuated one of the largest frauds in history, bilking investors out of billions of dollars. He is now serving a 150-year sentence in a federal prison facility.
Timothy A. Clary/AFP/Newscom.

INMATE POPULATIONS EXPLODE

The inmate population of the Bureau of Prisons numbered more than 216,073 as of February 2014 (approximately 80 percent of these inmates were confined in one of the 115 Bureau of Prisons–operated correctional institutions or detention centers) (see Figure 12.1). This is 137 percent of highest capacity.[7] The rest were confined through agreements with state and local governments and through contracts with privately operated community corrections centers, detention centers, prisons, and juvenile facilities. Inmate prison population increases are due to federal court sentencing of offenders to longer terms of confinement for serious crimes, the return of parole violators, and the effort to combat organized crime, drug trafficking, and illegal immigration (see Table 12.1). As of 2014, the percentage of inmates serving sentences for drug law violations was over 50 percent (see Figure 12.2). The Bureau of Prisons has opened at least 22 new correctional facilities since 2000. Four new medium-security facilities are under construction, and two are in the design phase. More than half of Bureau of Prison prisoners are in either low- or minimum-security institutions (see Figure 12.3).

figure 12.1

Inmate Population Report.

SOURCE: Federal Bureau of Prisons (2014), "Inmate Populations," http://www.bop.gov/about/statistics/population_statistics.jsp (accessed September 12, 2014).

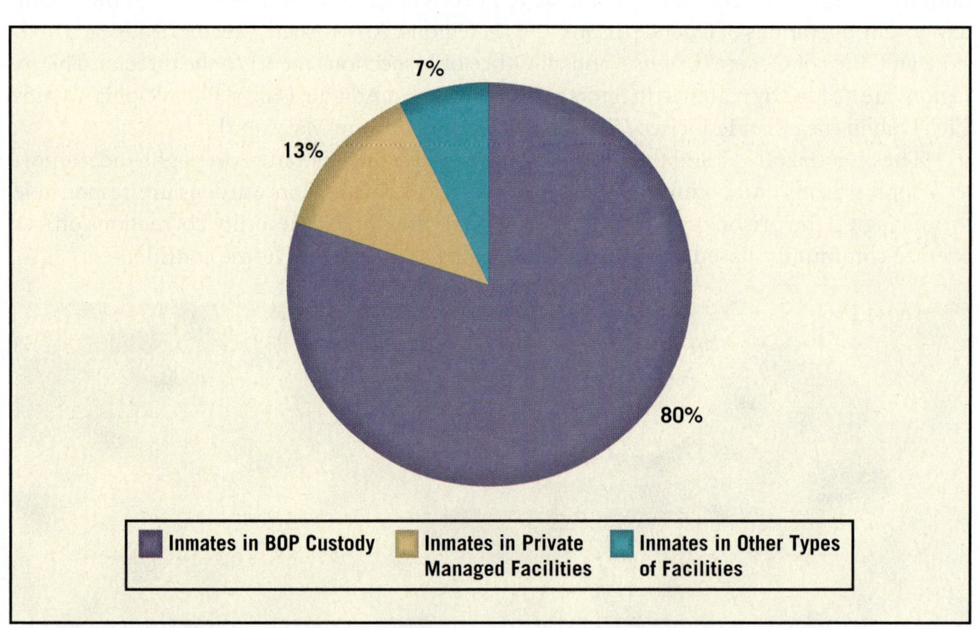

table 12.1 Source of Admissions of Adult Male Inmates

Source	State Institutions	Federal Bureau of Prisons
New Court Committed	282,353	50, 940
Parole Violators	131,468	4,508
Returned Escapes	1,473	0
Transferred in	1,406	1,011
Other	19,120	1
Total	438,258	56,460

SOURCE: American Correctional Association, *2012 Directory of Adult and Juvenile Correctional Departments, Institutions, Agencies, and Probation and Parole Authorities* (Alexandria, VA: American Correctional Association, 2012), pp. 42–43.

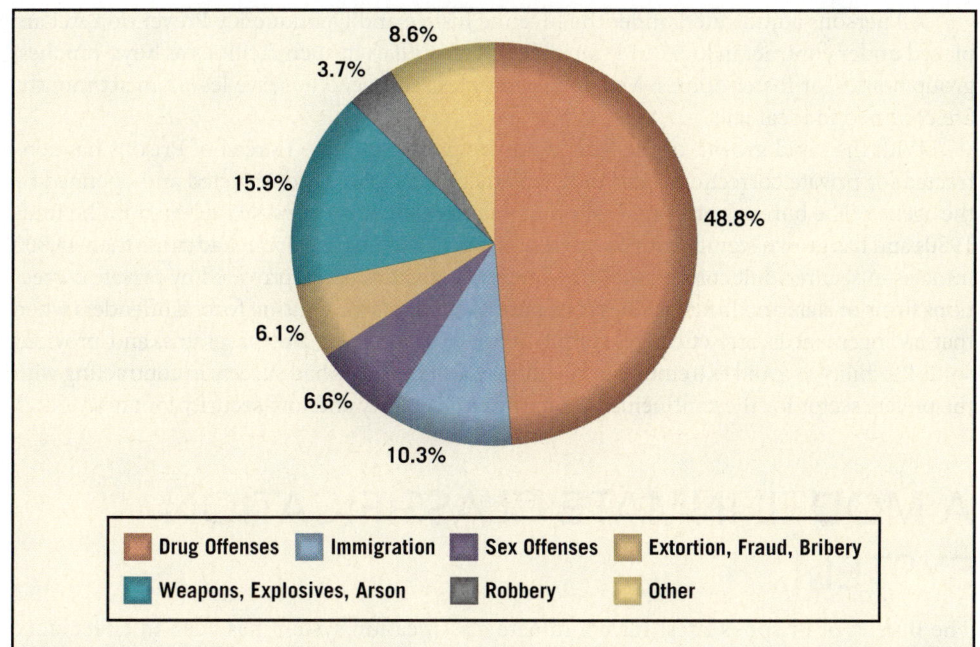

figure 12.2

Types of Offenses Committed by Bureau of Prisons Inmates, 2013.

SOURCE: Federal Bureau of Prisons (2014), Offenses," http://www.bop.gov/about/statistics/statistics_inmate_offenses.jsp (accessed September 12, 2014).

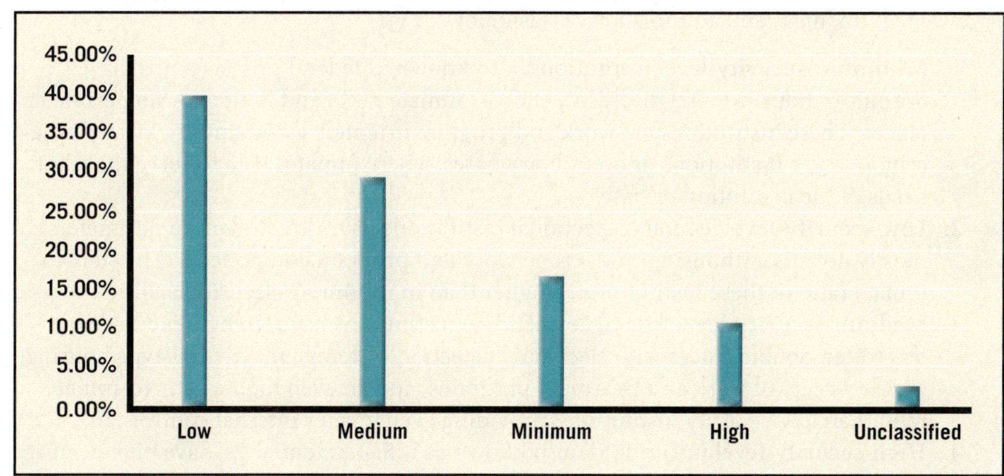

figure 12.3

SOURCE: Federal Bureau of Prisons (2014), "Prison Security Levels," http://www.bop.gov/about/statistics/statistics_inmate_sec_levels.jsp (accessed September 12, 2014).

COMMUNITY-BASED PROGRAMS AND CONTRACT FACILITIES

Prison space is a scarce and costly resource, to be used in situations when the interests of society must be protected. Because of the continuing record-high prison population growth in the federal system, the use of alternatives to incarceration for nonviolent offenders is essential. Almost 15 percent of prisoners are confined in the Bureau of Prisons's contract facilities. Approximately 75 percent of eligible offenders released to the community are regularly released through community treatment centers. Those centers are used for offenders near release as a transition back to home, job, and community. Time is used to find a job, locate a place to live, and reestablish family ties. Some adult inmates sentenced to less than six months are confined in halfway houses or local jails.

All persons adjudicated under the Juvenile Justice and Delinquency Prevention Act are placed under contract in local and state facilities as well as in such facilities as boys' ranches, group homes, or foster homes. Most adult inmates sentenced to serve less than six months are confined in local jails.

With the rapid growth of the federal inmate population, the Bureau of Prisons has contracted for private corrections beds to complement the facilities constructed and operated by the agency. The bureau's utilization of private sources for secure bed space began in the mid-1980s and has grown significantly in the recent past. In 2009, the bureau had more than 43,000 inmates in secure adult correctional and detention facilities being provided by private corrections firms or state and local facilities. The bureau contracts for housing federal offenders when that arrangement is cost effective, complements its operations and programs, and provides some flexibility to avoid extreme overcrowding. The bureau has had success in contracting with the private sector for the confinement of minimum-security and low-security inmates.

A MODEL INMATE CLASSIFICATION SYSTEM

key term

Minimum-security level
A lower level of custody that allows freedom to interact with other prisoners and programs consistent with the offender's imprisonment.

key term

Low-security level
A correctional assignment of prisoners permitting limited mobility and program participation consistent with their incarceration.

key term

Medium-security level
A correctional classification restricting offenders' movements and privileges while incarcerated.

key term

High-security level
A classification designation reducing inmate movement and treatment participation within the correctional facility; may also refer to "supermax," security housing units, or "close supervision."

key term

Administrative-security level
Facilities with special missions that might contain inmates from all custody levels.

The Bureau of Prisons's latest formal inmate classification system has been in effect since April 1979. Variables such as severity of offense, history of escapes or violence, expected length of incarceration, and type of prior commitments are used to determine an inmate's security level. The federal system groups its institutions into five security levels—minimum, low, medium, high, and administrative—as follows:

1. **Minimum-security-level** institutions, also known as federal prison camps, have dormitory housing, a relatively low staff-to-inmate ratio, and limited or no perimeter fences. These institutions are work and program oriented, and many are located adjacent to larger institutions or on military bases, where inmates help to serve the labor needs of the institution or base.
2. **Low-security-level** federal correctional institutions have double-fenced perimeters, mostly dormitory housing, and strong work and program components. The staff-to-inmate ratio in these institutions is higher than in minimum-security facilities.
3. **Medium-security-level** federal correctional institutions have strengthened perimeters (often double fences with electronic detection systems), mostly cell-type housing, a wide variety of work and treatment programs, and an even higher staff-to-inmate ratio than low-security institutions, providing even greater internal controls.
4. **High-security-level** institutions, also known as U.S. penitentiaries, have high-security perimeters (either walled or double fenced), multiple- and single-occupant cell housing, close staff supervision, and close control of inmate movement.
5. **Administrative-security-level** facilities are institutions with special missions, such as the detention of pretrial offenders, the treatment of inmates with serious or chronic medical problems, or the containment of extremely dangerous, violent, or escape-prone inmates. Administrative facilities are capable of holding inmates in all security categories.[8]

The Bureau of Prisons is responsible for carrying out the judgments of federal courts when a period of confinement is ordered. All sentenced offenders who are medically able are required to complete a regular daily work assignment. In addition, all offenders have opportunities to participate in educational, vocational training, work, religious, and counseling programs. In their major institutions, ranging from minimum to high security, more than 36,000 employees were at work in 2014. They were 72 percent male and 28 percent female. Addressing its growth projections, the Bureau of Prisons had more than more than 120 facilities online in February 2014, in hopes of providing for continued growth in the federal prison population. The sentences being served by Bureau of Prisons inmates can be found in Table 12.2.

table 12.2 **Sentences Imposed**

Sentence	Number of Inmates	Percentage of Inmates
Less than 1 year	4,494	2.3
1–3 years	23,157	11.7
3–5 years	27,787	14.0
5–10 years	57,134	28.7
10–15 years	40,754	20.5
15–20 years	18,986	9.6
More than 20 years	20,249	10.2
Life	6,115	3.1
Death	57	0.0

SOURCE: Federal Bureau of Prisons (2014), "Sentences Imposed," 2014, at http://www.bop.gov/about/statistics/statistics_inmate_sentences.jsp (accessed September 12, 2014).

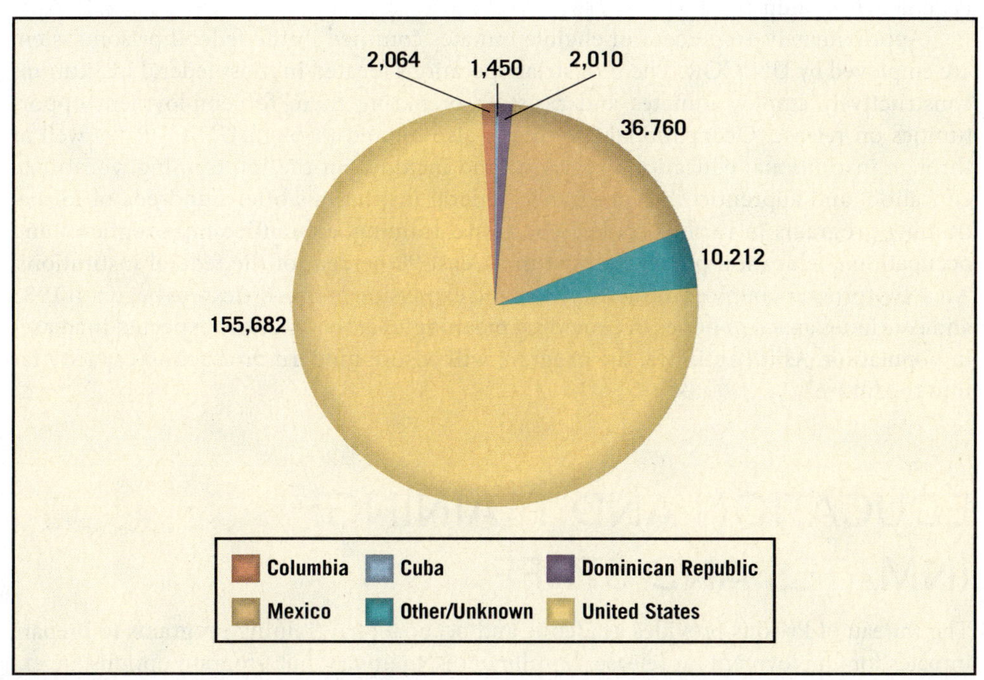

figure 12.4

Citizenship of Inmates by Country.

SOURCE: Federal Bureau of Prisons (2014), "Inmate Citizenship," http://www.bop.gov/about/statistics/statistics_inmate_citizenship.jsp (accessed September 12, 2014).

The classification system, designed to place offenders in the least restrictive institution possible that is closest to their homes, has been effective. Moving as many inmates as possible into such open institutions as prison camps results in higher-security-level institutions becoming more humane through reduced crowding. The citizenship of Bureau of Prisons inmates in 2014 is shown in Figure 12.4.

UNICOR: FEDERAL PRISON INDUSTRIES, INC.

Federal Prison Industries, Inc., with the corporate trade name **UNICOR**, is a wholly owned government corporation that sells its products and services to other federal agencies. UNICOR's mission is to support the Bureau of Prisons through the gainful employment of

key term

UNICOR

A wholly owned federal subsidiary that supports the Federal Bureau of Prisons through the gainful employment of inmates across a variety of work programs.

correctional practice 12.1

UNICOR: The Federal Prison Industries

FPI is, first and foremost, a correctional program. The whole impetus behind Federal Prison Industries is not about business but instead about inmate release preparation helping offenders acquire the skills necessary to successfully make that transition from prison to law-abiding, contributing members of society. The production of items and provision of services are merely by-products of those efforts.

Rigorous research demonstrates that participation in prison industries and vocational training programs has a positive effect on post-release employment and recidivism for up to 12 years following release. Inmates who worked in prison industries or completed vocational apprenticeship programs were 24 percent less likely to recidivate than nonprogram participants and 14 percent more likely to be gainfully employed. These programs had an even greater positive impact on minority offenders, who are at the greatest risk of recidivism.

SOURCE: UNICOR, http://www.unicor.gov/about/about_fpi_programs/ (accessed January 13, 2014).
Note: UNICOR is a federally owned subsidiary of the Federal Bureau of Prisons, and these two paragraphs were taken from the online source referenced above.

inmates in diversified work programs. Correctional Practice 12.1 provides an overview of Federal Prison Industries.

Approximately 16 percent of eligible inmates confined in the federal prison system are employed by UNICOR. The industrial operations located in most federal institutions constructively employ inmates and assist in preparing them for employment opportunities on release. Occupational training is also offered through UNICOR (as well as through institutional education programs) and includes on-the-job training, vocational education, and apprenticeship programs. Federal institutions offer hundreds of formal training programs in various trades. Vocational training, apprenticeship programs, and occupational education programs exist in at least 90 percent of the federal institutions. An active program of plant modernization and expansion of industries was begun in 1983 and continues apace in hopes of providing meaningful activity for the expected increases in population. As it continues, the program will ensure modern production capacity far into the future.

EDUCATION AND TRAINING: INMATES AND STAFF

The Bureau of Prisons provides academic and occupational training programs to prepare inmates for employment on release. Enrollment is voluntary, but program options are extensive, ranging from adult basic education (ABE) through college courses. Occupational training programs include accredited vocational training, apprenticeship programs, and preindustrial training.

A mandatory literacy program was implemented for inmates in 1983. It originally required all federal inmates to function at least at a sixth-grade educational level. Those who could not were required to enroll in the ABE program for a minimum of 90 days. In 1986, the standard was raised to an eighth-grade literacy level, the nationally accepted functional literacy level. In 1991, the Crime Control Act of 1990 (Public Law 101-647) directed the Bureau of Prisons to have a mandatory functional literacy program in place for all mentally capable inmates. The bureau voluntarily raised the standard to twelfth grade and required participation for a minimum of 240 hours or until participants obtain the general equivalency diploma (GED). All promotions in federal prison industries and in institution work assignments were made contingent on the inmate's achieving literacy. The Violent Crime Control and Law Enforcement Act of 1994 and the Prison Litigation Reform Act of 1995 link good-time credits to participation in the GED program.

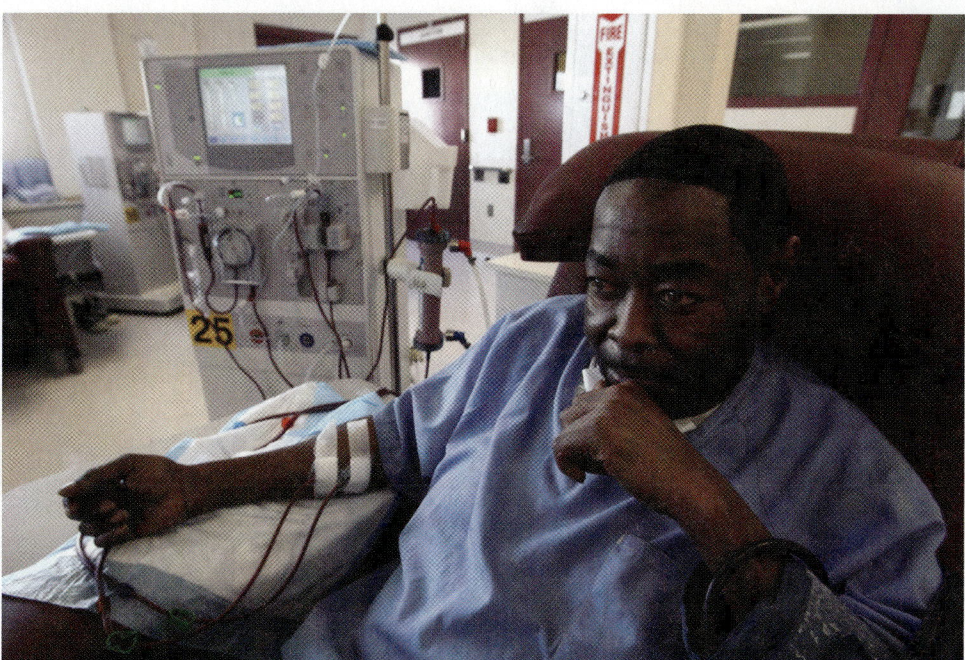

Photo 12.6
Prison inmate undergoing dialysis
Rich Pedroncelli/AP Images.

The ABE program has been quite successful. Certificates for completion of the GED program have been awarded to tens of thousands of inmates (at least 6,000 a year). English as a second language is also provided for all who need it. Other vocational training programs provide job training in such fields as computer sciences, business, diesel mechanics, construction and building trades, drafting and blueprints, and culinary arts.

Staff training provides every Bureau of Prisons employee with the knowledge, skills, and abilities required to ensure high standards of employee performance and conduct. The staff-training network consists of the Staff Training Academy at the Federal Law Enforcement Training Center in Glynco, Georgia, and the Management and Specialty Training Center in Denver, Colorado. Administrators in the Human Resource Management Division in Washington, D.C., oversee the program. All new employees are required to undergo three weeks of formal training during their first 60 days with the Bureau of Prisons as well as an institution familiarization program at their work site. The BOP employee staff data on gender and ethnicity can be found in Figures 12.5 and 12.6, respectively.

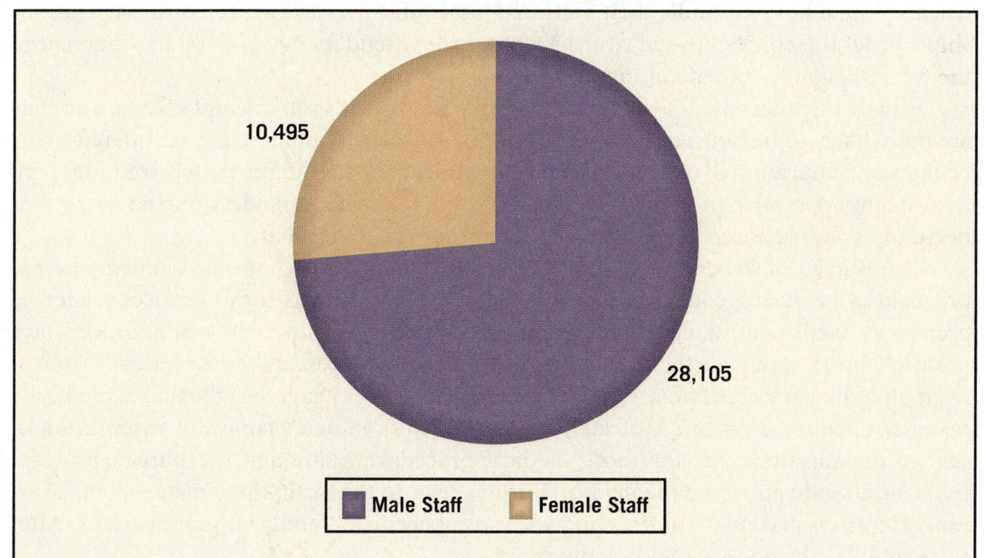

figure 12.5
Federal Bureau of Prisons Staff by Gender.

SOURCE: Federal Bureau of Prisons (2014), "Staff by Gender," http://www.bop.gov/about/statistics/statistics_staff_gender.jsp (accessed September 12 2014).

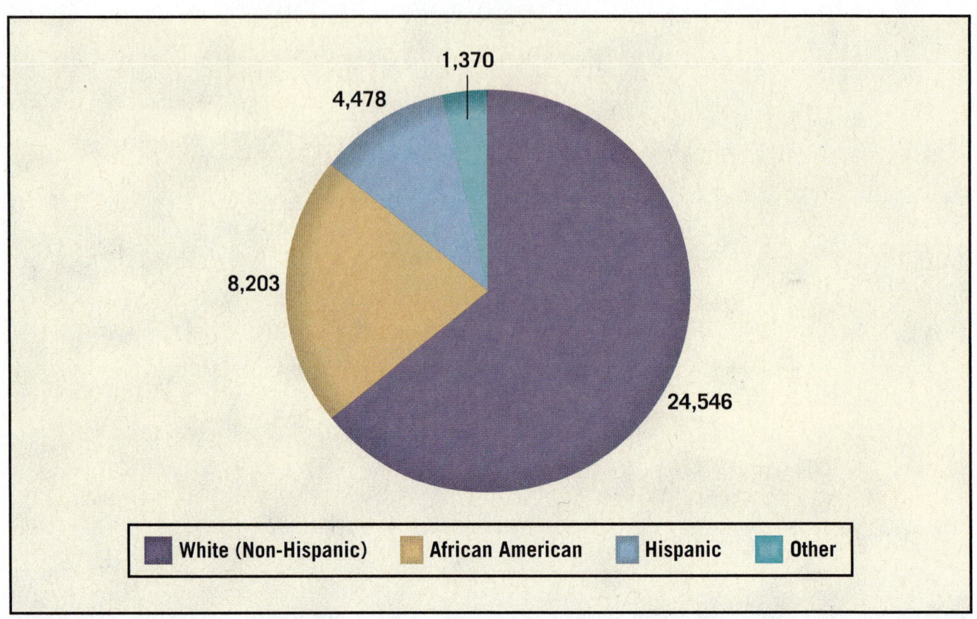

figure 12.6
Federal Bureau of Prisons Staff by Ethnicity.

SOURCE: Federal Bureau of Prisons (2014), "Staff by Race/Ethnicity," http://www.bop.gov/about/statistics/statistics_staff_ethnicity_race.jsp (accessed January 8, 2014).

FEDERAL FEMALE OFFENDERS

The Bureau of Prisons continues to focus on improving programs and services for female offenders. It operates a number of all-female facilities and at least 21 co-gender facilities. These facilities include stand-alone secure institutions and many prison camps adjacent to secure institutions.

The number of female offenders in the Bureau of Prisons's inmate population continues to increase. Recognizing that female offenders have different social, psychological, educational, family, and health-care needs, the bureau continues to design and implement special programs for female offenders. Programs include teaching women how to reduce stress; how to prevent, identify, obtain, and manage treatment for medical problems; and how to improve their personal relationships, be a better parent, and grieve over lost relationships. Several facilities also operate intensive treatment programs that focus on helping women who have histories of chronic sexual, emotional, or physical abuse by teaching them how to handle their victimization and learn ways to seek positive relationships. Federal facilities housed over 13,800 female offenders in 2014, about 7 percent of the total population of federal inmates.[9]

Female offenders are less likely than men to be violent or to attempt escape, and they are more likely to be housed in low- and minimum-security units. They are offered many of the same educational and recreational programs as male offenders. Job training, with subsequent apprentice programs, is intended to help female offenders pursue career opportunities after release.

The Bureau of Prisons offers a community residential program for women who are pregnant at or during confinement. This includes medical and social services related to pregnancy, birth control, child placement, and abortion. Child birth and abortions take place in a hospital outside the facility. Because current law prevents the federal government from providing any abortion assistance, the inmate (except when the abortion is medically necessary due to threat to life of the pregnant inmate), inmate's family, or external social service organizations pay for those medical procedures, although the bureau provides transportation to and from the medical facility. Prior to the birth, the inmate will make arrangements for placement of the child with social agencies, family, or grandparents. After three months, the bonded child is out-placed.

Photo 12.7

ADX Supermax Prison in Colorado.

Lizzie Himmel/Sygma/Corbis.

Pregnant inmates and other female inmates participate in programs, both pre- and postnatal classes, on a variety of topics that include childbirth, parenting, and coping skills. Other programs address chemical dependency, physical and sexual abuse counseling, treatment, budgeting classes, and educational and vocational programs.[10]

COMMUNITY CORRECTIONS IN THE FEDERAL SYSTEM

Community corrections is an integral component of the Bureau of Prisons's correctional programs. The bureau contracts with community corrections centers (also known as halfway houses) to provide assistance to inmates who are nearing release from prison. Community corrections centers provide a structured, supervised environment and support in job placement, counseling, and other services. Community corrections centers allow prerelease inmates to gradually rebuild their ties to the community, and they allow correctional staff to supervise offenders' activities during this readjustment phase. An important component of the community corrections center program is transitional drug abuse treatment for inmates who have completed residential substance abuse treatment while confined in a Bureau of Prisons institution.[11]

Some federal inmates are placed on home confinement for a brief period at the end of their prison terms. They serve this portion of their sentences at home under strict schedules and curfew requirements. Some community corrections centers enhance the accountability of inmates on home confinement through electronic monitoring.

Approximately 45 percent of federal offenders in community-based programs are housed in comprehensive sanctions centers. Comprehensive sanctions centers are similar to community corrections centers, but they have a more structured system for granting offenders gradual access to the community. They also require inmates to participate in more programs, and they formally involve the U.S. Probation Office in the release-planning process.

Through the community corrections program, the Bureau of Prisons has developed agreements with state and local governments and contracts with privately operated facilities for the confinement of juvenile offenders and for the detention or secure confinement of some federal inmates.

The Bureau of Prisons's community corrections program is administered by the staff in its central office, community corrections regional administrators, regional management teams in each of the bureau's six regional offices, and the employees of over 30 community corrections management field offices throughout the United States.

CHANGING POPULATION OF FEDERAL INSTITUTIONS

A former governor of Georgia, Lester Maddox, is credited with saying, when asked how to improve that state's correctional system, "What we need here is a better class of prisoner." The Bureau of Prisons was looked on for years as dealing with just the "cream of criminals." Whether true or apocryphal, times have changed, and the federal system has to deal with some real problem inmates today. The bureau is now experiencing some of the challenges associated with crowding and management of inmates with significant histories of violence and gang-related activities. In 1984, Congress passed a law that abolished federal parole, limited good-time credits, established a number of determinate sentences, and created the U.S. Sentencing Commission as an independent body, located in the judicial branch of the government. The commission began its work in 1985 and submitted new guidelines that have dramatically altered sentencing practices in the federal criminal justice system. Federal prison populations grew markedly by 2009, more as a result of the Anti-Drug Abuse Act of 1986 and the career offender provision of the Comprehensive Crime Control Act of 1984 than as a result of the guidelines. A summary of their impacts follows:[12]

1. "Straight" probationary sentences (i.e., sentences that require no form of confinement) were reduced significantly.
2. For especially serious crimes, such as drug offenses and crimes against persons, probationary sentences were no longer available.
3. For other crimes, such as property offenses, the proportion of sentences involving some form of probation did not change appreciably, although probation with a condition of confinement may have been substituted for straight probation.
4. Average time served for violent offenses increased substantially. For most property crimes, average time served remained largely unchanged. Exceptions include burglary and income tax fraud, for which average time served went up.

The changes have had a major impact on the correctional administrators in the Bureau of Prisons in the form of a massive increase in the numbers and types of inmates confined in federal institutions, which are already quite overcrowded.

Military Offenders

In addition to the federal offenders housed and handled by the Federal Bureau of Prisons, there is a large group of other offenders housed and managed by the U.S. military. They are known collectively as military offenders and are drawn from the five branches of the military: U.S. Air Force, Army, Marine Corps, Navy, and Coast Guard.

The number of prisoners under military jurisdiction, by branch of services, can be found in Table 12.3. These male offenders are housed in the U.S. Military Barracks at Fort Leavenworth, Kansas (see Correctional Practice 12.2). Female military offenders are housed at the Naval Consolidated Brig in San Diego, California.

Most civilians believe that the typical military prisoner is confined for offenses unique to the military, such as desertion, disrespect, espionage, malingering, adultery, disobedience, alcohol abuse, or absence without leave. Yet such offenses in total represent only one of seven of the offenses committed by military prisoners. Some 60 percent of military offenders committed crimes against the person or violent crimes, such as murder, rape, and sexual

table **12.3** **Prisoners under Military Jurisdiction by Branch of Service**

Branch of Service	2011
Total	1,527
Prisoners who served in . . .	
Air Force	285
Army	702
Marine Corps	299
Navy	235
Coast Guard	6

SOURCE: Erika Parks and Lauren E. Glaze, *Bureau of Justice Statistics Bulletin NC. 239972* (Washington, DC: Bureau of Justice Statistics, November 2012), p. 9.

assault. About one in eight committed drug offenses, and larceny was the most common property crime for which offenders were convicted.

In addition, major differences between civilian and military prisoners appear to be age, education, employment, jobs, training, and dangerousness. Most military prisoners are highly educated, young, and in good health and physical condition. They had a job at the time of arrest. They have skills and a work ethic (unlike many civilian prisoners); few need to learn a work ethic.

key term

Fort Leavenworth
Military post that contains a maximum-security prison facility for military services.

correctional **practice 12.2**

U.S. Military Barracks at Fort Leavenworth, Kansas

Fort Leavenworth is a U.S. Army installation and the oldest active U.S. Army post west of the nation's capital. Fort Leavenworth includes the Military Correctional Complex, which is composed of the Disciplinary Barracks (maximum security) and the Midwest Joint Regional Correctional Facility (low security). The Disciplinary Barracks is the only maximum-security prison for male military personnel serving a sentence of at least 10 years, regardless of type of military service. It is an institution (nicknamed "The Castle") with 515 beds but currently holding about 440 inmates, six of whom are on death row and 10 of whom are serving life without parole. It is to this institution that Chelsea (Bradley) Manning was sent to serve 35 years for leaking classified documents to the public. Such an assignment poses operational quagmires for the military as well as for Chelsea Manning, who is a transgendered inmate who wishes to be treated as a female and has adopted the name of Chelsea. Fort Leavenworth is treating Chelsea as a man. Lesbian, gay, bisexual, and transgender persons are 13 times more likely to be sexually abused in prison than are other inmates.

Custody grades, depending on the degree of supervision needed to avoid attacks on others, are installational trustee, minimum, minimum inside only, medium, and maximum. There is a "special housing unit" that houses inmates for up to 23 hours a day. When those inmates leave their cells, they are shackled and controlled by at least two correctional officers known as correctional specialists. A correctional goal is inmate change with increasing earned lower security levels.

Inmates spend an average of 19 years in the "big house." Thirteen rehabilitation programs exist, including routine educational programming and vocational training. Apprenticeship programs include carpentry, graphic design, welding, dental assistance, and screen printing. There is also a barbering license program. Pay is low in work programs, about 14 to 80 cents an hour, and inmates are restricted as to the amount of canteen purchasing allowed per month.

With rare exceptions, inmates are not career criminals. More than half the inmates are imprisoned for sexual offenses. The most recent execution was in 1961. The focus during incarceration is on safety and preparing the offender for community reentry. Compared to civilian imprisonment facilities, the Disciplinary Barracks probably falls into the category of the safest places for criminals to serve their sentence.

SOURCE: Army News Service, "Doing Time at Leavenworth," http://usmilitary.about.com/od/justicelawlegislation/a/leavenworth.htm (accessed January 14, 2014); Amanda Hess, "Chelsea Manning Is Now the Most Famous Transgender Inmate in America. Will She Be Treated Humanely?," http://www.slate.com/blogs/xx_factor/2013/08/22/chelsea_manning_is_now_the_most_famous_transgender_inmate_in_america_all.html.

They have the potential for dangerousness, even more so than institutional threat groups ("prison gangs"). They have good physical training. Most have been trained to defend themselves and to kill, whether with a weapon or bare-handed. Many have learned commando tactics, use of explosives, firearm competencies, escape strategies, and physical opposition to the enemy (prison staff). As such, custody issues abound and are countered by institutional intelligence, special management cells, and specific strategies. Managing officers have created secure facilities that emphasize rehabilitative and reentry skills that will be of immediate use by prisoners seeking to become productive and lawful citizens or military returns following release.[13]

Summary

Outline the Development of the Federal Prison System

The federal government system of corrections has expanded rapidly over the past century. The Bureau of Prisons (BOP) was created by an act of Congress in 1930. Prior to that act, violators of federal statutes were held in local jails or state prisons by agreement with those jurisdictions. Such an arrangement became infeasible with the creation of federal statutes for previously state crimes, such as interstate transportation of prostitutes, drug tax laws, vehicle theft, and related crimes. This previous arrangement was further exacerbated by state-level crime waves; those jurisdictions could no longer house federal offenders due to space limitations. At the height of this stress, Sanford Bates was appointed head of the almost nonexistent federal correctional system.

The system grew rapidly; prison facilities were built, and others were repurposed. Probation and parole services increased the scope of the federal system. Probation and parole systems produced supervision failures, leading to return of the "twice condemned" to incarcerative settings. Sanford Bates created and built federal institutions, providing Bureau of Prison guidance, leadership, and encouragement to others; the bureau became the leading correctional system. The bureau centralized and developed its structure, organizing itself into meaningful divisions and developing a suitable classification system.

The War on Drugs sharply increased the number of inmates, contributing to a growth curve that is still increasing. The Bureau of Prisons began its "bricks-and-mortar" effort to construct more prison cells and facilities, but changes in sentencing practices and lengths, imposition of a truth-in-sentencing policy requiring federal inmates to serve 85 percent of the initial sentence imposed, and reduction in the power of the federal parole board to control prison population growth have contributed to the steep increase.

In recent years, the Bureau of Prisons has relied on private-sector corrections to manage its least dangerous inmates as well as expanding the limits of confinement to include placement in the community. The retrenchment movement challenging the lengths of sentences and mandatory minimum sentences has slowed but not stopped prison inmate growth. We will need to examine the impacts of such strategies in reducing inmate overpopulation. This would be a welcomed development for the Bureau of Prisons.

Explain the Development of Federal Prison Facilities

Violators of federal criminal statutes were originally committed to prisons in the state in which their crimes occurred, and the federal government paid each state for housing its offenders. Later, the number of federal crimes was greatly expanded, resulting in heavy use of state prison facilities. States experienced crime increases that overpopulated their prisons and declined to house federal inmates, resulting in a thrust to build federal prison facilities. Military prisons were available, but the influx of civilian law violators demanded construction of penitentiaries. Additional numbers and security levels of prison facilities have led to a variety of prison facilities.

Describe and Illustrate the Use of Contract Facilities by the Federal Prison System

About one in six federal inmates is housed in contract facilities. The federal system directs felons nearing their release dates to serve about the last six months in pre-parole community control. Other inmates are housed in private-sector prison facilities contracting to provide a range of security levels and management of inmates.

Identify and Contrast the Federal Prison Security Levels

Once an inmate is classified, that offender will be assigned to an appropriate facility: minimum security, low security, medium security, high security, or administrative security.

The higher the security level, the more risky the inmates in that facility.

Explain the Operations of UNICOR

UNICOR is the industrial system for the federal prison system, and inmates produce a wide range of goods for use by other federal prisons and other federal groups. It trains inmates, provides hands-on experience, and generates profits for the federal prison system.

Compare and Contrast the Education and Training of Federal Inmates and Staff

Inmates are compelled to master basic English skills, to earn the GED degree, and to work within the prison system in either institutional upkeep or UNICOR. Participation in a mandatory literacy skill course is required. Staff training provides every Bureau of Prisons employee with the knowledge, skills, and abilities required to ensure high standards of employee performance and conduct.

Summarize the Characteristics of Female Federal Offenders

Female offenders have different social, psychological, educational, family, and health care needs. Inmates are housed in the federal prison institutions; the Bureau of Prisons continues to design and implement special programs for female offenders. Programs include teaching women how to reduce stress; how to prevent, identify, obtain, and manage treatment for medical problems; and how to improve their personal relationships, be a better parent, and grieve over lost relationships. Female inmates are less violent than are males and are less likely to attempt escape; they are typically housed in low- and minimum-security facilities.

Summarize the Organization of the Federal Prison System

The Federal Bureau of Prisons provides administration at the central office in Washington, D.C., and from six regional offices. The central office is responsible for establishing national policy, developing and reviewing programs, providing training and technical assistance to the field, and coordinating agency operations in the various disciplines.

An assistant director heads each regional division; an Office of General Counsel and an Office of Inspections report to the director. The regional offices and the central office provide administrative oversight and support to federal prisons and community corrections offices.

In addition to the Federal Bureau of Prisons, the nation's military has a prison system incarcerating military offenders. Such offenders have committed serious crimes and serve long sentences. They are closely controlled in a system emphasizing rehabilitation and reintegration. More recent longitudinal evaluations of the military prisons' success could improve the public's view of the adequacy of the current system.

Key Words

Review Questions

1. Explain the various kinds of institutions in the federal prison system.
2. What forces led to the shift in philosophy of the Federal Bureau of Prisons in the 1970s?
3. Outline the institutional security classification system.
4. Why does the Bureau of Prisons have such an advantage over state systems in generating programs?
5. Why has the prison population of the Bureau of Prisons increased during the past few years?
6. Characterize inmates in the Bureau of Prisons institutions.

Application Case Studies

1. Imagine you are a pregnant inmate in the Federal Bureau of Prisons. Your happy child warms your heart, and you feel comforted that your family is expanding. At the end of 90 days, your baby will be taken from you. What can you do to reduce the pain of this separation?
2. You are the prison facility warden, and, for probably the first time, you become convinced that there has been a miscarriage of justice in the conviction and commitment of an inmate under your care and control. You have no doubt: If there ever were an innocent person in prison, this would be the one. What, if anything, *could* you do? And what *would* you do?
3. An institutional snitch informs your intelligence team that one of the correctional officers has been targeted for death by a prison gang. She is a competent and well-liked correctional officer who caught a gang member on the range with an institutionally made knife ("shiv"), resulting in that inmate being placed into the special housing unit for 90 days. His gang brothers threaten the life of that officer. What would you do? And what would you do if the prison gang assassin kills her?

Endnotes

1. This chapter has drawn heavily from Bureau of Prisons annual reports and various other bureau publications. The authors appreciate the cooperation and assistance and especially the provision of historical and other photographs. For critical views, see Jim Coyne, *The Repugnant Warehouse: An Exposé of the Federal Prison System* (Clifton Park, NY: Elysium Publishing, 1995); D. Burton-Rose, D. Pens, P. Wright, et al., *The Celling of America: An Inside Look at the U.S. Prison Industry* (Monroe, ME: Common Courage Press, 1998); Michael Santos, *Life behind Bars in America* (New York: St. Martin's Press, 2006); and American Correctional Association, *2012 Directory* (Alexandria, VA: American Correctional Association, 2012), p. 171. See also James Ridgeway and Jean Casella, "Under Fire, the Federal Bureau of Prisons Audits Its Use of Solitary Confinement—and Buys a New Supermax Prison," http://solitarywatch.com/2013/10/18/fire-federal-bureau-prisons-audits-use-solitary-confinement-buys-new-supermax-prison/ (accessed January 14, 2014); Government Accounting Office, "Improvements Needed in Bureau's Monitoring and Evaluation of Impact of Segregated Housing," GAO-13-429, May 1, 2013; and CIR.CA News, "Compassionate Release Program for Federal Prisoners Criticized," http://cir.ca/news/compassionate-prison-release-report (accessed January 14, 2013).
2. The facility is now part of the prison system of Washington State.
3. This facility is currently an Ohio correctional institution. See American Correctional Association, *2012 Directory*, p. 587.
4. Between November 21 and 23, 1987, 89 federal prison staff were seized as hostages at the Atlanta Penitentiary and at the Alien Detention Center at Oakdale, Louisiana. The uprisings have been described as the most disruptive episodes in the history of the Bureau of Prisons. Hostages were eventually released after the attorney general agreed to review each case of the Marielitos, Cubans who arrived in the nation during the Mariel boatlift. See "After Atlanta and Oakdale," *Corrections Today* 50 (1988): 26, 64–65; Bert Useem, C. Camp, and G. Camp, *Resolution of Prison Riots* (South Salem, NY: Criminal Justice Institute, 1993); and Mike Rolland, *Descent into Madness* (Cincinnati, OH: Anderson Publishing, 1997). Coverage of smaller but more lethal riots in federal prisons has been increasing, particularly since 2008. See *The Colorado Independent*, "Bureau of Prisons," http://www.coloradoindependent.com/tag/bureau-of-prisons (accessed November 11, 2008).
5. See Harry Allen and Nick Gatz, "Abandoning the Medical Model in Corrections: Some Implications and Alternatives," *Prison Journal* 54 (Autumn 1974): 4–14, and Simon Dinitz, "Nothing Fails Like a Little Success," in Edward Sagarin, ed., *Criminology: New Concerns* (Beverly Hills, CA: Sage, 1979), pp. 105–118. But see also C. T. Lowenkamp and E. L. Latessa, "Developing

Successful Reentry Programs," *Corrections Today* 76:2 (2005), 72–77, and Pamela Lattimore, "The Challenges of Reentry," *Corrections Today* 69:2 (2007): 88–91.

6. Only McNeil Island has been closed and has since been sold to Washington State to help solve some of that state's prison overcrowding. The institutions at Atlanta and Leavenworth still serve the overcrowded system.
7. William Sabol, Heather Couture, and Paige Harrison, *Prisoners in 2006* (Washington, DC: Bureau of Justice Statistics, 2007), p. 20; the Federal Bureau of Prisons, *State of the Bureau 2007* (Washington, DC: Federal Bureau of Prisons, 2008).
8. Federal Bureau of Prisons, "Quick Facts," http://www.bop.gov/about/facts.jsp (accessed April 26, 2005).
9. Federal Bureau of Prisons, *State of the Bureau 2009* (Washington, DC: Federal Bureau of Prisons, 2009), p. 57.
10. Federal Bureau of Prisons, "Female Offenders," http://www.bop.gov/inmates/custody_and_care/female_offenders.jsp (accessed January 14, 2014).
11. Federal Bureau of the Prisons, "Release Preparation," http://www.bop.gov/inmate_programs/release_emp.jsp.
12. National Institute of Justice, "The Impact of Federal Sentencing Guidelines," in *NIJ Reports: Research in* Action (Washington, DC: National Institute of Justice, 1987), p. 52. But see also The Sentencing Project, "Congress Needs to Change Federal Nonviolent Drug Sentencing Policy," http://www.sentencingproject.org/detail/news.cfm?news_id=1741&id=167 (accessed January 14, 2014).
13. Ibid.

Zumaphotos/Newscom.

Objectives

- Describe the history of private-sector involvement in corrections.
- Identify the advantages that private-sector providers claim in meeting the needs of public state prisons.
- Describe how prison inmates were considered "slaves of the state."
- List five examples of how private-sector companies could benefit juvenile offenders.
- Identify five controversies surrounding private-sector prison providers.
- Compare and contrast gatekeepers and rainmakers.
- Summarize other prison systems and the privatization of prisons.

chapter 13

Private-Sector Systems

Outline

"Private-sector correctional facilities report that they can do the same things that public-sector facilities can, and cheaper. In the end, the public shoulders the costs of both private and public prisons. Both cost the taxpayer money."

—Harry E. Allen

Overview

The chapter-opening quote about **private-sector correctional facilities**, written in 2014, foretells the continuing overcrowding problem that has been as a constant issue throughout the correctional system in recent years. State, city, and federal correctional administrators wrestled with this issue when the population of their combined institutions was approximately one-third of what it is now. This chapter deals with what has become another major factor in trying to keep up with the wave of populations under the supervision of criminal justice agencies: privatization of correctional services and facilities.

As will be shown, privatization of institutions is not a new idea. The major challenge for privatization is to provide for the incarceration of convicted felons in long-term, secure facilities by a private, for-profit company. The state of Tennessee was the first to consider the privatization of its entire adult prison system. One of the first and largest of the providers of privately operated adult correctional facilities made an offer to take over the complete management and operations of the beleaguered Tennessee system. For a number of reasons, that proposal was not accepted, and Tennessee decided instead to pour millions into upgrading its current system. This chapter discusses the pros and cons of privatization and its vast growth in the past two decades. See Figure 13.1 for more detail. We have seen this issue grow from a single paragraph to an entire chapter in the past few editions of this text. It seems fitting that this chapter is the sixth in your overview of institutional corrections because it relates to almost every other topic in the text. Bear in mind that private-sector *prisons* remain the fourth-largest correctional system in the nation.

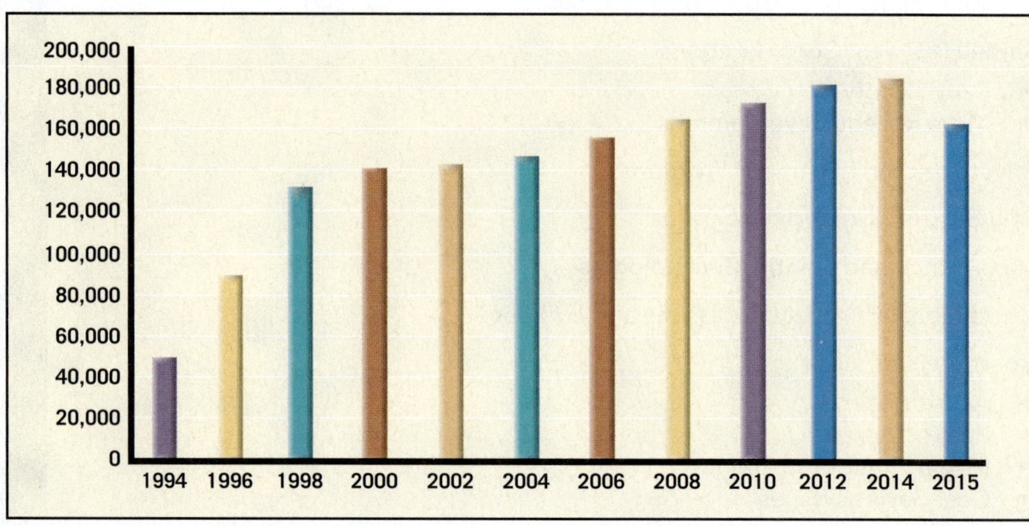

figure 13.1

Growth of Private-Sector Capacity (Beds).

SOURCE: Cody Mason (2012), "The Prison Project, Dollars and Detainees: The Growth of For-Profit Detention," http://sentencingproject.org/doc/publications/inc_prisonprivatization.pdf.

THE PRIVATE SECTOR IN COMMUNITY CORRECTIONS

key term

Private-sector correctional facility

Any *private* prison, for-profit prison, detention center, jail, or juvenile institution is a facility in which juveniles or adults are physically restricted, housed, or interned by a nongovernmental organization that is contracted by a public-sector government agency.

The idea of involving the private sector in providing management and operation of correctional facilities may come as a surprise to many students, but the concept of having government services provided by contracting with the private sector was actually the primary method of obtaining those services for the first hundred or so years of the existence of the United States. Transportation, fire protection, police, and even armies were often provided on contract. It was only in America's second century that services began to be provided through governmental bureaucratic agencies. In recent years, however, the cost of government-provided services has risen so high that many services are now moving "back to the future" to obtain correctional services being provided through the private sector.

The correctional field has experienced a number of privatization precedents: Health care, food service, education, mental health, transportation, and training have been provided by private contractors to many systems. From the time of John Augustus, most juvenile and adult halfway houses and other services have been provided by private for-profit, private nonprofit, or charitable organizations. As the need for more community corrections has grown, primarily due to overcrowded jails and prisons, many entrepreneurs in the private and private nonprofit sectors have become involved in the "boom" industry of community-oriented corrections. Almost 17 percent of confined adults are in privately owned or operated facilities.[1] Many of those entrepreneurs are now expanding across state borders and operating prisons, jails, and community services almost like a franchise. Only 19 states do not contract with private-sector prisons to house adult prisoners. Such agencies tend to ease their correctional problems by providing (1) alternatives to incarceration in the community, (2) meaningful programs inside the prisons to help prepare inmates for a better life when they are released, and (3) a bridge from incarceration to the free society that will assist in that difficult transition.

The main advantage of private service providers is their ability to expand and contract quickly when needs change. When a government invests in the operation of a community-based program or the building of a major correctional facility, it is often obliged to continue

Photo 13.1

Entry portal for a private sector facility.
Scott R. Galvin/AP Images.

to staff and operate the program or facility even if it is not cost effective to do so.[2] The entrepreneurs of community corrections can choose to modify an existing facility instead of building from the ground up, provide staff on a contract basis, utilize existing community resources for professional services, and close the facility when it is no longer needed and use it for another purpose. The private-sector community corrections programs and agencies of the federal courts and prisons house adult inmates in some 391 contracted community correctional centers as well as 1,141 facilities for juveniles. The number of privatized adult prisons and juvenile corrections facilities, by classification, is given in Table 13.1. Most states also contract for at least some of their community corrections, so this sector of business has continued to burgeon.

One of the major issues for the contractor concerns liability for potential public safety issues. Most government agencies are **self-insured**. This insurance protects them with the resources of the entire government entity—federal, state, county, or municipality. The private-sector operator, however, must have some type of liability insurance to cover the same problems. With the incredible growth of litigation in the United States, government agencies have become targets for opportunistic attorneys looking for new markets.[3] This feeding frenzy of litigation has caused insurance rates to skyrocket and has impacted operations in the private sector. The small operators have been put in a squeeze, and the large ones could be hurt as well.

key term

Self-insured
Government unit whose operations are not covered by external insurers.

table **13.1** Number of Privatized Adult Prisons and Juvenile Correction Facilities

Classification	Number of Adult Facilities	Number of Juvenile Facilities
Males	80	106
Females	10	27
Co-gender	11	84
Not classified	21	35
Total	122	252

SOURCE: American Correctional Association, *2012 Directory of Adult and Juvenile Correctional Departments, Institutions, Agencies, and Probation and Parole Authorities* (Alexandria, VA: American Correctional Association, 2012), pp. 26–27.

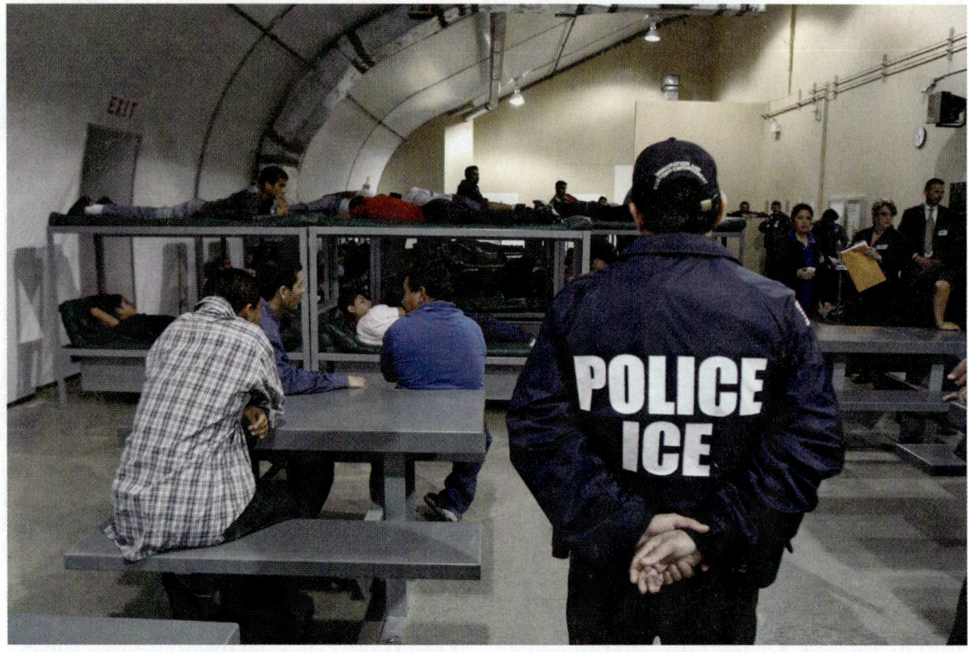

Photo 13.2

The privately run T. Don Hutto Residential Center is one of only two federal Immigration and Customs Enforcement detention centers for families with children in the United States. This prison, run by the Corrections Corporation of America, has come under fire for the alleged lack of education for children in the facility.

Jose Cabezas/Stringer/AFP/Getty Images.

In sum, the private sector is extensively involved in such correctional services as providing food, medical care, and training to facilities and agencies; filling gaps in services governmental agencies cannot or will not address (halfway houses, secure juvenile residential programs); and managing such correctional systems as high-security jails and prisons. Only the latter is the center of heated controversy, not only in light of liability issues but also concerning program inadequacies and potential use-of-force situations for which employees might not be adequately trained and competent. Other controversies are addressed near the end of this chapter.

SOME HISTORICAL CONSIDERATIONS

Early History

From a historical perspective, private involvement in corrections during the period from 1870 to 1930 was neither notable nor distinguished. Before this era, some states would lease out their entire prison populations to private bidders who would contract to provide food, custody, and clothing to inmates for a flat fee per inmate annually in return for the labor of the inmates. Contractors would use the inmates basically to farm or harvest crops, much like the **slaves of the master**. The state would make a profit and could avoid the cost of building additional and adequate facilities, hiring correctional staff, feeding and clothing inmates, and otherwise assuming such care, custody, and provisioning as would have been required. In brief, prisons became attractive "profit centers" for those states willing to lease out their convict populations. Costs incurred by contractors were significantly below those that would have been incurred if free-world labor had been hired or if, in the pre–Civil War era, more slaves had to be bought who would have had to be fed, clothed, housed, and disciplined more attentively than mere criminals.

key term

Slaves of the master
Inmates who are compelled to obey correctional managers and their staff.

During the period from 1870 to 1930, when industrialization was running under full steam in this nation, leasing out of inmates continued. Inmates were put to work building roads, railroads, and trestles or manufacturing wagons, shoes, boots, and many other consumables easily sold on the open market. To protect profit margins, contractors often

Photo 13.3
Inmate roadworker chain gang.
Underwood Archives/Contributor/Archive Photos/Getty Images.

would transport inmates in rolling cages, where they lived without sanitary and bathing facilities and were worked from dawn to dusk under the watchful eye of heavily armed guards ("overseers") who were not afraid to use brute force to achieve production quotas. Inmates attempting to escape were killed or beaten, placed in leg irons, forced to wear ball-and-chain restraints, dressed in distinctive garb, and had shortened life expectancies. Food was abysmal and in short supply, and health care was nonexistent. Seeking redress in court was impossible, and avenues of appeal and protest were closed.[4]

The suffering of inmates under these "chain-gang" conditions is common knowledge. What is not as well known is the large percentage of inmates leased out who died under contract arrangements, a figure frequently exceeding 50 percent in a given year. Loss of workers through death, however, had little consequence. Prison administrators were neither criticized nor condemned, and the media rarely covered those events. If a shortage of laborers occurred, prison administrators would lease out newly arrived prisoners who were quickly placed into harnesses and assigned to labor gangs. Not all states, of course, were this brutal in their approach to prisoners, and perhaps this description best fits only some states in the Deep South after the Civil War, when their prisons were filled with former slaves confined for law-violating behavior.[5] This was one of the most odious chapters in the early history of American corrections, and the residual feelings and sentiments about leasing inmates through private-sector involvement even now colors, even if unfairly, the arguments about privatization of corrections.

More Recent Developments

As noted, **privatization** is by no means a new concept in the field of corrections. Many services provided to state, federal, and local correctional facilities have come from the private sector almost from the beginning, and they have persevered. The criminal justice system often appears to be stumbling around like a clumsy giant. It can impose lengthy prison terms and even execute a few criminals. It can slap offenders on the wrist with fines and suspended sentences. It seems able to do little in between, however, although this condition

key term

Privatization
The provision of correctional services by private-sector purveyors.

is changing—but government moves very slowly. In the twentieth century, probation and parole were used as the most frequent alternative options to incarceration. The ability of these two types of sanctions to supervise and control offenders became the standard for the community. We have seen, however, that both of these options came under fire for charges of ineffectiveness.

As discussed in Chapter 8, the development of intermediate sanctions has provided three major options for direct private-sector involvement in corrections: (1) treatment programs, (2) supervised release and low-security custody, and (3) **technologies for surveillance** of offenders not incarcerated. These three options provide the greatest area of potential growth opportunity for private contractors as opposed to the operation of secure correctional facilities.

key term

Technologies for surveillance Application of electronic and other programs designed to allow for the identification of locations of offenders.

PRIVATE-SECTOR TREATMENT PROGRAMS

Supervised treatment programs, usually imposed as a condition of probation, include drug and alcohol abuse treatment and job-training programs. Virtually nonexistent 40 years ago, such programs are now common components of the criminal justice system. Almost all are private, and many are run for profit, deriving both their clients and their incomes from contracts with local governments. Some are designed as long-term residential facilities and others as outpatient clinics. Program philosophies vary widely:

- Some are organized with strict, military-like discipline.
- Others are based on religious beliefs.
- Some are devoted to group therapy.
- Others stress rugged individualism and self-reliance.
- Some are adopting evidence-based approaches.

The growing problem and critical need to respond to the widespread use of drugs creates a demand to treat drug abusers and has rekindled interest in these types of programs, and we can expect their numbers to increase.

Photo 13.4

Graduation ceremony for successful program participants and others in the program.
Marmaduke St. John/Alamy.

Private-sector programs handle a large number of criminal offenders. For every offender housed in a privately managed jail or prison, there are hundreds in privately operated noncustodial programs operating under contract with state and local governments. Despite their numbers and importance, these private programs are largely ignored in discussions of the privatization of corrections. This may be because such programs are regarded as merely service providers rather than penal programs or because their roles as agents of state control are obscured because client participation is sometimes voluntary.

Most private operators of prison facilities are for-profit corporations and are generally listed on stock exchanges as investments. As such, they can be seen as a **growth industry;** Some of the major private operators include Corrections Corporation of America (CCA); the GEO Group, Inc. (formerly Wackenhut Corrections); and Management and Training Corporation. Although CCA has been the largest, GEO's recent acquisition of Cornell and BI may change that.

key term

Growth industry
Any business venture whose volume of work systematically increases over time.

LOW-SECURITY CUSTODY PROGRAMS

Another important development in corrections in recent years has been the growth of low-security custodial facilities.[6] Many of the most innovative types of low-security facilities have been designed and implemented by advocates of privatization and, as such, are operated by private contractors. Today, this form of custody constitutes one of the fastest-growing areas of corrections and the most important segment in the business of private, for-profit corrections contractors.

The juvenile justice system, in particular, has come to rely on private contractors to provide such low-security custodial facilities. This in turn has both increased the government's flexibility in dealing with juveniles and expanded its capacity to commit them into custody. California, Florida, Massachusetts, Michigan, Pennsylvania, Rhode Island, and Washington, among other states, rely heavily on private contractors to care for their juvenile wards. In a number of states, placement in out-of-home settings constitutes a major component of the state's juvenile corrections policy; in some, private placements outnumber placements in public facilities. We should stress that these private custodial placements are not simply

Photo 13.5
Inmates at a privately run Santa Fe jail in California use the outdoor gym to take in some sun during their recreation time.
Ed Kashi/Corbis.

more efficient versions of state-run programs. Although these programs have diverted some and provided services to other juveniles who would otherwise have been placed in secure public institutions, they also target groups that once would not have been placed in custody at all. In short, such programs add a new intermediate level of sanctioning to the state's repertoire.

Private contractors have also played a similar role in developing low-security facilities for adult offenders, and there is a growing differentiation between what the private- and public-sector facilities have to offer. The private sector is developing more facilities at the low end of the spectrum, such as residential treatment facilities, community work release centers, prerelease centers, short-term detention facilities, restitution centers, return-to-custody facilities, parole revocation for chemical abuse, and the like. Nonetheless, private-sector providers also manage and provide services for secure jail and prison institutions.

Private-sector involvement in community corrections is increasing, and there are indications that it will continue to grow, especially if prison populations exceed capacity and pressures mount to increase alternatives that are more flexible and less costly. Time will tell if this "net-widening" effect of such expanded services will actually reach enough of the problem clients in the community who would not normally have been served.

SURVEILLANCE AND CONTROL TECHNOLOGIES

New technologies represent yet another area that has emerged in response to the heightened concern with crime. Only a few years ago, state laboratories performed chemical testing in a costly and time-consuming manner. Now private drug-testing companies across the nation can offer fast, cheap, and reliable tests to detect a large variety of illegal substances. But expanded use of cheap and reliable drug tests has also increased the likelihood of detection of illegal substances, which in turn has raised the number of probation and parole violators, helping to transform probation and parole officers from social workers to law enforcement officers. The upsurge in the numbers returned to custody has in turn generated demands for specialized low-security custodial facilities and new forms of confinement (such as in Texas and California). In short, new technology has placed burdens on the correctional system and affected its more traditional roles.

Private contractors have also introduced a variety of high-tech electronic devices that monitor the movement of people. These devices can be used for surveillance and offer the possibility of confinement without custody, as was also noted in Chapter 6. Developed by specialized security firms and now ubiquitous in application, **electronic monitoring** has vast potential as an effective and inexpensive intermediate form of punishment. For instance, it can supplement if not replace work-release facilities and be used to confine drunk drivers to their homes and places of work.

key term

Electronic monitoring
Any system or telemetry program that allows correctional staff to know the location of offenders.

CORRECTIONAL PRIVATIZATION: ISSUES AND EVIDENCE

It is now widely understood that, first, privatization arrangements cast the government and not a private firm as the entity that establishes public priorities and that, second, they involve the efforts to achieve public goals by reliance on private rather than public means. Importantly, one really cannot appreciate the significance of the privatization trends without having a basic understanding of what is so different today from as little as 30 years ago. In 1980, there was not a single privatized jail or prison here or abroad.

The precise moment when this concept of privatization of secure adult facilities was born is the subject of much debate. The foundation was probably laid on or near the date in 1983 when **Corrections Corporation of America (CCA)** was formed in Nashville, Tennessee. The first local contract for a secure county facility was awarded to CCA in 1984. Kentucky awarded the first state-level contract to **U.S. Corrections Corporation (USCC)** in 1985. The first federal-level contract of any size went to CCA from the Immigration and Naturalization Service in 1984. Soon there was a rush of private companies to get into this new field, and the number of beds and companies grew apace. The Texas Department of Corrections awarded contracts for four 500-bed facilities, to include their design, construction, and management. Two were awarded to CCA and two to the new Wackenhut Corrections Corporation (WCC), the forerunner of the **GEO Group**. This moved the private corrections industry into a much larger arena for privatization of correctional facilities. The first overseas venture involved a joint venture with the CCA and the Corrections Corporation of Australia and spread to the United Kingdom. The industry appeared to move from a novel idea to a viable alternative to publicly provided services. Resistance to privatization by correctional agencies has varied from experimentation to outright rejection, especially when privatization efforts were seen as an attack on job security.[7]

The result was rapid growth in this new niche of the private-services sector. In just the years between 1992 and 2010, the contract capacity for private, secure adult correctional facilities across the nation grew from 15,300 to an estimated 185,000, an increase of over 1,000 percent.

Privately managed adult facilities now house diverse prisoner populations in both small and large facilities. The number of jurisdictions electing to hold their prisoners in privately managed facilities has grown nationally at a substantial rate. Critics predicted that no maximum-security facility could be privatized, but CCA opened a privately managed maximum-security facility in Leavenworth, Kansas, in 1992. Numerous other privately managed facilities house significant numbers of maximum-security-classified prisoners. The evidence is mixed regarding control problems such as inmate-on-inmate assaults, inmate-on-staff assaults, minor disturbances, riots, and escapes and will be discussed later in the chapter.[8]

At least three of the companies that manage adult correctional facilities (CCA, GEO Group, and others) have also contracted for youthful offender programs. These programs deal primarily with older juveniles and put less emphasis on treatment, a focus in the typical residential programs that both Children Comprehensive Services and Youth Services operate. The youthful offender programs that are managed by adult corrections companies have lower per-diem charges on average (approximately $65 to $80 per day) when compared to residential programs run primarily by juvenile service providers ($85 to $180 per day). To date, private corrections companies concentrating on the adult market have chosen not to compete extensively with the companies that concentrate entirely on juvenile programs. See Table 13.2 for information on the states in which the number of prisoners is guaranteed to private companies.

At year-end 2012, privately operated prisons held more than 137,000 state and federal inmates. This figure includes 94,300 state inmates, 33,800 federal inmates, 14,814 U.S. Immigration and Customs Enforcement (ICE) inmates, and 17,154 inmates for the Marshal's Service.[9]

Correctional systems using private prison providers include 32 states, the District of Columbia, and the federal system. Among states, Texas (with 15,893 adult state inmates housed in private facilities) and Georgia and Florida (with about 10,000 each) reported the largest number in 2012.[10] Five states had at least 25 percent of their prison population housed in private facilities: New Mexico, Montana, Alaska, Wyoming, and Oklahoma. The use of private facilities was concentrated among southern and western states.

The recent recession has had an effect on the private prison industry as more and more states try to reduce their prison populations. Numerous private prisons have been closed, and it is reported that CCA has nearly 12,000 unfilled beds. Despite this setback, the private

key term

Corrections Corporation of America (CCA)
A private business seeking to provide correctional services to units of government; also known as the "parent of private-sector prison facilities."

key term

U.S. Corrections Corporation (USCC)
A private-sector correctional provider.

key term

GEO Group
A private-sector correctional provider formerly known as the Wackenhut group.

table **13.2** **States Where the Number of Prisoners Is Guaranteed* to Private Companies**

State	GEO	MTC	CCA
California	3	0	0
Arizona	2	2	2
New Mexico	2	0	1
Oklahoma	1	0	3
Louisiana	1	0	1
Mississippi	0	0	1
Florida	2	1	4
Georgia	1	0	3
Tennessee	0	0	1
Virginia	1	0	0
Indiana	1	0	0
Ohio	0	0	1

Note: *"Guaranteed" refers to 90 percent or more.
SOURCE: Kathy Hall and Jan Diehrm, "Where Prisoners Are Guaranteed," http://www.huffingtonpost.com/2013/09/19/private-prisons_n_3955686.html (accessed September 13, 2014).

prison industry appears to be a permanent fixture in American corrections. Recently, for example, Ohio announced it was entertaining a plan to sell four or five state prisons to a private contractor as means of reducing the state deficit.[11]

CONTROVERSIES

For the past three decades, there has been a steady and growing emphasis on using private-sector prisons in the management of juveniles, felons, and other offenders. Only in the past decade has there emerged a major pushback against this development. Critics and controversies abound in the area of private-sector involvement. Critics have addressed many issues and developments in the area; not all such private-sector evaluators or investigators have criticized every operation, facility, or program, and their criticisms no doubt do not apply to all private-sector providers. Yet there appears to be something of a groundswell in opinions and criticisms. In order to comprehend the meanings of controversies, it is necessary to start with the major assertions ("selling points") advanced by most private providers of detention and prison facilities that serve both juvenile and adult prisons as well as immigration violators.

Assertions

Generally, most providers make the following assertions:

1. Private-sector providers state that they can perform the same services as would be provided by state prisons.
2. They state that they can do the same tasks at less cost to the state.
3. Such providers state that they would be more effective in the prison services than are state providers of prisons, jails, and juvenile facilities.

4. Private providers report that they can service offenders from all levels of security assessment, including maximum-security prisons.
5. They report that they would enhance employment and resources for citizens in the local economy as well as the state.
6. Private-sector prison providers report that they can provide physical facilities cheaper and faster by seeking involvement of the private sector in gathering resources for the construction of facilities.

Public Interests

In state provider facilities, the public interest is containment of potential escapees, provision of services, enhanced public safety, maintaining security and safety within prisons, rehabilitation, and lessened recidivism. At the state level, the three major beneficiaries are the government, taxpayers, and offenders. The beneficiaries in the private-provider options would also include stockholders, investors, hedge funds, lobbyists, upper-level managers (salaries), corrupt public employees and politicians, and **rainmakers**, a general term describing the collaborating politicians with influence in securing the approval of the private-sector company contracts.

key term

Rainmakers
Powerful politicians and allies within governmental jurisdictions with sufficient influence to arrange approval of private-sector proposals to develop private prisons and continue their use in the local jurisdictions. The "rain" refers to monetary gain to the provider of private prisons and can also apply to personal political contributions by private-sector providers to the election of candidates friendly to the providers.

Illegal Immigration Issues

Some private prison corporations provide services, detention, and support to various state and federal agencies that detain individuals who have been arrested for immigration violations. Residing in this nation illegally is a civil code violation, not a criminal code offense. Because the accused cannot be punished criminally for their entry, it is not necessary to provide the *Miranda* warnings to them, and they are not entitled to legal representation. Ordinarily, they would be identified and fingerprinted and their records searched for criminal offenses; most would be deported to their last known home country. If, however, legal counsel can be arranged, about two in three who have counsel will have successful outcomes versus about 3 percent of those without legal counsel. Such illegal immigrants will be housed in detention cells by ICE and guarded by armed officers. These facilities hold approximately 30,000 immigrants; detention will most likely be provided by private-sector providers in ICE detention centers modeled after jails and prisons. If this is punishment, where is the conviction on which the detention is based?[12] The American Civil Liberties Union refers to such a process as "Banking on Bondage."

Cost-Savings Issues

The research and evaluations undertaken to date on the statement that private-sector providers can perform the same services at less cost than the public sector is not yet substantiated. Some studies show outcomes favorable to the private-sector providers, but the bulk of the costs studies find no difference or suggest just the opposite.[13] To date, we can conclude that such savings have not materialized for every jurisdiction contracting with private prison providers.

In considering the expenses of private-sector providers, it should be noted that profits are due to savings engendered through cost cutting and reduction in staff, restriction of basic supplies, reducing the quantity and quality of food, denial of medical services, hiring of nonunion workers, hiring staff at minimum wages, contract fraud, and guaranteed occupancy. Guaranteed occupancy means that the governmental entity contracting with the private-sector provider guarantees that a certain percentage of occupancy will be maintained by that agency, sometimes 95 to 97 percent full.[14] If the total number of inmates drops below that number, the state is required to pay for any empty beds at a cost predetermined in the contract. This has been likened to a "low-crime" tax. If the crime rate drops or changes in the criminal codes lead to less lengthy detention, the public jurisdiction is penalized for reducing the number of inmates under private-sector control. Costs can also be reduced by providing minimal benefits to staff, insufficient staff to manage every critical service point, reduction in the amount of available commodities, and other factors described later in this chapter.

Although there is a stress on guaranteed occupancy, it would strain the limit of logic to argue that private-sector providers maintain that rate through accepting all inmates sent to their facilities. In practice, inmates are mostly minimum- to medium-security offenders. It is not unknown for the private sector to return a maximum-security inmate to the public sector based on evidence of violence or dangerousness.[15] In addition, inmates accepted by the private provider are usually not very ill and not in need of costly medical treatment.[16]

Violence Issues

In general, the institutions managed by providers of private prisons and juvenile facilities have high levels of violence, much of which is not investigated, written up, or communicated to the public-sector contracting jurisdictions, as there are possible potentially negative outcomes.

Staff Recruitment and Turnover

Most facilities recruit potential staff who are hired at minimum-wage pay and with limited benefit packages. Efforts to unionize staff have met with resistance. Once hired, there is only minimal training and limited experience for new hires. This is a version of "fire one, hire another," previously seen in the decades immediately following the nation's Civil War, when chain gangs composed of previously indentured slaves were hired out. If one died, the response would be "One Dies? Hire another."

Staff turnover in some facilities is a high as 96 percent a year, well in excess of the highest rates within the public sector. High turnover means new hires might receive only minimal preservice training before assuming staff positions. It also implies that there is minimum industry memory of past events and improving the rates of successful intervention and supervision.[16] New hires seldom know critical supervision tactics. A high rate of new hires also implies that there may not be sufficient staff to fill every critical post 24/7. To fill minimal critical posts implies that staff may be asked to hold over for a second (or third) tour of duty. Tired security staff may not intervene when necessary, may ignore clues suggesting pending altercations, or may refuse to reenter a facility in which some inmates are rioting. This further implies more violent altercations between inmates, destruction of property, and loss of life.[17] Security must be sufficiently strong to deter such events.

Rehabilitation

Cost cutting can occur at many levels, but staff reduction and program termination are two possible ways to bring costs down and fatten the profit margin. Program cutting means, in part, less efficiency in the provision of rehabilitation. If rehabilitation leads to lesser recidivism, then it is in the public interest to expend time, money, and effort to secure it. One indicator of whether a facility is effective in the area of rehabilitation is to measure the criminal behavior committed by former inmates. Here the evidence is not encouraging. Comparisons of public with private prisons suggest that public safety is more clearly secured through the presence of rehabilitation programming, especially academic education, job training, vocational apprenticeships, and job placement on reentry. Critics generally agree that rehabilitation is best achieved in the public-sector institutions. Bear in mind that there is some evidence of **cherry picking** when evaluating private- and public-sector outcomes. Inmates in private-sector facilities are more likely to be minimum- and medium-security inmates, not the harder, more violent and disruptive maximum- or higher-security offenders concentrated in the public-sector facilities. Here is the argument in a nutshell: If you are working with lower-security offenders, you should have higher rates of success following inmate release. Alternatively, the highest-security-level inmates should have the highest levels of recidivism. The evidence to date is just the opposite. Justice employees, the general population, and other informed citizens should ask why that is. In addition, a Justice Department study in 2001 found that private prisons had assault rates 65 percent higher than those of public prisons. One study found that 40 percent of released youth from a Florida private prison were arrested and convicted within a year of release versus only 25 percent of youth from a New York public facility, a large difference.

key term

Cherry picking

In corrections, this is the process of selecting the best or most desirable of inmates for inclusion in a program or facility with the intention of securing the best possible favorable outcome.

Cost Cutting and Commodities

A commodity is, generally speaking, an item that is useful or valued, such as gold, food, automobiles, or homes. Some are obviously more valued than others. Commodities that can be consumed are, in confinement facilities, highly prized and can command high prices in the limited economy of the prison. This would include tobacco, alcohol, illicit drugs, knives, and so on. Such commodities should never be found within a prison, and considerable effort (at least in the public sector) is made to interdict such contraband. (Canada permits no tobacco on any prison campus, including parking lots.)

Other legal consumable commodities within a prison would include commissary items, water heaters ("stingers"), and personal effects. The private sector is expected to provide equivalent access to personal commodities, as there is little alternative source of provision. We focus here on a facility for female offenders. Juvenile wards and adult inmates need an adequate supply of certain commodities: food, toothpaste, deodorant, tampons, soap, toilet paper, and bras, for example. Parenthetically, the quality and quantity of commodities are expected to be adequate. Costs can be lowered through restricting necessary commodities, such as rationing toilet paper to no more than five sheets a day.

Food is a **hot-button item** for juvenile and adult inmates. Not only must there be enough food, but its quality must be acceptable. It is expected that food will be sufficient to meet the caloric needs of similarly placed offenders and sufficiently attractive so as not to lead to riot and disturbance. It is no surprise that the major disturbance location within a prison facility remains the dining room, with the recreation yard and exercise areas in which inmates concentrate a close second. Food full of maggots, served cold, and undercooked (such as chicken served up cold and still bloody); flies inside precooked dishes; and inedible food served in the midst of free-ranging rats, cockroaches, and mice does not meet the standards necessary for human consumption. In a confinement facility, disturbance, riot, and assault can easily be triggered by both the quantity and the quality of the food. In one instance, a fire inside the kitchen of the Ohio Penitentiary in 1971 knocked out the ability of the facility to feed inmates. The director of the state department of corrections immediately ordered sufficient sandwiches, drinks, and potatoes from a major food service chain to feed the 1,900 inmates, avoiding the considerable potential for a major disturbance. Instead of a riot, inmates were pleased to receive a break from institutional food and the resulting "picnic" atmosphere.

key term

Hot-button item

A topic in someone's mind that, when discussed, makes the individual offended or very passionate about the issue. Such topics can include people, religion, politics, possessions, criminals, or passions. In the correctional system, food is often a hot-button item for inmates.

Critics cite numerous examples of skimping on food service and the quality of foods. Such action poses the potential for major disturbances as well as increased hostility between the keepers and the kept.[18]

Corruption Issues

One of the ways to increase profit margins is to increase the volume of customers using your product, service, or opportunities. "Selling points" are easily identified, as noted earlier in this chapter. Rainmakers can be effective sources of increased enrollments, and **gatekeepers** can be recruited to refer or order clients to participate in desired services.

Most gatekeepers are honestly convinced that the referral or commitment of the offender to a service or facility would be the best resolution of a sentencing interest and/or the client or criminal. Such judges, in particular, frequently search for a public safety solution, one that would also benefit the client. Other gatekeeping judges can (and do) make decisions on sentences based on personal gain that can accrue to the sentencing judge. Such a replacement from the public interest to a personal gain is a form of **corruption.**[19]

The correctional field has had its share of corrupted gatekeepers. One such official was a governor who sold pardons for financial consideration; another was a police property room commander who stole seized illicit drugs for personal gain and made "evidence" disappear from the property room. Another gatekeeper would be the sentencing judge who committed juveniles to a private juvenile delinquent facility for financial consideration: a cash award for each juvenile committed to a private-sector operator. Such behavior puts profits far ahead of the public interest. The cash award is an incentive to lock up more offenders. In 2010 and 2011, two former juvenile court judges were arrested and convicted in a "kids-for-cash" scandal. They were instrumental in shutting down a public juvenile facility and steering juvenile wards to a newer private-sector facility in exchange for millions of dollars from the operator of the facility, constituting a **kickback.** Both are reported to now be serving long prison sentences. One critic described this approach as treating prisoners as commodities and describing inmates as "prisoners of profits."

We caution that despite the critics' assertions, court documents, convictions, evaluations, and input from former employees of private facilities, current evidence on private operations remains hard to muster. To allay or verify such criticisms, a federal or state investigative unit should conduct investigations of past practices and prospective operations. Unfair criticisms might well be identified.

key term

Gatekeeper
A criminal or juvenile justice professional (such as a prosecutor, parole board member, politician, or judge) who determines access to services, detention or confinement facilities, or commitment to prison or parole.

key term

Corruption
Dishonest or illegal behavior, especially by powerful people (such as government officials, judges, or police officers).

key term

Kickback
A return of a percentage of a sum of money already received, typically as a result of pressure, coercion, or a secret agreement; a percentage of income given to a person in a position of power or influence as payment for having made the income possible; usually considered improper, unethical, or illegal.

Summary

Describe the History of Private-Sector Involvement in Corrections

Most correctional services and agencies before 1980 involved private-sector providers, with services ranging from training and education to medical care and food to probation and parole services. In 1977, private-sector providers began to incorporate to provide privatized institutional facilities. Currently, private corporations hold about 17 percent of the nation's institutionalized offenders, but controversies around those arrangements are ongoing.

Identify the Advantages That Private-Sector Providers Claim in Meeting the Needs of Public State Prisons

Private providers report that they can service offenders from all security levels, build prison facilities faster and cheaper than the state might, and enhance the local economy by employing local workers. They also claim to be as effective as (or more so than) state prisons.

Describe How Prison Inmates Were Considered "Slaves of the State"

Before the end of the nineteenth century, states would lease inmates to the private sector for a fee paid to the state in exchange for inmate labor. Leased inmates would basically farm or harvest crops, much like the slaves of the master ("planter with plantation"). The state would make a profit and could avoid the cost of building additional and adequate facilities, hiring correctional staff, feeding and clothing inmates, and otherwise assuming such care, custody, and provisioning as would have been required. In brief, prisons became attractive "profit centers" for those states willing to lease out their convict populations to the private sector.

List Five Examples of How Private-Sector Companies Could Benefit Juvenile Offenders

Historically, it was common for government agencies to secure food, health care, education, mental health, transportation, and training services for juveniles through private-sector entities. During the period from the birth of the nation until about 1930, profit, nonprofit, and charitable organizations contracted with the state to provide all types of facilities and services for juvenile offenders. Private-sector providers benefit juvenile offenders by continuing these practices.

Identify Five Controversies Surrounding Private-Sector Prison Providers

Private-sector providers have been accused of staff cruelty, neglect, undue punishment, untrained and inferior staff, and high staff turnover resulting in loss of control in some facilities. Other controversies have arisen over alleged lack of rehabilitation, academic education, and vocational training and the high recidivism rates of their clients.

Compare and Contrast Gatekeepers and Rainmakers

Rainmakers are powerful politicians and allies within governmental jurisdictions with sufficient influence to arrange approval of private-sector proposals to develop private prisons and continue their use in the local jurisdictions. The "rain" refers to monetary gain to the provider of private prisons and can also apply to personal political contributions by private-sector providers to the election of candidates friendly to the providers.

Gatekeepers are justice officials who make decisions influencing the resolution of cases and arrange for the incarceration of offenders. Gatekeepers can be corrupted into committing large numbers of correctional clients to private-sector incarceration facilities, usually for kickbacks and private enrichment.

Summarize Other Prison Systems and the Privatization of Prisons

In this nation, public-sector prisons are tax-supported institutions designed to provide care, custody, and safety of offenders for intended social and penal objectives. Correctional leaders are responsive to the public interest and both the legislative and the executive branches of government. Their behaviors are controlled by policies and principles enunciated by the state and courts, including job termination and trials. Private-sector prisons are seldom as open to examination and investigations, and their effectiveness is seldom questioned. They are not directly responsive to the general public or state government and are usually profit generators.

Key Words

private-sector correctional facility, 280
self-insured, 281
slaves of the master, 282
privatization, 283
technologies for surveillance, 284
growth industry, 285
electronic monitoring, 286
Corrections Corporation of America (CCA), 287
U.S. Corrections Corporation (USCC), 287
GEO Group, 287
rainmakers, 289
cherry picking, 291
hot-button item, 291
gatekeeper, 292
corruption, 292
kickback, 292

Review Questions

1. What are the primary reasons for the private sector to become involved in prisons and jails?
2. How many beds are being supplied by the private sector in adult prisons?
3. What are the major arguments against privatization of adult jails and prisons?
4. What are the major arguments in favor of privatization of correctional services?
5. What vested interests are evident in the controversy over privatization of correctional facilities?

Application Case Studies

1. You are the director of your state's department of corrections, and a key aide to your governor calls you to her office. She informs you that three state senators will be introducing a bill to solicit bids from private prison providers to manage two new prisons they would propose to first build and then operate. She asks you whether you are in favor of this plan and how you would decide which type of offenders you would assign. How do you respond?
2. You are a county supervisor, and a trusted news reporter tells you in confidence that two juvenile court judges have been committing almost all of their wards to a private juvenile facility. He also tells you that an asset evaluation has been ongoing and that the two judges have made recent and new investments that, in total, exceed more than their total annual incomes from all known sources. What would you do?
3. You are the informant news reporter from Case Study 2, and a correctional staff member working in a private detention center tells you that a certain male juvenile ward has disappeared, but there was no announcement to that effect and there is no ongoing search for that juvenile. How would you proceed?

Endnotes

1. William Sabol, Heather Couture, and Paige Harrison, *Prisoners in 2008* (Washington, DC: Bureau of Justice Statistics, 2007), p. 1.
2. Joseph Jacoby, "The Endurance of Failing Correctional Institutions," *The Prison Journal* 82:2 (2002): 168–188.
3. Douglas McDonald, E. Fournier, E. Russell, et al., *Private Prisons in the United States* (Cambridge, MA: Abt Associates, 1998).
4. Harry E. Allen and J. Abril, "The New Chain Gang: Corrections in the Next Century," *American Journal of Criminal Justice* 22:1 (1997): 1–12; Matthew Mancini, *One Dies, Get Another: Convict Leasing in the American South* (Columbia: University of South Carolina Press, 1999). See also Major W. Cox, "Chain Gang's Newest Wedge," http://www.majorcox.com/columns/chains.htm (accessed November 16, 2008).
5. James Anderson, L. Dyson, and W. Brooks, "Alabama Prison Chain Gangs," *Western Journal of Black Studies* 24:1 (2000): 9–1; Timothy Dodge, "State Convict Road Gangs in Alabama," *The Alabama Review* 53:4 (2000): 243–270. See also Scott Henry, "How Do You Say 'Chain Gang' in Arabic?," http://blogs.creativeloafing.com/freshloaf/2008/02/14/how-do-you-say-chain-gang-in-Arabic?/ (accessed November 16, 2008).
6. For example, California has 13 contract correctional facilities providing minimum security and treatment. In 2007, 9 of these 10 units housed more than 7,900 offenders. American Correctional Association, *2007 Directory of Adult and Juvenile Correctional Departments, Institutions, Agencies, and Probation and Parole Authorities* (Lanham, MD: American Correctional Association, 2007), pp. 128–129.
7. Richard P. Seiter, "Private Corrections: A Review of the Issues," http://cca.com/Media/Default/documents/CCA-Resource-Center/Private_Corr_Review.pdf (accessed September 13, 2014).
8. A series of evaluation studies can be found at http://www.correctionscorp.com/researchfindings.html. None of the authors has any financial interest in any private-sector correctional group.
9. Cody Mason, (2012), "Dollars and Detainees: The Growth of For-ProfitDetetion," http://sentencingproject.org/doc/publications/inc_Dollars_and_Detainees.pdf (accessed January 26, 2014).

10. American Correctional Association, *2012 Directory* (Alexandria, VA: American Correctional Association, 2012), pp. 752–754.
11. After the bids were received, only two prisons were slated to be transferred to private operators.
12. Graham Kates (2013), "Fast Track to Deportation," http://www.thecrimereport.org/news/inside-criminal-justice/2013-09-fast-track-to-deportation (accessed September 13, 2013). See also Detention Night Watch, "The Influence of the Private Prison Industry in Immigration Detention," at http://www.detentionwatchwork,org/privateprisons (accessed May 18, 2013).
13. Cody Mason, *Too Good to Be True: Private Prisons in* America (Washington, DC: The Sentencing Project, 2012); American Civil Liberties Union, "Private Prisons," http://www.aclu.org/prisoners/rights/private-prisons (accessed November 12, 2012).
14. See Craig Harris, "Arizona Faces Growing Cost of Private Prisons," http://www.azcentral.com/news/arizona/articles/20131204arizona-private-prisons-growing-cost.html?nclick_check=1 (accessed December 31, 2014). The author argues that the guarantee of a high occupancy rate is a major contribution to a healthy bottom line at the expense of taxpayers, a "profit machine" for private businesses; the article includes quotes from correctional managers who argue that correctional facilities should be used to reduce recidivism among those eventually released. Is this "banking on bondage"? See also Brian Haas, "Tennessee Taxpayers Fund Empty CCA Prison Beds," http://www.tennessean.com/article/20131011/NEWS0201/310110126/ (accessed November 11, 2013).
15. See Chris Kirkham, "Private Prison for Juveniles in Mississippi Plagued by Violence, despite Federal Settlement," http://www.huffingtonpost.com/2012/06/14/private-prison-mississippi_n_1598293.html (accessed June 14, 2012).
16. Seth Wessler, "Did a Private Prison Corporation's Abuse of Inmates Spark a Deadly Riot in Mississippi?," http://www.alternet.org/story/155544/did_a_private_prison_corporation's_abuse_of_inmates_spark_a_deadly_riot_in_mississippi (accessed January 29, 2014).
17. Scott Cohn, "Private Prison Industry Grows despite Critics," http://www.nbcnews.com/id/44936562/ns/business-cnbc_tv/t/private-prison-industry-grows-despite-critics/ (accessed January 27, 2014). See also Chris Kirkham, "Private Prison Empire Rises despite Startling Record of Juvenile Abuse," http://projects.huffingtonpost.com/prisonersofprofit (accessed October 25, 2013).
18. Mason, *Too Good to Be True*, p. 10.
19. Jerry Linott, "Circle of Trust Broken," http://psdispatch.com/news/local-news/1143207/Much-has-changed-since-scandal-broke (accessed January 28, 2014). Two judges who pled guilty to corruption charges and who had received $2.8 in kickbacks from two private-sector prison providers in a case known commonly as "Kids for Cash" were sentenced to prison terms of 17 and 28 years, respectively, for the constitutional violations of the juveniles' rights. The Pennsylvania Supreme Court took a "remarkable" step in expunging the criminal records of over 2,400 juveniles handled by the two judges, as well as compensating the victims of the juvenile offenders. Most of the detained juveniles were quickly released.

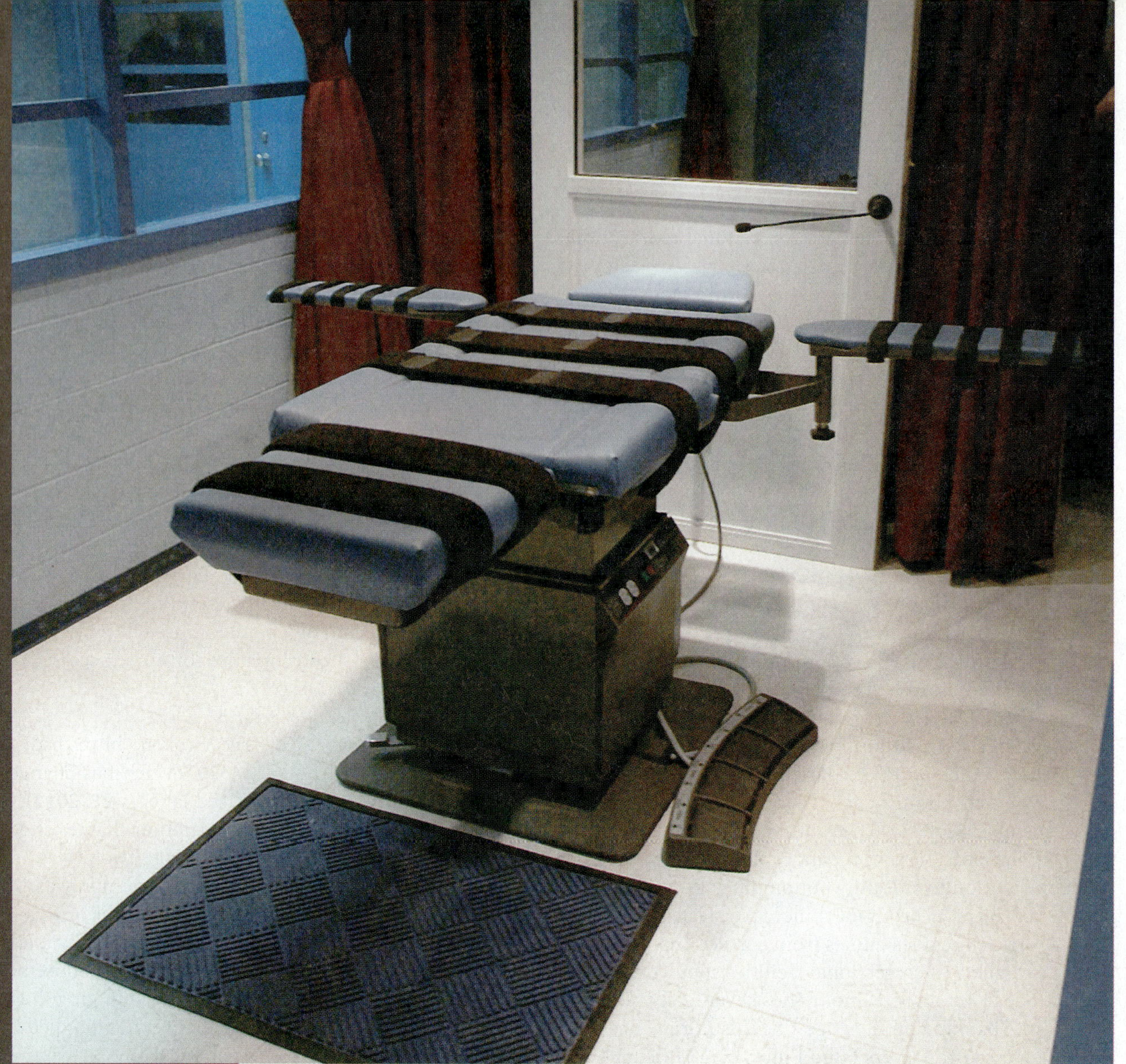

Bob Child/AP Images.

Objectives

- Outline the history of the death penalty in the nation and legal provisions for it.
- Describe forms of execution.
- Describe the effects of decisions of the U.S. Supreme Court on capital punishment.
- Summarize the Eight Amendment's impacts on the death penalty.
- Explain how prosecutorial discretion impacts the death penalty.
- Draw appropriate conclusions about the deterrent effects of the death penalty.
- Describe forms of capital punishment.
- Describe how executions are carried out and the problems associated with executions.
- Explain why there are so few females on death row in America.
- Compare and contrast the abolitionists and retentionists positions on the death penalty.
- Identify who may not be executed in the nation.
- Summarize the characteristics of current death row prisoners.
- Compare and contrast the costs of the death penalty and a sentence of life without parole.

chapter 14

The Death Penalty

Outline

"When the punishment of death is inflicted in a trivial number of cases in which it is legally available, the conclusion is virtually inescapable that it is being inflicted arbitrarily."

—*Furman v. Georgia*, 408 U.S. 238 (1976)

Overview

Perhaps no subject in the field of corrections has had as much controversy at the individual, judge, church, or administrator level than capital punishment. The arguments rage on, ranging from the aspects of morality to the fringes of justice to the core of retribution and revenge. Is it right to kill someone in the name of the state because that person killed someone? We have also changed the methods of execution to perhaps somehow make the act more acceptable to the general public. Popular films such as *Dead Man Walking*[1] attempt to show both sides of this controversial ultimate punishment.

This chapter explores the history, methods, application, and operation of the death penalty as well as the nature of crimes resulting in this sentence. Whether a person is for or against capital punishment often depends on who the offender is and who the victim(s) may be. The student must keep an open mind about the death penalty and realize that it has been around as long as societies have existed. Is it time to abolish the death penalty or make it more efficient, less gruesome, and more certain? We cover all the bases in this chapter, exploring a unique facet of American justice and a problem for corrections.

table **14.1** States without the Death Penalty (Year Abolished in Parentheses)

Alaska (1957)	Michigan (1846)	West Virginia (1965)
Connecticut (2012)	Minnesota (1911)	Wisconsin (1853)
Hawaii (1957)	New Jersey (2007)	ALSO: District of Colombia (1981)
Illinois (2011)	New Mexico (2009)	
Iowa (1965)	New York (2007)	
Maine (1887)	North Dakota (1973)	
Maryland (2013)	Rhode Island (1984)	
Massachusetts (1984)	Vermont (1964)	

SOURCE: Death Penalty Information Center (2014), "States with and without the Death Penalty," http://www.deathpenaltyinfo.org/states-and-without-death-penalty (accessed September 2014).

ORIGINS OF THE DEATH PENALTY

key term

Capital punishment
The imposition of a sentence of death by the state.

key term

Execution
The killing of an offender by the state.

In earlier chapters, we made brief references to some of the issues regarding capital punishment, or the death penalty. The frequency with which the topic comes up demonstrates how intertwined it is with the other aspects of criminal justice. The term **capital punishment** generally refers to the **execution**, in the name of the state, of a person convicted of certain crimes. The crimes for which this punishment has been imposed have varied over the centuries, but treason, murder, and rape have been the most common. In some states in the nation, death-eligible offenses also include train wrecking, treason, perjury causing execution, drug trafficking, aircraft piracy, and contract murder,[2] although no one has been executed in the United States for any crime except for murder since the death penalty was reinstated in 1975.The U.S. military, the federal government, and most states allow the death penalty; states without the death penalty are Alaska, the District of Columbia, Connecticut, Hawaii, Illinois, Iowa, Maine, Maryland, Massachusetts, Michigan, Minnesota, New Jersey, New Mexico, New York, North Dakota, Rhode Island, Vermont, West Virginia, and Wisconsin.[3] States without the death penalty and the years abolished are listed in Table 14.1.

The methods by which the punishment has been carried out have been even more varied and include being hanged, burned, boiled in oil, impaled, shot, strangled, beheaded, drawn and quartered, electrocuted, gassed, and now injected with lethal drugs. In the United States, contemporary techniques include the firing squad, hanging, the gas chamber, electrocution, and lethal injection. Lethal injection appears to be the most frequent and humane technique, although debate continues as to whether execution should be humane.[4]

In the nation's earliest history, executions were almost always administered as a public spectacle in the hope they would serve as a warning and a deterrent to others. It could be argued that the human desire to obtain retribution for crimes was transferred from the individual to the state in a way that finally became repugnant to many enlightened societies. Still, long after the elimination of the more bloody forms of capital vengeance, controversy still centers on the possible deterrent value of the death penalty. The arguments for and against the death penalty concern the issues of deterrence, excessive cruelty (Eighth Amendment arguments), equability (Sixth and Fourteenth Amendment considerations), and attitudes toward capital punishment.[5]

BETTER WAYS TO DIE?

Probably America's most innovative contribution to the various methods of execution was the invention of the electric chair. Although this invention was extolled as a more humanitarian way to kill the offender than the then-current ways (hanging and firing squad, for example), many considered it merely a promotional scheme of the New York electrical company that developed it. The first electrocution was conducted at the Auburn Penitentiary in

New York on August 6, 1890. The first person to die in this highly touted new device was William Kemmler, a convicted murderer from Buffalo, New York.

Opponents of the electric chair, including Thomas Edison, claimed that it must be excessively painful (a claim vehemently denied by prison administrators who used it).[6] The opposition advocated lethal gas as the most humane execution method. The first person to die in America in a prison gas chamber was a Chinese immigrant worker named Gee Jon. The crude system, gaining favor after a series of incredibly gruesome executions by electric chair, used cyanide gas. On February 8, 1924, in Nevada, Gee died in just six minutes.

In an effort to make the execution of condemned criminals easier and cleaner still, lethal injection gained favor in the 1970s and 1980s. It seems that many states thought they could reinstate the death penalty more easily if it was seen to be less cruel and unusual. Charles Brooks, a codefendant in a murder trial, was the first prisoner to die in this manner, executed on December 6, 1982, in Texas.

It is interesting to note that 35 states (some states authorize more than one method) and the federal government have passed legislation to use a lethal injection of chemicals as the latest, "most humane" form of execution as the primary or secondary option.[7] Since 1976, over 85 percent of executions have used lethal injection. Noteworthy is that physicians' associations are expressing concern that their members, whose profession it is to save lives, may be asked by the state to take lives, creating a conflict with the Hippocratic Oath. It seems we are still seeking a way to make the process, if not the practice, of execution more humane.

The physical pain of the execution is probably the smallest concern of the offenders during their prolonged wait in the death house, a wait that averages almost 11 years.[8] The longest time from being sentenced to death and execution appears to be 25 years. The mental anguish the condemned must endure, which that long wait can only intensify, has been a primary focus of the recent widespread controversy surrounding the death penalty, as the more industrialized societies have moved to abolish it.[9] The use of the death penalty in the United States peaked in the crime-laden 1930s, when a total of 1,513 prisoners were executed, an average of about 14 per month. The increased number of appeals and rising opposition to the death penalty peaked in the turbulent 1960s, and in 1972 the U.S. Supreme Court placed a moratorium on the death penalty while states considered legislation that could meet strict constitutional guidelines.[10] That moratorium was dissolved by the decision of ***Gregg* v. *Georgia*** in 1976, and executions began anew in 1977 with convicted murderer Gary Gilmore's cry of "Let's do it!" before being voluntarily executed before a firing squad in Utah. Today there are 18 states without the death penalty (listed earlier). In 2000, Governor George Ryan of Illinois imposed a moratorium on the state's death penalty. "We have now freed more people than we have put to death under our system—13 people have been exonerated and 12 have been put to death. There is a flaw in the system, without question, and it needs to be studied."[11] In 2003, Governor Ryan commuted the sentences of all 156 death row inmates to life. On March 9, 2011, Governor Quinn signed legislation abolishing the death penalty in Illinois.

key term

Gregg* v. *Georgia
The 1977 case that ended the moratorium on the death penalty.

ARBITRARY AND INFREQUENT PUNISHMENT

To better understand the magnitude of the death penalty issue, we must examine the somewhat incomplete records on the subject. The total number of executions between 1976 and May 2011 was 1,355, with the highest number in 1999 at 98. As mentioned earlier, the death penalty has most often been prescribed for murder and rape. One thus would reasonably expect a fairly high correlation between the number of such offenses and the number of executions. In the 1930s, the earliest period for which relatively reliable statistics are available, the average number of executions was about 165 per year. The number of murders and rapes reported per year during the 1930s averaged 3,500 and 3,800, respectively, a ratio of about 1 execution for every 44 **capital crimes** reported.[12]

key term

Capital crimes
Offenses for which an offender can receive the death penalty, usually murder and rape.

Also significant is the number of executions in different states and regions. Most executions have taken place in the South. Over 80 percent of the 1,355 executions between 1976 and midyear 2013 took place in the South, with Texas (507), Virginia (110), Oklahoma (106),

table **14.2** **Top 10 States for Executions, 1976–2013**

State	Total Executions
Texas	507
Virginia	110
Oklahoma	106
Florida	81
Missouri	68
Alabama	56
Georgia	53
Ohio	52
North Carolina	43
South Carolina	43

SOURCE: Death Penalty Information Center (2013), "Number of Executions by State," http://www.deathpenaltyinfo.org/number-executions-state-and-region-1976.

Florida (81), and Missouri (69) accounting for nearly two-thirds of all executions. Table 14.2 shows the top 10 states for executions since 1976. Midwestern states accounted for about 12 percent of the executions, the West about 6 percent, and the Northeast less than 3 percent. It is worth noting that 35 percent of those executed between 1976 and midyear 2013 were black, 7 percent were Hispanic, and 2 percent were Native Americans and Asians.[13]

The number of executions per year dropped to only 11 in 1988 (see Figure 14.1). The number since then has fluctuated, with 98 in 1999, down to 37 in 2008. When we consider the thousands of murders reported during that period, we must consider the comments of Justice William Brennan:

> When a country of over 200 million people inflicts an unusually severe punishment no more than fifty times a year, the inference is strong that the punishment is not being regularly and fairly applied. To dispel it would indeed require a clear showing of non-arbitrary infliction.[14]

Even if one agrees that the number of murders does not necessarily reflect the number for which the death penalty might have been imposed, the difference is still staggering. As Justice Potter Stewart explained in ***Furman* v. *Georgia***, the death penalty is "freakishly" or "spectacularly" rare in its occurrence. In an argument in *Furman*, Justice Brennan in 1972 summed up the **arbitrary** nature of the death penalty:

> When the punishment of death is inflicted in a trivial number of cases in which it is legally available, the conclusion is virtually inescapable that it is being inflicted arbitrarily. Indeed, it smacks of little more than a lottery system. The states claim, however, that this rarity is evidence not of arbitrariness, but of informed selectivity: Death is inflicted, they say, only in "extreme" cases.
>
> . . . When the rate of infliction is at this low level, it is highly implausible that only the worst criminals or the criminals who commit the worst crimes are selected for this punishment. No one has yet suggested a rational basis that could differentiate in those terms the few who die from the many who go to prison.[15]

It is also important to remember that the two crimes of murder and rape have accounted for nearly 99 percent of the executions in the United States since 1930, with over 87 percent of the total for murder alone. It appears that the original practice of *mandating* the death penalty for murder has become repugnant to American society as a whole. This is demonstrated by the reluctance of juries to convict in such cases despite the earlier efforts of state legislators to pass laws that call for mandatory executions for certain types of murder.

The concept of **intent to kill**, or **malice aforethought**,[16] usually an essential element of proof in the capital murder statutes, provided a rationale for juries to opt for a lesser penalty.

key term

Furman* v. *Georgia
The Supreme Court decision that the death penalty in Georgia was being applied arbitrarily and discriminatorily against minorities; as a result of this case, a moratorium on the death penalty was imposed throughout the United States.

key term

Arbitrary
Acting without criteria, usually in a discriminatory manner.

key term

Intent to kill
Malice aforethought; having the intent to kill prior to the crime; planned and premeditated crime.

key term

Malice aforethought
Having the intent to kill prior to the commission of the crime; planned and premeditated.

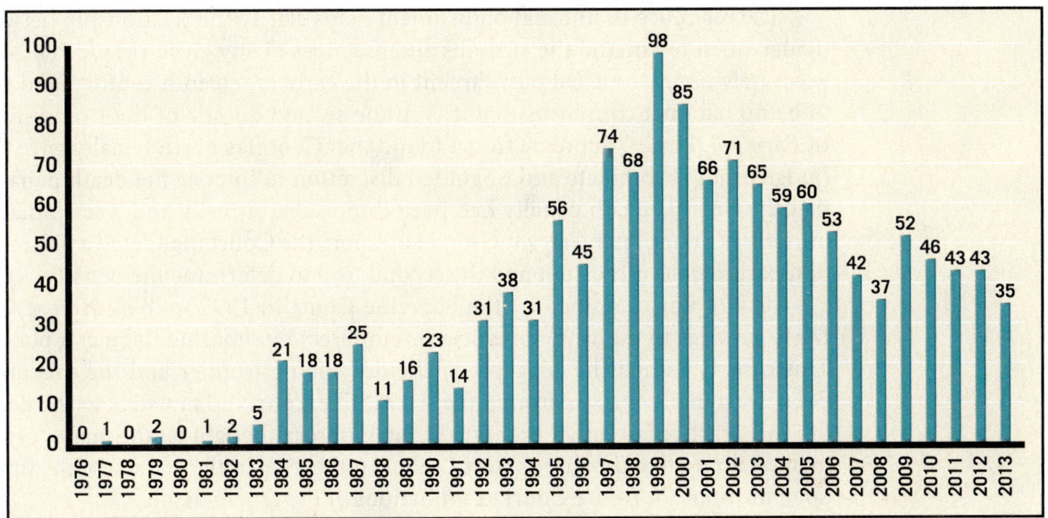

figure 14.1

Executions, 1982–2013.

Note: As of October of 2013, an additional 32 inmates have been executed.

SOURCE: Death Penalty Information Center (2014), http://www.deathpenaltyinfo.org.

Legislatures finally recognized that juries were using this concept to avoid the death penalty and passed statutes that attempted to differentiate between the degrees of various capital crimes (for example, first- and second-degree murder and first- and second-degree rape), thus trying to restrict mandatory execution to the first offenses. In response, juries simply refused to convict in cases in which they felt—arbitrarily—that the death penalty was inappropriate. The further refinement of the distinction between capital and noncapital cases was abandoned by legislation in many jurisdictions, and juries were given legal discretion to continue the practice they had already established in fact. The sentence of death is now discretionary in every jurisdiction in which it is still used, and it is the jury that must determine to impose death rather than another sentence.

In those states with capital punishment, the prosecutor must decide to seek the **death penalty**, using the vast discretion inherent in that office. If the decision is not to pursue a death-eligible charge, then the jury is usually prevented from imposing the sentence of death. Consistent (but not unchallenged) evidence suggests that race of the victim colors the prosecutor's decisions: Victim-based discrimination has been found to be an important determinant in Texas,[17] the Chattahoochee Judicial District (Georgia),[18] and Kentucky[19] but not in California.[20] Evaluations of prosecutorial discretion are ongoing.[21] We discuss the role of the prosecutor in more detail later.

key term

Death penalty
Execution of the offender by the state.

THE EIGHTH AMENDMENT AND THE DEATH PENALTY

American jurisprudence has borrowed much from the English law. The ban against **cruel and unusual punishment** embodied in the Eighth Amendment was lifted from the English Bill of Rights of 1689. As Justice Thurgood Marshall indicated in *Furman* v. *Georgia,*

> Perhaps the most important principle in analyzing "cruel and unusual" punishment questions is one that is reiterated again and again in the prior opinions of the Court: i.e., the cruel and unusual language "must draw its meaning from the evolving standards of decency that mark the progress of a maturing society." Thus, a penalty, which was permissible at one time in our nation's history, is not necessarily permissible today. The fact, therefore, that the Court, or individual justices, may have in the past expressed an opinion that the death penalty is constitutional is not now binding on us.[22]

key term

Cruel and unusual punishment
Prohibited by the Eighth Amendment to the Constitution.

The reference to unusual punishment helps clarify the relationship between this particular amendment and the customs and practices of any given period. The death penalty was surely not an unusual punishment in the early nineteenth century, and there appears to be no national consensus that it is in the second decade of the twenty-first century.[23] In *Furman,* the U.S. Supreme Court found that Georgia's death penalty gave the sentencer (judge or jury) complete and unguided discretion to impose the death penalty and ruled that the Georgia death penalty had been imposed arbitrarily and discriminatorily against minorities. In the later *Gregg* v. *Georgia* opinion, the Court mandated a bifurcated trial, the first part to determine guilt and the second trial to determine the penalty.

Cruelty was examined by the Supreme Court in 1878 in *Wilkerson* v. *Utah.*[24] It was Utah's practice to punish premeditated murderers by shooting them at a public execution. This case examined the concepts of the developing frontier and the execution practices being used in other areas around the world. The Court did not stick to the doctrine of traditional practice but rather examined contemporary thought on the matter of cruel punishment. It found that the case against Utah was not cruel in the context of the times, but it left open the door for future Court examinations of the cruelty issue:

> Difficulty would attend the effort to define with exactness the extent of the constitutional provision which provides that cruel and unusual punishments shall not be inflicted: but it is safe to affirm that punishments of torture . . . and all others in the same line of unnecessary cruelty, are forbidden by that amendment to the Constitution.[25]

Only with the introduction of the electric chair in New York was the issue of cruel and unusual punishment raised again. The 1890 case of *In re Kemmler* challenged the use of that new form of execution as cruel and unusual punishment, but the Court was unanimous in its decision that electrocution was not unconstitutional just because it was unusual. It also came very

Photo 14.1
Three ways to carry out a sentence.

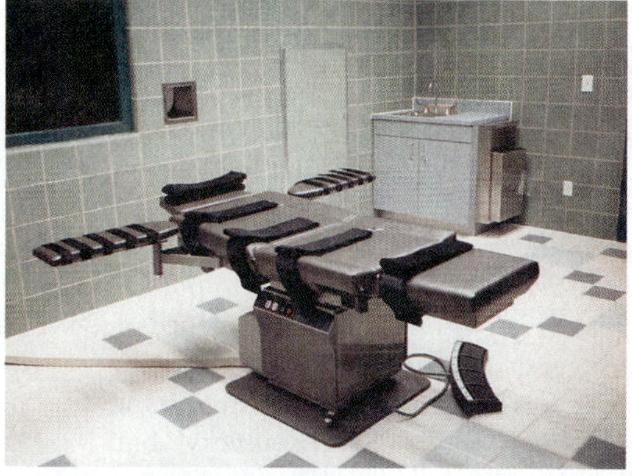

a. Lethal injection.
Chuck Robinson/AP Images.

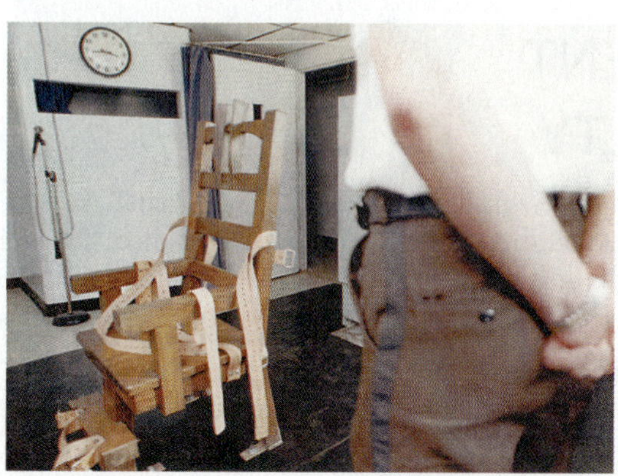

b. Electric chair.
Mark Foley/AP Images.

c. Gas chamber.
Julie Smith/AP Images.

close to employing the due process clause of the Fourteenth Amendment in the case, giving early warning that it might do so at a later, more substantial hearing. In the 1892 case of *O'Neil* v. *Vermont,* the court again affirmed that the Eighth Amendment did not apply to the states but with three strong dissenting opinions. One of the dissenting justices wrote the following:

> That designation [cruel and unusual], it is true, is usually applied to punishments which inflict torture, such as the rack, the thumbscrew, the iron boot, the stretching of limbs and the like, which are attended with acute pain and suffering. The inhibition is directed not only against punishments of the character mentioned, but against all punishments which by their excessive length or severity are greatly disproportionate to the offenses charged. The whole inhibition is against that which is excessive.[26]

This logic, although a minority attitude at the time, prevailed to dominate the 1910 landmark case of *Weems* v. *United States,*[27] the first time the Court invalidated a penalty because the Court found it excessive. Clearly, excessive punishment had become as objectionable to the Court as what was inherently cruel. Not until 1947 did the Court decide another significant case on the issue of whether the Eighth Amendment applied to the states. In the case of *Louisiana ex rel. Francis* v. *Resweber,*[28] the Court was virtually unanimous in its agreement that the infliction of unnecessary pain is forbidden by traditional Anglo-American legal practice. This unusual case involved a convicted murderer (Francis) who was sentenced to die in the electric chair. The electrical system malfunctioned at the execution, so Francis was not killed the first time the current passed through his body.[29] Pleading that a second attempt at electrocution would be cruel and unusual punishment, Francis took his case to the Supreme Court. Although the case brought out many of the crucial Eighth Amendment issues, the Court stopped short of enforcing that amendment on the states, and Francis lost his appeal on a 5-to-4 split. He thus was finally executed, but his case paved the way for several that came in the 1960s.

The next significant case we note is the landmark 1972 case on capital punishment, *Furman* v. *Georgia.* The Court's decision was 5 to 4 in favor of a ban on using capital punishment as it was currently being practiced. Indeed, the justices were so widely divided on the issue that each wrote a separate opinion. Only two of the justices (Brennan and Marshall) held that the death penalty was cruel and unusual punishment under all circumstances. The due process clause of the Fourteenth Amendment was evoked, leaving the states with the problem of passing legislation that met the Court's requirements, as described in the opinion of Chief Justice Warren Burger:

> The legislatures are free to eliminate capital punishment for specific crimes or to carve out limited exceptions to a general abolition of the penalty, without adherence to the conceptual strictures of the Eighth Amendment. The legislatures can and should make an assessment of the deterrent influence of capital punishment, both generally and as affecting the commission of specific types of crimes. If legislatures come to doubt the efficacy of capital punishment, they can abolish it either completely or on a selective basis. If new evidence persuades them that they acted unwisely, they can reverse their field and reinstate the penalty to the extent it is thought warranted. An Eighth Amendment ruling by judges cannot be made with such flexibility or discriminating precision.[30]

Although the minority opinion seemed to feel the Court had overstepped its jurisdiction, the tenor of the dissenting remarks made it clear the justices were willing to hear a new appeal when the findings in *Furman* were challenged. The high level of legislative activity in the states, seeking to reinstate the death penalty under the Court's new guidelines, suggested there would be a challenge in the near future. Although *Furman* gave a new lease on life[31] to the 600-plus men who had been sitting on death row,[32] new death sentences continue to be handed down, awaiting final resolution of the issue.

Two recent decisions by the Supreme Court have further limited the use of the death penalty. In ***Atkins* v. *Virginia***, the Court held that it is unconstitutional to execute defendants with mental retardation. This was followed in 2005 with *Roper* v. *Simmons,* in which the court struck down the use of the death penalty for juveniles. Since 1976, 22 defendants had been executed for crimes committed as juveniles.

PROSECUTOR'S DISCRETION

As yet unresolved is the controversial role of discretion in the decision to seek the death penalty. The prosecutor must enter a formal charge and may or may not seek the death penalty. One factor that affects the decision to seek the death penalty is the race of the victim. In South Carolina, for example, studies show that if the victim is white and the offender black, then the black offender is eight times as likely to face a death sentence as that same offender would face if the victim were black.[33] Keil and Vito found that, in Kentucky, blacks who killed whites, as compared to other homicide offenders, had a more-than-average chance of being charged with a death-eligible crime (by the prosecutor) and sentenced to die (by the jury). They also found 13 cases in their study's time frame in which whites murdered blacks and prosecutors failed to seek the death penalty even once. Prosecutors have a **gatekeeper function** in the judicial system: If they choose not to seek the death penalty, then the jury cannot impose it. Keil and Vito suggest the following:

key term

Gatekeeper function
Process by which the criminal justice official exercises authority to move the case to the next-higher level.

> It may be to the prosecutor's political and career advantage to treat murders in which the black kills a white more seriously than murders involving other racial combinations, even when such murders have the same legal attributes of seriousness. Juries may find it socially expedient to act in the same way in sentencing offenders to death.[34]

Radelet reaches a similar conclusion using status attributes (race, social class, economic status) in his study of executions since 1608.[35]

The effect of offender's race in light of the race of the victim suggested racism at work in the pre-*Furman* years. The death row population has since shifted from a majority black population to a more diverse population in which blacks are only about one-third of the offenders on death row. Yet the race of the victim continues to play a major role. More than 80 percent of the murder victims whose cases resulted in an execution were white; nationally, about half of the murder victims were white. Does racism jaundice the decisions of law enforcement, prosecutors, judges, and juries? The debate continues.

DETERRENCE OF THE DEATH PENALTY

key term

Deterrent
The hope that a criminal sanction will stop potential offenders by inflicting suffering on actual offenders.

Although there are substantial claims that the death penalty may act as a **deterrent** to others, depending on the ideological position of the debater, one should realize that if the death penalty were a deterrent, no crime would occur. Those who favor the death penalty ("retentionists") point out that a lighthouse sits beside a dangerous rock-strewn coastline to warn ships away. The fact that a few ill-fated ships run afoul of the dangers the lighthouse proclaims is no reason to tear the lighthouse down—or to abolish capital punishment. For those ships the lighthouse warns away, there is no evidence of deterrence, although deterrence has no doubt been in effect. Only the ones that ignore to their peril the lighthouse's warning will show up as "failures" of the deterrent effect.

It is also interesting to note that the South had the highest murder rate and also accounts for over 80 percent of the executions, whereas the Northeast, which accounts for less than 3 percent of all executions, had the lowest murder rate. Table 14.3 shows the murder rates per 100,000 population across various regions of the country.

Public Opinion and the Death Penalty

The American public's attitude toward the death penalty has fluctuated wildly, as reflected in public opinion polls. Although support for the death penalty has declined over the past decade, most polls continue to show support for the death penalty in the abstract (that is, if no alternative is considered)—with about 60 percent approval for cases involving murder—and several opinions are somewhat softened when the public is given viable alternatives. As shown in Figure 14.2, support for the death penalty falls to only 40 percent when the alternative is life

table 14.3 **Murder Rate per 100,000, 2002–2012**

	2002	2004	2006	2008	2010	2012	Executions since 1976
South	6.8	6.6	6.8	6.6	5.6	5.5	1106
West	5.7	5.7	5.6	5.0	4.2	4.2	84
Midwest	5.7	4.7	5.0	4.8	4.4	4.7	158
Northeast	4.1	4.2	4.5	4.2	4.2	3.8	4
National	5.6	5.5	5.7	5.4	4.8	4.7	

SOURCE: Death Penalty Information Center (2012), "Murder Rates by State and Nationally," http://www.deathpenaltyinfo.org/murder-rates-nationally-and-state.

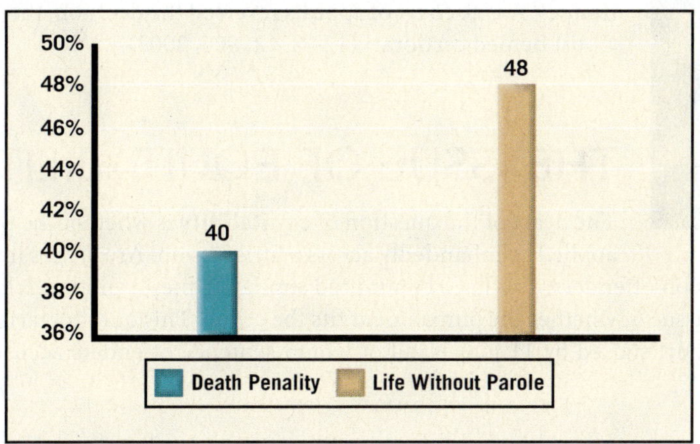

figure 14.2

Support for Life without Parole.

SOURCE: M. Lagos, "Field Poll: Less Voter Support for Death Penalty," *San Francisco Chronicle*, September 29, 2011, http://www.sfgate.com/crime/article/Field-Poll-Less-voter-support-for-death-penalty-2299084.php (accessed September 13, 2014).

without parole. However, this fact seems to have as little impact on death penalty legislation as public opinion has on gun control. Those who advocate the death penalty claim there is no viable alternative that provides equal protection for society. They would also argue that the seriousness of the crime requires the maximum penalty.[36] The 2010 survey shows that many would be supportive of a true life sentence. The number of offenders sentenced in the nation to life without parole has been markedly increasing since 1992 (see Table 14.4).

Many who oppose the life sentence as a replacement for the death penalty observe that the parole laws in many states make it possible for a "lifer" to get out in a relatively brief time.[37] Usually, those who receive life sentences become eligible for parole in about 13 years, but the national average served under a life sentence is currently about 25 years. The proposed answer to this argument is to remove the hope of parole from a prisoner given a life sentence (referred to as **life certain**).

key term

Life certain
Judge's sentence that precludes parole eligibility; order to incarcerate the offender until dead.

The chance that an innocent person might be convicted also detracts from the acceptability of the irreversible death penalty.[38] Since 1974, 135 death row inmates have been exonerated.

table 14.4 **Growth of Life without Parole**

Year	Life without Parole Sentences
1992	12,453
2003	33,633
2008	40,174
2012	49,180

SOURCE: Ashley Nellis, *The Prison Project, Life Goes On: The Historic Rise in Life Sentences in America* (Washington DC: TSP, 2013), p. 13.

Photo 14.2

Kerry Max Cook, recently exonerated by DNA after 22 years on death row in Texas.
Robin Marchant/Contributor/Getty Images Entertainment/Getty Images.

The Controversy Continues

Many death row inmates profess their innocence, and recently developed scientific techniques (such as DNA testing) have established the factual innocence of at least a dozen inmates on death row, some of whom were within days of executions and all of whom have subsequently been released.

In 2002, Justice Jed Rakoff, U.S. district judge in the Southern District of New York, addressed the problem of executing the innocent before they might establish their innocence. He concluded that this would deprive them of their opportunity to prove their innocence and thus would be a violation of rights under the Fifth Amendment. Judge Rakoff then declared the federal death penalty statute unconstitutional.[39] A U.S. court of appeals reversed the decision; the U.S. Supreme Court denied certiorari (124 S. Ct. 807, 2003).

THE ISSUE OF EQUITABILITY

The heart of the question of **equitability** is whether the punishment is applied evenhandedly across a jurisdiction. Are judges imposing similar sentences on offenders who have committed similar crimes? Another related question involves the issue of whether the punishment fits the crime. This question arises in the case of a single court staffed by 11 judges, all of whom sentence offenders accused of driving

correctional **practice 14.1**

The Execution Process Today in Ohio

About 24 hours before a condemned inmate is scheduled to be executed, he will be taken from the Ohio State Penitentiary, where the state keeps death row inmates, to the Southern Ohio Correctional Facility, where executions are carried out.

The inmate will then be able to order his "special meal," which is served about 4 p.m. the day before the execution is to be carried out. He is also given an examination to determine if the medical personnel on the state's execution team will have any difficulties locating suitable veins to insert the shunts that will carry the lethal drugs into the inmate's system.

The inmate is housed in the state's death house, located in the same small building where the execution will be carried out, and he has access to a television and a radio. He also is given visitation time with friends, family, spiritual advisers, and his attorneys the evening prior to his execution.

If the inmate is not awake by 6 a.m., prison staff will wake him up, and he will be offered the prison's breakfast as well as the chance to shower before donning his execution garb. He also will be allowed a final set of visits with family and others.

Shortly before the inmate is to enter the execution chamber, the prison's warden will read the death warrant, and medical personnel will insert the shunts for the drugs. The shunts are typically placed in the arms.

After the inmate is prepared, he will walk 17 steps down a hallway and be strapped to the injection table in the death chamber. Execution team members will examine the tubing that will carry the drugs into the inmate, and a low-pressure saline drip will begin to flow through the lines into the inmate. The drip will constantly flow throughout the process to ensure the lines remain open.

The warden will then offer the inmate the opportunity to make a final statement on which there is no set time limit. After the inmate's last words, the warden will signal the execution team members who are in control of the drugs, and the first drug, thiopental sodium, a sedative, will be injected into the inmate through the tubing. After the sedative has been administered, the warden will call the inmate's name, shake his shoulder, and pinch his arm to make sure he is unconscious. An execution team member also will examine the equipment to make sure it is functioning properly. If there is a problem with the lines or the inmate remains conscious, the lines may be moved and a second dose of the sedative administered. If the inmate is deemed unconscious, then the second drug will be administered. After the drug has been administered, a curtain will be closed, and the inmate will be checked for signs of life, typically by the Scioto County coroner. The curtain will then be reopened, and the warden will announce the inmate's time of death.

SOURCE: Brad Dicken, "The Last 24 Hours of a Condemned Inmate," *Chronicle Online*, June 3, 2009, http://chronicle.northcoastnow.com/2009/06/03/the-last-24-hours-of-a-condemned-inmate/.

under the influence of alcohol. One judge may routinely impose fines of $100 on all offenders to be sentenced; another sentencing judge may impose 30 days in jail plus 30 hours of community service. The other nine judges may place their offenders on probation, one condition of which may be compulsory attendance at meetings of Alcoholics Anonymous. Which one, if any, of these punishments best fits the crime: a fine, jail time plus community service, or probation with mandatory attendance in an alcohol-avoidance program?

key term

Equitability
Whether the punishment is applied evenhandedly across a jurisdiction.

In terms of the death penalty, perhaps the question could best be phrased like this: "Are blacks who kill white victims more likely to receive a death sentence than white killers who murder black victims?" As noted earlier, the answer is most certainly yes. Retentionists might argue that such selectivity is immaterial.

Behavioral science may not provide the most adequate basis for arguments against the equitable application of the death penalty, but available evidence suggests that the death penalty is not evenly applied and may be wanton and even freakish in its imposition. That conclusion, in more tentative form, can be found in a report by the General Accounting Office[40] as well as in the work of Keil and Vito, cited previously. The execution process is described in Correctional Practice 14.1.

Correctional Practice 14.1 walks through the steps of the execution process as currently practiced in Ohio, and our discussion now turns to another aspect of capital punishment: women and the death penalty.

WOMEN AND THE DEATH PENALTY

In general, both the sentencing-to-death rate and the death row population remain very small for women in comparison to those for men. Actual execution of female offenders is quite rare, with only 571 documented instances beginning with the first in 1632. These 571 female executions constitute less than 3 percent of the total of 20,425 confirmed executions in the United States since 1608. In the past 100 years, 40 women have been executed in the United States, and 13 female offenders have been executed since 1976. The most recent execution was on December 3, 2013, in Texas.

Death sentences for and actual executions of female offenders are also rare in comparison to such events for male offenders. In fact, women are more likely to be dropped out of the system the further the capital punishment process progresses. Following in summary outline form are the data indicating this screening-out effect:

- Women account for about 1 in 10 (10 percent) murder arrests.
- Women account for only 1 in 50 (2.0 percent) death sentences imposed at the trial level.
- Women account for only 1 in 67 (1.5 percent) persons presently on death row.
- Women account for only 1 in 100 (1 percent) persons actually executed since *Furman*.[41]

Homicides by women are less likely to involve the felony murders and other specific circumstances that are more likely to result in death sentences. Women usually kill friends and relatives, for which they are unlikely to get a sentence of death. Of the 3,108 inmates on death row at the start of 2008, only 61 offenders (or 1 of every 51 of the condemned on death row) were women, even though about 1 of 10 arrestees for murder is a woman.[42] Correctional Practice 14.2 tells the stories of 8 of the 13 women executed in the United States since 1976.

JUVENILES AND THE DEATH PENALTY

The United States still endorses capital punishment as a response to crime, particularly homicide. Fluctuating but substantial public support remains for the death penalty, particularly for homicide. In a 2010 Pew Research Center poll, some 62 percent of respondents endorsed the death penalty in general. There is noticeably less support for the death penalty for juveniles; 79 percent of the respondents in one 2003 survey opposed capital punishment for juvenile offenders.[43]

The U.S. Supreme Court ruled in 1988 that a death penalty for a person committing a crime while age 15 or under was "cruel and unusual punishment" and thus a violation of the Eighth Amendment.[44] A year later, the Court decided that the death penalty was not cruel and unusual if imposed on 16-year-old offenders.[45] In 2005, the Court held that the Eighth and Fourteenth Amendments forbid the execution of offenders who were under the age of 18 when their crime was committed.[46]

The Supreme Court has also ruled on the constitutionality of executing those with intellectual disability, as described in Policy Position 14.1, and Correctional Practice 14.3 notes the prevalence of intellectual disability in as well as other characteristics of death row inmates.

JUSTIFICATIONS

Nowhere else in the correctional system can the justifications for capital punishment be seen so clearly than in the area of the murderer. Three major justifications for the death penalty are collectively referred to as the **retentionist** position and include revenge, just deserts, and protection. Those advocating **revenge** as a justification argue that victims, survivors, and the state are entitled to "closure." In this view, only after the execution can psychological, emotional, and social wounds begin to heal. Executing the offender permits that closure. This argument is sometimes referred to as "life for a life."

Other proponents argue that some persons are beyond rehabilitation and that their acts are so egregious an affront to societal standards and humanity that the only adequate response is the penalty of death. This is sometimes referred to as the **just deserts argument**.

Finally is the **societal protection argument**. Once executed, the dead cannot continue their violent and frequently murderous life course. They can commit no further crime. In this sense, social defense is strengthened when the offender is permanently disabled through execution. Many members of society believe that all three arguments form a sufficient basis for retaining and imposing the death penalty, even on mentally retarded, mentally ill, and (previously) juvenile offenders. (In June 2002, the Supreme Court declared execution of persons with mental retardation unconstitutional.[47])

key term

Retentionist
Person seeking to retain the death penalty.

key term

Revenge
Seeking retribution for a harm inflicted.

key term

Just deserts argument
Argument that offenders should receive severe punishment because of the nature of the crime committed.

key term

Societal protection argument
The argument that once executed, the offender cannot commit another crime, thus protecting society.

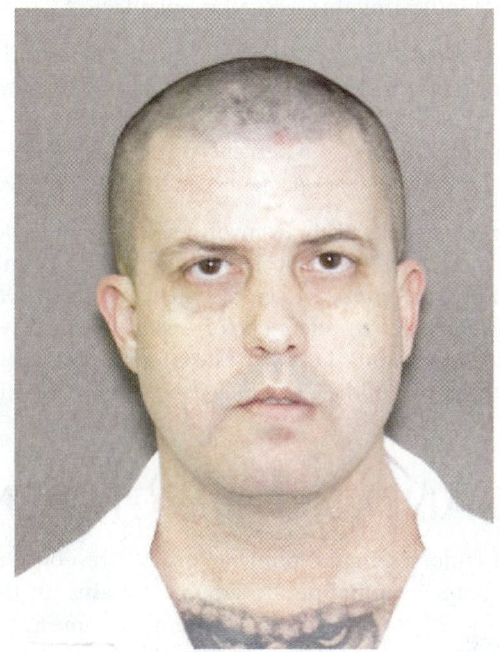

Photo 14.3
Jerry Martin was executed in Texas on December 3, 2013, for killing a correctional officer during an escape attempt in 2007.
Texas Department of Criminal Justice.

correctional **practice 14.2**

Executed Females

Thirteen females have been executed since 1976. Here are several of their stories:

- **Velma Barfield** in North Carolina on November 2, 1984. She was in a relationship with Stuart Taylor, who was a widower. She forged checks on Taylor's account to pay for her addiction. Fearing that she had been found out, she mixed an arsenic-based rat poison into his beer and tea. Taylor became very ill. As his condition worsened, she took him to the hospital, where he died a few days later. There was an autopsy that found the cause of Taylor's death was arsenic poisoning, and Velma was arrested and charged with his murder. At the trial, her defense pleaded insanity, but this was not accepted, and she was convicted. The jury recommended the death sentence. Velma appeared cold and uncaring on the stand and gave the district attorney a round of applause when he made his closing speech.
- **Karla Faye Tucker** in Texas on February 3, 1998. When she was 13, she began traveling with the Allman Brothers Band. In her early twenties, she started to hang out with bikers, and on June 13, 1983, she entered the home of another biker with two men to steal a motorcycle. During the robbery, two persons were killed, and one of the men and Tucker were convicted of committing murder with a pickaxe. This case entered the U.S. and international news because she had become a born-again Christian while in prison, and George W. Bush, then governor of Texas, had to decide on her request for clemency, which he ultimately denied.
- **Christina Riggs** in Arkansas on May 2, 2000. Riggs, a licensed nurse, was convicted of murder by smothering her two preschool-aged children in their beds at the family's Sherwood home. She wrote suicide notes saying, "I hope one day you will forgive me for taking my life and the life of my children. But I can't live like this anymore, and I couldn't bear to leave my children behind to be a burden on you or to be separated and raised apart from their fathers and live knowing their mother killed herself." Riggs then took 28 Elavil tablets, normally a lethal dose, and injected herself with enough undiluted potassium chloride to kill five people. The next day, police officers entered her apartment, found Riggs, and rushed her to the hospital. During the death penalty phase, Riggs would not allow attorneys to put on a defense, saying she wanted a death sentence. The jury obliged, and she was sentenced to death by lethal injection. Riggs said "Thank you" and squeezed her attorney's hand.
- **Wanda Jean Allen** in Oklahoma on January 11, 2001. She was sentenced to death in 1989 for killing her lover, Gloria Leathers, in Oklahoma City in 1988. The two women, who had met in prison, had a turbulent relationship. Leathers's death followed a protracted argument between the couple that began at a local shop, continued at their home, and culminated outside a police station. Allen maintained she had acted in self-defense, claiming that Leathers had struck her in the face with a hand rake during the confrontation at the house and that outside the police station Leathers had again come at her with the rake. Allen shot Leathers. The wound to Allen's face from the rake was still visible when she was photographed in jail. Later in 1995, a psychologist conducting a comprehensive evaluation of Wanda Jean Allen found "clear and convincing evidence of cognitive and sensory-motor deficits and brain dysfunction," possibly linked to an adolescent head injury.
- **Aileen Wuornos** in Florida on October 9, 2002. Wuornos was a prostitute and convicted serial killer who was sentenced to death by the state of Florida in 1992. She ultimately received five additional death sentences. Wuornos admitted to killing seven men, in separate incidents, all of whom she claimed raped her (or attempted to) while she was working as a prostitute. The 2003 movie *Monster*, starring Charlize Theron and Christina Ricci, tells Wuornos's story from the moment she met Selby Wall (based on Wuornos's lover and four-year companion, Tyria Moore) until her first conviction for murder.
- **Frances Newton** in Texas on September 14, 2005. She was executed for the April 7, 1987, murder of her 23-year-old her husband Adrian; her son Alton, 7; and daughter Farrah, 21 months. The prosecution suggested that the motive for the killings was to collect the $100,000 life insurance policy. Newton said that a drug dealer killed the three. The Houston police claimed that her husband, Adrian Newton, was a drug dealer and was in debt to his supplier. Newton maintained her innocence from her first interrogation in 1987 until her execution in 2005.
- **Teresa Lewis** in Virginia on September 23, 2010. She was executed for the October 30, 2002, murder of her husband and stepson in an attempt to claim life insurance money. The murder was carried out by two hired gunmen, both of whom were sentenced to life in prison. Lewis was regarded as the mastermind of the murders at the time of her trial, though later analysis would suggest that with her low IQ and dependency disorder, she was manipulated by the gunmen.
- **Kimberly McCarthy** in Texas on June 26, 2013.She was executed for the 1997 murder of a 71-year-old retired college professor who was her neighbor. Attorneys for McCarthy filed motions to stay her execution on the grounds that jury selection was tainted by racial bias and that McCarthy's original attorney did not provide adequate representation. McCarthy was the five-hundredth person executed in Texas since the reinstatement of the death penalty.

SOURCE: Death Penalty Information Center, "Women and the Death Penalty," http://www.deathpenaltyinfo.org/women-and-death-penalty (accessed September 13, 2014).

policy position 14.1

The Death Penalty and the Mentally Challenged

On June 20, 2002, the Supreme Court issued a landmark ruling ending the execution of those with intellectual disability. In *Atkins v. Virginia*, the Court held that it is a violation of the Eighth Amendment ban on cruel unusual punishment to execute death row inmates with "mental retardation." The decision reflects the national consensus which has formed on this issue.

In 1989, the U.S. Supreme Court had upheld (5 to 4) the constitutionality of executing those with intellectual disability in *Penry v. Lynaugh* (492 U.S. 302). The Court said that "mental retardation" should be a mitigating factor to be considered by the jury during sentencing. Writing for the majority, Justice Sandra Day O'Connor said that a "national consensus" had not developed against executing those with "mental retardation."

At the time, only two states, Maryland and Georgia, prohibited such executions. Between the *Penry* and *Atkins* decisions, 16 additional states enacted laws prohibiting the execution of the "mentally retarded." The federal death penalty statute also forbids such executions. Prior to *Atkins v. Virginia*, 18 states plus the federal government did not allow the execution of those with "mental retardation": Arizona, Arkansas, Colorado, Connecticut, Florida, Georgia, Indiana, Kansas, Kentucky, Maryland, Missouri, Nebraska, New Mexico, New York, North Carolina, South Dakota, Tennessee, and Washington.

Source: Death Penalty Information Center, "Intellectual Disability and the Death Penalty," http://www.deathpenaltyinfo.org/intellectual-disability-and-death-penalty#Atkins (accessed November 29, 2013).

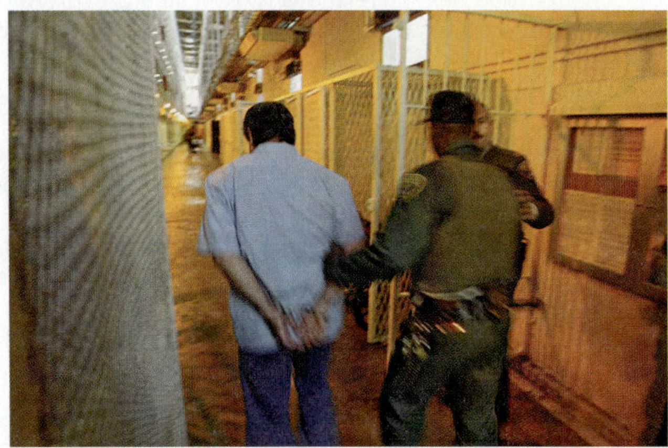

Photo 14.4

A prisoner on death row at San Quentin Prison, California, is led back to his cell in the East Block, holding 731 condemned inmates.
AP Images.

correctional practice 14.3

Characteristics of Death Row Inmates

Surprisingly, there are few studies of and resultantly little known about death row inmates. There are problems in using official institutional records, clinical studies, research, demographic information, and anecdotal commentaries to extrapolate such data. Thus, the major source of information appears to be the Death Penalty Information Center (http://www.deathpenaltyinfo.org/).

There were almost 3,100 death row inmates as of May 21, 2014. Such inmates are disproportionately southern males, a large proportion of whom have been sentenced for murder. Racial characteristics show the larger portion to be white males, but, as noted earlier in the chapter, the race of the victims remains controversial. Far fewer white males are on death row for killing black victims; blacks who kill whites are much more likely to be sentenced to death and thus sitting on death row. The race of the victim seems to be important in the sentencing decisions made by justice gatekeepers.

In general, death row inmates are academically deficient and score lower on tests measuring intellectual ability. They have high rates of neurological difficulties and disproportionate rates of substance abuse (both drug and alcohol), brain trauma, and broken childhood households. Psychological disorders are frequent and serious, and such disorders are made more difficult by the fact and experience of conditions of confinement as well as social isolation.

Yet the evidence suggests that death row inmates are not particularly violent in the institutions in which they are held. This may be due to the level of custody under which death row inmates are contained, but it may also reflect the absence of controlled substances in this environment, as many were under the influence of such substances when they committed their instant crimes.

As noted in Policy Position 14.1, the U.S. Supreme Court determined that intellectually disabled offenders (usually defined as scoring 70 or less on intelligence tests, although this value is higher in some states) are barred from execution (*Atkins v. Virginia*). Some states (such as Texas) are not eager to reveal existing intelligence quotients in their records regarding the intellectual disablement of their inmates (*In re Campbell*).

SOURCE: Mark Cunningham and Mark Vigen, "Death Row Inmate Characteristics, Adjustment, and Confinement: A Critical Review of the Literature," *Behavioral Sciences and the Law* 20 (2002): 191–210; Fifth Circuit, *In re Campbell*, No. 14-20293, May 12, 2014.

Other persons favoring the death penalty argue that capital punishment has a deterrent effect and that increasing the probabilities of being executed tends to *reduce* the crime rate.[48] Some retentionists argue that Christian scriptures mandate the death penalty;[49] others argue that society has a *duty* to impose the death penalty for heinous crimes because any other punishment would denigrate both the values that crime violates and the victim.

Finally, some retentionists argue that there are killers on death row who, if not executed but eventually released, would continue to kill other victims. Case studies of certain offenders whose death sentences were commuted to life in prison and were subsequently paroled only to kill again are used as examples that prove their dangerousness. This position is sometimes called the "mad dog" argument in favor of the death penalty.[50] The debate continues.

THE DEATH PENALTY AND TERRORISM

The federal government and the U.S. Code of Military Justice have death penalty statutes that permit capital punishment for designated offenses. The accused would be tried in either a federal court or a military tribunal, depending on the jurisdiction. If tried in federal court, the panoply of rights, immunities, and protections afforded under the U.S. Constitution would apply, including rules of procedure and evidence. The U.S. Code of Military Justice restricts many of the rights otherwise available to civilians. At the time of this writing, it is unclear which, if either, jurisdiction would be appropriate for terrorists.

By midyear 2005, a number of captured Taliban and al-Qaeda prisoners had been taken to military detention camp "X-ray" at Guantanamo Bay, Cuba. Such detainees are believed to pose a threat to the United States or have intelligence value. Exactly how many detainees have been imprisoned and their identities are unknown.

Detainees may face a military trial, a trial in U.S. courts, prosecution in their homelands if returned, or trial in an international court. The first two of those options could result in the death penalty.

The nation's policy toward this special group of offenders challenges national and international law as the government attempts to redefine criminal actions to avoid Articles of War and rights guaranteed under the Geneva Convention. If defendants were punished with limited or no due process, would there be secret trials? How could the accused call witnesses to offer evidence to refute the prosecutor's evidence? How could exculpatory evidence be offered? Will appeals be permitted? It is challenges such as these that not only sharpen the contrast between a government and citizenry under law but also validate the necessity of adhering firmly to the rights, liberties, and freedom guaranteed by the U.S. Constitution.

Photo 14.5

Death row inmates exercising in 8 × 12 cages, which they must enter and leave in handcuffs.

Penni Gladstone/San Francisco Chronicle/Corbis.

THE COST OF THE DEATH PENALTY

Although some may argue that it is cheaper to invoke the death penalty than to incarcerate an offender in prison for life, studies do not bear that out. For example, a study concluded that the cost of the death penalty in California has totaled over $4 billion since 1978.[51] This figure is over and above what it would have cost that state had it utilized life without parole instead of death. Some findings from various states are as follows:[52]

- Washington: At the trial level, death penalty cases are estimated to generate roughly $470,000 in additional costs to the prosecution and defense over the cost of trying the same case as an aggravated murder without the death penalty. On direct appeal, the cost of appellate defense averages $100,000 more in death penalty cases than in non–death penalty murder cases.

- Tennessee: Death penalty cases cost an average of 48 percent more than the average cost of trials in which prosecutors seek life imprisonment.
- Kansas: The investigation costs for death sentence cases were about three times greater than for non–death sentence cases. The appeal costs were 21 times greater.
- Indiana: The cost of the death penalty is 38 percent greater than the total costs of life-without-parole sentences.
- North Carolina: Death penalty cases cost $2.16 million more per execution than non–death penalty murder cases with a life sentence.
- Florida: The state would save $51 million each year by punishing all first-degree murderers with life in prison without parole.
- California: The death penalty costs $114 million a year beyond the cost of simply keeping the convicts locked up for life. This figure does not include the millions spent on court costs to prosecute capital cases.
- Ohio: Defending and prosecuting death row inmates cost taxpayers at least half a million dollars and sometimes more than $1 million per inmate.

Clearly, there is a high financial cost to the death penalty. Whereas some might argue that it is a cost that is worth bearing, others believe that this is one more reason to abolish the death penalty.

COMMITMENTS TO DEATH ROW CONTINUE

With 3,108 prisoners on death row across the nation (see Figure 14.3) and the number of executions still high, what will be the public's reaction if an unprecedented number of executions occurs in the next few years? Administrators, politicians, legislators, and the public wrestle with what to do about the backlog of incarcerated death row inmates awaiting execution.

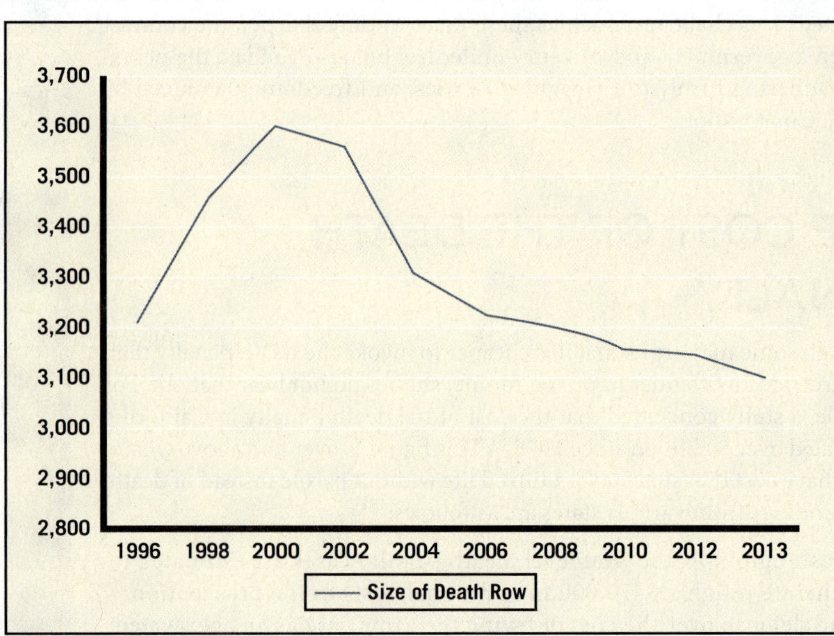

figure 14.3

Size of Death Row by State for Selected Years.

SOURCE: Death Penalty Information Center, "Death Row Inmates by State," http://www.deathpenaltyinfo.org/death-row-inmates-state-and-size-death-row-year.

Summary

Outline the History of the Death Penalty in the Nation and Legal Provisions for It

With the exception of the early Quakers in Pennsylvania, the original 13 states initially had the death penalty, the statutes for which frequently included biblical scriptures as justifications for those statutes. The U.S. Constitution and the Bill of Rights list defenses for improper justice processes. More recent U.S. Supreme Court decisions have placed limitations on the death penalty regarding who may be executed and the means for such executions.

Describe Forms of Execution

Historically, many countries executed death penalty offenders harshly and used a variety of methods, ranging from burning at the stake and drawing and quartering to shooting, hanging, crucifixion, impaling, and beheading. In this nation, shooting and hanging were early methods of execution, but electrocution, lethal gas, and lethal injections have been widely implemented in more recent years. Currently, the state of Tennessee now permits only electrocution as the sole procedure for executing offenders.

Describe the Effects of Decisions of the U.S. Supreme Court on Capital Punishment

In addition to the Bill of Rights and constitutional protections and procedures guaranteed to the accused, in regard to the death penalty the Supreme Court has generally addressed cruel and unusual punishment, prohibitions against torturous execution processes, and defining of limitations on who can be death eligible. The effect of these decisions is to lessen the probability of executing offenders by requiring adherence to constitutional muster and earlier case law as well as the emerging standards of decency in a developing society. Currently, there is controversy over the types and effects of drugs used in lethal injections, cruel and torturous death in the process of execution, forbidding execution of the intellectually challenged, and forbidding executions based on age of the offender at time of the death-eligible crime.

Summarize the Eighth Amendment's Impacts on the Death Penalty

The Eighth Amendment to the U.S. Constitution notes, "Excessive bail shall not be required, nor excessive fines imposed, nor cruel and unusual punishments inflicted." This amendment's immediate application in light of the death penalty is whether the death penalty is excessively cruel and whether the punishment is unusual. Signal cases in this area deal with such procedures as executing the offender by lethal injection if the drug dose does not immediately kill and if the person undergoing execution also suffered from a lingering and painful death, whether a blotched execution can be repeated, whether the intellectual competencies of the accused prevents the individual from understanding the meaning of his or her acts and the state's execution, and related questions. Court decisions have limited states in the application of the death penalty and in their procedures for doing so.

Explain How Prosecutorial Discretion Impacts the Death Penalty

The death penalty process generally requires that the government, through a prosecutor who favors the imposition of death, charge the accused with a death-eligible crime. If the prosecutor, as gatekeeper, does not charge the accused with a death-eligible crime, the accused cannot be executed. This makes for a few jurisdictions in which death sentences are frequent and whose criminals form most of the population of death row inmates. Said differently, some jurisdictions frequently seek the death penalty for the accused and subsequently produce the largest proportion of death row inmates. Behind every death row occupant is a prosecuting attorney who wanted to put the offender to death and used prosecutorial discretion to achieve that intent.

Draw Appropriate Conclusions about the Deterrent Effects of the Death Penalty

Deterrence is a major argument for the use of the death penalty. In general deterrence, the intent is to use the execution of one offender to demonstrate the will and strength of the jurisdiction to kill those who might commit certain crimes. Specific deterrence means that the offender was executed and will not be able to commit more such egregious crime. Investigations to date have failed to find sufficient evidence supporting the deterrence argument. Other researchers look at executions as having a brutalizing effect and propose that they act to encourage others to commit death-eligible crime.

Describe Forms of Capital Punishment

Lethal injection requires a mix of drugs that effectively end life with a "one-two" punch, stopping breathing and then stopping the heart from beating. Yet the most lethal drug combination requires importation of the necessary drugs to kill the perpetrator. Major drug manufacturers in America do not manufacture the most effective and highly desired chemicals; these are produced in European countries that reject the death penalty. As we go to press, the possible future of lethal injection appears to be in doubt. At this time, there is no agreement on which drugs to use in the lethal injection approach. Other means of execution are hanging, electrocution, firing squad, and lethal gas (gas chamber).

Describe How Executions Are Carried Out and the Problems Associated with Executions

When the death warrant is received by the prison administration, the offender is isolated and enters the death watch (inmates under death warrant are not permitted to kill themselves). The institution's execution team rehearses the execution to avoid errors, and the inmate enters the execution area (usually the death chamber). The warden or superintendent is legally authorized to signal to the execution team to proceed with the process. Witnesses as appropriate can view the execution, and a medical officer pronounces the inmate dead. The curtains are then closed, and the witnesses file out. The body is removed and transported as previously authorized.

Problems include a last-minute stay of execution that creates emotional issues for all parties to the execution, personal impact on witnesses, demonstrations outside the prison by both retentionists and abolitionists, reaction of the media to the event, and possible later exoneration after the fact.

Explain Why There are so Few Females on Death Row in America

Death sentences and executions for female offenders are rare in comparison to such events for male offenders. Women account for only 10 percent of murder arrests, some 2 percent of death sentences imposed after trial, and only about 1 percent of persons actually executed. In general, the further the females are processed into the justice system, the more likely they are to receive leniency.

Compare and Contrast the Abolitionist and Retentionist Positions on the Death Penalty

Retentionists believe that public safety is best served through execution of offenders, setting an example to deter other would-be murderers from committing that crime. They believe the state must uphold punishments for all crime and that murderers are free-acting and rational persons who willfully and deliberately commit premeditated murder. They argue that sacred scriptures justify and demand the death penalty: Such evil persons must be removed from society, and the death penalty is the final removal and action for increased public safety. Retentionists want to retain the death penalty.

Abolitionists argue that most death-eligible persons were not exercising free will during the time of their crimes and that most were at least somewhat incapacitated (high on drugs or alcohol, mentally ill, unable to determine right from wrong, or defending themselves from attach by their victims). They believe the death penalty to be excessive, cruel, highly selective, and infrequently deserved and that the state should not kill anyone, even those who kill. Abolitionists want to abolish the death penalty.

Identify Who May Not Be Executed in the Nation

The U.S. Supreme Court has determined that the mentally ill, mentally deficient, juveniles under age 18 when committing their crime, and those significantly impaired through excessive consumption of drugs or alcohol (or both) are not eligible to receive the death penalty. Other mitigating factors that make an offender ineligible are ineffective legal counsel, impaired legal counsel, and insanity, any of which raise constitutional issues and allow the possibility that such offenders could be excluded from being sentenced to death.

Summarize the Characteristics of Current Death Row Prisoners

The majority of inmates on death row are white men from the southern states, most of whom were convicted of murder. In terms of racial factors, African Americans who killed white residents are overrepresented; few white men on death row were convicted of killing an African American. Death-row inmates had disruptive and traumatic lives as children and evince mental and physical illnesses, which the isolation in death rows complicates and exacerbates. Many have low intelligence scores. In general, they are less violent while incarcerated than other inmates; the comparatively few female death row inmates are even less violent.

Compare and Contrast the Costs of the Death Penalty and a Sentence of Life without Parole

Trial of those charged with committing a death-eligible crime is, in its process, very expensive. Collateral attack, deposition expenses, defense strategies, and other legal costs are higher in death-eligible cases. Even when convicted, the offender can and more likely will appeal the conviction and sentence, sometimes more than once to the same appeals court on a variety of issues, one at a time. Eventually, most such convictions will result in imprisonment and high security costs; the staff-to-inmate ratio is low, and 24-hour-a-day maximum- and death row security procedures are necessary. Appeals could be continued from behind the prison walls, increasing the legal costs burden of the state and defenders. It is by far less expensive to the state to secure a sentence penalty of life (or life without parole, or the old "life and a day") than it is to shoulder the immense costs of attempting to execute a death-eligible inmate.

Key Words

capital punishment, 298
execution, 298
Gregg v. *Georgia*, 299
capital crimes, 299
Furman v. *Georgia*, 300
arbitrary, 300
intent to kill, 300
malice aforethought, 300
death penalty, 301
cruel and unusual punishment, 301
gatekeeper function, 304
Atkins v. Virginia, 303
deterrent, 304
life certain, 305
equitability, 306
retentionist, 308
revenge, 308
just deserts argument, 308
societal protection argument, 308

Review Questions

1. Explain the guidelines that came out of *Furman* v. *Georgia* and its related decisions.
2. Prepare an argument for the retention of the death penalty and then prepare an argument against it.
3. How does the race of the victim affect being charged with a capital crime?
4. Who were the first to die in America by electrocution, by the gas chamber, and by the use of lethal injection? What are your reactions to each form?
5. Make the case that the death penalty should be abolished.

Application Case Studies

1. Three outstanding religious clerics in the United States have proposed to debate the use of the death penalty. One is a fundamentalist minister espousing the "use of biblical law" argument. The other two are adherents to the argument that the death penalty should never be used because it violates the "thou shall not kill" rule as well as the "Great Commandment," which states that the one rule by which to live is to love your God with all your heart, all your strength, and all your soul and to love thy neighbor as thyself. Three major television networks have agreed to carry the debate live and to broadcast a 30-minute question-and-answer session. You get to choose one question. What would it be?
2. You are a prosecuting attorney, and you are asked to defend the death penalty to a group of religious leaders in your community. What arguments would you make?
3. You are appealing the case of a mentally challenged murderer on death row; however, his intelligence quotient does not meet the threshold established by the U.S. Supreme Court. What arguments would you make?

Endnotes

1. Tim Robbins, director, *Dead Man Walking* (Hollywood, CA: Grammercy/Polygram Film Productions, 1995). This film was nominated for a number of Academy Awards. Susan Sarandon played the nun who tried to help save a condemned man's soul by counseling him to admit to the crimes, and she won the best actress Oscar for 1995.
2. Death Penalty Information Center, "Crime Punishable by the Death Penalty," http://www.deathpenaltyinfo.org/capitaloffenses.html. See also Bureau of Justice Statistics, "Capital Punishment Statistics," http://www.ojp.usdoj.gov/bjs/cp.htm (accessed October 29, 2008).
3. States that have recently abolished the death penalty include New Mexico (2009), Maryland (2013), and Connecticut (2012). However, the repeal was not retroactive, and each has inmates remaining on death row. Death Penalty Information Center, "States without the Death Penalty," http://www.deathpenaltyinfo.org/states-and-without-death-penalty.
4. See Chris Little, "Bible Supports the Death Penalty," http://i2i.org/Publications/Op-Eds/Other/op971029.htm (accessed February 12, 2003). See also "Death Penalty Debate," http://www.lexingtonprosecutor.com/death_penalty_debate.htm; "Seventeen Arguments for the Death Penalty," http://yesdeathpenalty.com/argument_1.htm; and http://www.prodeathpenalty.com (accessed October 28, 2008).
5. The most readable discussion of these issues can be found in P. Lewis, Harry Allen, Henry Mannle, and Harold Vetter, "A Post-*Furman* Profile of Florida's Condemned—A Question of Discrimination in Terms of the Race of the Victim and a Comment

on *Spinkellink* v. *Wainwright,*" *Stetson Law Review* 9:4 (Fall 1979): 1–45. The general public strongly supports the death penalty. A 2013 Gallup poll reports that 60 percent of adults nationwide support the death penalty, which is the lowest rate in more than 40 years. Death Penalty Information Center, "Death Penalty," http://www.deathpenaltyinfo.org/documents/gallup-10-29-13.pdf. See also John Arthur, "Racial Attitudes about Capital Punishment," *International Journal of Comparative and Applied Criminal Justice* 22:1 (1998): 131–144, and J. D. Unner and F. T. Cullen, "The Racial Divide in Support of the Death Penalty," *Social Forces* 85 (2007): 281–301.

6. Personnel required to participate in an execution are an often-ignored component of capital punishment. See Robert Johnson, *Death Work: A Study on the Modern Execution Process* (Belmont, CA: Wadsworth, 1998).
7. In February 2008, the Nebraska Supreme Court ruled that electrocution, the state's sole execution method, was unconstitutional. Up until then, Nebraska was the only state that required electrocution.
8. Harry Barnes and Negley Teeters, *New Horizons in Criminology* (New York: Prentice Hall, 1948), p. 309. In 1988, the average wait from conviction to execution was six years and eight months, but by 2006 it had increased to almost 12 years. John Bonczar and Tracy Snell, "Capital Punishment 2003," http://www.ojp.usdoj.gov/bjs/pub/pdf/cp03.pdf, p. 12; Bureau of Justice Statistics, *Capital Punishment 2006* (Washington, DC: Bureau of Justice Statistics, 2007).
9. For a good reference on this controversy, see Ernest van den Haag and J. Conrad, *The Death Penalty: A Debate* (New York: Plenum, 1983). See also Roger Hood, "Capital Punishment—A Global Perspective," *Punishment and Society* 3:3 (2001): 331–354.
10. *Furman* v. *Georgia,* 408 U.S. 238 (1972).
11. See http://archives.cnn.com/2000/US/01/31/illinois.executions.02/.
12. J. Edgar Hoover, *Crime in the United States* (Washington, DC: U.S. Government Printing Office, 1931–1939). A rough average of such crimes known to the police is presented.
13. Death Penalty Information Center, "Race of Defendants Executed since 1976," http://www.deathpenaltyinfo.org/dpicrace.html.
14. Justice William J. Brennan, *Furman* v. *Georgia,* 408 U.S. 238 (1976).
15. Brennan, *Furman* v. *Georgia.* See also Susan Cho, "Capital Confusion: The Effect of Jury Instructions on the Decision to Impose Death," *Criminology* 36:3 (1998): 711–733.
16. Malice aforethought means malice in fact or implied malice in the intent of one who has had time to premeditate an act that is unlawful or harmful. This issue is wrapped around the plea of not guilty by reason of insanity. See William Schabas, "International Norms on Execution of the Insane and the Mentally Retarded," *Criminal Law Forum* 4:1 (1993): 95–117, and James Aker, R. Bohm, and S. Lanier, eds., *America's Experiments with Capital Punishment* (Durham: North Carolina University Press, 1998).
17. Paigh Ralph, J. Sorensen, and J. Marquart, "A Comparison of Death-Sentenced and Incarcerated Murderers in Pre-*Furman* Texas," *Justice Quarterly* 9:2 (1992): 185–209.
18. Death Penalty Information Center, *Chattahoochee Judicial District: Buckle on the Death Belt: The Death Penalty in Microcosm* (Washington, DC: Death Penalty Information Center, 1992); see also Death Penalty Information Center, *Killing Justice: Government Misconduct and the Death Penalty* (Washington, DC: Death Penalty Information Center, 1992).
19. Gennaro Vito and T. Keil, "Capital Sentencing in Kentucky: An Analysis of Factors Influencing Decision Making in the Post-*Gregg* Period," *Journal of Criminal Law and Criminology* 79:2 (1988): 483–508. See also Thomas Keil and G. Vito, "The Effects of the *Furman* and *Gregg* Decisions on Black–White Execution Ratios in the South," *Journal of Criminal Justice* 20:3 (1992): 217–226, and Richard Deiter, *The Death Penalty in Black and White* (Washington, DC: Death Penalty Information Center, 1998).
20. Stephen Klein and J. Ralph, "Relationship of Offender and Victim Race to the Death Penalty in California," *Jurimetrics Journal* 32:3 (1991): 33–48. But see Steven Shatz and N. Rivkind, "The California Death Penalty Scheme," *New York University Law Review* 72:6 (1997): 1283–1343.
21. Franklin Zimring, A. Sarat, R. Emerson, et al., "Symposium: Research on the Death Penalty," *Law and Society Review* 27:1 (1993): 9–175; Mark Small, "A Review of Death Penalty Caselaw: Future Directions for Program Evaluation," *Criminal Justice Policy Review* 5:2 (1991): 114–120; Thomas Keil and G. Vito, "Race and the Death Penalty in Kentucky Murder Trials: 1976–1991," *American Journal of Criminal Justice* 20:1 (1995): 17–35; John Whitehead, "'Good Ol' Boys' and the Chair," *Crime and Delinquency* 44:2 (1998): 245–256. On the possible impact of racial stereotyping and death eligibility, see Sara Steen, Rodney Enger, and Randy Gainey, "Images of Danger and Culpability: Racial Stereotyping, Case Processing and Criminal Sentencing," *Criminology* 45:2 (2005): 405–468.
22. Justice Thurgood Marshall, *Furman* v. *Georgia.* Actually, the U.S. Supreme Court shifted from the earlier standard (concerned only with historical techniques for imposing punishment) to the "emerging standards" doctrine in 1910 (*Weems* v. *United States,* 217 U.S. 349). See also Julia Fleming, "The Death Penalty: Another Threat to the Culture of Life," *Journal of Religion and Society* 4:3 (2008): 126–134.
23. *Atkins* v. *Virginia,* 536 U.S. 304 (2002).

24. *Wilkerson* v. *Utah,* 99 U.S. 130 (1878). The Utah Supreme Court upheld a lower-court decision sentencing a prisoner convicted of murder in the first degree to be shot publicly. See also Kay Gillespie, *The Unforgiven: Utah's Executed Men* (Salt Lake City, UT: Signature Books, 1991). See also *Baze et al.* v. *Rees, 553 U.S. Baze* v. *Rees,* 07-5439, U.S. (2008).
25. Justice Nathan Clifford, *Wilkerson* v. *Utah,* 99 U.S. 130 (1878). See also William Schabas, *The Death Penalty as Cruel and Unusual Torture* (Boston: Northeastern University Press, 1996).
26. Justice Stephen Field, *O'Neil* v. *Vermont,* 1944 U.S. 323 (1892). See also Faith Lutze and D. Brody, "Mental Abuse as Cruel and Unusual Punishment," *Crime and Delinquency* 45:2 (1999): 242–255.
27. *Weems* v. *United States,* 217 U.S. 349 (1910). This decision represented a broad interpretation of the Eighth Amendment, asserting that "cruel and unusual punishment" could apply to prison sentences of a length disproportionate to the offense.
28. *Louisiana ex rel. Francis* v. *Resweber,* 329 U.S. 459 (1947). The Louisiana Supreme Court denied a writ of habeas corpus against a second attempt to execute a prisoner convicted of murder, the first attempt at electrocution having failed because of mechanical difficulty.
29. See Death Penalty Information Center, "Post-*Furman* Botched Executions," http://www.deathpenaltyinfo.org/botched.html, and http://www.deathpenaltyinfo.org/some-examples-post-furman-botched-executions.
30. Burger, *Furman* v. *Georgia.*
31. Gennaro Vito and D. Wilson, "Back from the Dead: Tracking the Progress of Kentucky's *Furman*-Commuted Death Row Populations," *Justice Quarterly* 5:1 (1988): 101–111. Also see Gennaro F. Vito, Deborah Wilson, and Edward J. Latessa, "Comparison of the Dead: Attributes and Outcomes of *Furman* Convicted Death Row Inmates in Kentucky and Ohio," in *The Death Penalty in America: Current Research, ed. R. Bohm* (Cincinnati, OH: Anderson Publishing, 1990).
32. They included such notable figures as Sirhan Sirhan, the convicted killer of Senator Robert Kennedy, and Charles Manson, leader of the group of mass killers in California known as the "Family."
33. Raymond Paternoster and A. Kazyaka, "The Administration of the Death Penalty in South Carolina: Experience over the First Few Years," *South Carolina Law Review* 39:2 (1988): 245–411; Aker et al., *America's Experiments with Capital Punishment.*
34. Thomas Keil and G. Vito, "Race and the Death Penalty in Kentucky Murder Trials: An Analysis of Post-*Gregg* Outcomes," *Justice Quarterly* 7:1 (1990): 189–207. See also Amy Phillips, "Thou Shalt Not Kill Any Nice People," *American Criminal Law Review* 35:1 (1997): 93–118.
35. Michael Radelet, "Executions of Whites for Crimes against Blacks: Exceptions to the Rule?," *Sociological Quarterly* 30:4 (1989): 529–544. See also Keil and Vito, "The Effects of the *Furman* and *Gregg* Decisions." But see John DiIulio, "My Black Crime Problem, and Ours," *The City Journal* 6:2 (1996): 14–28.
36. In a telephone survey of respondents in Ohio, Skrovon et al. found disapproval of the death penalty being used on juveniles. Sandra Skovron, J. Scott, and F. Cullen, "The Death Penalty for Juveniles: An Assessment of Public Support," *Crime and Delinquency* 35:4 (1989): 546–561. William Carlsen reports that Californians solidly support the death penalty for adults (63 percent favor versus 33 percent opposed) but that life in prison without the possibility of parole as an alternative to capital punishment is favored by 67 percent of the respondents. William Carlsen, "Support for the Death Penalty—Sometimes," *San Francisco Chronicle,* March 28, 1990, p. A9. The war against drugs has been spread to the death penalty. See Charles Williams, "The Death Penalty for Drug-Related Killings," *Criminal Law Bulletin* 27:5 (1991): 387–415.
37. Richard Deiter (1993), "Sentencing for Life: Americans Embrace Alternatives to the Death Penalty," http://www.deathpenaltyinfo.org/article.php?scid-45&did-481. For the average time to be served, see Paula Dixon, *Truth in Sentencing in State Courts* (Washington, DC: U.S. Department of Justice, 1999), p. 7.
38. H. Bedeau and M. Radelet, "Miscarriages of Justice in Potentially Capital Cases," *Stanford Law Review* 40:1 (1987): 21–179. See also Elizabeth Rapaport, "The Death Penalty and Gender Discrimination," *Law and Society Review* 25:2 (1991): 367–383; Michael Radelet, H. Bedeau, and C. Putnam, *In Spite of Innocence: The Ordeal of 400 Americans Wrongly Convicted of Crimes Punishable by Death* (Boston: Northeastern University Press, 1992); and Michael Wein stock and G. Schwartz, "Executing the Innocent: Preventing the Ultimate Injustice," *Criminal Law Bulletin* 34:4 (1998): 328–347.
39. *United States of America* v. *Alan Quinones* (2002 U.S. Dist. Lexis 7320).
40. *Death Penalty Sentencing: Research Indicates Pattern of Racial Disparities* (Washington, DC: General Accounting Office, 1990).
41. Death Penalty Information Center, "Women and the Death Penalty," http://www.deathpenaltyinfo.org/.
42. Darrell Steffensmeier, J. Schwartz, H. Zhong, and J. Ackerman, "An Assessment of Recent Trends in Girls' Violence Using Diverse Longitudinal Sources: Is the Gender Gap Closing?," *Criminology* 43:2 (2005): 255–405. See also Jennifer Schwartz and Brian Rookey, "The Narrowing Gap in Arrests," *Criminology* 46:3 (2008): 637–672.

43. A poll conducted by ABC News revealed strong opposition to the death penalty for juveniles in general: only 21 percent were in favor of the death penalty for juveniles versus the 62 percent who preferred the sentence of life without parole. The poll was conducted December 10–14, 2003 (ABC News, December 19, 2003).
44. *Thompson* v. *Oklahoma,* 487 U.S. 815 (1988).
45. *Stanford* v. *Kentucky,* 492 U.S. 361 (1989).
46. *Roper* v. *Simons,* 03-633 (2005). See also *Atkins* v. *Virginia,* 536 U.S. 304 (2002).
47. Hashem Dezhbakhsh, Paul Rubin, and Joanna Mehlhop Shepherd, "Does Capital Punishment Have a Deterrent Effect?," http://www.ipta.net/pubs/emory.edu.
48. Dudley Sharp, "Death Penalty and Sentencing Information," http://www.prodeathpenalty.com/DP.html.
49. Ibid.
50. Clark County Prosecutor, "Robert Lee Massie," http://www.clarkprosecutor.org/html/death/US/massie703.htm. See also "Press Release: New Jerseyans for Alternatives to the Death Penalty, Nov. 21, 2005"; for full report, see http://www.njadp.org.
51. Judge Arthur L. Alarcón and Paula M. Mitchell, *Costs of Capital Punishment in California: Will Voters Choose Reform this November?,* 46 Loy. L.A. L. Rev. S1 (2012). The full text is available at http://digitalcommons.lmu.edu/llr/vol46/iss0/1. See also Death Penalty Information Center, "Financial Facts about the Death Penalty," http://www.deathpenaltyinfo.org/costs-death-penalty.
52. See Death Penalty Information Center, "Financial Facts about the Death Penalty," and Jon Craig, "Death Row Inmates Can Cost $1M Each," *Cincinnati Enquirer,* July 12, 2010.

Suggested Readings: Part 3

American Correctional Association. [Special theme issue] Reentry. *Corrections Today* 67:2 (2005).

———. [Special theme issue] Reentry. *Corrections Today* 69:2 (2007).

———. [Special theme issue] Offender Programs. *Corrections Today* 75:4 (2013).

Amnesty International. *Nigeria: Waiting for the Hangman.* New York: Amnesty International, 2008.

Bailey, William. "Deterrence, Brutalization and the Death Penalty: Another Examination of Oklahoma's Return to Capital Punishment." *Criminology* 36:4 (1998): 711–733.

Bureau of Justice Statistics. *Capital Punishment 2011.* Washington, DC: U.S. Department of Justice, 2012. http://www.bjs.gov/content/pub/pdf/cp11st.pdf.

———. "Prisoners Executed in the United States: 1930–1999." http://www.ojp.usdoj.gov/bjs.

———. *Prisoners Executed.* Washington, DC: U.S. Department of Justice, 2013. http://www.bjs.gov/index.cfm?ty=pbdetail&iid=2079.

Burke, Peggy. *Abolishing Parole: Why the Emperor Has No Clothes.* Lexington, KY: American Probation and Parole Association, 1995.

Council of State Governments. *Report of the Re-Entry Policy Committee.* Lexington, KY: Council of State Governments, 2004.

Cullen, Francis T., E. Latessa, and V. Burton Jr. "The Correctional Orientation of Prison Wardens: Is the Rehabilitative Ideal Supported?" *Criminology* 31:1 (1993): 69–92.

Currie, Elliott. *Crime and Punishment in America: Why the Solutions to America's Most Stubborn Social Crisis Have Not Worked—And What Will.* New York: Metropolitan Books, 1998.

Death Penalty Information Center. http://www.deathpenaltyinfo.org.

Ditton, Paula. *Mental Health and Treatment of Inmates and Probationers.* Washington, DC: Bureau of Justice Statistics, 1999.

Editors, Correctional News. "CCA Completes Initial Phases of 3,600-Bed Arizona Facility." *Corrections News* 14:6 (2008): 19.

———. Editors, Correctional News. "Marshals Service to House Inmates in GEO Group Facility in Georgia." *Corrections News* 14:2 (2008): 13.

English, Kim, S. Pullen, and L. Jones. *Managing Adult Sex Offenders in the Community: A Containment Approach.* Washington, DC: U.S. Department of Justice, 1997.

Feeley, Malcolm. "The Privatization of Prisons in Historical Perspective." *Criminal Justice Research Bulletin* 6:2 (1991): 6–8.

Finn, Peter. *Chicago's Safer Foundation: A Road Back for Ex-Offenders.* Washington, DC: U.S. Department of Justice, 1998.

———. Finn, Peter. *Successful Job Placement for Ex-Offenders.* Washington, DC: U.S. Department of Justice, 1998.

Glaze, Lauren, and L. Maruschak. *Parents in Prison and Their Minor Children.* Washington, DC: Bureau of Justice Statistics, 2008.

Hanrahan, Kate, J. Gibbs, and S. Zimmerman. "Parole and Revocation." *The Prison Journal* 85:3 (2005): 251–269.

Harris, George A., ed. *And Tough Customers: Counseling Unwilling Clients.* Laurel, MD: American Correctional Association, 1991.

Hassine, Victor. *Life without Parole.* New York: Oxford University Press, 2008.

Hughes, Timothy, and D. Wilson. *Reentry Trends in the United States.* Washington, DC: Bureau of Justice Statistics, 2005. http://www.ojp.usdoj.gov/bjs/reentry/reentry.htm.

Johnson, Robert. *Death Work: A Study of the Modern Execution Process.* Belmont, CA: Wadsworth, 1998.

Johnson, Robert, and H. Toch. *Crime and Punishment: Inside Views.* Los Angeles: Roxbury, 2000.

Kilpatrick, D., D. Beatty, and S. Howley. *The Rights of Crime Victims.* Washington, DC: U.S. Department of Justice, 1998.

Langan, Patrick, and David Levin. *Recidivism of Prisoners Released in 1994.* Washington, DC: Bureau of Justice Statistics, 2002.

Lanza-Kaduce, Lonn, K. Parker, and C. Thomas. "A Comparative Recidivism Analysis of Releasees from Private and Public Prisons." *Crime and Delinquency* 45:1 (1999): 28–47.

Latessa, Edward. J., S. Listwan, and D. Koetzle. *What Works (and Doesn't) in Reducing Recidivism.* Cincinnati, OH: Anderson Publishing, 2013.

Latessa, Edward. J., and P. Smith. *Corrections in the Community.* Cincinnati, OH: Anderson Publishing, 2011.

Lilly, J. Robert, and M. Deflem. "Profit and Penalty: An Analysis of the Corrections Commercial Complex." *Crime and Delinquency* 42:1 (1996): 3–20.

Love, Margaret. *Relief from Collateral Consequences of a Criminal Conviction.* Washington, DC: The Sentencing Project, 2008.

Lutze, Faith, and D. Brody, "Mental Abuse as Cruel and Unusual Punishment." *Crime and Delinquency* 45:2 (1999): 242–255.

Maruschak, Laura. *HIV in Prisons and Jails, 2006–2020.* Washington, DC: Bureau of Justice Statistics, 2013. http://www.bjs.gov/index.cfm?ty=pbdetail&iid=4452.

Maruschak, Laura, and A. Beck. *Medical Problems of Inmates, 2006.* Washington, DC: Bureau of Justice Statistics, 2008.

Maruschak, L., and E. Parks. *Probation and Parole in the United States 2012.* Washington, DC: Bureau of Justice Statistics, 2012.

Mumola, Christopher. *Substance Abuse and Treatment, State and Federal Prisoners, 1997.* Washington, DC: Bureau of Justice Statistics, 1999.

Mumola, Christopher, and J. Karberg. *Drug Use and Dependence, State and Federal Prisoners, 2005.* Washington, DC: Bureau of Justice Statistics, 2006.

Petrosino, Anthony, and C. Petrosino. "The Public Safety Potential of Megan's Law in Massachusetts." *Crime and Delinquency* 45:1 (1999): 122–139.

Scalia, John. *Prisoner Petitions Filed in U.S. District Courts, 2000.* Washington, DC: Bureau of Justice Statistics, 2004. http://www.ojp.usdoj.gov/bjs/pub/pdf/ppfusd00.pdf.

Seiter, Richard P. "Private Corrections: A Review of the Issues." http://www.correctionscorp.com/static/assets/Private_Corr_Review_of_Issues.pdf.

Sexton, George E. *Work in American Prisons: Joint Ventures with the Private Sector.* Washington, DC: U.S. Department of Justice, 1995.

Sorensen, Jon, and D. Wallace, "Prosecutorial Discretion in Seeking Death." *Justice Quarterly* 16:3 (1999): 559–578.

Sundt, Jody, and F. Cullen. "The Role of the Contemporary Prison Chaplain." The *Prison Journal* 78:3 (1998): 271–298.

Thomas, Charles W. *Correctional Privatization: The Issues and Evidence.* Toronto: The Fraser Institute, 1996.

———. Thomas, Charles W. "Prisoner Rights and Correctional Privatization: A Legal and Ethical Analysis." *Business and Professional Ethics Journal* 10:1 (1991): 3–45.

Tonry, Michael. "Crime and Human Rights: How Political Paranoia, Protestant Fundamentalism, and Constitutional Obsolescence Combined to Devastate Black America." *Criminology* 46:1 (2008): 1–34.

Turner, Susan, and J. Petersilia. "Work Release in Washington: Effects on Recidivism and Courtroom Costs." *Prison Journal* 76:2 (1996): 138–164.

Vaughn, Michael, and S. Carter Collins. "Medical Malpractice in Correctional Facilities: State Tort Remedies for Inappropriate and Inadequate Health Care Administered to Prisoners." *The Prison Journal* 84:4 (2004): 505–534.

Wilkinson, Reginald, and E. Rhine. "Confronting Recidivism." *Corrections Today* 67:5 (2005): 54–57.

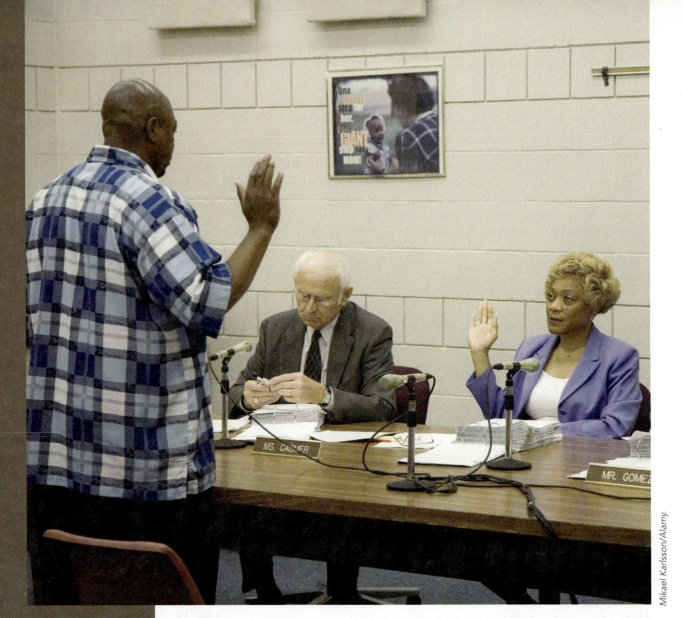

Mikael Karlsson/Alamy.

Objectives

- Outline the history of parole.
- Compare and contrast parole and pardon.
- Describe the current status of parole in the United States.
- Summarize the issues associated with prisoners reentering the community, including the stigma parolees face.
- Explain how parole is granted and the role of the parole board.
- Identify the conditions of parole.
- Summarize the role of parole officers.
- Explain how parole supervision is terminated, including revocation of parole.
- Describe the prisoner reentry process.
- Explain reentry courts.
- Explain the effectiveness of parole.

chapter 15 Parole and Reentry

Outline

The Development of Parole

- The Roots of American Parole
- Early Practices in Other Nations
- Parole Comes to the United States

Pardon and Parole: Two of the Ways Out of Prison

What Is Parole?

Parole Administration

The Parole Board

Parole Release

Parole Release Guidelines

Parole Conditions

Role of the Patrol Officer

Parole Revocation

Parole Remains a Major Segment of Corrections

Pardons

Reentry: The New Challenge

- Work-Release Programs
- Furlough Programs
- Halfway Houses
- Reentry Courts

Is Parole Effective?

"If inmates do not meet the standards the board has established for parole, their sentences are continued and they are 'flopped' as a failure of parole."

—Edward J. Latessa

Overview

The correctional process as described so far has followed offenders as they were filtered through the correctional system. We have seen how those who wind up in prison face both challenges and opportunities as they serve out their sentences and descend the classification ladder until they reach their minimum status and ultimate release date. This chapter now brings our focus to parole, traditionally the most common method for leaving prison and reentering society in a graduated manner. Parole (or earned early release) is a correctional process that has often found itself under attack as a method for inmates to easily gain early release from their stated sentences. The attitude that swept the nation in the past couple of decades as prison populations continued to soar was to make sentencing even harsher and to make the inmates serve as much of their sentences in a prison as possible.[1] Recently, however, there has been a subtle but important shift toward focusing more on those offenders returning to our communities. Although offenders have been "going home" as long as there have been prisons, new attention has been given to their reentry into the community. The student needs to understand the fact that many issues underlie the process of parole and reentry in today's environment, and therefore we need to reexamine the use of the time-tested tool of parole as well as other ways in which offenders exit prison. We begin with a brief history of parole.

THE DEVELOPMENT OF PAROLE

Parole is a correctional option that often evokes strong feelings. Some people argue that it should be abolished entirely, whereas others believe it provides men and women with an opportunity to demonstrate that they can reenter society and lead law-abiding and productive lives. Regardless of one's position, parole is an important part of the American correctional scene. Because more than 839,000 inmates were on parole in 2011, it is important that we understand the roots of parole and how it is granted.

The Roots of American Parole

Parole from prison, like the prison itself, is primarily an American innovation.[2] It emerged from a philosophical revolution and a resulting tradition of penal reform established in the late eighteenth century in the newly formed United States. As with many other new ideas that emerged in early America, parole had its roots in the practices of English and European penal systems.

In England, orders of transportation were thought to be a severe punishment. In the eighteenth century, banishment, a common penalty for the aristocracy or nobility for centuries, was imposed on the common offender for the first time. The judge would order the common offender transported to the colonies rather than to the gallows or pillory. The criminal would be allowed to go at liberty in the new land, sometimes for a period of indenture,[3] on the condition of not returning to England for a specified time period (such as 10 years), if at all.[4]

Criminologists commonly accept punishment by transportation as the principal forerunner of parole.[5] They argue that transportation was an organized, uniform process by which thousands of convicts were punished in a manner short of execution or corporal punishment because it was a system wherein offenders eventually obtained their freedom.

key term

Alexander Maconochie
Commander of Norfolk Island who devised a method for inmate ticket-of-leave that later contributed to Ireland's parole system.

key term

Irish system
Developed in Ireland, one of the first parole systems that permitted inmates to work their way into lower-security settings.

key term

Sir Walter Crofton
Director of the Irish penal system in 1846, he improved on the "ticket-of-leave" system developed by Maconochie; his system also had provisions for supervision by police, the first parole officers.

Early Practices in Other Nations

The governor of a prison in Spain started the first operational system of conditional release in 1835. Up to one-third of a prison sentence could be reduced by good behavior and a demonstrated desire to do better. A similar system was enacted in Bavaria in 1837, and many prison reformers in France in the 1840s advocated the adoption of similar conditional release systems. In fact, the term *parole* comes from the French *parole d'honneur*, or "word of honor," which characterized the French efforts to establish parole release. Prisoners would be released after showing good behavior and industry in the prison[6] and on their word of honor that they would obey the law.

Despite the fact that these efforts predate those of **Alexander Maconochie** (see Correctional Profile 15.1), it is he who is usually given credit as being the father of parole. In 1840, Captain Maconochie was put in charge of the English penal colony in New South Wales at Norfolk Island, about 1,000 miles off the coast of Australia. To this colony were sent the criminals who were "twice condemned." They had been shipped from England to Australia and then from Australia to Norfolk. Conditions were allegedly so bad at Norfolk Island that men reprieved from the death penalty wept and those who were to die thanked God.[7]

correctional **profile 15.1**

Alexander Maconochie

In March 1840, Maconochie took up duties as commandant of the penal settlement at Norfolk Island. Cruel punishments and degrading conditions abounded on the island when he arrived. It was under these conditions that Maconochie devised an elaborate method of granted conditional release and began to apply his penal policies.[8] Under his plan, prisoners were awarded marks and moved through stages of custody, each with increased responsibility, until finally earning release. Although Maconochie was soon removed from his position, the ideas he had formulated spread to Ireland and eventually the United States, and for this reason he is often regarded as the "father of parole." His influenced the **Irish system**, designed by **Sir Walter Crofton**, which permitted inmates to work their way into lower-security settings, earn a ticket-of-leave, and work and live outside the prison. Maconochie's ideas can also be seen in the current practice of "good-time credits," described in Correctional Practice 15.1.

correctional practice 15.1

Good-Time Laws

The term **good time** does not refer to having fun within prison walls. Instead, it involves taking days off an offender's sentence as a result of conduct and behavior in accordance with the institutional rules. In 1817, New York was the first state to pass a good-time statute. The rules throughout the nation were firm and fairly straightforward, even though they varied from state to state. New York's statute enabled the correctional administrator to reduce by one-fourth the time of any prisoner sentenced to imprisonment for not less than five years on certificate of the principal keeper and other satisfactory evidence that such prisoner had behaved well and had acquired, on the whole, the net sum of $15 or more per annum. Every state in the Union and the District of Columbia had passed some kind of good-time law by 1916. California began awarding good time in 1990 at a one-to-two ratio: one day of reduction for every two days of good time.

Parole Comes to the United States

In 1870, the first meeting of the American Prison Association was held in Cincinnati, Ohio. Reform was the battle cry of the day, and the meeting took on an almost evangelical fervor.[9] Both Sir Walter Crofton and American warden F. B. Sanborn advocated the Irish system.[10]

Armed with the success of the meeting, the focus of prison reformers shifted from incarceration as the answer to crime to a concentrated movement to return offenders to society. Prisons remained central, but they were now seen almost as a necessary evil, not as an end. Prison reformers everywhere began to advocate adoption and expansion of good-time laws, assistance to released prisoners, the adoption of the ticket-of-leave system, and parole. In 1869, the New York state legislature passed an act creating the Elmira Reformatory and an indeterminate sentence of "until reformation, not exceeding five years."

With the passage of this law, parole in the United States became a reality. It soon spread to other jurisdictions, and by 1944, every jurisdiction in the nation had a parole authority.[11]

PARDON AND PAROLE: TWO OF THE WAYS OUT OF PRISON

Most offenders who enter the prisons of America eventually end up back on the streets of their old neighborhoods. Unless prisoners die in prison (from natural or other causes), almost all will someday be released back into society. The cruelly long sentences of the nineteenth century usually meant that the few offenders who did leave the prisons were bitter, broken, or both. Today, many offenders leave prison on parole, sometimes long before the expiration of their maximum sentences. Until recent years, the number and percentage of prisoners **released on parole** exhibited a steady decline. In 1966, prisoners released on discretionary parole numbered 61 percent of the total, but that figure declined to 39 percent in 1990. Since the **truth-in-sentencing movement**,[12] the percentage has declined even more, down to an estimated 28 percent in 2009, but for the past couple years it has risen slightly and was at 31 percent in 2010. Although the use of discretionary parole release before sentence expiration has generally declined, many offenders whose sentences expire are now required to have a period of parole supervision (sometimes called *mandatory* or *postrelease control*). As a result, the U.S. total of persons under parole supervision increased from about 531,000 in 1990 to more than 883,900 by the beginning of 2012, over 16 percent of the total of those under correctional supervision.[13]

key term

Good time
Taking days off an inmate's sentence for good behavior while incarcerated.

key term

Release on parole
Release of an inmate from confinement to expiration of sentence on condition of good behavior and supervision in the community.

key term

Truth-in-sentencing movement
Begun in the 1990s, this movement required inmates to serve a significant portion of their sentences before consideration for release.

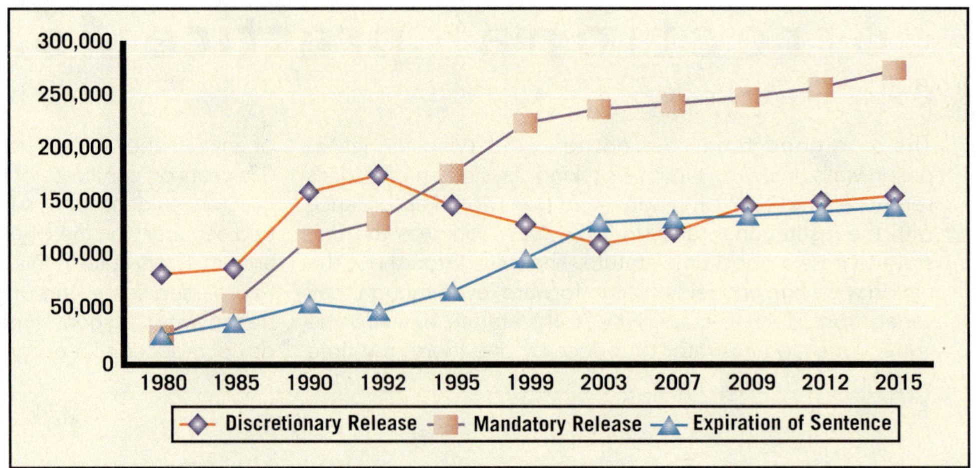

figure 15.1

Releases from State Prison by Method of Release, 1980–2015.

NOTE: Data for 2012 and 2015 are extrapolated.

SOURCE: T. Hughes, T. Wilson, and A. Beck, *Trends in State Parole, 1990–2000* (Washington, DC: Bureau of Justice Statistics, 2001); L. M. Maruschak and E. Parks, *Probation and Parole in the United States, 2011* (Washington, DC: Bureau of Justice Statistics, 2012).

The significance of parole is clear when we recognize that the only alternatives are clemency, commutation, completion of sentence, death, escape, or some form of shock probation. Information on avenues by which inmates leave prison is given in Figure 15.1. As can be seen in these data, conditional **discretionary release**, which is traditional parole release with supervision, has started to increase. Conditional **mandatory release** is when an offender is released prior to expiration of sentence (usually triggered after a set portion of the sentence has been served), with supervision in the community. This mechanism for release is the most common type of release but has been declining the past three years and is now at 46 percent, down from 51 percent in 2010. Unconditional release is when the sentence has expired ("expiration of sentence") and the offender is released without conditions or supervision. Table 15.1 shows the number of adult inmates released in 2011 under postincarceration supervision for the top 10 states and the U.S. Federal Bureau of Prisons. As shown, very few inmates in the federal system are released under conditional supervision.

key term

Discretionary release
Parole of an inmate from prison prior to expiration of his or her maximum sentence according to the boundaries set by the sentencing body or legislature.

key term

Mandatory release
The required release of an inmate from incarceration because the statutes mandate the release of any inmate who has served his or her maximum sentence.

key term

"Max out"
Release after serving the entire sentence.

key term

Executive clemency
A pardon, reduction of sentence, or release of an inmate by the governor or pardoning authority.

key term

Pardon
Exoneration of blame for the offense by the governor or paroling authority.

In the days of frequent capital punishment and life sentences, death in prison was always a strong possibility. The prisoner might die as a result of natural causes, an accident, suicide, or homicide inside the walls. Another way out, sometimes not much better from the offender's viewpoint, is to be forced to serve the entire maximum sentence before release (to "**max out**" a sentence). Infinitely better but rare is **executive clemency** in the form of a pardon or similar action by the governor. A full **pardon** usually means complete exoneration of blame for the offense and relieves the prisoner of the stigma of guilt. One version of the pardon is **amnesty**, which may be granted to a group or class of offenders. For example, the United States has a long tradition of granting amnesty to soldiers who deserted or avoided service in major wars. In countries where it is customary to imprison political dissidents, the government also may use mass amnesty to gain public favor. Executive power can also be used to grant a **reprieve**, usually in the case of the death penalty (a well-used plotline in grade B movies of the 1930s and 1940s in which the star is granted a last-minute reprieve while being strapped into the electric chair). Usually, a reprieve results not in a release but merely in a reduction in the severity of the punishment or a delay in its imposition. Punishment can also be lessened by **commutation**, shortening of the sentence by executive order. Usually the commutation is based on time already spent in jail and prison and results in almost immediate release of the petitioner. Another form of release, discussed in Chapter 4, results from some sort of appellate review action. These procedures, along with parole (and, of course, escape or natural death), cover the major ways a prisoner can expect to leave prison.

table 15.1 **Releasees from Prison 2011**

Jurisdiction	Expiration of Sentence	Postincarceration Supervision
California	2,439	117,250
Texas	30,558	40,848
Florida	22,822	12,425
New York	2,799	20,670
Louisiana	1,380	15,532
Indiana	2.073	14,502
Tennessee	4,629	10,218
Pennsylvania	2,901	10,409
Michigan	1,097	10,796
Maryland	3,634	7,567
Federal Bureau of Prisons	54,163	649

SOURCE: American Correctional Association, *2012 Directory of Adult and Juvenile Correctional Departments, Agencies, and Probation and Parole Authorities* (Alexandria, VA: American Correctional Association, 2012), pp. 44–45.

WHAT IS PAROLE?

The classic definition of **parole** is "release of an offender from a penal or correctional institution, after he has served a portion of his sentence, under the continued custody of the state and under conditions that permit his reincarceration in the event of misbehavior."[14] The definition given by the American Probation and Parole Association can be found in Policy Position 15.1. Parole has two major elements: the release of an offender from prison under specific guidelines and the supervision of the offender in the community.

key term

Amnesty
A form of pardon for a class of offenders, such as draft dodgers.

policy position 15.1

American Probation and Parole Association (APPA) Position Statement on Parole

The purpose of parole is to improve public safety by reducing the incidence and impact of crime committed by parolees. Parole is not leniency or clemency but a logical extension of the sentence to provide the opportunity to return offenders to society as productive and law-abiding citizens after a reasonable period of incarceration and at a time when they are assessed to have the capability and desire to succeed and live up to the responsibilities inherent in such a release. Conditions of parole and supervision services provided to conditionally released offenders are means by which the parole authority can assist the offender to successfully reintegrate into the community while providing a continuing measure of protection to society. The core services of parole are to provide investigation and reports to the paroling authority, to help offenders develop appropriate release plans and to supervise these persons released on parole. Parole authorities and supporting correctional agencies, in addition to fulfilling these responsibilities, may provide a wide variety of supporting pre-release and post-release programs and services, such as employment and life skills counseling, halfway house accommodation, counseling services, specialized community work programs and family services.

Parole is premised on the following beliefs:

- The majority of incarcerated offenders can benefit from a period of transition into the community prior to completion of their sentence.
- The protection of society is a primary objective of conditional release.

SOURCE: American Probation and Parole Association, https://www.appa-net.org/eweb/Dynamicpage.aspx?site=APPA_2&webcode=IB_PositionStatement&wps_key=e21e9312-056e-43be-8d55-dda3549dd7dc (accessed September 14, 2014).

table **15.2** U.S. Adult Residents under Community Supervision and Parole, 2002–2015*

	Per 100,000 U.S. Adults		U.S. Residents on—	
	Community Supervision	Parole	Community Supervision	Parole
2002	2,198	349	1 in 45	1 in 287
2004	2,226	351	1 in 45	1 in 285
2006	2,228	353	1 in 45	1 in 283
2008	2,203	358	1 in 45	1 in 279
2010	2,067	355	1 in 48	1 in 281
2012*	1,995	352	1 in 51	1 in 283
2014*	1,669	349	1 in 54	1 in 285
2015*	1,591	348	1 in 56	1 in 286

Note: *Data extrapolated.

SOURCE: Laura M. Maruschak and Erica Parks, *Probation and Parole in the United States, 2011* (Washington, DC: Bureau of Justice Statistics, 2012), p 4.

key term

Reprieve
A reduction in sentencing severity; sometimes used in death penalty cases when execution of the offender is at least temporarily stopped.

key term

Commutation
A reduction of the severity of the sentence by the executive branch of government.

key term

Parole
Release of the inmate from confinement after he or she has served a portion of the sentence under the continued custody of the state and under conditions that permit reincarceration in the event of misbehavior.

Today, all but two states have some system of parole supervision for released offenders, even though some 16 states and the federal government have eliminated parole board release ("discretionary parole"), and another four have abolished parole board authority for releasing certain violent offenders. In 1999, Wisconsin became the most recent state to abolish parole board release.[15]

Table 15.2 shows the rates of U.S. adults under community supervision and parole. Whereas the rate for community supervision has gone from 1 in 45 to 1 in 56, the rate for parole is virtually unchanged. Figure 15.2 identifies the most serious offense of adults on parole.

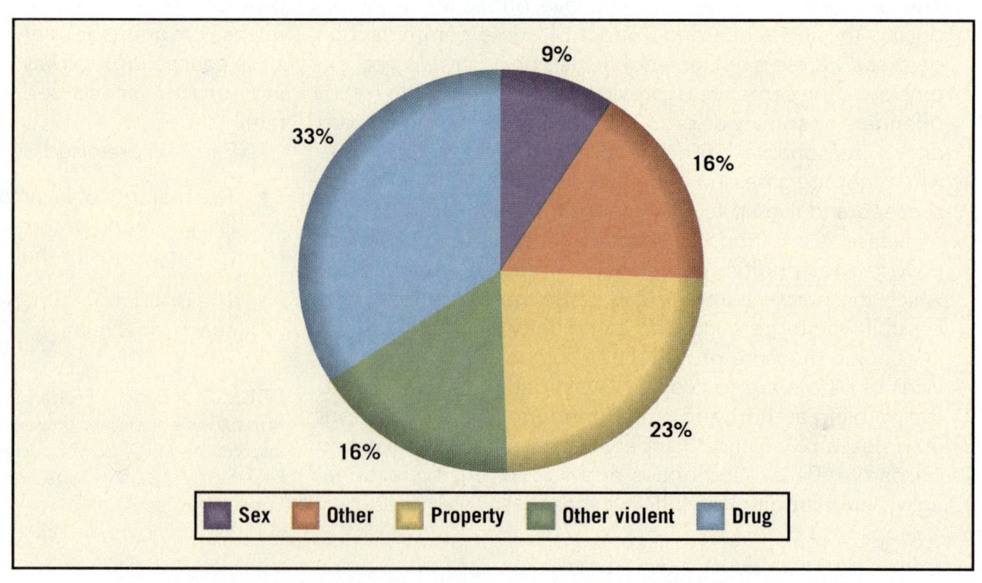

figure 15.2

Most Serious Offense of Adults on Parole, 2011.

SOURCE: Laura Maruschak and E. Parks, *Probation and Parole in the United States, 2011* (Washington, DC: Bureau of Justice Statistics, 2012), p. 17.

PAROLE ADMINISTRATION

If prisoners want to be released on parole, they must be recommended for it and their records reviewed by some procedure that will select them for that option. For this reason, how parole is administered and by whom is of vital concern to the prison population as well as to the rest of society.

Parole is a complex procedure and has many functions and processes that differ from one jurisdiction to another. Traditionally, parole includes five basic functions:

1. Selecting and placing prisoners on parole
2. Establishing conditions of supervision
3. Aiding, supervising, assisting, and controlling parolees in the community
4. Returning parolees to prison if the conditions of parole are not met
5. Discharging parolees when supervision is no longer necessary or when sentence is completed

The executive branch of government administers parole, unlike probation, which is a judicial function. As such, its form and operation vary from state to state.

THE PAROLE BOARD

Just who are the people who make these inmate release decisions? When parole selection procedures were first instituted, many states had a single commissioner of parole, appointed by the governor. That kind of political patronage soon led to corruption and controversy and was generally abandoned after World War II. Today most states have a **parole board** that serves the function formerly held by one person. Today, parole boards across the country vary greatly by size, operating procedures, independence, and selection. For example, New York has 19 members on the board, whereas three states have only three members.[16] In some states, parole board members are closely linked to or actually part of the correctional system staff; in other states, parole board members are appointed by the governor and are independent of correctional institutions and the administrators of the system. It is important to remember that even states that have abolished parole release will operate parole boards long into the future in order to hear cases that were sentenced under previous sentencing laws.

key term

Parole board
A correctional person or board that has the authority to release or parole offenders committed to prisons, to set conditions, to revoke parole, and to discharge from parole.

Although an independent board may well be more objective than the correctional bureaucracy in making parole recommendations, it does not provide the perfect system. The argument is sometimes made that independent systems tend to place on parole boards persons who have little training or experience in corrections, which in turn causes unnecessary conflict between prison authorities and the boards.

PAROLE RELEASE

How is an offender selected for parole? This question is important not only for the inmate being considered but also for the public.

Parole selection guidelines differ widely from state to state. The U.S. Supreme Court has consistently held parole to be a privilege and consequently held that a full complement of due process rights does not need to be afforded at parole-granting hearings.[17] As a result, the states have been given the opportunity to establish whatever inmate privileges they believe appropriate at parole-granting hearings.

Most states have established regulations as to the amount of time an inmate is required to serve prior to parole eligibility. In 16 states, eligibility is obtained on completion of the minimum sentence. In 10 states, eligibility is achieved on completion of one-third of the

Photo 15.1
Victims participate in a parole board meeting via videoconferencing.
Octavio Jones/Tampa Bay Times/ ZUMA Press, Inc./Alamy.

maximum sentence. Other states use the number of prior felony convictions and length of prior sentences to calculate eligibility rules. Even in the states that use the same eligibility guidelines, wide variation exists in the length of the minimum and maximum prison terms handed down for the same offense. In reality, there are literally as many variations in eligibility as there are parole jurisdictions.[18] In addition to time factors, some states restrict the use of parole for those convicted of various serious personal offenses, such as first-degree murder, kidnapping, and aggravated rape.[19] Many states now advise victims of pending parole hearings, especially if the inmate has been convicted of a violent crime. Victims are permitted to submit written commentary and attend (or send a representative to) the parole board hearing. Videoconferencing allows victims to participate without being threatened by their assailants. Evidence suggests that parole boards are heavily influenced by such communications.[20]

key term
"Flopped"
Inmate term for denial of parole.

If inmates do not meet the standards the board has established for parole, their sentences are continued, and they are "**flopped**." But if accepted, they are prepared for turnover to the parole authority for a period of supervision determined by the parole board.

Our discussion about parole has concerned the adult system; however, it should be noted that several states also operate parole boards for juveniles. For example, in Ohio, youth committed to the Ohio Department of Youth Services go before a Release Authority, which then decides the release date and conditions. The Release Authority acts very similarly to an adult parole board.

In addition to specific parole services for juveniles, some states also offer special programs for both male and female inmates that interface with parole, as described in Correctional Practice 15.2.

PAROLE RELEASE GUIDELINES

Critics of the parole process have commented on the release decision , characterizing it as arbitrary, capricious, prejudiced, lawless, and offering no meaningful future directions for inmates who have not been released. One response to those criticisms has been the development of parole guidelines. Today, 30 states have structured parole guidelines.[21]

correctional practice 15.2

Shock Incarceration and Parole

Shock incarceration facilities (or boot camp prisons for young adult females) have been developed in city, county, and state jurisdictions. These include the New York State program for youthful female offenders. A typical case is discussed here. Rita is an example of the type of offender who often ends up in a boot camp program. Her case is described to indicate how boot camps interface with parole.

Women in Shock Incarceration Rita finishes 50 sit-ups and springs to her feet. At 6 a.m., her platoon begins a five-mile run, the last portion of this morning's physical training. After five months in New York's Lakeview Shock Incarceration Correctional Facility, the morning workout is easy. Rita even enjoys it, taking pride in her physical conditioning.

When Rita graduates and returns to New York City, she will face six months of intensive supervision before moving to regular parole. More than two-fifths of Rita's platoon did not make it this far; some withdrew voluntarily, and the rest were removed for misconduct or failure to participate satisfactorily. By completing shock incarceration, she will enter parole 11 months before her minimum release date. The requirements for completing shock incarceration are the same for male and female inmates. The women live in a separate housing area of Lakeview. Otherwise, men and women participate in the same education, physical training, drill and ceremony, drug education, and counseling programs. Men and women are assigned to separate work details and attend "Network" group meetings held in inmates' living units.

The most common guideline system will factor in the seriousness of the crime and the traits and previous criminal behaviors the inmate brings to the current offense (that is, substance abuse history, prior record, work history) to construct a matrix that specifies the amount of time (within narrow bounds) an inmate would have to serve before release. Good-time and earned-time credits can reduce the anticipated prison sentence. Such an approach permits the offender to know immediately how long the sentence will be and what must be done to shorten it. This approach also reduces the anxiety and hostility of the on-the-spot decision-making process frequently found in other jurisdictions. Generally, guidelines attempt to structure discretion, not eliminate it, and although parole boards can deviate from the recommendations of the guidelines, they usually have to provide a rationale in writing.

PAROLE CONDITIONS

Parole is in essence a contract between the state and the offender. If the offender is able to abide by the terms of the contract, freedom is maintained. If a violation of these conditions occurs or if a parolee is charged with a new crime, the parole board may revoke parole and return the offender to prison. The offender must abide by the contract and stay under parole supervision for the period of time outlined by the parole board. Although every state has its own policies and procedures, parole usually lasts more than two but usually less than seven years. Some states may permit discharge from parole after a very short time as long as the offender has diligently adhered to the prerelease contract. Although the exact content of these contracts varies among states and individuals, Correctional Practice 15.3 shows a simple and commonsense **parole agreement**.

key term

Parole agreement
Conditions imposed by the paroling authority and offender agreement to those conditions.

ROLE OF THE PAROLE OFFICER

The parole officer has two major roles: assisting parolees in their reentry and surveillance of parolee behavior. In the former, parole officers counsel, advise, and encourage parolees in the reentry process and help them gain employment. They develop and subsequently

correctional practice 15.3

Statement of Parole Agreement

The Members of the Parole Board have agreed that you have earned the opportunity of parole and eventually a final release from your present conviction. The Parole Board is therefore ordering a Parole Release in your case.

Parole Status has a two-fold meaning: One is a trust status in which the Parole Board accepts your word you will do your best to abide by the Conditions of Parole that are set down in your case; the other, by state law, means the Adult Parole Authority has the legal duty to enforce the Conditions of Parole even to the extent of arrest and return to the institution should that become necessary.

1. Upon release from the institution, report as instructed to your Parole Officer (or any other person designated) and thereafter report as often as directed.
2. Secure written permission of the Adult Parole Authority before leaving the [said] state.
3. Obey all municipal ordinances, state and federal laws, and at all times conduct yourself as a responsible law-abiding citizen.
4. Never purchase, own, possess, use or have under your control, a deadly weapon or firearm.
5. Follow all instructions given you by your Parole Officer or other officials of the Adult Parole
6. Authority and abide by any special conditions imposed by the Adult Authority.
7. If you feel any of the Conditions or instructions are causing problems, you may request a meeting with your Parole Officer's supervisor. The request stating your reasons for the conference should be in writing when possible.
8. Special Conditions: (as determined). I have read, or have had read to me, the foregoing Conditions of my Parole. I fully understand them and I agree to observe and abide by my Parole Conditions.

Witness ______________

Parole Candidate ______________

Date ______________

SOURCE: State of Ohio, Department of Rehabilitation and Correction, Adult Parole Authority, *Statement of Parole Agreement APA. 271* (Columbus: State of Ohio).

find community resources, serve as a friendly advocate, and encourage community employers and service providers to assist in the reentry process. They often mediate disagreements between the parolee and other persons not under community supervision. And in their service, or supportive, role, they become a sounding board for parolee concerns, explaining the pitfalls of parole and providing direction in matters believed to be criminogenic.

Parole officers are also enforcers of the general parole orders and intervene in the activities of the client when it is believed that there is some danger of "backsliding," or the commission of new crimes. When there is evidence of illegal behavior, new crime, or the gross violation of the imposed conditions of parole, the parole officer may investigate the causes of the parolee's current behavior that is in violation of parole conditions, cause the parolee to be arrested, investigate the potential violation of crime or parole requirements, and submit a report to the parole board with recommendations for resolving the instant issues. Parole officers generally have the authority to arrest and have the parolee incarcerated pending action by the parole board, such as increasing the level of supervision, tightening the conditions of parole, ordering additional restrictions (known as "tourniquet tightening"), or revoking parole and returning the parolee to imprisonment.

Some parole officers specialize in handling certain types of offenders (such as drug users or sex offenders); others handle a general and mixed caseload. A few have a large "minimum surveillance" caseload, whereas others specialize in high-need or high-risk clients. Such specialization is believed to increase parolee success and maximize public safety.

key term

Technical violation
A violation of the conditions of release other than the conviction for a new crime that can result in the offender being returned to prison.

PAROLE REVOCATION

Parolees who violate the conditions of their release can be returned to prison for a **technical violation**. Because of arbitrary procedures used in earlier parole revocation

policy position 15.2

Perpetual Incarceration Machine

Beginning in the 1980s, there was unprecedented growth in jail and prison populations, driven in part by tougher sentencing laws and the War on Drugs. The number of citizens incarcerated tripled over the past three decades, and the current correctional costs have expanded. The average state cost per inmate per year ranges from $13,000 to $47,450.

The huge increase associated with the use of incarceration has meant there were huge increases in the number of inmates paroled each year. From 1980 to the end of 2010, the parole population increased from more than 220,000 to 840,700 adults. Many fail on parole supervision and are parole violators: Offenders returned to prison for violating the conditions of their release or for a new offense committed while under parole supervision. In any given year, some 40 percent of offenders on parole are returned to prison, and about one-fourth (25 percent) of parole returnees were for technical violations. Nationally, parole violations contributed about 35 percent to the total number of prison admissions. In some states, parolees returned to prison exceed 75 percent of all parolees, to be released and returned again later. Those states are what Vito, Higgins, and Tewksbury call "perpetual incarceration machines."

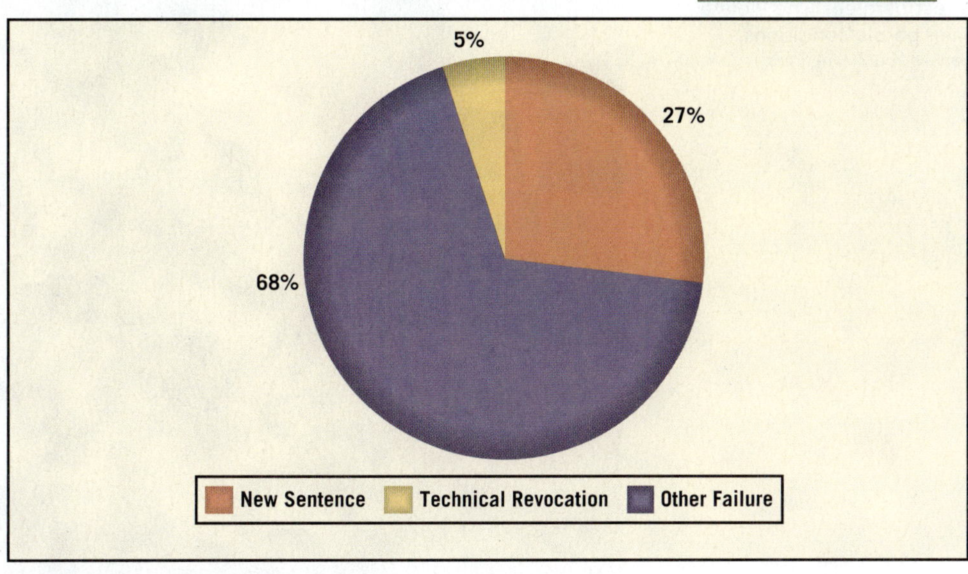

figure 15.3

Types of Failure for Parolees.

SOURCE: Laura M. Maruschak and E. Parks, *Probation and Parole in the United States, 2011* (Washington, DC: Bureau of Justice Statistics, 2012).

Due to the huge costs of corrections and dearth of state budgets, some states argue for alternative ways of processing technical parole violators. The argument is that the state cannot afford to house former parolees returned to prison for violation of the technical conditions of parole and that parolees should be incarcerated only for the commission of a new crime. Technical parole violations range from not observing curfews to not abstaining from alcohol and drug use and failing to contact a parole officer. The types of failure for parolees can be seen in Figure 15.3.

As a result of these counterforces, state and local jurisdictions advocate that intermediate sanctions be used to control nondangerous parole violators, such as house arrest, day reporting centers, "halfway-back" centers, intensive parole supervision, and jail time in lieu of prison time. For technical parole violators controlled by nonincarceration methods, therapeutic services and elements should be combined with supervision to maintain public safety. Some treatment service alternatives include programming and skill development, anger management programs, substance abuse programming, relapse prevention programming, mental health services, and related treatment alternatives.

In New Jersey, the halfway-back alternative to revocation for technical parole violators combines programming and skill development with residential facility control. These are commonly known as "violator centers" and use residential programming in lieu of return to prison. After extensive treatment, participants are returned to parole supervision. Parolees placed in the halfway-back centers had later survival rates (length of the period of time between release from prison and rearrest) that averaged longer than those of individuals placed in day reporting centers. Inmates who maxed out and were placed on parole did the worst. In addition, halfway-back parolees were 68 percent less likely than the max-out group to be reconvicted. Finally, for every 100 halfway-back parole participants, that state generated over $1.3 million in savings.

Vito, Higgins, and Tewksbury argue that parole violators should be reimprisoned only for new felony convictions, be held in local jails rather than a prison facility, and be given credit against their original sentences for all time served on parole.

SOURCES: Gennaro Vito, George Higgins, and Richard Tewksbury, "Characteristics of Parole Violators in Kentucky," *Federal Probation* 76:1 (2002), http://www.uscourts.gov/viewer.aspx?doc=/uscourts/FederalCourts/PPS/Fedprob/2012-06/index.html (accessed November 28, 2012); Office of Justice Programs, "Crime Solutions," http://www.crimesolutions.gov/ProgramDetails.aspx?ID=111 (accessed November 28, 2012). All public domain. Policy Position written by textbook authors.

Photo 15.2

If necessary, parole agents can arrest parolees who violate their parole conditions.
Bart Ah You/ZUMA Press, Inc./Alamy.

key term

Morrissey v. Brewer The U.S. Supreme Court decision that spells out the rights of an offender at a parole revocation hearing.

hearings, the U.S. Supreme Court in 1971 defined the basic rights of parolees at a parole revocation hearing in ***Morrissey* v. *Brewer*** (408 U.S. 271). Parolees must be notified in writing of the charges they face at least 24 hours before the preliminary hearing ("probable cause"). Revocation candidates have a right to hear the evidence against them, to cross-examine, and to refute the testimony. Furthermore, they can present their own evidence, and they have the right to a written report from the hearing that must be held before a neutral third party. Some states mandate legal counsel at this stage. At the second hearing, usually before a representative or member(s) of a parole board, the same rights are continued.

Parole revocation is a major issue facing corrections, and some the contributing factors are discussed in Policy Position 15.2.

PAROLE REMAINS A MAJOR SEGMENT OF CORRECTIONS

Despite growing pressures for the determinate sentence and the elimination of supervision on release, parole is still a growing segment of community corrections and a critical element in the correctional system. Although many prisoners are now released unconditionally back to the community, many are still released to community supervision. In some states, the title of *parole officer* has been changed to *community control officer* to reflect a custodial leaning, but the inmates remain under essentially the same controls as before.

Both parole and probation have a similar history, and even though they occur at opposite ends of the correctional process, their clients are supervised in much the same way. Thirty-four states have combined the administration of probation and parole into a single agency. Even probation, which had traditionally been a preincarceration option, now takes place in many cases after a brief period of jail or prison time. The main difference remains the method by which the offender is placed under either option. Probation remains a direct sentence by the court, whereas parole is a function of the executive branch, with discretionary parole being granted by the parole board and mandatory parole by corrections agencies under the governor. These parole agencies provide a variety of services.

PARDONS

Across the nation, parole boards are often directly involved in the consideration for a pardon, recommending this act of clemency to the state's governor. Although pardons are relatively rare, they can lessen social stigma and restore rights.[22] No mention of parole boards would be complete without mentioning their role in pardons. Some states restore civil rights when parole is granted; others do the same when the offender is released from parole. In still others, it is necessary for a governor to restore all rights, usually through a pardon. Some parole boards (such as those in Alabama) exercise pardon authority. Correctional Practice 15.4 provides more information on pardons.

California's **procedures for pardon** illustrate the process. What is required for a pardon in California? Generally, the offender must have led a crime-free existence for 10 years following release from parole. The offender must initiate a petition for pardon in a superior court (also called a court of common pleas in other jurisdictions). A formal hearing is held, and the presiding judge solicits opinions from the local district attorney and chief law enforcement officer in the jurisdiction. A computer search is made for any arrests and convictions. The local probation department prepares a pre-pardon hearing report. If the preponderance of evidence is favorable and no arrest or conviction record is found, the petition is approved by the superior court and forwarded to the governor's office. The governor may then order the equivalent of a parole board (Board of Prison Terms) to prepare an investigation that would contain a recommendation for pardon. If the report is favorable, the governor may pardon the petitioner, thereby restoring to him or her all of the rights and immunities of an ordinary citizen. It is evident that most ex-offenders, although no doubt preferring a pardon, may favor even more having the crime and conviction put as far behind them as possible. They may also not have the perseverance to endure such an involved and expensive procedure. Finally, statistics show that most ex-offenders are rearrested within the 10-year time period, even without further action by criminal justice system officials. No wonder so few ex-offenders seek and receive pardons.

key term

Procedures for pardon
Legal steps for a pardon, such as being crime free and meeting other conditions set by the state.

correctional **practice 15.4**

Pardon

Pardon is defined as an act of executive clemency that absolves the party in part or in full from the legal consequences of the crime and conviction. For the accused, pardon stops further criminal justice proceedings. Pardons can be full or conditional; the former generally applies to both the punishment and the guilt of the offender and blots out the existence of guilt in the eyes of the law. It also removes an offender's disabilities and restores civil rights. The conditional pardon usually falls short of the remedies available in the full pardon, is an expression of guilt, may restrict some freedoms, and does not obliterate the conviction but may restore civil rights.

Perhaps the most famous pardon was granted to former President Richard Nixon by President Gerald Ford. Many believe that this decision cost Ford the 1976 election. More recently, President Bill Clinton was widely criticized for his end-of-term pardons.

Photo 15.3

A drug lifer offender pleads for parole in the community under a relaxed lifer law in Plymouth, Michigan.

© Mikael Karlsson/Alamy.

REENTRY: THE NEW CHALLENGE

The large number of incarcerated offenders in the United States has led to the inevitable result that numerous offenders will reenter society each year. In fact, reentry has become the new buzzword used by policymakers to describe the process by which offenders come back into the community. Some have argued that parole is essential to this process,[23] whereas others[24] believe that because a high percentage of offenders pose minimal risk to public safety, parole supervision should be eliminated or shortened to about six months. Given estimates that a significant percentage of offenders who will be returning to the community have a number of pressing needs,[25] little doubt remains that services and treatment in the community should be an important part of the reentry process. Indeed, most states have created reentry programs designed to coordinate efforts and services between the institution, parole, and community correctional programs and treatment providers. Recently, the federal government committed funds to states to assist with the reentry process and to help ensure that offenders receive the services and treatment necessary to help them remain crime free. Signed into law on April 9, 2008, the Second Chance Act was designed to improve outcomes for persons returning to communities from prisons and jails. This first-of-its-kind legislation authorizes federal grants to government agencies and nonprofit organizations to provide employment assistance, substance abuse treatment, housing, family programming, mentoring, victim support, and other services that can help reduce recidivism. Discussed next are some of the programs that have been traditionally used for offender reentry into the community from the institution, and Correctional Practice 15.5 describes the challenges of reentry.

key term

Work release

A program in which inmates are allowed to work in the community with minimal restrictions but must return to confinement during nonworking hours.

Work-Release Programs

One of the earliest programs for releasing prisoners before their full sentences expired was the result of the first **work-release** legislation. The use of offenders for community work programs had its origins in ancient Rome, where prisoners aided in the construction of massive public works. Those workers, however, had no hope for release; their work was just another form of slave labor but with a new label. This has been the fate

correctional **practice 15.5**

Reentry Issues

Parolees face a variety of issues and challenges in the reentry process. Although their parole release may have been approved, certain hurdles remain before release. Inmates are required to have a residence before release, and some states require employment before exiting prison. Many parolees no longer have family members or friends willing to assist them when returning home. Some have been incarcerated so long that culture shock will arise over costs that the parolee has not addressed over the years, including the impacts of inflation and shifts in technology. Few will have medical insurance. Some parolees are more afraid of the outside than living in the correctional facilities, and some community members may be afraid of the parolee, especially those offenders convicted of sexual crimes, including child molestation.

Parolees returning to the community must find employment on release (or, as noted, prior to in some states). Finding work is a slow process. Parolees also face employment continuance issues, such as finding a home, overcoming stigma, and the immediate temptations of available drugs and alcohol in their own neighborhoods. Many return to the street gangs they left when incarcerated and are quickly caught up in illegal activities and crime, sometimes known as "back to the past."

Parolees often are uncertain about how effective they will be as spouses and in parenting. They probably will not have a bank account or credit. When they receive that first paycheck after finding employment, they might not know how to spend it or meet financial obligations. Transportation will be a major problem for most. Finally, they will have to learn better time management skills, as prisons revolve around total scheduling of all inmate time, a form of infantilization. Now parolees will have to set goals, create a free-world schedule, and learn how to maximize their time to maintain new options.

of many new efforts by penologists over the history of correctional efforts. The work-release philosophy, which permits inmates to work on their own in the free community, dates back to a 1913 Wisconsin statute that allowed misdemeanants to continue to work at their jobs while serving short sentences in jail. North Carolina applied the principles of the Wisconsin statute to felony offenders in 1957 under limited conditions; Michigan and Maryland soon followed suit with similar acts. In 1965, Congress passed the Federal Prisoner Rehabilitation Act, which provided for work release, furloughs, and community treatment centers for federal prisoners. This act served as a model for many states.

Photo 15.4

Work-release facilities provide a place to grow and even have a meaningful job on parole.
Mikael Karlsson/Alamy.

Institutional work release is not intended to be a substitute for parole, but it can be a valuable tool for the correctional administrator and the parole officer who must eventually supervise an individual who has participated in work release. The work-release program is not really an alternative to incarceration. Rather, it is a chance for offenders to develop and test their work skills, job discipline, and personal control over their behavior in the community—and it allows them to spend the major part of the day away from the institution. Because offenders must still return to the institution, the work-release program may be considered only a partial alternative that gives limited relief from the negative pressures of incarceration. Reentry can be an extreme challenge.

Work release has other benefits besides allowing inmates to be outside the walls for a period of time each day. The income derived from the work can be used in a number of ways: If the inmates have families, the earnings can be used to keep them off welfare rolls or to augment the assistance they might be receiving, inmates can reimburse victims for their loss, if the judge has required it,[26] or they may be able to build a nest egg for the time when they will be released. In many cases, the inmates can contribute toward their cost of housing and sustenance as well. This teaches them valuable budgeting and money management skills. One of the main fringe benefits is that their community becomes aware of their ability to maintain a job without creating problems for themselves or others. Also, their association with stable coworkers in the free world may give them support and guidance[27] that they could not find inside the prison walls. In the American tradition, the ability to do a good day's work both heightens the offenders' self-worth and commands respect from others. Scandinavian prisons have some kind of work facility attached to them, allowing inmates to work at real-world jobs for pay equal to that earned by a similarly skilled outside worker.

Furlough Programs

key term

Furlough
A prison-release program permitting the inmate to pursue education, vocational training, or employment in the community.

key term

Reintegration
The planned transition of an inmate from prison to the community.

Another form of partial incarceration is the **furlough**. Both work release and furlough extend the limits of confinement to include unsupervised absences from the institution. Furloughs and home visits have been allowed for many years. The death of a family member or some other crisis situation at home ("emergency furlough") was the most common reason for the home furlough. As states have passed legislation making furloughs a legal correctional tool, furloughs have been used for a number of purposes, including a home visit during holidays or just before release ("meritorious furlough"), so the return to the free world is a graduated process and includes **reintegration**. One benefit of home furloughs, obviously, is decreased sexual tension in institutions. A major roadblock to progress in such programs has been a few highly publicized and sensational failures. Those failures,[28] combined with the generally increasing numbers of violent and dangerous inmates coming out of the prisons, have made it difficult to promote any kind of furlough program.[29]

Halfway Houses

key term

Halfway house
A residential house or facility for offenders in the community; often used for inmates prior to final release to parole.

The search for ways to assist offenders transitioning from prison has pumped new life into an old option: the **halfway house**.[30] The interest in the halfway house as an important part of the reentry process has grown in the past few decades. Although earlier halfway houses served as residences for homeless men and women released from prison, they have since been used for a variety of purposes. Small residences offering shelter have been managed by prison aid societies since the early 1800s. In recent years, more attention has been given to halfway houses as the possible nuclei of community-based networks of residential treatment centers, as drug-free and alcohol-free living spaces, or as prerelease guidance centers.[31]

There are different patterns of referral to halfway house programs, the most frequent of which occurs when an inmate is granted a conditional release (such as parole, shock

Photo 15.5
Parolees at work helping urban residents garden for food.
© Jim West/Alamy.

parole, or shock probation) and is required to enter a halfway house during at least the initial period following release. This provides services to and surveillance of parolees who need support during this period. Time of residency may be specified before referral but usually is a shared decision to be made collaboratively by the supervision officer, client, and house staff. This decision is frequently based on such factors as resident's readiness to leave the house, employment, fine and restitution payments, savings, and alternative residential plan (see Correctional Practice 15.6). The offender generally continues on supervision after leaving the halfway house.

Another source of residents is those inmates whose release plans call for placement in a halfway house as the initial phase of their release procedure. Unlike the first option, however, halfway house residency occurs prior to formal granting of parole and subsequent supervision as a release or parolee. These inmates typically have a definite release date before they move from the prison to the halfway house. Note that these clients remain inmates who will serve the remainder of their sentences while residing in a halfway house. For these residents, halfway houses provide needed and significant assistance and direction in the transition from prison to community.[32] Additional benefits include continuation of jurisdiction by the referring correctional agency,[33] ability to return the inmate to incarceration without formal violation of parole, development of a more positive attitude toward the halfway house by the resident, lessening of loneliness and sense of isolation,[34] and less expensive aftercare service that can be more legitimately compared to imprisonment rather than the costs of parole.[35] The U.S. Bureau of Prisons was a leader in initiating this model for using halfway houses and continues to use this model on a prerelease basis.

The third avenue for residents to enter a halfway house differs by time of placement into the program; most offenders under probation and parole supervision do not initially reside in a halfway house. However, if such clients revert to criminal behavior or encounter unanticipated problems that could be resolved by program services or by a period of residency in a halfway house, the supervising agency may remand the offender to short-term residency in such a community corrections program. For example, in one study of halfway houses, it was found that parole violators who were placed in a halfway house had a 12 percent lower recidivism rate than those returned to prison.[36]

correctional **practice 15.6**

Housing for Returning Prisoners

As was noted in Chapter 7, offenders released from confinement face a number of challenges that contribute to recidivism and return to incarceration. These include lack of employment, alcohol and drug abuse histories, absence of housing, lack of supportive services, and homelessness. Many have developmental disorders, behavioral health problems, and disabilities. These challenges collectively contribute to failure of reentry and, when two or more challenges occur together, increase the brevity of time from release to reincarceration (shortened "survival periods").

Due to prison overcrowding, criminal justice costs, and budgetary limitations, policymakers are increasingly interested in cost containment and reducing prison populations. Legislatures, corrections administrators, judges, and law enforcement agencies tend to agree that changes are necessary, that some offenders need to be incarcerated for longer periods, and that there are too many low- and medium-risk offenders in the jails and prisons of the nation. The "mantra" seems to be "We can increase public safety and reduce prison populations by reserving scarce prison space for the 'truly dangerous.'"

The lack of offender housing is one barrier facing offenders leaving prison. Several states have begun or expanded efforts to secure housing for multiple-problem offenders emerging from confinement. These efforts can be found at the parole, work-release, mental health, and treatment program levels.

First, some parole boards may decide that inmates are eligible for parole but impose a prerelease condition that the reentry inmate must have a residential plan. This effort to provide housing options implies that the parole board has authorized their release but that the offenders cannot meet the required residence condition. The offender needs short-term financial assistance to enhance the effort to remain crime free to firm up the individual's reentry process. The Georgia Department of Corrections, for example, has instituted the Re-Entry Partnership Housing (RPH) program, which guarantees private-sector housing providers compensation (at $600 per month for three months for room and board) for otherwise eligible offenders. All offenders released on RPH have a parole officer whose duty it is to oversee the service provision and ensure offender compliance with the conditions of release.

Second, some offenders are released from prison on work release. Still technically inmates, work releasees locate employment, report to facility managers, earn salaries, and secure both training and employment. Work release generally leads to short periods of supervision, followed by parole. Work-release facilities provide access to a place to stay while work releasees become established and find employment. Some states also release inmates to a work-release center, although such inmates are not technically on work release. Some earn money (paychecks being sent to the housing unit) and pay restitution, family support, fines, and per diem charges with any remainder sum being issued to reentry offenders when they meet the release requirements. West Virginia has several such facilities.

Jails and prisons also hold offenders who have, for whatever reason, failed on probation or on parole. Typically, the cause of the failure is a technical violation of the conditions of supervision. Again, for West Virginia, about half the parole violators and almost 6 in 10 probation violators are there for technical revocations. Yet if your agency mission is to reduce the prison population while increasing public safety and it is believed that critical resources should be directed at high-risk offenders, committing low-risk technical supervision failures to incarcerative settings will generally work against your mission. Many states have specific institutions for certain problem inmates (for example, drug abusers), and these institutions deliver evidence-based treatments that will reduce recidivism and release inmates back into reentry. California has eight such facilities.

Finally, some states have or propose to develop reentry programs for offenders with disabilities, the homeless, and those with mental health problems. Such programs are designed to link offender needs with supportive housing. Ohio has developed supportive housing, a combination of permanent affordable housing with supportive services, such as coordinated case management, health and mental health services, substance abuse treatment programs, and job and vocational programs. This program—Returning Home-Ohio (or RHO)—focuses on prisoners at risk of returning to the Ohio Department of Rehabilitation and Correction. The RHO targets inmates close to their release date but who have a disability, are homeless at the time of their arrest, or have high risk of homelessness after release. Ohio provides resources for the care and treatment of these disabled returning prisoners. Results from the pilot program are very encouraging. In contrast to a control group, consider the following:

a. RHO participants were some 40 percent less likely to be rearrested.

b. More than 60 percent were less likely to be incarcerated.

c. They had longer periods of release before rearrest ("survival period").

d. Services paid for by the state were generally available to the treatment group.

Providing treatment services increased the cost of the RHO program and resulted in clear reductions along several major recidivism measures.

SOURCES: Georgia Department of Community Affairs (2012), "Re-Entry Partnership Housing," http://www.dca/state.ga.us/housing/specialneeds/programs/rph.asp (accessed August 30, 2012); Jared Hunt (2012), "Parole Violations Add to Jail Woes," http://www.dailymail.com/News/statenews/201208060176 (accessed September 17, 2012); Urban Institute, *Supportive Housing for Returning Prisoners* (Washington, DC: Urban Institute, 2012). Written by textbook authors.

policy position 15.3

California Realignment

In April 2011, California Governor Jerry Brown signed AB 109, also known as California Realignment, whereby some criminal justice responsibilities shift from the state prisons and parole board to local county officials and superior courts. Effective October 1, 2011, counties were required to take over the supervision of prisoners placed on parole whose last offense was not a violent crime or a sex offense. There are certain exceptions to this rule if the offender is judged to be "high risk." In addition, newly convicted offenders who are deemed to be nonviolent, nonserious, and non–sex offenders will be placed on probation or in local jails in lieu of sentences to state prison. Whereas high-risk, sex, and violent offenders remain under state supervision, lower-risk parole violators will be kept at the local level.

SOURCE: California Realignment Organization, http://www.calrealignment.org/realignment-overview.html.

At the federal level, the U.S. Bureau of Prisons established prerelease guidance centers in major metropolitan areas during 1961. The offender is sent to those centers from a correctional institution several months before he or she is eligible for parole. The offender is allowed to work and attend school in the community without supervision, and he or she participates in a number of programs in the halfway house itself. This approach has been copied by many states and appears to be a viable program when properly staffed and supervised. As possible uses for the halfway house are explored and outcomes are verified,[37] such units will offer not only short-term residency before the prisoner's placement on parole but also noninstitutional residence facilities[38] for a number of different categories of offenders.[39] At that point, **community residential centers** will constitute the first real alternative to institutional incarceration that works well in the community. In California, a surge of parole releasees resulted from that state's "realignment effort" (see Policy Position 15.3).

key term

Community residential center
Any correctional facility existing to provide services and maximize reintegration of the offender back into the community.

Reentry Courts

Following the popularity of drug courts, a new movement has taken root in which local courts have become more involved in the **reentry** of offenders back into the community. **Reentry courts** are specialized courts that are designed to reduce recidivism and improve public safety through the use of judicial oversight. The responsibilities generally assigned to reentry courts include (1) review offenders' reentry progress and problems, (2) order offenders to participate in various treatment and reintegration programs, (3) use drug and alcohol testing and other checks to monitor compliance, (4) apply graduated sanctions to offenders who do not comply with treatment requirements, and (5) provide modest incentive rewards for sustained clean drug tests and other positive behaviors.[40]

key term

Reentry
Process of inmates' return to the community and their adjustment to society ("free world").

key term

Reentry courts
Specialized courts designed to reduce recidivism and improve public safety through judicial oversight of those offenders released from prison.

The emergence of reentry courts is a major departure from traditional practice, where the responsibility of the court to an offender ended when the offender was sentenced by a judge. Judges typically have no role in the broad array of activities that carry out the terms of the sentence, the preparation of the offender for release, or the transition of the offender back into the community. The failure of traditional "solo" approaches, in which the agency or system operated independently, and the realization that offenders leaving prison are returning to the community have led to the development of this innovative approach to offender reentry. Although research is just emerging on the effectiveness of reentry courts, a recent study conducted by the Center for Court Innovation on the Harlem Parole Reentry Court found mixed results. Reentry court parolees were less likely to be reconvicted but more likely to have their parole revoked and be returned to prison. The researchers attributed this to the intensive nature of the program and the increased likelihood of detecting violations.[41] Although research has just begun to examine the effectiveness of this strategy, hopes are high that the approach will produce positive results (see Correctional Practice 15.7 for more on reentry courts).

correctional **practice 15.7**

Reentry Courts

Reentry courts represent a new form of jurisprudence that has elevated the partnership between courts and corrections in seeking the common goal of successful offender reintegration. The concept of the reentry court necessitates considerable cooperation between corrections and local judiciaries because it requires the coordination of the work of prisons in preparing offenders for release and actively involving community corrections agencies and various community resources in transitioning offenders back into the community through active judicial oversight.

As with the drug court concept, active judicial authority is applied to the reentry court to provide graduated sanctions and positive reinforcement and to marshal resources for offender support. Central to this effort is the development of a three fold strategy that seeks to improve the supervision of offenders, prepare communities to address public safety concerns, and provide services to aid offenders in reentering society. Despite being in its infancy with pilot sites in California, Colorado, Delaware, Florida, Iowa, Kentucky, New York, Ohio, and West Virginia, several core elements are present in each of these reentry court initiatives. According to the Office of Justice Programs, these core elements include the following:

- *Assessment and planning* that involves the offender, corrections department, and judiciary to identify the needs and develop a plan to begin building linkages in the community to support successful reintegration.
- *Active oversight*, whereby the reentry court meets with the offender at a high degree of frequency; meetings also include other relevant supporters or representatives from the supervising agency, family, and community. The underlying premise is for the judge to meet with offenders who are making progress as well as those who have failed to perform.
- *Management of supportive services* marshaled by the court to draw on community resources. The reentry court must have a broad array of supportive resources, including substance abuse treatment, job training programs, faith institutions, and housing services.
- *Accountability to community* through the development and involvement of citizen advisory boards, crime victims' organizations, and neighborhood groups. Accountability mechanisms may include ongoing restitution orders and participation in victim impact panels.
- *Graduated and parsimonious sanctions* established by the court that involve a predetermined range of sanctions for violations of the conditions of release. Paralleling drug courts, an array of relatively low-level sanctions that could be swiftly, predictably, and universally applied is developed.
- *Rewards for success* that incorporate positive judicial reinforcement, such as negotiating early release from parole after established goals are achieved or by conducting graduation ceremonies similar to those used in drug courts.

The major goal of the reentry court is the establishment of a seamless system of offender accountability and support services throughout the reentry process, using both the continuum-of-care and the wraparound services models. Using face-to-face scheduled meetings between the court judge and client, reentry courts establish individualized treatment and control strategies, coupled with both graduated sanctions and rewards, without resorting to incarceration, the most expensive punishment for parolee failures.

Reentry courts may authorize parole agents to refer parolees with a history of mental illness or substance abuse. Enabling legislation grants the court team authority over parole supervision in the instant case and determines the appropriate conditions of parole, orders treatment and rehabilitation services, identifies appropriate sanctions, lifts parole holds, and determines appropriate responses to alleged violations. Evaluations monitor program effectiveness. Initial, preliminary evaluations indicate that reentry clients are more successful, in terms of recidivism, than are others similarly situated but not under reentry court jurisdiction.

SOURCES: Judicial Council of California (2011), "Parole Reentry Court Program," http://www.courts.ca.gov/documents/prcp.pdf (accessed November 26, 2012); Office of Justice Programs (2012), "Reentry Courts," http://www.ojjdp.gov/mpg/progTypesReentryCourt.aspx (accessed November 26, 2012). See also Reginald Wilkinson and Gregory Bucholtz, "Prison Reform through Offender Reentry: A Partnership between Courts and Corrections," unpublished paper submitted to Pace Law School on the "Symposium on Prison Reform Law," October 2003.

IS PAROLE EFFECTIVE?

The most critical question asked of parole and other post release programs is whether they are effective. Outcome measures can include cost, humaneness, employment, and family reunification, just to name a few; however, the most important measure is public safety. Public safety is usually operationalized in corrections as recidivism, which, although it has

policy **position** 15.4

Effective Correctional Reentry

The development of services for those reentering society varies widely across the nation. Whereas some jurisdictions or even states have spent considerable time and money developing services for parolees as they are released back into their communities, others are forced to rely on a more fragmented approach to service delivery. We still know relatively little about the overall effectiveness of parole and even less about the effectiveness of the "newer" reentry programs.

According to Taxman and her colleagues, in an ideal model, reentry programs should include three or more phases designed to transition the inmate into the community. The first phase would begin in the institution, with service delivery congruent with the inmate's needs. The second phase would begin as the inmate is released from the institution. The inmates' risks and needs may change significantly as they enter the community context. Ideally, the individuals would continue in their treatment services, and case plans would be updated as needed. The final phase is an aftercare or relapse prevention phase where clients would receive ongoing support and services to address their needs. Although this model may provide the overall structure necessary to implement an effective reentry program, the processes and services offered by these programs are key to their success.

SOURCE: Excerpted from Shelly Listwan, Francis Cullen, and Edward J. Latessa, "How to Prevent Prisoner Re-Entry Programs from Failing: Insights from Evidence-Based Corrections," *Federal Probation* 70:3 (2006): 19–25.

some inherent limitations, is the ultimate indicator of a correctional program's success. The indicators used to measure recidivism, such as how it is defined (that is, arrest, conviction, incarceration), the lengths of follow-up, and the source of data (official, self-report), are all factors that can affect reported recidivism rates. Indeed, the best way to ensure a low recidivism rate may be to define it very narrowly (for example, incarceration in a state penal institution) and to utilize a very short follow-up period. Despite these challenges, recidivism remains the most important outcome of a correctional sanction. Policy Position 15.4 explores evidence-based correctional reentry programs.

Despite its widespread use, little is actually known about whether parole reduces recidivism. We do know that about half of parole discharges successfully complete parole. In a 2005 study of parole, the Urban Institute concluded that parole supervision has little

policy **position** 15.5

One Out of Five Arrests Involves a Probationer or Parolee

It has been a long-held assumption that people on probation and parole contribute disproportionately to crime as measured by arrests. To validate this assumption, the Council of State Government's Justice Center collaborated with four California chiefs of police to undertake a massive effort to establish the extent to which probationers and parolees contribute to crime. This involved collecting and matching more that 2.5 million arrest, probation, and parole records. Three major findings emerged:

1. Most adult felony and misdemeanor arrests were of people who were not on probation or parole status.
2. Probation and parole offenders accounted for only one in six arrests for violent crime and one in three arrests for drug violations.
3. During the 3.5 years in study period, total arrests dropped by 18 percent, the number of arrests of offenders under probation supervision dropped by 26 percent, and the number of arrests involving parole supervision declined by 61 percent.

Although law enforcement agencies recognize that all probationers and parolees are not alike, each individual poses a different level of risk to local communities. Community safety will increase by identifying offenders who merit justice agency attention and additional supervision as well as by closer coordination between law enforcement and correctional agencies.

SOURCE: Justice Center, Council of State Governments (2012), "The Impact of Probation and Parole Populations on Arrests in Four California Cities," http://www.pacenterofexcellence.pitt.edu/documents/CAL_CHIEFS_REPORT_FINAL.pdf (accessed February 12, 2013). Policy Position written by textbook authors.

effect on rearrest rates of released prisoners.[42] However, others have criticized the study, noting that it included only 15 states, including California, skewing the results.[43] Policy Position 15.5 investigates the common belief that parolees commit a disproportionate share of crimes. The debate about the effectiveness of parole will certainly continue into the future, and only more research will answer this important question.

In a recent study of parole violators in Pennsylvania,[44] researchers found a number of factors related to failure. Those parolees who had their parole violated were characterized as follows:

- Were more likely to hang around with individuals with criminal backgrounds
- Were less likely to live with a spouse
- Were less likely to be in a stable supportive relationship
- Were less likely to identify someone in their life who served in a mentoring capacity
- Were less likely to have job stability
- Were less likely to be satisfied with employment
- Were less likely to take low-end jobs and work toward a higher position
- Were more likely to have negative attitudes toward employment and unrealistic job expectations
- Were less likely to have a bank account
- Were more likely to report that they are "barely making it" (yet those in the success group reported over double median debt)
- Were more likely to report use of alcohol or drugs while on parole (but no difference in prior assessment of dependency problem)
- Had poor stress management skills, a primary contributing factor to relapse
- Had unrealistic expectations about what life would be like outside of prison
- Had poor problem-solving or coping skills
- Did not anticipate long-term consequences of behavior
- Failed to utilize resources to help themselves
- Acted impulsively to immediate situations
- Felt they were not in control
- Were more likely to maintain antisocial attitudes
- Viewed violations as an exceptional option to situation
- Maintained general lack of empathy
- Shifted blame or denied responsibility

In addition, success and failure groups did not differ in difficulty of finding a place to live after release, and both groups were equally likely to report eventually obtaining a job.

These findings are consistent with other research that has shown that criminogenic factors are the most important indicators of recidivism. Only by adequately addressing these factors will correctional professionals improve the outcomes of offenders.

Summary

Outline the History of Parole

Parole has its origins in the foresight and determination of Alexander Maconochie and Sir Walter Crofton, each of whom developed a program for early release and supervision of inmates under their charge during the nineteenth century. Correctional experiments and trailblazing eventually constructed the practice of parole now current in the United States.

Compare and Contrast Parole and Pardon

Parole is the release from incarceration prior to expiration of sentence, designed to effect reentry of the client to supervised return to the community. It almost always requires a parole officer charged with helping the offender find job placement, advising and counseling, and surveillance, with the possibility of parole revocation and return to imprisonment.

Pardons come in two major forms: conditional pardon and full pardon. A full pardon usually means complete exoneration of blame for the offense and relieves the prisoner of the stigma of guilt. One version of the pardon is amnesty, which may be granted to a group or class of offenders. Conditional pardons relieve some but not all of the limitations offenders suffer and, depending on the jurisdiction, might require continued interaction with a justice official.

Describe the Current Status of Parole in the United States

Parole as a process assumes that offenders can and will cease their deprecatory acts if motivated to do so, that almost all humans can be bettered, that the state has a responsibility to protect the public, and that some method exists of determining when beneficial change has readied the convict for release, hopefully back as a solid citizen. The parole board makes that determination and can effect the transition to the free society by providing control and guidance by professional parole agents or parole officers. Supervision usually ends when the parolee demonstrates capability to cease crime.

Summarize the Issues Associated with Prisoners Reentering the Community, Including the Stigma Parolees Face

Parole as a process is not linear. There is no magical potion or treatment that alone can lead the returning citizen to changing from past derelictions to model behavior. It is necessary to conceive of parole as a process and to recognize that parolees are not perfect. Some will violate the conditions of their parole, typically by alcohol or drug consumption, association with stronger offenders, or out of desperation and despair. The general public fears parolees, who subsequently face much stigma and blocked opportunities.

Most of these are violations of the rules of parole as determined by the parole board and parole officer. When criminogenic factors appear and the parolee seems to be "back-sliding," parole officers can arrest or deliver the offender up to the parole board for a consideration of the evidence. Most of the evidence appears to be violations of the rules of conduct rather than commission of new crimes. The board weighs the evidence provided by the parole agent and can act by threatening to commit or return the parolee to prison to serve the remainder of the original sentence, by tourniquet tightening, by imposing a brief jail time, or by assignment to a more intense supervision setting. If the parolee does not conform to expectations, parole might be revoked, and incarceration could result.

Explain How Parole Is Granted and the Role of the Parole Board

The parole board routinely considers inmates for possible parole, assaying program participation and success, assessing inmate risk posed if released, investigating community reactions to the possibility of parole of each offender, and conducting a prerelease investigation of that inmate and any possible parole plan, among other responsibilities. If the board is satisfied that the benefits of incarceration have been reached and change is evident, the board could release the inmate to the community, creating parole reentry. The board will decide what conditions the exiting inmate must observe, authorizing release usually on completion of a reentry plan. If the offender violates those conditions or is arrested for a new crime, the parole board may revoke conditional release and order the parolee returned to prison as an inmate.

Identify the Conditions of Parole

Parole is a contract between the state and the offender. If the offender abides by the terms of the contract, he or she remains free. If a violation of these conditions occurs or if a parolee is charged with a new crime, the parole board may revoke parole and return the offender to prison. The offender must abide by the contract and stay under parole supervision for the period of time specified by the parole board.

Summarize the Role of Parole Officers

Institutional parole officers undertake institutional prerelease investigations and can provide the parole board with recommendations for conditions of parole. This is an investigatory role. When the parolee begins reentry, those officers provide both service and surveillance functions. In cases of violations of parole conditions or the commission of new offenses, the parole officer offers insights, history, and recommendations as appropriate for parole board action.

Explain How Parole Supervision Is Terminated, Including Revocation of Parole

Parole usually lasts more than two but usually less than seven years. Some states may permit discharge from parole after a very short time if the offender has diligently adhered to the prerelease contract. Parolees who violate the conditions of their release can be returned to prison for a technical violation. Some states have medical release and compassionate release programs, which the parole officer would supervise.

Describe the Prisoner Reentry Process

The major challenges parolees face revolve around residence, employment, and human interactions. Some states underwrite the residence challenge by a short-term subvention for housing or assignment to a halfway house. Securing prerelease employment is a usual requirement that parole boards can impose. Finally, the parole officer must guard against the parolees' association with other criminals who are not ready to become free of crime.

Finally, we should note that not all inmates will be released by parole or through programs that extend the limits of confinement to include the community. Some inmates will "max out" and be released on compulsory release under supervision. Others will serve their sentences to the day. And some will fail repeatedly on parole, regardless of the efforts of the best officers and supervising parole board. The bright indicator of the effectiveness of parole is the fact that almost half of the released inmates will satisfactorily complete their community supervision and desist in criminal activity.

Explain Reentry Courts

Built on specialty courts research and experience, a reentry court is a specialized court for offenders who leave prison early and "reenter" society. Its purpose is to make the transition from incarceration to tax-paying citizen more likely. Over the past decade, these courts have been scrutinized by independent and governmental agencies and have been found to produce better results than traditional approaches, including incarceration.

Explain the Effectiveness of Parole

Offenders placed on parole are supervised by parole officers and mandated to reenter society as law-abiding citizens. Officers are equipped with authority to monitor and evaluate parolees and recommend to the parole board that failing parolees be returned to prison. The board can require law-abiding behavior and increase the level of surveillance. When parole is coupled with the reentry court, parolees generally conform, and more than 6 in 10 successfully complete the reentry process.

Key Words

Alexander Maconochie, 322
Irish system, 322
Sir Walter Crofton, 322
Good time, 323
Release on parole, 323
Truth-in-sentencing movement, 323
Discretionary release, 324
Mandatory release, 324
"Max out," 324
Executive clemency, 324
Pardon, 324
Amnesty, 324
Reprieve, 324
Commutation, 324
Parole, 325
Parole board, 327
Flopped, 328
Parole agreement, 329
Technical violation, 330
Morrissey v. *Brewer*, 332
Procedures for pardon, 333
Work release, 334
Furlough, 336
Reintegration, 336
Halfway house, 336
Community residential center, 339
Reentry, 339
Reentry courts, 339

Review Questions

1. What are the main models of parole boards?
2. What are the main differences between parole and probation?
3. Should parole boards be independent of institutions? Why or why not?
4. If you were responsible for reentry services in your state, how would you design a model reentry process?
5. What are parole guidelines, and how do they structure discretion?
6. Should parole supervision be abolished?
7. Do you favor mandatory release with supervision or discretionary release with supervision?
8. If you were the governor and were selecting parole board members, what qualifications would you look for?
9. Why is graduated release so beneficial to both the community and the offender?
10. What are reentry courts?
11. How can the effectiveness of a correctional program be measured?

Application Case Studies

1. John Doe is up for parole, and you are a member of the parole board considering his case. John has been incarcerated for 12 years for first-degree manslaughter, a crime he committed when he was 22 years old. John has been a model prisoner and has completed his general equivalency diploma and vocational training in electrical work, but the family of the victim is vehemently opposed to release. Would you vote for release? Why or why not?
2. You are the state director of corrections, and the federal courts have just ordered you to reduce your prison population by 10,000 inmates. Describe how you would select inmates for release and what steps you would put in place to keep the community safe.
3. You are a sitting member of your state's parole board. A man known to belong to a large prison gang comes up to you when you are eating alone and asks for a favorable consideration for release of the gang's president, currently in supermax segregation. Your standard "send me a letter and I'll investigate before taking action" is abruptly brushed away. The gang representative tells you the names of your wife and three children and asks if you love them. It is clearly a "do-or-die" threat. What would you do?

Endnotes

1. Restrictions on early release from prison and other reforms to reduce the discrepancy between sentence imposed and actual sentence served in prison have come to be known as "truth in sentencing." See Thomas Bonczar and L. Glaze, *Probation and Parole in the United States, 1998* (Washington, DC: U.S. Department of Justice, 1999), p. 6.
2. Various forms of conditional release from incarceration were developed in other countries before any American state adopted a parole system; however, the core elements of a parole system administrative board making release decisions and granting conditional, supervised release with the authority to revoke it were first created by legislation in New York State (1869).
3. A. Pisciotta, "Saving the Children: The Promise and Practice of Parens Patria, 1838–1898," *Crime and Delinquency*, 28:3 (1982): 410–425.
4. K. O. Hawkins, "Parole Selection: The American Experience" (unpublished doctoral diss., Cambridge University, 1971).
5. Ibid.
6. R. M. Carter, R. A. McGee, and K. E. Nelson, *Corrections in America* (Philadelphia: J. B. Lippincott, 1975).
7. See Ellen Chayet, "Correctional Good Time as a Means of Early Release," *Criminal Justice Abstracts* 26:3 (1994): 521–538.
8. J. V. Barry, "Captain Alexander Maconochie," *Victorian Historical Magazine* 27:1 (June 1957): 1–18. For a history of the American Correctional Association, see A. Travisono and M. Hawkes, *Building a Voice: The American Correctional Association, 125 Years of History* (Landham, MD: American Correctional Association, 1995), http://www.corrections.com/aca/history/html.
9. D. Fogel, *We Are the Living Proof*... (Cincinnati, OH: Anderson Publishing, 1975).
10. John Langbein, "The Historical Origins of the Sanction of Imprisonment for Serious Crime," *Journal of Legal Studies* 5 (1976): 35–60.
11. Hawkins, "Parole Selection: The American Experience."
12. Probation and Parole Statistics, in *Summary Findings* (Washington, DC: Bureau of Justice Statistics, U.S. Department of Justice, 2002).
13. *Probation and Parole in the United States, 2011* (Washington, DC: U.S. Department of Justice, 2012).
14. Wayne Morse, *The Attorney General's Survey of Release Procedures* (Washington, DC: U.S. Government Printing Office, 1939), p. 23.
15. Paula Ditton and Doris Wilson, *Truth in Sentencing in State Prisons* (Washington, DC: Bureau of Justice Statistics, 2004), p. 3.
16. Camille Camp and G. Camp, *The Corrections Yearbook, Adult Corrections 2002* (South Salem, NY: Criminal Justice Institute, 2002).
17. *Greenholtz* v. *Inmates of the Nebraska Penal and Correctional Complex*, 99 S. Ct. 2100 (1979).
18. No presidential pardon was awarded from 1994 to 1998, but 12 conditional pardons were awarded in 1999.
19. U.S. Office of the Pardon Attorney, *Civil Disabilities of Convicted Felons: A State-by-State Survey* (Washington, DC: U.S. Office of the Pardon Attorney, 1996).
20. Brent Smith, E. Watkins, and K. Morgan, "The Effect of Victim Participation on Parole Decisions," *Criminal Justice Policy Review* 8:1 (1997): 57–74.
21. J. Runda, E. Rhine, and R. Wetter, *The Practice of Parole Boards* (Lexington, KY: Council of State Governments, 1994).
22. U.S. Office of the Pardon Attorney, *Civil Disabilities of Convicted Felons.*
23. J. Travis and J. Petersilia, "Reentry Reconsidered: A New Look at an Old Problem," *Crime and Delinquency* 47 (2001): 291–313. See also Shelley Listwan, F. Cullen, and E. Latessa, "How to Prevent Prisoner Re-Entry Programs from Failing: Insights from Evidence-Based Corrections," *Federal Probation* 70:3 (2006): 19–25.

24. J. Austin, "Prisoner Reentry: Current Trends, Practices, and Issues," *Crime and Delinquency* 47 (2001): 314–334.
25. A. J. Lurigio, "Effective Services for Parolees with Mental Illnesses," *Crime and Delinquency* 47 (2001): 446–461.
26. Cece Hill, "Inmate Fee-for-Service Programs," *Corrections Compendium* 23:8 (1998): 7–16. See also Editors, "Rising Medical Costs Encourage States to Release Sick, Dying Inmates," *Correctional News* 14:6 (2008): 16; Christian Mason, Tod Burke, and Stephen Owen, "On the Road Again: The Dangers of Transporting Ailing Inmates," *Corrections Today* 75:5 (2013): 76-81; and Mark Foxall et al., "Meeting the Needs of the Mentally Ill: A Jail's Perspective," *Corrections Today* 75:5 (2013): 64–67.
27. The longer a work-release participant remains employed in the same work-release job after earning parole status, the greater the potential for parole success. Kyu Man Lee, *The Wichita Work Release Center: An Evaluative Study* (Ann Arbor, MI: University Microfilms International, 1983). See also Richard Jones, ed., "Conditions of Confinement," *Journal of Contemporary Criminal Justice* 13:1 (1997): 3–72.
28. David Anderson, *Crime and the Politics of Hysteria: How the Willie Horton Story Changed American Justice* (New York: Random House, 1995); Tali Mendelberg, "Executing Horizons: Racial Crime in the 1988 Presidential Campaign," *Public Opinion Quarterly* 61:1 (1997): 134–157.
29. The failure rate (both new crimes and failure to return) in furlough programs is remarkably low: about 1 percent. Camille Camp and G. Camp, *The Corrections Yearbook, Adult Corrections 2000* (South Salem, NY: Criminal Justice Institute), p. 148.
30. James Bonta and L. Motiuk, "The Diversion of Incarcerated Offenders to Correctional Halfway Houses," *Journal of Research in Crime and Delinquency* 24:3 (1987): 302–323; Edward Latessa and L. Travis, "Residential Community Correctional Programs," in *Smart Sentencing? An Examination of the Emergence of Intermediate Sanctions, ed.* James Byrne and A. Lurigio (Beverly Hills, CA: Sage, 1991); Sarah Twill, L. Nackerud, E. Risler, et al., "Changes in Measured Loneliness, Control and Social Support among Parolees in a Halfway House," *Journal of Offender Rehabilitation* 27:3/4 (1998): 77–92.
31. Additional information may be obtained from the International Community Corrections Association, http://www.iccaweb.org/.
32. Carolyn Tucker, K. Herman, B. Brady, et al., "Operation Positive Expression: A Behavioral Change Program for Adolescent Halfway House Residents," *Residential Treatment for Children and Youth* 13:2 (1995): 67–80.
33. Brian Grant, L. Motiuk, L. Brunet, et al., *Day Parole Program Review* (Ottawa: Correctional Service of Canada, 1996).
34. Twill et al., "Changes in Measured Loneliness."
35. Camp and Camp report that the cost per resident for private halfway house providers is 14 percent less than that provided by state departments of corrections. Camille Camp and G. Camp, *The Corrections Yearbook 1998* (Middletown, CT: Criminal Justice Institute), p. 123.
36. C. T. Lowenkamp and E. J. Latessa, *Evaluation of Ohio's Halfway Houses and Community-Based Correctional Facilities* (Cincinnati, OH: University of Cincinnati, 2002).
37. Marc Levinson, "In South Carolina, Community Corrections Means the Alston Wilkes Society," *Corrections Magazine* 9:1 (1983): 41–46. See also Bobbie Huskey and A. Lurigio, "An Examination of Privately-Operated Intermediate Punishments in the United States," *Corrections Compendium* 17:12 (1992): 1, 3–8, and Joseph Callahan and K. Koenning, "The Comprehensive Sanctions Center in the Northern District of Ohio," *Federal Probation* 59:3 (1995): 52–57.
38. Daniel Glaser, "Supervising Offenders Outside Prisons," in *Crime and Public Policy*, ed. James Wilson (San Francisco: Institute for Contemporary Studies, 1983), p. 212.
39. James Beck, "An Evaluation of Federal Community Treatment Centers," *Federal Probation* 43:5 (1979): 36–41; Paul Gendreau, M. Shilton, and P. Clark, "Intermediate Sanctions: Making the Right Move," *Corrections Today* 57:1 (1995): 28–65.
40. For more information on reentry courts, see http://reentrypolicy.org/announcements/reentry_courts_emerging_trend.
41. Z. Hamilton (2010), "Do Reentry Courts Reduce Recidivism? Results from the Harlem Parole Reentry Court," http://www.courtinnovation.org/sites/default/files/Reentry_Evaluation.pdf (accessed December 3, 2013).
42. A. L. Solomon, V. Kachnowski, and B. Avinash, *Does Parole Work?* (Washington, DC: Urban Institute, 2005).
43. For a summary of the criticism, see American Probation and Parole Association, http://www.appa-net.org/eweb/Dynamicpage.aspx?site=APPA_2&webcode=IE_NewsRelease&wps_key=50163cb7-737c-483f-8405-6cb0ca50e079.
44. Kristofer Bret Bucklen and Gary Zajac, "But Some of Them Don't Come Back (to Prison!): Resource Deprivation and Thinking Errors as Determinants of Parole Success and Failure," *Prison Journal* 89:3 (2009): 239–264. See also Gary Zajac, "But Some of Them Don't Come Back (to Prison): Determinants of Parole Success," http://www.portal.state.pa.us/portal/server.pt/document/1060758/determinants_of_parolee_success_pdf (accessed December 3, 2013).

part 4

Correctional Clients

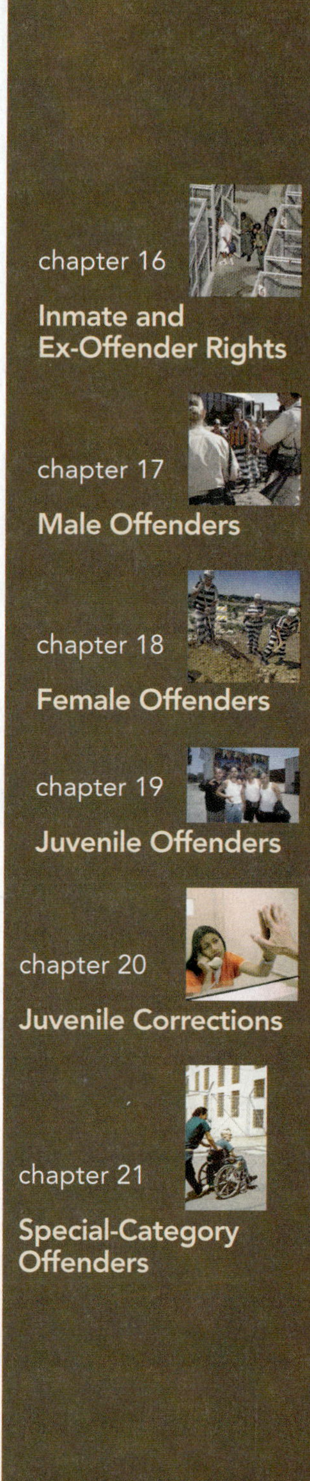

Overview

Part 4 (Chapters 16–21) deals with correctional systems and correctional functions, and the legal environment in which they operate. The last four chapters deal with the human beings incarcerated in institutions. In particular, we deal with male and female offenders, juvenile inmates, and special categories of inmates. Among the latter are groups of inmates with more problems than the other offenders in the mainstream of criminal behavior: the mentally disordered offender, the developmentally challenged offender, the sex offender, HIV-infected inmates, and geriatric inmates. Together, these categories represent the spectrum of the individual offenders under the custody and treatment of corrections administrators.

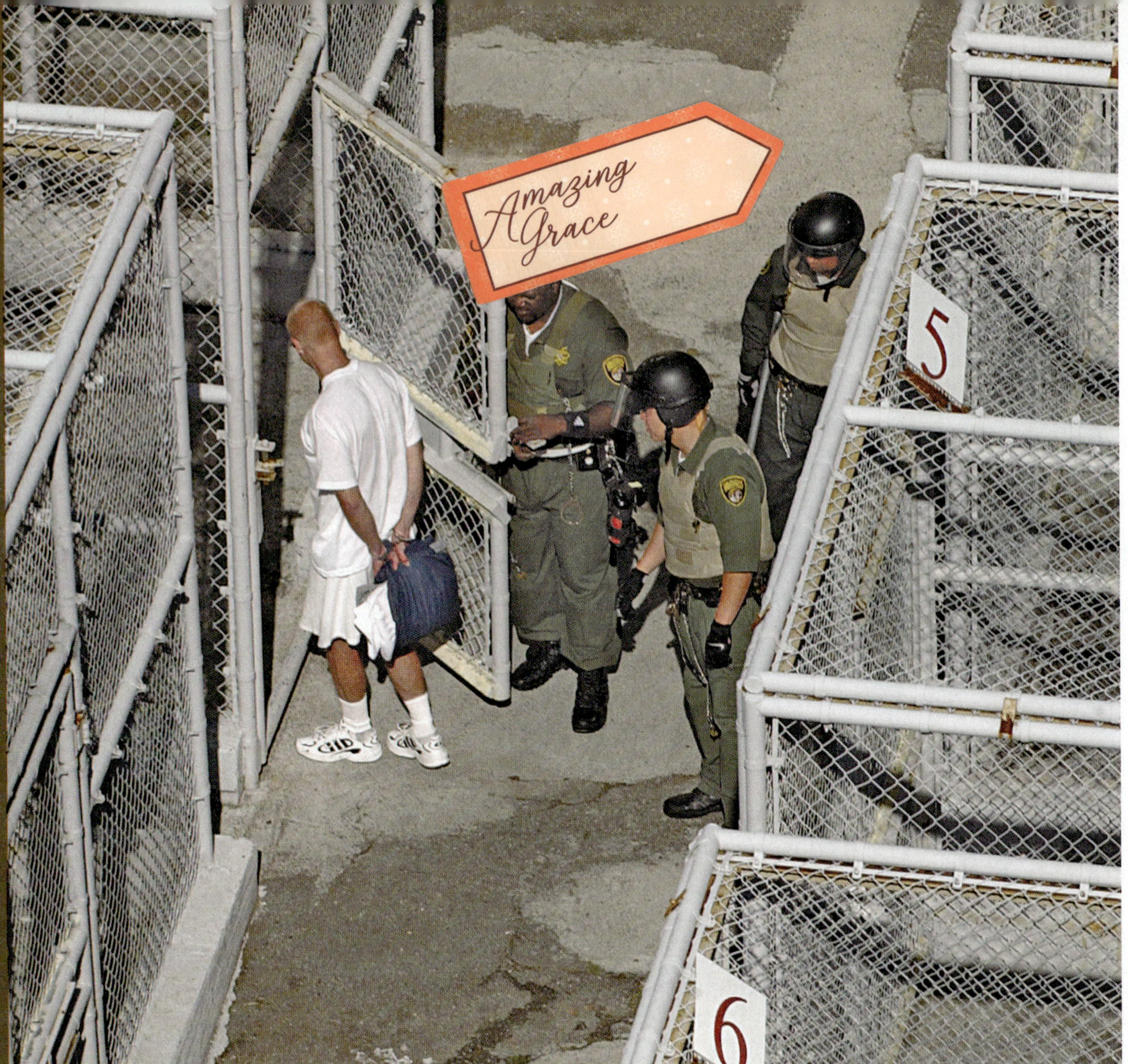

Clay Mclachlan/Corbis.

Objectives

- Summarize the issues associated with the stigma of being a prisoner and with the loss and restoration of civil rights.
- Describe the status of the convicted offender.
- Identify basic inmate rights.
- Compare and contrast the right to work with the need to work.
- Explain why restricted trades are barriers to employment.
- Describe the problem with having a record.

chapter 16
Inmate and Ex-Offender Rights

Outline

"Both federal and state courts in which litigation over correctional issues has been filed may appoint a servant of the court (court master) whose task it is to assist the court in whatever manner the court directs."

—Harry E. Allen

Overview

Ask the average person on the street what "rights" prisoners have coming to them when in confinement—or eventually when released after their sentences have been served. After a few seconds of a blank stare, most would answer, "What do you mean rights? They don't have any." In this chapter, we present in some detail the misunderstood world of those rights that apply to inmates and ex-offenders. The incredible amount of litigation in institutions, the long battles for the lives of what appear to be heinous animals who deserve to die, and the problems with the ex-prisoner trying to deal with society and carrying a heavy record for life cause us to wonder how this all came about.

The rights of inmates and offenders are important, and the courts and rights advocates carefully monitor them. When those persons have finally done their time and now find themselves back in their former neighborhoods—burdened by a record and a stigma that are hard to overcome—they still have rights as well. Literally millions of citizens on the streets of America have been convicted of a crime and placed under correctional supervision at some point in their lives. (Nearly 7 million inmates and ex-offenders are under active correctional supervision, from probation to incarceration to parole.) This chapter deals with the sometimes gray area of the offender and the problems offenders face while incarcerated and while trying to reintegrate into society. This task is one that has many bumps in the road back to being a productive and useful citizen, but many more make that trip and succeed than we often acknowledge. This chapter considers the restrictions on inmates and ex-offenders and the current status of efforts to provide additional rights. We start with some of the myths and legends about these efforts.

correctional **practice 16.1**

Court Masters in Corrections

Both federal and state courts in which litigation over correctional issues has been filed may appoint a servant of the court, or court master, a functional adjunct whose task is to assist the court in whatever manner the court directs. Typically, the master oversees the day-to-day compliance of the institution or institutional system to the decree of the court or the consent decree. A decree of the court implies that the defendant (correctional unit) lost the case and the court has issued orders that are to be implemented. A consent decree occurs where the complainants (inmates) or defendants agree to a set of actions that both would find acceptable.

Generally, masters monitor the lawsuit, report to the court, investigate complaints by inmates, have access to prisoners and their files, hold hearings, and write reports that inform the appointing judge about progress in the settlement of the orders. They also advise the court (through their special expertise in corrections, in particular) and help arrange compromises between the extremes of the demands of the inmates and the realities of prison administration.

When a master is appointed, correctional administrators tend to resist the intrusion of the master into the routine affairs of the institution. Some masters have their own reform agenda or fail to represent the correctional unit in securing compromise. Finally, the defendant (correctional system) must pay for the master and any staff, and there usually is little disincentive to the master's office running up long hours of work at high rates of compensation. Currently, masters are seen as providing correctional expertise to a court that has no competence in correctional administration. Future correctional administrators will need to develop positive working relationships with the court and negotiate with all parties to define clearly the powers, role, and scope of the master to minimize any negative fallout from the appointment of an intervention agent.

In 2007, the entire systems of nine states or territories were under consent orders, and another 224 institutions were under consent decrees.

SOURCE: Based on data from American Correctional Association, *2007 Directory* (Alexandria, VA: American Correctional Association, 2007), p. 15.

THE STATUS OF THE CONVICTED OFFENDER

key term

Convicted offender
Guilty law violator who has exhausted all appeals of conviction and sentencing.

When defendants have gone through the whole criminal justice process, including all appeals, and their sentences have been upheld, they officially acquire the status of **convicted offender**. They may already have spent a long time in jail or prison as their appeals made their tedious way through the courts. But with the final guilty verdict in, the offender's relationship to the correctional system undergoes a significant change. In this section, we examine the offender's new status and his or her rights during and after incarceration. Over the years, a body of folklore has grown about the rights of prisoners and ex-prisoners. We hope this chapter will dispel some of those myths and clarify recent developments.

With almost 7 million people[1] subject to the control of some kind of correctional authority in America each day, the status of those convicted offenders poses a significant problem. Correctional officials have been slow to draw up internal policies and procedures to guide their administrators in protecting the offenders' rights. Under the "hands-off" policy mentioned in Chapter 4, the courts were reluctant to criticize decisions and procedures developed by correctional administrators. That policy was abandoned in the mid-1960s, opening the door to case after case regarding prisoners' rights, with no end in sight. There are even some state departments of corrections under judicial review, several with a court-appointed monitor, or **court master** (see Correctional Practice 16.1), who supervises conformity to the court's order. Let us start with the basic rights of the confined inmate.

key term

Court master
Representative of the court ordered to monitor correctional compliance with a court's orders.

BASIC INMATE RIGHTS

Visiting and Community Ties

key term

Civil death
State of being physically alive but without rights.

You should recall from Chapter 1 that penal punishments included **civil death**, which meant that the offender's property was confiscated in the name of the state and his wife declared a widow, eligible to remarry. To society, the offender was, in effect, dead. The vestiges of

Photo 16.1

Couple visit by telephone in jail, separated by a glass partition.
Spencer Grant/PhotoEdit.

civil death are probably most visible in correctional practices that pertain to the privilege of having visitors. Debate continues about whether having visitors is actually a privilege or is in fact a right. The practice of having visitors is not new. Occasional visitors were allowed even as early as 1790 in the Walnut Street Jail. If a prisoner were diligent and good, a visit was allowed from a close family member—but only once every three months, for 15 minutes, through two grills, and under the scrutiny of a keeper.[2] This procedure may seem absurdly strict, but is not too far from the current practice in some high-security correctional institutions. The overriding security focus at most prisons dictates that visits be limited, subject to highly regimented conditions, and likely to discourage close physical or emotional contact. The dehumanizing rules and procedures for visiting do not accord with modern goals of rehabilitation and correction. Although security is important in maximum-security prisons, it could be tempered with humanity in such a personal thing as a visit from a friend or family member.

Limitations on visiting hours, restricted visitor lists,[3] overcrowded visiting rooms, and the overwhelming presence of guards contribute to the inmate's difficulty in maintaining ties with family and the outside world.[4] Most institutions are located far from large urban centers (where most inmates' families live), requiring long hours of travel and expense for visitors. Not only family ties but also friendships wither quickly under such conditions. This alienation creates serious problems for both the inmate and the institution. Typically, an inmate is allowed to receive a visitor once a week (in some places as seldom as once a month), usually a member of his or her immediate family. This is hardly representative of social life in contemporary America.

For the married inmate, family ties are inevitably weakened by long separation. With divorce frequent, the social consequences to the family, community, and institution are incalculable; imprisonment itself is grounds for divorce in some jurisdictions.[5] Institution officials often face severe problems caused by the deterioration of an inmate's family situation. When, for example, a wife does not write or the inmate hears through the grapevine that she has a lover, violence can and often does result—expressed in attacks against prison personnel,[6] another prisoner,[7] or attempts to escape.

Deprived of even a semblance of normal relations with the outside, the inmate turns to the other inmates and the inmate subculture for solace. It seems ironic that inmates are cut off from both friends and relatives and must depend almost entirely on the company

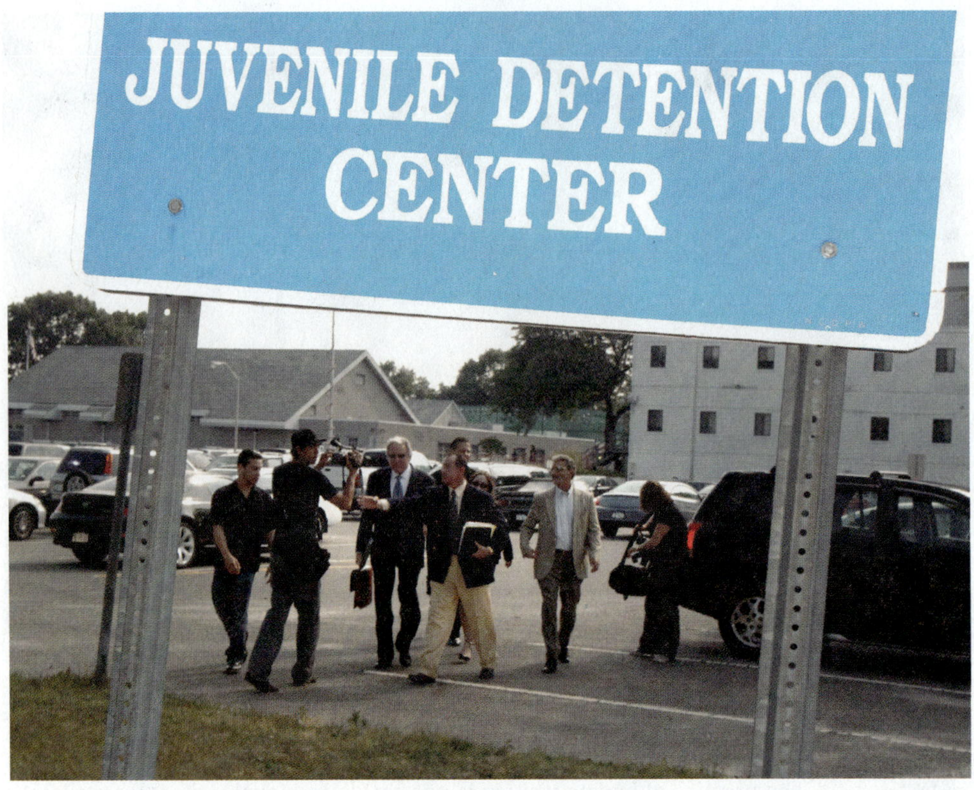

Photo 16.2

Juvenile rights must be protected by lawyers, here seen leaving a juvenile detention center after arguing to protect their clients' rights.
Richard Beetham/Newscom.

of criminals. Yet when finally released on parole, some parole rules forbid the parolee to associate with known ex-offenders. Such paradoxical situations seem to run counter to the basic premises of American corrections. There is no better way to combat the inmate social system and prepare an inmate for freedom than by strengthening his or her ties with the outside world through visitations, family or conjugal visits (see Correctional Practice 16.2),[8] home furloughs, telephone access, and mail.

Use of Mail

The mail system is closely tied to visitation as another way to maintain essential contact with the outside world. As in the case of visits, stated reasons for the limitation and censorship of mail are tied either to security or to the prison's orderly administration. Although the use of the mail system is a right, case law has established that correctional administrators can place reasonable restrictions on prisoners in the exercise of that right if there is a "clear and present danger" or compelling state need. As with most situations behind the walls, in the past, mail rules were systematically stiffened to facilitate the institutions' smooth operation. If it became too great an administrative burden to read all the incoming and outgoing mail, the number of letters or the list of correspondents was reduced. Eventually, a small maximum of allowed letters and very restrictive lists of correspondents became the standard. As long as the prisoners could not turn to the courts, this practice did not create a stir. When the attorneys appointed to help prisoners began to see the unjustness of restrictions concerning mail and other so-called privileges, they began to question the rules and reestablish those privileges as rights.

How much mail should a prisoner receive? Administrators have usually restricted it to an amount that can readily be censored. During personnel shortages (for example, in wars), the amount of mail was often limited to one letter a month. Outgoing mail was similarly restricted. Communications with an attorney could be opened and read but not censored

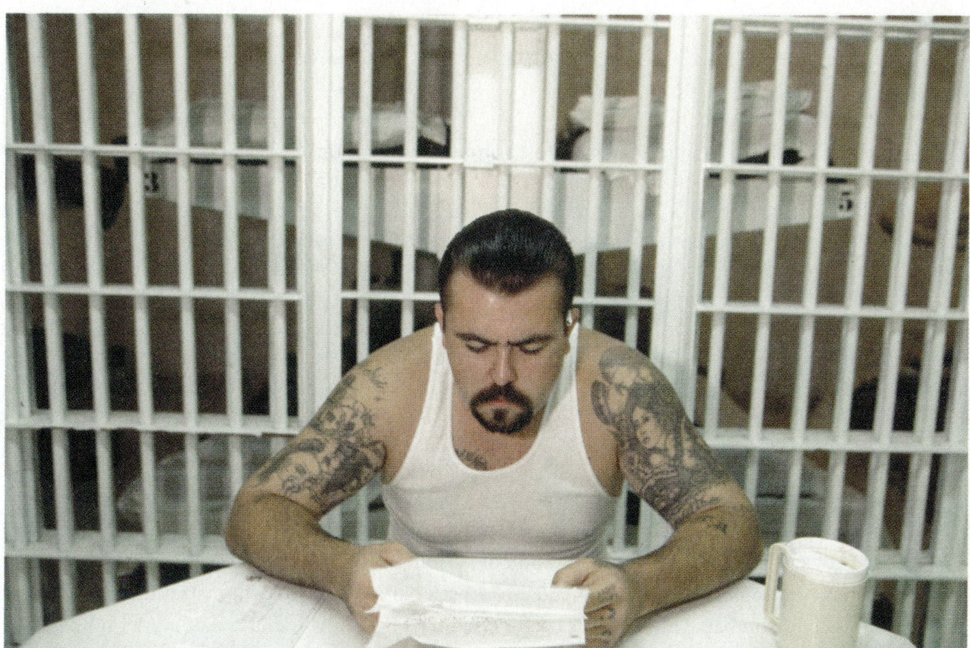

Photo 16.3

Incarcerated inmates are seldom allowed to communicate with the free world by e-mail.
A. Ramey/PhotoEdit.

unless the correspondence referred to plans for illegal activity[9] or contained contraband. More recently, court decisions have found that most censorship of communications between inmates and their lawyers is unconstitutional;[10] this direction also appears in decisions regarding communications with the news media.[11]

Death row inmates frequently receive only photocopies of correspondence sent to them from persons other than attorneys. There is a clear and present danger of poisoning from chemicals sprayed on stationery at the inmate's request. Stamps can also be affixed to envelopes with a liquid poison or drugs. Finally, lethal poison can also be suspended in ink. Ironically, death row inmates cannot be allowed to kill themselves before their execution, although many do commit suicide.[12]

Contraband and Mail

In the past, contraband was commonly described as "any material that might be used for an escape or used to take advantage of other prisoners." Such items as matches, money, pornographic pictures, guns, knives, lubricants, drugs, and tools are generally considered contraband. Any item could have been placed on the contraband list if it was seen as a threat to the prison's orderly operation.

The more recent definition of contraband is any item found on the prisoner or in his or her cell that is not specifically authorized by the administration in written rules. This helps simplify the process and eliminate any controversy as to what is or is not contraband. (For example, if written rules state that a prisoner is authorized two blankets and three are found in a cell inspection, the third blanket is, by definition, contraband and subject to removal.)

When an inmate wishes to communicate with a second inmate, either a friend or a jailhouse lawyer who is incarcerated at another institution, the courts have stuck to a hands-off policy, leaving that problem to the discretion of the correctional administrators. The general policy has been to prohibit the passage of any correspondence between inmates. This policy continues to be under attack, however, and has been rejected by some states.[13] In most court cases, the test for permissibility of mail and literature has been the **clear and present danger** standard:

key term

Clear and present danger
Test used in corrections to justify restricting the rights of inmates.

correctional practice 16.2

Family/Conjugal Visits

A conjugal visit is a scheduled extended visit during which an inmate is permitted to spend several hours or days in private, usually with a legal spouse. Although common in some countries, there are only five states in the United States that allow conjugal visits. These are California, Connecticut, New Mexico, New York, and Washington. Seen as a way to increase family ties, conjugal visits can also be a very effective prison management tool, as the incentive of conjugal visits means that inmates are strongly motivated to comply with the various day-to-day rules and regulations of the prison. As a result, inmates consciously avoid any rule violations that might disqualify them from having a conjugal visit. Although some see it as softening the prison experience and unfair to unmarried inmates, others, including Dr. Allen Ault, former director of corrections in Mississippi, believed it was one of the most powerful tools at his disposal for managing inmates. Throughout its history, the Mississippi Department of Corrections had allowed conjugal or "family" visits. Visits usually take place in a structure provided for that purpose, usually a caravan but sometimes a trailer or small cabin.

We accept the premise that certain literature may pose such a clear and present danger to the security of a prison, or to the rehabilitation of prisoners, that it should be censored. To take an extreme example, if there were mailed to a prisoner a brochure demonstrating in detail how to saw prison bars with utensils used in the mess hall, how to make a bomb, or how to provoke a prison riot, it would properly be screened. A magazine detailing for incarcerated drug addicts how they might obtain a euphoric "high," comparable to that experienced from heroin, by sniffing aerosol or glue available for other purposes within the prison walls, would likewise be censored as restraining effective rehabilitation. Furthermore, it is undoubtedly true that in the volatile atmosphere of a prison, where a large number of men, many with criminal tendencies, live in close proximity to each other, violence can be fomented by the printed word much more easily than in the outside world. Some censorship or prior restraint on inflammatory literature sent into prisons is, therefore, necessary to prevent such literature from being used to cause disruption or violence within the prison. It may well be that in some prisons where the prisoners' flash-point is low, articles regarding

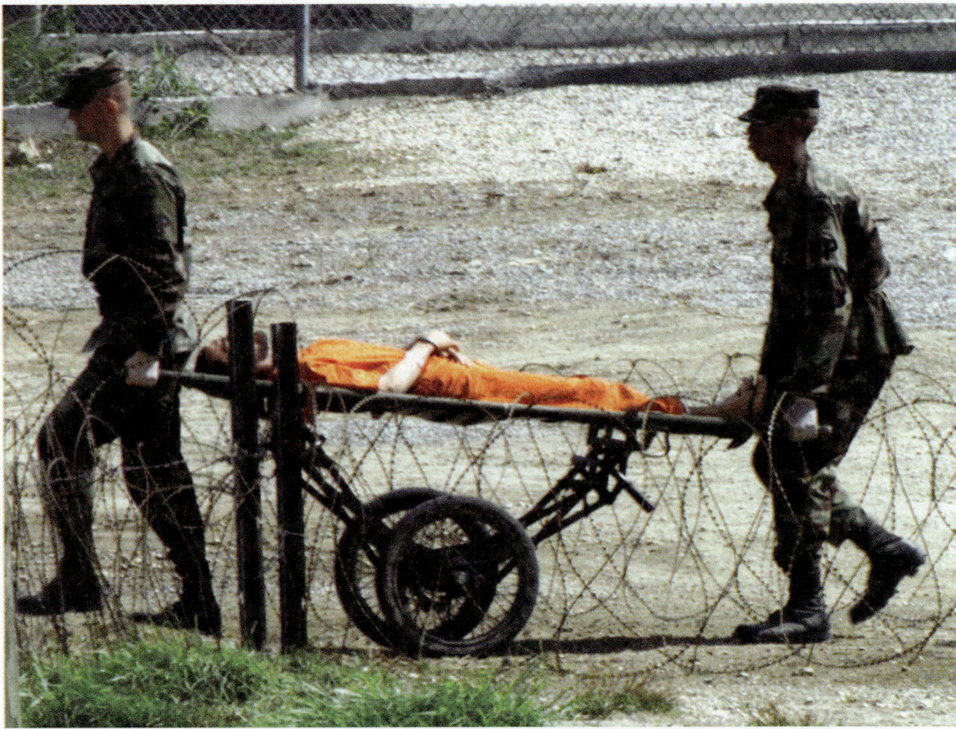

Photo 16.4
A detainee is carried by military police after being interrogated by officials at "camp X-ray" at the U.S. Naval Base at Guantanamo Bay, Cuba.
Marc Serota/Reuters.

> bombing, prison riots, or the like, which would be harmless when sold on the corner newsstand, would be too dangerous for release to the prison population. The courts have also upheld restrictions on incoming newspapers and magazines that would permit receipt of such mail if "only the publisher" is the sender.[14]

Ohio took the lead in the reform of mail censorship, eliminating all of it in Ohio's prisons on August 3, 1973.[15] Under the Ohio system, both incoming and outgoing mail is merely inspected for contraband and delivered unread. Each inmate may write and receive an unlimited number of items of mail. The adoption of those standards has caused few if any problems. Most states, however, still inspect, electronically, incoming packages and open letters to look for contraband. Currently, 27 states have begun offering a form of e-mail for inmates. This program does *not* provide inmates with direct e-mail access; however, it does allow those who wish to correspond with an inmate to enter into a subscription through a third-party website at a cost substantially less than the Postal Service.

Religious Rights in Prison

The idea underlying the penitentiary was drawn from religious precepts. It thus seems ironic that there would be any conflict in providing freedom of religion in prisons, but this has indeed been the case. The early efforts to restore the criminal through penitence and prayer were conducted in small homogeneous communities. As immigration to America expanded, it became the most heterogeneous nation in the world. Because the United States was founded on a belief that freedom of worship could not be infringed by the government, the First Amendment addressed those issues: "Congress shall make no law respecting an establishment of religion, or prohibiting the free exercise thereof." It is the conflict between what constitutes an established religion and the individual's right to exercise it that has caused grief in the nation's prisons.

A clear example of this problem was the **Black Muslim** decision, which has dominated case law for more than two decades. After a long string of cases,[16] the courts finally held that the Black Muslim faith did constitute an established religion and that the Black Muslims were therefore entitled to follow the practices the religion prescribed.[17] The resolution of the Black Muslim issue meant the standards applied there could be applied to any duly recognized religion.[18] This puts a strain on the prison administrator, who must allow equal protection for all inmates. The question of whether the state really grants each inmate "free exercise" simply by ensuring access to a minister of his or her particular faith is still unsettled.

key term

Black Muslims
American religious group based on Muslim theological concepts.

Access to Court and Counsel

Access to the federal courts was not established as a constitutional right for inmates until 1940 in a case called *Ex parte Hull.* In that decision, the U.S. Supreme Court established that "the state and its officers may not abridge or impair a petitioner's right to apply to a federal court for a writ of habeas corpus." Despite that clear ruling, the courts still maintained a strict hands-off policy in this regard until the 1964 case of *Cooper* v. *Pate.*[19]

Once the prisoners' right to use jailhouse lawyers was established in *Johnson* v. *Avery*,[20] inmates needed to be assured of an adequate supply of legal research materials; in 1971, the case of *Younger* v. *Gilmore*[21] guaranteed the inmate writ writers such assistance. But the extent of provided materials has varied considerably, from complete law libraries[22] in the state prisons to the bare essentials elsewhere.[23] Meanwhile, other states allow law students to run legal clinics inside institutions under the supervision of a law school faculty member qualified to practice in that jurisdiction. It seems the courts must continue to require that correctional administrations offer adequate legal counsel to inmates, or they will have to live with the continued use of jailhouse lawyers and the problems that result.

The right to consult with counsel has been clearly established.[24] The problem, before *Gideon* and the cases it generated, was that most inmates could not afford a lawyer to defend

key term

Jailhouse lawyer
An inmate who provides legal services to other inmates.

them or prepare later appeals.[25] Early prison rules restricted the use of **jailhouse lawyers**, those inmates who learn something about the law and use their skills to assist other inmates to file suits against correctional administrators and facilities. Restricting jailhouse lawyers from helping other inmates meant that few prisoners were able to file writs in the federal courts. After the courts established the right to counsel in *Gideon*, *Johnson* v. *Avery* covered those administrative agencies that could not or would not comply. Although not all jurisdictions have been able to provide counsel for all inmates, the remedies incorporated in the court decisions have helped fill the void—while incidentally creating a flood of writs that have washed over the civil and appeals courts. During the past two decades, the petitions filed in the U.S. district courts by federal prisoners increased 64 percent, and those by state prisoners increased 238 percent. The latter's civil rights suits increased by a whopping 389 percent. As a result of this steep increase, Congress enacted two legislative initiatives that sought to limit prisoners' ability to file petition in federal courts: the Prison Litigation Reform Act and the Antiterrorism and Effective Death Penalty Act. Together, these initiatives have sharply reduced inmate civil rights petitions.[26]

The Right to Medical Treatment and Care

The issue of adequate medical care in our prisons has finally prompted a decision from the U.S. Supreme Court. Only when a constitutionally guaranteed right has been violated has the Court become involved in the provision of medical care. Because both medical programs and the backgrounds of prison medical personnel are extremely diversified, the quality of medical aid varies among institutions.[27] Ironically, a nation that demands adequate medical care for all inmates is, at this writing, still struggling with providing adequate medical care for all of its citizens.

key term

Estelle* v. *Gamble
First U.S. Supreme Court case dealing with prison medical treatment.

The U.S. Supreme Court has taken the position that inmates in state prisons should seek remedy in the state courts. In the 1976 case of ***Estelle* v. *Gamble***,[28] that position was made even clearer. Although suits in the past have shown that prisoners' rights to proper diagnosis and medical treatment of illness have been violated on a grand scale, the courts have moved slowly in that area. In *Estelle*, however, the Court stated, "We therefore conclude that *deliberate indifference* [emphasis added] to serious medical needs of prisoners constitutes the unnecessary and wanton infliction of pain proscribed by the Eighth Amendment. This is true whether the indifference is manifested by prison doctors in their response to the prisoner's needs or by prison guards in intentionally denying or delaying access to medical care or intentionally interfering with the treatment once prescribed."[29] This was a giant step forward in the provision of medical treatment, but it still falls short of the individual remedies provided by decisions in other areas. For example, the U.S. First Circuit Court of Appeals has ruled that inmates must receive "adequate medical care" but do not necessarily deserve "the most sophisticated care that money can buy."[30] Medical care in prison in relationship to the AIDS problem has been described as "a national disgrace."[31]

key term

Deliberate indifference
Total deprivation of medical services.

Estelle stated a position of sympathy for complaints about the systemwide failure to provide adequate and humane medical care. The test of **deliberate indifference**, however, a requirement for evoking the Eighth Amendment, seems to be a major hurdle for most who choose to use *Estelle* as a basis for action (see Policy Position 16.1). Mere negligence or malpractice leaves the prisoner with remedy only in a state civil case. Total deprivation of medical service seems to be the current standard for application of constitutional prohibitions. One such example is the long-term solitary confinement of a large group of mentally ill inmates in a "supermax" prison.

One example of state failure to provide adequate health care services was seen in the state of California. In 2002, a federal judge determined that the California Department of Corrections system that provided health care to roughly 164,000 inmates was unconstitutional. He ordered major medical reforms, but the state failed to comply. As many as 64 preventable deaths of inmates a year (and injury to many others) due to medical malfeasance led to the Court's 2005 decision to order a receiver to take control of California's prison health care system.[32] In May 2011, the U.S. Supreme Court ordered California to reduce the population

policy position 16.1

The Deliberate Indifference Standard, *Farmer* v. *Brennan*

For a claim to be presented, the inmate must show that he or she was incarcerated under conditions posing a substantial risk of serious harm. This is the objective test, the *Rhodes* test: "Was the deprivation sufficiently serious?" If a plaintiff is able to establish a sufficiently serious deprivation, he or she must next satisfy the *Farmer* test, the "deliberate indifference" test: "Did the officials act with a sufficiently culpable state of mind?" (*Farmer* v. *Brennan*, 511 U.S. 825, 114 S. Ct. 1970 [1994]).

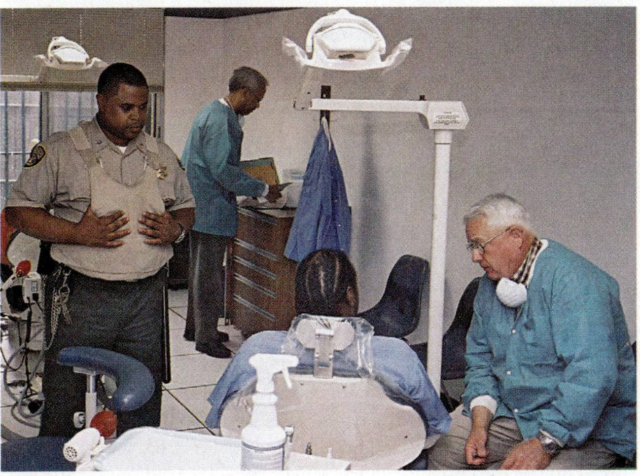

Photo 16.5

Inmates must rely on the prison to provide medical and dental services. Institutional guards must be present to protect the dentists and prevent theft of medical supplies.
Adam Tanner/Corbis.

Before the 1994 *Farmer* case, courts looked to an objective standard to determine if a prison official violated a prisoner's rights. The *Farmer* decision of 1994 set entirely different and personally responsible standards:

> For a claim . . . based on a failure to prevent harm, [Plaintiff] must show that [the inmate] [was] incarcerated under conditions posing a substantial risk of serious harm. [The objective test] The state of mind requirement follows from the several Supreme Court holdings that only the unnecessary and wanton infliction of pain implicates the Eighth Amendment. To violate the Cruel and Unusual Punishments Clause, a prison official must have a sufficiently culpable state of mind. [The subjective test]. The subjective component is the equivalent of criminal recklessness, much more than negligence or even malice. It is not similar to; it is criminal conduct that is required to be proven.
>
> "Subjective recklessness" as used in the criminal law is a familiar and workable standard that is consistent with the Cruel and Unusual Punishments Clause as interpreted in our cases, and we adopt it as the test for "deliberate indifference" under the Eighth Amendment. (*Farmer*, 511 U.S. at 838, 114 S. Ct. at 1980)

SOURCE: Personal communications with Deputy Attorney General Martin Basiszla, Office of the Attorney General, State of Hawaii, Honolulu, 1999; Mary Sylla, "HIV Treatment in U.S. Jails and Prisons," http://www.sfaf.org/files/site1/asset/beta_2008_win_jails_prisons.pdf (accessed November 18, 2008).

of its jammed prisons by more than 30,000 in two years to repair a health care system that lower courts found was defying constitutional standards and endangering guards as well as inmates. This ruling clearly has ramifications for other overcrowded correctional systems.

Because of the relative ineffectiveness of using state and tort courts to remedy inadequate medical services and treatment in institutions, inmates have more recently begun to sue correctional administrators through **Section 1983** of the U.S. Code. This section, passed in 1871 to protect the civil rights of recently freed slaves, allows petitioners to sue in a federal court without having first exhausted all existing state courts' remedies. The federal district and circuit courts are currently deciding a number of important cases, and some of those will eventually come before the U.S. Supreme Court.

key term

Section 1983
Legal statute for seeking redress regarding deprivation of legal rights of prisoners.

Civil Rights Act "1983" Suits

Title 42, Section 1983, of the U.S. Code, commonly known as the Civil Rights Act, reads as follows:

> Every person who, under color of any statute, ordinance, regulation, custom, or usage, or any state, or territory, subjects or causes to be subjected, any citizen of the United States or other person within the jurisdiction thereof to the deprivation of any rights, privileges, or immunities secured by the Constitution and laws, shall be liable to the party injured in an action at law, suit in equity, or other proper proceedings for redress.

correctional practice 16.3

Alternatives to Litigation

Civil litigation abounds over correctional issues such as prison overcrowding, compensation for lost personal property, need for a special diet, and restoration of good-time credits, increasing every year at great expense and time consumed by institutional managers. Further, court litigation is not a speedy technique for resolving inmate needs. Finally, correctional administrators have become increasingly concerned with the impact of lawsuits on the institution, including the reluctance of correctional staff to take actions, decline in staff morale, officer stress, and general reluctance to comply with discretionary duties. In the search for alternatives to litigation, four basic approaches have been proposed: grievance boards, inmate grievance procedures, the ombudsman, and mediators.

The grievance board is usually staffed by institutional employees or an occasional concerned citizen and is tasked to accept and investigate inmate complaints and then propose solutions, as relevant, to correctional administrators.

The inmate grievance procedure is similar to the grievance board, except that inmates are selected to serve as part of the grievance committee, a procedure many correctional managers find unacceptable because it might strengthen the influence of inmate grievance committee members over staff and other inmates.

The third alternative is the ombudsman, a public official who investigates complaints against correctional personnel, practices, policies, and customs and who is empowered to recommend corrective solutions and measures. Empowered to investigate, the ombudsman has access to files, inmates, records, and staff. The ombudsman (and office staff) tends to be impartial, have special expertise, and be independent of the correctional administrator. Reports are filed not only with the institutional manager but also with the correctional department director and funding agent for the office of the ombudsman. At least 17 correctional systems in the nation operate with the ombudsman to protect inmates.

Mediators are relatively new on the correctional scene and represent a third party skilled in correctional work who agrees to hear differences and to render a decision to remedy the condition that would be binding on both parties. Maryland, Rhode Island, Arkansas, and South Carolina have experimented with this approach.

An inmate might file a lawsuit in conjunction with any of these alternatives. The methods are seen as promising ways to avoid litigation over correctional issues. Federal prisoners are required to seek administrative remedies before filing a civil rights lawsuit.

SOURCE: Tracey Kyckelhahn and Thomas Cohen, *Civil Rights Complaints in U.S. District Courts, 1990–2006* (Washington, DC: Bureau of Justice Statistics), pp. 1, 8. Instructions for filing a complaint by inmate can be found at http://www.ncwd.uscourts.gov/sites/default/files/forms/PRISONER_CIVIL_RIGHTS_COMPLAINT_May2013.pdf (accessed December 11, 2013).

One example of the use of Section 1983 to redress medical malpractice and mistreatment can be seen in *Tucker* v. *Hutto*,[33] a Virginia case in which Tucker's arms and legs became permanently paralyzed as a result of improper use of antipsychotic drugs while he was a patient at the Virginia State Penitentiary Hospital. The suit was initiated by the National Prison Project[34] and settled out of court for $518,000. Section 1983 suits can be an effective although usually unwelcome avenue for defining and improving prisoner rights while under confinement. Many times the federal courts have been forced to overlook the issue of constitutional rights in order to correct situations involving a flagrant disregard of the need for adequate medical service. That disregard has often produced prison riots in the past, and it will continue to be a factor in right-to-treatment cases during the 2010s. Right to treatment is covered in detail in Chapter 21.

Alternatives to litigation, such as grievance boards and procedures, are discussed in Correctional Practice 16.3.

REMEDIES FOR VIOLATIONS OF RIGHTS

The first steps to remedy the almost standard practice of depriving convicted offenders of most rights have been taken, starting with the recognition that the Constitution does entitle those individuals to retain a substantial portion of their rights, even while incarcerated. The push for that recognition has come from the offenders themselves, often with the assistance of jailhouse lawyers, and has resulted in active and sympathetic judicial intervention.[35] The *writ of habeas corpus*, designed as a tool for prisoners to test the legality of their confinement, has been the main weapon in the battle for prisoner rights.[36] In 2002, the U.S. Supreme Court struck down Alabama's hitching post restraints as cruel and unusual punishment (*Hope* v. *Pelzer,* 536 U.S. 730 [2002]). The battle continues today, especially with regard to increased maintenance of community ties and the abolition of the death penalty.

The role of the federal courts in responding to inmate complaints is significant. The number of complaints filed in state and federal courts over jail and prison conditions, violations of inmate civil rights, due process violations, mistreatment, and lack of treatment of inmates has increased every year for the past two decades. Clearly, the rights of prisoners have become a driving factor in planning by administrators, legislators, and jurists in regard to operations and conditions in America's jails and prisons. Next we examine the plight of the ex-offender and the problems faced with a record that may result in a number of rights being either taken away or restored.

THE LEGEND OF THE EX-CON

The highly stylized version of the **ex-con** presented in the movies and on television usually depicts a tough, streetwise, scar-faced thug who is able to survive on wits and muscle, with a good-looking, submissive, and willing woman not too far in the background. The ex-con is often depicted as a person to be feared and never trusted. With a granite jaw and shifty eyes, he talks out of the corner of his mouth and prefers a life of crime. The real-life ex-offender, of course, is something quite different from our legendary ex-con of movie and mystery novel fame. The typical newly released ex-offenders found in most cities are often young, with little life experience outside prison walls; they are male or female, poor, with only the funds they managed to acquire while in prison; uneducated, generally with less than a high school diploma; former illicit drug users; and frightened, most having spent several years away from a rapidly changing world. After release from prison, these individuals must start a new life and make it in the free world while being watched by the correctional authorities, local police, employers, curious neighbors using computerized offender data banks, friends, and family. They often return to the same social and environmental conditions that gave rise to their trouble in the first place. The wonder is not that so many ex-offenders recidivate—but that more do not do so. If we add to this already heavy burden the legal and administrative restrictions placed on ex-offenders, it becomes evident that the happy-go-lucky ex-con is indeed a legend invented for the reading and viewing public.[37]

key term

Ex-con
Formerly institutionalized offender who has now given up a life as a criminal.

CONSEQUENCES OF A CONVICTION

Conviction for an offense carries with it the punishment imposed by statute. In addition, the convicted offender must carry several other disabilities and disqualifications that result from the conviction per se. Many state and federal statutes restrict some of the rights and privileges ordinarily available to law-abiding citizens in the nation. They include the rights to vote, to hold offices of private and public trust, to assist in parenting, to be on jury duty, to own firearms, to remain married, and to have privacy. Those and other rights may be lost on conviction. They are collectively called **collateral consequences** of criminal conviction. Just how many citizens face collateral consequences is unknown, but a conservative estimate is that there are at least 50 million persons living in our society who have been arrested for some offense in the nation, and at least 14 million of them have been convicted of a felony.

Even after offenders have served their sentences,[38] these secondary handicaps continue to plague them in the form of **social stigma**, loss of civil rights, and administrative and legislative restrictions. Each of those areas interacts with the others, and their overall

key term

Collateral consequences
Disabilities imposed on an offender on the basis of conviction.

key term

Social stigma
Mark of dishonor or shame.

effect is to prevent the successful reintegration of ex-offenders into the free community. The greatest dilemma faced by the ex-offender in search of a job is obvious—stigma, as discussed next.

key term

Stigma
Mark of dishonor or shame attached to a person based on crime or criminal status and behavior.

Stigma

The **stigma** of a prison record is to ex-offenders like a millstone to be worn around their necks until death. Although we pride ourselves that we have mostly advanced beyond the eye-for-an-eye mentality of the past, we do not show it in the treatment of our offenders who have allegedly paid their debt to society. Aaron Nussbaum pointed out some of the problems of stigma for the discharged prisoner:

> It is a grim fact that total punishment for crime never ends with the courts or jails. None can deny that a criminal record is a life-long handicap, and its subject a "marked man" in our society. No matter how genuine the reformation, nor how sincere and complete the inner resolution to revert to lawful behavior, the criminal offender is and remains a prisoner of his past record long after the crime is expiated by the punishment fixed under the criminal codes.
>
> This traditional prejudice and distrust stalks him at every turn no matter what crime he may have committed or the nature of the punishment meted out to him. It strikes at the first offender as ruthlessly, and with as deadly effect, as upon the inveterate repeater or the professional criminal. It pursues those alike who have served time in imprisonment, of long or short duration, and those who have been merely cloaked with a criminal record in the form of a suspended sentence, a dis-charge on probation, or even a fine.[39]

key term

Self-efficacy
Ability of offenders to assume direction of their lives.

One needs **self-efficacy** to survive in the competitive atmosphere of the free world. Thus, the diminished self-efficacy of the offender makes it difficult to bridge the gap between institutional life and the community.[40] It is the search for self-efficacy and status that leads many ex-offenders back to the circle of acquaintances that first led them afoul of the law. The personal disintegration encouraged by the fortress prisons of America makes many a discharged offender both a social and an economic cripple. We can only hope that the new techniques in corrections, designed to strengthen competencies and produce reasonable readjustment in the community, will help offset that effect, as will increased use of community corrections.

Loss of Civil Rights

Although most people recognize that released prisoners do not automatically regain all of their civil rights that were lost in prison, there is widespread confusion as to which rights are permanently lost and which suspended and what machinery is available to regain them. Sol Rubin, a lawyer and writer on penology, discussed the offender's loss of the rights to vote and engage in certain kinds of employment:

> [W]hen a convicted defendant is not sentenced to commitment, but is placed on probation, and receives a suspended sentence, he should lose no civil rights. This is a recommendation of the Standard Probation and Parole Act published as long ago as 1955. It is a contradiction of the purposes of probation and parole that this view does not prevail. A California case cites the following instruction to a new parolee: "Your civil rights have been suspended. Therefore, you may not enter into any contract, marry, engage in business, or execute a contract without the restoration of such civil rights by the Adult Authority." A look at the rights restored by the Adult Authority at the time of release on parole is just as sad, hardly more than that on release he may be at large. He may rent a habitation, he is told, buy food, clothing, and transportation, and tools for a job; and he is advised that he has the benefit of rights under Workman's Compensation, Unemployment Insurance, etc.

> When the sentence is commitment, the principle of *Coffin* v. *Reichard* ought to apply, that a prisoner retains (or should retain) all rights of an ordinary citizen except those expressly or by necessary implication taken away by law.[41]

The issue of restoring the rights of disenfranchised felony offenders in the nation is hotly debated, led in part by the Sentencing Project.[42]

Legal Consequences of a Felony Conviction

Under federal law and the laws of many states, conviction of a felony has consequences that may continue long after a sentence has been served. For example, convicted felons may lose essential rights of citizenship, such as the rights to vote and to hold public office, and may be restricted in their ability to obtain occupational or professional licenses. Under the federal gun control laws and under the laws of virtually all states, felons lose their firearms privileges. These and other collateral consequences of a felony conviction are burdens that follow from conviction in addition to any prison sentence, probation, or fine imposed by a court. Restoration of one or more of these rights frequently can be achieved, either automatically by the passage of time or by the occurrence of an event, such as completion of sentence or through some affirmative executive or judicial act that may be based on evidence of rehabilitation.

Although it may come as a surprise to many, state rather than federal law imposes a number of significant disabilities on conviction, even when the conviction is for a federal rather than state offense. The losses of the rights to vote, to hold state office, and to sit on a state jury are chief examples of such disabilities. Just as state law imposes a disability on a federal felon, so too a federal felon may be able to employ a state procedure to remove the disability instead of employing the only presently available federal restoration mechanism: presidential pardon.

The Office of the Pardon Attorney in the U.S. Department of Justice conducted research on federal statutes and the principal laws of all 50 states and the District of Columbia that deal with the effect of a felony conviction on the rights to vote, to hold office, to sit as a juror, and to possess firearms. It revealed that the laws governing the same rights and privileges vary widely from state to state, making something of a national crazy quilt of disqualifications and restoration procedures. It also showed that there were disagreements among agencies about how the law in a particular jurisdiction should be interpreted and applied. More important, the uncertain state of the law in various jurisdictions raises questions about a convicted felon's ability to determine his or her legal rights and responsibilities, which obviously can have serious consequences for affected individuals, particularly in connection with some felons' legal ability under federal law to possess firearms.

Not all states have paid consistent attention to the place of federal offenders in the state's scheme for loss and restoration of civil rights. While some state statutes expressly address federal offenses, both as to the loss of rights and as to the availability of restoration procedures, many do not. The disabilities imposed on felons under state law generally are assumed to apply with the same force whether the conviction is a state or federal one; in only a few states have particular disabilities been held not to apply to federal offenders. Similarly, state laws dealing with restoration of rights do not always address how federal felons' rights may be regained, particularly when state law disabilities for state offenders can be removed only by a state pardon. In at least 16 states, federal offenders cannot avail themselves of the state procedure for restoring one or more of their civil rights, either because state law restores that right to state offenders only through a pardon and federal offenders are ineligible for a state pardon or because a state procedure to restore rights to state offenders is unavailable to federal offenders.

There is considerable variation among the states as to whether loss or denial of a license or permit based on a conviction is mandatory or discretionary. Under some **occupational disability** statutes, revocation and/or denial of a license or permit are mandatory for certain

key term

Occupational disability Offenders are forbidden to practice designated occupations due to fact of conviction of crime.

offenses and/or for certain occupations. For example, revocation and denial of a teaching certificate may be mandatory for someone convicted of a drug offense or of a sex offense involving children. Nearly all states have enacted statutes requiring the registration of sex offenders.

key term

Firearms disability
Loss of rights of ex-felons to own, possess, or exercise control over firearms.

The federal **firearms disability** on convicted felons raises particularly complex issues for state offenders because the applicability of the federal disability turns on the extent to which the state felon's "civil rights have been restored" under state law and the extent to which the restoration "expressly provides that the person may not ship, transport, possess, or receive firearms." Although federal firearms laws seem to assume that restoration of civil rights is a monolithic concept with a specific meaning, that premise is belied by practice. Federal courts have grappled with whether and to what extent the federal firearms disability applies to state felons who lost no civil rights under state law as a result of their conviction compared to state felons who lost civil rights on conviction but who had them automatically restored by operation of state law. State felons, despite restoration of their political rights and certain firearms privileges, are still prohibited by state law from exercising other firearms privileges.

RIGHT TO WORK VERSUS NEED TO WORK

Ex-offenders are often faced with the cruel paradox that they must have employment to remain free, even though the system denies them employment because they have a record.[43] Many studies have shown that opportunity for employment is one of the most important factors in the successful reintegration of ex-offenders into the community. In the past, ex-offenders could move on to new territory and establish a new identity, thus escaping the stigmatization that goes with a prison record. On the advancing frontiers of early America, the new settlers asked few questions and judged individuals on their present actions rather than past records. But today, computers record every aspect of our lives, and privacy has become less a right than a very rare privilege.

To many people, the informational expansion is a boon. To ex-offenders, it often represents a mystery and potential catastrophe. Even citizens who find themselves involved in an arrest that does not result in conviction may suffer the worst consequences of a record, including the failure to obtain a job—or the loss of a current one.

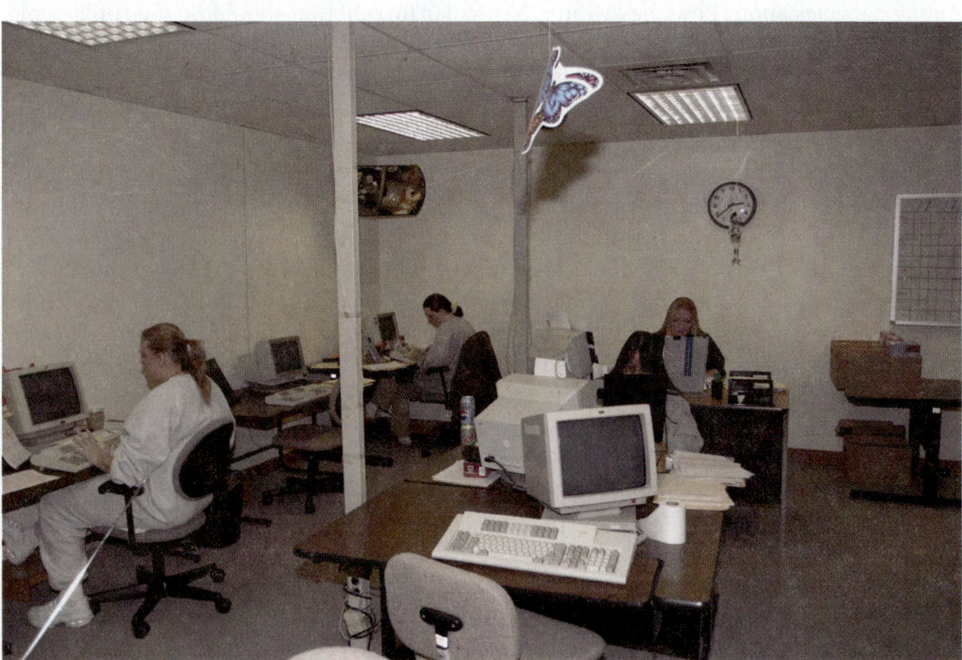

Photo 16.6
Inmates employed by a hotel chain making reservations for hotel guests. Many paroled inmates are subsequently hired by their contract hotel.
Mikael Karlsson/Alamy.

There appear to be two levels where action is necessary to alleviate this crushing burden for the ex-offender. At the community level, barriers to employment that work against the poor and uneducated must be overcome; that is, more realistic educational requirements for jobs must be negotiated. (Degrees and diplomas are often used as screening devices for jobs that do not require them in order to keep out most ex-offenders.) A structural framework must be created in which the community has jobs to fill, training to give, and a willingness to offer both to inmates and ex-offenders. Those conditions can be met only by basic changes in society, not by programs for the individual.

At the individual level, the offender must overcome any personal handicaps. Many recent programs are aimed at the employability of the inmate and the ex-offender, often the young, the unemployed, and the unskilled (frequently also members of minority groups), who make up the bulk of official U.S. arrest statistics. In community-based programs to help in the employment of inmates and ex-offenders, it must be assumed that the person has the capability for regular employment but is unfamiliar with and inexperienced in certain of the required behavioral skills. In other words, behavioral training rather than therapy is needed. It must also be assumed that if inmates learn to handle themselves in the community while under correctional control, they will be able to do so when those controls have been lifted. In planning employment assistance for inmates and ex-offenders who may need it, program planners are faced with the following questions:

- Should supportive services be provided in-house or be contracted?
- How good of a job should be sought ("dead end," having job mobility, on a career ladder, etc.)?
- Who should be trained, and what kind of training should be offered?
- What kind of and how much training should be provided in the institutions? When?

To answer these questions, a comprehensive service program should include the following:

- Assessment of the client's skills and abilities
- Training in job hunting and job readiness skills and in acquiring acceptable work attitudes
- Job training and basic education, if necessary
- Job development and job placement
- Follow-up with employee and employer after placement
- Other supportive services, as required (medical or legal aid)

key term

Certificate of Qualification for Employment
A certificate issued by the Ohio Department of Correction and Rehabilitation that the ex-inmate has completed job training and a certified prison program and is now qualified for employment. The certificate prevents the employer being sued due to hiring negligence.

correctional **practice 16.4**

Certificates of Qualifications for Employment

In July 2012, Gary Mohr, director of the Ohio Department of Rehabilitation and Correction, signed three **Certificates of Qualifications for Employment** (CQEs). A CQE is a way to indicate that a soon-to-be-released inmate or person under post release control has performed exceptionally while incarcerated in Ohio. To be eligible applicants must have completed the following:

a. An accredited in-prison vocational program

b. An accredited behavioral-modification program

c. Community service hours

There are two legal effects of the certificate:

1. It helps overcome the civil impacts of criminal convictions.
2. It protects employers from negligent hiring liability.

One of the most common reasons employers will not employ people **with** criminal records is because they fear being later sued for negligent hiring. The CQE provides legal protection from these lawsuits. This and other steps have been taken by Ohio to reduce the cotllateral consequences that ex-offenders often face.

SOURCE: Ohio Justice and Policy Center, http://www.ohiojpc.org; Ohio Department of Rehabilitation and Correction, "Addressing Collateral Consequences in Ohio," http://www.drc.ohio.gov/web/collcons1.pdf; Frank James, Lawrence Travis, Angela Reitler, Natalie Goulette, and Whitney Flesher, *Collateral Consequences of Conviction in Ohio* (Cincinnati, OH: Center for Criminal Justice Research, School of Criminal Justice, University of Cincinnati, 2011).

Recently, some states have begun experimenting with a "certificate of employability" for eligible offenders that is designed to give potential employers some peace of mind when hiring ex-cons.[44] Correctional Practice 16.4 describes the Certificates of Qualifications for Employment as used in Ohio. Only time will tell whether this idea will take hold and whether it will make a dent in the employability problems of ex-offenders.

RESTRICTED TRADES: BARRIERS TO EMPLOYMENT

key term

Employment restrictions Denial of employment opportunities due to being an ex-offender.

Although barriers to employment still exist in general for ex-offenders, today's standards are more likely to apply to the individual and his or her offense. Ex-offenders as an identified class (or minority) are appealing more to the courts. The 1990s continued to work toward improvements in that area, especially in the removal of **employment restrictions** for ex-offenders based simply on their being ex-offenders.[45] It is the general unemployment picture that most severely affects the ex-offender. When work is scarce for all, the ex-offender finds it more difficult to find any kind of employment. This tends to highlight the overall problem in all aspects of society that results from a criminal record. Slowly decreasing levels of crime and incarceration have brightened the picture for the present.

The National Alliance for Business and the Probation Division of the Administrative Office of the U.S. Courts operate a partnership venture designed to test a delivery system for ex-offender training services and employment. The model is designed to use existing resources that are coordinated to attain the model's objectives. The alliance provides technical assistance to localities attempting to implement the model, and it is proving to be a promising operation.[46]

THE PROBLEM WITH A RECORD

As we have seen, the person with a record of conviction is at a major disadvantage when trying to reintegrate into the community. The deprivation of rights and bars to employment are related to that record, so it is vital to know what having a record means in the age of information. It seems that a record, even a record of mere contact with the criminal justice system, is extremely difficult to shed once it has been acquired. This record becomes the basis for special attention by the police and difficulty with credit agencies. Once the record has been placed in the computers, it can be retrieved when requested by an authorized agency and, inevitably, by some unauthorized agencies.

The problem with having a criminal record in this country is especially critical when an arrest does not result in a conviction. In most foreign countries, an arrest with no conviction cannot be used against the person in later actions. In the United States, in most jurisdictions, employment applications can include questions about an arrest regardless of whether a conviction followed. Even a pardon, exonerating the suspect from guilt, does not remove the incident from the record. Not surprisingly, current attacks on this perpetual record are based on the cruel and unusual punishment clause of the Eighth Amendment.[47] Another legal approach is reflected in recent suits claiming that prisoners and ex-offenders are being discriminated against as a class instead of being treated on the basis of individual merit: It is a truism that we find hard to accept that the protections of the Bill of Rights against police and other official abuse are for all of the criminals, the noncriminals, and us. But when we consider that perhaps as many as 50 million people have a record of arrest, it is clear that the civil rights of those who are in conflict with the law are, indeed, in the most pragmatic way, the interest of all. We are in an era of struggle for civil rights—for blacks, for Latinos, for women, for those with mental illnesses, for the young, and even for the delinquent young.

We are well into a period of civil rights for homosexuals and others whose sexual practices are unreasonably subject to legal condemnation.

It is timely, indeed, that we awake to the excesses in punishing those in conflict with the law. It is a field of great discrimination and must be remedied just as much as other discriminations must be remedied. Not all people with a criminal record are vicious or degraded to begin with or, if their crime was vicious, doomed to remain as they were—unless, of course, we strive by discrimination and rejection to make them so.[48] Too often the way the public deals with ex-offenders is like driving a car by looking in the rearview mirror—eventually there will be a serious crash.

Registration of Criminals

Registration of criminals has been a practice ever since society started imprisoning individuals. In ancient times, registration was used to identify prisoners in penal servitude: Prisoners were branded or marked to decrease their already minimal chances of escape. Because penal slaves had no hope of ever being free, the markings were a sign of their permanent status. The **"yellow card"** was later used in European countries to identify former prisoners who were lucky enough to have lived through their sentences.[49] The registration of felons has also been a widespread practice in America, especially at the local level. A problem with local registration is that it tends to single out offenders for special attention from authorities to which they would not otherwise be subject. Most of those requirements are obsolete today. As information on offenders and arrested persons is placed into computer data banks, a public official can easily query the computer to check the status of almost anyone.

key term

Registration of criminals
Requirement imposed by government that all offenders be registered with local law enforcement agencies.

key term

"Yellow card"
European identification card, yellow in color, that signifies the carrier has been convicted of a crime.

Registration of Ex-Offenders

The most common form of local registration concerns sex-related offenses. The **sex offender file** is used to check out former offenders in the event of similar crimes. Such a file is no doubt an asset to law enforcement, but it becomes a real problem for the ex-offender who is seriously trying to reform. Such inquiries are legitimate for law enforcement personnel; however, the discretion with which they are conducted can make a great difference to the ex-offender.

key term

Sex offender file
Official documents containing information on sex offenders and their previous crimes.

This problem was recently highlighted in Washington State, where legislation allows for community notification when a predatory sex criminal is about to be released and considered to be still dangerous under the state's **Community Protection Act**, passed and implemented in 1990. The release of Joseph Gallardo, a convicted sex offender, with police notification to the community under the act and the citizen anger it engendered apparently resulted in the arson of the ex-offender's home and his being badgered out of the state and, subsequently, out of a second state. No matter how one might feel about the crimes committed by such offenders, it seems clear that the practices used to notify (and often inflame) communities often make reentry much more difficult. The practice of registering felons seems to be matter of interest again, mainly because of the mobility of our present American society, and is now in force in all jurisdictions. Registration may be much more subtle than the practice of branding with a scarlet letter,[50] but it also has the potential to become a permanent stigma, especially with the Internet. There is now even an "app for that" that allows one to track sex offenders on phones and other mobile devices.

key term

Community Protection Act
Legislation requiring offenders to register and live under public scrutiny.

In 1994, Megan Kanka was killed in New Jersey by a paroled sex offender who had twice been committed to prison for sex offending. His criminal history was unknown to the local community before he killed the child. Her mother led a movement to enact a sex offender and community notification law that, in conjunction with federal statutes, coalesced into a national movement to require registration of predatory sex offenders. All 50 states have now

key term

Megan's Law
Legislation requiring sex offenders to inform local police agencies of their location and the nature of their prior convictions.

key term

Adam Walsh Act
National legislation creating a national sex offender registry and organizing sex offenders into three tiers with increasing restrictions based on level.

key term

Expungement
Process by which a record of crime conviction is destroyed or sealed after expiration of a statutorily required period of time; also refers to the act of physically destroying information—including criminal records—in files, computers, or other depositories.

passed such laws (**Megan's Law**, named after the slain girl), and at least 47 of the states have included community notification components.[51] This was followed in 2006 by the passing of the **Adam Walsh Act**, which established a national sex offender registry and created three tiers for sex offenders, ranging from a lifetime registration to 15 years. Ohio and West Virginia were the first states to adopt the law to include juveniles. Figure 16.1 shows the number of registered sex offenders in the United States per 100,000 population. Whether such laws will lead to increased public safety and whether identified offenders will be displaced to other communities are not known, and these assumptions should be continuously assessed.

Expungement as a Response

Clearly the debilitating effect of a criminal conviction is often heightened rather than reduced when the ex-offender returns to the free society. Some states have recognized that fact and attempted to develop **expungement** statutes, which erase the history of criminal

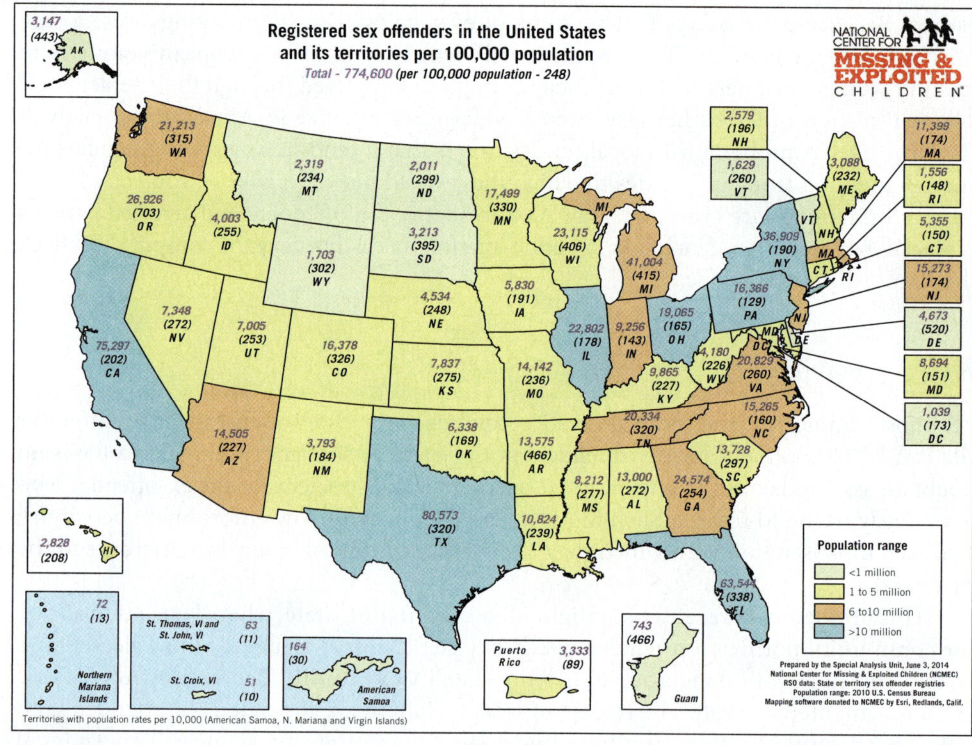

figure 16.1

Registered Sex Offenders in the United States per 100,000 Population.

Note:

- Data obtained via phone survey of the individual sex offender registries in the 50 states, District of Columbia, and five U.S. territories (American Samoa, Guam, Northern Mariana Islands, Puerto Rico, and the Virgin Islands). The U.S. Virgin Islands, Saint Thomas, and Saint Croix maintain separate sex offender registries, bringing the total number of registries surveyed to 57.
- The total number of registered sex offenders has been compared to U.S. Census data to determine the number of sex offenders per 100,000 total population in that state.
- Displayed on each state and territory is the total number of registered sex offenders in red with the number per 100,000 total population just below in parentheses in black.
- Colors indicate the range of where states and territories fall based on the total number of registered offenders per 100,000 total population in that state. This range is explained in the legend of the map.
- Included in the totals of 38 states or territories are offenders who have been deported, are currently incarcerated, or have moved to another state. The 19 states or territories that do not include these types of offenders in their totals are designated by hash marks.

SOURCE: National Center for Missing and Exploited Children, "Map of Registered Sex Offenders in the United State," http://www.missingkids.com/en_US/documents/Sex_Offenders_Map.pdf (accessed September 14, 2014).

conviction and completely restore the ex-offender's rights, thus removing the stigma of a criminal record. This idea was first developed in 1956 at the National Conference on Parole:

> The expunging of a criminal record should be authorized on a discretionary basis. The court of disposition should be empowered to expunge the record of conviction and disposition through an order by which the individual shall be deemed not to have been convicted. Such action may be taken at the point of discharge from suspended sentence, probation, or the institution upon expiration of a term of commitment. When such action is taken the civil and political rights of the of-fender are restored.[52]

Note that not all states restore rights at expungement; in others (such as Louisiana), a pardon remains necessary for full restoration of rights. Almost three decades ago, the American Bar Association Project on Standards for Criminal Justice made the following points regarding the need to remove the record stigma. These statements are still valid, but their general adoption has been agonizingly slow:

> Every jurisdiction should have a method by which the collateral effects of a criminal record can be avoided or mitigated following the successful completion of a term on probation and during its service.
>
> The Advisory Committee is not as concerned with the form which such attitudes take as it is with the principle that flexibility should be built into the system and that effective ways should be devised to mitigate the scarlet letter effect of a conviction once the offender has satisfactorily adjusted.
>
> Clearly, there is growing support for the principle that ex-offenders (especially those who have demonstrated they are in fact reformed) should be given a means of eliminating the brand of the felon. Though expungement is not the only answer to the problem of the burden and consequences of a criminal record, a sensible approach to the method is sorely needed.[53]

policy **position** 16.2

California Pardon Procedures

California's procedures illustrate some of the steps required for a pardon. Generally, the offender must have led a crime-free existence for 10 years following release from parole. The offender must initiate a petition for pardon in a superior court (also called a court of common pleas in other jurisdictions). A formal hearing is held, and the presiding judge solicits opinions from the local district attorney and chief law enforcement officer in the jurisdiction. A computer search is made for any arrests and convictions. The local probation department prepares a pre-pardon hearing report.

If the preponderance of evidence is favorable and no arrest or conviction record is found, the petition is approved by the superior court and is forwarded to the governor's office. The governor may then order the equivalent of a parole board (Board of Prison Terms) to prepare an investigation that would contain a recommendation for pardon. If the report is favorable, the governor may pardon the petitioner, thereby restoring to the petitioner all of the rights and immunities of an ordinary citizen. It is evident that most ex-offenders, although no doubt preferring a pardon, may favor even more having the crime and conviction put as far behind them as possible. They may also not have the perseverance to endure such an involved and expensive procedure. Finally, statistics show that almost all ex-offenders are rearrested within the 10-year time period, even if there is no further action by criminal justice system officials. No wonder so few ex-offenders seek and receive pardons!

Pardons can be full or conditional; the former generally applies to both the punishment and the guilt of the offender and blots out the existence of guilt in the eyes of the law. It also removes an offender's disabilities and restores civil rights. The conditional pardon usually falls short of the remedies available in the full pardon, is an expression of guilt, and does not obliterate the conviction but may restore civil rights.

The U.S. Supreme Court decisions on pardons and their effects are directly contradictory, and thus state laws usually govern pardons. Although pardons are not frequent in the nation at this time, it is reasonable to expect they may become more frequent as prison overcrowding becomes more critical. In 2003, Illinois Governor George Ryan pardoned four inmates he was convinced had been tortured into confessing to murder. President George W. Bush pardoned 15 individuals when he left office in 2008, and President Barack Obama pardoned 17 in the first year of his second term. See Correctional Practice 16.5 for more on presidential pardons and clemency.

key term

Pardon
Executive clemency restoring at least some rights to the offender.

RESTORING OFFENDERS' RIGHTS

Some states restore civil rights when parole is granted; others do so when the offender is released from parole. In still others, it is necessary for a governor to restore all rights, usually through a **pardon.**[54] California's procedures for pardon illustrate the latter, as explained in the Policy Position 16.2. What is required for a pardon in California?

correctional practice 16.5

Clemency and the President

The U.S. Constitution (Article II, Section 2) authorizes the president to grant executive clemency for federal offenses. Petitions are received and reviewed by a pardons attorney who makes recommendations. Clemency may be a reprieve, revision of a fine or penalty, commutation of a sentence, or a full pardon. A pardon, which is generally considered only after the completion of a sentence, restores all basic civil rights and may aid in the restoration of professional credentials and licenses that were lost due to the conviction. A commutation is a significant reduction in the sentence. Outcomes for clemency applications are listed on the right for the years shown in the accompanying table.

SOURCE: Office of the Pardon Attorney, "Presidential Actions," http://www.usdoj.gov/pardon/actions_administration.htm (accessed December 1, 2013).

Executive Clemency Granted/Denied

Year	Pardons	Commutation	Denied
1980	155	11	500
1985	32	3	279
1990	0	0	289
1994	0	0	785
1998	21	0	378
2000	59	3	601
2002	0	0	1,985
2004	12	2	960
2006	39	0	1,402
2008	44	2	2,695
2011*	0	0	1,288
2013	17	UNK	UNK

* Six months.

Summary

Summarize the Issues Associated with the Stigma of Being a Prisoner and with the Loss and Restoration of Civil Rights

Inmates and ex-offenders face significant problems resulting from conviction. For those sentenced to incarceration, many civil rights are reduced. Correctional administrators require an orderly facility and nonviolent inmates to the extent possible. Controls are necessary to limit violence, escape potential, competition for control of the institution, and correctional officer safety. Contraband must be interdicted and escape plans thwarted. Guns, alcohol, weapons, and even drugs must be interdicted or detected and destroyed. These are reasonable precautions with clear correctional purposes.

Although reasonable reductions on civil rights can be articulated and become objectives that a facility or program might want to achieve, inmates are seldom allowed to leave the facility or seek alternatives for medical, dental, and mental health issues. Inmates are isolated from civilian services outside the facility. They are therefore dependent on the correctional system to provide services of this nature. Not all correctional systems achieve adequate provision of needed services, particularly in the mental health and other medical areas. Ongoing lawsuits against states and local corrections facilities are rife, and as a result, the courts, particularly the federal courts, have insisted on the improvement of medical services. Some state systems (such as California) are currently under court orders to improve medical service or shrink the population to be served until such time that available services would be adequate. In other states and the federal prison system, court orders may pertain to only one institution in one correctional system. In these cases, inmates and their legal representatives have sued against denial of needed services. Such collateral consequences can be seen as additional punishments.

Parole and postrelease inmates also face legal challenges. Some are denied rights and privileges available to citizens in their jurisdiction but denied to similarly situated offenders. Some employment opportunities are denied parolees (and some probationers) due to the arrest or conviction record. Other convicted offenders may not approach within 500 feet of a school campus. In all state jurisdictions, there are laws requiring public notification of the release of a convicted sex offender in their jurisdiction, even if that offender has completed satisfactorily all the correction conditions imposed.

Such challenges have largely contributed to the efforts of some offenders to become "invisible," seek certificates of rehabilitation, attempt to convince the executive branch that a pardon (of some sort) is possible, or use available rehabilitation certifications to allow potential employees to hire the offender when released. Such efforts may bring access to employment and housing and eligibility for other services, but the speed at which desired goals are attainable is agonizingly slow. Such reticence and delay, as well as cost, discourage the rehabilitated from pursuing a law-abiding life, negating constructive efforts to reduce recidivism and leading to the return of parolees to prison. This is an area ripe for improvement.

Describe the Status of the Convicted Offender

When all appeals have been exhausted, the offender is now "convicted" and subject to rules and regulations of the corrections system. Institutional regulations were seldom examined by courts in order to avoid interfering with the acumen of correctional staff. In the 1960s, courts began to consider and then order changes in the ways and avenues of prison and reentry and established court masters to monitor the responsiveness of correctional practice.

Identify Basic Inmate Rights

In the 1960s, courts recognized that the U.S. Constitution applied to convicted and imprisoned inmates, and rights were defined in the areas of mail, visitation, contraband, religion, access to court and counsel, and medical treatment and care. Deliberate indifference became a major issue occurring in litigation. Remedies for inmates were created through Section 1983 of the U.S. Code, requiring an ombudsman system, mandated review of prison altercations, and tort suits.

Compare and Contrast the Right to Work with the Need to Work

In reentry, parolees are required to earn their living but find that the general public is unwilling to hire parolees and others with a criminal record. Parolees need to work but usually have no right to employment as viewed by potential employers.

Explain Why Restricted Trades Are Barriers to Employment

Inmates may have had training and licensure in a variety of trades and jobs, but many licensing authorities do not permit convicted offenders to be relicensed. Other occupations and organizations have "no-hire" policies, creating significant barriers in a returning inmate's search for employment.

Describe the Problem with Having a Record

In the era of computerized information, it is difficult for parolees and returning citizens to reclaim previous work, housing, travel, and monetary rights. These collateral consequences of conviction follow offenders throughout their lives, increasing the probability of recidivism.

Key Words

convicted offender, 350
court master, 350
civil death, 350
clear and present danger, 353
Black Muslims, 355
jailhouse lawyer, 356
Estelle v. *Gamble*, 356
deliberate indifference, 356
Section 1983, 357
ex-con, 359
collateral consequences, 359
social stigma, 360
stigma, 360
self-efficacy, 360
occupational disability, 361
Certificate of Qualification for Employment, 363
firearms disability, 362
employment restrictions, 364
registration of criminals, 365
"yellow card," 365
sex offender file, 365
Community Protection Act, 365
Megan's Law, 366
Adam Walsh Act, 366
expungement, 366
pardon, 368

Review Questions

1. Discuss the collateral consequences of a conviction.
2. How could expungement improve the reintegration process for ex-offenders?
3. Why does registration of criminals have such a drastic effect on the ex-offender? What are the alternatives?
4. What are the potential outcomes of registration of predatory sex offenders? How do you feel about this practice?
5. Why is it important for offenders to retain their ties with the community?
6. What are the advantages and disadvantages of having a court master?
7. Explain Megan's Law.
8. Explain the Adam Walsh Act.
9. What is the name of the writ that tests the legality of confinement?
10. How have the courts developed offender rights?
11. What are four alternatives to litigation that inmates might use to secure their rights?
12. What have been the impacts of the more conservative courts on the definition of inmate rights?

Application Case Studies

1. If you were an employer, would you hire an ex-offender? Would it make a difference if he or she had a Certificate of Qualification for Employment?
2. A friend of yours was recently convicted of drug possession. The friend wants to apply for a job at the company you work for, and the application form asks if the applicant has ever been convicted of a crime. What advice would you give your friend?
3. You recently moved into a new apartment and learn that there is a registered sex offender in the same building. What precautions will you take to ensure your safety and that of your family?

Endnotes

1. Lauren E. Glaze and Erika Parks, *Correctional Populations in the United States 2011* (Washington, DC: Bureau of Justice Statistics, 2012).
2. Harry Barnes and N. Teeters, *New Horizons in Criminology,* 3rd ed. (Englewood Cliffs, NJ: Prentice Hall, 1959), p. 505.
3. Visiting lists may be restricted, and persons who have violated visiting regulations may be removed from the lists. See *Patterson* v. *Walters,* 363 F. Supp. 486 (W.D. Pa. 1973). In addition, any person who previously attempted to help an inmate escape may be required to visit via noncontact means. See *In re Bell,* 168 Cal. Rptr. 100 (App. 1980).
4. See the evaluation of the New York Family Reunion Program in Bonnie Carlson and Neil Cervera, *Inmates and Their Wives: Incarceration and Family Life* (Westport, CT: Greenwood, 1992). See also Sara Unnutia, "Words Travel," *Corrections Today* 66:2

(2004): 80–83; Taylor Dueker, “Video Visitation: A Boon at Omaha,” *American Jails* 18:5 (2004): 65–67; and Lauren Glaze and Laura Maruschak, *Parents in Prison and Their Children* (Washington, DC: Bureau of Justice Statistics, 2008).

5. Velmer Burton, Francis Cullen, and Lawrence Travis, “The Collateral Consequences of a Felony Conviction: A National Study of State Statutes,” *Federal Probation* 51 (1987): 52–60.
6. James Stephan, *Prison Rule Violators* (Washington, DC: U.S. Department of Justice, 1989); Andrea Toepell and L. Greaves, “Experience of Abuse among Women Visiting Incarcerated Partners,” *Violence against Women* 7:1 (2001): 80–109.
7. R. W. Dumond, “The Sexual Assault of Many Inmates in Incarcerated Settings,” *International Journal of the Sociology of Law* 20:2 (1992): 135–158; Victor Hassine, *Life without Parole* (New York: Oxford University Press, 2008), pp. 71–76; Allen Beck and Paige Harrison, *Sexual Victimization in State and Federal Prisons Reported by Inmates, 2007* (Washington, DC: Bureau of Justice Statistics, 2008).
8. George Kiser, “Female Inmates and Their Families,” *Federal Probation* 55:3 (1991): 56–63; Minnesota Department of Corrections (2012), “The Effects of Prison Visitation on Offender Recidivism,” http://www.doc.state.mn.ur/publications/documents-11-11MNPriosnVisitationStudy.pdf (accessed June 21, 2013); Leo Degard (2013), “A New role for Technology: The Impact of Video Visitation on Corrections Staff, Inmates, and Their Families,” http://www.vera.org.blog/new-role-technology-impact-video-visitation-co (accessed December 10, 2013).
9. Gary Klivans, “Gang Codes: Gang Identity Theft,” *American Jails* 22:4 (2008): 70–77.
10. *Palmigiano* v. *Travisono,* 317 F. Supp. 776 (D.R.I. 1970).
11. William Gilbertson, “Irked by Focus on Inmates, California Bans Interviews,” *New York Times,* December 29, 1995, p. A4.
12. Alan Johnson, “Director Views Inmate Suicides as Failures; New Steps to Be Taken,” *Columbus Dispatch,* September 28, 2013, http://www.dispatch.com/content/stories/local/2013/09/28/director-views-inmate-suicides-as-failures-new-steps-being-taken.html (accessed December 10, 2013).
13. Some courts have upheld the restriction of communications between inmates at different institutions for security reasons. *Schlobohm* v. *U.S. Attorney General,* 479 F. Supp. 401 (M.D. Pa. 1979).
14. *Guajardo* v. *Estelle,* 580 F. 2d 748 (5th Cir. 1978). See also Joseph Bouchard and A. Winnicki, “‘You Found What in a Book?’ Contraband Control in a Prison Library,” *Library and Archival Security* 17:1 (2002): 9–16.
15. Executive Order Number 814 for incoming mail, 814A for outgoing mail. Office of the Governor, State of Ohio, August 3, 1972.
16. *Sewell* v. *Pegelow,* 304 F. 2d 670 (4th Cir. 1962); *Banks* v. *Havener,* 234 F. Supp. 27 (E.D. Va. 1964); *Knuckles* v. *Prasse,* 435 F. 2d 1255 (3rd Cir. 1970). These three cases dealt with the right of Black Muslim inmates to freedom of religion. In *Knuckles* v. *Prasse,* the court of appeals held that prison officials were not required to make available to prisoners Black Muslim publications that urged defiance of prison authorities and thus threatened prison security unless properly interpreted by a trained Muslim minister. In the *Sewell* decision, a clear instance of discrimination against a Black Muslim prisoner was brought before the court of appeals, which dismissed the case on the grounds that it properly came under the jurisdiction of the district court. In *Banks* v. *Havener,* responding to a petition under the Civil Rights Act by Black Muslim prisoners, the district court held that the antipathy of inmates and staff occasioned by the belief of Black Muslims in black supremacy was alone not sufficient to justify suppression of the practice of the belief of Black Muslim religion. See also *Hasan Jamal Abdul Majid* v. *Henderson,* 533 F. Supp. 1257 (N.D. N.Y., March 11, 1982).
17. Although correctional personnel originally feared them, the Black Muslims are paradoxically now viewed as a source of stability among inmates. See Keith Butler, “The Muslims Are No Longer an Unknown Quality,” *Corrections Magazine* 4 (June 1978): 55–65. But see Elaine Ganley, “Manual Outlines Muslim Radicalization in Prisons,” http://www.sfgate.com/cgi-bin/article.cgi?f=/n/a/10/01/international/132258D37.DTL (accessed October 1, 2008).
18. Access to a minister is a constitutional right. See *Cruz* v. *Beto,* 405 U.S. 319 (1972).
19. *Cooper* v. *Pate.* See also Rudolph Alexander, “Slamming the Federal Courthouse Door on Inmates,” *Journal of Criminal Justice* 21:2 (1993): 103–116.
20. *Johnson* v. *Avery,* 393 U.S. 483, 484 (1969). Through a writ of certiorari, a court of appeals decision was reversed in favor of an inmate who had been disciplined for violating a prison regulation that prohibited inmates from assisting other prisoners in preparing writs. The court of appeals had reversed a district court decision that voided the regulation because it had the effect of barring illiterate prisoners from access to general habeas corpus.
21. *Younger* v. *Gilmore,* 92 S. Ct. 250 (1971).

22. Alexander Parker and Dana Schwertfeger, "A College Library and Research Center in a Correctional Facility," *Journal of Offender Rehabilitation* 17:1/2 (1991): 167–179.
23. Gene Teirelbaum, *Inspecting a Prison Law Library* (New Albany, IN: W. Homer Press, 1989); American Association of Law Libraries, *Correctional Facility Law Libraries: An A to Z Resource Guide* (Laurel, MD: American Correctional Association, 1991). See also Craig Hemmens, Barbara Belbot, and Katherine Bennett, *Significant Cases in Corrections* (Los Angeles: Roxbury, 2004).
24. The U.S. Supreme Court has determined that death row inmates wishing to challenge their convictions and sentences have no constitutional right to a court-appointed counsel. For arguments in favor of such as right, see Michael Mello, "Is There a Federal Constitutional Right to Counsel in Capital Post-Conviction Proceedings?," *Journal of Criminal Law and Criminology* 79 (1990): 1065–1104. The other side is addressed by Donald Zeithaml, "Sixth and Fourteenth Amendments—Constitutional Right to State Capital Collateral Appeal: The Due Process of Executing a Convict without Attorney Representation," *Journal of Criminal Law and Criminology* 80 (Winter 1990): 1123–1144. The case is *Murray* v. *Giarranto*, 109 S. Ct. 2675 (1989). See also "High Court Overturns Another Death Penalty Case," *USA Today*, http://www.usatoday.com/news/Washington/2005-06-20-scotus-wrap_x.htm (accessed November 23, 2009).
25. Jennifer Gararda Brown, "Posner, Prisoners and Pragmatism," *Tulane Law Review* 66:5 (1992): 1117–1178.
26. Tracey Kyckelhahn and Thomas Cohen, *Civil Rights Complaints in U.S. District Courts, 1999–2006* (Washington, DC: Bureau of Justice Statistics, 2008), p. 8.
27. Editors, "California Prison Health Czar Heads to Court," *Correctional News* 14:6 (2008): 8; Editors, "Rising Medical Care Costs Encourage States to Release Sick, Dying Inmates," *Correctional News* 14:6 (2008): 16; Joseph Jackson (2013), "Mentally Ill Ex-Inmates Lack Treatment," http://urbanmilwaukee.com/2013/11/12/mentally-ill-ex-inmates-lack-treatment/ (accessed December 11, 2013).
28. *Estelle* v. *Gamble*, 97 S. Ct. 285 (1976). The standard for judging the adequacy of medical treatment is the level of care offered to free people in the same locality. The prison must furnish comparable services, and inmates may collect damages for inadequate medical treatment. See *Newman* v. *Alabama*, 559 F. 2d. 283 (1977). Medical treatment in jails is generally less adequate than that in prisons. See also American College of Physicians, National Commission on Correctional Care, "The Crisis in Correctional Health Care: The Impact of the National Drug Control Strategy on Correctional Health Services," *Annals of Internal Medicine* 117:1 (1992): 71–77. See also Kipnis Kenneth et al., "Correctional Health Care—In Critical Condition," *Corrections Today* 54:7 (1992): 92–120, and B. Jayne Anno, *Prison Health Care: Guidelines for the Management of an Adequate Delivery System* (Washington, DC: U.S. National Institute of Corrections, 1991).
29. Ibid. In 1995, the U.S. district court in San Francisco ruled that the California Pelican Bay Prison inflicted unconstitutional cruel and unusual punishment on prisoners. See Bill Wallace, "Pelican Bay Prison Ruled Too Harsh," *San Francisco Chronicle*, January 12, 1995, p. A7.
30. *United States* v. *DeColegro*, 821 F. 2d, 1st Cir. (1987).
31. Frederick Millen, "AIDS in Prison—A National Disgrace," *San Francisco Sentinel*, March 8, 1990, p. 7. See also Howard Messing, "AIDS in Jail," *Northern Illinois University Law Review* 11:2/3 (1991): 297–317. Especially useful is John R. Austin and Rebecca S. Trammell, "AIDS and the Criminal Justice System," *Northern Illinois University Law Review* 11:2/3 (1991): 481–527. See also Susan Jacobs, "AIDS in Correctional Facilities: Current Status of Legal Issues Critical to Policy Development," *Journal of Criminal Justice* 23:2 (1995): 209–221, and the special theme issue "Pandemic Disease: Are Jails Prepared?," *American Jails* 12:3 (2008).
32. James Sterngold, "Judge Orders Takeover of State's Prison Health Care System," *San Francisco Chronicle*, June 30, 2005, p. 1. See also James Sterngold, "U.S. Seizes State Prison Health Care; Judge Cites Preventable Deaths, 'Depravity of System,'" http://sfgate.com/cgi-bin/article.cgi?f=/c/a/2005/07/01/MNGOCDHPP71.DTL&hw=prison+medicine&sn=001&sc=1000 (accessed July 1, 2005).
33. In *Tucker* v. *Hutto*, entered as a civil case under 78-0161-R, Eastern District of Virginia, the trial judge approved the out-of-court settlement on January 5, 1979, just five days before the trial was to open. See also R. Allinson, "Inmate Receives $518,000 Damage Award," *Criminal Justice Newsletter* 10 (January 15, 1979): 7.
34. The National Prison Project, American Civil Liberties Union Foundation, 1346 Connecticut Avenue NW, Washington, DC 20036.
35. Office of Legal Policy, *Report to the Attorney General: Federal Habeas Corpus Review of State Judgments* (Washington, DC: U.S. Department of Justice, 1988).
36. Sue Davis and Donald Songer, "The Changing Role of the United States Court of Appeals: The Flow of

Litigation Revisited," *Justice System Journal* 13 (1989): 323–340.

37. Dennis Massey, *Doing Time in American Prisons: A Study of Modern Novels* (Westport, CT: Greenwood Press, 1989). See also Hassine, *Life without Parole.*
38. Gabriel Chin, "Felon Disenfranchisement and Democracy in the Late Jim Crow Era," *Ohio State University Journal of Criminal Law* 5:2 (2007): 329–340. See also Stephen Janis, "Ex-Felons Register for the Right to Vote," http://www.examiner.com/a-810882~Ex_felons_register_for_the_right_to_vote.html (accessed November 23, 2008), and Applied Research Center, "Compact for Racial Justice," http://www.sentencingproject.org/NewsDetails.aspx?NewsID=717.
39. As cited in Barnes and Teeters, *New Horizons in Criminology*, p. 544.
40. Michael Braswell, "Correctional Treatment and the Human Spirit: A Focus on Relationship," *Federal Probation* 53:2 (1989): 49–60. See also Michael T. French and Gary A. Zarkin, "Effects of Drug Abuse on Legal and Illegal Earnings," *Contemporary Policy Issues* 10:2 (1992): 98–110 (compares the impact of length of time in drug treatment and posttreatment legal and illegal earnings).
41. Sol Rubin, "The Man with a Record: A Civil Rights Problem," *Federal Probation,* September 1971, p. 4. See also A. J. Klick, "Should Ex-Cons Have Their Rights Restored?," http://www.tucsoncitizen.com/daily/local/56389.php (accessed November 22, 2008).
42. The Sentencing Project (2013), "Presumed Guilty," http://www.sentencingproject.org/detail/news.cfm?news_id=1681&id=133 (accessed December 11, 2013).
43. Kathleen Dean Moore, *Pardons: Justice, Mercy, and the Public Interest* (New York: Oxford University Press, 1989). See also "Obama Pardons 17 Felons, First in His Second Term," *New York Times*, March 2, 2013, http://www.nytimes.com/2013/03/02/us/politics/obama-pardons-17-felons-first-in-his-second-term.html?_r=0 (accessed December 11, 2013).
44. As of 2012, Illinois, New York, Iowa, and Ohio were the four states to allow ex-inmates to receive a certificate of employability.
45. There is a potential liability in disclosing a parolee's background to a prospective employer if it results in the client not getting the job. See Rolando del Carmen and Eve Trook-White, *Liability Issues in Community Service Sanctions* (Washington, DC: U.S. Department of Justice, 1986), pp. 19–21. See also Davis E. Barlow, Melissa Hickman Barlow, and Theodore G. Chiricos, "Long Economic Cycles and the Criminal Justice System," *Crime, Law, and Social Change* 19:2 (1993): 143–169 (examines the relationship between long cycles of capitalist activity and formation of public policy on criminal justice).
46. For a discouraging note on the impact of fiscal constraints on ex-offender programs, see Danesh Yousef, "Baton Rouge Ex-Offenders' Clearinghouse: A Casualty of Misguided Savings," *International Journal of Offender Therapy and Comparative Criminology* 33 (1989): 207–214. See also Ted Chiricos, Kelle Barrick, William Bales, and Stephani Bontrager, "The Labeling of Convicted Felons and Its Consequences for Recidivism," *Criminology* 45:3 (2007): 547–581.
47. "Excessive bail shall not be required, nor excessive fines imposed, nor cruel and unusual punishment inflicted."
48. Rubin, *The Man with a Record*, pp. 6–7.
49. The scarlet letter was a scarlet "A" that the Puritans required known female adulterers to wear around the neck as a punitive mark. The practice is fully described in Nathaniel Hawthorne's novel *The Scarlet Letter.*
50. Other visible indicators include branding the forehead, slitting the ears, and removing the nose.
51. It should be noted that some states have not enacted all of the requirements of Walsh Act, balking at the requirement that some juvenile sex offenders be required to register for life.
52. Georgetown University Law School, *The Closed Door: The Effect of a Criminal Record on Employment with State and Local Public Agencies* (Springfield, VA: National Technical Information Service, 1972), p. v.
53. American Bar Association, *Laws, Licenses and the Offender's Right to Work* (Washington, DC: American Bar Association, 1973), p. 7.
54. For a discussion of executive clemency, see Center for Policy Research and Analysis, *Guide to Executive Clemency among American States* (Washington, DC: National Governors' Association, 1988).

A. Ramey/PhotoEdit.

Objectives

- Summarize the trends in the adult prison population.
- Describe the issues adult prison inmates face.
- Describe the prison population increase.
- Compare and contrast jail and prison inmates.
- Explain what might be done to reduce functional illiteracy among prison inmates.
- Explain the consequences of prisonization.
- Explain rape and sexual assault in all-male institutions.
- Identify five outcomes of the graying of American prison populations.

chapter 17 Male Offenders

Outline

"Keeping track of the rapidly fluctuating adult male prison population is like trying to paint a moving bus."

—Harry E. Allen

Overview

In the next chapter, we will acquire an understanding of the variety of female offenders who are dealt with as "clients" of the jail and prison systems of America. As we saw in Part 1, until very recently, earlier incarceration practices were not intended to "correct" the behavior of inmates. Consequently, the young and the old, the sick and the well, the women and the men, and the dangerous and the helpless were housed and placed indiscriminately in a single, all-inclusive facility. As the concepts of penitence and corrections were developed, men and women were segregated into separate institutions. Later, institutions became further specialized, with different kinds of institutions for the younger inmates, who were separated from the more hardened felons (although these groups are still sometimes hard to tell apart), and a separate system was created for juveniles (see Chapter 20).

In this chapter, we examine the processes used with and conditions of men who have been convicted and sentenced to the adult prisons of America and probably placed there following some length of exposure to the conditions of jail life. If corrections and prisons can be considered businesses, we continue our analogy by considering adult male inmate groups as clients with different needs, problems, and demands than other types of clients. Using a business analogy, we can describe corrections in all areas as a growth industry. As this chapter unfolds, you will see the crimes for which inmates are committed, problems inmates pose to staff and correctional officers, the inmate culture into which they settle, the realities of danger and death in prison, and the challenges of the aged prisoner. Inmates face widespread boredom, lack of contact with the outside world, dulling routine, and bland and frequently repetitive food. Most institutions are loud, cheerless, and (sometimes) fraught with dangers that range from sexual assault to unwarranted punishment from correctional officers to gangs, "crazies," and foes. This is the environment into which many inmates step when they are sent to prison.

This chapter deals with several questions. Who are the male prison inmates? What are their needs, and what programs should be devised to address those needs? What should we know about their backgrounds? What happens to the men in the prisons of America?

Photo 17.1

A lot of "doing time" results in dead time.

PRISON POPULATION TRENDS

Keeping track of the rapidly fluctuating adult male prison population is like trying to paint a moving bus. The number of male offenders housed in America's prisons rose at an alarming rate, along with the total prison population, until just recently. The population rose from 883,500 in 1993 to the staggering figure of 1,250,000 in the beginning of 2013. Fortunately, the prison and jail populations appear to be leveling off and actually decreasing (see Figure 17.1). This does not include almost 83,600 males sentenced to state prisons by the courts but who were, at the time, "holdbacks," that is, inmates being held in county jail facilities because of prison overcrowding.

Some 88 percent of male inmates were incarcerated in state prisons, and slightly more than 12 percent were in federal prisons. Another 29,500 inmates were being held in other adult long-term institutions (for example, the Cook County Department of Corrections, the New York City Department of Corrections, and the Philadelphia Prison System). In total,

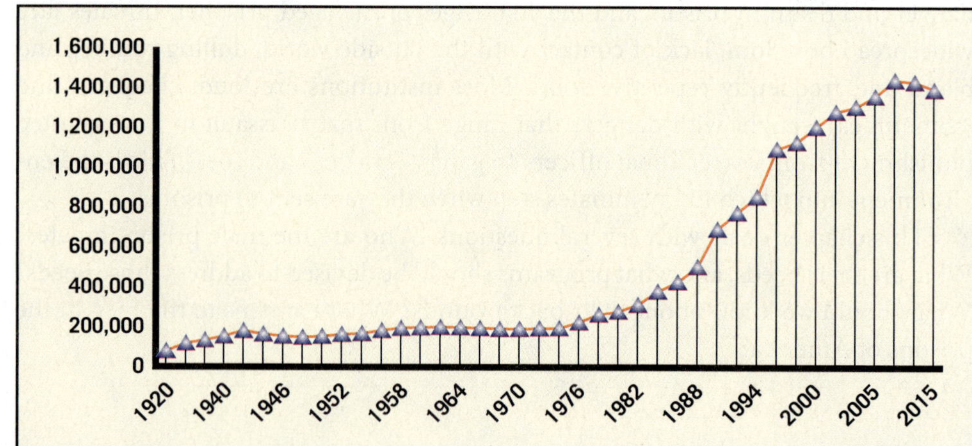

figure 17.1

Number of Incarcerated Male Offenders, 1920–2015.

Note: Data for 2015 are extrapolated.

SOURCE: E. Ann Carson and Daniela Colinelli, *Prisoners in 2012—Advance Counts* (Washington, DC: Bureau of Justice Statistics, 2013).

there are approximately 927 male inmates in adult prisons for every 100,000 male residents in the country. Said differently, almost 1 percent of the adult males in the nation were in prison on a given day in 2012.

PRISONER POPULATION

Criminal History

Male prisoners have committed a broad range of criminal acts, and many are recidivists. Violent offenses account for more than half (53.5 percent) of the crimes for which males were sentenced to state prison, and these include homicide, manslaughter, rape, robbery, aggravated assault, and sexual assault. Drug law violations (possession, possession for sale, and trafficking) accounted for about 17 percent of males in state correctional facilities. All other crimes, ranging from forgery, fraud, embezzlement, theft, and motor vehicle theft to public order offenses, accounted for just one in three male inmates (see Figure 17.2).

We must remember that those sentenced and actually incarcerated in adult prisons are at the bottom of the correctional filter. As a group, men in prisons are undereducated and underemployed, primarily because of their social class and lack of opportunity.

Two-thirds are from minority **racial and ethnic groupings**, are poor, and have been unable to cope with the complexities of urban life. Black men are incarcerated at six times the rate of whites, and as of 2012, one in six black men had been incarcerated.

key term

Racial and ethnic groupings Division of prisoners based on racial or ethnic characteristics.

Explanations of this vast disparity include law enforcement bias, selective incapacitation, saturation policing of black neighborhoods, lack of social services and employment opportunities, zero-tolerance policies, and law enforcement focusing on low-end drug sales. Approximately 17 percent of black males ages 20 to 29 were in prisons in 2012.[1] It is also interesting to note that about 99,000 of all inmates in the United States were foreigners, the majority from Mexico.[2] See Correctional Practice 17.1 for more on the characteristics of jail inmates.

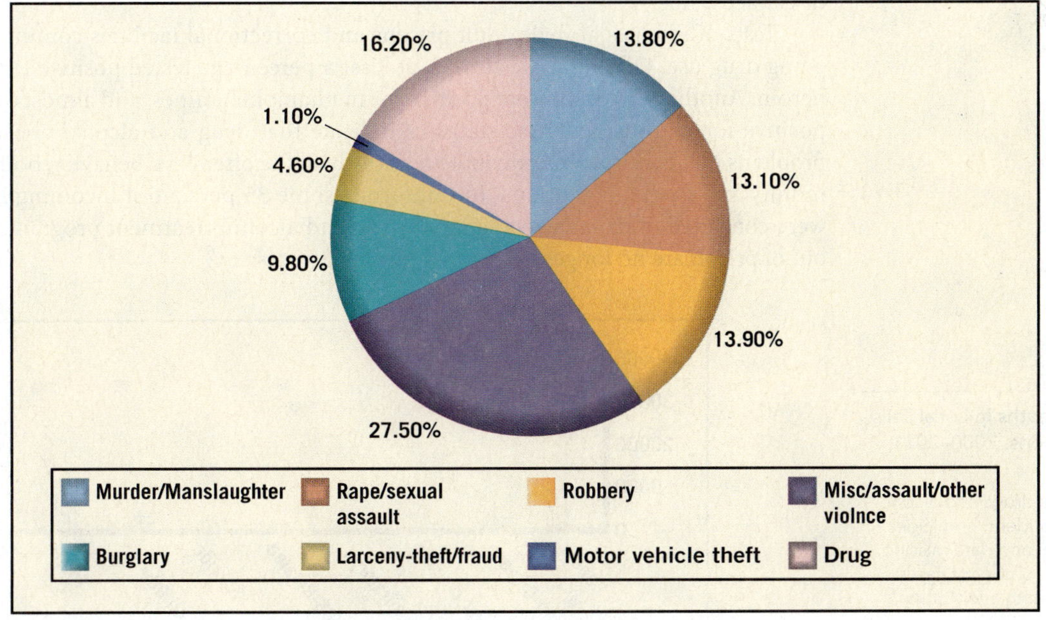

figure 17.2

Offenses of Male Offenders Sentenced to State Prisons.

SOURCE: E. Ann Carson and Daniela Golinelli, *Prisoners in 2012—Advance Counts* (Washington, DC: Bureau of Justice statistics, 2013), p. 10.

Dangerousness

Adult male prisons (and almost all other detention facilities) are often overcrowded to the danger point,[3] and it is obvious that the present systems will be unable to meet the increasing demands. Some male offenders are extremely dangerous and must be isolated from others. In the 1970s, it was estimated that only some 15 to 25 percent of the male population in prison fell into this category. That situation, however, has changed; overcrowding and citizen alarm about violence in the community have tended to force correctional administrators to find ways to release those men considered least dangerous back into the community. This has left an increasing percentage of violent offenders in maximum-security prisons and also led to the creation of the supermax prison. In some states, the number of violent offenders in maximum-security prisons who committed crimes against the person is close to 62 percent and growing, as property offenders are given alternatives to incarceration. The presence of prison gangs (**institutional threat groups**) heightens anxiety, triggers lawsuits, and poses potential personal threat to other inmates.[4] Deaths of prison inmates are detailed in Figure 17.3. Although the vast majority die from natural causes, homicides and suicides also occur all too frequently. For an excellent PowerPoint presentation on jail suicide, conduct an Internet search using the key terms "U.S. Marshal Service with suicide prevention in jails with basics."

key term

Institutional threat groups Prison gangs.

Drugs and Alcohol

As stated earlier, male offenders tend to be heavy users of alcohol and drugs. One study, for example, found that almost one-third of the men in prison had been drinking at the time of their current offense and that more than one-third were under the influence of drugs. That pattern has changed only in the acquisition of a broader catalog of ever more powerful **"designer" drugs**, such as methamphetamine and Ecstasy, many of which can induce violent behavior. Recently, heroin has reemerged as a drug, ravishing communities. For example, the medical examiner in Cuyahoga County (Cleveland, Ohio) reported that there were 170 heroin overdose deaths in 2013—more than deaths due to homicides or car accidents.[5]

key term

"Designer" drugs Analogues of controlled substances manufactured by underground chemists.

Tests of inmates at male adult prisons and correctional facilities continue to find ongoing drug use. Of all inmates tested, at least a percentage tested positive for cocaine and heroin. Another 2 percent were positive for methamphetamines, and almost 6 percent were positive for marijuana. These statistics indicate that drug and alcohol abuse are serious problems that continue to contribute negatively to the offenders' behavior, both in the community and in the institutions. In California, some 35 percent of incoming male inmates were convicted of drug law violations. Drug and alcohol treatment programs both in and out of prison are no longer a luxury—they are a necessity.[6]

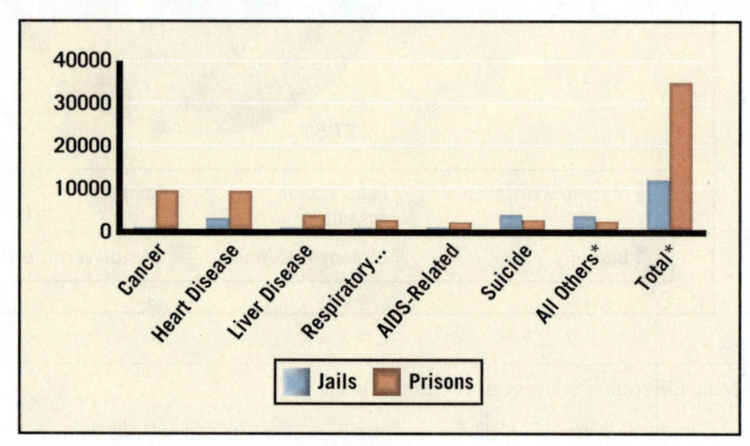

figure 17.3

Number of Deaths in Local Jails and State Prisons, 2000–2011, by Cause.

Note: *Includes drugs and alcohol intoxication, accident, homicide, other/unknown, and data missing. In 2007, a high number of cases were missing death information.

SOURCE: Margret E. Noonan and Scott Ginder, *Mortality in Local Jails and State Prisons, 2000–2011* (Washington, DC: Bureau of Justice Statistics 2013).

correctional practice 17.1

Characteristics of Jail Inmates

There were more than 645,900 male jail inmates in 2012, a majority of whom were black (42.5 percent) or Hispanic (17 percent) and almost 61 percent of whom had not been convicted. Almost half of jail inmates in 2012 were under correctional or court supervision at the time of their most recent arrest, almost a third on probation, an eighth on parole, and 7 percent on bail or bond. More than 7 out of 10 male inmates had prior sentences to probation or incarceration, over 4 in 10 had served at least three sentences, and almost one in three were violent recidivists.

Almost 7 in 10 convicted male inmates reported they consumed alcohol (beer, wine, or liquor) regularly, and one in three said they had used alcohol at the time of their instant offense. When drug use and alcohol use are combined, more than half of the convicted male inmates were using drugs or alcohol (or both) at the time of the offense. In 2005, male jail inmates reported life experiences they had after using alcohol and drugs, and about half said that through use of alcohol or drugs, they had threatened their own or others' lives, had damaged relationships with other people, or had marred their personal and work histories. Nearly two-thirds confessed to driving a motor vehicle after drinking or drug use, including almost one in five who had been in a subsequent accident. Almost half had been in a physical fight after substance consumption.

More than one in five had lost a job because of substance abuse. In another study, 10 percent of sampled jail inmates were positive for one or more drugs consumed while in jail. More than one-third of male inmates reported they had a physical, mental, or emotional condition or difficulty seeing, learning, hearing, or speaking. Over their lifetime, more than 4 in 10 had developed an illness, injury, or medical condition that needed professional medical attention. A third had a medical problem in jail (such as a cold or the flu). One in 20 had been injured in a fight or assault after admission to jail. Some one in four had at least once received treatment for a mental or emotional problem other than drug or alcohol abuse. In addition, one in six men was defined as mentally ill, a third of the mentally ill jail inmates were alcohol dependent, and more than one in four received mental health services while in jail.

The picture that emerges over time from the characteristics of men in jail suggests a group of "problemed" men in need of a variety of remedial and interventional programs designed to lessen their criminal activities and proclivities. They appear to be particularly in need of drug and alcohol treatment programs, employment services, residential treatment programs, detoxification, antabuse treatment, or related programming. Despite some cynicism about enforced substance abuse treatment, there is accelerating evidence that such treatment works in lessening recidivism.

Many of these unconvicted defendants will later be committed to prison, where they will receive mostly inadequate or insufficient treatment for their underlying conditions.

SOURCE: Darrell Gilliard, *Prison and Jail Inmates 1998* (Washington, DC: U.S. Department of Justice, 1999); Caroline Wolf Harlow, *Profile of Jail Inmates 1996* (Washington, DC: U.S. Department of Justice, 1998); Paula Ditton, *Mental Health and Treatment of Inmates and Probationers* (Washington, DC: U.S. Department of Justice, 1999); Doris Wilson, *Drug Use, Testing and Treatment in Jails* (Washington, DC: U.S. Department of Justice, 2000); Doris James, *Profile of Jail Inmates, 2002* (Washington, DC: Bureau of Justice Statistics, 2004); Jennifer Karberg and Doris James, *Substance Dependence, Abuse, and Treatment of Jail Inmates, 2002* (Washington, DC: Bureau of Justice Statistics, 2005); Todd Minton, *Jail Inmates at Midyear 2012* (Washington, DC: U.S. Department of Justice, 2013).

Another troubling problem is examined in Correctional Practice 17.2—suicide in confinement facilities.

Education and Work

Education is an important factor in American society; it is viewed by many as an essential prerequisite for economic stability and success. In a high-tech society such as that of the United States, education is crucial for getting a job and earning an adequate income. Despite this need for education, the most recent national survey found that one in five Americans can be considered **functionally illiterate**.[7] As a group, male state prison inmates are less educated than their counterparts in the civilian population. Sixty-three percent of the inmates have not received a high school diploma, in contrast with 36 percent of the general population 18 years of age or older. This sad situation may become worse if youths pass through our public school systems without being properly prepared to function with developed problem-solving skills in an urban environment. It is not too surprising that crime is

key term

Functionally Illiterate
Prisoners with low-level education skills who are unable to read and follow written instructions.

correctional practice 17.2

Suicide in Confinement Facilities

The number of suicides in California's jails increased dramatically in 2012 to a record high of 38, or a rate of 52 per 100,000 jail inmates. Most died of strangulation by using socks, shoelaces, or jail bedding. The California state prison rate was much lower: 19 per 100,000 prisoners. Nationally, the 2012 suicide rate in jails was 36 per 100,000 inmates, almost twice the rate in state prisons.

This jail suicide rate was the highest since 1983, before wrongful death and liability suits led to jail reforms and prevention programs for potentially suicidal inmates. This may be a reflection of the number of mentally ill inmates in jail. The number of mentally ill jail inmates receiving treatment has more than doubled in the past five years.

Many first-time prisoners may become unstable in a confinement environment. The public has increasingly become intolerant of quality-of-life crimes such as aggressive panhandling ("unarmed robbery") and public drunkenness. At the same time, the number of community mental health services and treatment facilities has been drastically reduced, leaving no alternative to jail detention and punishment.

Nationally, there are between 400 and 600 jail suicides each year, about 9 in 10 by hanging. Suicide is the leading cause of deaths in most jails. The rate (per 100,000 inmates) is four times greater than in the community. There are almost 310 prison suicides each year, a rate that is close to that in the community. Violent offenders in both local jails (192 per 100,000 population) and state prisons (19 per 100,000 prison inmates) had suicide rates over twice as high as those of nonviolent offenders. Male jail inmates were also 1.6 times more likely to commit suicide than female inmates. Fortunately, suicide rates in confinement facilities have been steadily decreasing, in part due to liability issues and subsequent training of correctional staff.

SOURCE: Margaret Noonan, *Mortality in Local Jails and State Prisons, 2000–2011* (Washington, DC: U.S. Department of Justice, 2013); "In California's County Jails, Suicides Are Up Sharply," http://www.bakersfield.com/24hour/healthscience/v-print/story/436652p-3494415c.html (accessed July 16, 2002); Lindsay Hayes, "Scope of a National Public Health Problem," *Preventing Suicide* 2:4 (2002): 3; National Center on Institutions and Alternatives, "Liability for Custodial Suicide: A Look Back," http://www.ncianet.org/suicideprevention/study.asp (accessed October 18, 2008); U.S. Marshals Service, http://www.usmarshals.gov/prisoner/jail_suicide.pdf (accessed September 14, 2014).

often chosen as one alternative for survival under those circumstances. It is not enough that many inmates are now given a chance to earn a high school education in prison; the nation as a whole must insist that the education provided by our public school systems supplies the skills needed to keep these men out of prison.

Finally, almost one in four imprisoned men are eligible to be furloughed into an early-release procedure, but fewer than half of those eligible are given the opportunity to take such a furlough. Most inmates (69 percent) have some kind of **institutional work assignment**, but the average pay is less than $1 per hour for their work. It is hard to motivate an incarcerated man to make a serious effort to learn a trade while he is working in prison for such low wages when the same man has made up to $500 a day illegally in his community—and knows it can be done again.

key term

Institutional work assignment
Prison industry jobs based on institutional operational needs, community projects, or prison industry programs.

Reasons for the Soaring Prison Populations

As discussed in Chapter 18, the increase in female inmates in prison has been heavily impacted by the War on Drugs and violence. This is true also of male inmates. This factor was discussed in Chapter 3 in terms of a pendulum swing toward strong enforcement and the opening up of the floodgates into adult male prisons. Violent offenses accounted for 54 percent of the prison population increase from 1990 to 2012; drug offenses were the second-largest category.[8] More than one in five male state prison inmates and 5 in 10 federal male prison inmates are serving time for a drug law violation or drug-related crime. A decline in the prison release rate (down from 37 to 31 per 100 state prisoners) and an increase in the number of parole violators returned to prison account for most of the rest of the portion of the prison population growth. Table 17.1 shows prison admission data for 2012. Almost 30 percent of state prison admissions were parole violators.

table 17.1 Male Adult Inmate Population—Admissions in 2012

		FBOP
New Court Committed	282,353	50,940
Parole violators	131,468	4,508
Returned escapes	1,473	161
Transferred in	1,406	1,011
Other	19,120	1
Total	438,258	56,460

SOURCE: American Correctional Association, *2012 Directory of Adult and Juvenile Correctional Departments, Institutions, Agencies, and Probation and Parole Authorities* (Alexandria, VA: American Correctional Association, 2012), pp. 42–43.

As discussed, until just recently, prison populations had sharply increased, much to the dismay of both prisoner advocates and concerned correctional administrators. There are multiple reasons given for the population boom. Some correctional personnel are quick to note that the police and courts may have become more efficient more quickly than the correctional subsystem did. Not only did law enforcement increase in efficiency, but expanded use of plea bargaining by prosecutors may also have led to more commitments to prison. Court administration procedures were enhanced by using computers and other technology, further feeding the growth of prison populations.

Others identified the hardening of public opinion as a factor, pointing out that judges were often under considerable local pressure to commit offenders rather than use other alternatives. Still others have pointed to the increase in the **population at risk**,[9] those males in the age range of 18 to 29. Inasmuch as crime is a young person's occupation and considering the fact that the number of persons in the high-crime-rate ages doubled between 1965 and 1985, one would expect the factor of age to contribute heavily to the overpopulation of American prisons. The **age-at-risk** problem was made worse by a population shift over the past 15 years, during which families with young sons moved to urban areas from rural environments. The rural settings had provided more control and more wholesome outlets for young men. Historically, such population shifts—regardless of the population group in motion—meant that the second generation engaged in more frequent criminal behavior. In that case, recent population shifts coincided with an increase in the population at risk, and we can therefore expect the committed population to rise for several more years.

Three other factors have contributed to the growth in male prison populations, although the amount of effect is not precisely known. First, sentence enhancements were enacted by many states and include lengthening of prison sentences, enactment of three-strikes legislation (in some states mandating 20 years to be served in prison before possibility of parole release), and "prior imprisonment" statutes, which mandate prison terms for any subsequent felony conviction, even if the first disposition was not incarceration.

Second, Congress enacted a "truth-in-sentencing" program that provides funds for states to construct new prisons provided that the state enacts legislation requiring inmates to serve 85 percent of the imposed sentence. Male offenders are serving greater portions of their sentences, thus slowing the "turnover" rate.

Policy Position 17.1 further examines growth in the federal prison population.

Finally, prosecutor appear determined to focus on crimes of violence in their communities, seeking imprisonment as a sentencing outcome

key term

Population at risk
Those offenders more likely to offend, usually expressed as high-level potential for committing a crime.

key term

Age at risk
Those potential offenders likely to offend, segregated by age categories.

Photo 17.2
Inmates unpacking computer equipment prior to its installation.
Marmaduke St. John/Alamy.

policy position 17.1

Growth in the Federal Prison Population

The major reason for the dramatic federal prison population growth is that more people are sentenced to prison and for longer periods of time. For example, in 2011, over 90 percent of convicted federal offenders were sentenced to prison, whereas only about 10 percent received probation. By comparison, in 1986, only 50 percent received a prison sentence, with the rest receiving probation or a fine.

In 2011, the average federal prison sentence was 52 months, which is higher than the average at the state level for similar crime types. However, this difference is magnified by the fact that at the federal level, all offenders must serve at least 85 percent of their sentences, whereas at the state level, most serve a lower percentage, with nonviolent offenders often serving less than 50 percent of their sentences.

Although the number of inmates sentenced for immigration crimes in the federal system has also risen, it is drug sentences that are the main driver of the population's growth; in 2011, drug trafficking sentences averaged 74 months, and mandatory minimum sentences have kept even nonviolent drug offenders behind bars for a long time.

Source: Lauren E. Glaze and Erinn J. Herberman, *Correctional Populations in the United States, 2012* (Washington, DC: Bureau of Justice Statistics, 2013); Julie Samuels, Nancy La Vignea, and Samuel Taxy (2013), "Stemming the Tide: Strategies to Reduce the Growth and Cut the Cost of the Federal Prison System," http://www.urban.org/UploadedPDF/412932-stemming-the-tide.pdf (accessed March 2, 2014).

and stiffening plea negotiations by raising the minimum period of incarceration recommended to sentencing judges. A collateral consequence of such a strategy is that a subsequent second felony conviction, in some states, imposes a mandatory sentence of imprisonment that would be twice as long as if the offender had never been convicted.

It certainly seems that America has been determined to resolve its crime problems with a philosophy of "lock 'em up and throw away the key."[10] Although incapacitation may be an effective way to prevent crime temporarily, helping offenders expand their opportunities and enter the mainstream of American society might be a more permanent way of lowering crime rates and the collateral national costs of incarceration.[11]

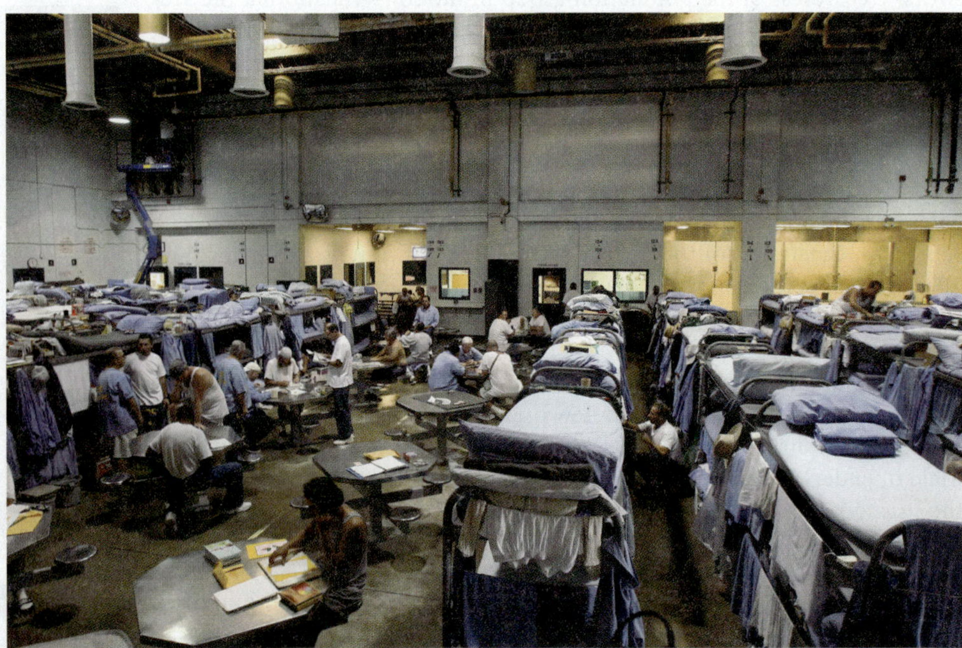

Photo 17.3
Inmate overcrowding results in all available space being converted to living quarters.
Justin Sullivan/Staff/Getty Images News/Getty Images.

PRISONIZATION PLAYS A ROLE

Every venture intended to elevate humanity (or at least to encourage improvement) has as many unplanned and unwanted effects as it has desired effects. Efforts to give male offenders a setting in which to do penance and be "reformed" have resulted in a number of unwanted side effects, ranging from the mental and physical deterioration caused by extreme solitary confinement at Sing Sing to a more contemporary unwanted phenomenon called **prisonization**. The originator of the term, Donald Clemmer, described this process as "the taking on in greater or less degree of the folkways, mores, customs, and general culture of the penitentiary."[12] Clemmer observed that acculturation into the prison community subjects the inmate to certain influences that either breed or deepen criminal behaviors, causing the prisoner to learn the criminal ideology of the prison, that is, to become "prisonized." Prisonization is a process that includes accepting the subordinate role into which one is thrust as an inmate; developing new habits of sleeping, dressing, eating, and working; undergoing status degradation; adopting a new language; and learning that one is dependent on others (including one's fellow inmates) for the scarce pleasures found in incarceration, including food, work assignment, freedom from assault, and privileges. Students of prisonization believe this process not only leads the inmate to further identify with criminal codes, goals, and behaviors but also serves to undercut reintegration programs and to lessen the offender's ability to adjust to society after release.[13]

key term

Prisonization
The process by which the newly committed inmates (and some prison staff) are introduced into the culture of the society of captives and learn to live within that inmate culture.

Many inmates have come to develop a set of social beliefs, attitudes, and conception of destiny from experiences in their younger and formative years as well as hearing such negative comments and orientations from peers and, to some extent, parents. They believe, for example, that a victim of theft has insurance and will not be harmed, thus devaluing and dehumanizing the victim, and that most of the people they assault were about to assault them first or owed them money and the only way to secure it was the use of physical force. Others think life owes them a living because they never got any "breaks" when growing up. They also learn quickly to deny responsibility for their behavior, assigning responsibility to the "stupid person who tried to jack me up" and who "failed to show respect." Such offenders have poor self-control, are often self-centered, and possess distorted perceptions of the world. Most have almost no skills in management of aggression and lack appropriate assertiveness. They have low victim empathy and little impulse control and undertake behavior that sets themselves up in a high-risk situation. These are cognitive beliefs that assure the offender that criminal behavior makes sense. In some ways, no amount of boot camp programming will remove this socially disruptive behavior or dissolve this negative approach, address cognitive defects, or erase poor parenting. This treatment approach (cognitive skill building) has been repeatedly shown to significantly reduce criminal reoffending. The point here is that prisonization is a ubiquitous process and mechanism of reinforcing antisocial patterns of reasoning.

The phenomenon of prisonization appears to exist in all prisons, not just the large gothic bastions that testify to archaic prison philosophies. Former inmates can bring it into the prison, but even in new prisons that receive first-time offenders, the inmates' pains of imprisonment can generate the prisonization process.

Because prisonization occurs in every institution, although to varying degrees, it is necessary to understand the benefits that accrue to the men who adhere to the inmate codes. The future correctional administrator must also understand the pains of imprisonment that encourage socialization into the inmate subculture. Those pains are status deprivation, sexual deprivation, material deprivation, and enforced intimacy with other and more dangerous offenders. Another aspect of prison culture is inmate slang, described in Correctional Practice 17.3.

If the institutional administrator and staff emphasize individual and group treatment rather than custody and discipline, if a pattern of cooperation can be developed between informal inmate leaders and institutional authorities, if a medium- or minimum-custody level can be achieved, and if violators of rules governing the use of force by the correctional

correctional **practice 17.3**

Inmate Slang

Male prisons are a society unto themselves, separated almost totally from the free society. Under these conditions, prison slang, a form of dialect, is developed. Slang has emerged partly as an expression of community for the inmates and also as an effort to confuse the correctional staff. We include some examples of inmate slang terminology, which may or may not be in use in every institution:

- All day: a life sentence, as in "I'm doin' all day"
- Backdoor parole: to die in prison
- The barn: a large, open dorm
- Box: radio
- Brake fluid: psychiatric meds
- Brown shirt: correctional officer
- Dead man walking: inmate on way to execution
- Fire in the hole: correctional officer approaching
- Hack: guard
- Duck: a new guard
- Fish: a new inmate
- Home boy: someone from the same city
- One time: stash the drugs, guard on floor
- The man: usually the warden, can be a captain
- Pack the rabbit: hide object in rectum
- Shank: homemade knife
- Snitch: informant
- Stinger: homemade electric apparatus for heating water
- Tailor-mades: factory-made cigarettes
- Thump: to fight
- Keester it: hide object in rectum
- Pruno: homemade alcohol
- Range queen: inmate who takes a woman's role

staff are consistently reprimanded, then the prison culture and the prisonization process can be markedly reduced. Some researchers have suggested that shorter prison terms tend to undercut the power of the prison culture because inmates can and do participate in "anticipatory socialization" as they near the end of their prison sentences and begin to

Photo 17.4

Los Angeles sheriff's deputies escort mentally ill patients to a new facility.
Chris Pizzello/AP Images.

prepare for their participation in the activities of the free world. It thus is reasonable to assume that short, fixed periods of incarceration would help reduce the negative effects of prisonization.

Rape and Sexual Assault in All-Male Institutions

In 2003, President Bush signed the **Prison Rape Elimination Act**, the first U.S. government law passed to deal with sexual assault behind bars (see Policy Position 17.2). The law calls for the gathering of national statistics about the problem, the development of guidelines for states about how to address prisoner rape, the creation of a review panel to hold annual hearings, and the provision of grants to states to combat the problem. Estimates are that one in five men in prison has been sexually abused, often by other inmates. Rates for women, who are most likely to be abused by male staff, reach as high as one in four in some facilities.

key term

Prison Rape Elimination Act of 2003
United States federal law designed to reduce prison sexual assaults.

In a detailed study of aggression among men behind prison walls, Anthony Scacco posited that sex is a vehicle for exploitation rather than an expression of pathological personality or situational frustration.[14] The sexual assaults that occur within prisons and jails cannot be categorized solely as **homosexual attacks**;[15] rather, they are often assaults made by heterosexually oriented males for political reasons—that is, to show power and dominance over other human beings. It is a depressing fact that victimization, degradation, racism, and humiliation of victims are the foremost reasons that sexual assaults are perpetrated on men in this setting. As Victor Hassine, himself an inmate (who purportedly committed suicide in prison), noted,

key term

Homosexual attacks
Sexual assaults on potential victim inmates, usually by heterosexual prisoners.

> Gang bangers often rely on rape in prison to generate fear and to maintain power over the general population. While street gangs use gunplay and murder to gain power, prison gangs use the threat of rape to dominate inmates and to ensure the repayment of even small debts. Some prison gangs require new inmates to commit rape as a gang initiation ritual. The act of raping another inmate is viewed as a way for gang members to demonstrate courage, strength, and cunning.[16]

In institutions for only male felons, homosexual behavior between consenting adults has been a recurrent phenomenon, as in other such unisexual settings as naval ships and religious monasteries. It is unreasonable to expect inmates to abandon sexual behavior in prison, particularly when they face increasingly long sentences. As Peter Buffum noted,

> [The present pattern of homosexuality in prisons] means that as long as the prison is an environment, which is largely devoid of situations where legitimate affectional ties can be established, there will be a tendency for the formation of homosexual relationships, especially among those persons serving long sentences who have concomitantly lost contact with meaningful persons in the free community. If in addition the prison does not allow legitimate attempts of the inmates to control their own lives and does not give an opportunity for expressions of masculinity and self-assertion that are meaningful among men at this social level, there will be homosexual relationships created to fulfill this need.[17]

Especially among younger inmates and those who accept passive roles, homosexual behaviors and relationships could impair future commitments to heterosexuality as well as create exploitative situations. When such relationships create jealousy among inmates, the potential for serious violence and administrative problems increases. If a third inmate becomes involved in a dyadic relationship or there is a transfer of affection, extreme violence can occur. The once frequent pattern of transferring the passive partner to another institution is no longer an adequate or constitutional response by prison management. Segregating passive partners may cause the active inmates to coerce others into sexual behavior as well as to raise legal issues of inmate rights and to create the potential for lawsuits arising from such isolation.

policy position 17.2

Eliminating Violence

The Prison Rape Elimination Act of 2003 is the first U.S. federal law passed dealing with assault of prisoners, requiring "the gathering of national statistics about the problem; the development of guidelines for states about how to address prisoner rape; the creation of a review panel to hold annual hearings; and the provision of grants to states to combat the problem." It was partly a response to a Human Rights Watch report on prison rape in U.S. prisons. In 2012, of the 11 facilities with the highest prevalence of sexual victimization, three were in Texas and two were in Florida.

Source: Allen J. Beck, Marcus Berkofsky, and Christopher Krebs, *Sexual Victimization in State and Federal Prisons Reported by Inmates, 2011–12* (Washington, DC: Bureau of Justice Statistics, 2013).

key term

Family (conjugal) visits
Prison program designed to reinforce family ties through unsupervised contact, usually between husband and wife.

Prison administrators will need to consider and implement home visits at known intervals for those under long sentences as well as provide activities and programs that will attack the real problems. At the beginning of 2005, however, only six states reported permitting inmates to have **family (conjugal) visits**. This allowed inmates to have some control over their own lives and maintain affectionate relationships and stable interpersonal interaction. Encouraging correspondence with and visits from relatives and family helps reduce the pains of imprisonment and helps family reunification. Conjugal visits are programs in California, Connecticut, New Mexico, New York, and Washington. Mississippi, the first state to allow conjugal visitation starting over a century ago, terminated the privilege in 2014.

THE GRAYING OF AMERICA'S MALE PRISONERS

The proportion of prisoners in the nation's institutions who are elderly is rapidly increasing, in large part due to the tougher long-term sentences inherent in the "get-tough-on-crime" stance. It has been estimated that about 1 in 12 inmates are age 50 or over (121,800). There were more than 26,000 prisoners ages 65 and older in all prison institutions in the nation in 2012.

The growth rate of "geriatric inmates" (age 50 or above) is particularly acute in California, Texas, and Florida, which have large prison populations. For example, in California, the population of prisoners over 55 doubled in the years from 1997 to 2006. About 20 percent of California prisoners are serving life sentences, and over 10 percent are serving life without the possibility of parole. Louisiana's prison system now holds more than 5,000 people over the age of 50—a three fold increase in the past 12 years. In Florida, the growth rate of older offenders already exceeds that of younger offenders; in California, over 29,000 men are serving sentences of 25 years to life for conviction of a "third-strike" felony.[18] Nationwide, the number of inmates serving life sentences is over 159,000, and those serving life without parole is over 49,000.[19] As these inmates age, the cost of incarceration will skyrocket. In New York, the annual cost per inmate exceeds $59,000 (see Chapter 21).

key term

Elderly inmates
All prisoners over a specific age, usually 55 years old.

Elderly inmates are *more* likely than other prisoners to have committed crimes such as homicide and manslaughter as well as sexual offenses. They are *less likely* than other inmates to be imprisoned for robbery and burglary. Because of their significantly longer sentences, elderly inmates may be concentrated in prisons well beyond their proportions in the civilian population, which will pose problems for them as well as prison administrators.

First, they will have health care concerns and need preventive health care programs that, if not provided, could be a source of considerable and, for correctional administrators, substantial litigation costs. At the least, these inmates will suffer from depression and differing nutritional needs (less protein, fewer calories, and more soft food and fiber).

Photo 17.5

A geriatric unit in Estelle Prison, Texas.
Andrew Lichtenstein/The Image Works.

In addition, growing old in prison will mean having to avoid exploitation and violence by younger inmates,[20] having to adjust new personal needs to prison life, and not having suitable programs (recreational, educational, or housing). Vulnerability to victimization, frailty, and isolation from outside relatives and friends will take their toll, as will fear of death, hopelessness, and being unable to cope when released.

Health care costs increase significantly as a result of treatment for hypertension, diabetes, stroke, cancer, and emphysema. Glasses, dentures, kidney dialysis, and heart surgery are also required. In 2001, the medical costs for prisoners exceeded $4.2 billion, and a recent study analyzed inflation-adjusted correctional health care from 44 states and

Photo 17.6

A psychiatrist evaluates a celled prisoner to gauge his suicide potential.
Kin Man Hui/ZUMAPRESS/Newscom.

key term
Geriatric center
Correctional facility for elderly inmates.

estimated that these states spent $6.5 billion on inmate health care. It has been estimated that by 2015, health care costs for elderly inmates will increase 14-fold.[21] Many prisons will become **geriatric centers**,[22] and special staff and staff training will be necessary to treat this unique-needs segment of the nation's offenders. Perhaps a nation that can explore outer space can find the necessary compassion to care for the increasing group of elderly inmates during this second decade of the new century. Executive clemency, including pardons, may once again become a frequent act as government struggles with the problems of elderly inmates. The new federally mandated insurance coverage legislation (currently referred to as "Obamacare") may encourage the early release of elderly inmates into a community in which medical care would be available.

Summary

Summarize the Trends in Prison Population

The U.S. adult male prison population has increased sharply over the past four decades, reaching a population total some five times higher than that in 1986. This increase has been attributed to enhanced sentencing lengths, a shift in requiring inmates to serve some 85 percent of the length of sentence pronounced by the sentencing judge, an influx of rurally oriented immigrants whose sons overcontribute to the burgeoning prison population, the War on Drugs, a frightened populace and a resulting "get-tough" political stance, and other factors revolving around illegal drugs and their importation.

Describe the Issues Adult Prison Inmates Face

Male prisoners are basically drawn from the more disadvantaged citizenry whose education, work skills, substance abuse histories, physical and mental health, and vocational futures are negative. In terms of corrections, they also tend to be both high-risk and high-need clients. Institutional programs that would address these limitations and reduce recidivism are sparse, although many states have solid programs. If the inmate can successfully complete education and vocational training and utilize evidence-based programs, they would be basically prepared to assume lives outside of prison. When they exit prison or are paroled, they have then to face the challenge of finding both housing and work.

Describe the Prison Population Increase

The male inmate population has soared over the past three decades, although there have been slight reductions in populations in the past three years. Most incarcerated males are in prison, which houses more than twice the number in jails. The jail population also contains many "holdbacks" awaiting transfer to prisons when space becomes available. The increase has been fueled by law enforcement's focus on drug trafficking, illegal immigration, and crimes of violence. Even while the crime rate in the nation has retreated to pre-1972 levels (and juvenile offending has been almost halved in the last decade), the number of incarcerated offenders continues to leap forward.

Compare and Contrast Jail and Prison Inmates

Most jail and prison inmates are minority and undereducated, and most received poor parenting in their more formative years. Most lack job skills and have a spotty employment history. Still others have become addicted to illegal drugs and have heavily contributed to the revolving-door phenomenon found in correctional facilities; others have moved into urban environs in which education and training are required in order to earn a decent living. This set of underlying causes is offered not to excuse the predations of the incarcerated but to point out the unequal access of some groups to the American dream.

Some mental characteristics influencing the illegal behaviors of inmates revolve around failure, inaccurate assumptions about the nature of living in a technologically advanced culture, a sense of anger and poor anger management skills, a self-centered view of reality, and a lack of ability to defer gratification. In one sense, many such inmates have not been socialized into constructive roles and views of selves. In certain jurisdictions, street gangs have formed, precursors of institutional threat groups or prison gangs that pose management and safety issues for correctional managers and prison staff.

In the past few decades, community-based correctional resources have increased, and administrators have made coordinated efforts to utilize such opportunities to avoid incarcerating the least dangerous and low-threat individuals and groups. The search for effective and data-based treatment options is beginning to provide result-proven treatment options that, over time, will decrease the number of offenders who would graduate to long-term sentences.

In terms of correctional policy, major changes are appearing due to decreased funding available to jails and prisons, the emergence of evidence-based effective treatments, public advocacy, and the emerging consensus that although some offenders are truly dangerous, most can be treated through alternatives to incarceration. The strain on available resources will lead to changes in policy related to geriatric inmates, whose medical expenses will probably quadruple in the next two decades. Court decisions on the quality of life within prisons, availability of medical and mental health services, and prison overcrowding are compelling some state correctional systems and state government officials to significantly reduce the number of incarcerated inmates. Promising strategies are emerging, and the total number of incarcerated offenders is beginning a slow decrease. The important point is to determine the dangerousness inmates pose, to use alternatives to incarceration for the less dangerous and rehabilitated, and to implement evidence-based treatment programs. Much remains to be done.

Explain What Might Be Done to Reduce Functional Illiteracy among Prison Inmates

Functional illiteracy generally means that a person cannot read, write, and understand the basics of the English language, often due to inadequate or discarded educational programs. Prisons can compel inmates to achieve functional literacy through institutional programs, mandated educational achievement prior to parole consideration, and use of relevant subject matter to reduce illiteracy.

Explain the Consequences of Prisonization

Inmates take on the culture of the prison and any institutional threat groups as part of the socialization of being an inmate. This includes rationalizations and neutralizations for their crimes, thought patterns found among other offenders, language describing the roles of staff and victims, anticipations for more criminal behavior following release, and the roles certain inmates assume while imprisoned. Taken together, they lessen the potential for reintegration, increase danger in prison, and contribute to recidivism after release.

Explain Rape and Sexual Assault in All-Male Institutions

Both rape and sexual assault among inmates are seldom homosexual acts but instead are driven by efforts of non-homosexual men to prove manhood, exert inmate power and increase fear among potential victims, and force other inmates to pay debts. Homosexual rape in prison is about the power of one prisoner over another.

Identify Five Outcomes of the Graying of American Prison Populations

The graying phenomenon is a result of increased sentence length and mandatory minimum regulations requiring serving a higher proportion of the sentence imposed by the court. Fewer inmates are being released through parole. As a result, the graying of the prison population will continue. This phenomenon means staff will have to be retrained, prisons will have to be redesigned, penal institutions will have to be dedicated to geriatric inmates, inmates will be less able to correctly respond to orders by correctional officers, inmates will face increasing physical and mental problems, and the costs of medical treatment will sharply escalate. Some of these costs can be reduced by medical parole and compassionate release, particularly of the less dangerous and older inmates.

Key Words

racial and ethnic groupings, 377
institutional threat groups, 378
"designer" drugs, 378
functionally illiterate, 379
institutional work assignment, 380
population at risk, 381
age at risk, 381
prisonization, 383
Prison Rape Elimination Act, 385
homosexual attacks, 385
family (conjugal) visits, 386
elderly inmates, 386
geriatric center, 388

Review Questions

1. Explain the dynamics of rape in a male prison.
2. What factors contribute to prisonization?
3. What can be done to reduce sexual assaults in prisons?
4. How should male inmates be sentenced?
5. Why are so many prisoners members of minority groups?
6. What problems do elderly inmates pose and face?
7. How can corrections address the problems of elderly offenders?
8. What impacts do street and prison gangs have on prison management?
9. Debate: Offenders should be released to community control when they reach age 70.

Application Case Studies

1. You are the director of corrections in your state and have been asked by the governor to give her three ways to reduce the prison population. What would you say?
2. You have just been appointed warden, and the prison you are about to take over is listed as being among those with the highest rates of sexual victimization. What changes will you make?
3. You are a warden, and there has recently been several suicides at your facility. What steps will you take?

Endnotes

1. E. Ann Carson and William J. Sabol, *Prisoners in 2011* (Washington, DC: Bureau of Justice Statistics, 2012).
2. Nick Miroff, "Controversial Quota Drives Immigration Detention Boom," *Washington Post,* October 13, 2013, http://www.washingtonpost.com/world/controversial-quota-drives-immigration-detention-boom/2013/10/13/09bb689e-214c-11e3-ad1a-1a919f2ed890_story.html (accessed March 2, 2014).
3. Prison administrators argue that reserve capacity is needed to operate a prison effectively. Prison dormitories and cells need to be repaired and maintained periodically. Additional space may be needed for emergencies. Special housing (such as protective custody and punitive segregation) and administrative units (such as prison recreation, intake, and program space) are required. The federal prison system is running over137 percent of capacity, and 21 states are over at least their lowest capacity, some (such as Alabama) by as much as 193 percent of capacity. E. Ann Carson and Daniela Golinelli, *Prisoners in 2012* (Washington, DC: Bureau of Justice Statistics, 2013).
4. Dan Eckhart, "Civil Actions Related to Prison Gangs," *Corrections Management Quarterly* 5:1 (2001): 9–64. See also Frank Marcell, "Security Threat Group Effect on Corrections during the Past Decade," *Corrections Today* 68:2 (2006): 56–59.
5. "The Heroin Epidemic: Cuyahoga County Logs Record-Breaking Death Toll in 2013," *Cleveland Plaindealer*, December 29, 2013.
6. Caroline Wolf Beck, *Drug Enforcement and Treatment in Prison, 1990* (Washington, DC: U.S. Department of Justice, 1992). See also Harry Wexler, "The Success of Therapeutic Communities for Substance Abuse in American Prisons," *The Prison Journal* 75:1 (1995): 57–66; Dorothy Lockwood, J. McCorkle, and J. Inciardi, "Developing Comprehensive Prison-Based Therapeutic Community Treatment for Women," *Drugs and Society* 13:1/2 (1998): 193–212; and Michael Prendergast et al., "Reducing Substance Abuse in Prisons," *The Prison Journal* 84:2 (2004): 265–280.
7. Charles Bailey, "Prison Populations Surging, and Not Just Because of the Nation's Economic Slowdown," *Corrections Digest* 7:2 (1976): 9. See also Miriam Williford, *A Contradiction in Terms?* (Phoenix, AZ: Oryx Press, 1994), and Elliott Currie, *Crime and Punishment in America: Why the Solutions to America's Most Stubborn Social Crisis Have Not Worked—And What Will* (New York: Metropolitan Books, 1998).
8. Carson and Golinelli, *Prisoners in 2012.*
9. Rob Wilson, "U.S. Prison Population Sets Another Record," *Corrections Magazine* 4:2 (1980): 5; Currie, *Crime and Punishment in America.* But see Grant Stitt, Donia Giascopassi, and Mark Nichols, "The Effect of Casino Gambling on Crime in New Casino Jurisdictions," *Journal of Crime and Justice* 23:1 (2000): 1–23.
10. A term developed in the 1930s. See also Joan Petersilia, "California's Prison Policy: Causes, Costs, and Consequences," *The Prison Journal* 72:1/2 (1992): 8–36, and Theodore Sasson, *Crime Talk: How Citizens Construct a Social Problem* (Hawthorne, NY: Aldine, 1995).
11. See Currie, *Crime and Punishment; in America* and John Donahue and P. Siegelman, "Allocating Resources among Prisons and Social Programs in the Battle against Crime," *Journal of Legal Studies* 27:1 (1998): 1–43.

12. Donald Clemmer, *The Prison Community* (New York: Rinehart, 1940), p. 8. See also Barbara Peat and T. Winfree, "Reducing the Intra-Institutional Effects of 'Prisonization': A Study of a Therapeutic Community for Drug-Using Inmates," *Criminal Justice Behavior* 19:2 (1992): 206–225; Hans Toch, "Inmate Involvement in Prison Governance," *Federal Probation* 59:2 (1995): 34–39; and Darren Lawson, C. Segrin, and T. Ward, "The Relationship between Prisonization and Social Skills among Prison Inmates," *The Prison Journal* 76:3 (1996): 293–301.
13. Kenneth Adams, "Adjusting to Prison Life," in *Crime and Justice: A Review of Research,* ed. Michael Tonry (Chicago: University of Chicago Press, 1993), pp. 275–359; Paula Faulkner and W. Faulkner, "Effects of Organizational Change on Inmate Status and the Inmate Code of Conduct," *Journal of Crime and Justice* 20:1 (1997): 55–72.
14. Anthony Scacco, *Rape in Prison* (Springfield, IL: Charles C Thomas, 1975); Michael Scarce, *Male on Male Rape* (New York: Plenum, 1997); Thomas Fagan, D. Wennerstrom, and J. Miller, "Sexual Assault of Male Inmates," *Journal of Correctional Health Care* 3:1 (1996): 49–65; Christine Saum, H. Surratt, and J. Inciardi, "Sex in Prison: Exploring the Myth and Realities," *The Prison Journal* 75:4 (1995): 413–430. But see Richard Tewksbury, "Measures of Sexual Behavior in an Ohio Prison," *Sociology and Social Research* 74:1 (1989): 34–39; Richard Tewksbury and Elizabeth Mustaine," Lifestyle Factors Associated with the Sexual Assault of Men," *Journal of Men's Studies* 9:2 (2001): 23–42; and Christopher Hensley and Richard Tewksbury, "Wardens' Perceptions of Inmate Fear of Sexual Assault," *The Prison Journal* 85:2 (2005): 198–203.
15. Helen Eigenberg, "Homosexuality in Male Prisons: Demonstrating the Need for a Social Constructionist Approach," *Criminal Justice Review* 17:2 (1992): 219–234. See also Genesis 19: 1–9, in which non-gay men planned to sexually assault angels. The "Sodomites" are heterosexual men with a hatred of outsiders and who intend to violate cultural mores by attacking the angels. The "sin" is breaking the hospitality rules.
16. Victor Hassine, *Life without Parole* (New York: Oxford University Press, 2008), p. 138.
17. Peter Buffum, *Homosexuality in Prisons* (Washington, DC: U.S. Government Printing Office, 1972), p. 28. See also James Stephan, *Prison Rule Violators* (Washington, DC: Bureau of Justice Statistics, 1989); David Hallpren, "Sexual Assault of New South Wales Prisoners," *Current Issues in Criminal Justice* 6:3 (1995): 327–334; and Saum et al., "Sex in Prison."
18. Harry E. Allen and Bruce S. Ponder, "Three Strikes Legislation and Racial Disparity in California: 1994–2001," paper presented at the annual meeting of the Academy of Criminal Justice Sciences, Anaheim, CA, March 8, 2002; California Department of Corrections, "Second and Third Strike Felons in the Adult Institution Population," http://www.cdcr.ca.gov/Reports_Research/Offender_Information_Services_Branch/Quarterly/Strike1Archive.html (accessed October 17, 2008).
19. The Sentencing Project, "Trends in Corrections," http://sentencingproject.org/doc/publications/inc_Trends_in_Corrections_Fact_sheet.pdf.
20. Richard Dagger, "The Graying of America's Prisons," *Corrections Today* 50:3 (1988): 26–34; Ronald Day, "Golden Years behind Bars," *Federal Probation* 58:2 (1994): 47–54.
21. American Correctional Association, *2010 Directory* (Lanham, MD: American Correctional Association, 2010). See also Sarah Bradley, "Graying of Inmate Population Spurs Corrections Challenges," *On the Line* 13:2 (March 1990): 5. The average costs for imprisoning elderly inmates is high because they suffer from an average of three chronic illnesses during their incarceration. In New York, these costs range from $50,000 to $75,000 a year. Rozann Greco, "The Future of Aging in New York State," http://aging.state.ny.us/explore/project2015/briefs04.htm (accessed February 16, 2005).
22. Gennaro Vito and D. Wilson, "Forgotten People: Elderly Inmates," *Federal Probation* 49:2 (1985): 18–24; Deborah Wilson and G. Vito, "Long-Term Inmates: Special Need and Management Considerations," *Federal Probation* 52:3 (1988): 21–26. At least 22 states already have special geriatric prison wings or housing units for their older inmates. See also Todd Edwards, *The Aging Inmate Population* (Atlanta, GA: Council of State Governments, 1998), and Project for Older Prisoners, California Department of Corrections, "A Look at Other States' Programs for Older Inmates," http://www.sfgate.com/cgi-bin/article.cgi?file=/news/archive/2003/02/25/state2034EST0156.DTL (accessed December 16, 2004).

Objectives

- Summarize the characteristics and trends of the adult female prison population.
- Describe the characteristics of female inmates and issues, challenges, and barriers faced by female inmates.
- Outline the history of women's prisons.
- Describe the culture in women's prisons.
- Explain the concept of co-gender institutions.
- Draw appropriate conclusions concerning the use of community corrections for female offenders.

chapter 18

Female Offenders

Outline

"Drug-addicted women tend to come from families with a high incidence of mental illness, suicide, and alcohol or drug dependence."

—Harry E. Allen

Overview

Although male offenders (Chapter 17) do provide the lion's share of adult prisoners (93 percent), the female inmate population has been increasing at a higher annual rate of growth. In this chapter, we examine that phenomenon as well as those similar processes and conditions with which females must contend. We look at the kinds of women and the crimes that place them in state, federal, and other adult female prisons and correctional institutions. You will find that many female offenders are moving away from "woman crime" and becoming more mainstream in their criminal behaviors and levels of violence, posing new challenges to old approaches.

To compare the relative levels of incarceration between female and male prisoners, we first examine the crime rates for both categories and look at the differing patterns of conviction and sentencing rates for those crimes. The "steel ceiling" that has traditionally tended to divert females from long-term incarceration in correctional facilities into community mental health and correctional alternatives seems to have cracked somewhat recently; different trends are emerging for female prisoners. The student is presented with information about problems specific to female offenders that may cause them to need special treatment. What happens to female offenders in the prisons of America?

FEMALE CRIME AND INCARCERATION RATES

As shown in Figure 18.1, the number of female prisoners in adult facilities has grown rapidly and has just recently begun to level off. Although this grand total represents just less than 8 percent of the U.S. prison population overall, it is a significant and worrisome trend. Although the total number of male prisoners has grown by about 48 percent since 1995, the number of female prisoners grew by nearly 64 percent, continuing a long trend of higher rate of growth for female inmates. They constitute over 13 percent of the jail population on a given day.[1] To get a better understanding of just who these prisoners are and why the rate and numbers are increasing, one has to look closer at the kinds of crimes, regionally and nationally, being committed by females.

The period from 1970 through the 1990s included the years when women's equality and civil rights were asserted, if not established, on almost every front.[2] Yet only recently has there been a movement to push for the rights of female prisoners in corrections. In a way, females still receive differential, sometimes even preferential, treatment at almost every station of the criminal justice system, partly in deference to traditional female gender roles (except in the area of drug arrests).[3] We now examine the more common kinds of crime index (see Chapter 4) offenses committed by females and compare some of the dispositions to institutions for females in a rapidly changing environment.

Although the criminal statistics contained in the Uniform Crime Reports of the Federal Bureau of Investigation are somewhat limited and "soft," especially for crimes involving females, they are the best available and can at least be accepted as indicators of trends.[4] A comparison of the total **arrests by gender** in 2012 for the eight major (index) crimes can be found in Table 18.1 Women commit far less crimes of violence than do men. The eight index crimes do not include drug offenses. As Figure 18.1 illustrates, women are arrested three times more frequently for drug offenses than for crimes of violence.[5]

These figures clearly indicate the growing role of the female offender in the entire criminal justice system. As we note later, **preferential treatment** of females seems to be disappearing for those females arrested for nontraditional crimes (crimes of violence and crimes committed with one or more other female offenders). For example, between 1991 and 2011, new court commitments of females to state prisons for violent offenders increased 83 percent.[6] We may have to take a new look at the **"traditional" female crimes** as we continue to examine the "new" female offender of the twenty-first century.

key term

Arrests by gender
Comparison of arrest data between male and female offenders.

key term

Preferential treatment
Argument that female offenders receive more lenient treatment at all phases of the criminal justice system.

key term

"Traditional" female crimes
Those criminal offenses particular to the female gender (prostitution and infanticide, for example).

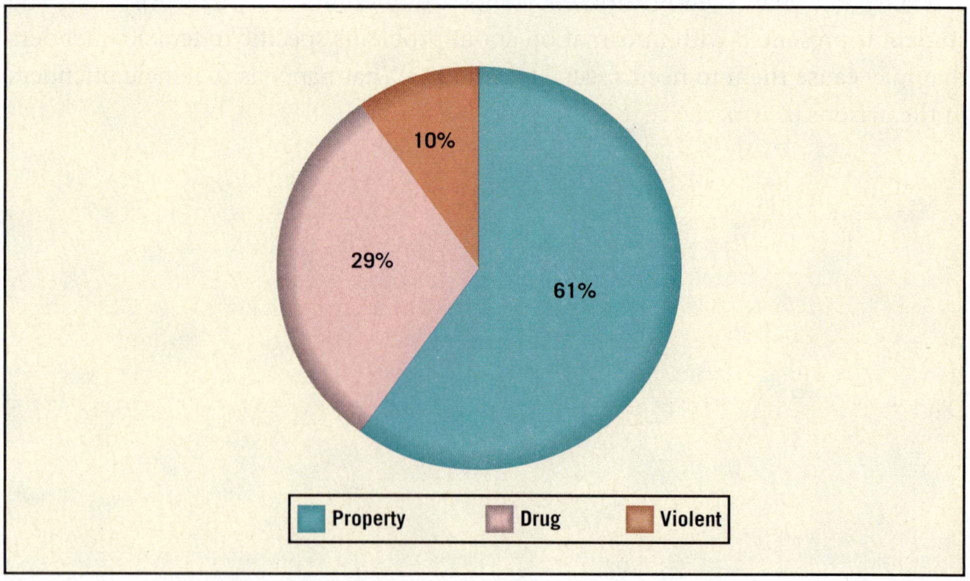

figure 18.1
Major Crimes for Which Females Were Arrested (in percent)

SOURCE: Federal Bureau of Investigation, *Crime in the United States 2012* (Washington, DC: U.S. Department of Justice, 2013), chart 32.

table 18.1 Arrests of Females by Type of Part I Crime, 2012

Offense Charged	Total	Female Crimes	Percentage Female
Total: All index crimes	972,218	486,107	33.3
Murder and nonnegligent manslaughter	6,3037	830	11.6
Forcible rape	11,782	109	0.009
Robbery	50,033	9,032	13.2
Aggravated assault	201,049	59,103	22.7
Burglary	161,450	32,432	16.7
Larceny-theft	488,888	374,332	43.3
Motor vehicle theft	37,327	8,833	19
Arson	6,476	1,436	18
Violent crime	278,167	69,074	19.8
Property crime	694,051	417,033	37.5

SOURCE: Federal Bureau of Investigation, *Crime in the United States 2012* (Washington, DC: U.S. Department of Justice, 2013).

The general increase in female criminality may also be seen as reflecting the changing patterns of criminal opportunity for females. It is interesting that arrests for prostitution, the crime Freda Adler calls "the oldest and newest profession,"[7] declined nearly 40 percent between 2003 and 2012.[8] Whether this relates to more and better jobs for females, the growth of AIDS awareness, or a changing moral climate we leave for others to determine.[9]

The arrest figures for prostitution, however, are only the tip of the iceberg. Because prostitution is one of the so-called **victimless crimes**[10] and clients seldom complain because they would be implicating themselves, the number of arrests for prostitution usually reflects only cases of flagrant solicitation, rampant disease, or a local cleanup campaign.[11] Considerable folklore surrounds prostitution, most of it with no basis in fact. Those who profit from prostitution (almost never the prostitutes themselves) are not about to compile statistics or seek publicity. It is a business that thrives on sexual appetite, with the ultimate motive being simple profit.

key term

Victimless crimes
Offenses in which the victim does not seem to appear, or is equaled to the offender (prostitution and drug abuse, for example).

A Differential Justice System for Females?

The previous scarcity of research in the area of female equality in general and the role of females in the criminal justice system in particular makes this area the current gold mine for researchers and writers.[12] It is unfortunate that much of the earlier literature was a warmed-over version of the old myths and inaccuracies of the 1940s and 1950s.

The first point at which the female offender comes into contact with the criminal justice system is the point of arrest. Although arrest may be a traumatic experience for the male offender, it has special problems for the female. It is estimated that 80 percent of the female offenders in America have dependent children at home and that a percentage of those children have no one else to care for them.[13] About 80,000 females in jails and prisons have an estimated 200,000 children under age 18[14] (see Table 18.2). Concern for the children and a tendency among officers to identify female offenders with their own mothers or sisters may cause arresting officers to use more discretion than they might with a male in the same situation. A recognition of the need to provide more pretrial services for female offenders has prompted many communities to develop volunteer programs to assist with the female

table 18.2 Estimated Number of Female Parents in Prison, 2011 (Top 10 States)

State	Mothers
Texas	7,533
California	4,970
Florida	4,410
Ohio	2,410
Georgia	2,310
Arizona	2,020
Illinois	1,770
Virginia	1,730
Pennsylvania	1,690
Missouri	1,590
Total	**30,433**

SOURCE: The Sentencing Project, *Parents in State Prisons* (Washington, DC: The Sentencing Project, 2012).

problems at home. It is important to remember that the children of female offenders often are placed with relatives or foster parents or become residents of juvenile residential facilities as a result of their mothers' actions. To the juveniles who are removed from the community and placed in what they perceive as a facility for other juveniles who have committed offenses, it becomes hard to accept that protection, not punishment, is the state's motivation (see Chapter 18). The incoming pregnant female resident whose child is removed from her care at or immediately following birth may find it hard to believe that her child will grow up without bonding with her.

An officer's reluctance to arrest females for traditional crimes is also the result of age-old customs, mores, and laws that have created great distinctions between men and women under apprehension.[15] Although police officers seldom hesitate to place a male offender "up against the wall" and to respond to force with equal force, they often loathe doing so with a female. Most police departments have strict rules and regulations regarding the apprehension, search, and detention of females. In most cases, a female officer or matron is assigned to detain females and conduct searches of their persons.

The female offender seldom spends much time in detention before trial. Concern for the family and the lack of adequate female detention facilities or female personnel in the police department almost demand pretrial release for females.[16] Until quite recently, female offenders also usually committed less serious offenses and could therefore be released on bail or on their own recognizance. Beginning in the 1980s, however, females have been committing more serious crimes and, perhaps owing to the move to equalize punishments for codefendants, have been receiving more severe sentences However, as females are arrested in greater numbers for crimes that have been committed primarily by men in the past, they can expect the **paternalistic attitude of judges**—if such an attitude now exists—to diminish rapidly.[17] As Meda Chesney-Lind notes, the male model of prisons is being superimposed on female prisoners in the rush to vengeful equity.[18]

key term

Paternalistic attitude of judges
Sentiments found in a system under which an authority undertakes to supply needs or regulate conduct of those under its control, particularly for female offenders.

The differential treatment accorded to females in many cases does not automatically mean better treatment or consideration. Moreover, as an alternative to differential treatment, the model of the male prison is sometimes copied, even to the point of ignoring the female inmates' obvious physical differences.[19]

For those and other reasons, female offenders had traditionally received discretionary treatment by police and prosecutors. Females brought to court now are still apt to receive

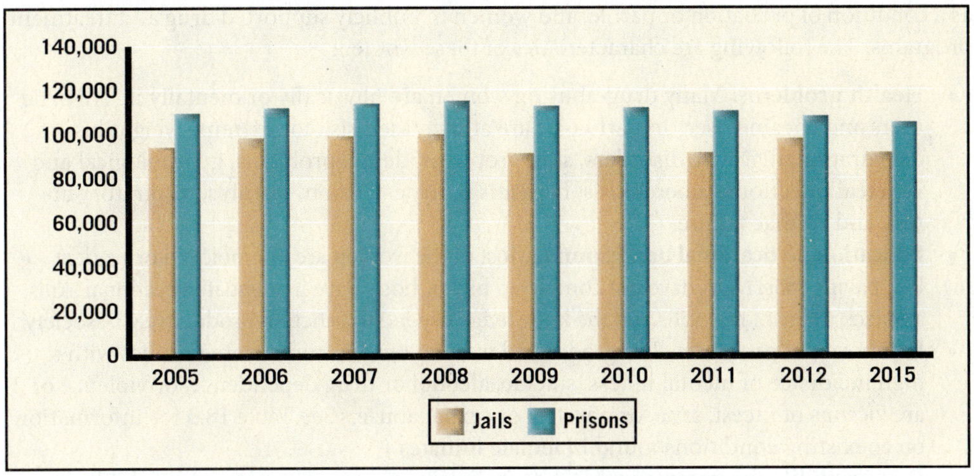

figure 18.2

Females in State and Federal Prisons and Local Jails, 2005–2015. Data for 2015 extrapolated.

SOURCE: Todd Minton, *Jail Inmates at Midyear 2012* (Washington, DC: Bureau of Justice Statistics, 2013), p. 5; E. Ann Carson and Daniela Golinelli, *Prisoners in 2012—Advance Counts* (Washington, DC: Bureau of Justice Statistics, 2013), p. 2.

consideration for probation, fines, and suspended sentences more often than are men who commit comparable crimes. Of course, female offenders are less likely to have long criminal offense records and to commit violent crimes.

Statistics on the growth of female prisoners in state prisons and their offenses between 1999 and 2015 can be found in Figure 18.2.[20] It appears that the greatest change has been in the area of females committed for violent and property offenses. With regard to violent crime, the numbers are still significantly lower than for males. The War on Drugs has become a war on females and has materially contributed to the exploding growth of female prisoners. Yet they are not the "major players" in the drug trade; at least one-third are jailed for drug possession. In one sense, they can be seen as "prisoners" of the War on Drugs; in the federal prison system, drug offenders exceed 50 percent of the prison population.

Why has the female prison population increased so sharply? No one knows for certain, but some of the reasons given are that females have more opportunities to commit crime than ever before, they are committing more serious crimes, and they are being sentenced more severely by judges. Many state drug statutes mandate imprisonment and restrict the sentencing discretion of the judge. Other theories are that presentence investigators and the judiciary, influenced by the **women's liberation movement**, are less likely to give favorable sentencing considerations than they were in the past, that parole boards are using uniform sentencing guidelines that force female inmates to serve more time, and that females are getting their "just deserts" under the conservative backlash to treat all offenders more severely. Others argue that the War on Drugs has sent many more female drug addicts into prisons than in the past and that excessively long sentences for possession of controlled substances to which the offender is addicted (a medical problem) has had a disproportionate effect on females. For example, one researcher recently called Oklahoma's drug laws "mean" and overly punitive and said the state's tough-on-crime sentencing guidelines are to blame for women serving lengthy sentences.[21]

key term

Women's liberation movement
A series of social movements intended to narrow the gaps between rights and privileges accorded to males and to free females from oppressive minority status.

There are many theories but not much data, and it is not unreasonable to assume that there are probably multiple reasons for the increase.

Characteristics of Drug-Abusing Female Offenders

To gain a picture of the special needs of drug-abusing women offenders, information was taken from several sources covering women arrestees, women incarcerated in jails and prisons, women offenders diverted into community-based treatment instead of incarceration or as a condition of probation or parole, and women in publicly supported drug and treatment programs. The following are characteristics of these women:

- **Health problems.** Many drug-abusing women are physically or mentally ill. All drug users and cocaine users in particular are at increased risk for extreme weight loss, dehydration, digestive disorders, skin problems, dental problems, gynecological and venereal infections, tuberculosis, hepatitis B, hypertension, seizures, respiratory arrest, and cardiac failure.
- **Educational/vocational background.** Most of the women are unemployed or work at low-paying jobs. Most have not completed high school, have inadequate vocational skills, and lack many of the skills and the knowledge needed to function productively in society.
- **Psychosocial problems.** Drug-addicted women tend to come from families with a high incidence of mental illness, suicide, alcohol or drug dependence, or violence or are victims of incest, rape, or physical or sexual abuse. (See Table 18.3 for information on coexisting conditions found in female inmates.)
- **Responsibility for parenting.** Most drug-abusing women offenders are of childbearing age, already have children, and are single mothers. Many of them receive little or no help from the children's father(s), lack supportive family and social networks, and have limited or no financial resources. Often their children become drug abusers themselves, thereby perpetuating both drug abuse and dysfunctional parenting across generations.
- **Drug use and treatment.** Most drug-abusing women offenders started abusing drugs and alcohol at an early age, and many used drugs, especially cocaine, on a daily basis prior to incarceration. In one survey of women in prison, 46 percent of respondents reported they had used drugs and/or alcohol at the time of their offense. Approximately 25 percent of adult women offenders have spent some time in a drug/alcohol treatment program, which, however, has most likely been of limited duration and intensity.
- **Criminal justice and child protective services involvement.** A percentage of drug-abusing women who seek treatment have had some involvement with the criminal justice system or with child protective services. One study reported that an estimated 60 to 80 percent of child abuse and neglect cases were from substance-abusing families.

Although these characteristics have been found to typify the population of drug-abusing women offenders, they have different implications for programs. Individual women will differ in the manifestations and severity of these characteristics and attendant problems. Such diversity calls for an assessment of specific clients' needs and the provision of services designed to meet those needs. If a program lacks a well-developed assessment procedure, clients are less likely to receive appropriate services, such as treatment in a style matched to cultural identity and cognitive level and of adequate intensity and duration.[22]

table 18.3 Coexisting Conditions Found in Female Inmates

Condition	Percent
Physical/sexual abuse	70
Current medical problem	53
Depression/mental health issues	74
Any substance abuse problem	70
High school graduate	<50
Homeless in year before arrest	16

SOURCE: Lauren Glaze and Laura Maruschak, *Parents in Prison and Their Minor Children* (Washington, DC: Bureau of Justice Statistics, 2008), http://www.bjs.gov/content/pub/pdf/pptmc.pdf (accessed September 14, 2014). See also Jennifer Sullivan and Miyoko Wolf, "Women behind Bars: State Takes a New Approach," *Seattle Times*, November 3, 2013.

The plight of the woman behind jail or prison bars is often a difficult one. In terms of institutions, the male-oriented criminal justice system may totally ignore the special requirements of the female offender.[23] The nature of punishment for female offenders has come a long way from the time when they were thrown into the gaols as diversions for the incarcerated male felons, but more needs to be done before treatment of the female offender can be said to be an integrated part of corrections.[24]

FEMALES IN JAIL

Females have never been a large portion of the inmates of jails in the nation, but the War on Drugs has contributed significantly to the number arrested and placed in jails and detention centers and has also increased the proportion of all inmates who are female. The number of females held in America's jails has increased dramatically during the past 30 years and is up over 300 percent since 1996.[25] The characteristics of current female jail inmates are generally the same, except for drug-related crime increases, as those found in an earlier survey of jails. More than 80 percent had used drugs in their lives, and more than half of the convicted inmates had used drugs in the month prior to the current offense that brought them to jail; almost 40 percent had used drugs daily. Some 24 percent of the female jail inmates had used cocaine or crack in the month before their current offense. About one in six convicted females in jail reported they had committed their current offense for money to buy drugs. Better than one in three convicted female inmates reported being under the influence of alcohol at the time of their offense.

A profile of jail inmates illustrates other important demographic and criminal characteristics of females in jail, including the following:[26]

- About 12 percent of the female inmates were in jail for a violent offense.
- Female jail inmates were more likely than males to be drug offenders, 29 percent versus 24 percent.
- More than 49 percent of the females were first-time offenders, compared to 37 percent for men.
- Female jail inmates were less likely to be employed in the month prior to their arrest than males, 40 percent versus 60 percent.

Photo 18.1

Female in her cell with her three children

Josef Sloup/age fotostock Spain, S.L./Alamy.

Photo 18.2
Female prisoners in stripes take a break from work in a tent detention center in Maricopa County, Arizona.
A. Ramey/PhotoEdit.

- Around 16 percent of female jail inmates had sustained an injury following an assault.
- More than 55 percent of females reported they had been sexually abused in their past, up from 47.5 percent in 1996. Of these, more than 20 percent reported the abuse had occurred prior to age 18. Women were also more likely to have been abused by an intimate partner (68 percent) than men (11 percent), and 26 percent said they had been abused by a parent or guardian and 34 percent by a friend.
- More than 46 percent were using drugs or alcohol at the time of their offense, and more than 55 percent admitted to drinking regularly.
- Low income was typical of almost all inmates.

One study of women in jail found high rates of lifetime trauma exposure (98 percent), current mental health disorders (36 percent), and drug and alcohol problems (almost three out of four). Most were deficient in parenting skills.[27]

This brief overview of female jail inmates suggests that they generally are not drawn from mainstream America, come from deprived and unstable backgrounds, have been extensively abused over time, and face significant employment, financial, psychological, emotional, and social barriers in their efforts to live in and seek reintegration into their local communities.[28] Most of these jail inmates are not dangerous but need assistance in existence and living. Incarceration in jail or prison may achieve punishment; societal goals would probably be better achieved if these high-problem female offenders were sentenced to community alternatives and received extensive treatment and service delivery. This is particularly true of abused females who enter the correctional system.[29]

FEMALES IN PRISON

As noted, despite the earlier preferential treatment of female offenders, the number of incarcerated females in the United States started to rise sharply in the 1980s. Today, California, Texas, Florida, and the federal system hold 4 out of every 10 female inmates, and Oklahoma leads the country in the incarceration rate for females at 121 per 100,000.[30] Figure 18.3 shows the 10 states with the most incarcerated females.

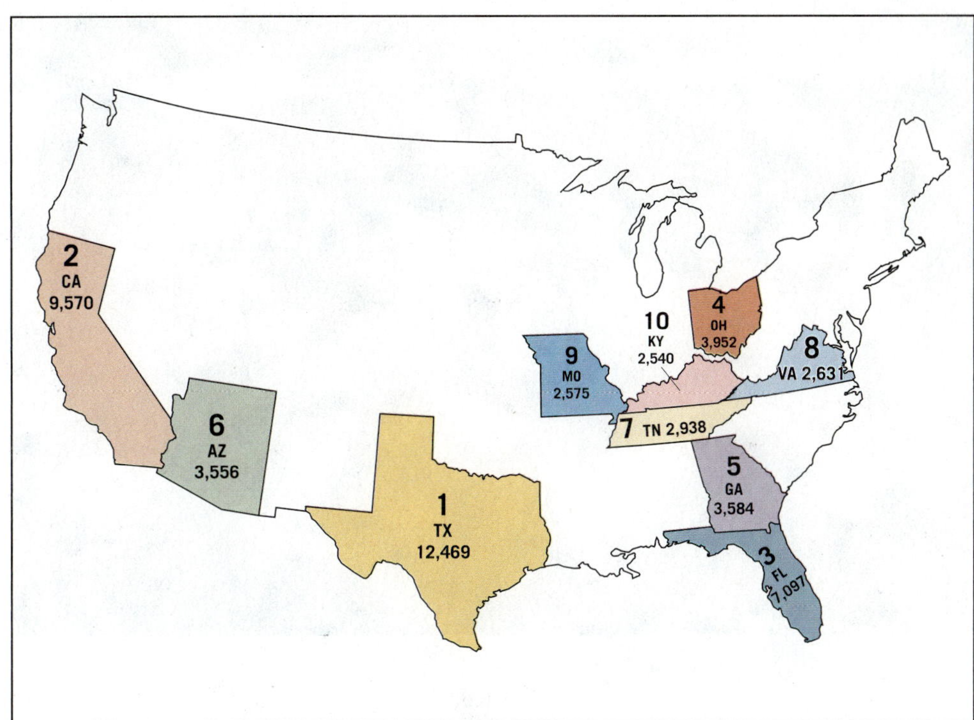

figure 18.3

Ten States with the Highest Female Inmate Population and Percentage of Females to Total State Inmate Population.

SOURCE: American Correctional Association, *2012 Directory of Adult and Juvenile Correctional Departments, Institutions, Agencies, and Probation and Parole Authorities* (Alexandria, VA: American Correctional Association, 2012), pp. 36–37.

Overall, the rate of growth for female prison inmates over the past 30 years has been phenomenal. Between1980 and 2012, the female population increased 587 percent, growing from 15,118 to 111,387. The rate of growth for females since 2000 has been about double the rate of men. Although the rate of incarceration for females is still considerably lower than that of males (68 per 100,000 females in the nation versus 955 per 100,000 for males), the gap is narrowing.[31] Not all groups of females are incarcerated at the same rate in America. Black women are incarcerated at 2.5 times the rate of white women, and Hispanic women are incarcerated at 1.4 times the rate. Between 2000 and 2010, the rate of incarceration decreased by 35 percent for black women and increased 28 percent for Hispanic women and 38 percent for white women. Figure 18.4 shows the rates of incarceration over this period of time.

The typical female prisoner is black, non-Hispanic, and age 35 to 39; has never been married; has some high school education; and was not employed at the time of arrest. She has likely been sentenced for a nonviolent crime and is a recidivist (either

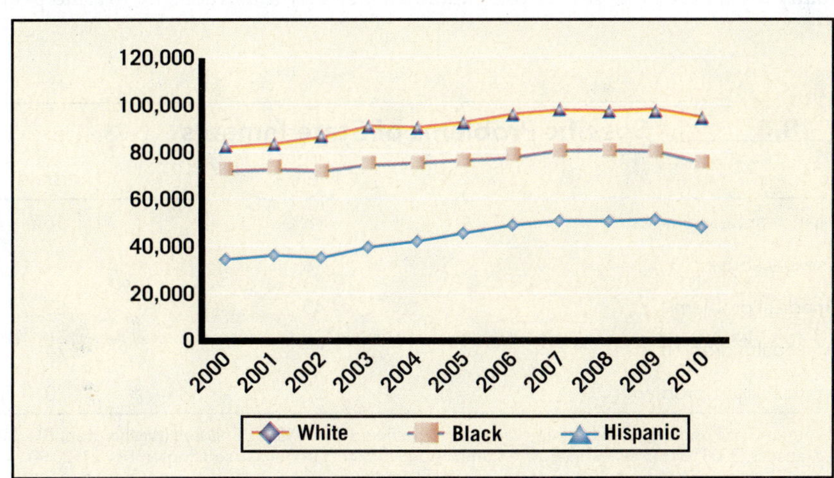

figure 18.4

Female Incarcerations, 2000–2010, by Ethnicity.

SOURCE: Data from Paul Guerino, Paige M. Harrison, and William J. Sabol, *Prisoners in 2010* (Washington, DC: Bureau of Justice Statistics, 2011), p. 16, and The Sentencing Project, *Incarcerated Women, 2013* (Washington, DC: The Sentencing Project, 2013), p. 2.

Photo 18.3

Female inmates at Julia Tutwiler Prison, Alabama, relaxing in their unattractive dormitory.
A. Ramey/PhotoEdit.

sentenced to probation or previously incarcerated as a juvenile or an adult). A third of all female inmates reported they were under the influence of a drug at the time of their offenses. Overall, just over half of the females in prison had been using drugs or alcohol or both at the time the imprisonment offense occurred. An estimated 84 percent of the females in state prisons had used drugs at some time in their lives prior to admission, fairly close to 80 percent of the men. Some 40 percent of the female inmates had participated in a drug treatment program at some point in their lives.[32] Women in prison are more likely than men to be the victims of staff sexual assault, with more than three-quarters of all reported staff sexual misconduct involving women who were victimized by male correctional staff.[33]

key term

Abused females
Female victims of usually violent acts that may be physical or psychological in damage or both.

Prior abuse by spouse, family member, parent, and significant other (boyfriend or girlfriend) creates consequences for the abused.[34] Childhood and adult victimization of females is frequently a precursor to female criminality. Many **abused females** are left with emotional scars and diminished self-confidence. More than 61 percent of female prisoners are mothers, and two in three have children under age 18.[35] Female prisoners reported that more than 80 percent of their children under age 18 were living with a relative, usually the maternal grandmother. Table 18.4 clearly illustrates the myriad problems

table **18.4** Specific Problems of State Inmates

Abused	Male	Female
Homeless in year before arrest	8%	16%
Physical/sexual abuse	8	64
Current medical problem	40	53
Any mental health problem	55	74
Any substance abuse problem	67	70

SOURCE: Lauren Glaze and Laura Maruschak, *Parents in Prison and Their Minor Children* (Washington, DC: Bureau of Justice Statistics, 2008), http://www.bjs.gov/content/pub/pdf/pptmc.pdf (accessed September 14, 2014).

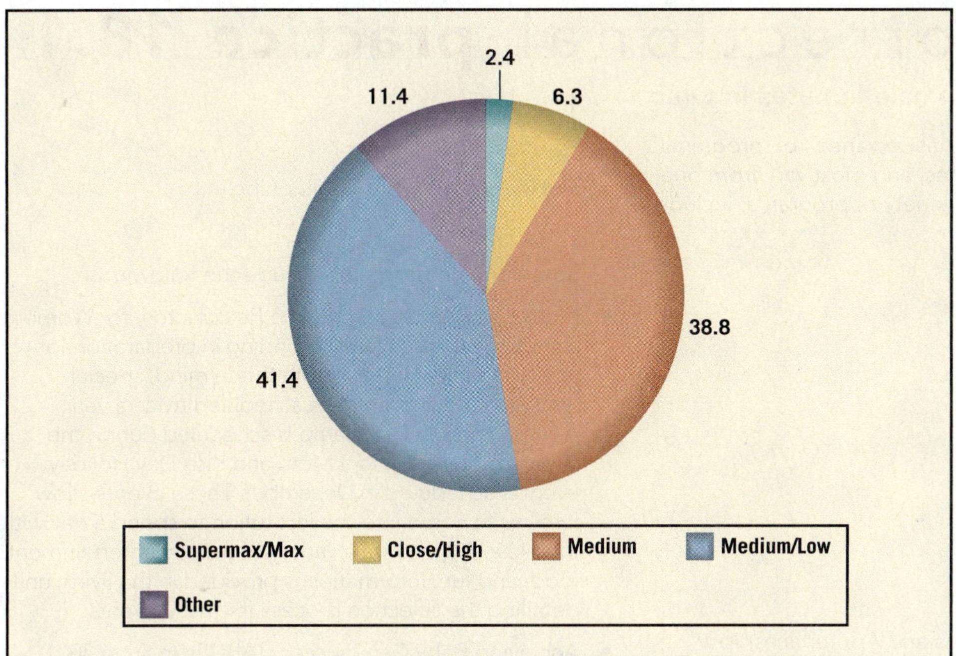

figure 18.5
Adult Female Inmate Populations by Security Level.

SOURCE: American Correctional Association, *Adult Inmate Population by Gender and Security Level* (Alexandria, VA: American Correctional Association, 2012), pp. 40–41.

that female inmates reported. For male prison inmates, almost 90 percent of their children under age 18 are living with the children's mothers. This is an important difference that we discuss later.

Female inmates are housed in a variety of facilities. About half of these facilities are penal institutions, known by a variety of names: prisons, reformatories, penitentiaries, correctional facilities, and prison camps. Most are housed in minimum- to low-security units (see Figure 18.5).

This profile of the imprisoned female inmate hardly reflects a dangerous offender for whom incarceration in prison is required. Instead, many such offenders could probably be handled more effectively,[36] less expensively, and more humanely in alternatives to prison. Unfortunately, this situation most likely reflects probable national practice throughout the country. The Pew Trust recently argued that using a broader range of sanctions can protect communities, punish law violators, and conserve tax resources for other pressing public needs, such as schools or transportation.[37]

FEMALE INSTITUTIONS

The American Correctional Association (ACA) found a range of adult and juvenile institutions headed by both male and female administrators. Some headed facilities for adults, for delinquents, or both.[38]

In 2012, male wardens supervised 780 adult male institutions, 32 adult male co-gender institutions, and 59 adult co-gender facilities. They also supervised 45 juvenile female institutions, 121 juvenile co-gender institutions, and 919 juvenile male institutions. Female wardens supervised 189 adult male, 26 co-gender, and 67 adult female facilities as well as 237 juvenile male, 65 juvenile co-gender, and 38 juvenile female facilities.

The picture with regard to the administration of these female prisons has changed greatly in recent years. In 1966, female correctional administrators headed only 10 of the nation's institutions. The 2010 *ACA Directory* showed that 2,551 of the 7,778 correctional administrators of adult and juvenile institutions were females.[39] Female correctional administrators tend to be managing male as well as female co-correctional

correctional practice 18.1

Programs Available to Female Inmates in Ohio

Each correctional jurisdiction has a variety of programs made available to female inmates, and most vary from one another. Ohio provides a wide variety of programs, including the following:

- Therapeutic Community
- Money Smart
- Thinking for a Change
- Victim Awareness
- Pre-GED
- GED
- Adult Basic Education
- College Classes
- Various Vocational Programs and Apprenticeships:
    - Administrative Office Technology
    - Building Maintenance
    - Horticulture
    - Web Design
    - Animal Trainer
    - Boiler Operator
    - Cosmetology
    - Electrician
    - Optician
    - Heating and Air Conditioning
    - Janitorial

Some unique programs include the following:

- Mom and Kids Day: The Ohio Reformatory for Women strives to promote family bonding in preparation for family reunification, and with this in mind, special family-oriented events are scheduled twice a year. A Mom and Me Day Camp is scheduled during the summer months, and a Mom and Kids Day Holiday event is scheduled in December. These events allow families to come into the institution to spend a day with their loved ones with a variety of events, entertainment, food, and fun. Information is provided in the living units detailing the selection process for these events.
- Achieving Baby Care Success (ABCS): In June 2001, the Ohio Reformatory for Women opened Ohio's only nursery program within an institution. The ABCS program allows incarcerated pregnant inmates to maintain custody of their infants after they are born. Each participant has an individualized treatment plan so that the problems that resulted in her incarceration are thoroughly addressed. Hands-on parenting instruction is available for every mother in the program. Eligible mothers for the program are screened and must be serving a short-term sentence for a nonviolent crime. The criteria for the program ensure that the mothers and infants leave the institution together.

institutions or community and minimum-custody facilities. As a matter of fact, the president of the ACA from 2004 to 2006 was Gwendolyn Chunn, the seventh female president of that prestigious organization. The first state-level prison exclusively for women was the Indiana Reformatory for Women. The first female warden was Mary Belle Harris at the Federal Correctional Institute at Alderson, West Virginia, when it opened in 1925.[40]

Because conditions in female institutions vary greatly, it would be fruitless to attempt to describe them individually. They are not all horror stories; it is sufficient to state that the best and the worst aspects of the male institution are also in evidenced in the female prison, the only major differences being the variations based on the traits unique to each gender and the varied training and education programs available to males. Correctional Practice 18.1 provides a list of the correctional programs available in Ohio for female inmates.

One notable difference between prisons for males and females lies in the fact that many states only have one major facility for females compared to many prisons, for males. As a result, a state's female prison will often house every classification level—high, close, medium, and minimum—all within one compound. Unlike in the male prison, where one or two levels may be present, the range of classification levels within female institutions poses unique management issues.

SPECIAL PROBLEMS FOR INCARCERATED FEMALES

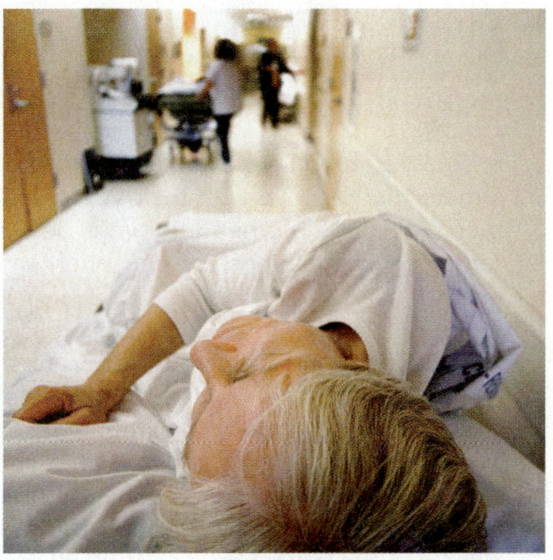

Photo 18.4

The health care needs of incarcerated women are inadequately addressed by many jails and prisons due to lack of financial resources.
Spencer Grant/PhotoEdit.

Among the many problems female inmates face when in prison are pregnancy, loss of family ties, and aging behind the walls. We start this discussion with the pregnant inmate entering prison. Earlier studies suggest that some one in four adult females entering prison either were pregnant or had given birth to an infant within the last 12 months.[41] It is estimated that 1 in 25 women in state prison are pregnant when admitted, and more than 1,400 babies are born in prison each year.[42] Medical care, resources, and programs, although varying across institutions, are thought to be inadequate for such inmates. A primary explanation for the lack of programs has been the relatively small size of the female offender population and the expense involved in special programming for the small segment of prisoners that female inmates represent. The size argument, however valid in past decades, does not hold in current correctional scenes. Although female inmates remain a small portion of the total prison populations, their numbers have increased to the point that new policies are needed.

Pregnant inmates need special diets, lighter work assignments, supportive programs, and a less stressful environment. Programs and resources are needed for miscarriages, premature birth, and deliveries. Until recently,[43] the major options were abortion, placing children with relatives, putting the children up for adoption, or foster care. Not only do such forced separation policy options pose severe emotional anguish and problems for mothers, but separation of the newborn child from the mother can create severe emotional and developmental problems for the infant.[44] Many prisons are now starting to provide family services as well as classes in child development and parenting, parental functioning, and stress management. Some female prisons have even started programs that allow young infants to remain with their mothers. For example, Washington State has a nursery program at its female prison in Gig Harbor that includes an Early Head Start component. Inmate mothers are accountable for the 24-hour care of their children while living in a supervised environment.[45] California's Community Prisoner Mother Program is operated by the state's department of corrections and is described in Correctional Practice 18.2.[46] Other states have policies that permit babies to live with their mothers for up to a year, require immediate foster care placement, or do not permit the mother to see the baby.

key term

Pregnant inmates
Female inmates who at time of detention are carrying a fetus or enter that condition while incarcerated.

In addition, research on female inmates documents that females are more family oriented than male inmates and that as many as 62 percent of imprisoned females are mothers to minor children.[47] Evidence of the significance that children play in the lives of female inmates can be seen in pictures displayed on desks or taped behind prison identification badges, articles in prison newspapers, the frequency with which children are discussed, and the general concern evident about the well-being of their individual children. Many females feel that their families and friends have abandoned them when they are sent to prison, just when their needs for support and friendship are highest and inmates are at the lowest point of their lives: ashamed, incarcerated, lonely, depressed, guilt ridden, acutely worried about their children, scared, and with tarnished self-esteem. Family members are particularly central at this time, as they can care for the inmate's children and bring them to visit, send money and special foods, write and call, guard their property, and take up their cause if mistreated by institutional staff. Thus, visiting is of crucial importance to female inmates who sense—if not know—that their role as mother is weak, and their incarceration and absence can lead to a child's behavioral problems (obsessive crying, deterioration in relations with peers and schoolwork, withdrawal from relatives and reality, and so on).

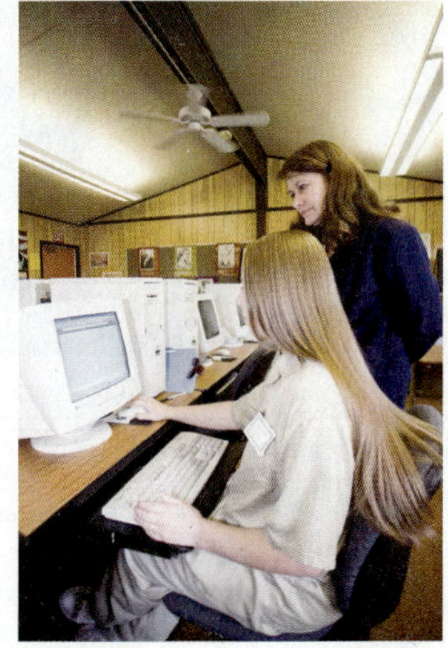

Photo 18.5

Training in Computer-Aided-Design (CAD) in prison.
Mikael Karlsson/Alamy.

Although failure of relatives to visit is a great hardship for most incarcerated mothers, often it results more from physical and institutional barriers than lack of care and concern on the part of relatives. Many institutions are located far away from the urban centers from

correctional practice 18.2

California Community Prisoner Mother Program

In small, community-based facilities throughout California, inmate mothers live with their young children. The Community Prisoner Mother Program is designed to build better parenting relationships and brighter futures while the inmates serve their time.

While in the program, mothers reestablish bonds with their children and prepare to return to the community as working, productive members. The homelike facilities provide a stable caregiving environment. At the same time, mothers learn valuable skills. In preemployment training, they gain practical information and tips about applying for, landing, and keeping a job. In specialized parenting classes, they learn how to talk with and relate to their children and how to discipline effectively. Both mothers and children also may receive counseling. Because the majority of the mothers have had some sort of chemical dependency in the past, they also attend drug education classes geared to keep them from returning to their old habits, make them aware of the dangers of drug addiction, and show them how drugs impair both in their lives and in the lives of their children.

SOURCE: California Department of Rehabilitation and Corrections, "California Community Prisoner Mother Program," http://www.cdcr.ca.gov/Adult_operations/FOPS/Community_Prisoner_Mother_Program.html.

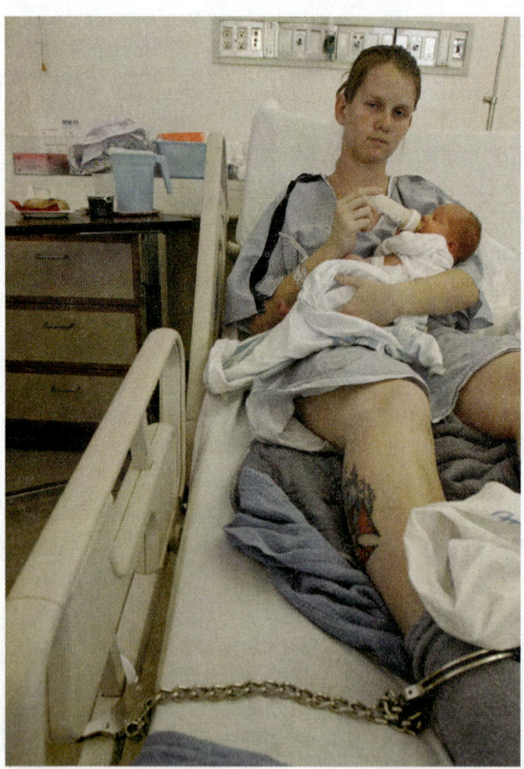

Photo 18.6

A young mother in prison feeds her infant after just giving birth.
Mark Allen Johnson/ZUMAPRESS/Newscom.

which most female inmates originate, and travel and related expenses are hurdles to be overcome. Many relatives do not own cars and must depend on the kindness of neighbors for travel. Other discouraging factors include having to submit to searches before visiting, being too poor to afford overnight accommodations, or having work schedules too tight to permit frequent or lengthy visits. Some institutions are not "visitor friendly," with visits limited in frequency to once a month, provision of only one large room for visitations of all families, having no children's toys or a playground, and presenting an unfriendly and hostile setting. Better-managed institutions (such as in Nebraska and New York) have children's nurseries, play areas, and equipment; allow conjugal and family visits; and provide accommodations for mothers to plan, cook for, and feed their children in separate visiting rooms and trailers. Weekend passes, home visits, home furloughs, halfway house placements, and frequent visiting privileges not only ease parenting problems but also lessen the probability that the children will become innocent victims. Clearly, there is a need for institutions to establish policies that encourage **family cohesion** and strengthen ties for the mother when she is eventually released.

The third major problem is aging in prison. The graying of America is reflected in prison populations, as seen in Table 18.5. This is particularly a problem with the older female inmates undergoing social, psychological, emotional, and physical changes within the institutional walls.[48] Females in America tend to live longer than men (about seven or eight years) and make up about 60 percent of older Americans. In prison, they are "forgotten" inmates and have been little studied or recognized. Incarceration encourages dependency and passivity, factors that tend to shorten life expectancy under any circumstance. Visual, physical, and muscular impairments pose particular problems for elderly female inmates. Not only will staff have to be specifically trained and programs individualized, but gerontology consultants and medical programs also will be required that address issues such as dealing with menopause, breast cancer, hysterectomies, eye cataracts, and hip, spine, and back impairments. By 2015, an estimated 8,436 female inmates will be age 55 or older. As the numbers of elderly female inmates swell, physical plants will need to be retrofitted, including color coding

key term

Family cohesion
Term describing the relationship between offenders and their families, as in sticking together tightly.

table **18.5** **Female Inmates over Age 55 in State Prisons, 1988–2011**

Year	Females
1988	511
1990	709
1992	875
1994	1,141
1998	2,043
2000	1,900
2004	3,792
2007	3,604
2009	4,203
2011	5,616
Percent change	1,099%

SOURCE: American Correctional Association, *2012 Directory of Adult and Juvenile Correctional Departments, Institutions, Agencies, and Probation and Parole Authorities* (Alexandria, VA: American Correctional Association, 2012), pp. 38–39.

of floors and buildings, adding wall handrails and wheelchair ramps, widening door frames and entries, providing rest areas for more challenged inmates, and revamping space to include nursing and convalescent rooms and services. Special diets, medications, nursing patterns, and physical therapy will need to be initiated and expanded. It is clear that a correctional crisis is in the making and that prisons are not conducive to caring for the elderly (age 65 and over), aged (age 75 plus), or very old (age 85 and over). Alternative sentencing, timely and compassionate release, and community correctional centers are more realistic options for those who pose no threat to the community or self. Correctional action now may avoid costly programming and extensive legal issues and lawsuits in the decades to come. Deliberate indifference to medical needs has been declared a violation of constitutionally guaranteed rights (Eighth Amendment). Indeed, one recent study of medical care in a large jail facility likened the care inmates received to "torture."[49]

Homosexual Behavior and the Pseudo family

The **single-sex experience** and long-term deprivation of heterosexual outlets create the same kinds of problems in female institutions as are found in male prisons. The recommendations for co-gender institutions may seem extreme to the uninitiated, but the leavening effect of a system that allows at least nonsexual social contact in daily activity with members of the opposite sex is considerable. Excessive administrative concern about overt signs of friendship that may be indicative of possible homosexual activity conflicts with many standard practices for females outside the walls. If two males were observed holding hands as they walked down the street, they would be suspected of being gay. That same behavior, although not considered at all strange for females (and particularly girls) on the outside, is viewed with great suspicion inside the walls for girls and adult females alike. Some female inmates were gay or bisexual before entering a correctional institution and do not change their behaviors under incarceration. Others were heterosexual before imprisonment but enter into romantic alliances within correctional facilities. It is believed that most of the latter return to heterosexual relationships after release, but

key term

Single-sex experience Inmate behavior involving other persons of the same sex in either a homogenital or a homosocial relationship.

some continue their lesbian behavior after imprisonment ("jailhouse turnouts"). An inmate graphically described the situation:

> It's tough to be natural. The thing that most of us are trying to accomplish here, we're trying to get our minds at a point to where we can handle whatever comes our way, to get our emotions balanced, to maybe straighten up our way of thinking. You know, it just makes it hard when you're trying to be a natural person—to react to things normally—when the staff won't let you be normal—when you do a normal thing that being a woman makes it normal, and then have them say no, you can't do that because if you do, that's personal contact and that's homosexuality. So there's our mental hassle.
>
> I know that when females are thrown together without men or without the companionship of men it makes it pretty rough on them—females being the emotional people that they are. They have to have a certain amount of affection and close companionship. You know, a woman, if she's with a man she'll put her hand on him or maybe she'll reach up and touch him. This is something that a woman does naturally without thinking, and so if a woman has a good friend, or an affair, she does the same thing because this is her nature. The thing of it is—like I have a friend at the cottage—neither one of us have ever played. We're never gonna play. And if somebody tried to force us into it, we couldn't, wouldn't, or what have you. But being a woman and after being here for quite a while, we put our arms around each other, we don't think there's anything the matter with it, because there's nothing there—it's a friendship. We're walking down the hall, our records are both spotless, she's a council girl, I'm Minimum A [minimum-custody classification]. I've never had anything on my record that was bad and my god, the supervisor comes out and says, "Now, now girls, you know we don't allow that sort of thing here." And we look at her and say, "What sort of thing?" "This personal contact." And yet this same supervisor, we saw her up at the corner putting her arm around another supervisor the same way we were doing. So this is where part of our mental hassle comes in.[50]

The redefinition of the natural acts just described into something considered evil and proscribed is another reason that institutionalization is so crippling to the long-term female prisoner. As inmates, male or female, learn that simple signs of friendship are prohibited, they learn to re-press their impulses toward interpersonal warmth when they get out. The kind of behavior that makes them acceptable on the inside makes them appear hard (unfeeling, unresponsive) on the outside. In the male, this kind of coldness can be viewed as "tough" or "macho" but is sometimes considered unattractive when displayed by females.

Until recently, very few studies have been conducted on the homosexuality of female prisoners. Much conjecture is found in the literature, but true scientific research is rare. Even the monumental effort to compile statistics on female offenders in Sheldon and Eleanor Glueck's *500 Delinquent Women*[51] did not consider homosexuality, but gender and sex role research is increasing.[52]

The demands of institutional management make it difficult to prevent homosexual activity. There are never enough personnel to watch all of the inmates, so lovers get together despite the staff's efforts. In many institutions, the staff adopts the attitude of "looking the other way" with regard to the female inmates' sexual activity. (The same is true in many men's institutions;[53] see Chapter 17.) It is possible that homosexuality and homosociality are even more prevalent in female institutions than in those for men because a high percentage of the inmates have been so misused by men[54] that they have already turned to other females to fulfill their emotional needs on the outside. In addition, prisons for females are generally less secure and less compartmentalized, making it easier for women to interact. It is also quite possible that the impact of imprisonment is significantly different for females, tending to encourage a homosexual response. Women may also feel a stronger need to create a pseudo family inside the walls to help replace the one they have lost. Females appear more likely to view arrest, jailing, the court trial, and commitment to prison in highly personal terms. This personalized reaction could harden antisocial attitudes and lead to further illegal behavior. One study has identified three **psychological deprivations** that might contribute to homosexual behavior:[55]

1. Affection starvation and need for understanding
2. Isolation from previous symbiotic interpersonal relations
3. Need for continued intimate relationships with a person

It is hard to imagine an incarcerated felon (male or female) who does not suffer these deprivations to some degree.

key term

Psychological deprivation
Loss of or failure to develop emotional cohesion, support, or love through failure to provide emotional or physical caring.

THE CO-GENDER CORRECTIONAL INSTITUTION

The co-gender, or co-correctional, prison is a new development in corrections. Two were opened in 1971 in the Federal Bureau of Prisons system. Since that time, there have been many coed adult state and federal facilities; at least 418 state-level co-gender facilities for adults existed in 2012. An unknown number of co-gender private institutions exists, and 25 states did not report on their facilities for juveniles in 2012.[56] John Smykla and J. Williams defined adult co-corrections (co-gender) as adult institutions, the major purpose of which is the institutional confinement of felons. Each is managed by one institutional administration and has regular programs or areas in which female and male inmates have daily opportunities for interaction.[57] The general concept of **co-gender institutions** is as follows:[58]

Photo 18.7
Correctional staff counsels inmates within their jail pods.
Mikael Karlsson/Alamy.

1. To reduce the dehumanizing and destructive aspects of confinement by allowing continuity or resumption of heterosexual relationships
2. To reduce the institutional control problems through the weakening of disruptive homosexual systems, the reduction of predatory homosexual activity, the lessening of assaultive behavior, and the diversion of inmate interests and activities
3. To protect inmates likely to be involved in "trouble" were they in a same-sex institution
4. To provide an additional tool for creating a more normal, less institutionalized atmosphere
5. To cushion the shock of adjustment for releasees by reducing the number and intensity of adjustments to be made
6. To realize economies of scale in terms of more efficient utilization of available space, staff, and programs
7. To provide relief of immediate or anticipated overcrowding, sometimes of emergency proportions
8. To reduce the need for civilian labor by provision of both light and heavy inmate workforces
9. To increase diversification and flexibility of program offerings and equal access for males and females
10. To expand treatment potentials for working with inmates having "sexual problems" and development of positive heterosexual relationships and coping skills
11. To provide relief from immediate or anticipated legal pressures to provide equal access to programs and services to both sexes
12. To expand career opportunities for females, previously often "boxed into" the single state female institutions, as co-correctional staff

key term

Co-gender institution
A co-educational prison housing both male and female inmates interacting under a single institutional administration.

The question of whether these objectives have been met cannot yet be answered, primarily because most evaluations of their effectiveness continue to be weak at best.[59]

COMMUNITY CORRECTIONS AND FEMALE OFFENDERS

Our review of the problems posed by female offenders as well as problems female inmates face due to incarceration has suggested that most female offenders pose little danger to public safety, that substance abuse underlies much of their criminal behavior, and that much damage to inmates and their families may be done through incarcerating those whose basic problem is alcohol and/or drug abuse.

Institutions for females are not known for the long-term effectiveness of their "inside-the-walls" treatment programs, which tend to be limited in number and occur in an artificial environment, thus reducing their effectiveness.[60] What is needed are more reasonable risk reduction programs that speak to the underlying problems that have led to criminal behavior and incarceration. Those are, of course, generally found in the community and include halfway houses, group homes, residential treatment facilities, mental health and substance-abuse programs, probation, and other intermediate sanctions as discussed in more detail in the chapters on probation, intermediate sanctions and parole, and reentry. Such programs have long been recommended for nonviolent offenders and were strongly advocated by the American Bar Association's Sentencing Project as well as the National Council on Crime and Delinquency.[61]

There are now more than 946,000 females on probation (24 percent of adult probationers) and an additional 98,000 on parole (14 percent of all parolees).[62] Unfortunately, gender-specific programs are often lacking, and residential programs specifically designated for females are often found only in the largest urban areas. Because female offenders seldom pose much threat to public safety and are seldom violent, managing them in a community-wide, coordinated correctional system with graduated degrees of supervision in the community is a viable option for this correctional population. For those females who are incarcerated, it is equally important to develop and expand family-based programming to allow them to maintain contact with their children.[63]

Summary

Summarize the Characteristics and Trends of the Adult Female Prison Population

Female inmates represent only about 7 percent of prison inmates, yet their numbers are continuously increasing (despite the welcomed but precipitous decline of crime in the nation). Although no one is exactly sure why this might be, the arguments range from the breakdown of the paternalistic attitudes of sentencing judges to an increase in committing of crimes more typical of male inmates and thus not crimes females might have committed some two decades ago. Yet few female offenders commit violent crime, are eager to escape confinement, and are violent in confinement facilities. Thus, most female offenders are concentrated in minimum- and low-security facilities. For most jurisdictions, the small number of female inmates typically means there is only one prison available to receive female offenders and fewer vocational, educational, and training opportunities and programs available to female inmates.

Describe the Characteristics of Female Inmates and Issues, Challenges, and Barriers Faced by Female Inmates

The smaller number of female inmates, in contrast to male inmates, usually means the institution is far away from concentrations of populations in which these offenders lived prior to commitment. This severely impacts the number and length of visitations of family and friends, interactions with children, feelings of loss of love and attention by family, and increased isolation. For female offenders whose definition of self is drawn from interactions with significant others, such distances undercut a sense of worth and self-efficacy. Out of such losses, female inmates tend to look for solace and family within the population of that facility, and the development of substitute families or pseudo families results. Most women in prisons and jails are drawn from a deprived and unstable background, have been extensively abused over time, and face significant employment, financial, psychological, emotional, and social barriers in their efforts to live in and seek reintegration into their local communities. The typical female prisoner is black, non-Hispanic, and age 35 to 39; has never been married; has with some high school education; and was not employed at the time of arrest. Most are also single mothers with frequently missing husbands and receive little to no financial support from the fathers of their children.

Outline the History of Women's Prisons

The history of women's prisons is, relative to male facilities, quite brief. Prior to the nineteenth century, few prison institutions existed for female offenders. The first major development was the creation of an institution devoted exclusively to female offenders (the Indiana Reformatory for Women, established in 1873), and the first female warden was Mary Belle Harris at the Federal Correctional Reformatory for Women, opened by the Federal Bureau of Prisons in 1925.

Describe the Culture in Women's Prisons

The culture of female institutions varies. Much of the pain associated with single-sex prison communities can be decreased through the use of co-gender institutions, and the number of such institutions is gradually increasing, particularly among private-sector providers of co-gendered facilities. Yet female prisoners as a group suffer from the negative double impact of imprisonment and benign neglect (in some jurisdictions). The growth in the number of female offenders in the next decade probably will contribute to the construction of more facilities, contracting with community and private-sector providers, and an increase in the number of treatment services and community reintegration programs.

Explain the Concept of Co-Gender Institutions

Co-correctional prison institutions are facilities in which both male and female offenders are housed, usually living in a facility that permits interactions and joint treatment programs. They are more relaxed, typify the free world, and are structured to normalize life within prisons.

Draw Appropriate Conclusions Concerning the Use of Community Corrections for Female Offenders

Few female offenders pose significant danger to others, and females are usually high-need and low-risk offenders. Community corrections provide opportunities for lowering risky behaviors (particularly drug and alcohol abuse) and learning alternative behaviors in environments that could result in criminal behavior. Community correction is viewed as at least as effective as imprisonment, uses available treatment and service providers in the community, and is believed to be significantly less expensive than imprisonment.

Key Words

arrests by gender, 394
preferential treatment, 394
"traditional" female crimes, 394
victimless crimes, 395
paternalistic attitude of judges, 396
women's liberation movement, 397
abused females, 402
pregnant inmates, 405
family cohesion, 406
single-sex experience, 407
psychological deprivation, 409
co-gender institution, 409

Review Questions

1. What are the major crimes for which females are convicted? Explain why.
2. Why have females been treated so differently in the correctional system?
3. What impact does incarceration have on "mothering" of children?
4. Develop a model for handling the female offender that would have differing degrees of social control and offer female criminals an opportunity to stop criminal activity.
5. Describe the typical female inmate.
6. Identify three groups of special-problem female offenders and their specific needs.

7. How has the War on Drugs impacted corrections and specifically female offenders?
8. What should be done with the pregnant female prison inmate? With her baby?
9. What special problems do female offenders who have been victims of prior abuse face when they are imprisoned?

Application Case Studies

1. If you were the warden of a female prison, what are some of the programs you would create for the inmates?
2. A female offender convicted of fraud is before the judge for sentencing. You are her attorney and would like to make an argument for probation, but this is her third offense, and she has failed probation in the past. What options would you suggest at the sentencing hearing? Would your argument change if she were pregnant?
3. List three of the barriers that women face when leaving prison. Design a reentry program that would help to address these needs.

Endnotes

1. Todd D. Minton, *Jail Inmates at Midyear 2012* (Washington, DC: Bureau of Justice Statistics, 2013).
2. Michael Tonry, "Why Are U.S. Incarceration Rates So High?," *Overcrowded Times* 10:3 (1999): 1, 8–16. See particularly p. 8.
3. Most apprehended drug couriers ("mules") are female. If arrested in New York City's John F. Kennedy Airport, they could be sentenced under New York statutes for a minimum penalty of three years' to life imprisonment, but the sentence may be reduced to lifetime probation if the mule provides "material assistance" leading to the arrest of a drug dealer or higher-placed drug entrepreneur. Few mules can offer "material assistance" of any prosecutorial value because they are so marginally involved (if at all) with the ongoing criminal enterprise. In 1999, U.S. district courts granted almost 8,000 "substantial assistance reductions" to 44 percent of defendants in federal courts, most of which were granted to drug offenders. Few were granted to females. John Scalia, *Federal Drug Offenders, 1999 with Trends from 1984–1999* (Washington, DC: Bureau of Justice Statistics, 2001), p. 10.
4. Federal Bureau of Investigation, *Crime in the United States 2012* (Washington, DC: U.S. Department of Justice, 2013).
5. Ibid.
6. E. Ann Carson and Daniela Golinelli, *Prisoners in 2012: Trends in Admissions and Releases, 1991–2012* (Washington, DC: Bureau of Justice Statistics, 2013).
7. Freda Adler, *Sisters in Crime* (New York: McGraw-Hill, 1975). See also Bernard Schissel and K. Fedec, "The Selling of Innocence," *Canadian Journal of Criminology* 41:1 (1994): 33–56.
8. Federal Bureau of Investigation, *Crime in the United States 2009* (Washington, DC: U.S. Department of Justice, 2010). See also Jacqueline Boles and K. Elifson, "Sexual Identity and HIV: The Male Prostitute," *Journal of Sex Research* 31:1 (1994): 39–46; Thomas Calhoun and G. Weaver, "Rational Decision-Making among Male Street Prostitutes," *Deviant Behavior* 17:2 (1996): 209–227; and Leon Pettiway, *Honey, Honey Miss Thang: Being Black, Gay and on the Streets* (Philadelphia: Temple University Press, 1996).
9. Studies of lifetime prevalence of intimate partner abuse suggest that at least 4 in 10 females will be physically and sexually abused during their lifetimes. There is some evidence that rates of physical and sexual abuse may be highest for females ages 18 to 39, with monthly income of less than $1,000, children under age 18 being at home, and those ending a relationship within the past 12 months. Stephen Dearwater, J. Coben, J. Campbell, et al., "Prevalence of Intimate Partner Abuse in Women Treated at Community Hospital Emergency Departments," *Journal of the American Medical Association* 280:5 (1998): 433–438. See also Bureau of Justice Statistics, *Family Violence Statistics Including Statistics on Strangers and Acquaintances*, http://www.fbi.gov/about-us/cjis/ucr/crime-in-the-u.s/2012/crime-in-the-u.s.-2012/persons-arrested/persons-arrested (accessed September 14, 2014).
10. Robert Meier and G. Geis, *Victimless Crime? Prostitution, Drugs, Homosexuality and Abortion* (Los Angeles: Roxbury Publishing, 1997); Barrie Flowers, *The Prostitution of Women and Girls* (Jefferson, NC: McFarland, 1998); Karen Stout and B. McPhail, *Confronting Sexism and Violence against Women: A Challenge for Social Work* (New York: Longman, 1998); Melissa Farley, "Unequal," http://crime.about.com (accessed February 28, 2008).

11. See Ira Sommers, D. Baskin, and J. Fagan, "The Structural Relationship between Drug Use, Drug Dealing and Other Income Support Activities among Women Drug Users," *Journal of Drug Issues* 26:4 (1996): 975–1006; John Potterat, R. Rothenberg, S. Muth, et al., "Pathways to Prostitution," *Journal of Sex Research* 35:4 (1998): 333–340; and Tove P. Tiby, "The Production and Reproduction of Prostitutions," *Journal of Scandinavian Studies in Crime and Crime Prevention* 3:2 (2003): 154–172.
12. Joanne Belknap, *The Invisible Woman: Gender, Crime and Justice* (Belmont, CA: Wadsworth, 2007).
13. Cynthia Seymour, ed., "Children with Parents in Prison," *Child Welfare* 77:5 (1998): 469–639; James Boudouris, *Parents in Prison* (Lanham, MD: American Correctional Association, 1996); Ken Gosnell, "Fathers Successfully Returning Home," *Corrections Today* 69:2 (2007): 46–50.
14. Amnesty International, "Mothers behind Bars," http://www.amnesty-usa.org/rightsforall/women/report-101.html (accessed February 28, 2008).
15. As early as 1984, Candace Kruttschnitt and D. Green were debunking the chivalry assumptions in their "The Sex-Sanctioning Issue: Is It History?," *American Sociological Review* 49:4 (1984): 541–551. See also Ellen Steury and F. Nancy, "Gender Bias and Pretrial Release: More Pieces of the Puzzle," *Journal of Criminal Justice* 18:5 (1990): 417–432; Randall Shelden, "Confronting the Ghost of Mary Ann Crouse: Gender Bias in the Juvenile Justice System," *Juvenile and Family Court Journal* 49:1 (1998): 11–26; and Marie Grabe, K. Trager, Melissa Lear, and Jennifer Raush, "Gender in Crime News," *Mass Communication and Society* 9:2 (2007): 137–163.
16. Mark Pogrebin and E. Poole, "Sex, Gender and Work: The Case of Women Jail Officers," in *Sociology of Crime, Law and Deviance, ed.* Jeffrey Ulmer (Stamford, CT: JAI Press, 1998), pp. 105–126; Timothy Griffin and John Wooldredge, "Sex-Based Disparities in Felony Dispositions before and after Sentencing Reform in Ohio," *Criminology* 44:4 (2006): 893–923.
17. B. Farnsworth and R. Teske, "Gender Differences in Felony Court Processing," *Women and Criminal Justice* 6:2 (1995): 23–44.
18. Meda Chesney-Lind, "Women in Prison: From Partial Justice to Vengeful Equity," *Corrections Today* 60:7 (1998): 66–73.
19. Susan Crawford and R. Williams, "Critical Issues in Managing Female Offenders," *Corrections Today* 60:7 (1998): 130–134; Editors, "L.A. County Makes Room for Female Prisoners," *Correctional News* 13:3 (2007): 17.
20. Bureau of Justice Statistics, *Correctional Populations in the United States, 2009* (Washington, DC: Bureau of Justice Statistics, 2010); William Sabol Heather Couture, *Prisoners in 2006* (Washington, DC: Bureau of Justice Statistics, 2007), p. 24.
21. Andrew Knittle, "Oklahoma's 'Mean' Laws Are to Blame for High Female Incarceration Rate, Sociologist Says," http://newsok.com/oklahomas-mean-laws-to-blame-for-high-female-incarceration-rate-sociologist-says/article/3891614 (accessed January 1, 2013).
22. Jean Wellisch, Michael Prendergast, and Douglas Anglin, *Drug-Abusing Women Offenders: Results of a National Survey* (Washington, DC: Bureau of Justice Statistics, 1995). See also Jennifer Karberg and Doris James, *Substance Dependence, Abuse and Treatment of Jail Inmates, 2002* (Washington, DC: Bureau of Justice Statistics, 2005), and National Association of Drug Court Professionals, "Drug Courts Are Effective," http://www.nadcp.org/Drug%20courts%20are20effective (accessed August 25, 2013).
23. Louise Bill, "The Victimization and Revictimization of Female Offenders," *Corrections Today* 60:7 (1998): 106–112.
24. Donna Kerr, "Substance Abuse among Female Offenders," *Corrections Today* 60:7 (1998): 114–120. See also Michelle Staples-Horne, "Addressing Specific Health Care Needs of Female Adolescents," *Corrections Today* 69:5 (2007): 426.
25. Bureau of Justice Statistics, *Correctional Populations in the United States, 2009*. See also Bureau of Justice Statistics, "Jail Inmates at Midyear 2013," http://www.bjs.gov/content/pub/pdf/jim13st.pdf (accessed September 14, 2014).
26. Doris J. James, *Profile of Jail Inmates, 2002* (Washington, DC: Bureau of Justice Statistics, 2004).
27. Bonnie Green, J. Miranda, A. Daroowalla, and J. Siddique, "Trauma, Mental Health Functioning, and Program Needs of Women in Jail," *Crime and Delinquency* 51:1 (2005): 131–151. See also Correctional Association of New York, "Women in the Criminal Justice System," http://www.correctionalassociation.org/issue/women (accessed January 18, 2014), and "Nearly 150 Incarcerated Women Forced into Sterilization Procedures in California Prisons," http://www.correctionalassociation.org/news/more-than-100-incarcerated-women-endured-forced-sterilized-in-california-prisons (accessed January 14, 2014).
28. Virginia McCoy, J. Inciardi, and L. Metch, "Women, Crack and Crime," *Contemporary Drug Issues* 22:3 (1995): 435–451; Meda Chesney-Lind, *The Female Offender: Girls, Women and Crime* (Thousand Oaks, CA: Sage, 1997). See also the theme issue "Female Offenders," *Corrections Today* 60:7 (1998).
29. Boot camps, with their requirements of absolute obedience to authority, may be harmful to female

offenders who have been in abusive relationships. See Doris MacKenzie, L. Ellis, S. Simpson, et al., *Female Offenders in Boot Camp* (College Park: University of Maryland, 1994).

30. Bureau of Justice Statistics, *Correctional Populations in the United States, 2009.*
31. Ibid.
32. L.I.S., Inc., *Profiles of Correctional Substance Abuse Treatment Programs* (Langmont, CO: National Institute of Corrections, 1994); Christopher Mumola, *Substance Abuse and Treatment, State and Federal Prisoners, 1997* (Washington, DC: U.S. Department of Justice, 1999), p. 13.
33. A. Beck, *PREA Data Collection Activities, 2012* (Washington, DC: Bureau of Justice Statistics, 2013).
34. Caroline Wolf Harlow, *Prior Abuse Reported by Inmates and Probationers* (Washington, DC: U.S. Department of Justice, 1999). For data on abuse across the nation, see Patricia Tjaden and N. Thoennes, *Prevalence, Incidence and Consequences of Violence against Women* (Washington, DC: U.S. Department of Justice, 1998). See also American Civil Liberties Union, "Words from Prison: Sexual Abuse in Prison," https://www.aclu.org/womens-rights/words-prison-sexual-abuse-prison (accessed September 14, 2014).
35. Lauren Glaze and L. Maruschal, *Parents in Prison and Their Minor Children* (Washington, DC: Bureau of Justice Statistics, 2008).
36. Natalie Pearl, "Use of Community-Based Social Services to Reduce Recidivism in Female Parolees," *Women and Criminal Justice* 10:1 (1998): 27–52.
37. Pew Charitable Trusts, *One in 100: Behind Bars in America 2008* (Washington, DC: Pew Charitable Trusts, 2008), p. 4.
38. American Correctional Association, *Directory 2012* (Alexandria, VA: American Correctional Association, 2012), pp. 64–65. Twenty-five states did not report the number of their facilities and programs for juveniles.
39. Ibid, pp. 40–41. Five states did not report on wardens and superintendents in adult institutions.
40. Excellent chronicles of female correctional managers can be found in *Women and Criminal Justice.* See in particular Mary Hawkes, "Edna Mahan: Sustaining the Reformatory Tradition," *Women and Criminal Justice* 9:3 (1998): 1–21, and Joann Morton, "Martha E. Wheeler: Redefining Women in Corrections," *Women and Criminal Justice* 5:2 (1994): 3–20. See also Joann Morton, ed., "Women in Corrections," *Corrections Today* 54:6 (1992): 76–180, and the theme issues on "Best in the Business," *Corrections Today* (yearly).
41. George Church, "The View from behind Bars," *Time*, September 22, 1990, pp. 20–22.
42. See Laura M. Maruschak (2006), "Medical Problems of Jail Inmates," http://www.bjs.gov/, and Correctional Association of New York, *Women in Prison Fact Sheet*, downloaded November 5, 2014 from http://www.correctionalassociation.org/wp-content/uploads/2012/05/Wome_in_Prison_Fact_Sheet_2009_FINAL.pdf. For data on babies born to jail inmates, see Oliver Lee, "What Happens to Babies Born in Jail?," http://www.takepart.com/article/2012/05/28/what-happens-babies-born-jail (accessed September 14, 2014). See also Kisa Miela Santiago, "Babies Born behind Bars: Motherly Love or Abuse?," http://www.hlntv.com/article/2013/05/10/prison-nursery (accessed September 14, 2014).
43. John Wooldredge and K. Masters, "Confronting Problems Faced by Pregnant Inmates in State Prisons," *Crime and Delinquency* 39:3 (1993): 195–203; Jessica Pearson and N. Thoennes, "What Happens to Pregnant Substance Abusers and Their Babies?," *Juvenile and Family Court Journal* 47:2 (1996): 15–28.
44. Joann Morton and D. Williams, "Mother/Child Bonding," *Corrections Today* 60:7 (1998): 98–105; Paula Dressel, J. Porterfield, and S. Barnhill, "Mothers behind Bars," *Corrections Today* 60:7 (1998): 90–94; Win Sisson, "Don't Forget about the Children," *Corrections Today* 68:7 (2006): 54–57.
45. Washington Correctional Center for Women, "Washington Department of Corrections," http://www.doc.wa.gov/facilities/Washingtoncc-women.asp. See also Jeanne Woodford, "Women and Parole," http://www.ihc.ca.gov/ihcdir/womenparole/woodruffApr04.pdf.
46. California Department of Corrections, "Community Prisoner Mother Program (CPMP)," http://info.sen.ca.gov/pub/07-08/bill/asm/ab_0051-0100/ab_76_cfa_20070226_094043_asmcomm.html. See also California Department of Corrections and Rehabilitation, "California Department of Corrections and Rehabilitation Opens New Family Foundations Program Facility in Fresno," http://www.cdcr.ca.gov/news/2008_Press_Release/January_25/index.html (accessed March 8, 2008).
47. Lauren E. Glaze and Laura M. Maruschak, *Parents in Prison and Their Minor Children* (Washington, DC: Bureau of Justice Statistics, 2010); Morton and Williams, "Mother/Child Bonding"; Dressel et al., "Mothers behind Bars."
48. See also Phyllis Ross and J. Lawrence, "Health Care for Women Offenders," *Corrections Today* 60:7 (1998): 122–129, and Susan Crawford and R. Williams, "Critical Issues in Managing Female Offenders," *Corrections Today* 60:7 (1998): 130–134.
49. *Estelle* v. *Gamble*, 97 S. Ct. 285 (1976). See also Michael Vaughn and L. Carroll, "Separate but Unequal: Prison versus Free-World Medical Care," *Justice Quarterly* 15:1 (1998): 3–40; Kristine Shields and C. de Moya,

"Correctional Health Care Nurses' Attitudes toward Inmates," *Journal of Correctional Health Care* 4:1 (1997): 37–59; Michael S. Vaughn and Linda G. Smith, "Practicing Penal Harm Medicine in the United States: Prisoners' Voices from Jail," *Justice Quarterly* 16 (1999): 175–232; Michael Vaughn and Sue Collins, "Medical Malpractice in Correctional Facilities," *The Prison Journal* 84:4 (2004): 505–534; Paul von Zielbauer, "Private Health Care in Jails Can Be a Death Sentence," *New York Times*, February 27, 2005, p. A7; and Editors, "California Receiver Issues Status Report on Prison Medical Systems," *Correctional News* 13:7 (2007): 14.

50. David Ward and Gene Kassenbaum, "Sexual Tension in a Woman's Prison," in *The Criminal in Confinement*, ed. M. Wolfgang and L. Savitz (New York: Basic Books, 1971), pp. 149–150; Candace Kruttschnitt, "Race Relations and the Female Inmate," *Crime and Delinquency* 29:4 (1983): 577–592.
51. Sheldon Glueck and Eleanor Glueck, *500 Delinquent Women* (New York: Knopf, 1934).
52. John Smykla, *Co-Corrections: A Case Study of a Co-Ed Federal Prison* (Washington, DC: University Press of America, 1979). See also Christopher Uggen and C. Kruttsnitt, "Crime in the Breaking: Gender Differences in Desistance," *Law and Society Review* 33:2 (1998): 339–366, and Charlotte Bright, Scott Decker, and Andrea Burch, "Gender and Justice in the Progressive Era," *Justice Quarterly* 24:7 (2007): 657–678.
53. Victor Hassine, *Life without Parole: Living in Prison Today* (Los Angeles: Roxbury, 2002); Robert Johnson and H. Toch, *Crime and Punishment: Inside Views* (New York: Oxford University Press, 2008); Christopher Hensley and Richard Tewksbury, "Warden's Perceptions of Prison Sex," *The Prison Journal* 85:2 (2005): 127–144; Editors, "California to Trial Condoms in Prisons," *Correctional News* 14:1 (2008): 32.
54. Tjaden and Thoennes, *Prevalence, Incidence, and Consequences of Violence against Women*; Bonita Versey, K. de Cou, and L. Prescott, "Effective Management of Female Jail Detainees with Histories of Physical and Sexual Abuse," *American Jails* 16:2 (1998): 50–54; Shannon Catalano, "Intimate Partner Violence in the United States," http://www.ojp.usdoj.gov/bjs/intimate/ipv.htm (accessed March 8, 2008).
55. Leslie Acoca and J. Austin, *The Crisis: The Women Offender Sentencing Study and Alternative Sentencing* (Washington, DC: National Council on Crime and Delinquency, 1996).
56. American Correctional Association, *2012 Directory,* pp. 60–61.
57. John Smykla and J. Williams, "Co-Corrections in the United States of America, 1970–1990: Two Decades of Disadvantages for Women Prisoners," *Women and Criminal Justice* 8:1 (1996): 61–76.
58. Pamela Schram, "Stereotypes about Vocational Programming for Female Inmates," *The Prison Journal* 78:3 (1998): 255–270.
59. Smykla and Williams, "Co-Corrections in the United States of America, 1970–1990."
60. Paul Gendreau, Shelia A. French, and Angela Taylor, *What Works (What Doesn't Work): The Principles of Effective Correctional Treatment,* International Community Corrections Association Monograph Series (La Crosse, WI: International Community Corrections Association, 2002).
61. The Sentencing Project, *Women in the Criminal Justice System* (Washington, DC: The Sentencing Project, 2007); Christopher Hartney, *The Nation's Most Punitive States for Women* (Oakland, CA: National Council on Crime and Delinquency, 2007).
62. Bureau of Justice Statistics, *Prisoners in 2006* (Washington, DC: Bureau of Justice Statistics, 2007).
63. Family Strengthening Policy Center, "Supporting Families with Incarcerated Parents," http://www.nassembly.org/fspc/practice/documents/brief8.pdf (accessed May 28, 2008).

Rob Lacey/vividstock.net/Alamy.

Objectives

- Outline the development of the juvenile justice system.
- List the categories and characteristics of juvenile offenders.
- Summarize trends in juvenile crime.
- Explain the decline in criminal behavior as the offender ages.
- Explain how juveniles may be transferred to adult court and describe issues regarding juvenile offenders in adult criminal courts.
- Describe community-based treatment programs for juvenile offenders.
- Summarize juvenile rights and the cases that have impacted them.
- Describe juvenile gangs.
- Explain the concept of the super-predator.

chapter 19 Juvenile Offenders

Outline

"Data on the relationship between crime and age indicate that crime is a young man's game."

—Edward J. Latessa

Overview

The previous two chapters and the one that follows describe the variety of "clients" that usually are formed into separate groups for sentencing and incarceration following arrest and detention. In the early history of American justice, the distinctions of sex, age, or personal infirmities were given little thought, and "offenders" were lumped into a single category—prisoners. Institutional inmates needed only be classified as convicted, and even that distinction was often overlooked in society's haste to punish actual or alleged miscreants. Over the decades, many different paths were developed for various categories of offenders; jails were separated into male and female sections, and those convicted were sent to different, specialized kinds of institutions to serve out their sentences and have their special needs met. But what about those offenders classified, by age, as juveniles? What became of them in the adult systems?

This chapter digresses somewhat from the general pattern because the process of handling juvenile offenders has grown into an entirely separate system of justice. Therefore, we develop the history of juvenile justice in more detail than was covered earlier in the text to show how juvenile procedures have developed almost independently from adult justice and are designed to assist wayward youth. The juvenile justice system has now grown into an entirely separate "industry." This is especially timely as we follow the activities of street gangs, children who murder other children, and all the punitive and neoclassical efforts to again try juveniles in adult courts as "super-predators."[1] We hope to provide the student, in this single chapter, with a basic understanding of juvenile involvement in crime, arrest and prosecution procedures, and commitment to juvenile correctional facilities.

This is not meant to be an exhaustive or a complete treatise on juvenile offenders but simply a base on which to build an understanding of the origins and current practices in this separate and unique correctional system as well as an introduction to juvenile corrections.

WHERE DOES THE JUVENILE FIT IN?

key term

Common law
Law based on judges' decisions and custom as distinct from written laws.

key term

Parens patriae
A Latin term that refers to the duty of the state to protect those unable to protect themselves, particularly juveniles and the mentally disordered.

key term

Ward
A minor subject to wardship or protection by the state; may also refer to other persons protected by court order or legal status.

key term

Chancery court
One of the five divisions of the High Court of Justice of Great Britain, presided over by the Lord High Chancellor and that serves as a legal protector of the rights of minors.

How did we go from wayward youth to super-predators in such a short time? Like most of America's criminal justice system, our juvenile justice system derives from the **common law** of England, as brought to the United States by our forefathers. With regard to criminal responsibility, the English common law made three assumptions concerning age and criminal responsibility:

1. Children under the age of seven were presumed to be incapable of holding criminal intent.
2. From the ages of 7 to 14, offenders were not held responsible unless the state could prove they could clearly distinguish between right and wrong.
3. If offenders were 14 or older, they were assumed to be responsible for their acts and therefore deserving of punishment. Here, the burden was on the defendants to prove they were not responsible.

The king was considered the father of his country (***parens patriae***), who assumed responsibility for protecting all dependent children. *Parens patriae* is a legal philosophy by which the state assumes the role of the parent of the child: *The parent is the state.* In England, that responsibility was fulfilled by the chancery court,[2] in which the needful child became a **ward** of the state under the protection of *parens patriae.* The **chancery court** was designed to act more flexibly than the more rigid criminal courts. The main concern was for the welfare of the child; legal procedures that might hamper the court in its beneficial actions were either circumvented or ignored. Thus, there were two concepts under the common law: that children under certain ages were not responsible for their actions and that a certain category of children was in need of protection by the state. It was not until the ages of possible responsibility were raised to 16 and 18 that those two concepts merged into the concept of juvenile delinquency.

CRIMINAL BEHAVIOR DECLINES WITH AGE

Data on the relationship between crime and age indicate that crime is a young person's game. It seems to peak at age 17, then begins to drop. Younger people may be more likely to be arrested because of inexperience and ineptness in crime. Young people also commit crimes that more easily result in arrest, such as shoplifting, purse snatching, and drug selling. Also, youths tend to commit crimes in groups, and the resolution of a single crime (such as a car theft) may result in several arrests. The decline by age could also be an artifact of incapacitating repeat offenders by imposing longer sentences; such offenders then grow older in prison. Habitual offenders also seem to become less likely to be caught and arrested. Therefore, older prisoners who do return to crime tend to have longer periods before rearrest ("survival periods") and enjoy longer periods of freedom between incarcerations. The most serious offenses for which juveniles were arrested from 2003 through 2012 are noted in Table 19.1.

The juvenile crime rate declined over 37 percent during the past 10 years. This could be a result of the shrinking of the population at risk (12- to 18-year-old youths), or it could mean that real progress is being made in the juvenile justice system. But, as we will show, juveniles contribute to a significant portion of the crime problem. Juveniles are persons subject to juvenile court proceedings because a statutorily defined event was alleged to have occurred while their ages were below the statutorily specified limit of original jurisdiction of a juvenile court. A juvenile delinquent, then, has been adjudicated by an officer of a juvenile court for law violations that would be crimes if an adult had committed them. Figure 19.1 shows the percentages of arrests involving juveniles.

table 19.1 Most Serious Offense for Which Juveniles Were Arrested, 2003–2012

Most Serious Offense	Total Number of Juvenile Arrests	Percent Change, 2003–2012
Total	**1,403,497**	**− 37.0**
Violent Crime Index	**38,444**	**− 36.0**
Murder and nonnegligent manslaughter	443	−37.0
Forcible rape	1,682	−36.0
Robbery	13,200	−19.5
Aggravated assault	23,119	−42.7
Property Crime Index	**200,824**	**−36.0**
Burglary	36,424	−36.5
Larceny-theft	152,983	−31.7
Motor vehicle theft	8,403	−69.0
Arson	3,014	−46.1

SOURCE: Federal Bureau of Investigation, "Crime in the United States, 2012," table 32, http://www.fbi.gov/about-us/cjis/ucr/crime-in-the-u.s/2012/crime-in-the-u.s.-2012/tables/32tabledatadecoverviewpdf (accessed January 18, 2014).

Because a very large percentage of incarcerated felons were first incarcerated as juveniles in training institutions and schools for delinquents, we look briefly at the development and function of the juvenile court and the juvenile justice system, starting with the philosophy that produced them.

Despite concern for their children's welfare, most communities have a tolerance point for juveniles' disruptive behavior. When children go beyond that point, they can be taken

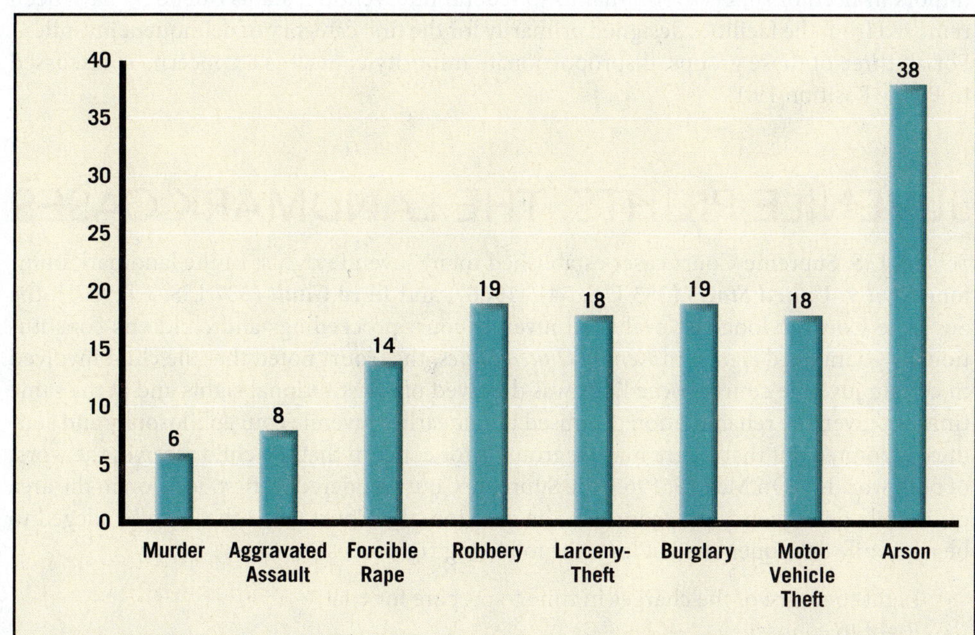

figure 19.1 Percentages of Arrests Involving Juveniles.

SOURCE: Federal Bureau of Investigation, *Uniform Crime Report, 2012*, http://www.fbi.gov/about-us/cjis/ucr/crime-in-the-u.s/2012/crime-in-the-u.s.-2012/tables/34 tabledatadecoverviewpdf (accessed September 15, 2014).

into custody and recorded as delinquents. The mixing of juvenile offenders and adult felons was a practice that had existed for centuries but in America's early history was looked on as repugnant. In 1899, children in trouble, dependent children, and delinquent juveniles began to receive differential attention in the courts. The first juvenile court was established in that year in Chicago, and the delinquent joined the dependent and neglected child as a ward of the state. Serious delinquents were the last category to come to the attention of the juvenile court. When the juvenile delinquent was thus placed under the cloak of *parens patriae*, he or she was removed entirely from the formal criminal justice system.

key term

Dependent
Any child without parents or guardians or whose parents are unable to provide such care, treatment, or custody that should be afforded to a child.

key term

Neglected
General term referring to a child who is not receiving the care that ought to be afforded by parents or guardians.

key term

Delinquent juveniles
Juveniles who have committed a criminal act that if committed by an adult would be a crime.

key term

Status offenders
Juveniles who have committed acts that are law violations by virtue of the child's age but would not be criminal if committed by an adult (such as running away, incorrigibility, defiance).

key term

Incorrigible (unruly) juveniles
Unruly juveniles whose behavior is not controlled by their parents.

key term

Kent* v. *United States
A U.S. Supreme Court decision that courts must provide the "essentials of due process" in transferring juveniles to the adult system.

key term

In re Gault
A U.S. Supreme Court decision that juveniles have four basic constitutional rights in hearings that could result in commitment to an institution.

CATEGORIES OF JUVENILE OFFENDERS

Essentially three kinds of children come into contact with the juvenile court system—a significant event in their lives. The children in two of those categories have committed no offense; they are either **dependent** (without family or support) or **neglected** (having a family situation that is harmful to them). The only category that involves an offense is the **delinquent juvenile**.

The care of neglected and dependent children is important, of course, but the juvenile courts were established primarily to handle delinquent juveniles. For judicial purposes, delinquents are divided into three categories:

1. Children who have allegedly committed an offense that would be a crime if an adult had committed it. This group now comprises more than 75 percent of the population of the state institutions for delinquent juveniles.
2. **Status offenders** who have allegedly violated regulations that apply only to juveniles: curfew restrictions, required school attendance, and similar rules and ordinances. (A "status offender" is generally accepted as a juvenile who has come into contact with the juvenile authorities based on conduct that is an offense only when committed by a juvenile—such as runaways, violations of curfews, and refusal to conform to parental guidance.)
3. **Incorrigible (unruly) juveniles** who have been declared unmanageable by their parents and the court.

The second and third groups are often referred to as persons in need of supervision or minors in need of supervision. Thanks to federal intervention, status offenders have been removed from the facilities designed primarily for the first category of delinquent juveniles.[3] For all three of these groups, disproportionate minority contact is a concern, as discussed in Policy Position 19.1.

JUVENILE RIGHTS: THE LANDMARK CASES

Several U.S. Supreme Court cases established many juvenile rights. In the landmark opinions ***Kent* v. *United States*** (383 U.S. 541 [1966]) and ***In re Gault*** (387 U.S. 1 [1967]), the Supreme Court at long last evaluated juvenile court proceedings and children's constitutionally guaranteed rights. In *Kent* v. *United States*, the Court noted that the child involved in certain juvenile court proceedings was deprived of constitutional rights and at the same time not given the rehabilitation promised under earlier juvenile court philosophy and statutes. It pointed out that "there may be grounds for concern that the child receives the worst of both worlds."[4] On May 15, 1967, the Supreme Court rendered its first decision in the area of juvenile delinquency procedure. In the decision, the Court ruled that a child alleged to be a juvenile delinquent had at least the following rights:

- Right to notice of the charges in time to prepare for trial
- Right to counsel

policy position 19.1

Disproportionate Minority Contact

Disproportionate minority contact (DMC) refers to the disproportionate number of minority youth who come into contact with the juvenile justice system. The federal government requires states to develop and implement plans to reduce the proportion of minority youth detained or confined in secure detention facilities, secure correctional facilities, jails, and lockups if they exceed the percentage of minority youth in the general local population. The purpose of this requirement is to ensure equal and fair treatment for every youth in the juvenile justice system regardless of race and ethnicity.

Minority youth have much more frequent contacts with the juvenile justice system than do white youth. This difference is partly the result of differences in frequency, types, and seriousness of involvement with delinquency, but differential involvement does not fully explain the DMC. Youth of color remain in the juvenile justice system longer than do white youth. Black youth represent about 17 percent of the general youth population, 28 percent of juvenile arrests, and more than 50 percent of youth committed to state adult correctional facilities. They are over represented at every point in the spectrum of juvenile delinquency.

Differential involvement may explain a small part of this equation, but additional factors, singularly and combined, function together to enlarge DMC in the juvenile justice system. Some of those factors are the following:

- School "zero-tolerance" policies of districts that exist in urban low-income communities that contain a high concentration of DMC, such as criminalizing school infractions for drug possession, alcohol ingestion, and district campus loitering
- Varying alternatives for treatment that might also be related to low-income districts
- Institutionalized racism
- Uneven access to effective legal counsel
- Income-related barriers to treatment
- Risk assessment instruments standardized on more economically viable white juveniles
- Differential command of language competencies

Contact with the juvenile justice system has significant collateral damages, as such contact will reduce options for education, housing, employment, and job placement. Additional contacts reduce the stability of communities and deepen the divide between whites and nonwhites.

Reducing DMC is both a daunting challenge and a difficult process. Initial steps are to identify and define the problem, develop local service providers, encourage transparency, and implement phases of reductions. Community support is crucial and must include stakeholders that have been impacted by minority involvement. Long-term involvement is also crucial and directions for change can emerge from both successes and failures. Referrals to the police for school-based incidents as a policy might be researched, and detention alternatives could be developed. Finally, county agencies could work with the school district to develop and manage school-based conflict resolution plans. In general, DMC must become a priority for communities in order to sustain drops in overrepresentation.

SOURCE: Office of Juvenile Justice and Delinquency Prevention (2012), "Disproportionate Minority Contact," http://www.ojjdp.gov/pubs/239457.pdf (accessed December 10, 2012); and The Sentencing Project, "Disproportionate Minority Contact," http://www.sentencingproject.org/doc/publications/jj_DMCfactsheet.pdf (accessed November 30, 2012).

- Right to confrontation and cross-examination of his or her accusers
- Privilege against self-incrimination, at least in court

The *Gault* decision ended the presumption that the juvenile courts were beyond the scope or purview of due process protection. With *In re Winship* (397 U.S. 358 [1970]), the Supreme Court held that to justify a court finding of delinquency against a juvenile, the proof must be beyond a reasonable doubt that the juvenile committed the alleged delinquent act. *McKeiver* v. *Pennsylvania* (403 U.S. 528 [1971]) implied that the due process standard of "fundamental fairness" applied; the Court rejected the concept of trial by jury for juveniles. The Court contended that the "juvenile proceeding has not yet been held to be a 'criminal prosecution' within the meaning and reach of the Sixth Amendment."[5] Since *McKeiver*, more and more rights have been extended to the juvenile process while still trying to keep it separate.[6]

The Supreme Court has not been the only source of change in the area of juvenile rights, however. Federal acts and legislation have also played an important role. Until the Uniform Juvenile Court Act of 1968, police or others could still take a child into custody in a situation in which the Fourth Amendment would have exempted an adult. In 1974, the U.S. Congress

key term

Juvenile Justice and Delinquency Prevention Act
Act requiring a comprehensive assessment of the juvenile justice system to identify those youth who are victimized or otherwise troubled but have not committed criminal offenses.

key term

Roper* v. *Simmons
A U.S. Supreme Court decision that made it unconstitutional to impose capital punishment for a crime committed while under the age of 18.

key term

Graham* v. *Florida
A 2010 U.S. Supreme Court decision holding that juveniles cannot be sentenced to life imprisonment without parole for nonhomicide offenses.

key term

Miller* v. *Alabama
In 2012, the Supreme Court held that mandatory sentences of life without the possibility of parole are unconstitutional for juvenile offenders.

key term

Diversion
The halting or suspension of a juvenile from further involvement with the justice system in return for approved behaviors.

key term

Decriminalization
To remove or reduce the criminal classification or status of a formerly criminal act.

key term

Deinstitutionalization
The return of a patient from a mental hospital into the community.

passed the **Juvenile Justice and Delinquency Prevention Act** (Public Law 93-415). This act required a comprehensive assessment regarding the effectiveness of the existing juvenile justice system. The intent of the act was to clearly identify those youth who are victimized or otherwise troubled but have not committed criminal offenses and to divert such youth from institutionalization. Simultaneously, the act was intended to promote the utilization of resources within the juvenile justice system to more effectively deal with youthful criminal offenders.

Thus far, the procedural rights guaranteed to a juvenile in court proceedings are as follows:

1. The right to adequate notice of charges against him or her
2. The right to counsel and to have counsel provided if the child is indigent
3. The right to confrontation and cross-examination of witnesses
4. The right to refuse to do anything that would be self-incriminatory
5. The right to due process, prior to the transfer of a juvenile to an adult court[7]
6. The right to be considered innocent until proven guilty beyond a reasonable doubt

More recently the court has taken up the issue of severe punishment for juveniles. In 2005, the court decided in ***Roper* v. *Simmons*** (543 U.S. 551) that is was unconstitutional to impose capital punishment for crime committed while under the age of 18. This decision overturned prior law that allowed for youth 16 or older to be executed. Although not without controversy, the 5-to-4 decision paved the way for the ***Graham* v. *Florida*** (560 U.S. 48) decision in 2010 that held that juveniles cannot be sentenced to life imprisonment without parole for nonhomicide offenses. Extending beyond *Graham v. Florida*, in 2012 the Supreme Court, in ***Miller* v. *Alabama*** (567 U.S.), held that mandatory sentences of life without the possibility of parole are unconstitutional for juvenile offenders. These three important cases have helped turn back the more punitive sentences that juveniles were subjected to over the years. Juveniles still face lifelong terms despite these rulings because some states mete out criminal sentences so long that they achieve the mandatory life sentence length and impact. The Supreme Court has also ruled on extreme punishments for juveniles, as described in Correctional Practice 19.1.

Decisions of the U.S. Supreme Court have led to four major trends in the handling of juveniles: diversion, decriminalization, deinstitutionalization of status offenders, and decarceration.

Diversion is the official halting or suspension, at any legally prescribed processing point after a recorded justice system entry, of formal juvenile (or criminal) proceedings against an alleged offender and referral of that person to a treatment or care program administered by a non–justice agency or private agency. Sometimes no referral is given. Diversion programs function to divert juveniles out of the juvenile justice system, encourage the use of existing private correctional agencies and facilities for such youths, and avoid formal contact with the juvenile court. Those programs include remedial education programs, foster homes, group homes, and local counseling facilities and centers. The effectiveness of such programs has not yet been demonstrated, but they are being closely evaluated.

Decriminalization does just what it sounds like it does—it makes the act not criminal anymore. The principal aim in the juvenile and criminal justice systems is to remove from the scope of law and social control certain types of currently proscribed behaviors that pose little perceived danger to society. Those behaviors are frequently seen as "deviant" rather than illegal and thus "not the law's business."[8] The decriminalization movement, then, would delete deviant behavior from juvenile laws and proceedings and leave to social agencies the task of providing assistance if and when requested.

One category of juveniles that falls under the aegis of the juvenile court is the status offender. These youths commit offenses that are based only on the offender's status as a juvenile. These offenses include ungovernability, running away, unruliness, school truancy, disregard for or abuse of lawful parental authority, and repeated use of alcoholic beverages.

correctional practice 19.1

Extreme Punishments for Youths

The U.S. Supreme Court has issued three major opinions in the past decade that have significantly changed the applications of extreme punishments for juveniles. First, in 2005, the Court prohibited *imposing* the death penalty on minors. Second, the Court forbade the imposition of the sentence of life without parole for all crimes except *homicide*. Finally, in 2012, it outlawed the imposition of *mandatory* life without parole sentences for juveniles. The 2012 ruling now allows sentencing judges to consider *mitigating* circumstances and to impose a lesser punishment.

In 2012, the governor of California signed a bill that reshaped the sentence of life without parole for minors whose crimes were committed when they were juveniles. The California law now requires those inmates to serve a minimum of 25 years in prison before becoming eligible for parole. Those youth under the "life, no parole" sentence may request a reduced sentence of 25 years to life, and the law now authorizes several alternatives to serving that lengthy sentence. If those inmates have served a minimum of 15 years and show signs of remorse and rehabilitation, they may request a reduced sentence. A second option revolves around the presence of an adult codefendant when the youth's crime was committed. Some 300 juvenile inmates in the California Department of Corrections and Rehabilitation are serving a "life, no parole" sentence.

SOURCE: Editors, "Calif. Gov. Jerry Brown Signs SB 9," *Correctional News* 18:7 (2012): 9.

The nation has moved away from putting status offenders into secure institutional settings, a concept known as **deinstitutionalization**.[9]

Decarceration removes as many juveniles from custody as possible and treats them in an open environment. This option, given the violent nature of some incarcerated juveniles, seems to still be waiting for its time to come.

These recommendations reflect the earlier intent of the Juvenile Justice and Delinquency Prevention Act to divert status offenders to shelter facilities rather than juvenile detention centers or jails as well as not to detain or confine status offenders in any institution in which they would have regular contact with adult offenders. The leading figure in the deinstitutionalization movement is Jerome Miller (1928–), who convinced the governor of Massachusetts to close all but one correctional institution.

key term

Decarceration
Process of releasing offenders from institutional facilities, primarily by closing those facilities.

key term

Statutory exclusion
Principle that requires a category juvenile offender to be bound over as an adult, based on the type of offense committed. All such juveniles committing an identified offense must be transferred to adult court.

key term

Juvenile waiver
Juvenile court transfer of alleged delinquents to adult court for more intensive and lengthy punishment.

key term

Direct filing
Prosecutorial decision to refer the case to an adult criminal court rather than to a juvenile court.

WHO IS A JUVENILE TODAY?

The "upper age of jurisdiction" is the key factor in this first decade of the twenty-first century. It is the oldest age at which a juvenile court has original jurisdiction over an individual for law-violating behavior. State statutes define which youth are under the original jurisdiction of the juvenile court. These definitions are based primarily on age criteria. In most states, the juvenile court has original jurisdiction over all youth charged with a criminal law violation who were below the age of 18 at the time of the offense, arrest, or referral to court. Many states have higher upper ages of juvenile court jurisdiction in status offense, abuse, neglect, or dependency matters, often through age 20. All states plus the District of Columbia have at least one provision for transferring juveniles to the criminal court for which no minimum age is specified. Many states have statutory exceptions to basic age criteria. The exceptions, related to the youth's age, alleged offense, and/or prior court history, place certain youth under the original jurisdiction of the criminal court, known as **statutory exclusion**. In some states, a combination of the youth's age, offense, and prior record places the youth under the original jurisdiction of both the juvenile and the criminal courts. In these situations where the courts have concurrent jurisdiction, the prosecutor is given the authority to decide which court will initially handle the case. This is known as concurrent jurisdiction, prosecutor discretion, **juvenile waiver**, certification to adult criminal court, or **direct filing**.[10] The number of delinquency cases judicially waived to criminal court in 2009 was 45 percent less than in 1994, when it peaked.

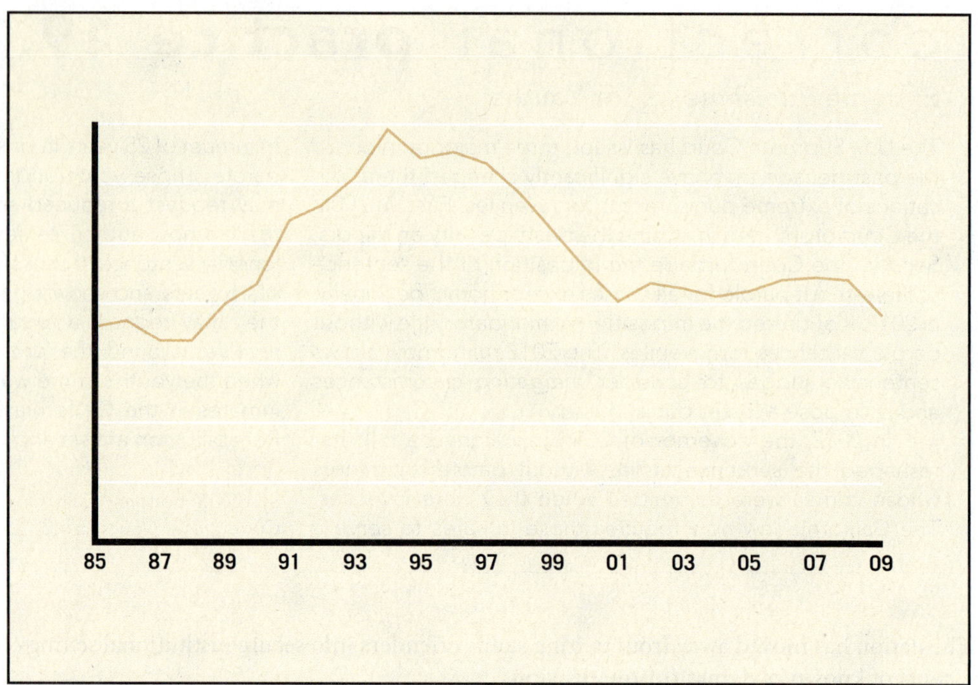

figure 19.2

Delinquency Cases Judicially Waived to Criminal Court, 2009.

SOURCE: Benjamin Adams and Sean Addle, *Delinquency Cases Waived to Criminal Court 2009* (Washington, DC: Office of Justice Programs, 2012).

Figure 19.2 shows the number of cases between 1985 and 2009. Not surprisingly, personal offenses account for about half of juvenile cases that are waived to adult court.[11] Currently, there are over 1,500 youth age 17 or under in adult prisons.[12] Figure 19.3 shows the types of dispositions of cases from 1993 to 2015. Policy Position 19.2 describes juvenile transfers to adult court.

The most recent national survey of juvenile defendants in crime courts in the largest 40 cities notes the following:

1. An estimated 7,100 juvenile defendants were charged with felonies in adult criminal court.
2. Juveniles (64 percent) were more likely than adults (24 percent) to be charged with a violent felony.
3. These juvenile defendants were generally treated as serious offenders, as 52 percent did not receive pretrial release; 63 percent were convicted of a felony, and 43 percent received a prison sentence averaging 90 months.[13]

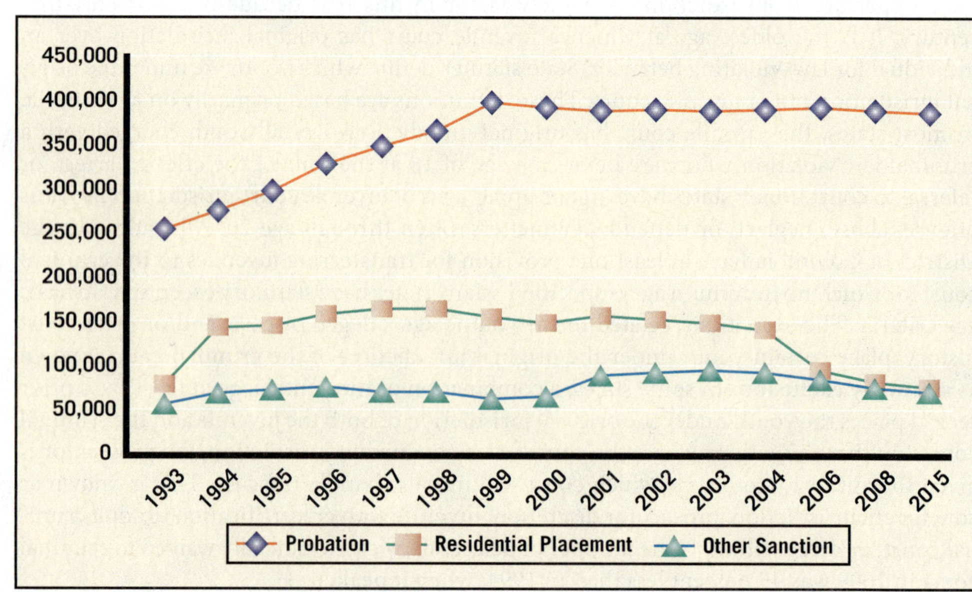

figure 19.3

Adjudicated Delinquency Cases by Disposition, 1993–2015.

Note: Data for 2015 are extrapolated.

SOURCE: Office of Juvenile Justice and Delinquency Prevention, *Statistical Briefing Book 2012* (Washington, DC: Office of Juvenile Justice and Delinquency Prevention).

policy position 19.2

Transfer of Juveniles to Adult Court

During the years 1980–1995, the nation experienced a sharp rise in violent crime as well as numerous highly publicized cases whether juveniles committing repetitive violent and other serious crimes. The public and policymakers began to wonder whether the juvenile court could provide sufficiently for public safety and whether societal protection could be increased by transferring juveniles to adult court. Rhetoric, later proven to be unsubstantiated, arose about the pending successive waves of juvenile "super-predators" characterized by both heartlessness and resistance to interventions. In such an environment, some states debated the wisdom of retaining such adolescents in juvenile court and began to authorize transfer to adult court through certification, automatic waiver, or direct filing by the prosecutor to the adult court. Lists of crimes were developed that required automatic transfer, and age limits were lowered for such transfers. In effect, the focus shifted from the actor to the act and from rehabilitation to retribution.

Estimates of the proportion of prison inmates who are under age 18 range from 1.2 to 2.3 percent of prison populations. Supreme Court Justice Elena Kagan estimated 2,000 teenagers were sentenced to life without parole in that Court's decision in 2012 to ban mandatory life sentences without the possibility of parole for offenders younger than age 18.

Questions about the fairness of transfer of juveniles have arisen. First is the major question of fairness: Does transfer to adult court inflict conditions and punishments that are unduly harsh? The second major question is, Does transfer actually reduce crime in comparison to placement in juvenile court?

One of the possible collateral consequences of transfer is that juveniles could serve longer sentences as adults than as juveniles. Evidence is that about 20 percent of transferred adolescents receive a sentence of probation. In California, transferred juveniles served a shorter period of time than youth sentenced for the same offense in the juvenile justice system. Another possible detrimental effect is that other inmates or correctional staff might subject adolescent offenders to physical, sexual, or psychological victimization. Evidence to date is that adolescents in adult facilities are five times more likely to be sexually assaulted, and the risk of assault for an adolescent in an adult facility is significantly greater than that for adults in the same facility.

Does transfer reduce crime through locking up serious offenders (incapacitation), deter future crime by imposing harsh punishment (individual deterrence), or signal other juveniles to not commit crime because of harsher penalties that could be inflicted (general deterrence)? There is not much agreement amongst authorities that any of these three effects are achieved, and the amount of research supporting or refuting these effects is quite sparse and generally inconclusive. There is some evidence that transferred juveniles are more likely to recidivate, recidivate at a higher rate, and be arrested for more serious offenses than those who remain in the juvenile justice system.

SOURCE: Edward Mulvey and Carol Schubert (2012), "Transfer of Juveniles to Adult Court," http://www.ojjdp.gov/pubs/232932.pdf (accessed December 11, 2012); David Tanenhaus, "The Court's Liberal Turn on Juvenile Justice," *New York Times,* June 27, 2012, http://www.nytimes.com/2012/06/27/opinion/the-roberts-courts-liberal-turn-on-juvenile-justice.html?pagewanted=print&_r=0 (accessed December 10, 2013).

THE JUVENILE CRIME PROBLEM

It has been estimated that approximately one of every six boys and 1 of every 12 girls in the United States will be referred to a juvenile court before their 18th birthday. The previous rise in juvenile crime has been considered the most serious aspect of the crime problem in the nation; however, recently there has been a significant decline in the juvenile crime rate. In 2003, approximately 1.4 million arrests were made of persons under the age of 18, and in 2012 that number had dropped to about 881,000, a 37 percent reduction. As noted in Figure 19.2, the rate at which juveniles are involved in serious crimes varies from a low of 6 percent for murder to a high of 38 percent for arson.

Law enforcement agencies in 2012 made 443 arrests of juveniles for murder and nonnegligent manslaughter, 13,200 arrests of persons under 18 for robbery, 23,119 arrests for aggravated assault, and 1,682 for rape, as reported in the Violent Crime Index of the Federal Bureau of Investigation's Uniform Crime Report. These figures were down considerably from the previous decade. The number of juvenile homicides was over 50 percent below the peak year of 1993 and at its lowest level since the mid-1980s.[14] It would be simplistic but arguably correct to say that the nation is suffering from an outbreak of crime reduction.

JUVENILE VIOLENCE AND OTHER CRIMES IN DECLINE

As was suggested, across the nation, the amount of violent crime involving juveniles as offenders or victims is on a decline. This is good news, as from about the time of the emergence of crack cocaine in the mid-1980s, the use of violence has become a part of juvenile gang culture, and these crimes seem to have also spread to many youths who are not gang members. Between 2003 and 2012, violent crime for juvenile offenders dropped over 37 percent. Unfortunately, despite the reduction in juvenile crime, the increase in the 1980s and early 1990s, combined with some high-profile cases, has caused society as a whole and the juvenile courts as well to develop a "get-tough" attitude toward violent crime by juveniles. Despite the drops, juveniles still accounted for 11 percent of all arrests in 2012, more than 11 percent of all violent crimes, and 18 percent of property crimes.[15]

JUVENILE VICTIMS OF VIOLENCE

Contrary to popular perceptions of the risk of violent crime, teenagers are victimized at rates that are nearly as high as those of adults. The following shows some of the findings concerning victimization:

- In 2012, 48 percent of those victimized by violent crimes were juveniles, with nearly 10 percent being the most serious violent offenses.
- Between 1980 and 2015, over 48,000 juveniles were murdered in the United States.
- The serious violent victimization of juveniles ages 12 to 17 increased from 1985 to 1993 but then dropped substantially.
- Until their teenage years, boys and girls are equally likely to be victims of murder.
- Between 1980 and 2009, most murdered children younger than age six were killed by a family member, whereas older juveniles were more likely to be killed by an acquaintance or stranger.
- In one-third of all sexual assaults reported to law enforcement, the victim was younger than age 12.[16]

It is important to note that the juveniles who are charged with violent crimes represent 11 percent of the total crimes committed by juveniles. Despite these relatively small numbers, such crimes of violence as drive-by shootings, casual murder, intrafamilial murder, and senseless abuse of other children create a hard-line attitude in the American public. The courts have been recognizing this perception and have been responding with more severe dispositions, including referring those who commit such violent crimes to stand trial as adults (through waiver to adult court).

REDUCING RECIDIVISM WITH SERIOUS JUVENILE OFFENDERS

Violent crime has been and will remain a problem; however, there is evidence that even adolescents who have committed serious offenses are not necessarily going to have an adult criminal career.[17] Decades of research[18] on delinquent careers and prevention have identified the following risk factors as contributing to serious, violent, and chronic juvenile crime:

- Weak family attachments
- Lack of consistent discipline
- Physical abuse and neglect
- Poor school performance

- Delinquent peer groups
- Substance abuse
- High-crime neighborhoods

The **U.S. Office of Juvenile Justice and Delinquency Prevention** proposed six strategies for preventing and reducing at-risk behavior and juvenile delinquency:[19]

1. Strengthen families in their role of providing guidance, discipline, and strong values as their children's first teacher.
2. Support core social institutions, including schools, churches, and other community-based organizations, to alleviate risk factors and help children develop to their full potential.
3. Promote prevention strategies that reduce the impact of negative risk factors and enhance protective factors.
4. Intervene immediately when delinquent behavior first occurs.
5. Establish a broad range of graduated sanctions that provides both accountability and a continuum of services to respond appropriately to the needs of each delinquent offender.
6. Identify and control the small percentage of juvenile offenders who are serious, violent, and chronic offenders.

Adaptations and new programs continue to be developed today. In the 1990s, we saw a rise in the number of military-style boot camps designed to drill discipline and coax self-worth into juveniles. Although boot camps were popular with the public and politicians, research on their effectiveness has generally found that they are not effective in reducing recidivism. In fact, there is some evidence that juvenile boot camps actually lead to higher failure rates. Some believe this is because the social learning in most boot camps actually teaches and models aggressive behavior.

key term

U.S. Office of Juvenile Justice and Delinquency Prevention
A branch of the U.S. Department of Justice that seeks to improve knowledge about juvenile offenders and evaluate both exploratory and prevention research and is capable of providing grants to researchers and administrators who would focus on solution of a major juvenile offense.

correctional **practice 19.2**

What Works with Youthful Offenders?

Two national assessments of the effectiveness of literally hundreds of intervention programs for treating and handling juvenile offenders found interesting and surprising results. The most effective approaches are behavioral in nature and include the following types of interventions:

- Structured social learning programs that teach new skills (how to interact with the opposite sex, problem-solving skills, etc.) and reinforce behavior and attitudes
- Cognitive behavioral programs that target attitudes, values, peers, substance abuse, anger, and so on
- Family-based interventions that train family on appropriate behavioral techniques

Perhaps the most important results dealt with what does not work with youthful offenders:

- Drug prevention classes focused on fear and other emotional appeals (e.g., DARE)
- Drug education programs
- Talking cures
- Nondirective interventions
- Self-help programs
- Increasing cohesion of criminal groups
- Targeting non-crime-producing factors
- Fostering self-regard (self-esteem)
- Radical nonintervention (doing nothing)
- Targeting low-risk offenders
- Correctional boot camps using traditional military basic training
- School-based leisure-time enrichment programs
- "Scared Straight" programs in which juvenile offenders visit adult prisons
- Home detention with electronic monitoring
- Rehabilitation programs using vague, unstructured counseling
- Residential programs for juvenile offenders using challenging experiences in rural settings

SOURCE: National Institute of Corrections, "Promoting Public Safety Using Effective Interventions with Offenders," http://www.nicic.org, accessed 2001; Lawrence Sherman et al., *Preventing Crime: What Works, What Doesn't, What's Promising* (Washington, DC: National Institute of Justice, 1998).

correctional practice 19.3

Mentoring

Mentoring involves a relationship between more experienced adults (mentors) and an unrelated younger mentee wherein continuous support, guidance, and instruction from the mentor is designed to improve the character, characteristics, and life skills of the mentee. Mentoring is a low-cost delinquency prevention and intervention strategy that builds on the resources and leadership of local communities and caring individuals.

Mentoring is based on the premise that predictable, consistent relationships with stable, competent adults can help youth cope with challenges and steer clear of high-risk behaviors. In a mentoring relationship, mentors provide guidance and support to help young people build self-confidence, learn positive behaviors, stay in school, and avoid such pitfalls as drugs and gangs.

Mentors can be teachers, peers, or community leaders, and mentees can be young people from all socioeconomic backgrounds, ethnicities, and cultures. Mentoring services are offered in schools, community centers, religious institutions, school-to-work programs, and other youth-oriented facilities.

Of the 17.6 million young people who could benefit from having a mentor in 2005, only 2.5 million were in formal, one-to-one mentoring relationships. Most mentoring relationships last on average nine months, but more than one in three mentors spent at least 12 months with their mentees. Only 16 percent of mentors had mentees in the juvenile justice system. Little brothers and little sisters of the Big Brothers Big Sisters of America program were 46 percent *less* likely than their peers without mentors to initiate drug use during their study period.

SOURCE: Office of Justice Programs, U.S. Department of Justice (2011), "Mentoring," http://www.ojp.usdoj.gov/newsroomfactsheets/ojpfs_mentoring.html (accessed November 28, 2012).

Fortunately, much research has demonstrated that well-designed treatment programs for youth can be effective in reducing delinquent behavior. Research on effective programs for youth has found that the most effective approaches are behavioral interventions, where offenders learn to replace their delinquent behavior through prosocial modeling and reinforcement. Those programs found not to be effective include, among other things, boot camps, fostering self-regard, home detention with electronic monitoring, and drug education programs. Correctional Practice 19.2 further explores treatment programs for juveniles, and Correctional Practice 19.3 describes the promising approach of mentoring.

The offending of juveniles is not the only concern. Young people are disproportionately the victims of violence as well. Violence impacts the quality of life for these children in their developing years.

JUVENILE GANGS

The U.S. Juvenile Justice and Delinquency Prevention unit defines a gang as a group of juveniles or young adults in a police jurisdiction that responsible officers would be willing to identify as a "gang." Excluded here are motorcycle gangs, hate or ideological groups, prison gangs (see Chapter 8), and exclusively adult gangs.[20]

It is estimated that in 2011, **youth gangs** were active in more than 3,300 jurisdictions. It is also estimated that approximately 782,500 gang members and 29,000 gangs were active in the United States in 2011. As alarming as these figures are, the good news is that the number of reported gang-related homicides decreased from 2,020 in 2010 to 1,824 in 2011.[21]

key term

Youth gang
A continuing criminal enterprise by juveniles and young adults that commits violence and other criminal acts to sustain itself.

The presence of youth gangs and gang problems must be recognized before anything meaningful can be done to address the gang problem. Identifying the manifest and underlying factors contributing to the problem is also important. Promising approaches include the following:

1. Targeting, arresting, and incarcerating gang leaders and repeat gang offenders
2. Referring fringe members ("wannabees") and their parents to youth services for counseling and guidance
3. Providing preventive services for youths who are clearly at risk

Photo 19.1

Many street gangs embrace drug use, physical strength and handguns by gang members.
Axel Koester/Corbis News/Corbis.

4. Crisis intervention or mediation of gang fights
5. Patrols of community "hot spots"
6. Close supervision of gang offenders by criminal justice and community-based agencies
7. Remedial education for targeted youth gang members, especially in middle school
8. Job orientation, training, placement, and monitoring for older youth gang members
9. Safe zones around schools
10. Vertical prosecution, close supervision, and enhanced sentences for hard-core youth gang members (Vertical, or hard-core, prosecution puts the same prosecutor in charge of all aspects of a case from charging to sentencing.)[22]

Photo 19.2

Crack cocaine destined for street sale by a youth gang.
Scott Keeler/ZUMA Press, Inc./Alamy.

key term

Crack cocaine
An illegal drug derived from powder cocaine and consumed primarily by smoking.

Although these approaches are promising, not until the underlying reasons for belonging to a gang are found will appropriate solutions be developed.

Gangs have been part of the urban scene for decades, but it took the advent of cocaine, especially **crack cocaine**, to create gangs whose only real motivation is money. One law enforcement survey of gangs reports that more than half of the documented gang members in their jurisdiction had migrated from other areas. However, about 6 in 10 agencies reported few or no such migrants. Among agencies that experienced a high percentage of migration, 45 percent reported that social reasons (such as members moving with their families and pursuit of legitimate employment opportunities) affected local migration "very much." Drug market opportunities (23 percent), avoidance of law enforcement crackdowns (21 percent), and participation in other illegal ventures (18 percent) were also reported as reasons for migration.[23] Gangs vary in and often are composed by ethnicity and race: white, Asian, Hispanic, African American, and Pacific Rim gangs abound. The factors influencing local gang violence center around drugs, inter- and intragang conflict, gang members returning from confinement, and gang member migration (both within and from outside the United States).[24]

THE NEW BREED: DISPELLING THE MYTH OF THE SUPER-PREDATOR

key term

Super-predator
Aggressive juvenile offender believed to engage in frequent and dangerous behaviors.

In the past, many of the juveniles in the system were not considered hardened criminals but simply wayward youngsters who had strayed from the right path. In the mid-1990s, several criminologists began to predict that the United States was on the verge of a crime wave perpetuated by a new breed of juvenile offenders. Buzzwords such as **super-predator** were used increasingly in the press and by politicians to describe this new type of youthful offender, ruthless young men and women who saw crime as a way of life and who it was believed were unconcerned about the consequences of their actions, more likely to engage in crime and violence, and less likely to be deterred by the threat of harsh punishment. Advocates of pursuing a "hard line" with the super-predators were quick to call for increased punishment and tougher laws to deal with this upcoming scourge.[25]

Governmental units rushed to pass laws to deal with super-predators, but, in fact, they have not emerged. Such laws were touted as benefiting public safety. The evidence today is that treating juveniles as adults increases the probabilities that such young people will continue to reoffend.[26] These dire predictions never came to pass, but the myth of excessive youth violence contributed to the public's belief that the juvenile crime rate was increasing and that youth accounted for a large proportion of overall crime.

RESTORATIVE JUSTICE

key term

Restorative justice
System of punishments designed to repair the damage to victims, community, and offender caused by the offender's criminal act.

Restorative Justice Online defines **restorative justice** as follows:

> A theory of justice that emphasizes repairing the harm caused or revealed by criminal justice. It is best accomplished through cooperative processes that include all stakeholders.

Practices and programs reflecting restorative purposes will respond to crime by doing the following:

1. Identifying and taking steps to repair harm
2. Involving all stakeholders
3. Transforming the traditional relationship between communities and their governments in responding to crime[27]

correctional practice 19.4

Teen Court

A teen court is a problem-solving court designed to interrupt any developing pattern of criminal behavior in juveniles. A teen court is a court run by teens for teens. Also known as peer courts and youth courts, most promote self-esteem, self-improvement, and a healthier attitude toward authority. Offenders are forced to assume responsibility for their misbehavior and must accept the consequences of their actions. The ultimate objective is to suppress the commission of a subsequent offense and, by example, to deter more first-time offenders.

Juveniles eligible for processing in the teen court are typically between the ages of 13 and 17, have committed misdemeanors or violations, and are otherwise eligible for diversion. Typical offenses include the following:

- Petty theft
- Possession of alcohol or drugs
- Criminal mischief
- Cyberbullying
- Burglary
- Driving offenses
- Curfew violations
- Trespassing
- Graffiti
- Vandalism
- Battering
- Reckless burning
- Harassment

Photo 19.3
Juveniles engaging in breaking and entering, frequently resulting in grand theft.
Ace Stock Limited/Alamy.

Depending on agreements with local courts, offenders might be cited to court by law enforcement officers or referred by local schools and/or by local community organizations (such as the YMCA and YWCA). Juveniles must admit guilt or plead no contest. Eligibility for acceptance into a juvenile court is typically determined by a teen court coordinator during a pretrial review of the case with the juvenile and his or her parent/guardian. If accepted, the juvenile must sign an agreement to comply with the sentence imposed by a jury of his or her peers.

All functions of the teen court are carried out by teens, with the exception of the presiding judge. They may operate quite similarly to traditional adult courts and hold hearings before a judge or jury, with the jury imposing an appropriate disposition. Another court model is to empanel a jury of youth judges who collectively evaluate the case, hear evidence, deliberate, and sentence the juvenile offender. Sentence sanctions could include restitution, verbal or written apologies to the victim, community service, attending educational workshops, writing an essay, attending a victim impact panel, attending anger management classes, and undergoing drug/alcohol evaluations and following any recommendations. A teen court coordinator monitors each case. If the juvenile is not complying, the case is referred back to the formal juvenile court for alternative disposition. Other restorative justice sanctions include restitution, work details, community service, and other creative ways of helping juvenile offenders make amends for their misbehavior.

Once the sentence is completed, the defendant may make formal application to a superior court to have his or her case/record expunged. Teen courts pursue restorative justice and reintegration of the youth to the community for community protection, competency development, and accountability. This is done by addressing the root causes of juvenile violations. Teen courts also aim to reduce recidivism. Recidivism ranges from 6 to 10 percent (depending on the program), about half the rate for juvenile offenders handled in traditional ways.

SOURCE: City of Calabasas, California, "Calabasas City Teen Court," http://www.ci.calabasas.ca.us/teen-court.html (accessed November 26, 2012).

key term

Teen court
Courts staffed by juveniles who adjudicate juvenile problems and have the authority to enforce those adjudications.

Restorative justice is seen as one way to deal with less serious juvenile delinquents and to minimize, if possible, their involvement in the juvenile justice system. One example of restorative justice at work in the juvenile delinquency dispositional phase of correcting a juvenile is the **teen court**, also known as the *youth court.* In most cases, the teen court is a diversion program for the first-time unruly and misdemeanor offenses, such as shoplifting, disorderly conduct, destruction of property, and possession of alcohol. In almost all cases, the problem being addressed is a nonviolent crime generally committed by a first-time offender. Volunteer juveniles perform the roles of prosecuting and defense attorneys, bailiff, clerk, and jury, with an adult judge presiding. Teen court demands that the delinquents accept responsibility for their actions and holds them accountable for their offenses. Teen court defendants have already admitted to their personal crimes.

Teen jurors hear the case and determine what sentence will be imposed. Sentencing conditions may include performing community service, making financial reimbursement to the victim for the damage the delinquent has inflicted, making a written or oral apology, attending educational programs, obtaining counseling, writing an essay, or performing future teen court service on another case. The jury, of course, may require multiple conditions. Successful completion of all sentence requirements results in the avoidance of a court record and conviction by the juvenile. The restorative justice principles are thus achieved: The offender must make amends to the victim and community, providing opportunities for both victims and community members to participate in the process and provide valuable input in decision making.

The Sioux Falls, South Dakota, teen court, working through Scouting America, indicates national recidivism rates from 3 to 8 percent. The Anne Arundel (Maryland) teen court reports a 10 percent recidivism rate; the teen court in Columbus, Ohio, reports a recidivism rate of 4 percent. If the disposition is not completed in a timely fashion, the case is returned to the referring agency for formal processing.[28] Correctional Practice 19.4 gives more details on teen courts.

Although the number of violent juveniles arrested in a given year is still quite small (estimates are 0.5 percent of youth), the perception of the dangerous youth remains. This accounts for the pressure to punish juveniles for their crimes by waiving them to criminal courts. People have been looking for a silver-bullet answer to juvenile crime, and the current focus is more on locking them up than on treatment.

Many experts in juvenile justice stress the need to work with families and communities to diffuse problems before they get out of hand. Most experts dismiss the "get-tough" approach with juvenile offenders as a waste of money and as an ineffective approach to increasing public safety.[29] Those who work with young offenders often see the results of a failed school system and the lure of the streets. Early intervention and working with communities and families are not always easy, but in the long run they may produce the best results.

Summary

Outline the Development of the Juvenile Justice System

The "juvenile court" emerged from the advocacy of concerned citizens who backed the development of the juvenile court in Chicago, Illinois, in the late 1800s. By 1926, every state had juvenile probation as a diversion from detention. States were quick to protect juveniles from the harshness then found in the adult courts and to render such care, custody, and treatment that ought to be provided by parents. In the 1980s, a movement to minimize constitutional guarantees provided by juvenile courts developed, leading eventually to movement for the binding over of juveniles to adult courts for punishment rather than rehabilitation. Cases brought to the U.S. Supreme Court eventually resulted in the strengthening of juvenile court procedures. For example, persons under the age of 18 cannot be executed in the United States.

Currently, juvenile courts provide services and rehabilitation and deal with status offenders, persons in need of supervision, minors in need of supervision, delinquents, and juvenile super-predators. The latter are few in number. Such courts accept the fact that juveniles need to be handled differently from adult offenders, that detention should be used as a last resort, that the rules of evidence and guilt determination must be favorable to the juvenile, and that treatment leading to rehabilitation is the ultimate goal.

List the Categories and Characteristics of Juvenile Offenders

Most juvenile offenders are from minority and working-class backgrounds, have limited resources, received inadequate tutoring and parenting, and do not do well in grade school. They are quick to drop out of school, and few have meaningful employment. They are not the super-predators popular in writings about juvenile offenders in the 1990s; they are troubled youth for whom society's services were inadequate and for whom guidance and instruction were weak. Drug experimentation decreases the involvement of juveniles with meaningful pursuit of the future and can lead to eventual detention if services and programs are not provided.

Summarize Trends in Juvenile Crime

Juvenile offenders represent a decreasing element of the overall crime problem in the nation, although they represent a significant group of arrests, particularly for the offense of arson. Yet many social and justice policies are based on emotional and irrational rather than treatment outcome concepts. Many stereotypes about juvenile offenders were generated, for whatever reason, by advocates for heavier punishment, individual deterrence through punishment, and an articulated but incorrect view of the super-predator juvenile.

One welcomed trend is the sharp reduction of crimes committed by juveniles, likened to an outbreak of lawfulness in the nation. Innovative programs and practices have emerged, such as teen courts, restorative justice, mentoring, and programs designed to strengthen the power of the family to reduce if not control the misbehavior of their sons and daughters.

Explain the Decline in Criminal Behavior as the Offender Ages

Data show that crime peaks at age 17. Younger people may be more likely to be arrested because of inexperience and ineptness in crime. Young people also commit crimes that more easily result in arrest, such as shoplifting, purse snatching, and drug selling. Also, youths tend to commit crimes in groups, and the resolution of a single crime (such as a car theft) may result in several arrests. The decline by age could also be an artifact of incapacitating repeat offenders by imposing longer sentences; such offenders then grow older in prison. Habitual offenders also seem to become less likely to be caught and arrested.

Explain How Juveniles May Be Transferred to Adult Court and Describe Issues regarding Juvenile Offenders in Adult Criminal Courts

Some states debated the wisdom of retaining such adolescents in juvenile court and began to authorize transfer to adult court through certification, automatic waiver, or direct filing by the prosecutor to the adult court.

Questions about the fairness of transfer of juveniles have arisen, and authorities disagree on the answers. Does transfer to adult court inflict conditions and punishments that are unduly harsh? Does transfer actually reduce crime in comparison to placement in juvenile court? Does transfer reduce crime through locking up serious offenders (incapacitation), deter future crime by imposing harsh punishment (individual deterrence), or signal other juveniles to not commit crime because of harsher penalties that could be inflicted (general deterrence)? Answers to these questions are not clear, and more research is needed.

Describe Community-Based Treatment Programs for Juvenile Offenders

The juvenile court accepts the proposal that community-based treatment will work for almost all juveniles who come before the court. Such treatments include warnings, curfews, community work orders, restitution, restorative justice programming, foster placement, probation, and aftercare. Most state juvenile courts practice tourniquet sentencing, but the tightened conditions imposed on the ward are designed to encourage cooperation with court-ordered treatments.

Summarize Juvenile Rights and the Cases That Have Impacted Them

In *Kent* v. *United States,* the U.S. Supreme Court noted that the child involved in certain juvenile court proceedings was deprived of constitutional rights and at the same time not given the rehabilitation promised under earlier juvenile court philosophy and statutes.

In re Gault ended the presumption that the juvenile courts were beyond the scope or purview of due process protection. With *In re Winship,* the Supreme Court held that to justify a court finding of delinquency against a juvenile, the proof must be beyond a reasonable doubt that the juvenile committed the alleged delinquent act.

McKeiver v. *Pennsylvania* implied that the due process standard of "fundamental fairness" applied; the Supreme

Court rejected the concept of trial by jury for juveniles. However, since *McKeiver,* more and more rights have been extended to the juvenile process.

Describe Juvenile Gangs

Another deleterious influence is the development of local groups of similarly situated juveniles frequently aggregating into local street gangs and, for many, continuance into adult gangs, most of which operate for the development of resources, money, and influence. The effect is probably more frequently seen contemporarily in minority neighborhoods or cultural islands, including those from agrarian or subsistence farming backgrounds. Juvenile gangs frequently sell illegal or illicit chemical compounds or drugs, are frequently armed, and strive for the pursuit of money and respect. Some will eventually seek membership in and be accepted by ongoing criminal syndicates known as adult gangs. The gang phenomenon and violence associated with gangs have helped to create a thrust to use punishment to break up, control, or eliminate gang influences.

Explain the Concept of the Super-Predator

In the 1990s, scholars and practitioners identified a new type of juvenile offender emerging as a crime problem, the super-predator. Alleged to be violent, predatory, and gang related, super-predators were defined as needing more control than that available through the juvenile court. Special laws and policies were proposed and usually adopted, but the super-predator did not emerge. It is debated whether this term could be a social construct with limited reality or another example of correctional quackery.

Key Words

common law, 418
parens patriae, 418
ward, 418
chancery court, 418
dependent, 420
neglected, 420
delinquent juveniles, 420
status offenders, 420
incorrigible (unruly) juveniles, 420
Kent v. *United States*, 420
In re Gault, 420
Juvenile Justice and Delinquency Prevention Act, 422
Roper v. *Simmons*, 422
Graham v. *Florida*, 422
diversion, 422
decriminalization, 422
deinstitutionalization, 423
decarceration, 423
statutory exclusion, 423
juvenile waiver, 423
direct filing, 423
U.S. Office of Juvenile Justice and Delinquency Prevention, 427
youth gang, 428
crack cocaine, 430
super-predator, 430
restorative justice, 430
teen court, 432
Miller v. *Alabama*, 422

Review Questions

1. Explain the concept of *parens patriae.* How does it apply today?
2. Describe and differentiate between the three kinds of children who come into contact with the juvenile courts.
3. What were the major findings in the case of *In re Gault?*
4. What are the major trends in the juvenile justice system?
5. Explain the effect of diversion on the correctional funnel for juveniles.
6. Define *restorative justice* and explain how teen courts implement those procedures.
7. What are five promising approaches to dealing with youth gangs?
8. Debate: Super-predator juveniles should be bound over to the adult courts to be tried as adults.
9. What are the most effective treatment models for juvenile offenders? The least effective?
10. What are the advantages of teen courts?
11. How can restorative justice reduce recidivism?

Application Case Studies

1. Debate: Should juveniles who commit murder be given life in prison without parole?
2. If you were a juvenile court judge and your local school superintendent asked you to assist him in reducing the truancy problem, what programs would you recommend?
3. Your local juvenile court judge wants to start a boot camp for juvenile delinquents, and you have been asked to meet with him to discuss the program. What would you tell him?
4. You have been asked by the local police chief to help design a strategy for dealing with juvenile gangs in your community. Help her design a strategy.

Endnotes

1. Only about 6 percent of juvenile gang members in adult and juvenile institutions meet the basic criteria of "super-predator." See George Knox, J. Harris, T. McCurrie, et al., *The Facts about Gang Life in America Today* (Chicago: National Gang Crime Research Center, 1997). See also Liz Ryan and Seth Turner, "New Report Highlights the Impact of Incarcerating Youth in Adult Facilities and Strategies for Reform," *American Jails* 21:2 (2007): 59–65.
2. Chancery courts date back to England's feudal era. They traditionally had broad power over the welfare of children but exercised that authority almost exclusively on behalf of minors whose property rights were in jeopardy. In America, this authority was extended to minors in danger of both personal and property attacks.
3. Irving Spergel, R. Chance, K. Ehrensaft, et al. *Gang Suppression and Intervention: Community Models* (Washington, DC: Office of Juvenile Justice and Delinquency Prevention, 1994), pp. 3–4.
4. *In re Gault*, 387 U.S. 1, 27 (1967).
5. *McKeiver v. Pennsylvania*, 403 U.S. 541 (1971).
6. See Christopher Manfredi, *The Supreme Court and Juvenile Justice* (Lawrence: University Press of Kansas, 1998).
7. Robert Meier and Gilbert Geis, *Victimless Crimes?* (Los Angeles: Roxbury Publishing, 1997). See also Erik Eckholm, "Juveniles Facing Lifelong Terms despite Rulings," *New York Times*, http://www.nytimes.com/2014/01/20/us/juveniles-facing-lifelong-terms-despite-rulings.html?_r=0 (accessed September 15, 2014).
8. Philip Secret and J. Johnston, "The Effect of Race in Juvenile Justice Decision-Making in Nebraska," *Justice Quarterly* 14:3 (1997): 445–478.
9. *In re Gault*. See also Adhikain Para and Karaspang Pambata, "Research on the Situation of Children in Conflict with the Law in Selected Metra Manilia Cities," http://resourcecentre.savethechildren.se/sites/default/files/documents/3147.pdf (accessed September 15, 2014).
10. Liz Ryan and Jason Ziedenberg, "The Consequences Aren't Minor—The Impact of Trying Youth as Adults and Strategies of Reform," http://www.justicepolicy.org/images/.../07-03_C4YJConsequences_JJ.pdf (accessed September 15, 2014).
11. Benjamin Adams and Sean Addle, "Delinquency Cases Waived to Criminal Court, 2009," http://www.ojjdp.gov/pubs/239080.pdf (accessed September 15, 2014).
12. American Correctional Association, *2012 Directory of Adult and Juvenile Correctional Departments, Institutions, Agencies, and Probation and Parole Authorities* (Alexandria, VA: American Correctional Association, 2012). It should also be noted that although most states consider anyone under the age of 18 a juvenile, some states, such as New York and North Carolina, use under 17 years of age.
13. Bureau of Justice Statistics, "Criminal Case Processing Statutes," http://www.ojp.usdoj.gov/bjs/cases.htm#juvenil (accessed February 8, 2008).
14. Federal Bureau of Investigation, "Uniform Crime Report 2012," http://www.fbi.gov/about-us/cjis/ucr/crime-in-the-u.s/2012/crime-in-the-u.s.-2012 (accessed September 15, 2014).
15. Howard Snyder and Melissa Sickmund, "Juvenile Offenders and Victims: 2006 National Report," http://ojjdp.ncjrs.org/ojstatbb.nr2006/downloads/NR2006.pdf (accessed February 8, 2008).
16. Carl McCurley and Howard N. Snyder, "Victims of Violent Juvenile Crime," *Juvenile Justice Bulletin*, July 2004; Paul Harms and Howard Snyder, "Trends in the Murder of Juveniles: 1980–2000," *Juvenile Justice Bulletin*, September 2004; *Juvenile Offenders and Victims: 1995 National Report* (Washington, DC: Office of Juvenile Justice Delinquency and Prevention, 1995). The 2006 data are from Office of Juvenile Justice and Delinquency Prevention, "Statistical Briefing Book 2006," http://www.ojjdp.ncjrs.org/ojstatbb/index.html (accessed February 8, 2008).
17. Edward Mulvey, "Highlights from Pathways to Desistance: A Longitudinal Study of Serious Adolescent

Offenders," https://ncjrs.gov/pdffiles1/ojjdp/230971.pdf (accessed September 14, 2014).

18. See the excellent review by David Farrington, "Predictors, Causes and Correlates of Male Youth Violence," in *Youth Violence: Crime and Justice, a Review of Research,* vol. 24, ed. M. Tonry and M. H. Moore (Chicago: University of Chicago Press, 1998), pp. 421–475; National Institute of Corrections, "Promoting Public Safety Using Effective Interventions with Offenders," http://www.nicic.org (accessed September 2001); Lawrence Sherman et al., *Preventing Crime: What Works, What Doesn't, What's Promising* (Washington, DC: National Institute of Justice, 1998); and Margit Weisner, D. M. Capaladi, and H. K. Kim, "Arrest Trajectories across a 12-Year Span," *Criminology* 45:4 (2007): 835–864. Evidence-based correctional practices are explored in great detail in the December 2007 issue of *Corrections Today* 69:6.
19. Lawrence Sherman, "Preventing Crime: What Works, What Doesn't, What's Promising. Office of Juvenile Justice and Delinquency Prevention, Highlights of the 2004 National Youth Gang Surveys," https://www.ncjrs.gov/works/wholedoc.htm (accessed September 15, 2014).
20. Jeffrey Butts and D. Conners, *The Juvenile Court's Response to Violent Offenders: 1985–1989* (Washington, DC: U.S. Department of Justice, 1993), pp. 14–15.
21. Arlen Egley and James C. Howell, *Major Highlights of the 2012 National Youth Gang Survey,* OJJDP Fact Sheet (Washington, DC: Office of Juvenile Justice and Delinquency Prevention, 2013).
22. Barbara Allen-Hagen and M. Sickmund, *Juveniles and Violence: Juvenile Offending and Victimization* (Washington, DC: U.S. Department of Justice, 1993), p. 4.
23. Arlen Egley, James Howell, and Aline Major, eds., *National Youth Gang Survey Summary: 1991–2001* (Washington, DC: Office of Juvenile Justice and Delinquency Prevention, 2006).
24. *In re Gault.*
25. Arlen Egley and James C. Howell, *Highlights of the 2011 National Youth Gang Survey*, Juvenile Justice Fact Sheet (Washington, DC: Office of Juvenile Justice and Delinquency Prevention, 2013).
26. Peter Hamill, "Only Man Seems Capable," *New York Post*, April 25, 1989.
27. Restorative Justice Online, "Introduction," http://www.restorativejustice.org (accessed September 15, 2014).
28. Manuel Martinez, "Teen Court," http://www.fccourts.org/DRJ/teenct.html (accessed February 16, 2008). See also Brandi Miller, "Low Recidivism Rate for Teen Court Participants," http://www.siouxempireunitedway.org/NewsReleases/2007/TeenCourt.pdf (accessed February 17, 2008).
29. Stephen Gluck, "Wayward Youth, Super Predator: An Evolutionary Tale of Juvenile Delinquency from the 1950s to the Present," *Corrections Today* 59:3 (1997): 62–66. See also "The Myth of the Super Predator," http://rethinkingreentry.blogspot.com/2014/04/the-myth-of-super-predator.html, and http://rethinkingreentry.blogspot.com/2014/04/the-myth-of-super-predator.html (accessed September 2014). Linked to these URLs are a video and a larger article.

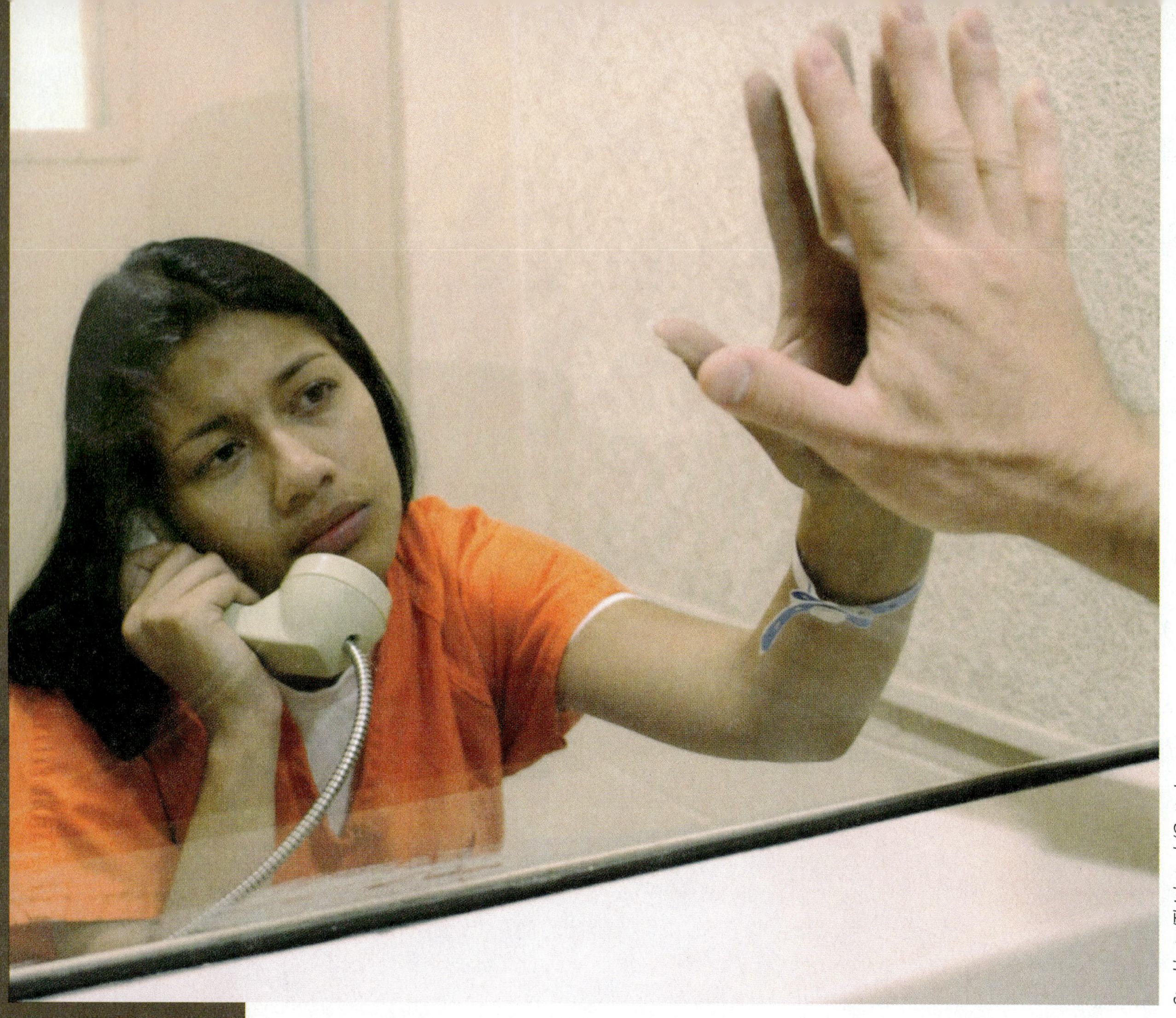

Stockbyte/Thinkstock/Getty Images.

Objectives

- Describe the types of facilities that house juvenile offenders.
- Explain the role and characteristics of juvenile group homes and why there is no standard definition.
- Describe the effectiveness of group homes and explore some of the reasons that these facilities can actually increase failure for the youth placed in them.
- Describe juvenile detention centers, their purpose, how they are used, and steps being taken to reduce detention of youth.
- Explore the use of residential treatment centers and some of the different types of programs they offer.
- Describe training schools and the types of programs offered in these facilities.
- Explore sexual victimization of incarcerated youth and learn about the scope of the problem.
- Explain some of the ways states are attempting to reduce the number of youth housed in training facilities.

chapter 20 Facilities for Juveniles

Outline

Youth Held in Custody and Types of Facilities

Juvenile Group Homes

- Lack of a Standard Definition
- Characteristics of Group Homes
- Effectiveness of Group Homes

Juvenile Detention Centers

- Reducing Juvenile Detention

Residential Treatment Centers

Training Schools for Youth

- Institutional Treatment and Rehabilitation
- Sexual Victimization of Incarcerated Youth

Reducing Commitments

"Youth may be placed in a group home for a variety of reasons, including parental abuse or neglect, behavioral problems, and delinquent behavior."

—Edward J. Latessa

Overview

The previous chapter reviewed the types of juvenile offenders and some of the crimes that they commit. This chapter focuses on the types of correctional facilities that are used to house them. These range from group homes that sometimes resemble family living arrangements to secure institutions that are more like adult prison facilities. Although serious juvenile offenders can legally be housed in the adult system, this chapter centers on those facilities that have been specifically designed to house juvenile offenders. This chapter also looks at some of the more creative ways that states have reduced their institutional populations as well as some of the programs and treatments offered within these facilities.

YOUTH HELD IN CUSTODY AND TYPES OF FACILITIES

The Office of Juvenile Justice and Delinquency Prevention has identified a wide range of juvenile facilities, including group homes, detention shelters, camps, training schools, and residential treatment facilities. Detention centers tend to be locally operated, training schools tend to be state facilities, and group homes tend to be privately managed. Table 20.1 shows the number of different types of juvenile facilities in the United States. Detention centers, group homes, and residential treatment centers make up about 95 percent of all juvenile facilities. Table 20.2 shows the number of facilities as well as the number of youth. The most recent census found more than 66,000 youth held in juvenile facilities, with the smallest (1 to 10 residents) accounting for more than 32 percent of all facilities but only 5 percent of all youth held in custody. Conversely, the largest facilities (over 201 residents) held 16 percent of all youth but represented only 2 percent of all facilities. The good news is that, overall, the juvenile custody population dropped 18 percent from 2008 to 2010 and over 34 percent between 2006 and 2011, and the trend appears to be continuing. Figure 20.1 shows the number of youth held in juvenile correctional facilities between 1998 and 2010.

table **20.1** **Number and Type of Juvenile Facilities**

Type	Number of Facilities
Detention center	705
Shelter	137
Reception center	72
Group home	528
Ranch/wilderness camp	68
Training school	188
Residential treatment center	763
Total	2,111

SOURCE: S. Hockenberry, M. Sickmund, and A. Sladky, *Juvenile Residential Facility Census, 2010: Selected Findings* (Washington, DC: U.S. Department of Justice, Office of Juvenile Justice and Delinquency Prevention, 2013), http://www.reginfo.gov/public/do/DownloadDocument?documentID=423760&version=0 (accessed February 14, 2014).

table **20.2** **Facility Size and Number of Youth Residents**

Facility Size	Number of Facilities	Number of Youth
1–10	676	3,500
11–20	481	6,220
21–50	563	16,340
51–100	243	15,705
101–200	108	13,928
201+	40	10,629
Total:	1,868	66,322

SOURCE: S. Hockenberry, M. Sickmund, and A. Sladky, *Juvenile Residential Facility Census, 2010: Selected Findings* (Washington, DC: U.S. Department of Justice, Office of Juvenile Justice and Delinquency Prevention, 2013), http://www.reginfo.gov/public/do/DownloadDocument?documentID=423760&version=0 (accessed February 14, 2014).

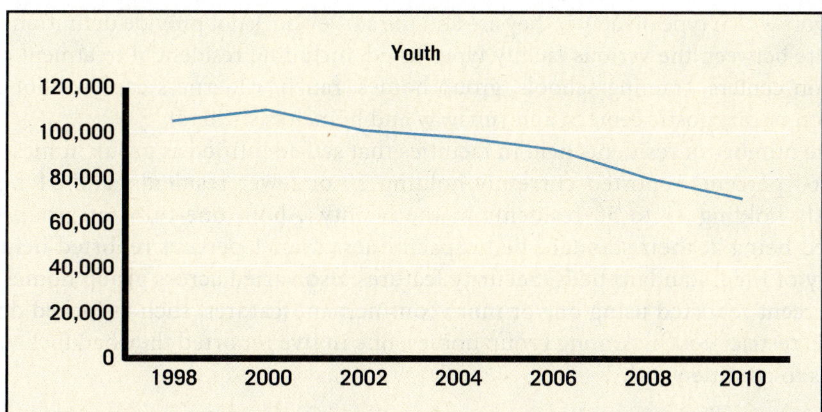

figure 20.1

Number of Youth Held in Juvenile Facilities, 1998–2010.

SOURCE: Adapted from M. Sickmund, *Juveniles in Residential Placement, 1997–2008, OJJDP Fact Sheet* (Washington, DC: Office of Juvenile Justice and Delinquency Prevention, 2010), and S. Hockenberry, M. Sickmund, and A. Sladky, *Juvenile Residential Facility Census, 2010: Selected Findings* (Washington, DC: U.S. Department of Justice, Office of Juvenile Justice and Delinquency Prevention, 2013), http://www.reginfo.gov/public/do/DownloadDocument?documentID=423760&version=0 (accessed February 14, 2014).

JUVENILE GROUP HOMES

In the juvenile justice system, halfway houses are often referred to as group homes. A group home is a residential placement for juveniles that operates in a homelike setting in which a number of unrelated youth live for varying time periods. Juvenile **group homes** tend to be much smaller than adult halfway houses, and a typical group homes houses between 5 and 16 youth. Some group homes operate similar to adult halfway houses with a program director and staff, whereas others may have one set of "house parents" or a rotating staff. Some therapeutic or treatment group homes also employ specially trained staff to assist youth with emotional or behavioral difficulties. Group homes are considered less restrictive than juvenile detention centers, and they are generally staff-secured as opposed to locked facilities. There are generally fewer restraints on how youth can interact with the community, and they often attend school in the community.

key term

Group home

A residential placement option that operates as a homelike setting in which a number of unrelated youth live for varying time periods.

Lack of a Standard Definition

Group homes typically fall under the category of residential group care. Although there are differences between group homes and other types of residential care (such as residential treatment centers), the research literature provides few clear differentiations between the different types of placements used for juveniles and at-risk youth.[1] In the **Juvenile Residential Facilities Census**,[2] a biennial survey conducted by the Office of Juvenile Justice and Delinquency Prevention, over 100 facilities self-identified as both residential treatment centers and group homes (the group home/residential treatment center combination was the most common facility-type combination).[3] The lack of standardized definitions and the variability in program characteristics make it problematic to try to generalize findings from evaluation research. Youth may be placed in a group home for a variety of reasons, including parental abuse or neglect, behavioral problems, and delinquent behavior.

key term

Juvenile Residential Facility Census

A biennial survey conducted by the Office of Juvenile Justice and Delinquency Prevention to gauge the number and use of youth residential placements.

Characteristics of Group Homes

The Juvenile Residential Facility Census found that more than 660 facilities identified themselves as group homes. Group homes constituted 27 percent of all reporting facilities and held 10 percent of juvenile offenders in placement on the census date.[4] Group homes and residential treatment centers outnumbered all other types of facilities included on the survey (although this finding may be misleading, as residential facilities are asked to self-report which type of facility they are and the survey does not provide definitions to differentiate between the various facility types listed, including residential treatment centers, detention centers, training schools, group homes, ranch/wilderness camps, boot camps, reception or diagnostic centers, and runaway and homeless shelters).

The number of residents held in facilities that self-identified as group homes varied. Most (64 percent) reported currently holding 10 or fewer residents, and 31 reported currently holding 11 to 50 residents in the facility. About one-third of group homes reported being at their standard bed capacity; less than 1 percent reported being over capacity of their standard beds. Security features also varied across group homes. Thirteen percent reported using one or more confinement features, such as locked doors or gates, to restrict youth. Among group homes, one in five reported they had locked doors or gates to confine youth.[5]

Effectiveness of Group Homes

Given the diversity of the populations served and the lack of standardization for group homes for juveniles, it is difficult to evaluate their effectiveness. Some studies suggest that adolescents placed in therapeutic group homes do experience positive effects on their behavior while they are in homes, but there is little, if any, evidence to suggest that treatment outcomes are sustained over time.[6] Overall, there is little research to support the overall effectiveness of group homes, and the research available does have several limitations. One explanation for the disappointing long-term outcomes of therapeutic group homes may be the psychological profiles of their clients. Group homes are frequently seen as the "last stop" before secure detention, and the youth referred to them often suffer from serious mental or behavioral problems that have prevented successful placement in other settings.[7] To increase the likelihood of long-term positive effects, it is important for group homes to be seen as only one step in a continuum of care—a continuum that emphasizes sustained treatment after discharge from the home.[8]

In addition, many researchers believe that small group settings that encourage fraternization among delinquents may actually promote disruptive and deviant behavior.[9] Association with deviant peers within a group home setting could increase antisocial attitudes and problem behaviors, leading to a variety of negative outcomes for youth through adolescence and into adulthood. Additional rigorous research is needed to determine the effectiveness of group homes to address problem behaviors of youth and reduce risks of delinquency and the possible deleterious effects of placement with deviant peers.

JUVENILE DETENTION CENTERS

key term

Juvenile detention center ("juvie")
An institution where youth are detained when suspected of a juvenile offense, awaiting hearing or case disposition, found to be a youthful offender, or for treatment or rehabilitation. Also called "juvies."

Juvenile detention centers, also called juvenile halls in California (or "**juvies**"), are usually reserved for shorter periods of incarceration, although there are some exceptions.[10] For many youth, the detention center is the first stop following an arrest. For some youth, the stay can be hours or until a parent arrives to take them home, whereas for others the stay may be considerably longer. Some may be sentenced to detention; however, for many youth, this is where they are held pending a hearing in juvenile court. These facilities are usually secure and can include programs, school, and other activities associated with a correction facility. Most these facilities are locally operated, although some are regional facilities that serve multiple counties.

Reducing Juvenile Detention

Evidence suggests that even a short stay in detention can have a harmful effect on youth, and although some high-risk youth may need to be in detention, the vast majority of youth detained are nonviolent offenders.[11] In order to assist jurisdictions in reducing the use of detention, in 1992 the Annie E. Casey Foundation launched the **Juvenile Detention Alternatives Initiative (JDAI)** to reverse the troubling trends in juvenile justice and demonstrate that juvenile detention and corrections populations could be substantially and safely reduced.[12] JDAI has developed some core strategies to assist in reducing the use of detention. These include the following:

- **Collaboration** between the major juvenile justice agencies, other governmental entities, and community organizations is essential.
- **Use of accurate data**, both to diagnose the system's problems and proclivities and to assess the impact of various reforms, is critical.
- **Objective admissions criteria and instruments** must be developed to replace subjective decision making at all points where choices to place children in secure custody are made.
- **New or enhanced nonsecure alternatives to detention** must be implemented in order to increase the options available for arrested youth. These programs must be careful to target only youth who would otherwise be locked up. Whenever possible, they should be based in those neighborhoods where detention cases are concentrated and operated by local organizations.
- **Case processing reforms** must be introduced to expedite the flow of cases through the system. These changes reduce lengths of stay in custody, expand the availability of nonsecure program slots, and ensure that interventions with youth are timely and appropriate.
- **Special detention cases**—youth in custody as a result of probation violations, writs, and warrants, as well as those awaiting placement—must be reexamined and new practices implemented to minimize their presence in secure facilities.
- **Reducing racial disparities** requires specific strategies (in addition to those just listed) aimed at eliminating bias and ensuring a level playing field for youth of color.
- **Improving conditions of confinement** is most likely to occur when facilities are routinely inspected by knowledgeable individuals applying rigorous protocols and ambitious standards.

Through the efforts of JDAI, many jurisdictions have significantly reduced the number of youth held in detention centers, thus lessening their harmful effects on juveniles and saving a considerable amount of money.

key term

Juvenile Detention Alternatives Initiative (JDAI)
A program of the Annie E. Casey Foundation designed to help jurisdictions reduce the use of detention.

RESIDENTIAL TREATMENT CENTERS

Although some group homes are also identified as **residential treatment centers**, many of these facilities are larger and in some cases secure. For example, in Ohio there are 12 **community correctional facilities (CCFs)** established throughout the state. These facilities are designed to provide a dispositional alternative to juvenile and family court judges when committing youth adjudicated for a felony offense. These facilities range from 16 to 50 beds and include both secure and staff-secure facilities, with the average stay of juveniles being about six months. These facilities offer a wide range of programs, including school; group, family, and individual counseling; and treatment for sexual offenders, chemical dependency, mental health, anger, aggression, and thinking errors. Research on the Ohio CCFs reveals that those facilities with high-quality programs were more effective at reducing recidivism. In addition, those CCFs that served higher-risk youth, targeted dynamic risk factors with cognitive-behavioral modalities, and employed trained and qualified staff were found have stronger effects on recidivism than those that did not.[13] Correctional Practice 20.1 describes Ohio's Youth Development Center.

key term

Residential treatment centers
Centers that house youths with significant psychiatric, psychological, behavioral, or substance abuse problems who have been unsuccessful in outpatient treatment or have proved too ill or unruly to be housed in foster care, day treatment programs, and other nonsecure environments but who do not yet merit commitment to a psychiatric hospital or secure correctional facility.

key term

Community correctional facility (CFC)
A form of residential treatment center found in Ohio that offers a wide range of programs and services to youth.

key term

Juvenile camps and ranches Residential treatment centers in California that offer a wide range of programs and services to youth.

One form of residential programs for youth can be found in California, with 28 counties in the state operating 67 **juvenile camps and ranches**. Los Angeles has the most, with 19, and in 2013 there were about 4,500 youth served in these facilities statewide. These county camps and ranches serve primarily a juvenile population that has been adjudicated (sentenced) by the court to detention. They provide one-third of county juvenile probation beds.

correctional **practice 20.1**

The Youth Development Center

The Youth Development Center (YDC) is a 16-bed residential treatment center for boys operated by Lighthouse for Youth located in Cincinnati, Ohio. YDC is a therapeutic community-based program for teenage boys who suffer from emotional or behavioral disorders or who have been unsuccessful in other out-of-home placements. Residents focus on developing age-appropriate life skills as well as addressing issues regarding their emotional and behavioral well-being. YDC makes every effort to involve families when they are available so that youth can work toward reunification or a sustained positive family relationship.

Program Philosophy YDC promotes a holistic and collaborative therapeutic approach to helping adolescents recognize and achieve their full potential, becoming healthy, responsible and self-reliant individuals. YDC works with youth and their families to identify strengths in their relationships and make commitments to change. The primary goal is to provide a safe, therapeutic environment for male youth until they return home or are stepped down to a less restrictive placement.

Profile of Youth The following is the current profile of youth and families in YDC:

- Residents are male adolescents ages 12 to 18.
- Many residents have histories of sexual and/or physical abuse and/or neglect.
- Many residents have histories of multiple unsuccessful placements.
- Many residents have histories of criminal or delinquent behavior, including running away and truancy.
- Typically, youth are victims of physical and sexual abuse and/or may suffer from emotional and mental health problems, including depression, suicidal behavior, self-mutilating behavior, sexual acting out, borderline and other personality disorders, posttraumatic stress disorder, anxiety disorders, conduct disorders, oppositional-defiant disorder, and developmental disabilities.
- Families often lack support and have few resources for meeting children's needs. They are often single-parent families that provide inadequate structure and supervision. Family mental health issues include depression, personality disorders, substance abuse disorders, and chronic stress.
- Social skills deficits of residents include poor communication, misinterpretation of social cues, poor peer and interpersonal relationship skills, difficulty dealing with disappointment and loss, and lack of self-sufficiency skills.
- Self-management issues of residents include poor self-concept, impulse control difficulties, anger management deficits, poor problem-solving and decision-making skills, and lack of effective coping skills.
- School difficulties of residents include academic and behavioral problems, school failure, learning disabilities, developmental disabilities, and truancy.

Daily Activity Schedule:

Monday through Friday	
6:00–8:00 a.m.	Wake up, shower, clean room, eat breakfast
7:00–9:00 a.m.	Residents out to school or educational program
2:00–4:00 p.m.	Return from school, room visit, laundry, free time, snack
3:00–7:00 p.m.	Scheduled individual and family counseling sessions
4:30–6:00 p.m.	Monday: Group Therapy
	Thursday: Group Therapy
	Wednesday: House Meeting
	Friday: Recreation

SOURCE: Thanks to the Lighthouse for Youth for providing the information. This feature was created by the authors.

TRAINING SCHOOLS FOR YOUTH

The equivalent of the adult prison is the **training school for youth**, also called juvenile correctional facilities. These institutions are usually reserved for youth who have been committed by a judge for a serious offense, although some states still incarcerate juveniles who have committed misdemeanors.

key term

Training school for youth
A secure correctional institution for the custody, control, and reeducation of juvenile delinquents, usually housing more serious offenders sentenced to incarceration.

In the landmark *In re Gault* decision, the U.S. Supreme Court emphasized the reality of institutionalization for a juvenile:

> Ultimately, however, we confront the reality. A boy is charged with misconduct. The boy is committed to an institution where he may be restrained of liberty for years. It is of no constitutional consequence and of limited practical meaning that the institution to which he is committed is called an Industrial School. The fact of the matter is that, however euphemistic the title, a "receiving home" or an "industrial school" for juveniles is an institution of confinement in which the child is incarcerated for a greater or lesser time. His world becomes "a building with whitewashed walls, regimented routine and institutional hours." Instead of mother and father and sisters and brothers and friends and classmates, guards, custodians, state employees people his world, and delinquents confined with him for anything from waywardness to rape and homicide.[14]

Facilities designated exclusively for juvenile incarceration often resemble adult prisons; however, given the population, there are some significant differences. In adult institutions, the emphasis is on custody, and the same preoccupation with security can also shape the programs and general environment in juvenile facilities; however, most have a mission that requires rehabilitation and services.

The youths are placed in dormitory-style housing (or single cells in some cases), often with the fixed furniture and dreary interiors that are typical of adult institutions. The average cost for juvenile institutional confinement is more than $250 per resident per day, although the cost of small and highly specialized state facilities can easily exceed $600 per resident per day.[15] A list of the 10 states with the highest juvenile correctional populations is given in Table 20.3, and Correctional Practice 20.2 provides one youth's perspective on his stay in an Ohio correctional facility.

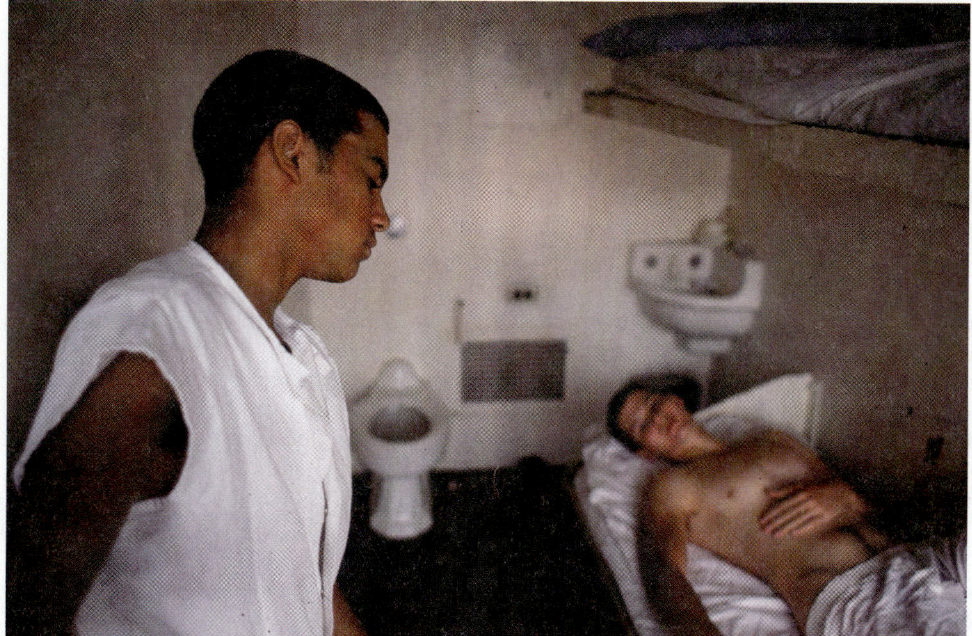

Photo 20.1

Juveniles are treated like adult offenders in some of the old custody control facilities, made to feel small and unworthy like the "scum" in prison.
Andrew Lichtenstein/Corbis News/Corbis.

table 20.3 **Ten States with the Highest Number of Juveniles under Supervision**

State	Juveniles under Supervision
Georgia	3,708
Maryland	1,756
Tennessee	1,364
California	1,158
Massachusetts	1,133
Texas	1,009
Colorado	970
Utah	943
South Carolina	866
Oregon	738

SOURCE: American Correctional Association, *2012 Directory of Adult and Juvenile Correctional Departments, Institutions, Agencies, and Probation and Parole Authorities* (Alexandria, VA: American Correctional Association, 2012), pp. 50–51.

Institutional Treatment and Rehabilitation

Over 40 years ago, the Commission on Criminal Justice Standards and Goals offered extensive guidelines and standards to assist the juvenile institutions in their reexamination of educational and vocational training programs.[16] Unfortunately, in spite of those standards and guidelines, actual experience has shown that many youths committed to juvenile institutions are just "doing time."[17] Instead of being a constructive and maturing experience, incarceration in a juvenile institution is likely to be harmful for the juvenile. All juvenile institutions require youth to attend school, but beyond that, the treatment and services offered vary considerably from state to state and facility to facility. One example of a state that is trying to improve the treatment and services offered to incarcerated youth is California.

correctional **practice 20.2**

From One Youth's Perspective

Youth J shares some of his thoughts about his stay at an Ohio Department of Youth Services correctional facility and parole experience:

I spent 20 months at Indian River JCF, and I was on parole supervision with the Cleveland Region for about 3 months. What made a difference for me was the staff that actually noticed the good things I was doing. It made a difference when staff didn't treat me like an inmate and treated me with respect. Some treated me like I was family. This made me comfortable. This made my days better. This made me want to keep doing good. While I was in a facility, the mentoring program gave me a sense of leadership. The Youth Council motivated me to be a good leader and do the right thing. My school experience was difficult but also nice. It made a difference having teachers who looked out for me. They have a hard job with things being crazy, but if you want to learn, they will make sure that they give you attention. My Transition Coordinator helped me fill out my FAFSA and create a resume. Now I'm in college. One of the things I learned is that I am responsible. I don't need people to tell me what to do; I can just be responsible for myself. My mom helped me during all of this. She sent me letters every day. When there was pressure to be part of a gang, she encouraged me to stay strong and do the right thing. The one message that I have for staff is this: don't judge a book by its cover. Some kids look like troublemakers. Look past that. If you take the time, and don't overlook a person, then they will be able to do great things.

SOURCE: The authors would like to thank the Ohio Department of Youth Services for sharing this material and granting permission to use it.

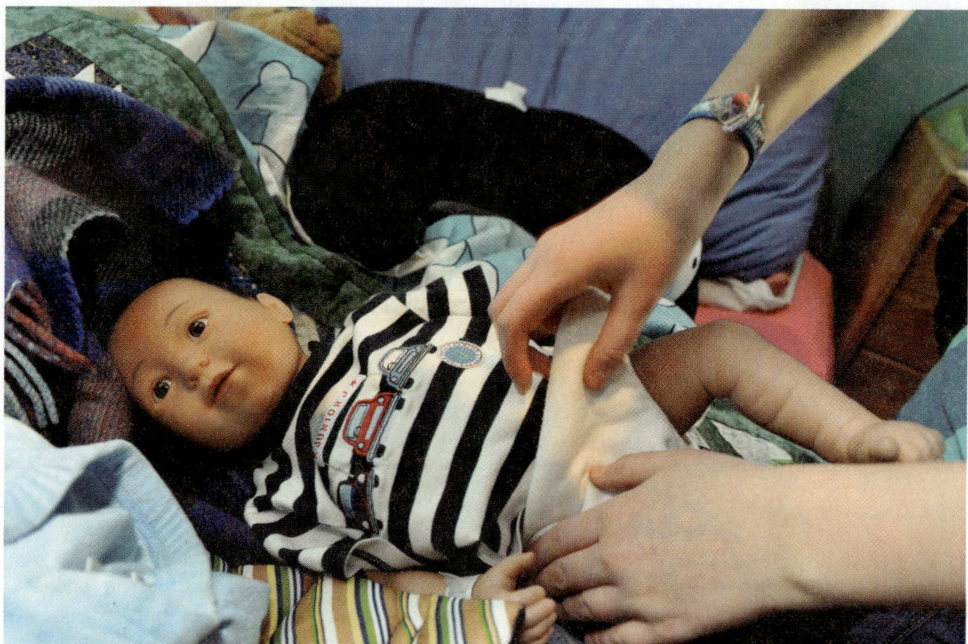

Photo 20.2

Parenting skills are learned with a mechanical baby in the Baby, Think Twice program.
Paula Solloway/Alamy.

After years of reform through court intervention, the California Division of Juvenile Justice (DJJ) has dramatically reduced the number of youth incarcerated, closed facilities, and improved the programs and services offered youth. The DJJ provides academic and vocational education, treatment programs that address violent and criminogenic behavior, sex offender behavior, substance abuse and mental health problems, and medical care while attempting to maintain a safe and secure environment conducive to learning. Treatment is guided by a series of plans supervised by the Alameda Superior Court as per a settlement agreement in a lawsuit known as *Farrell*.

In California's DJJ, youth are assigned living units based on their age, gender, risk of institutional violence, and specialized treatment needs. The population in each living unit is limited, and staffing levels ensure that each youth receives effective attention and

Photo 20.3

Juvenile offenders in Los Angeles work with children with severe disabilities at the El Camino School as part of their jail time and rehabilitation program.
Tony Savino/The Image Works.

rehabilitative programming. The framework for DJJ's programs is the Integrated Behavior Treatment Model. It is designed to reduce institutional violence and future criminal behavior by teaching anticriminal attitudes and providing personal skills for youth to better manage their environment. DJJ staff from every professional discipline work as a team to assess the unique needs of each youth and to develop an individualized treatment program to address them. Through collaboration with the youth, the team administers a case plan that takes advantage of each youth's personal strengths to maximize treatment in other areas of the individual's life to reduce the risk of reoffending.[18]

Another promising program, focusing on cognitive-behavioral programming, is described in Correctional Practice 20.3.

correctional **practice 20.3**

Treatment of Juveniles in Custody

The New Directions Program is a 24-bed cognitive behavioral program for higher-risk youth revoked from parole and returned to the Ohio Department of Youth Services. The program is designed to provide a secure, intensive, high-fidelity, evidence-based treatment program and to reduce recidivism rates. Each youth receives over 200 hours of programming in structured groups designed to teach new pro-social skills, and each youth is expected to meet defined behavioral goals as he progresses through the program. Therapeutic targets include the following dynamic criminogenic needs:

- Teaching and practicing noncriminal alternative behavior in risky situations
- Building problem-solving, self-management, anger management, and coping skills
- Reducing antisocial cognitions, enhancing recognition of risky thinking and feelings, and developing alternative less risky thinking and feelings
- Reducing associations with antisocial peers by teaching youth to recognize and avoid negative influences (people, places, things), practicing new skills (like being assertive instead of passive), and maintaining relationships without getting into trouble
- Reducing conflict, building nurturance and/or caring positive relationships, and improving communication and problem-solving skills with family members
- Enhancing school performance, rewards, and satisfaction
- Enhancing involvement and satisfaction in pro-social leisure activities
- Reducing the personal and interpersonal supports for substance-abusing behavior and enhancing alternatives to substance abuse

Initial data indicated that the program reduced recidivism as well as institutional misconduct. As shown in the accompanying tables, recidivism and institutional misconduct were reduced by 46 percent. In general, the medium-risk groups were more successful in terms of program completion. The successful termination rate for community-based correctional facilities was 79 percent but only 56 percent for the halfway-house group.

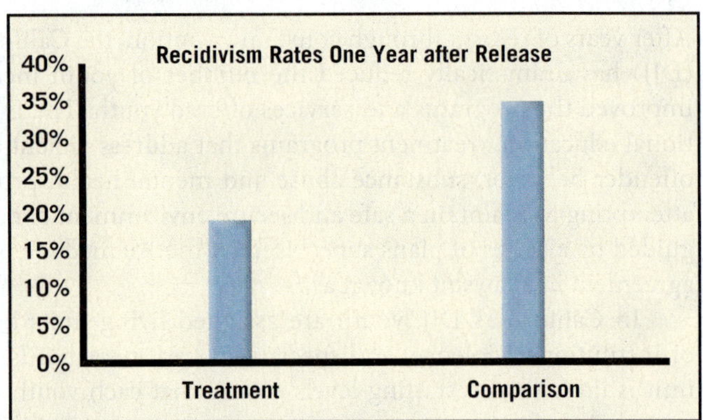

Recidivism Rates One Year after Release

SOURCE: Edward Latessa, *Evaluation of New Directions Program* (Cincinnati, OH: School of Criminal Justice, University of Cincinnati, 2013).

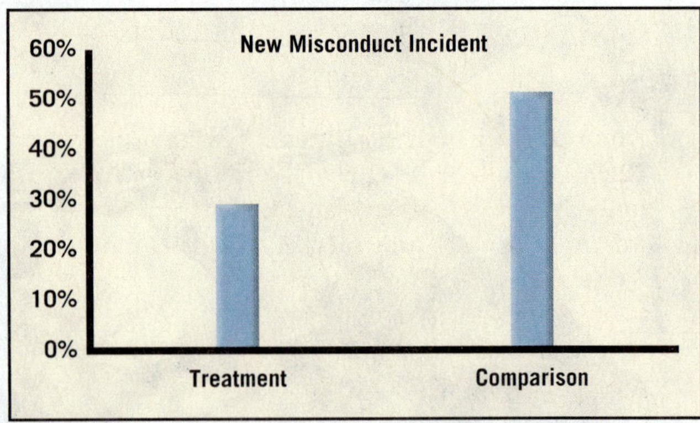

Institutional Misconduct

SOURCE: Edward Latessa, *Evaluation of New Directions Program* (Cincinnati, OH: School of Criminal Justice, University of Cincinnati, 2013).

correctional practice 20.4

The Missouri Model

In the early 1970s, Jerome Miller, director of juvenile justice in Massachusetts, took the bold step of closing the state's training schools and juvenile facilities. In the early 1980s, the state of Missouri followed suit and also closed its troubled training schools and large juvenile facilities and decided to build a different system. Known as the Missouri Model, this approach emphasizes small regional residential facilities closer to a youth's home and a philosophy of treatment rather than punishment. The Missouri Model is based on some key principles:

1. Small and non-prison-like facilities, close to home
2. Individual care within a group treatment model
3. Safety through relationships and supervision, not correctional coercion
4. Building skills for success
5. Families as partners
6. Focus on aftercare

Research shows that behavior is greatly improved, including fewer assaults, less use of restraints and isolation, and reduced recidivism.

SOURCE: Adapted from Richard A. Mendel, *The Missouri Model: Reinventing the Practice of Rehabilitating Youthful Offenders* (Baltimore, MD: The Annie E. Casey Foundation, 2010).

Other states have tried to reduce or eliminate large facilities, most notably Massachusetts and Missouri. Correctional Practice 20.4 describes the **Missouri Model** of treatment. Many are also working to improve the treatment and services offered to incarcerated youth, but much remains to be done.

key term

Missouri Model
An approach developed in Missouri that involves the use of small residential facilities that provide treatment in a homelike environment.

Sexual Victimization of Incarcerated Youth

As part of the 2012 Bureau of Justice Statistics National Survey of Youth in Custody, researchers examined the prevalence of **sexual victimization** in juvenile institutions. The major findings included the following:[19]

key term

Sexual victimization
An umbrella term that includes any nonconsensual sexual activity that is committed by force or fear or mental or physical incapacitation, including through the use of alcohol or drugs.

- An estimated 9.5 percent of adjudicated youth in state juvenile facilities and state contract facilities (representing 1,720 youth nationwide) reported experiencing one or more incidents of sexual victimization by another youth or staff in the past 12 months or since admission if less than 12 months.
- About 2.5 percent of youth (450 nationwide) reported an incident involving another youth, and 7.7 percent (1,390) reported an incident involving facility staff.
- An estimated 3.5 percent of youth reported having sex or other sexual contact with facility staff as a result of force or other forms of coercion, whereas 4.7 percent of youth reported sexual contact with staff without any force, threat, or explicit form of coercion.
- Among state juvenile facilities, the rate of sexual victimization declined from 12.6 percent in 2008–2009 (when the first survey was conducted) to 9.9 percent in 2012. The decline in state facilities was linked to a decline in staff sexual misconduct with force (declining from 4.5 percent of youth in 2008–2009 to 3.6 percent in 2012) and staff sexual misconduct without force (declining from 6.7 percent to 5.1 percent).
- Of males, 8.2 percent reported sexual activity with staff, and 2.8 percent of females reported sexual activity with staff.
- Of females, 5.4 percent reported forced sexual activity with another youth at a facility, and 2.2 percent of males reported forced sexual activity with another youth at a facility.
- White youth reported sexual victimization by another youth (4.0 percent) more often than black youth (1.4 percent) or Hispanic youth (2.1 percent).

key term

Posttraumatic stress disorder (PTSD)
A mental health condition that is triggered by a terrifying event; a common disorder of juveniles in detention.

correctional practice 20.5

Posttraumatic Stress Disorder, Trauma, and Comorbid Psychiatric Disorders among Detained Youth

There are approximately 2.11 million arrests of youth annually. Youth means both children and teenagers but not adults. Altogether, these arrests account for one in six of all violent crime and more than one in four property crime arrests. It should be no surprise than over 80,000 youth are detained on any given day. The percentage of youth with psychiatric disorders is a major public health issue. In brief, some two-thirds of young males and three-quarters of young females in juvenile detention have one or more psychiatric disorders.

Posttraumatic stress disorder (PTSD) may be more common in youth in the juvenile justice system than in those in the free society. This anxiety disorder can be caused by traumatic events, such as severe injury or threat of death, or witnessing someone being killed. Presenting symptoms may be emotional numbing, increased arousal, flashbacks, and avoidance of reminders and scenes of the trauma. The deeper the youth's entry into the juvenile justice system, the higher the proportion of PTSD. One-third of incarcerated male youth have PTSD.

PTSD often occurs with other psychiatric disorders, known as comorbid disorders. Youth with comorbid disorders exhibit significantly more health and behavioral problems than other youth and have greater impaired interpersonal relations with family, peers, and the justice system. Some frequent comorbid psychiatric disorders include substance abuse disorder, depression, and conduct disorders. Those with comorbid disorders are more difficult to treat and may act out against authority.

A significant study of detained youth was released in June 2013. The study found that among detained youth, almost all (93 percent) had experienced at least one trauma, and almost 6 in 10 had been exposed to trauma at least six times. The most common trauma was witnessing violence. Among detained youth with PTSD, over 90 percent had at least one comorbid psychiatric disorder. Identifying youth with PTSD and comorbid disorders is difficult, as standard interview screens usually do not detect such problems. Treatment for comorbidity may worsen the presenting problems. In only a few detention facilities are comorbid disorders identified and treated.

Some routine law enforcement practices can exacerbate symptoms of mental disorders, such as handcuffing and searching. These may result in increased anxiety, aggression, depression, and numbing of emotions. Institutional practice should include diagnosis of PTSD, identification of traumatized youth, and individualized treatment. Our nation's youth are probably among its most traumatized; the resources to treat them by punishment must be balanced with the necessary resources to treat them individually.

SOURCE: Office of Juvenile Justice and Delinquency Prevention (2013), "PTSD, Trauma, and Comorbid Disorders in Detained Youth," http://www.ojjdp.gov/pubs/239603.pdf (accessed June 4, 2013).

correctional practice 20.6

Residential Treatment Centers

Residential treatment centers are programs and sites that provide treatment, rehabilitation, guidance, and education for juvenile offenders. In terms of numbers, most are in the private sector, and some permit movement within the community (especially for education and training purposes). In general, their treatment goals are providing job training, helping juveniles learn how to avoid illegal activity and relapse to former drug and alcohol use, providing assistance to juveniles in earning the general equivalency diploma, facilitating family reconciliation, and assisting juveniles in finding appropriate work on reintegration and release.

Such treatment centers may be privately or publicly funded, especially by contract with the state, juvenile courts, and private sectors. They are known by a variety of terms—halfway houses, community corrections centers, and youth development centers, among others. State-supported programs may be totally supported by the state and service clients from juvenile courts or state training institutions or probationers at risk of revocation and placement in a state juvenile correctional institution. Many permit only limited circulation within the community. Contract facilities are more likely to be state supported and under contract, although there are many private-sector halfway houses not necessarily contracted with units of local jurisdictions. The unifying threads are treatment, rehabilitation education, conflict resolution, family reconciliation, victim compensation, and relapse prevention.

- Black youth reported a higher rate of sexual victimization by facility staff (9.6 percent) than white youth (6.4 percent) or Hispanic youth (6.4 percent).
- Youth who identified their sexual orientation as gay, lesbian, bisexual, or other reported a substantially higher rate of youth-on-youth victimization (10.3 percent) than heterosexual youth (1.5 percent).

The survey also identified 13 facilities with high rates of sexual victimization of youth. Two of these facilities (one in Georgia and one in Ohio) had rates of 30 percent or higher.

Correctional Practice 20.5 describes other issues faced by detained juveniles, such as trauma and posttraumatic stress disorder, and Correctional Practice 20.6 summarizes residential treatment centers.

REDUCING COMMITMENTS

As mentioned, over the past several years the number of youth incarcerated in juvenile facilities has declined significantly. Many reasons given for this decline: a lower crime rate among youth, court intervention, increased public support for alternatives, state and county budget cuts, and specific strategies designed to keep youth in their communities. One example of an initiative that has successfully reduced the number of youth held in institutions is Ohio's **RECLAIM** (Reasoned and Equitable Community and Local Alternatives to the Incarceration of Minors). One of the purposes of RECLAIM was to provide funding to local jurisdictions to develop community programming so that fewer youth would be committed to state facilities. Since 1995 when RECLAIM went statewide, well over $350 million has been distributed, and the effects on admissions to state institutions have been significant. Figure 20.2 shows the impact of this innovative policy shift on admissions, down well over 50 percent since the program was implemented in 1994. In 2010, Ohio initiated Targeted RECLAIM, which focused on the six largest counties in the state, and in 2012 seven more counties were added. The results have been very promising, and Ohio has been able to close seven juvenile facilities. Recently, Illinois began REDEPLOY Illinois, modeled after Ohio's program. Only time will tell if it has an impact on that state's juvenile offender population.

key term

RECLAIM
Ohio initiative designed to reduce admissions to the state's juvenile institutions through grants to local governments to underwrite such diversion.

An independent evaluation conducted by the University of Cincinnati found Ohio's RECLAIM and CCF programs to be cost effective when compared to placement in any

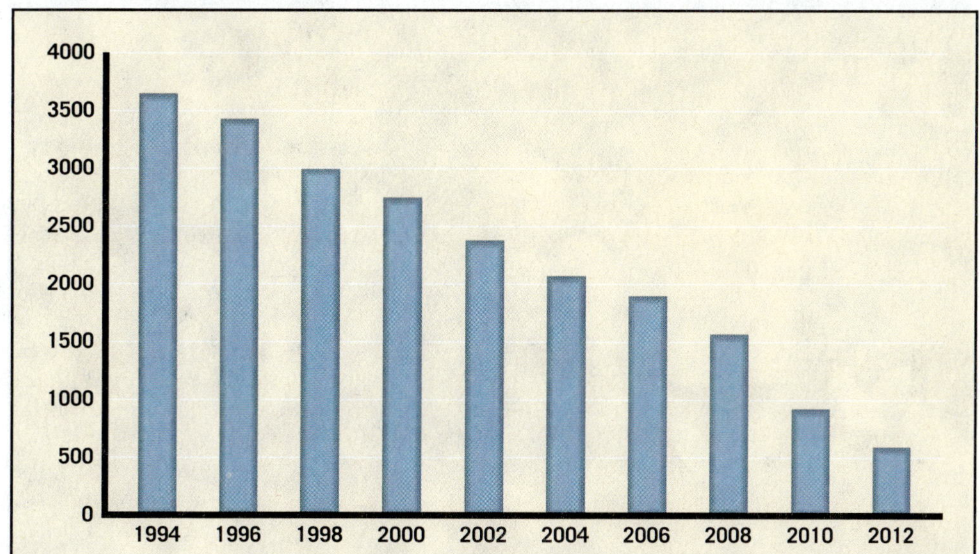

figure 20.2
Ohio Department of Youth Services Admissions, 1994–2012.

SOURCE: L. Brusman-Lovins, *Evaluation of New Directions Program* (Cincinnati, OH: Center for Criminal Justice Research, University of Cincinnati, 2010).

figure 20.3

Any Indicator of Failure by Risk and Placement Type.

SOURCE: E. J. Latessa, B. Lovins, and J. Lux, *Evaluation of Ohio's RECLAIM Programs* (Cincinnati, OH: University of Cincinnati School of Criminal Justice, 2013).

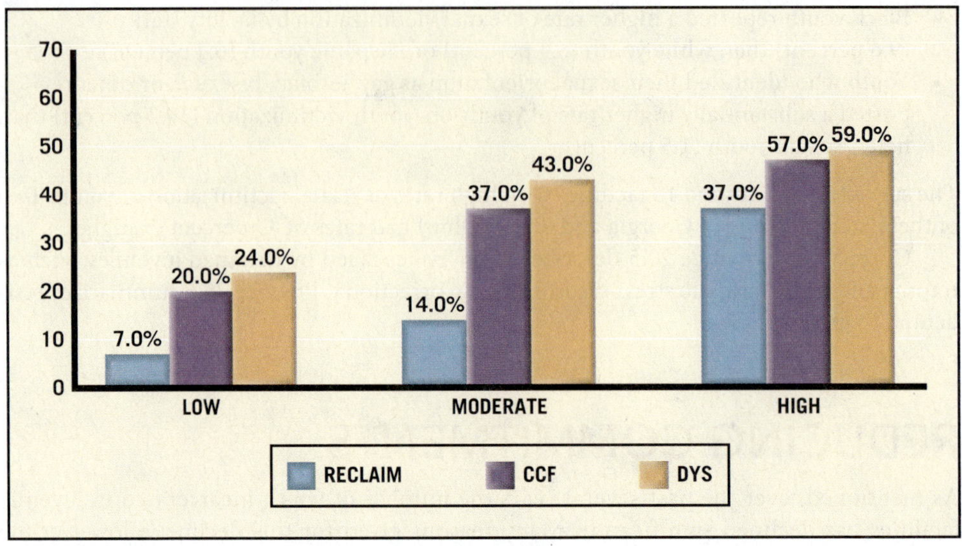

Ohio Department of Youth Services (ODYS) institution. To measure effectiveness, juveniles were classified as lower- to moderate-risk youth and high-risk youth. High-risk offenders performed better in the program's CCFs, with an estimated cost almost $30,000 per resident year, significantly lower than the cost of other ODYS institutions (over $51,000 per resident year). The cost of $1,960 per youth for RECLAIM programming was significantly less than that for the other two alternatives, as RECLAIM provides out-of-home placement, probation, intensive supervised probation, restitution, and county services made available by RECLAIM funding.[20] In a 2013 study of 2,000 youth in Ohio, comparison was made between youth placed in a RECLAIM program versus a CCF or a juvenile correctional facility. This

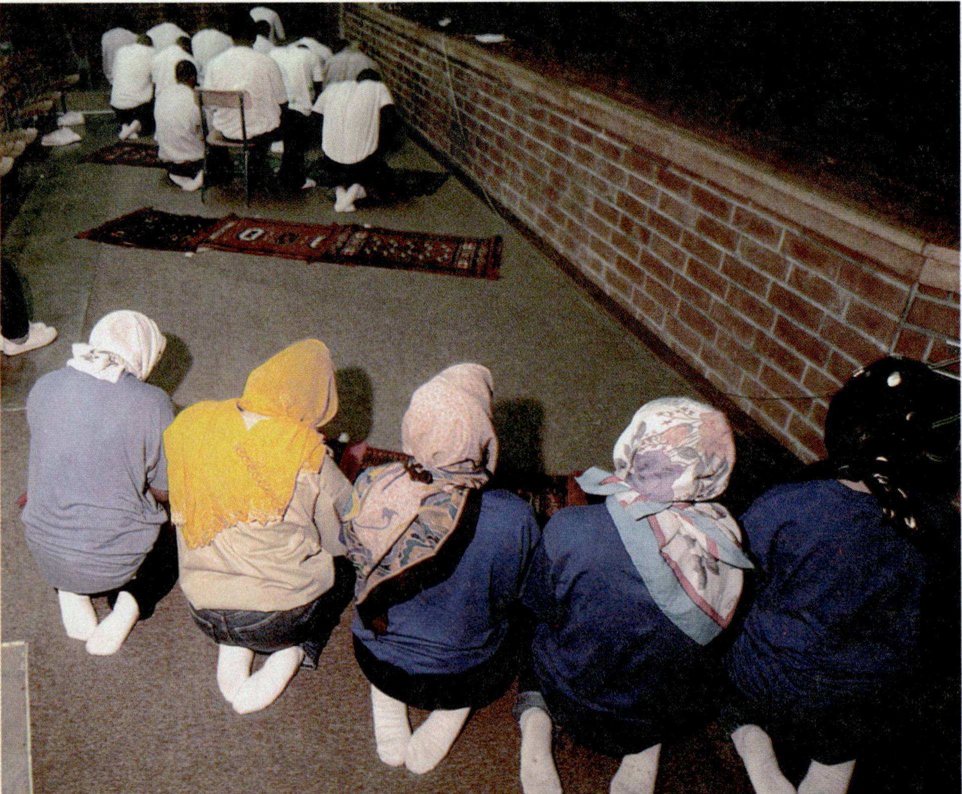

Photo 20.4

Muslim wards pray in the auditorium at the California Department of Juvenile Justice, Ventura, California.
A- Ramey/PhotoEdit.

study highlights the negative effects of more restrictive placements, especially for low-risk youth. Figure 20.3 show the recidivism rates based on the risk level of the youth and the type of placement.

Institutions are the most expensive and least successful method of handling juvenile offenders, but until more services needed for supervision and treatment in the community are forthcoming, judges often have no other choice but to commit offenders. The junior prisons are not all bad, but the custody philosophy creates the same problems as such philosophies at the adult level.

Summary

Describe the Types of Facilities That House Juvenile Offenders

Juvenile offenders are housed in a wide range of facilities, some resembling adult prisons, and others having a more homelike environment. Although many are operated locally, more serious juvenile offenders are usually sent to state-run facilities often called training schools. National data indicate that the number of youth incarcerated across the range of facilities has been declining.

Explain the Role and Characteristics of Juvenile Group Homes and Why There Is No Standard Definition

Group homes are like adult halfway houses but are usually smaller and often have a more homelike environment. Youth are usually allowed to attend local schools and other programs are often provided. One of the challenges is that there is no set definition for residential facilities for youth, which makes it difficult to study and evaluate them. Most group homes are small, with 10 or fewer residents.

Describe the Effectiveness of Group Homes and Explore Some of the Reasons That These Facilities Can Actually Increase Failure for the Youth Placed in Them

Although many youth exhibit positive behavior when in placement in group homes, research indicates that the effects usually do not last. One explanation is the range of youth placed in these types of facilities, such as mixing delinquent youth with others who have been abused and neglected.

Describe Juvenile Detention Centers, Their Purpose, How They Are Used, and Steps Being Taken to Reduce Detention of Youth

Juvenile detention centers are often used for short-term incarceration; these centers are often where police take youth who have been arrested. Most are locally operated. Efforts by the Annie E. Casey Foundation through its Juvenile Detention Alternatives Initiative have been designed to reduce the use of detention. Strategies include collaboration, use of data, admission criteria and screening, development of nonsecure alternatives, and better case processing. These efforts have been successful in jurisdictions that have employed them.

Explore the Use of Residential Treatment Centers and Some of the Different Types of Programs They Offer

Residential treatment centers are usually larger than group homes and are often secure. Ohio has developed a number of such facilities called community correctional facilities, whereas in California they are often referred to as camps or ranches. Many of the youths in these facilities have been sentenced by the court, and they usually receive a wide range of programs and services.

Describe Training Schools and the Types of Programs Offered in These Facilities

Training schools are usually reserved for the more serious juvenile offender, and stays can be much longer than in other types of juvenile facilities. These facilities often resemble adult prisons, and costs can average more than $250 per day per juvenile. Although some training schools have a punitive orientation, most are trying to provide more programs and services. California is an example of a state that, through court intervention, has reformed its juvenile institutions and has moved toward a more rehabilitative orientation.

Explore Sexual Victimization of Incarcerated Youth and Learn about the Scope of the Problem

Sexual victimization is always a concern and justifiably so. National data on incidents have highlighted inappropriate sexual behavior between staff and youth and youth and other youth.

Explain Some of the Ways States Are Attempting to Reduce the Number of Youth Housed in Training Facilities

Through a number of initiatives, states have attempted to reduce their commitment of youth to residential placement. Data indicate that these attempts have been successful, as the numbers continue to drop. Some states, like Ohio, have seen a dramatic reduction in the number of youth housed in state institutions, mainly through funding of local alternatives.

Key Words

group home, 441
Juvenile Residential Facilities Census, 441
juvenile detention center ("juvie"), 442
Juvenile Detention Alternatives Initiative (JDAI), 443
residential treatment center, 443
community correctional facility (CCF), 443
juvenile camps and ranches, 444
training school for youth, 445
Missouri Model, 449
sexual victimization, 449
posttraumatic stress disorder (PTSD), 450
RECLAIM, 451

Review Questions

1. What are some of the explanations for why the number of juveniles in residential facilities has declined over the past several years?
2. Compare and contrast juvenile group homes and training schools.
3. Detention facilities are often used for short-term sentences or youth awaiting a court hearing. If you were asked to reduce the number of youth in your local detention facility, what are some of the strategies you might use to accomplish this task?
4. How has Ohio reduced the commitment rate of juveniles to state facilities?
5. Judges often send youth to residential programs such as group homes because they are abused or neglected; however, this often places them with higher-risk delinquent youth. Given what we know about the harmful effects of placing low- and high-risk youth together, what other strategy might you recommend to a judge?
6. If your state was considering the Missouri Model, what do you think would be some of the political challenges that would have to be overcome?

Application Case Studies

1. You are the director of a juvenile facility, and your program evaluations indicate substantial frequency of sexual victimization of juvenile wards. What would you do to lessen these predatory sexual activities?
2. A major lawsuit against the state department of youth services that you direct resulted in a federal court imposing a court monitor to correct violations of the wards' constitutional rights. The monitor requires you to develop a management plan that would maximize services to medium-risk juvenile wards. What five steps would you take?
3. The state association of juvenile court justices invites you to make a short presentation on new approaches to the ongoing overcrowding of your juvenile facilities. What five points would you try to make in your presentation?

Endnotes

1. P. A. Curtis, G. Alexander, and L. A. Lunghofer, "A Literature Review Comparing the Outcomes of Residential Group Care and Therapeutic Foster Care." *Child & Adolescent Social Work Journal* 18:5 (2001): 377–392.
2. Office of Juvenile Justice Delinquency Prevention, *2008 Juvenile Residential Facilities Census* (Washington, DC: Office of Juvenile Justice Delinquency Prevention, 2009).
3. S. Hockenberry, M. Sickmund, and A. Sladky, *Juvenile Residential Facility Census, 2010: Selected Findings,*

OJJDP National Report Series Bulletin (Washington, DC: National Center for Juvenile Justice, 2011).

4. Ibid.
5. Ibid.
6. See K. A. Kirigin, C. J. Braukmann, J. D. Atwater, and M. M. Wolf, "Evaluation of Teaching-Family (Achievement Place) Group Homes for Juvenile Offenders," *Journal of Applied Behavior Analysis* 15:1 (1982): 1–16, and J. P. Ryan, J. M. Marshall, D. Herz, and P. M. Hernandez, "Juvenile Delinquency in Group Welfare: Investigating Group Home Effects," *Children and Youth Services Review* 30 (2008): 1088–1099. For a more recent study, see P. Chamberlain and J. B. Reid, "Using a Specialized Foster Care Community Treatment Model for Children and Adolescents Leaving the State Mental Hospital," *Journal of Community Psychology* 19 (1991): 226–276.
7. D. Satcher, *Mental Health: A Report of the Surgeon General* (Washington, DC: U.S. Department of Health and Human Services, 1999).
8. J. C. Howell and M. Lipsey, "Promising Sanctions Programs in a Graduated System," *Juvenile Sanctions Center Training and Technical Assistance Bulletin* 1:4 (2004): 1–7 (Washington, DC: National Council of Juvenile and Family Court Judges).
9. T. J. Dishion, K. M. Spracklen, D. W. Andrews, and G. R. Patterson, "Deviancy in Training in Male Adolescent Friendships," *Behavior Therapy* 27 (1996): 327–390.
10. There are some exceptions, especially in California, where juvenile halls can include youth who are serving sentences and are housed for an extended period of time.
11. See Barry Holman and Jason Ziedenberg (2006), "The Dangers of Detention: The Impact of Incarcerating Youth in Detention and Other Secure Facilities," http://www.justicepolicy.org/images/upload/06-11_rep_dangersofdetention_jj.pdf (accessed February 19, 2014).
12. For information about the JDAI initiative, see http://www.aecf.org/MajorInitiatives/JuvenileDetentionAlternativesInitiative.aspx.
13. Christopher Lowenkamp, Matthew D. Makarios, Edward J. Latessa, Richard Lemke, and Paula Smith, "Community Corrections Facilities for Juvenile Offenders in Ohio: An Examination of Treatment Integrity and Recidivism," *Criminal Justice and Behavior,* 37:6 (2010): 695-708.
14. Michael Tonry, ed., *The Handbook of Crime and Punishment* (New York: Oxford University Press, 1998). See also Don Gibbons, "Review Essay: Changing Lawbreakers: What Have We Learned since the 1950s?," *Crime and Delinquency* 45:2 (1999): 272–293; Sharon Levrant, F. Cullen, B. Fulton, and J. Wozniak, "Reconsidering Restorative Justice: Adolescence and Early Childhood," *Crime and Delinquency* 45:3 (1999): 3–27.
15. American Correctional Association, *2007 Directory* (Alexandria, VA: American Correctional Association, 2007), p. 24. See also American Correctional Association, *2012 Directory* (Alexandria, VA: American Correctional Association, 2012), pp. 50–51.
16. *Law Enforcement Assistance Administration, Corrections—Report of the National Advisory Commission on Criminal Justice Standards and Goals* (Washington, DC: Law Enforcement Assistance Administration, 1973).
17. But see M. Hagan, M. Cho, J. Jensen, et al., "An Assessment of the Effectiveness of an Intensive Treatment Program for Severely Mentally Disturbed Juvenile Offenders," *International Journal of Offender Therapy and Comparative Criminology* 41:4 (1997): 340–350.
18. For a review of the progress made, see Barry Krisberg (2011), "Criminal Justice: The Long and Winding Road: Juvenile Corrections Reform in California," http://www.law.berkeley.edu/files/Long_and_Winding_Road_Publication-final.pdf (accessed February 15, 2014).
19. Alan J. Beck, David Cantor, John Hartge, and Tim Smith, *Sexual Victimization in Juvenile Facilities Reported by Youth, 2012* (Washington, DC: Bureau of Justice Statistics, 2013).
20. Data provided by the Ohio Department of Youth Services.

Sharon Gekoski-Kimmel/KRT/Newscom.

Objectives

- Summarize the issues regarding offenders who are mentally ill.
- Summarize the issues regarding offenders who are developmentally challenged.
- Summarize the issues regarding sex offenders.
- Explain how AIDS and infectious diseases have affected prisons.
- Explain how prison officials handle transgender inmates.
- Summarize the issues regarding aging offenders.

chapter 21
Special-Category Offenders

Outline

"Prisoners tend to be in poor mental health, and a large percentage of male and female prisoners will, over their lifetime, have at least one psychiatric disorder."

—Bruce S. Ponder

Overview

Now we come to the chapter that deals with those offenders who have many more problems than other offenders in the mainstream of criminal behavior. We examine some of the so-called rejects of society who are too often found in America's jails and correctional facilities.[1] Many of these individuals are handicapped by their mental processes, and others are labeled by their specific problems, extreme behavior, or personal background.

Of the many categories that could be examined, we have chosen to discuss the mentally disordered offender, the developmentally challenged offender, the sex offender, HIV-infected inmates, transgender inmates, and geriatric inmates. Although these categories do not constitute an exhaustive list of the possible types of special-category offenders, we feel they represent a fair spectrum of the problems faced by correctional administrators and the individual offenders who are in their custody and treatment. We first delve a little into the history and development of categories of mentally disordered (mentally ill) offenders to provide a proper framework for examination of these special inmates.

Since 1970, the closing of 90 percent of the mental health facilities and centers in local counties and their state-funded counterparts has diverted the mentally disordered into correctional facilities (jails and prisons), a process called **transincarceration**. The increasing and unrestrained overcrowding continues to place these stigmatized offenders into the correctional bureaucratic system, where their special needs are more often ignored than met. What their needs are and how they are met are discussed in this chapter. We also assess the growing numbers of these special-category offenders and how our systems are coping with this problem. After finishing this final chapter in Part 4, the student will have been exposed to most of the clients found in the criminal justice and juvenile justice systems.

key term

Transincarceration
Movement of offenders diverted from mental health institutions to prisons.

THE MENTALLY DISORDERED OFFENDER

What kind of illness would civilized people find so repulsive that they would reject the sufferers in the most barbaric fashion and brand them with a stigma that would remain with them for a lifetime, even if a cure were achieved? Those unfortunates, persons with mental disability (mentally disturbed and disordered), were once scorned, banished, and even burned alive, as they were considered evil. But, in more enlightened times, we built backwoods fortresses for them, presumably to protect ourselves from contagion. They have been executed as witches, subjected to exorcisms, chained, and even thrown into gatehouses and prisons to furnish as a horrible diversion for the other prisoners.[2]

key term

Mentally disturbed
Persons with a mental illness.

Before the Middle Ages, persons with a mental illness (**mentally disturbed**) were generally tolerated and usually cared for locally by members of their own family, tribal system, or primitive society. However, the advent of widespread poverty, disease, and religious fanaticism seemed to trigger intolerance for any unexplainable deviation from the norm. People who were mentally disturbed were thought to be possessed by devils and demons and were punished harshly because of it. As mentioned in Chapter 1, they were subjected to having "the Devil beaten out of them." In that era, those who were deemed insane were driven out of society, but later they were confined in asylums, another form of isolation from society.

key term

Asylum
Institution for the care and custody of mentally ill societal members.

The first insane **asylum** was constructed in Europe in 1408.[3] From that date until recently, the asylum was a "dumping ground" for all of the mentally disordered people who could be neither understood nor cured. In the United States, one after another of the individual states responded to that compelling method of ridding society of misfits by building numerous institutions during the mid-1800s. The inflated claims of cures for mental illness could not stand up against the process of institutionalization, however, and long-term commitments, often for a lifetime, not cures, became the rule of the day.

Asylums became yet another "invisible empire" in America, with the punitive excesses and lack of care or caring ignored by society. "Out of sight, out of mind" was the catchphrase for these unfortunates. With the discovery of tranquilizing drugs, these "snake pits" became places where patients were put into a controllable stupor, until the "magic bullet," a cure for mental illness, could be found. Longer and longer periods of institutionalization, often ordered at the request of family members, finally got the attention of the courts.

In the 1960s, the rights of all citizens, including the mentally ill and convicts, were being reexamined at every level. The abuses in the back wards of the asylums were brought to light, and the counterreaction was extreme. In the early 1970s, state after state adopted policies under the Community Mental Health Act that swept the country. The essential goal was to release, or **deinstitutionalize**, all inmates of the asylums who were not a "clear and present danger" to themselves and society.

key term

Deinstitutionalization
The return of a mentally ill person following release from a mental hospital facility.

key term

Transinstitutionalism
Process referring to the transfer of the mentally ill to the justice system facilities, particularly jails and prisons.

Although benign in their intents, these acts flooded the central cities of America with tens of thousands of street people with mental impairments and created the need for poorhouses. The response by most jurisdictions was to transfer the problem to the criminal justice system, filling the jails and correctional institutions of America, a process known as **transinstitutionalization.**[4] In the early 1980s in Seattle, Randy Revelle, a former King County executive, was fond of saying that the King County Jail was the "third largest mental health facility in the state. The first being the Western State Hospital, the second the section of I-5 [freeway] between the jail and the hospital."[5]

Mentally Ill Inmates

From the 1960s to the 1980s, the deinstitutionalization movement demanded that people with mental illnesses be treated in the community, using new drug therapies that appeared to control even the most extreme behaviors of people with mental illnesses. People with mental illnesses such as depression, schizophrenia, and anxiety disorders suffer from one or more brain

Photo 21.1
A unit for mentally disturbed inmates at the Los Angeles County Jail, built in 1998.
Chris Pizzello/AP Images.

dysfunctions that are often successfully treated with such medications as Prozac and Zoloft. This liberation of psychiatric patients was reinforced by court decisions that awarded certain legal rights to people who were mentally ill, but few community-based programs were developed to treat psychiatric patients effectively. Released to the community without adequate support and treatment services, people with mental illnesses gravitated to criminal confinement facilities for offenders, particularly to jails but also to the prisons of the United States.

Although exact numbers are not known, it is estimated that perhaps 20 percent of offenders imprisoned at any time have severe or acute mental illnesses, such as schizophrenia, manic depression, and depression. Approximately 10 to 15 percent of persons with these three illnesses will die by suicide. Yet current treatment is extremely effective, if given.[6]

Prisoners tend to be in poor mental health, and a large percentage of male and female prisoners will, over the lifetime, have at least one psychiatric disorder. The greater the level of disability while in prison, the more likely the inmate is to receive mental health services. In practice, proportionately more female prisoners use mental health services than do males, and whites are more likely to seek or secure prison mental health services than others. It is estimated that at least half of the inmates who need such treatment go without it.

Although the U.S. Supreme Court has not found that inmates have a constitutional right to treatment, it has ruled that an inmate's constitutional right to medical treatment includes the right to treatment for serious emotional illness. The corrections system is caught in the middle. Institutions are not required to provide services simply because their clients are criminals and thus have shifted critical funds to other uses (such as increased security staffing). On the other hand, the threat of potential litigation or having a court-appointed correctional master has meant that some revision and provision of mental health services for seriously ill inmates is necessary.[7]

As people with mental illnesses became a larger segment of the population in jails and prisons, professionals in the mental health field became essential to correctional administrators. Although the ratio of mental health practitioners to inmates remains much too low, there has been some progress. Because many institutions must deal with mental health issues on a priority basis, few to no services are provided for the majority who do not exhibit violent or bizarre behavior. It is a practical fact that in corrections, "the squeaky wheel gets the grease."[8]

correctional practice 21.1

Criminal Thinking and Mental Illness

In a recent study Morgan, Fisher, and Wolff (2010) studied 414 adult offenders with mental illness (265 males, 149 females) and found the following:

- Of the study group, 66 percent had belief systems supportive of a criminal lifestyle based on the Psychological Inventory of Criminal Thinking Scale.
- When compared to other offender samples, male offenders with mental illness scored similar to or higher than non-mentally-disordered offenders.
- On the Criminal Sentiments Scale–Revised, 85 percent of men and 72 percent of women with mental illness had antisocial attitudes, values, and beliefs—higher than the percentages of the incarcerated sample without mental illness.

Morgan et al. concluded that criminal thinking styles differentiated people who commit crimes from those who do not, independent of mental illness. They went on to say that incarcerated persons with mental illness are both mentally ill *and* criminal, and therefore these should be treated as co-occurring problems.

SOURCE: Center for Behavioral Health Services Criminal Justice Research Policy Brief, April 2010, Rutgers University.

It appears that the relationship between crime and mental disorder (at least in *groups*, as shown in one study) has no real causal effect.[9] Correctional Practice 21.1 describes the results of a recent study exploring the connection between mental illness and criminal thinking. It is essential for society to learn more about distinguishing between different kinds of mental illness and their impacts on safe and secure administration of correctional institutions. It is important to remember that the real link to look for is one that indicates the potential for harm to the mentally ill person and others. It may be a long time before such options are available to the already overcrowded corrections systems in the United States.

key term

Not guilty by reason of insanity (NGRI)
Defense of offenders not to deny the commission of the crime but to assert they lacked the capacity to understand the nature of the crime or that it was wrong.

Two Ways to Escape Criminal Responsibility

There are two justifications that defendants can invoke in an attempt to relieve themselves of criminal responsibility for a criminal act. The first is **not guilty by reason of insanity (NGRI)**; the second is **incompetent to stand trial**. In the first instance, offenders do not deny the commission of the act but assert they lacked the capacity to understand the nature of the act or that it was wrong. The second instance is based on the common law criterion that defendants must be able to understand the charges against them and to cooperate with their counsel in the preparation of their own defense. The procedures for determining competency vary considerably among jurisdictions, but most make it a court decision based on psychiatric testimony. If defendants are found incompetent to stand trial, then they are usually committed to a mental institution until declared competent.

key term

Incompetent to stand trial
Legal defense asserting that defendants must be able to understand the charges against them and to assist legal counsel in the preparation of their own defense.

The Criminally Insane

With the advent of legal insanity and legal incompetence as defenses against criminal conviction came the development of special asylums for the **criminally insane**, in most cases just another form of prison without due process protections. A visiting student from Italy once remarked to the authors, when visiting a hospital for the criminally insane, "How can a person be criminally insane? If you are criminally responsible, you cannot be insane; if you are insane, you cannot be criminally responsible." That question is difficult to answer directly; such institutions are usually reserved for the following categories of offenders:[10]

1. Persons adjudicated incompetent to enter a plea or stand trial
2. Defendants found not guilty by reason of insanity

key term

Criminally insane
Mentally ill inmates who are diagnosed as incompetent to plead or stand trial or not guilty by reason of insanity who became mentally ill while incarcerated or other potentially hazardous mentally ill persons requiring special security.

3. Persons adjudicated under special statutes (e.g., "sexually dangerous persons," "defective delinquents," or "sexual psychopaths")
4. Convicted and sentenced offenders who have become mentally disturbed while serving a prison sentence and have been transferred to a mental health facility
5. Other potentially hazardous mentally ill persons requiring special security during the course of their evaluation and treatment

In more recent years, those claiming to be NGRI have been the subjects of considerable debate.[11] President Nixon sought to have the NGRI defense abolished. More informed criminologists point to such problems with the insanity defense as excessive media coverage, suspicion of malingering by the defendant, and conflicting and suspicious testimony by mental health professionals testifying for either the defense or the prosecution.

The insanity defense is used in less than 1 percent of all felony cases, and of those, only one in four defendants is found to be NGRI. One study found only the most emotionally and behaviorally disturbed defendants to be successful in their plea and that the successful petitioners had committed more serious offenses. The decision to acquit is more frequently made in court by prosecutors, defense attorneys, and the judge and less frequently by jury members. Persons acquitted by NGRI are generally found to be less likely than their cohort of convicted offenders to commit crimes after release.[12]

Prosecutors often hope that those accused offenders acquitted through the plea of NGRI will be institutionalized for a period sufficient to reduce their dangerousness and to provide both public safety and some retribution. The debate continues. Perhaps the most reasonable solution would be to determine guilt first and then shift the issue of diminished capacity (insanity, in this case) to the sentencing or case disposition stage. The American Psychiatric Association, following the attack by John Hinckley on the life of President Reagan, recognized that position.

As a response, by 1986, 12 states abolished the insanity defense entirely, then created **guilty but mentally ill (GBMI)** statutes in its place.[13] Under those statutes, an offender's mental illness is acknowledged but not seen as sufficient reason to allow him or her to escape criminal responsibility. If convicted, offenders are committed to prison. Some states will provide mental health treatment in the prison setting, but others may transfer the offender to a mental health facility for treatment. In Georgia, defendants who entered insanity pleas but were determined GBMI received harsher sentences than their counterparts whose guilt was determined in trial, suggesting increased punishment for the disturbed offender.[14]

key term

Guilty but mentally ill (GBMI)
Plea entered by the defendant acknowledging guilt but asserting a lack of capacity to understand the nature of the act or that it was wrong.

The position of the American Psychiatric Association is that significant changes in the legislation should be made to deal with the disposition of violent persons acquitted by NGRI:[15]

1. Special legislation should be designed for those persons charged with violent offenses who have been found not guilty by reason of insanity.
2. Confinement and release decisions should be made by a board including both psychiatrists and other professionals representing the criminal justice system and akin to a parole board.
3. Release should be conditional on having a treatment supervision plan in place, with the necessary resources available to implement it.
4. The board having jurisdiction over the released insanity acquittees should also have the authority to reconfine them.
5. When psychiatric treatment in a hospital setting has obtained the maximal treatment benefit possible but the board believes that for other reasons confinement is still necessary, the insanity acquittee should be transferred to the most appropriate nonhospital facility (prison).

While the public remains upset by a seemingly gaping loophole in the net of justice, the courts continue to seek equitable ways to deal with the offender who has diminished mental capacity.

The Problems of Prediction

key term

Predict potential dangerousness
Process by which treatment staff assess dangerousness, the offender's risk for future dangerous offenses.

It is unfortunate that the long indeterminate sentences often given to mentally disordered offenders reflect a fear that those committed might be a problem in the future. It is the expectation that someone is capable of predicting criminal inclination that makes the programs for treating those who are mentally disordered so questionable. Who can **predict potential dangerousness** with any degree of accuracy? Noted psychiatrist Bernard Rubin stated, "The belief in the psychiatrist's ability to predict the likely dangerousness of a patient's future behavior is almost universally held, yet it lacks empirical support." He added, "Labeling of deviancy as mental illness or predicting dangerousness is just a convention to get someone to treatment. Once in treatment the concept of dangerousness is forgotten."[16]

So we see the paradox of requiring psychiatrists to predict behavior and to attach a label to offenders, when that might result in an indefinite or even lifelong commitment to a mental institution for someone who is not really dangerous (a false-positive prediction). Further, the individual is then labeled for custody and treatment in a special area within that institution. When we consider the wealth of folklore surrounding mental institutions, it becomes clear that a dreadful lifelong stigma accompanies the label of "criminally insane."

THE DEVELOPMENTALLY CHALLENGED OFFENDER

key term

Developmentally challenged
A term denoting intellectual disabilities, sometimes referred to as mental retardation.

Within the correctional system are offenders who, although considered legally sane and competent to stand trial, are **developmentally challenged**. (An IQ score of 69 or below on a standardized test is the generally accepted measure for identifying the developmentally challenged, with exceptions.) Their intellectual level and social adaptability measure well below average, yet they are adjudged legally responsible for their actions. Some 4 to 9 percent of the prison population is composed of developmentally challenged inmates.

Photo 21.2
Developmentally challenged inmates using computers to master learning objectives.
Andrew Aitchison/Alamy.

In addition to the developmentally challenged, prisons contain an unknown but larger number of lower-functioning inmates with fewer intellectual abilities (compared to the general prison population) and IQs that may approach 70 but who do not technically meet the requirements of mental retardation They have diminished intellectual abilities, but a diagnosis of mental retardation is not warranted. Unlike mental illnesses, the developmentally challenged and lower-functioning inmates are not treated with medication but may learn both skills and coping mechanisms that would allow them to lead more satisfactory and productive lives.

In their guidelines for incarcerated developmentally challenged offenders, Santamour and West address the problems encountered:[17]

1. In prison, the developmentally challenged offender is slower to adjust to routine, has more difficulty in learning regulations, and accumulates more rule infractions which, in turn, affect housing, parole, and other related matters.
2. Retarded [developmentally challenged] inmates rarely take part in rehabilitation programs because of their desire to mask their deficiencies.
3. They often suffer the brunt of practical jokes and sexual harassment.
4. Such inmates are more often denied parole, serving on the average two or three years longer than other prisoners for the same offense.

Administrators from both fields (corrections and mental health) have a tendency to regard the developmentally challenged offender as a misfit in their system of services. (People with developmental challenges tend to have higher rates of involvement in violent incidents in prison.[18]) Well-meaning administrators from both systems look to one another to assume responsibility for programming and funding. Because of the few resources available to each system and even more pressing concerns, the result is often very limited programming.

The special needs of the developmentally challenged offender are unique, and the program models are few. Those models that do exist are limited primarily to special education programs geared more to the needs of the individual with learning disabilities than to those of the developmentally challenged person. One promising model concerned with these offenders on a county level focuses on substance abuse, psychological needs, and both vocational and educational improvement.[19]

Historical Perspective

In reviewing historical and philosophical trends in the study of the developmentally challenged offender, it is noteworthy that before the late nineteenth century, little attempt was made to differentiate between the developmentally challenged individual and anyone who committed a crime.

Currently, there is less reluctance to associate "developmentally challenged " directly with delinquency. Much of the revived interest from the 1960s to date has been generated by the legal community and not by criminologists. Such a phenomenon stems from a growing awareness that the preponderance of developmentally challenged individuals in the criminal justice system may be more an administrative and legal artifact than evidence for a causal relationship between the developmentally challenged and criminality.

The landmark ***Ruiz* v. *Estellez*** decision has also set the tone for judicial consideration of the developmentally challenged inmate.[20] This class-action suit involved issues of overcrowding, medical care, inmate trustees as guards, and other conditions in Texas facilities; the federal court declared the Texas prison system to be unconstitutional. Judge Justice found that between 10 and 15 percent of the Texas Department of Corrections inmates were developmentally challenged and that they were distributed throughout the system. The judge echoed Santamour and West concerning the developmentally challenged inmates' special problems and added the following:

1. They are abnormally prone to injuries, many of which are job related.
2. They are decidedly disadvantaged when appearing before a disciplinary committee.

key term

Ruiz* v. *Estellez
U.S. Supreme Court decision that prisons must provide treatment to the developmentally challenged, assessing the conditions in the Texas Department of Corrections.

This raises basic problems of fairness and the special need for assistance.[21] It seems obvious that the issue of the developmentally challenged inmate is slowly coming to the forefront, led by the decisions of the courts.

Recent litigation has determined emerging rights of the developmentally challenged inmate. In 1981, *Green* v. *Johnson* (512 F. Supp. 965) established that developmentally challenged inmates under age 22 have a right to receive special education. In *Atkins* v. *Virginia* (536 U.S. 304, 2002), the U.S. Supreme Court ruled that developmentally challenged inmates cannot be executed. In 2007, the U.S. Supreme Court decided that incompetent prison inmates could not be executed in *Panetti* v. *Quarterman* (551 U.S. 2007; 127 S.Ct. 2842, 2007). The Americans with Disabilities Act requires all correctional agencies to establish procedures to screen for developmentally challenged inmates and provide rehabilitation programs specifically designed for them (see Chapter 9).

Developmentally challenged offenders are often individuals who have never been accepted by society at large. Becoming a part of the "society of captives" is often their first experience of acceptance and thus has a pervasive impact. At Bridgewater State Hospital and Prison in Massachusetts, personnel commenting on the strengths of the association between developmentally challenged inmates and the prison culture noted that only the developmentally challenged inmates returned to prison for social visits. Are developmentally challenged offenders in need of special consideration in regard to criminal responsibility? As noted by Richard C. Allen,

> Historically, society has pursued three alternative courses with the developmentally challenged offender: we have ignored his limitations and special needs; or we have sought to tailor traditional criminal law processes to fit them; we have grouped him with psychopaths, sociopaths, and sex deviates in a kind of conventicle of the outcast and hopeless.[22]

One way to accomplish such consideration would be with a special court, similar to a juvenile court, where the developmentally challenged offenders are handled both for the crime and for their condition.

SEX OFFENDERS

Common Sex Offenses

Any analysis of sex offenses is complicated because state legislatures are often too inhibited to describe specifically the acts they are seeking to punish. Thus, punishment may be decreed for "lewd and lascivious conduct," "acts against nature," "carnal knowledge," "imperiling the morals of a minor," and so on. Almost any sexual activity can be prosecuted under one or another of those vague and overly broad rubrics. The same term, moreover, means different things in different states. Thus, **sodomy**, which in many states would refer primarily to male homosexual acts, might also be applied to heterosexual oral or anal intercourse or to sexual contacts with animals.

key term

Sodomy

Anal or oral copulation with a member of the same or opposite sex or copulation with an animal; the U.S. Supreme Court recently struck down sodomy law application to consenting adults in private.

key term

Sex offense

A violation of laws that control sexual intercourse or crimes of a carnal nature, including attempts at such crimes.

Highly misleading terms may be used, such as *statutory rape* for an offense that is not rape at all but rather sexual intercourse with a fully consenting female who has not yet reached the age of legal consent (18 in some states). Discussions of **sex offenses** are further complicated by the fact that a man charged with a serious offense such as rape may be permitted, in the course of plea bargaining, to plead guilty to a lesser offense; hence, men who are in fact rapists may be lodged in correctional institutions for such apparently nonsexual offenses as breaking and entering or assault. In the following discussion, we consider the actual offenses committed rather than the vague legal terminology often used or the lesser offenses to which an offender may plead. Trends in reported forcible rape can be found in Figure 21.1.

Until the past few years, the term *sex offense* commonly called to mind a lust-murder of the most irrational and heinous type. More recently, the intense and proper concern of the women's movement with rape and related crimes, such as assault with intent to commit

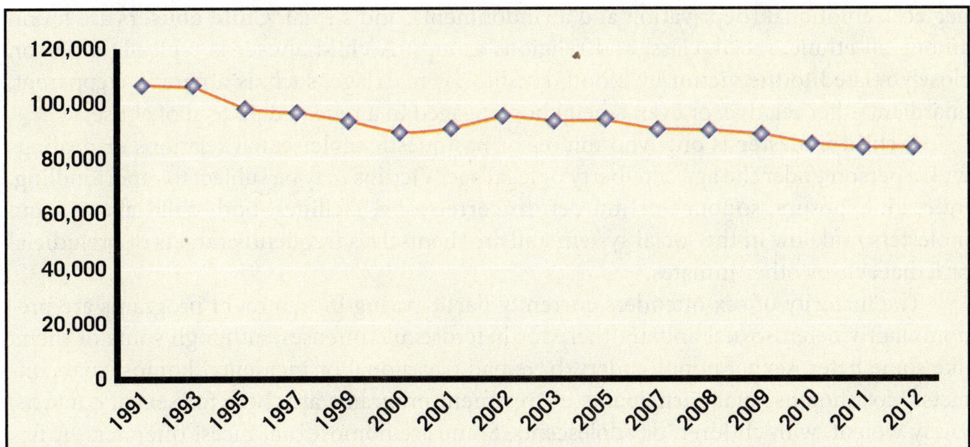

figure 21.1

Reported Female Rapes, 1991–2012.

SOURCE: Federal Bureau of Investigation, *Uniform Crime Report 2012*, http://www.fbi.gov/about-us/cjis/ucr/crime-in-the-u.s/2012/crime-in-the-u.s.-2012/violent-crime/rape (accessed September 18, 2014).

rape, has tended to make rape the predominant sex offense in the minds of many people. Many experts believe that heterosexual rape, in its more violent forms, is not a sex crime at all but a crime of power and dominance over women.[23]

Laws governing public indecency and solicitation for prostitution are still enforced in many jurisdictions, but they commonly lead to fines, probation, or short sentences in local correctional institutions. The remaining five categories of sex offenses account for the overwhelming majority of treatment program participants:

1. Rape, attempted rape, assault with intent to rape, and the like[24]
2. Child molestation[25]
3. Incest[26]
4. Exhibitionism and voyeurism
5. Miscellaneous offenses (breaking and entering, arson, and the like) in cases involving a sexual motivation

Child abuse is any act of commission or omission that endangers or impairs a child's physical or emotional health and development. The major forms are physical (such as

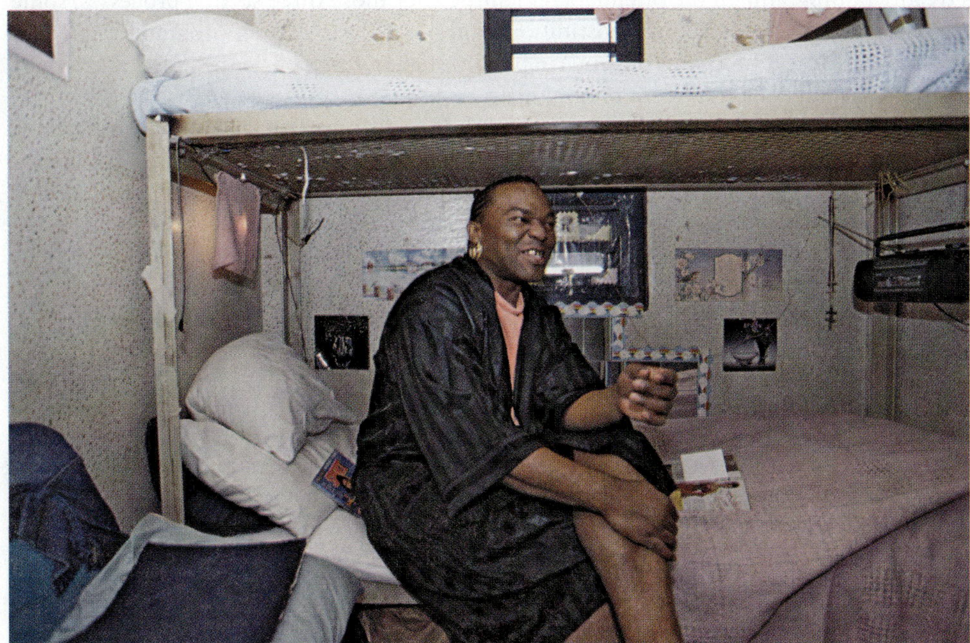

Photo 21.3

Gay inmate "Jacquie" lives well at the maximum-security Buckingham Correctional Institution in Virginia.
Shepard Sherbell/Corbis.

key term

Child abuser
A person who mentally or physically abuses a child.

key term

Child molester
An adult charged with criminal and civil offenses in which the adult engages in sexual activity with a minor or exploits a minor for the purpose of sexual gratification.

neglect), emotional (deprivation and abandonment), and sexual. **Child abusers** are found among all ethnic, racial, class, and religious groups. A child abuser is typically a person closely related to the victim by blood, kinship, or marriage, such as a parent, stepparent, guardian, other relative, or even a neighbor, engaged in a repeated pattern of abuse.

A **child molester** is one who injures or has questionable sexual relations or dealings with a person under the age of puberty or legal age. Victims may be subject to rape, fondling, indecent exposure, sodomy, or murder. In correctional facilities, both child abusers and molesters rank low in the social system and are themselves frequently targets of prejudicial or lethal acts by other inmates.

The majority of sex offenders currently participating in treatment programs are predominantly heterosexual and are there for heterosexual offenses, although some of them, like some heterosexual nonoffenders, have had occasional or incidental homosexual contacts. Most homosexual participants in treatment programs are there for sexual contacts, rarely violent, with children or adolescents. Some are homosexual incest offenders. A few have committed homosexual rape or rape-related offenses.

Almost all sex offenses *prosecuted* in the United States today (except for prostitution-related offenses and offenses involving indecent public performances) are committed by men. The only significant exceptions are the rare cases of child molestation in which a woman is prosecuted along with a man, often her husband or significant other, as an accessory or in child pornography. As a rough estimate, 200 or 300 males are prosecuted for sex offenses for every female prosecuted. It is probable, of course, that the ratio of offenses committed by females is much higher than the ratio of prosecutions.

Most sex offenders in treatment programs are 18 to 35 years of age. A significant minority (mostly child molesters, those offenders whose contacts with children are of a sexual nature) is past 50. How do the sex offenders enrolled in treatment programs differ from the remainder of sex offenders? At least five "sorting processes" distinguish the two groups. Some sex offenses are reported to the police; others are not. Most rapes and a wide range of lesser offenses go unreported. No man ends up in a treatment program as a result of an unreported offense. After an offense is reported, the perpetrator may or may not be apprehended and prosecuted. Those who escape arrest and prosecution no doubt differ in significant respects from those who reach the courts.

Of those prosecuted, small numbers are found not guilty, and many (mostly minor offenders) receive suspended sentences or are placed on probation without assignment to a treatment program. Of the offenders remaining after those three sorting processes, some are sent to ordinary correctional institutions and others to treatment programs. Who will be sent to treatment programs depends in part on state law, in part on the judge, and in part on the availability of a treatment program.[27]

Finally, most treatment programs can (and do) reject or transfer to other institutions those offenders they deem unsuitable for treatment. The net effect of these five sorting processes is a population of program participants from which most of the very serious offenders and most of the very minor offenders have been screened.

Sex Offenders and Probation

Probation officers are generally underprepared or undertrained to work with sex offenders because such preparatory efforts are complex, expensive, and time intensive. Most officers lack specific training in the required interpersonal and professional skills. Often caseload size inhibits effective supervision; probation linkages with other social service agencies and providers are not optimal. Often female officers feel concerned about their own safety, and most sex offenders are "high-need" cases.

Probation officers, to control sex offenders, increasingly use enhanced probation services, through specialized caseload and electronic monitoring, Global Positioning System (GPS) monitoring (see Correctional Practice 21.2), and intensive supervision. Probation and

correctional practice 21.2

Monitoring High-Risk Sex Offenders with GPS Technology

Offenders committing sex crimes are frequently the subject of considerable controversy as well as potential violence. Reactions of generally law-abiding citizens to sex offenders and their recidivism can take the form of physical assault, arson directed at the offender's residence or vehicle, and other vigilante events. This is true for parolees in general, sex offenders, and sex offenders on GPS monitoring. If the sex offender commits a heinous sex crime (such as the kidnapping, rape, and murder of a child), public reaction is intense. These events lead to fear, violence, and demands to create policies that will protect the vulnerable. Few citizens will deny the irrefutable damage caused to victims of sex offenses.

Legislatures have tended to mandate imprisonment, increase the penalties for sex offenses, require completion of sex-offender treatment programs, authorize exclusion zones ("parolee may not come within 500 feet of a school campus"), and create sex-offender registries, among other policies. In the past two decades, some states have instituted and require electronic monitoring programs. California is one of those states.

In June 2006, California voters approved a proposition mandating that all sex offenders be placed on GPS supervision for life and that state parole officers enforce the terms and compliance while a sex-offender parolee is under the state's jurisdiction. By 2011, sex-offender parolees constituted almost 10 percent of all parolees in California.

Until very recently, the effectiveness of GPS monitoring of high-risk sex offenders in terms of increasing offender compliance with parole requirements or reducing recidivism (rearrest, reconviction, and return to incarceration) was not clear. The underlying policy question is how effective GPS monitoring is in ensuring public safety and at what cost.

The study of California high-risk sex offenders found that the GPS group did significantly better than a comparison group of subjects who received parole supervision (about 38 percent lower rates for parole revocation and return-to-custody events). The GPS group demonstrated significantly better outcomes on compliance and recidivism.

A cost analysis found that imprisonment costs $129 per day per inmate, traditional parole supervision costs $27 per day per parolee, and the GPS program costs almost $36 per day per parolee. The conclusion is that the GPS monitoring system is more expensive than traditional parole supervision but is significantly more effective than traditional supervision. Continued incarceration is 350 percent more expensive than GPS monitoring!

More outcome effectiveness data are needed and should address better classification of sex offenders to detect any differential risks among them, effective enforcement of parolee attendance at sex-offender treatment programs, imposition of graduated sanctions for noncomplying offenders (such as home curfew or house arrest), and universal imposition of the requirement of exclusion zones for high-risk sex offenders.

SOURCE: Stephen Gies et al. (2012), "Monitoring High-Risk Sex Offenders with GPS Technology," https://www.ncjrs.gov/pdffiles1/nij/grants/238481.pdf (accessed October 20, 2012).

parole agencies also contract with privately run community correctional centers to provide treatment programs for sex offenders as an adjunct to community control (see Chapter 13). As these strategies are more widely implemented across the nation, a smaller proportion of treatable sex offenders will be committed to prison facilities.

It is possible, of course, that tomorrow an alumnus of one of those treatment programs may commit a heinous lust-murder; however, an alumnus of a local high school or a member of a church choir could do the same. Treatment programs are specifically designed to minimize the likelihood that an offender will commit any sex offense following release, either a crime of the grossly offensive type or a lesser offense similar to the ones the offender committed in the past.

Sex Offenders in Prison

Attitudes toward sex offenders widely held by the public[28] as well as by legislators,[29] judges,[30] corrections officers,[31] and others in positions of power are influenced largely by traditional beliefs and continue to change. The number of sex offenders who are prisoners in state corrections systems continues to climb.

In correctional facilities providing more comprehensive treatment services to sex-offender populations, treatment program elements (modalities) are usually combined.

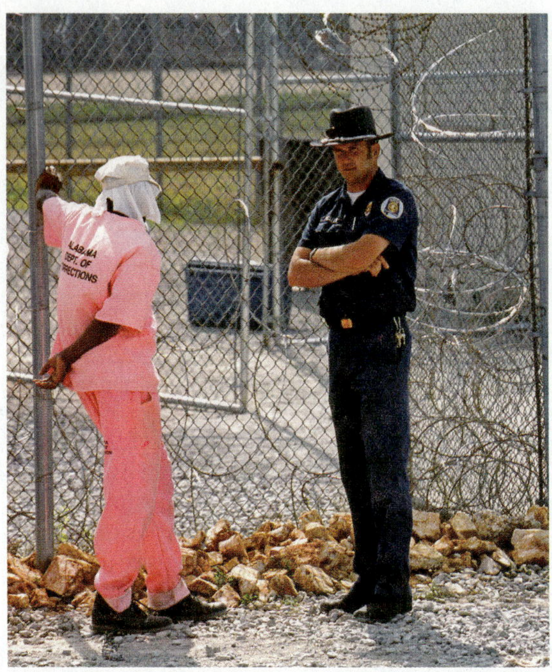

Photo 21.4

A security guard talks to a "pink-garbed" sex offender at the Limestone Facility, Capshaw, Alabama.
A. Ramey/PhotoEdit.

Such modalities can include cognitive-behavioral treatment; sex education, human sexuality, stress and anger management, social skills, and substance-abuse programs; and training in identifying and avoiding high-risk situations, relapse prevention, and coping skills.

Long-term programs generally provide intensive and highly structured programs of at least two years, aftercare (up to a year), and follow-up services. Clients can be returned for refresher treatment ("tune-ups"), if necessary.

Studies of the effectiveness of treatment for sex offenders are favorable, with strong evidence supporting a cognitive-behavioral approach. Using this method, distorted thinking is challenged, and sex offenders are taught how to avoid or manage high-risk situations. There is also some evidence that hormonal treatment can be effective with certain types of sex offenders.[32] Treatment with the so-called castration drug (Depo Provera) provides the same effect as castration, without the need for surgery. Although its use is not common, it might be used as an adjunct to supervision. For example, Texas, which used Depo Provera as an adjunct to individual and group treatment, showed relapse rates for Depo Provera–treated subjects to be one-third that for comparison offenders not treated and about 40 percent less than comparison cases after the drug was withdrawn. The Texas evaluation concludes that maintenance-level Depo Provera drug treatment is beneficial for the compulsive sex offender.[33]

The attitude toward the child molester, particularly those who use ritual child abuse and mutilation in cults,[34] has activated many states to legislate extreme increases in the range of punishment for such offenses. Such attitudes are reinforced by the continued recidivism reported almost daily with regard to these "headline" offenders. The history of the success with sexual offenders was initially poor, and the future is bleak if additional new approaches to this age-old problem are not developed, tested, and tried.

Involuntary Commitment of Sex Offenders

key term

Involuntary commitment
Laws that allow predatory sex offenders to be incarcerated in mental health facilities after their sentence has been served.

Due to changes in sentencing laws and several well-publicized cases in the 1990s, at least 17 states have passed various versions of what has come to be called "sexual predator" legislation. These laws allow for indefinite **involuntary commitment** of sex offenders to mental health treatment facilities after they complete prison terms for serious sex offenses. The impetus for this legislation was the repeal of the indeterminate sentencing laws under which serious sex offenders previously were confined in prison until prison officials were satisfied that they were no longer dangerous and the highly publicized accounts of a number of people who, on release from prison for sex crimes, committed additional heinous crimes, in some cases against children. The U.S. Supreme Court narrowly approved sexual predator laws in a 1997 decision, *Kansas v. Hendricks* (521 U.S. 346 [1997]); however, the courts remain divided on this issue, and some mental health organizations have taken a strong stand against such practices.[35]

AIDS IN PRISONS

The AIDS pandemic growing in the United States has of course reached prisons, particularly through offenders with histories of injecting drugs, sharing needles, and engaging in unprotected sexual activities. Estimates of the extent of infection vary across states and institutions, but by 2010, 20,093 inmates had been diagnosed HIV or AIDS (of which 1,756 were females), and 72 deaths were attributed to the disease. Almost 25 percent of HIV-positive inmates had AIDS, and inmates held in California, New York, Texas, and Florida accounted for 51 percent of this population. Prisoner-to-prisoner (intraprisoner) transmission is also a factor, but the rate appears to be low.[36] One factor that may contribute to the low rates of transmission is the availability of condoms and extensive AIDS education programs in some confinement facilities. Three jails in California and at least two state prison systems (Vermont and Oregon) make condoms available to inmates.

AIDS is a medical term describing terminal phases of **HIV infection**. It indicates an acquired immune system deficiency in which the human body is progressively unable to ward off common diseases and illnesses that would normally be quickly overcome. First, the War on Drugs has serious implications for concentration of HIV-positive cases in prisons. As the National Commission on AIDS pointed out, "By choosing mass imprisonment as the federal and state governments' response to the use of drugs, we have created a de facto policy of incarcerating more and more individuals with HIV infection." That trend is shown in Figure 21.2.[37] While the rate of AIDS infection has declined steadily over the past decade, it remains a problem for correctional administrators for many reasons.

Photo 21.5

As the sizeable "Baby Boomer" population ages, elderly inmates are becoming more common.

Robin Nelson/ZUMApress/Newscom.

HIV infection and resulting AIDS cases pose particular problems for corrections in terms of staff and inmates. Staff have been alarmed by the introduction of AIDS into prison, and initially little was done through education or training to reduce levels of irrational fear. Institutional policies had to be developed and reconsidered in the areas of diagnosing, managing, and treating HIV infection.[38] Additional policy development and implementation were also necessary in the areas of staff training and education, inmate counseling, pretest and posttest counseling, voluntary (versus mandatory) testing, medical parole, and discharge and aftercare services (for parole and community supervision). Infection control policies have also become necessary for dentists, nurses, physicians, security staff, and treatment personnel. Some HIV transmission and risk factors and precautionary and preventive measures are as follows:

- High-risk behaviors for HIV transmission—sex, drug use, sharing of injection materials, and tattooing—occur in correctional facilities.
- HIV transmission among correctional inmates has been shown to occur.
- Comprehensive and intensive education and prevention programs represent the best response to these facts, although the precise content of such programs is controversial.
- Rape and coerced sexual activity also occur in correctional facilities but require a different response, one based on inmate classification, housing, and supervision.

key term

AIDS
Medical term describing terminal phases of HIV infection.

key term

HIV infection
An acquired infection that compromises the body's ability to arrest or overcome common diseases and other illnesses.

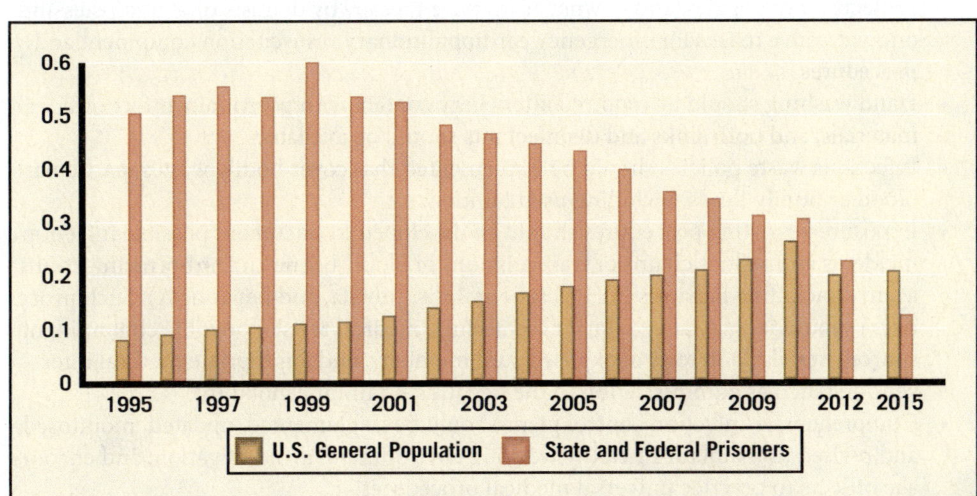

figure 21.2

Population with Confirmed AIDS, 1995–2012 (in percent).

SOURCE: Laura Maruschack, *HIV in Prisons, 2001–2010* (Washington, DC: Bureau of Justice Statistics, 2012); Centers for Disease Control, Division of HIV/AIDS Prevention (2013), "HIV in the United States: At a Glance," http://www.cdc.gov/hiv/pdf/statistics_basics_factsheet.pdf (accessed November 29, 2013).
Note: Data for 2015 are extrapolated.

Photo 21.6
An AIDS patient sits on the floor of his cell in punitive administrative isolation from other inmates.
A. Ramey/PhotoEdit.

- The implementation of "standard precautions" represents the heart of a correctional infection control program and the first line of defense against the occupational transmission of HIV.
- Condom distribution and other harm reduction strategies have not been widely adopted in American correctional systems.
- Experience with harm reduction in correctional facilities in Europe and elsewhere may warrant the attention of U.S. correctional administrators.[39]

AIDS and Custody Staff

Rebecca Craig identified five communicable diseases frequently found in correctional facilities: hepatitis A and B, HIV, rubella, and tuberculosis. She presented procedures thought necessary to address HIV infection.[40] These include the following:

- Avoid blind pocket searches and reaching into blind crevices to lessen the possibility of needlesticks and other puncture wounds; instead, use flashlights, mirrors, and other visual aids.
- Protective equipment should be provided and used, including latex gloves, masks, protective eye goggles, and gowns for invasive therapy by dentists or at autopsies and one-way valve masks for emergency cardiopulmonary resuscitation equipment and procedures.
- Hand washing should be required after every contact with potentially infectious materials, and both sinks and disinfectants should be available.
- Infectious waste policies should be implemented that cover bodily wastes, particularly blood or bodily fluids, including used tampons.
- Exposure-reporting procedures should be developed to document possible infection incidents and reduce chains of transmissions of blood-borne and airborne infectious agents (including hepatitis B, HIV, tuberculosis, rubella, and hepatitis A). Such procedures should include after-contact counseling, medical tests of possible contaminant sources, serial blood tests of exposed staff members, and appropriate medical intervention (such as administration of the hepatitis B immune globulin).
- Comprehensive infection control plans should be implemented, updated, monitored, and revised to maintain a healthy working environment, avoid litigation, and encourage officers to practice universal medical procedures.

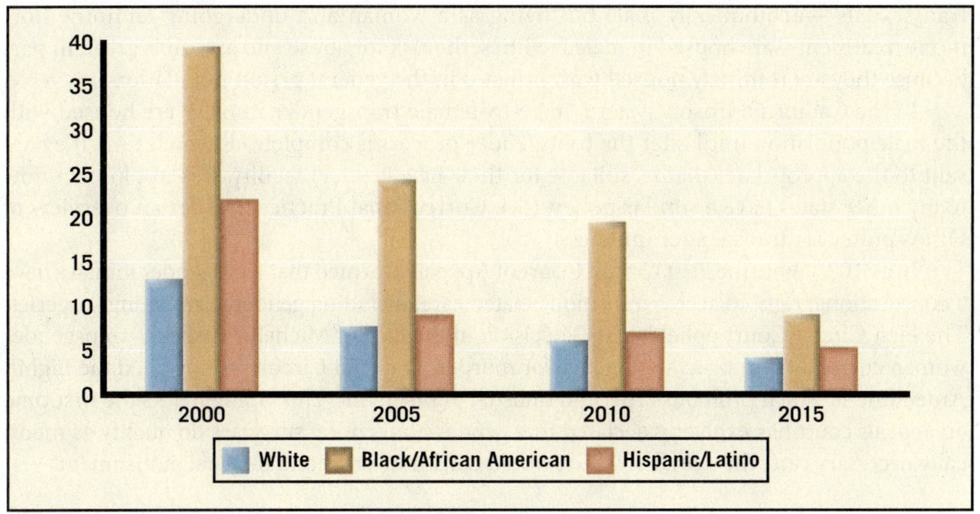

figure 21.3

Rate of AIDS-Related Deaths, 2000–2015 (per 100,000 inmates).

SOURCE: Laura Maruschak, *HIV in Prisons, 2001–2010* (Washington, DC: Bureau of Justice Statistics, 2012), p. 1. Note: Data for 2015 are extrapolated.

Adopting these policies will go a long way toward easing staff anxiety and tension in prison settings.

AIDS and Inmates

Perhaps the best single approach for managing HIV infections revolves around educational programs to inform inmates of necessary behaviors. Consensus on appropriate medical treatment within prison settings is that prisons should adopt existing community treatment as the standard of care.[41] At a minimum, special infirmaries should be established to prevent AIDS patients from becoming further victims of airborne infections.[42] Infirmaries[43] should also have drug treatment protocols that specify **antiviral drugs** such as AZT and protease inhibitors (usually taken together and with other antiviral drugs as "cocktails") and drug therapy for such opportunistic infections as tuberculosis and pneumonia. The AIDS death rate is dropping in prisons (see Figure 21.3), perhaps in part due to implementation of such policies and protocols.

key term

Antiviral drugs
Special antiviral pharmaceuticals used to lessen the levels and virulence of HIV infections.

Correctional administrators should propose and encourage a medical-parole mechanism for AIDS patients who are no longer a threat to the public safety for early release back into the community by paroling authorities. Prerelease counseling[44] well in advance of the proposed release date would help inmates identify resources and service providers in the communities to which they will be released. Ideally, each institution should identify a community-based support group of HIV-positive volunteers for inmate referral and ease of transition.

The cost of HIV and AIDS treatment in prison is unknown, but California approximates its costs as being as much as $86,000 per inmate per year. Existing Social Security and related medical insurance coverage would pay most of these costs if the offender were in a community setting. (Many correctional systems are arranging for parolees to receive "Obamacare" medical insurance at the point of their release from confinement.) By managing medical care, corrections could develop an efficient health care system in prison, lessen stigma, reduce paranoia and staff–inmate tensions, and sharply curtail the potential for costly litigation.[45] Innovation and leadership are required to overcome these problems.

TRANSGENDER INMATES

Although no one knows how many **transgender inmates** are housed in prisons and jails, this population poses an especially difficult problem for correctional officials. Access to medical procedures, housing considerations, and safety are some of the major issues faced by prison administrators. For example, although most male "preoperative

key term

Transgender inmate
An inmate having a gender identity that is different from the assigned sex at birth.

transsexuals"—anatomically male but living as a woman and undergoing feminine hormone treatment—are housed in male facilities, the risk for abuse and assault is great, in part because they are routinely housed with inmates in the general prison population.

In the California prison system, male-to-female transgender inmates are housed with the male population until after the transgender process is complete, at which time they are sent to the appropriate (that is, suitable for their new gender) facility. It is not known how many other states have a similar policy. (See Correctional Practice 21.3 for an overview of Ohio's policy for transgender inmates.)

In a 2103 ruling, the First Circuit Court of Appeals affirmed that transgender inmates have a constitutional right to access transition-related care, including gender-confirming surgeries. The First Circuit Court upheld a 2012 decision in the case of Michelle Kosilek, a transgender woman currently serving a life sentence for murder. The First Circuit's ruling cited the Eighth Amendment, which prohibits cruel and unusual punishment. This ruling marks the first time an appeals court has explicitly declared that gender-confirming surgeries do qualify as medically necessary care, the denial of which would constitute cruel and unusual punishment.

correctional **practice 21.3**

How the Ohio Department of Rehabilitation and Correction (ODRC) Handles Transgender Inmates

Several questions were posed to correctional officials in Ohio regarding transgender inmates, and the following was obtained:

1. **Does Ohio pay for hormone therapy and sex-change surgery?**

   All inmates, including transgendered inmates, receive a comprehensive reception evaluation to determine needs. The plan of care (whether this would include hormone treatment and/or surgery) is handled on a case-by-case basis by a multidisciplinary team of medical and mental health professionals. Hormone treatment and all surgeries, whether it be sex change or any surgery, require approval of the state medical director or his or her designee. Ohio has continued and paid for hormone treatments that were started prior to incarceration for those patients for whom stopping the treatment would have a negative outcome for the patient. To date, hormone therapy has not been initiated during incarceration solely due to a transgender diagnosis. To date, ODRC has never authorized a sex-change surgery during incarceration. In general, ODRC does not approve or fund elective surgeries or treatments. However, we continue to evaluate our policy and treatment modalities for transgendered inmates as the literature and evidence-based practice guidelines evolve. We review these on a case-by-case basis and develop a plan of care appropriately. The ODRC pays for any treatment that we approve for our patients.

2. **Are all transgender inmates placed in protective housing, or are some in the general population?**

   No, transgender inmates are not automatically placed in protective housing. Transgendered inmates may reside in both settings within the ODRC. The ODRC has always followed the requirements of the Prison Rape Elimination Act (PREA) and has developed screening, tracking, reporting, assessment, and case management systems for transgendered inmates to achieve compliance with recent PREA standard changes. Our system has the capability to identify needs for protective housing for transgendered and other at-risk populations, and we use protective housing accordingly based on our needs assessment.

3. **If a male-to-female sex change has been completed, does the ODRC house the inmate in a female prison?**

   Although the ODRC has never approved/authorized sex-change surgery for an inmate to date, we have received inmates who have undergone sex change prior to incarceration. These inmates are reviewed on a case-by-case basis for appropriate placement. There is review and input by medical, mental health, legal, and unit management/custody staff. Generally inmates in these situations are placed in housing that is consistent with their genitalia at that point in time (male to male prison, female to female prison). Again, how-ever, this is done on an individual basis with consideration of where the inmate can best live, adapt, and be safe/secure.

SOURCE: Special thanks to Deputy Director Sara Andrews and Director of Nursing Jennifer A. Clayton, Ohio Department of Rehabilitation and Correction.

GERIATRIC INMATES: THE GRAYING OF AMERICAN PRISONS

As was mentioned in Chapter 17, the proportion of prisoners in the nation's institutions who are elderly is rapidly increasing, in part due to the tougher long-term sentences inherent in the current "get-tough-on-crime" stance but also because of the aging of the general population in America. By 2012, there were over 125,000 male and 6,906 female inmates over 55 years of age housed in state and federal institutions.[46] This trend, which appears likely to continue, will have a significant impact on correctional administration and budgets in this new century. It is estimated that by 2015, at least one in six, or over 160,000, inmates will be

key term

Elderly inmate
An inmate of an age that exceeds the jurisdiction's definition of elderly inmates, frequently age 55 and above.

policy position 21.1

Mass Incarceration of the Elderly

In terms of the incarceration rate, the United States leads the world. Due to lengthy sentencing, mandatory minimum sentences, and "tough-on-crime" and War on Drugs policies, incarceration has often been the option of choice. As sentences have gotten longer, so has the prison population grown older. Currently, one in six prison inmates are age 55 or older. If current trends continue, that proportion will rise to one in three incarcerated offenders by 2030, according to the estimates of the American Civil Liberties Union (ACLU). The extreme sentencing policies and growing number of life sentences have turned many of our correctional facilities into prison nursing homes.

The increasing concentration of the "old" and "elderly" is not a direct result of a burgeoning crime wave committed by "graysters." Instead, it is more a direct result of imprisoning offenders for longer periods of time, life sentences to prison, rapid revocation of parole, and sentences imposing life without parole. This development over the past quarter of a century in the nation's history has increased prison populations over 400 percent, in contrast to the 36 percent growth rate of the general population. If current trends continue, we could see 400,000 elderly inmates by 2030.

Prison costs have also skyrocketed. The ACLU estimates the costs of an average prisoner to be just over $34,000 per year. Housing a prisoner age 50 and older requires over $68,000. This difference in large part is a result of a lack of sufficient health care and inaccessibility of healthy living prior to imprisonment, elderly inmate deterioration and rapid aging due to heavy stresses behind bars, and the costs of health care for more seriously challenged elderly inmates. Many states are now forced to deal with the demonstrated fact of massive spending on incarceration of the elderly, which is fiscally difficult to sustain and, in terms of public safety, unnecessary.

Releasing and paroling of aging inmates, along with extending the limits of confinement to include family placement or subsidized housing providers or even to community corrections residential centers, would be significantly less expensive that the mass incarceration of elderly prisoners.

Some states, such as Louisiana and California, have legislated effective and cost-saving reforms in response to crime and criminals, acknowledging that it is inappropriate and ineffective to continue this one-size-fits-all model of massive incarceration. Others are exploring changes to sentence length, minimum mandatory sentences, three-strikes sentences, compassionate release programs, and limits on revocation of parole due to technical violations. The general goal is to depopulate the elderly inmates from prison and focus correctional control on high-risk offenders.

Research clearly shows that by age 50, most people have significantly outlived their crime years, and the arrest rate of those over 65 years of age is extremely low. Public safety is not enhanced by continued incarceration of geriatric inmates. Releasing geriatric inmates is not going to trigger an "elderly crime wave."

Recommendations for depopulating aging prisoners include the following:

1. Grant conditional release to aging prisoners whose safety risk is low.
2. Expand and frequently use medical parole.
3. Maximize both the accountability and transparency of parole boards.
4. Authorize and expand the Federal Prisoner Aging Release process.
5. Repeal "truth-in-sentencing" laws.
6. Require the "third strike" to be a crime of violence.
7. Repeal habitual offender and three-strikes sentencing laws.
8. Repeal minimum mandatory sentencing laws.

Source: American Civil Liberties Union (2012), "At America's Expense: The Mass Incarceration of the Elderly," http://www.aclu.org/criminal-law-reform/Americas-expense-mass-incarceration-elderly (accessed October 23, 2012).

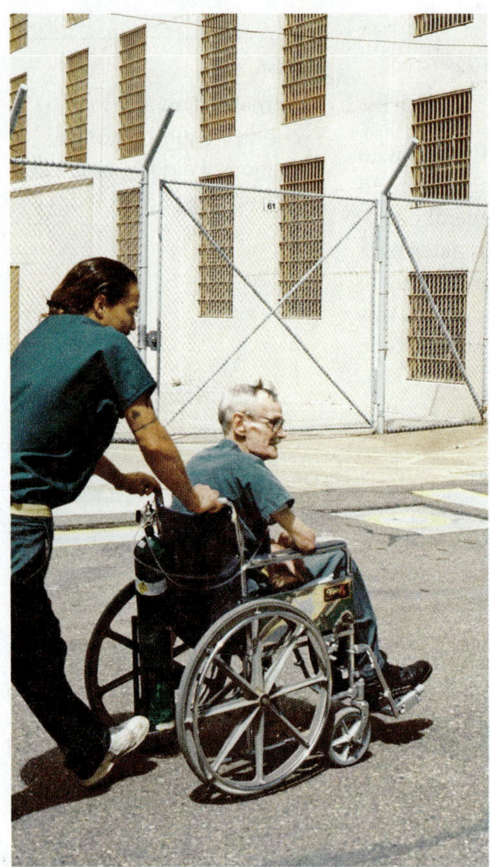

Photo 21.7
Robert Lee Lilley, a convicted sex offender, is wheeled into the yard at Territorial Prison (Colorado). The then-70-year-old Lilley (at the time of the photograph), who has numerous health problems, requires an inmate attendant. Lilley has been denied parole twice and will likely die in prison. His case highlights the public health costs associated with elderly prisoners throughout the country.
Sean Cayton/The Image Works.

age 50 or over. The number of older inmates (age 55 or above) in Florida is now over 16 percent of all prisoners, and in New York, although the overall prison population declined 11.6 percent between 2007 and 2012, the elderly population increased by nearly 28 percent. Policy Position 21.1 further examines the issue of the elderly in America's prisons.

Elderly inmates are more likely than other prisoners to have committed crimes such as homicide and manslaughter as well as sexual offenses. They are less likely than younger inmates to be imprisoned for robbery and burglary. Because of their significantly longer sentences, elderly inmates may be concentrated in prisons well beyond their proportions in the civilian population, which will pose problems for them as well as prison administrators. First, they will have health care concerns and need preventive health care programs that, if not provided, could be a source of considerable and, for correctional administrators, substantial litigation costs. At the least, inmates will suffer from depression and differing nutritional needs (less protein, fewer calories, and more soft food and fiber). Because taste sensations decline with aging, the elderly will request food richer in seasonings and will have a decrease in gastric acid and increase in gas production and constipation. Special diets will be needed.

In addition, growing old in prison will mean having to avoid exploitation and violence by younger inmates, having to adjust new personal needs to prison life, and not having suitable programs (recreational, educational, or housing). Vulnerability to victimization, frailty, and isolation from outside relatives and friends will take their toll, as will fear of death, hopelessness, and being unable to cope when released. (See Correctional Practice 21.4 for more on the challenges faced by elderly inmates.) Some departments of corrections have concentrated all "elderly inmates" into one or two specific facilities and reassigned younger inmates to other units in order to develop sufficient cell space for this purpose. Some states define the population to be protected as over age 35. Assault rates are reported to have dropped for the protected inmates.

Health care costs will increase significantly for treatment of conditions such as hypertension, diabetes, stroke, cancer, Alzheimer's disease, and emphysema. Glasses, dentures, kidney dialysis, and heart surgery will be required. It has been estimated that in 10 years, annual health care costs for elderly inmates ($69,000 in 1997 and $86,000 in California) will increase by 14-fold.[47] Many smaller prisons will become geriatric centers, or special centers for elderly inmates will be built, and special staff as well as staff training will be necessary to treat this special category of the nation's offenders. Perhaps a nation that can explore outer space can find the necessary compassion to care for this small but increasing group as we continue into this new century. Executive clemency, including pardons, may become a frequent act, if for nothing else than to save money on prisoners who are probably no longer a danger to society.[48] Released inmates will become eligible for low- or no-cost medical care.

Preliminary data from the U.S. Census Bureau's annual State Government Finance Census indicate that states spent $48.5 billion on corrections in 2010, about 6 percent less than in 2009. The average state corrections expenditure per inmate was $28,323 in 2010, although a quarter of states spent $40,175 or more. By 2015, total cost for corrections in America will exceed $73 billion.

The Federal Bureau of the Prisons expended $6.9 billion. The average cost of imprisoning a state inmate was over $31,000. States spent over $3.3 billion for medical care of inmates, averaging over $5,200 per inmate. The state of California spent the most for medical services for each inmate ($11,986), and Illinois spent the least ($2,217). The national average percentage for medical care was 15 percent of operating expenditures.[49]

The **geriatric inmate**, sentenced to life with little hope of parole, could live many years in the prisons of America—long after his or her dangerousness has passed. The courts of the land will be checking carefully to ensure that the person's rights are not violated, and it is certain that imprisonment costs will soar. Geriatric prisoners are "special people" and must be thought of as such when considering sentences that are too long (beyond what is cost effective).

key term

Geriatric inmate
An older elderly inmate whose physical or mental disabilities require more extensive medical and treatment care.

correctional **practice 21.4**

Challenges Geriatric Inmates Face in Prisons

Most prison systems in the nation have not yet adapted to the needs of inmates over age 50. Age 50 (or age 55 in some jurisdictions) is commonly used as the defining point at which inmates are known as "geriatric inmates"(or "geries"). Prisons were not designed for geriatric inmates, and as a result there are many challenges.

To maintain independence, inmates must be able to perform unique physical behaviors, some of which (bathing, dressing, and using bathroom facilities) are shared across all geriatric persons, whether in prison or in the free world. There are also unique additional activities that must be performed in the prison setting. These include the following:

- Jumping off the bed to the floor when an alarm is sounded, as all inmates must
- Dropping to the floor immediately so staff can count and control inmates
- Climbing into and out of the top bunk in dormitory settings
- Hearing and responding to orders from correctional personnel
- Standing in line for long periods of time (as in waiting to be served food and inmate counts)
- Walking to the dining room or other areas of the facility

In some prisons, wheelchair-bound inmates are expected to drop to the floor and stand for the count or get out of their wheelchairs when the alarm sounds. Others with brittle bones or having trouble walking may find a drop to the "boots-to-the-floor" order hazardous. In addition, falls are hazardous and can be a quick route to becoming a wheelchair- or bed-bound inmate.

Medical challenges that geriatric inmates face revolve around the absence of health care services available when they were in the free world. These act to compound medical problems in prison, including arthritis, hypertension, renal insufficiencies, asthma, and inability to sleep. Our prison systems were never designed for a geriatric population, and it has been estimated that by 2030, some one in three prisoners could be geriatric inmates. What are some basic prison changes needed for geriatric inmates in the short haul? (Changes in the long haul are explored in Policy Position 21.1.) In no particular order, recommendations are as follows:

a. All geriatric inmates should be assigned to the lower bunks unless the inmate requests another "home," such as top bunk or single cell.

b. Such cells should have grab bars in reach of toilet facilities.

c. Geriatric inmates should be celled near dining facilities.

d. More time should be allocated for geriatrics for dropping to the floor during alarms.

e. Showers should be retrofitted with grab bars in and immediately beside the entry point.

f. Nonskid rubber mats should be in place on shower and other wet floors.

With most states facing demands for services that cannot be provided, what should and can be done for the geriatric inmate with dementia so profound that he or she cannot even remember his or her name, much less the day and month of the year or who the president of the nation is? Or for the near-end inmate who has suffered one or more strokes and is partially or totally paralyzed? Should prisons be geriatric hospitals? These questions have no easy answers but will require increased attention as America's prisons continue to gray.

SOURCE: Steve Tokar (2006), "Geriatric Inmates Face Challenges Unique to Prison," http://www.ucsf.edu/news/2006/03/5398/geriatric-inmates-face-challenges-unique-prison (accessed October 23, 2012).

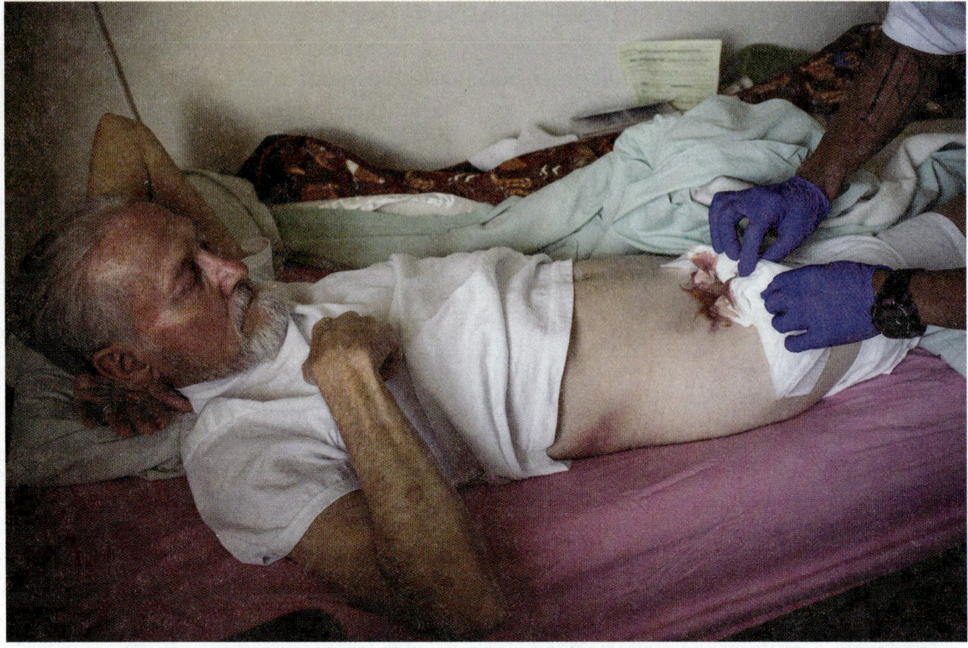

Photo 21.8

Medical staff treating a geriatric inmate for an open wound in his groin. Note bedsore above right hip.
Andrew Burton/Staff/Getty Images News/Getty Images.

Summary

Summarize the Issues Regarding Offenders Who Are Mentally Ill

Since the 1970s, major changes have been made in the handling of clients in the mental health facilities in local and state correctional facilities. Significant U.S. Supreme Court decisions focused on incarcerated inmates have contributed to the general cultural belief that treatment of correctional offenders is not constitutionally required. Successive court cases, however, resulted in legal dicta: If you detain a person for mental health issues, dangerousness, and potential criminal acts, you must provide treatment services. Failure to do so can lead to expenditure of significant financial and political resources if offender rights are violated.

Underlying the shift to incarceration of the "mad, bad, and sick" was an incorrect assumption. Major strides in the medical prescription armature and demonstration projects served to convince most mental health leaders that community treatment using pharmaceutical interventions on the local level would provide the much-needed solution to the needs of such offenders. They may be criminals, but they are also sick. Such community services never materialized, primarily for economic reasons but also for the fact that many of the ill were also criminal, and criminals were believed to be the least worthy of Americans to receive beneficial treatment.

Summarize the Issues Regarding Offenders Who Are Developmentally Challenged

The evisceration of facilities for the mentally and developmentally challenged contributed to the concentration of both groups in correctional confinement centers (jails and prisons). The future of corrections in the nation lies in significant revision of criminal sentences, reduced reliance on incarceration, buttressing of community-based services, and use of evidence-based practices. Younger, enthused, informed, and dedicated justice professionals are required for this resolution.

Summarize the Issues regarding Sex Offenders

Sex offenders are not liked in the public or in prison and suffer from a large number of dangers, such as assaults and vigilante justice, and sometimes receive no assistance from community supervision officers who frequently do not know appropriate management techniques.

Explain How AIDS and Infectious Diseases Have Affected Prisons

Infectious diseases such as hepatitis A and B, HIV, rubella, and tuberculosis plague all correctional facilities but especially the higher-custody units, such as prisons and penitentiaries. HIV, untreated, can result in AIDS, and treatment for both stages does not prevent death. Infectious diseases are very expensive to treat and manage, easily spread, and feared by corrrectional staff. Coupled with long-term imprisonment and an aging population in prisons, these diseases require expensive management and treatment efforts, resulting in a larger proportion of the institutions' financial resources being required for treatment. Compassionate release and medical parole, when implemented, result in less drain on correctional finances.

Explain How Prison Officials Handle Transgender Inmates

Transgender inmates are housed with the general population; however, placement is often made on a case-by-case basis.

Summarize the Issues regarding Aging Offenders

Due to lengthy sentencing, mandatory minimum sentences, and "tough-on-crime" and War on Drugs policies, incarceration has often been the option of choice. As sentences have gotten longer, so has the prison population grown older. Together, these have significantly slowed the exit of inmates from confinement and created a large population of geriatric inmates who require increasingly costly medical care as well as special considerations that are difficult for facilities to implement. The challenges presented and faced by geriatric inmates will increase as this population continues to grow.

Key Words

transincarceration, 457
mentally disturbed, 458
asylum, 458
deinstitutionalization, 458
transinstitutionalization, 458
not guilty by reason of insanity (NGRI), 460
incompetent to stand trial, 460
criminally insane, 460
guilty but mentally ill (GBMI), 461
predict potential dangerousness, 462
developmentally challenged, 462
Ruiz v. *Estelle*, 463
sodomy, 464
sex offense, 464
child abuser, 466
child molester, 466
AIDS, 469
HIV infection, 469
antiviral drugs, 471
transgender inmate, 471
elderly inmate, 474
geriatric inmate, 475
involuntary commitment, 468

Review Questions

1. What spurred the growth of asylums in America?
2. How can one avoid criminal responsibility?
3. What are the most common sex offenses?
4. What would the American Psychiatric Association do with insanity acquittees?
5. What problems do developmentally challenged offenders pose for correctional administrators?
6. What recommendations have been offered for correctional processing of developmentally challenged offenders?
7. Can sex offenders be treated?
8. What can be done to reduce staff fear of AIDS?
9. What can be done to reduce AIDS in prison?
10. What should be done with geriatric prisoners?
11. Why does inmate health care cost more than that of the general public?
12. Debate: Inmates over age 70 should be released to community supervision.
13. Why are there so many mentally disordered offenders in prison?
14. What problems does the prison pose for developmentally challenged inmates?
15. Has the GBMI statute approach solved the dilemma of protecting society while providing treatment to disturbed offenders?

Application Case Studies

1. Following a highly publicized case, your state is considering involuntary commitments for sex offenders. You have been asked to testify before the legislative committee considering the bill. State your position and outline your testimony.
2. You are the chief probation officer in your county (congratulations) and have decided to use GPS monitoring for all serious sex offenders. Draft a one-page memo to your staff that outlines the goal of this new policy, how it will be operated, and what indicators will be used to determine its effectiveness.
3. You have been asked by the director of corrections in your state to develop some new policies for better handling the growing number of geriatric inmates housed in the state prisons. Before you begin, however, you need more information. What information would you collect, and why?
4. You are the warden of a prison, and one of your male inmates comes to you and tells you that he is transgender and wants to continue treatment for a sex change. What special steps would you take to ensure his safety?

Endnotes

1. Kenneth Adams, "Who Are the Clients? Characteristics of Inmates Referred for Mental Health Treatment," *The Prison Journal* 72:1/2 (1992): 120–141. See also Richard Bembo, H. Cervenka, B. Hunter, et al., "Engaging High-Risk Families in Community-Based Intervention Services," *Aggression and Violent Behavior* 4:1 (1999): 41–58.
2. G. Ives, *A History of Penal Methods* (London: S. Paul, 1914). Exploitation of incarcerated developmentally challenged offenders by more aggressive and stronger inmates remains a problem in all facilities: mental institutions, juvenile centers, nursing homes, jails, and prisons. In 1980, Congress passed the Civil Rights of Institutionalized Persons Act, authorizing the attorney general to intervene in correctional settings if violations of inmates' civil rights are suspected. For an example of juvenile victimization, see C. Bartollas, S. Miller, and S. Dinitz, *Juvenile Victimization: The Institutional Paradox* (New York: Holsted Press, 1976), pp. 53–76. See also Freda Briggs, *From Victim to Offender: How Child Sexual Abuse Victims Become Offenders* (St. Leonards, Australia: Allen and Unwin, 1995). For a study of missed opportunity, see Luke Birmingham, D. Mason, and D. Grubin, " A Follow-Up Study of Mentally Disordered Men Remanded to Prison," *Criminal Behavior and Mental Health* 8:3 (1998): 202–213.
3. J. Wilpers, "Animal, Vegetable or Human Being?," *Government Executive,* May 1973, p. 3. See also Terry Kupers, "Trauma and Its Sequelae in Male Prisoners: Effects of Confinement, Overcrowding and Diminished Services," *American Journal of Orthopsychiatry* 66:2 (1996): 189–196.
4. Bruce Arrigo, "Transcarceration: A Constructive Ethnology of Mentally-Ill 'Offenders,'" *The Prison Journal* 81:2 (2002): 162–186.
5. Randy Revelle, former King County executive, while accepting the National Association of Counties award for the "6 East" project for mentally ill inmates at the King County Jail, 1982.
6. Chris Sigurdson, "The Mad, the Bad and the Abandoned: The Mentally Ill in Prisons and Jails," *Corrections Today* 62:7 (2001): 162–186. See also Brian Dawe, "Managing the 'Other' Inmates," http://www.corrections.com/news/articles/16946 (accessed January 17, 2008), and Corrections News, "Prisoners in Finland Suffer High Rates of Mental Illness," *Corrections News* 13:6 (2007): 34.
7. Corrections News, "California Receiver Issues Status Report on Prison Medical System," *Corrections News* 13:7 (2007): 14; Doris James and Lauren Blaze, *Mental Health Problems of Prison and Jail Inmates* (Washington, DC: Bureau of Justice Statistics, 2006), p. 1.
8. In 1999, Los Angles County had to appropriate more than $8 million as a supplemental allocation to improve mental health care in its jails. Chris Sigurdson, "The Mad, the Bad and the Abandoned," http://search.aol.com/aol/search?enabled_terms=&s_it=wscreen50-bb&q=Los+Angeles+with+The+Mad%2C+the+Bad+and+the+Abandoned.
9. Although the issue of mental illness as a risk factor for criminal conduct is still debated, most empirical research indicates that mental illness is not strongly correlated with criminal conduct. See J. Bonta, M. Law, and R. K. Hanson, "The Prediction of Criminal and Violent Recidivism among Mentally Disordered Offenders: A Meta-Analysis," *Psychological Bulletin* 123 (1998): 123–142. See also S. Wessely and P. J. Taylor, "Madness and Crime: Criminology versus Psychiatry," *Criminal Justice and Mental Health* 1:3 (1991): 193–228. See also Mary Ann Finn, "Prison Misconduct among

Developmentally Challenged Inmates," *Criminal Justice and Mental Health* 2:3 (1992): 287–299; Lynette Feder, "A Comparison of the Community Adjustment of Mentally Ill Offenders with Those from the General Prison Population," *Law and Human Behavior* 15:5 (1991): 477–493; and Bruce Link, Howard Andrews, and Francis Cullen, "The Violent and Illegal Behavior of Mental Patients Reconsidered," *American Sociological Review* 57:2 (1992): 275–292. But see Barry Wright, I. McKenzie, J. Stace, et al., eds., "Adult Criminality in Previously Hospitalized Child Psychiatric Patients," *Criminal Behavior and Mental Health* 8:1 (1998): 19–38.

10. National Institute of Mental Health, *Directory of Institutions for the Mentally Disordered Offenders* (Washington, DC: U.S. Government Printing Office, 1972); Anthony Walsh, *Correctional Assessment, Casework and Counseling* (Lanham, MD: American Correctional Association, 1997).
11. Valerie Hans, "An Analysis of Public Attitudes toward the Insanity Defense," *Criminology* 24:3 (1986): 393–413. Among her more interesting findings were that the public wants insane lawbreakers punished, believes that insanity defense procedures fail to protect the general public, and wildly overestimates the use and effectiveness of the insanity defense. See also Bruce Arrigo, *The Contours of Psychiatric Justice* (New York: Garland, 1996), and Caton Roberts and S. Golding, "The Social Construction of Criminal Responsibility and Insanity," *Law and Human Behavior* 15:4 (1991): 349–376.
12. Marnie Rice, Grant Harris, and Carol Lang, "Recidivism among Male Insanity Acquittees," *Journal of Psychiatry and the Law* 18:3/4 (1990): 379–403; Richard Pasework, B. Parnell, and J. Rock, "Insanity Defense: Shifting the Burden of Proof," *Journal of Police Science and Criminal Psychology* 10:1 (1994): 1–4.
13. John Klofas and Ralph Weisheit, "Guilty but Mentally Ill: Reform of the Insanity Defense in Illinois," *Justice Quarterly* 4:1 (1987): 40–50. The effects of the GBMI statutes are discussed in Kurt Bumby, "Reviewing the Guilty but Mentally Ill Alternatives," *Journal of Psychiatry and the Law* 21:2 (1993): 191–220.
14. Lisa Callahan, Margaret McGreevy, Carmen Cirincione, et al., "Measuring the Effects of the Guilty but Mentally Ill (GBMI) Verdict: Georgia's 1982 GBMI Reform," *Law and Human Behavior* 16:4 (1992): 447–462; Carmen Cirincione, H. Steadman, and M. McGreevy, "Rates of Insanity Acquittals and the Factors Associated with Successful Insanity Pleas," *Bulletin of the American Academy of Psychiatry and the Law* 23:2 (1995): 339–409.
15. American Psychiatric Association, *Standards for Psychiatric Facilities* (Washington, DC: American Psychiatric Association, 1981), pp. 17–18. But see Washington State Department of Corrections, *Mentally Ill Offenders: Community Release Outcome Study* (Olympia: Washington State Department of Corrections, 1997).
16. Bernard Rubin, "Prediction of Dangerousness in Mentally Ill Criminals," *Archives of General Psychiatry* 27:1 (September 1972): 397–407; Robert Prentky, A. Lee, R. Knight, et al., eds., "Recidivism Rates among Child Molesters and Rapists," *Law and Human Behavior* 21:6 (1998): 635–659; Michael Ross, "Reflections from Death Row," in *Crime and Punishment: Inside Views*, ed. Robert Johnson and H. Toch (Los Angeles: Roxbury, 2000).
17. Miles Santamour and Bernadette West, *Sourcebook on the Mentally Disordered Prisoner* (Washington, DC: U.S. Department of Justice, 1985), p. 70. See also Joan Petersilia, "Justice for All? Offenders with Mental Retardation and the California Corrections System," *The Prison Journal* 77:4 (1997): 358–380, in which Petersilia estimates the mentally retarded offender in California as 2 percent of all probationers and 4 percent of all incarcerated persons.
18. Finn, "Prison Misconduct among Developmentally Challenged Inmates," p. 296. See also Allen Beck, Paige Harrison, and Devon Adams, *Sexual Violence Reported by Correctional Authorities* (Washington, DC: Bureau of Justice Statistics, 2006).
19. Severson identifies 10 basic services necessary for inmate mental health. Margaret Severson, "Refining the Boundaries of Mental Health Services: A Holistic Approach to Inmate Mental Health," *Federal Probation* 56:3 (1992): 57–63; Rudolph Alexander, "Incarcerated Juvenile Offenders' Right to Rehabilitation," *Criminal Justice Policy Review* 7:2 (1995): 202–213.
20. *Ruiz* v. *Estelle,* 503 F. Supp. 1265 (S. D. Tex. 1980), *aff'd in part,* 679 F. 2d 1115 (5th Cir. 1982), *cert. denied,* 103 S. Ct. 1438 (1983) at 1344. See Rolando Del Carmen, B. Witt, W. Hume, et al., *Texas Jails: Law Practice* (Huntsville, TX: Sam Houston Press, 1990); John Sharp, *Behind the Walls: The Price and Performance of the Texas Department of Criminal Justice* (Austin: Texas Comptroller of Public Accounts, 1994).
21. Joan Petersilia, *Doing Justice: Criminal Offenders with Development Disabilities* (Berkeley: University of California Press 2000).
22. Richard C. Allen, "Reaction to S. Fox: The Criminal Reform Movement," in *The Developmentally Challenged Citizen and the Law*, ed. M. Kindred (Washington, DC: U.S. Government Printing Office, 1976), p. 645. See also Mark Nichols, L. Bench, E. Morlok, and K. Liston, "Analysis of Mentally Retarded and Lower-Functioning Offender Correctional Programs," *Corrections Today* 65:2 (2003): 119–121.

23. Mary Dickson, *Rape, the Most Intimate of Crimes*, http://www.pbs.org/kued/nosafeplace/articles/rapefeat.html (accessed October 5, 2014).
24. See Patricia Cluss et al., "The Rape Victim: Psychological Correlates of Participation in the Legal Process," *Criminal Justice and Behavior* 10:3 (1983): 342–357, and Patricia Mahoney and L. Williams, "Sexual Assault in Marriage: Wife Rape," in *Partner Violence*, ed. Jana Jasinski and L. Williams (Thousand Oaks, CA: Sage, 1998), pp. 113–162.
25. David Finkelor, "Removing the Child—Prosecuting the Offender in Cases of Sexual Abuse: Evidence from the National Reporting System for Child Abuse and Neglect," *Child Abuse and Neglect* 7:2 (1983): 195–205. But see Philip Jenkins, *Moral Panic: Changing Concepts of the Child Molester in Modern America* (New Haven, CT: Yale University Press, 1998).
26. Jean Goodwin et al., *Sexual Abuse: Incest Victims and Their Families* (Boston: John Wright, 1982). See also Katherine Beckett, "Culture and the Politics of Signification: The Case of Child Abuse," *Social Problems* 43:1 (1996): 57–76, and Joann Brown and G. Brown, "Characteristics and Treatment of Incest Offenders," *Journal of Aggression Maltreatment and Trauma* 1:1 (1997): 335–354.
27. Ross Cheit, R. Freeman-Longo, M. Greenberg, et al., "Symposium on the Treatment of Sex Offenders," *New England Journal of Criminal and Civil Confinement* 23:2 (1997): 267–462. See also Abe Macher, "Pedophiles and the Sexual Transmission of HIV to Children," *American Jails* 11:2 (2007): 33–36.
28. Richard McCorkle, "Research Note: Punish or Rehabilitate: Public Attitudes toward Six Common Crimes," *Crime and Delinquency* 39:2 (1993): 250–252; Joel Rudin, "Megan's Law: Can It Stop Sexual Predators?," *Criminal Justice* 11:3 (1996): 2–10, 60–63.
29. Timothy Flanagan, P. Brennan, and D. Cohen, "Conservatism and Capital Punishment in the State Capitol: Lawmakers and the Death Penalty," *The Prison Journal* 72:1/2 (1992): 37–56.
30. Anthony Walsh, "Placebo Justice: Victim Recommendations and Offender Sentences in Sexual Assault Cases," *Journal of Criminal Law and Criminology* 77:4 (1986): 1126–1141; Federal Bureau of Investigation, *Crime in the United States 1994* (Washington, DC: U.S. Department of Justice, 1995), p. 225.
31. John Weeks, G. Pelletier, and D. Beaulette, "Correctional Officers: How Do They Perceive Sex Offenders?," *International Journal of Offender Therapy and Comparative Criminology* 35:1 (1995): 55–61; American Correctional Association, *Point/Counterpoint* (Lanham, MD: American Correctional Association, 1997).
32. For a review of the effects of different types of treatment for sex offenders, see Gordon C. Nagayama Hall, "Sexual Offender Recidivism Revisited: A Meta-Analysis of Recent Treatment Studies," *Journal of Consulting and Clinical Psychology* 63:5 (1985): 802–809.
33. E. Brecher, *Treatment Programs for Sex Offenders*, prepared for the National Institute of Law Enforcement and Criminal Justice (Washington, DC: U.S. Government Printing Office, 1978), pp. 1–12. The material for this section has been extracted from this document and reflects the current literature on the subject. See also Walter Meyer, C. Cole, and D. Lipton, "Links between Biology and Crime," *Journal of Offender Rehabilitation* 25:3/4 (1997): 1–34.
34. Steven Glass, "An Overview of Satanism and Ritualized Child Abuse," *Journal of Police and Criminal Psychology* 7:2 (1991): 43–50; Ben Crouch and K. Damphouse, "Newspapers and the Antisatanism Movement: A Content Analysis," *Sociological Spectrum* 12:1 (1992): 1–20; William Bernet and C. Chang, "The Differential Diagnosis of Ritual Abuse Allegations," *Journal of Forensic Sciences* 42:1 (1997): 32–38.
35. See, for example, http://www.mentalhealthamerica.net/.
36. Laura Maruschak, *HIV in Prisons 2001–2010* (Washington, DC: Bureau of Justice Statistics, 2012).
37. National Commission on Acquired Immune Deficiency Syndrome, *Report: HIV Disease in Correctional Facilities* (Washington, DC: U.S. Department of Justice, 1992), p. 5. See also James Marquart, V. Brewer, J. Mullins, et al., "The Implication of Crime Control Policy on HIV/AIDS-Related Risk among Women Prisoners," *Crime and Delinquency* 45:1 (1999): 82–98.
38. Caroline Wolf Harlow, *Drug Enforcement and Treatment in Prisons, 1990* (Washington, DC: U.S. Department of Justice, 1992), p. 1. See also Meyer et al., "Links between Biology and Crime."
39. There are no confirmed cases of a correctional officer whose workplace exposure resulted in HIV infection. Jeanne Flavin, "Police and HIV/AIDS: The Risk, the Reality, the Response," *American Journal of Criminal Justice* 23:1 (1998): 33–58.
40. Rebecca Craig, "Six Steps to Stop the Spread of Communicable Diseases," *Corrections Today* 54:7 (1992): 104–109. See also Mary Coplin, "Managing the Challenge of HIV," *Corrections Today* 54:8 (1992): 104–107.
41. Robert Reeves, "Approaching 2000: Finding Solutions to the Most Pressing Issues Facing the Corrections Community," *Corrections Today* 54:3 (1998): 74, 76–79.
42. Abe Macher, "Esophageal Candidiasis in Patients with Primary HIV Infection," *American Jails* 11:1 (2007): 43–46; Abe Macher, "Issues in Correctional HIV Care," *American Jails* 11:3 (2007): 45–48.
43. Joseph Paris, "Why an AIDS Unit?," in *The State of Corrections: Proceedings of the 1991 Annual Conferences*

(Laurel, MD: American Correctional Association, 1992), pp. 3–56.

44. Donald McVinney, "Counseling Incarcerated Individuals with HIV Disease and Chemical Dependency," *Journal of Chemical Dependency Treatment* 4:2 (1991): 105–118.
45. Patricia Satterfield, "A Strategy for Controlling Health Care Costs," *Corrections Today* 54:2 (1992): 190–194. But see Margaret Norris and M. May, "Screening for Malingering in a Correctional Setting," *Law and Human Behavior* 22:3 (1998): 315–323.
46. American Correctional Association, *2012 Directory* (Lanham, MD: American Correctional Association, 2010). Seven states did not report the ages of their inmates, so these are minimum numbers.
47. Sarah Bradley, "Graying of Inmate Population Spurs Corrections Challenges," *On the Line* 13 (March 1990): 5; Ronald Aday, "Golden Years behind Bars," *Federal Probation* 58:2 (1994): 47–54.
48. Mari Herreras, "Threw Away the Key?," *Tucson Weekly*, January 17, 2008 http://www.tucsonweekly.com/gbase/Currents/content?oid=oid%3A105444 (accessed January 18, 2008).
49. See American Correctional Association, *2012 Directory*, and Kristen Hughes, *Justice Expenditures and Employment in 2003* (Washington, DC: Bureau of Justice Statistics, 2006).

Suggested Readings: Part 4

American Jail Association. *American Jails*. Quarterly publication of the American Jail Association.

Carson, Ann E., and Daniela Golinelli. *Prisoners in 2012*. Washington, DC: Bureau of Justice Statistics, 2013.

Center on Juvenile and Criminal Justice. "California Youth Crime Declines: The Untold Story. http://www.cjcj.org (accessed January 18, 2008).

———. "Crime Rates and Youth Incarceration in Texas and California Compared: Public Safety or Public Waste?" http://www.cjcj.org (accessed January 18, 2007).

Donziger, Steven. *The Real War on Crime*. New York: HarperCollins, 1996.

Harlow, Caroline Wolf. *Prior Abuse Reported by Inmates and Probationers*. Washington, DC: U.S. Department of Justice, 1999.

Harrel, Erica. *Black Victims of Violent Crime*. Washington, DC: Bureau of Justice Statistics, 2007.

Hassine, Victor. *Life without Parole: Living in Prison Today*. New York: Oxford University Press, 2012.

Hayes, Lindsay, and Eric Blaauw, eds. "Prison Suicide." Special issue of *Crisis* 18:4 (1997): 146–189.

Heidi, Kathleen. *Young Killers: The Challenge of Juvenile Homicide*. Thousand Oaks, CA: Sage, 1999.

James, Doris, and Lauren Glaze. *Mental Health Problems of Prison and Jail Inmates*. Washington, DC: Bureau of Justice Statistics, 2006.

Maruschak, Laura. *HIV in Prisons and Jails, 2002*. Washington, DC: Bureau of Justice Statistics, 2004.

———. *Medical Problems of Jail Inmates*. Washington, DC: Bureau of Justice Statistics, 2006.

———. *HIV in Prisons, 2001–2010*. Washington, DC: Bureau of Justice Statistics, 2012.

Mauer, Mark. *Mandatory Minimum Sentencing Laws—The Issues*. Washington, DC: The Sentencing Project, 2007.

———. "Racial Impact Statements as a Means of Reducing Unwarranted Sentencing Disparities." *Ohio State Journal of Criminal Law* 5:19 (2007): 19–46.

McCoy, Clyde, and James Inciardi. *Sex, Drugs, and the Continuing Spread of AIDS*. Los Angeles: Roxbury, 1995.

Nichols, Mark, L. Bench, E. Morlok, and K. Liston. "Analysis of Mentally Retarded and Lower-Functioning Offender Correctional Programs." *Corrections Today* 65:2 (2003): 119–121.

Noonan, Margaret, and Scott Ginder, *Mortality in Local Jails and State Prisons, 2000–2011*. Washington, DC: U.S. Department of Justice, Bureau of Justice Statistics, 2013.

Pew Center on the States. *Prison Count 2010*. http://www.pewtrusts.org/en/search#q=Prison%20Count%202010.

Ross, Jeffrey Ian. "Supermax Prisons." *Society* 44:3 (2006): 60–64.

Sheppard, David, and Patricia Kelly. *Juvenile Gun Courts*. Washington, DC: Office of Justice Programs, 2002.

Snyder, Howard, and Melissa Sickman. *Juvenile Offenders and Victims 2006*. Washington, DC: Office of Justice Programs, 2006.

The Sentencing Project. *Women in the Criminal Justice System: An Overview*. Washington, DC: The Sentencing Project, 2007.

Uzoaba, Julius. *Managing Older Offenders: Where Do We Stand?* Ottawa: Correctional Service of Canada, 1998.

Wahlin, Lottie. "New Restorative Approach to Sex Crimes." http://www.restorativejustice.org/editions/2006/july2006/restore (accessed January 17, 2008).

———.Wahlin, Lottie. "Victim Offender Mediation in Sweden." http://www.restorativejustice.org/editions/2006/august2006/vomsweden (accessed January 17, 2008).

appendix careers in corrections

INTRODUCTION

For those who are considering working in corrections but have not yet made a decision as to which type of approach to make toward a meaningful and rewarding career, we list here some of the major options for employment. Additional information can be garnered through discussion with your instructor or an information search using the Internet. We suggest to our online students that they search for background data using key employment terms from the course and the name of their state or local jurisdiction as the secondary search term. A career in corrections offers an opportunity to leverage your talent and become the leader you were meant to be.

We would be remiss if we did not point out that job descriptions and performance vary by jurisdiction. What might be listed as "Correctional Cook" may or may not require certification as a correctional officer. You will find this appendix not only informational but also powerful as a broad approach to the spectrum of careers in corrections.

Accountant

Accountants classify and evaluate financial data; record transactions in financial records; prepare and analyze financial statements, records, and reports; and supervise the maintenance of inmate accounts.

Anger Management Specialist

Anger management specialists operate treatment programs within a correctional system designed to help offenders rein in their anger and aggression by understanding how and why anger arises and rehearsing alternative nonviolent expressions.

Bail Release Officer

A bail release officer is a court employee empowered with the authority to order the pretrial release of the person on personal recognizance on execution of an unsecured appearance bond in an amount specified by the court. This judicial officer typically utilizes a structured interview scale on which the characteristics and history of the suspect are measured and decisions made to release or hold for court appearance.

Case Manager

Case managers (also known as correctional treatment specialists) perform correctional casework in an institutional setting; develop, evaluate, and analyze program needs and other data about inmates; evaluate progress of individual offenders in the institution; coordinate and integrate inmate training programs; develop social histories; evaluate positive and negative aspects in each case situation; and develop release plans.

Chaplain

A prison chaplain provides spiritual growth and education programs for inmates, counsels inmates preparing for release, coordinates special programs, and trains volunteers. A chaplain spends considerable time circulating through the prison, making him- or herself available when needed to listen or counsel inmates or staff. A chaplain arranges emergency phone calls for inmates, notifies inmates of deaths of family members, attends funerals, and provides grief counseling to inmates who have experienced loss. A prison chaplain generally provides services within his or her own faith but is also responsible for ensuring that incarcerated people have a chance to practice according to their own religious and spiritual beliefs, including minority faiths.

Correctional Auditor

Correctional auditors are experienced correctional professionals who are usually approved by the American Correctional Association or licensing authorities. The average auditor has worked in corrections for more than 18 years and has experience supervising and evaluating the type of programs being reviewed (especially for accreditation). Auditors are also utilized for field consultation, re-audits, and monitoring visits to accredited or certified programs.

Correctional Lieutenant

A correctional lieutenant is an officer who serves as lieutenant, managing and supervising a force of correctional personnel in the execution of a variety of correctional and counseling duties. The correctional lieutenant deploys personnel in locations to ensure productive and effective supervision of inmates and staff; supervises shift operations, ensuring assignments are posted and carried out; conducts roll call, making sure staff is aware of changes in operational security; inspects zone and other assignments for safety/health hazards; and counsels nonsupervisory staff on a variety of correctional duties related to security and inmate conduct and safety, cleanliness, and maintenance in the correctional setting. A correctional lieutenant ensures and/or assists in ensuring that adequate operational efficiency is maximized; provides supervisory review of sanitation, cleanliness, and safety conditions in assigned areas: identifies health hazards in the area; initiates corrective action and ensures employee awareness of such hazards; and makes appropriate notifications through the chain of command. A correctional lieutenant promptly reports violations and/or on-the-job injuries and ensures that medical attention is provided as requested by established guidelines. A correctional lieutenant submits reports on extraordinary occurrences /critical incidents, individual job performance, proposed adverse/corrective actions, awards and commendations, and other duties that may be assigned.

Correctional Officer

A correctional officer supervises adult offenders while in custody; conducts thorough inspections and searches of inmates, buildings, and grounds; performs security observation; prepares documentation regarding institutional matters; operates security equipment; recognizes critical behavior; restrains and controls offenders; responds to emergencies; enforces and follows rules and regulations, including written and/or oral directives; oversees all aspects of the basic needs and welfare of residents; participates in case management and classification procedures; and provides intervention for residents in the custody of the jurisdiction by facilitating and/or overseeing counseling, medical care, first aid, clothing and laundry, janitorial and housekeeping supplies, transportation of inmates, meals, movement, jobs, and other services as required.

Court Master

A court master is a representative of the court ordered to monitor correctional compliance with the court's orders.

Dental Hygienist

A dental hygienist assists prison dentists in their practice by performing preventive and therapeutic treatment procedures and by instructing patients in oral self-care techniques.

Detention Officers

Detention officers are usually employed in jail facilities and are not usually deputy sheriffs. They frequently process inmates, maintain jail security, serve meals, and transport inmates. In addition, they receive and process inmates into the custody of the institution, search prisoners, and take charge of personal property. They frequently provide inmates opportunity to call an attorney or relative, advise inmates on institutional rules and regulations, and patrol jail areas periodically to ensure security and maintain order. They may receive, count, record, and wash all laundry in the jail and distribute medication to inmates as prescribed or indicated. Finally, they perform related tasks as required.

Drug Treatment Specialists

Drug treatment specialists conduct interviews to determine inmate treatment eligibility, conduct drug education classes for groups of inmates, provide group and individual counseling to inmates with substance use disorders, write treatment plans and psychosocial histories, and write treatment summaries that are used to develop aftercare plans on inmate release to the community. These specialists are also found in various community correctional programs.

Family Counselors

Family correctional counselors work with inmates toward their goals in rehabilitation. They help offenders develop relapse prevention plans, steer them toward acquiring education, provide counseling, and teach job skills. Although most correctional counselors work in state or federal prisons, some work in nursing and residential care facilities treating inmates who are physically infirm. Still others work with offenders who have been released from incarceration and are referred by social assistance programs. Correctional counselors often work with clients who are dangerous. Some counselors specialize in unifying family ties and strengthening family cohesion and communication. Others encourage family visitation of incarcerated inmates, encourage the resumption of employment opportunities, and work with establishment of the required residential plan of eligible parolees.

Federal Probation and Pretrial Services Officer

U.S. probation and pretrial services officers and officer assistants are U.S. district court employees. They provide services that protect the community and help the federal courts ensure the fair administration of justice. They are also federal law enforcement officers. They hold the responsibility to investigate and supervise persons charged with and convicted of crimes against the United States.

Human Resource Specialists

Human resource specialists provide support and technical assistance in all areas of personnel, including staffing, classification, employee relations, salary and wage administration, labor/management relations, and training/development alternatives.

Institutional Parole Officer

Institutional parole officers complete interviews and case summaries of all offenders who are eligible for review. They also provide information to offenders on voting panel decisions and the reasons for approval or denial.

Internal Investigator

The internal investigator protects and serves the public, employees, and offenders by gathering information, examining operations, enforcing departmental standards and laws through audits and investigations, and recommending solutions. Such officers coordinate, collaborate, assimilate, and disseminate information, findings, and intelligence to the leadership and staff of the correctional facility.

Juvenile Intake Officer

Juvenile intake officers conduct assessments of youths to determine whether they are in need of assistance or disciplinary measures. They take into account a juvenile's history, mental health, family situation, and other factors when determining how to handle an issue. These issues are often brought before them by either law enforcement or families and include truancy, drug and alcohol use, destructive behavior, misdemeanors, and felonies. Once the officer understands a minor's history and actions, he or she can recommend detention and treatment options.

Nurse

The registered nurse plans and provides comprehensive nursing care including but not limited to executing physician's orders, dispensing and administering medications, and assisting physicians in examinations and treatment of patients. The nurse applies nursing and supervisory techniques required in the care, treatment, and referrals of inmates/residents and performs all technical/clinical procedures within the scope of his or her education and licensure.

Nurse Practitioner

A nurse practitioner provides primary care that focuses on assessment, health management, education, advocacy, and prevention. Roles that might be assumed include conducting physical exams, prescribing medication, diagnosing and treating illness, interpreting lab tests, and counseling patients on health care options.

Ombudsman

The mission of the ombudsman office/inmate affairs unit is to promote fairness, accountability, and integrity by investigating public and offender grievances, appeals, and inquiries regarding unfair practices and noncompliance of policy. The ombudsman accomplishes that task by investigating allegations of violations of state policies and procedures, monitoring problems in the correctional system in a fair and consistent manner, and addressing offender and general public concerns in an unbiased, impartial, and courteous manner.

Online Educator/Trainer

Correctional personnel with experience and success in operations frequently turn to using online resources to train and educate less experienced workers. This frequently (but not always) involves using computer technology that allows multiple reviews of the content, group study, program practice, and best practices in corrections. The most frequently used technology is probably the PowerPoint slide presentation. Trainers with extensive experience usually become outstanding educators on a part-time or second-career online basis.

Operational Readiness

An umbrella term encompassing various necessary employment skills in prison operations, all designed to prevent a breakdown of operability of prison facilities. The three major job categories include carpenter, painter, and electrician. Also known as training instructors, they usually administer the vocational training program for inmates in correctional institutions. Positions in these classes conduct or supervise the erection, maintenance, and repair of various buildings and structures; the drawing of working sketches and preparation of cost estimates; the maintenance of tools, materials, and equipment in good repair; and the preparation of simple reports. They may instruct, lead, or supervise inmates, wards, residents, or patients of the correctional facilities; prevent escapes and injury by these persons to themselves or others or to property; maintain security of working areas and work materials; and inspect premises and search inmates for contraband, such as weapons or illegal drugs.

Parole Board Member

Parole board members are corrections staff whose primary statutory duties include conducting release consideration hearings on all parole-eligible inmates and providing clemency recommendations to the governor. Members are empowered to revoke granted parole, recommend the reduction of prison sentences, consider medical and clemency release, and otherwise ease the reentry of inmates who are granted parole.

Parole Officer

A parole officer evaluates offender progress and recommends intensity of supervision based on observations from time of conviction through the period of adjustment after release from an institution, assists offenders in securing jobs, maintains contacts with business organizations and employment agencies, and arranges for employment interviews. He or she also counsels and refers offenders to specialized treatment services at guidance clinics, mental health clinics, and related organizations and records offender restitution payments, cost of supervision, court costs, and other related payments. He or she maintains an awareness of offenders' daily activities and evaluates desirability to remain at liberty and represents the department of corrections in all parole hearings for inmates assigned to caseload. The parole officer appears as a witness at parole or probation revocation hearings is responsible for the case management of all assigned inmates, serves as a team leader or member in all case reviews to determine the direction for each case, and serves as team chairman or member of all disciplinary due process hearings for inmates assigned to caseload. He or she evaluates information from reports, interviews, and correspondence and prepares case histories for recommendations for inmate classification and job assignment.

Physician (Primary Care)

Primary care is that care provided by physicians specifically trained for and skilled in comprehensive first contact and continuing care for persons with any undiagnosed sign, symptom, or health concern. Primary care includes health promotion, disease prevention, health maintenance, counseling, patient education, and diagnosis and treatment of acute and chronic illnesses in juvenile and adult confinement facilities. Primary care is performed and managed by a personal physician, often in collaboration with other health professionals.

Presentence Investigation Officer

This court-related officer undertakes a presentence investigation of eligible offenders. Its reports include an agent's evaluation of the offender, the circumstances of the offense, a personal and criminal history of the offender, and a sentencing recommendation. Victims also have an opportunity to provide information on what impact the crime has had on their lives and may express their opinions regarding the appropriate sentence.

Prison Cook

Under supervision, the cook prepares, cooks, and serves food at a detention facility; supervises food service workers, inmates, or juveniles in routine food preparation and cleaning activities; and undertakes other work as required. Cooks work without immediate supervision are required to perform the full range of cooking assignments and are responsible for the preparation of food for assigned shifts while supervising lower-level food service personnel, inmates, or juveniles in semiskilled kitchen tasks. Some jurisdictions require that the cook be a certified correctional officer.

Prison Intake Officer

A prison intake officer conducts assessments of new admissions to correctional facilities to determine criminal, personal, educational, employment, and mental health issues; verifies historical information; and assesses escape and dangerousness potentials. The intake officer, usually working with a team of representatives from major posts in the facility, determines inmate needs, establishes required treatments and level of custody, and makes assignment to appropriate confinement facility.

Prison Intelligence Officer

A prison intelligence officer is an institutional gang investigator who gathers information for analysis of individuals and gangs, supervises intelligence analysts, and oversees their daily activities, including development of intelligence analyses and products. He or she conducts complex operational information/intelligence gathering and investigations involving parolees, wards, and inmates suspected of major organized criminal enterprise/gang activity and interviews suspects, witnesses, and victims in reference to violations committed by persons under correctional control. A prison intelligence officer establishes and maintains ongoing liaisons with local, state, and federal law enforcement agencies to assist with investigations relating to gang/criminal activity as well as the resolution of criminal activity and resulting criminal prosecutions.

Probation Officer: Adult Offenders

Probation officers (and correctional treatment specialists) typically do the following: evaluate offenders to determine the best course of rehabilitation; provide offenders with resources, such as job training; test offenders for drugs and offer substance abuse counseling; monitor offenders and help with their progress; conduct meetings with offenders and their family and friends; and write reports on the progress of offenders. A primary duty is the preparation of a presentence investigation report for court use.

Probation Officer: Juvenile Offenders

Duties of probation officers for juvenile offenders include developing disposition reports for court use, supervising the conduct and behavior of minors, maintaining necessary order and discipline, directing minors in constructive activities, attempting to modify antisocial behavior, and assisting minors in adjusting to detention situations. They are also involved in instructing and encouraging good manners, sportsmanship, and proper attitudes toward work, play, and citizenship and planning organized recreation and group activities and leisure-time activities, such as games, athletics, and crafts. They also prepare observation reports on the attitude, behavior, appearance, interest, skills, progress, and needs of the juveniles under their supervision and report to the juvenile court on progress and development of positive and negative behavior.

Program Evaluator

A program evaluator investigates the effectiveness of a correctional program or practice in achieving its stated objectives. This typically involves undertaking new research or amassing information on the participants' outcomes following program involvement. Such evaluators help in maximizing the impact of the resources available to corrections in enhancing public safety.

Psychiatric Orderly

A psychiatric orderly provides nursing care to mentally ill, emotionally disturbed, or mentally retarded patients in a psychiatric hospital, mental health clinic, or prison unit/lockdown facility and participates in rehabilitation and treatment programs. He or she helps patients/inmates with their personal hygiene (e.g., bathing, grooming, and keeping beds, clothing, and living areas clean); administers oral medications and hypodermic injections following the physician's prescriptions and hospital procedures; takes and records measures of a patient's general physical condition, such as pulse, temperature, and respiration, to provide daily information; observes patients to detect behavior patterns and reports observations to medical staff; and intervenes to restrain violent or potentially violent or suicidal patients by verbal or physical means as required.

Psychiatrist

A psychiatrist is a medical practitioner who supervises and manages the daily operations of a mental health clinic, serves on committees as appropriate, and conducts staff in-service training. A psychiatrist assesses inmates' mental status and medical needs, directs the formulation of treatment plans based on diagnosis, monitors patient progress and modifies treatment plans as indicated, and communicates medical orders to the nursing staff. He or she also delivers direct and emergency patient psychotherapy services in group and/or individual therapy as appropriate, participates in case disposition and follow-up planning, and provides medical case supervision and consultation. The psychiatrist maintains records and provides documentation associated with services delivered, certifies patients for inpatient hospital or acute care psychiatric facilities as appropriate, and provides evaluations as required by the courts.

Psychologist

Correctional psychologists play a crucial role within the mental health industry. Correctional psychologists face the daunting task of providing mental health treatment to those placed in custodial correctional settings. The main responsibility of a correctional psychologist is to rehabilitate inmates and to help them transition from prison back into the free world. Correctional psychologists also use their skills to create a safer atmosphere for staff dealing with inmates. These professionals attempt to lessen the likelihood of physical violence against those working in prisons. In addition to these responsibilities, correctional psychologists often weigh in on parole recommendations and conduct psychological evaluations of inmates.

Quick-Response Team

The quick response team consists of on-duty staff properly trained and capable of immediately responding to spontaneous emergencies or containing a situation until an emergency squad can be assembled if needed.

Recreational Specialists

Recreation specialists plan, organize, and administer recreational programs and activities for inmates in both juvenile and adult correctional institutions.

Reentry Coordinator

A reentry coordinator assists individuals being released from jails and prisons to successfully reintegrate into the community by helping them receive community-based services, such as substance abuse treatment and support groups, employment, education/training, housing, and family reunification.

Situation Control Team (SITCON)

SITCON is a specially trained facility team that is activated during high or anticipated top-level emergencies to conduct negotiations during hostage situations or in situations requiring the use of negotiation tactics (e.g., barricaded suspects).

Substance Abuse Counselor

Substance abuse and behavioral disorder counselors advise people who suffer from alcoholism, drug addiction, eating disorders, or other behavioral problems. They provide treatment and support to help the client recover from addiction or modify problem behaviors.

Superintendent (see Warden/Superintendent)

Teachers

Teachers must be able to teach inmates, including those having environmental, cultural, and economic disadvantages. Special requirements and skills are necessitated by the learning objectives employed to teach particular disadvantaged groups. Knowledge and the ability to implement a variety of innovative or advanced instructional techniques are essential. Teachers must possess professional knowledge of the principles, theories, practices, and techniques of education in combination with a thorough knowledge of one or more subject matters in which instruction is given.

Victims' Rights Advocate

Victim advocates are professionals trained to support victims of crime. Advocates offer victims information and emotional support and help finding resources and filling out paperwork. Sometimes, advocates go to court with victims. Advocates may also contact organizations, such as criminal justice or social service agencies, to get help or information for victims. Some advocates staff crisis hotlines, run support groups, or provide in-person counseling. Victim advocates may also be called victim service providers, victim/witness coordinators, or victim/witness specialists.

Warden/Superintendent

Prison wardens ensure that prisons operate efficiently, safely, and securely. They oversee all staff in a prison, monitoring that applicable laws, rules, standards, and facility-specific policies are followed. Jail wardens perform similar duties but work with offenders in short-term detention. In larger facilities, wardens are assisted by deputy wardens performing specific duties. As the chief executive officer of the prison, the warden has management responsibility for attaining mission goals. The warden's primary responsibility is to manage the operations, supervisory staff, support staff, and inmates. The warden is usually assisted by several deputy wardens, typically one each for management, custody, industry, and treatment programs. The warden manages the correctional facility and interacts with external local, state, and federal entities and agencies.

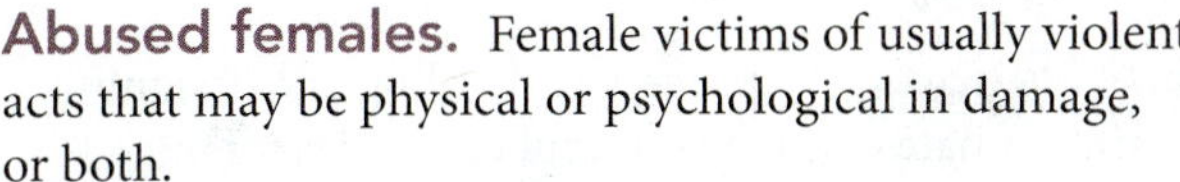

glossary

Abused females. Female victims of usually violent acts that may be physical or psychological in damage, or both.

Adam Walsh Act. National legislation creating a national sex offender registry and organizing sex offenders into three tiers with increasing restrictions based on level.

Administrative-security level. Facilities with special missions that might contain inmates from all custody levels.

Administrative sentencing. Process by which the actual length of the sentence is left up to the administrators of the correctional system, as seen in such processes as good-time credit, probation, parole, and program participation; the actual sentence served is set by the executive branch rather than the judicial.

Affirm. Appeal court's decision that due processes have not been violated by the government.

Age at risk. Those potential offenders likely to offend, segregated by age categories.

Age of Enlightenment. A philosophic movement of the eighteenth century marked by a rejection of traditional social, religious, and political ideas and an emphasis on rationalism.

Agricultural prison. Any prison whose main products are agricultural and whose institutional value is the foodstuffs and produce grown.

AIDS. Medical term describing terminal phases of HIV infection.

Alcatraz. A supermax island prison for inmates in the San Francisco Bay Area and part of the U.S. Bureau of Prisons until its closing; also known as "the Rock."

Alderson. The first federal institution for female offenders.

Alternative to death and flogging. Any correctional punishment less than the death penalty, such as imprisonment, probation, diversion, and so on.

Amnesty. A form of pardon for a class of offenders, such as draft dodgers.

Anger management. Treatment programs within a correctional system designed to help offenders rein in their anger and aggression by understanding how and why anger arises, and rehearsing alternative nonviolent expressions.

Antiviral drugs. Special antiviral pharmaceuticals used to lessen the levels and virulence of HIV infections.

Appeal. Petition to higher courts to reverse procedures and protect offenders based on due process issues.

Arbitrary. Acting without criteria, usually in a discriminatory manner.

Arrests by gender. Comparison of arrest data between male and female offenders.

Ashurst–Sumners Act. Federal legislation requiring "truth of manufacturing, transportation and interstate shipment of prison-made goods" by requirement that the packages be plainly and clearly marked.

Asylum. Institution for the care and custody of mentally ill societal members.

Auburn system. Prison model consisting of small individual cells, large work area for group labor, and enforced silence.

Back-end solutions. Strategies for reducing prison population overcrowding by early release programs, such as parole, shock parole, and expanded good-time credits.

Backfilled. Management strategy to meet minimum critical staffing by asking corrections officers to work the next tour of duty.

"Bad news list". The list of gang members or even correctional staff who fail to conform from which free-world associates are to enforce gang discipline.

Banishment. To remove by authority from a state or country; the sentence to cast out of a local residence or country due to criminal behavior on the offender's part.

Benefit of clergy. The exclusion of offenders from the death penalty if able to read particular segments of ancient texts.

Black Muslims. American religious group based on Muslim theological concepts.

Blood feud or vendetta. An often-prolonged series of retaliatory, vengeful, or hostile acts or exchange of such acts.

Boot camp. Modeled after military boot camps, offenders are required to engage in strict discipline and a physical regimen.

"Blue flu". Ploy used by correctional officers to strengthen their hands in negotiations with command officers.

Brank. A birdcage-like instrument placed on the offender's head with sharp-edged iron plates that would cut tongues and mouths of the gossipers.

Bridewell. A workhouse created for the employment and housing of London's unemployed or underemployed working classes.

Broken windows probation. Concept that the probation officer is asked to communicate with victim(s) and the community, hold the offender accountable, and improve the leadership of probation.

Bureaucratic control. Predominant public administration format for prison operations.

Capital crimes. Offenses for which an offender can receive the death penalty, usually murder and rape.

Capital punishment. The imposition of a sentence of death by the state.

Cat-o'-nine-tails. Torture device for whipping or flogging.

Cell blocks. Multitier living cells usually stacked one atop the other, built within a hollow building and not touching exterior walls.

Certificate of qualification for employment. A certificate issued by some Departments of Corrections to eligible offenders that is designed to give potential employers some peace of mind when hiring ex-cons.

Chancery court. One of the five divisions of the High Court of Justice of Great Britain, presided over by the Lord High Chancellor and that serves as a legal protector of the rights of minors.

Cherry picking. In corrections, this is the process of selecting the best or most desirable of inmates for inclusion in a program or facility, with the intention of securing the best possible favorable outcome.

Child abuser. A person who mentally or physically abuses a child.

Child molester. An adult charged with criminal and civil offenses in which the adult engages in sexual activity with a minor or exploits a minor for the purpose of sexual gratification.

Civil death. State of being physically alive but without rights; the status of a living person equivalent in its legal consequences to natural death; loss of all rights and powers as if dead.

Civil rights. Those rights defined in the U.S. Constitution or accorded through judicial decisions.

Classical school. Approach to understanding crime and social policy for offenders.

Classification. The process of dividing and assigning incoming inmates into meaningful categories for assignment to institutions and programs.

Classification process. The process by which offenders are assigned to types of custody and treatment programs, based on such factors as offense category, escape potential, substance abuse patterns, previous experience with the criminal justice system, and so on.

Clear and present danger. Test used in corrections to justify restricting the rights of inmates.

Co-gender institution. A coeducational prison housing both male and female inmates interacting under a single institutional administration.

Cognitive. Mental processes that generally hinder change in prisoners but can be corrected by various thinking, speaking, and conceptual treatments.

Cognitive-behavioral intervention. A structured process that attempts to change how an offender thinks and sees the world through cognitive restructuring (what they think) and behavioral rehearsal (how they think).

Collateral attack. The process of raising additional legal questions in other courts but before case disposition.

Collateral consequences. Disabilities imposed on an offender on the basis of conviction.

Common law. Law based on judges' decisions and custom, as distinct from written laws.

Community correctional facility (CFC). A form of residential treatment center found in Ohio that offers a wide range of programs and services to youth.

Community corrections. A model of corrections based on the assumption that the offender should be reintegrated into the community through existing and potential community services.

Community corrections acts (CCAs). Legislation that funds local community correctional programs designed to divert offenders from prison.

Community Protection Act. Legislation requiring offenders to register and live under public scrutiny.

Community residential center. Any correctional facility existing to provide services and maximize reintegration of the offender back into the community.

Community residential treatment center. Also known as a halfway house, a residential facility that provides room and board as well as rehabilitation programming.

Community work order. Requiring offenders to provide service to the community to help repair the harm they have committed.

Commutation. A reduction of the severity of the sentence by the executive branch of government.

Comorbidity. Two or more occurring medical treatment needs for one inmate.

Conditional liberty. A prisoner release scheme that allows the penitent inmate to be released to the community under specific conditions that can be revoked; a system commonly known as "parole."

Congregate system. Prison modeled on the Auburn system with inmate work and feeding done en masse, in total silence.

Contraband. Any object forbidden in prison.

Convict bogey. Irrational fear of prison inmates who can only be managed through head counts, locking, and recounting.

Convicted offender. Guilty law violator who has exhausted all appeals of conviction and sentencing.

Corporal punishment. Any physical pain inflicted short of death; common methods include crucifixion, whipping, torture, mutilation, branding, and caning.

Correctional chaplaincy. A program of recruiting clergy who minister to the religious needs of inmates.

Correctional ideology. Systematic body of ideas and practices that pertain to the processing of offenders.

Correctional officer corruption. A form of misconduct by correctional officers in which officers seek personal gain, such as money or protection from inmate violence, through the abuse of power, such as accepting bribes in exchange for not pursuing an investigation or not writing up an inmate for proscribed behavior. Includes criminal acts forbidden by the prison, such as smuggling drugs or alcohol or excessive use of force for vengeance.

Correctional officers. Line prison officers working directly with the inmate population.

Corrections Corporation of America (CCA). A private business seeking to provide correctional services to units of government; also known as the "parent of private-sector prison facilities."

Corruption. Dishonest or illegal behavior, especially by powerful people (such as government officials, judges, or police officers).

Count. Method used to verify that all inmates are present in prison.

Court master. Representative of the court ordered to monitor correctional compliance with a court's orders.

Court of appeals. Any higher court with post-conviction authority; any court authorized to treat with contempt decisions made by the lower court.

Court of last resort. The highest appeal court having jurisdiction within that particular geographical area.

Crack cocaine. An illegal drug derived from powder cocaine and consumed primarily by smoking.

Criminal gang. An organized criminal syndicate intent on pursuing illegal behavior for the benefit of all members.

Criminal history data. Information related to an offender's prior arrests and convictions.

Criminally insane. Mentally ill inmates who are diagnosed as incompetent to plead or stand trial or not guilty by reason of insanity or who became mentally ill while incarcerated or other potentially hazardous mentally ill persons requiring special security.

Criminology. Looks at the reasons for and consequences of crime.

Cruel and unusual punishment. Prohibited by the Eighth Amendment to the Constitution.

Custody. Term referring to the level of immediate control exercised over offenders within correctional institutions.

Day reporting center. Facility to which offenders are sent for scheduling and monitoring of their activities.

Death penalty. Execution of the offender by the state.

Decarceration. Process of releasing offenders from institutional facilities, primarily by closing those facilities.

Decriminalization. To remove or reduce the criminal classification or status of a formerly criminal act.

Deinstitutionalization. The return of a mentally ill person following release from a mental hospital facility.

Deinstitutionalization. The return of a patient from a mental hospital into the community.

Deliberate indifference. Total deprivation of medical services.

Delinquent juveniles. Juveniles who have committed a criminal act that, if committed by an adult, would be a crime.

Dependent. Any child without parents or guardians or whose parents are unable to provide such care, treatment, or custody that should be afforded to a child.

"Designer" drugs. Analogues of controlled substances manufactured by underground chemists.

Desistance. Ceasing of criminal behavior by the offender. Can also imply lessening of the severity of criminal offenses.

Determinate sentencing. A flat sentence of punishment imposed by the sentencing court; judge-imposed fixed term of incarceration with the expectation the inmate will serve that amount of time.

Deterrence by sentencing. Discouraging the individual and the public's propensity to commit additional crimes by imposition of harsh punishment; the goal is crime reduction.

Deterrent. The hope that a criminal sanction will stop potential offenders by inflicting suffering on actual offenders.

Deterrent effect. The extent of crime control by incapacitation, threat of punishment, or announced potential criminal sanction.

Developmentally challenged. A term denoting intellectual disabilities, sometimes referred to as mental retardation.

Direct filing. Prosecutorial decision to refer the case to an adult criminal court rather than to a juvenile court.

Disciplinarian. Prison administrator usually using harsh punishments to reinforce institutional rules.

Discretionary release. Parole of an inmate from prison prior to expiration of his or her maximum sentence according to the boundaries set by the sentencing body or legislature.

Diversion. Minimizing offender processing through the justice system by imposing treatment, supervision, and referral of offenders to service providers outside of the justice system; the halting or suspension of a juvenile from further involvement with the justice system in return for approved behaviors; minimizing penetration into the criminal justice system through police, community, or court programs.

Domestic terrorist group. Terrorist group that operates within the nation or commits crime in the local law enforcement jurisdiction.

Double jeopardy. The second trying of a suspected offender for the same crime as originally charged.

Drug court. Problem-solving court that requires drug offenders to participate in court-mandated treatment programs.

Due process. Legal requirement that constitutional rights of the accused and correctional clients will conform to guaranteed constitutional protection minimums.

Eastern Penitentiary. Prison facility designed on the Pennsylvania system with rows of individual cells attached to corridors and outside cells.

Educational doctrine. Correctional approach seeking to provide crime prevention by education, emphasizing vocational and educational skills, and teaching inmates to discipline themselves.

Elderly inmate. An inmate of an age that exceeds the jurisdiction's definition of elderly inmates, frequently age 55, although it can vary depending on the jurisdiction.

Electronic monitoring. Any system or telemetry program that allows correctional staff to know the location of offenders; tracking of offender whereabouts electronically.

Electronic parole. Community supervision technique that uses electronic devices to maintain surveillance on parolees. Can also include GPS surveillance.

Employment restrictions. Denial of employment opportunities due to being an ex-offender.

Equitability. Whether the punishment is applied even-handedly across a jurisdiction.

Escape. Flight from prison facilities and illegal absences from institutions.

Estelle v. Gamble. First U.S. Supreme Court case dealing with prison medical treatment.

Evidence-based classification system. A practical criminological procedure intended to identify the behavioral characteristics of certain offenders and use of those attributes to classify inmates as gang members or not.

Ex-con. Formerly institutionalized offender who has now given up a life as a criminal.

Execution. The killing of an offender by the state.

Executive clemency. A pardon, reduction of sentence, or release of an inmate by the governor or pardoning authority.

Expungement. Process by which a record of crime conviction is destroyed or sealed after expiration of a statutorily required period of time; also refers to the act of physically destroying information—including criminal records—in files, computers, or other depositories.

External classification. Process leading managers to assign inmates to an institution.

Family (conjugal) visits. Prison program designed to reinforce family ties through unsupervised contact, usually between husband and wife.

Family cohesion. Term describing the relationship between offenders and their families, as in sticking together tightly.

Federal Bureau of Prisons. The federal correctional system located within the Department of Justice.

Fee system. Fees charged to state and federal prison systems to house inmates in local jails.

Felony. Serious criminal violation, sometimes punished by death or sentence of at least one year in prison.

Felony probation. The offender is placed on probation for committing a felony.

Firearms disability. Loss of rights of ex-felons to own, possess, or exercise control over firearms.

"Flopped". Inmate term for denial of parole.

Fort Leavenworth. Military post that contains a maximum-security prison facility for military services.

Friedensgeld. The practice of paying restitution for crime to both the victim and the Crown.

Frisk search. Process of detecting inmate contraband by manual search of the bodies of inmates.

Front-end solutions. Options for controlling the number of inmates being sent to prison.

Functionally illiterate. Prisoners with low-level education skills who are unable to read and follow written instructions; Unable to read, write, or spell above the third-grade level.

Furlough. A prison-release program permitting the inmate to pursue education, vocational training, or employment in the community; program of temporary leave from a prison for educational, work, or emergency purposes.

Furman v. Georgia. The Supreme Court decision that the death penalty in Georgia was being applied arbitrarily and discriminatorily against minorities; as a result of this case, a moratorium on the death penalty was imposed throughout the United States.

Gagnon v. Scarpelli. U.S. Supreme Court decision that held probation is a privilege, not a right, but, once granted, the probationer has an interest in remaining on probation.

Gaols. Places of confinement in England for persons held in lawful custody; *specifically*: such a place under the jurisdiction of a local government (as a county) for the confinement of persons awaiting trial or those convicted of minor crimes.

Gatekeeper. A criminal or juvenile justice professional (such as a prosecutor, parole board member, politician or judge) who determines access to services, detention or confinement facilities, or commitment to prison or parole.

Gatekeeper function. Process by which the criminal justice official exercises authority to move the case to the next higher level.

GED. General equivalency diploma certifying inmate's achievement of the equivalent of a high school diploma.

General deterrence. Preventing potential criminal behavior by making examples of offenders openly; the message here would be "See what will happen to you if you commit crime."

General population. Prisoners not restricted to tighter controls than other inmates.

GEO Group. A private-sector correctional provider formerly known as the Wackenhut group.

Geriatric center. Correctional facility for elderly inmates.

Geriatric inmate. An older elderly inmate whose physical or mental disabilities require more extensive medical and treatment care.

"Get right with God". Directive that the offender must make peace with God through repentance and atonement.

"Get-tough" laws. Belief that offenders should be punished to prevent criminal recidivism; such laws would lengthen the term of incarceration and minimize use of community resources; two important law programs are using the determinate sentence and compelling the inmate to serve a large percentage of the imposed sentence.

Goldbrickers. Inmates seeking sick calls for other than medical needs.

Good time. Taking days off an inmate's sentence for good behavior while incarcerated.

Good-time policies. Administrative mechanism reducing sentence length by crediting inmates for good behavior, extra work, or other statutory policies.

Gradualism approach. A "go-slow" approach to design and implementation of new programs.

Graduated release. Programs bridging inmate status from imprisonment to community control.

Graffiti. Unauthorized writing or drawing on a public surface, such as a wall, building, fence, and so on, defacing it.

***Graham* v. *Florida*.** A 2010 U.S. Supreme Court decision holding that juveniles cannot be sentenced to life imprisonment without parole for nonhomicide offenses.

***Gregg* v. *Georgia*.** The 1977 case that ended the moratorium on the death penalty.

Group home. A residential placement option that operates as a homelike setting in which a number of unrelated youth live for varying time periods.

Growth industry. Any business venture whose volume of work systematically increases over time.

Guilty but mentally ill (GBMI). Plea entered by the defendant acknowledging guilt but asserting a lack of capacity to understand the nature of the act or that it was wrong.

Halfway house. A residential house or facility for offenders in the community; often used for inmates prior to final release to parole.

Hawes–Cooper Act. Federal legislation that forbids the manufacture and transportation of prison goods made by convicts and prisoners.

Hedonistic calculus. Jeremy Bentham's argument that the main objective of an intelligent person is to maximize pleasure while minimizing pain; it was believed that individual's behavior could be influenced in a scientific manner.

Hepatitis A and B. Viral infections resistant to medical treatments.

High-security level. A classification designation reducing inmate movement and treatment participation within the correctional facility; may also refer to "supermax," security housing units, or "close supervision."

Hispanic STG. The U.S. government has defined *Hispanic or Latino* persons as being "persons who trace their origin or descent to Mexico, Puerto Rico, Cuba, Central and South America (except for Brazil), and other Spanish cultures."

HIV infection. An acquired infection that compromises the body's ability to arrest or overcome common diseases and other illnesses.

"Holdback" jail inmates. Inmates held in jail awaiting transportation to a federal or state prison.

Home detention. Sentence whereby offenders serve at least some of their sentence in their own domicile.

Homosexual attacks. Sexual assaults on potential victim inmates, usually by heterosexual prisoners.

Hospice de San Miguel. A corrections facility designed for incorrigible boys and youth that included silence, large work areas, and separate sleeping cells. Both expiation and reform were intended goals.

Hot-button item. A topic in someone's mind that, when discussed, makes the individual offended or very passionate about the issue. Such topics can include people, religion, politics, possessions, criminals, or passions. In the correctional system, food is often a hot-button item for inmates.

House arrest. Being confined to one's home except when permission is granted to leave.

Hulks. Abandoned or unusable transport ships anchored in rivers and harbors that confined criminal offenders.

Ideology. Systematic body of ideas and practices.

***In re Gault*.** U.S. Supreme Court decision that juveniles have four basic constitutional rights in hearings that could result in commitment to an institution.

Incapacitation. Depriving offenders of the ability to commit additional crime, usually through imprisonment.

Incompetent to stand trial. Legal defense asserting that defendants must be able to understand the charges against them and to assist legal counsel in the preparation of their own defense.

Incorrigible (unruly) juveniles. Unruly juveniles whose behavior is not controlled by their parents.

Indeterminate sentence. A period of confinement with specified minimum and maximum length, allowing a parole board to release the inmate when rehabilitation has been achieved.

Indeterminate sentencing. Judge imposes a minimum and maximum period of incarceration time under the assumption that a parole board will identify the maximum benefit from imprisonment and subsequently release the inmate.

Industrial prison. Any penal institution whose main objective is the use of inmate labor to produce marketable products for prison profit.

Initial classification. The initial process by which offenders are assigned to level of custody, work assignment, and treatments.

Inquisition. A former Roman Catholic tribunal for the discovery and punishment of heresy; an investigation conducted with little regard for individual rights through a severe questioning.

Inside cells. Prison cells that do not touch the outside walls of the cell block.

Institutional gang investigator. An institutional gang investigator is a trained individual whose primary or sole function is to gather information on institutional security threat groups and individuals and propose isolation or control of such so as to neutralize potential disruptive behavior.

Institutional needs. Basic and mandatory functions for assigning prisoners to support institutional objectives.

Institutional threat groups. Prison gangs.

Institutional work assignment. Prison industry jobs based on institutional operational needs, community projects, or prison industry programs.

Intelligence. Secret information that a government agency collects about a suspect, inmate, or group.

Intensive supervised probation (ISP). Intermediate sanction requiring increased supervision for probationers.

Intent to kill. Malice aforethought; having the intent to kill prior to the crime; planned and premeditated crime.

Interdiction. Any law enforcement practice designed to confront and halt the activities, advance, or entry of members of a security threat group or contraband.

Intermediate sanctions. Correctional programs that fall somewhere between probation and prison.

Internal classification. Process of assigning inmates to types of programs and work and cell locations.

Involuntary commitment. Laws that allow predatory sex offenders to be incarcerated in mental health facilities after their sentence has been served.

Irish system. A prison management scheme with multiple stages of control, allowing the inmate to earn higher stages until released when penitence was achieved; release was on a revocable "ticket of leave" or conditional pardon.

Irish system. Developed in Ireland, one of the first parole systems that permitted inmates to work their way into lower-security settings.

Isolationism and withdrawal. Implementing programs without a systematic, rational scheme.

Jail. A local secure facility designed to house offenders, usually for one year or less.

Jail inmates. Offenders housed in a local facility, including those waiting for trial, those awaiting transport to a state or federal prison, and those convicted of a crime, usually punishable by less than one year.

Jailhouse lawyer. An inmate who provides legal services to other inmates.

Just deserts. Sentencing ideology that stresses that any punishment to be applied must be dependent on the culpability of the offender and the seriousness of the offense.

Just deserts argument. Argument that offenders should receive severe punishment because of the nature of the crime committed.

Justice Department. The unit of the federal government in which the Federal Bureau of Prisons is located.

Juvenile camps and ranches. Residential treatment centers in California that offer a wide range of programs and services to youth.

Juvenile Detention Alternatives Initiative (JDAI). A program of the Annie E. Casey Foundation designed to help jurisdictions reduce the use of detention.

Juvenile detention center ("juvie"). An institution where youth are detained when suspected of a juvenile offense, awaiting hearing or case disposition, found to be a youthful offender, or for treatment or rehabilitation. Also called "juvies."

Juvenile Justice and Delinquency Prevention Act. Act requiring a comprehensive assessment of the juvenile justice system to identify those youth who are victimized or otherwise troubled but have not committed criminal offenses.

Juvenile Residential Facility Census. A biennial survey conducted by the Office of Juvenile Justice and Delinquency Prevention to gauge the number and use of youth residential placements.

Juvenile waiver. Juvenile court transfer of alleged delinquents to adult court for more intensive and lengthy punishment.

"Keester". To hide contraband objects within the rectum or vagina of prison inmates.

Kent v. United States. A U.S. Supreme Court decision that courts must provide the "essentials of due process" in transferring juveniles to the adult system.

Kickback. A return of a percentage of a sum of money already received, typically as a result of pressure, coercion, or a secret agreement; a percentage of income given to a person in a position of power or influence as payment for having made the income possible; usually considered improper, unethical, or illegal.

Lease system. The hiring of inmates to perform work details managed by private entrepreneurs, either while out of or still incarcerated in prison facilities.

Lex salica. The custom of atonement for wrongs against a victim by payment to appease the victim's family.

Lex talionis. The act of repaying in kind, such as "an eye for an eye, a tooth for a tooth."

Life certain. Judge's sentence that precludes parole eligibility; order to incarcerate the offender until dead.

Lock psychosis. Term denoting overconcentration of prison administrators with security and community protection, to be accomplished through extensive use of locks, head counts, and internal control of inmates.

Lockdowns. Control of prison and inmates by not permitting inmates to leave their cells or rooms.

Lockstep formation. Lines of inmates marching closely behind their leader, with hands on top of shoulders or under the armpits. Requires shuffling and muteness in march from one area of the prison to another.

Low-security level. A correctional assignment of prisoners permitting limited mobility and program participation consistent with their incarceration.

Maison de force. A Belgian workhouse for beggars and miscreants, designed to make a profit by an enforced pattern of hard work and both discipline and silence. An important rule: "If a man will not work, neither let him eat."

Malice aforethought. Having the intent to kill prior to the commission of the crime; planned and premeditated.

Mamertine prison. An early place of confinement in Rome using primitive dungeons built under the main sewer.

Mandatory release. The required release of an inmate from incarceration because the statutes mandate the release of any inmate who has served his or her maximum sentence.

"Max out". Release after serving the entire sentence.

Medical model. Model that sees the causes of crime as lying within the individual and that stresses providing treatment and therapy until the offender is well. Leaders in the medical model were Sanford Bates and the Federal Bureau of Prisons.

Medical services. Any treatment programs designed to treat physical or psychological maladies of inmates.

Medium-security level. A correctional classification restricting offenders' movements and privileges while incarcerated.

Megan's Law. Legislation requiring sex offenders to inform local police agencies of their location and the nature of their prior convictions.

Mental health issues. A range of diagnosed mental illnesses that often afflict jail inmates.

Mentally disturbed. Persons with a mental illness.

Meta-analysis. A quantitative statistical analysis that is applied to separate but similar experiments of different and usually independent researchers and that involves pooling the data and using the pooled data to test the effectiveness of the results, such as the effectiveness of education in reducing recidivism.

Mexican Mafia. La Eme, or the Mexican Mafia, a gang populated mainly by Hispanics but has some Caucasian members. They are allied with the Aryan Brotherhood. Their major enemy is the *Nuestra Familia* (in Spanish, "our family").

Miller v. Alabama. In 2012, the Supreme Court held that mandatory sentences of life without the possibility of parole are unconstitutional for juvenile offenders.

Minimum-security level. A lower level of custody that allows freedom to interact with other prisoners and programs consistent with the offender's imprisonment.

Misdemeanor. A relatively minor violation of the criminal law, usually punishable by no more than one year in confinement.

Missouri model. An approach developed in Missouri that involves the use of small residential facilities that provide treatment in a homelike environment.

Modify. Appeal court order requiring change in the trial court's legal decision on guilt or other rights.

***Morrissey* v. *Brewer*.** The U.S. Supreme Court decision that spells out the rights of an offender at a parole revocation hearing.

Neglected. General term referring to a child who is not receiving the care that ought to be afforded by parents or guardians.

Neighborhood/local street gang. Those gangs confined to specific neighborhoods and jurisdictions that often imitate larger, more powerful national gangs. The primary purpose for many neighborhood gangs is drug distribution and sales.

New-generation jail. Developed in the 1970s, a new-generation jail is a facility designed for maximum interaction between the staff and inmates.

Not guilty by reason of insanity (NGRI). Defense of offenders not to deny the commission of the crime but to assert they lacked the capacity to understand the nature of the crime or that it was wrong.

Occupational disability. Offenders are forbidden to practice designated occupations due to fact of conviction of crime.

Ombudsman. Correctional overseer who investigates reported complaints (as from inmates, prison personnel, and prison staff), reports findings, and helps to achieve equitable settlements.

One percenter OMG. Some motorcycle gangs can be distinguished by a "1%" patch worn on the colors. This is claimed to be a reference to a comment made by the American Motorcyclist Association in which they stated that 99 percent of motorcyclists were law-abiding citizens, implying that the last 1 percent were outlaws

Outlaw. Declared to be outside the law of the tribe (nation, family).

Outlaw motorcycle gang (OMG). OMGs are organizations whose members use their motorcycle clubs as conduits for criminal enterprises.

Outside cells. Prison cells attached to a corridor with the back of the cell extending outward toward a peripheral wall.

Own recognizance. When an arrestee is released from jail under promise that he or she will return for his or her court hearing.

Paramilitary model. Organization of custody staff into ranks of armed forces.

Pardon. Executive clemency restoring at least some rights to the offender.

Pardon. Exoneration of blame for the offense by the governor or paroling authority.

***Parens patriae*.** A Latin term that refers to the duty of the state to protect those unable to protect themselves, particularly juveniles and the mentally disordered.

Parole. Release of the inmate from confinement after he or she has served a portion of the sentence, under the continued custody of the state and under conditions that permit reincarceration in the event of misbehavior.

Parole agreement. Conditions imposed by the paroling authority and offender agreement to those conditions.

Parole board. A correctional person or board that has the authority to release or parole offenders committed to prisons, to set conditions, to revoke parole, and to discharge from parole.

Paternalistic attitude of judges. Sentiments found in a system under which an authority undertakes to supply needs or regulate conduct of those under its control, particularly for female offenders.

Penitentiary. Originally a detention center in which inmates could do penance and repent or turn away from crime; now any larger penal institution for detention of inmates.

Penitentiary system. Prison designed to enforce penitence and prisoner anonymity, with individual manual labor in inmate cells.

Pennsylvania system. The system of prison discipline using isolation or solitary confinement with both a work requirement and moral and religious instruction.

Plea bargaining. Process by which the defendant agrees to plead guilty for prosecutorial consideration.

Podular/direct supervision. With podular/direct-supervision housing units, inmates have interaction with staff and other inmates through day rooms or common areas.

Political prisoner. A political prisoner is someone who is imprisoned for his or her participation in political activity.

Population at risk. Those offenders more likely to offend, usually expressed as high-level potential for committing a crime.

Posttraumatic stress disorder (PTSD). A mental health condition that is triggered by a terrifying event; a common disorder of juveniles in detention.

Predict potential dangerousness. Process by which treatment staff assess dangerousness, the offender's risk for future dangerous offenses.

Preferential treatment. Argument that female offenders receive more lenient treatment at all phases of the criminal justice system.

Pregnant inmates. Female inmates who at time of detention are carrying a fetus or enter that condition while incarcerated.

Presentence investigation (PSI) report. Document that results from an investigation undertaken by a court-authorized officer or agency, designed to provide information on the defendant so the judge can make an informed sentencing decision.

Presentence report. Document prepared by agent of the court that investigates the offender's background for judicial determination of punishment.

Presumption of innocence. Under the U.S. Constitution, those charged with a crime are presumed innocent until convicted in a court of law.

Presumptive sentencing. A sentencing mechanism fixed by a sentencing commission or legislature that identifies maximum and minimum sentences for punishment to be imposed by the judge but permitting adjustment for special circumstances.

Pretrial alternatives. Programs and sanctions designed to release those jail inmates who are awaiting trial; alternatives can include electronic monitoring, supervision, treatment programs, house arrest, and other creative options designed to reduce jail populations.

Pretrial intervention programs. Requiring defendants awaiting trial to report to a supervision officer.

Pretrial jail incarceration. Holding someone accused of a crime who cannot make bail.

Prevention ideology. Avoidance or reduction of criminal behavior using methods and programs that contribute to crime prevention.

Price-tag justice. A term used by inmates to refer to fines imposed as a result of a criminal conviction.

Prison gang. A group of inmates that band together for protection or to carry out criminal activities. Prison gang are often highly structured and operate under a specific "constitution" or set of rules and are usually comprised almost exclusively of offenders from the same racial background, place of birth, or residence.

Prison Rape Elimination Act of 2003. United States federal law designed to reinforce prison sexual assaults.

Prison rules. Written documents designed to control inmate behaviors.

Prison stripes. Prison uniforms with horizontal black bands and white stripes, frequently colored to designate inmate classification.

Prisonization. The process by which the newly committed inmates (and some prison staff) are introduced into the culture of the society of captives and learn to live within that inmate culture; the process of adopting the culture of the prison.

Private-sector correctional facility. Any *private* prison, for-profit prison, detention center, jail, or juvenile institution is a facility in which juveniles or adults are physically restricted, housed, or interned by a nongovernmental organization that is contracted by a public-sector government agency.

Privatization. The provision of correctional services by private-sector purveyors.

Proactive supervision. Treatment strategy serving to prepare for, intervene in, or control an expected occurrence or situation by offenders on probation, especially a negative or difficult one.

Probation. A court sentence to release the offender to the community under supervision, with possible revocation of sentence if conditions warrant.

Probation revocation. Change of sentence from probation to another correctional control status, due to violation of the conditions of probation.

Procedures for pardon. Legal steps for a pardon, such as being crime free and meeting other conditions set by the state.

Programming. Implementation of a specific set of activities carried out according to guidelines to achieve a defined purpose, such as encouragement of inmates to earn a GED certificate as one activity that would reduce offender recidivism.

Project Newgate. Prison treatment program stressing full-time college work, group counseling, and aftercare following parole.

Psychological deprivation. Loss of or failure to develop emotional cohesion, support, or love through failure to provide emotional or physical caring.

Punishment ideology. Painful sanction applied to the offender, who is seen as an enemy of society.

Racial and ethnic groupings. Division of prisoners based on racial or ethnic characteristics.

Racially or ethnicity-oriented prison gang. Prison gang comprised almost exclusively of offenders from the same racial background or place of birth.

Railroading. The formal or even informal violation of the civil rights of the accused that leads to incapacitation or other unjustified punishment.

Rainmakers. Powerful politicians and allies within governmental jurisdictions with sufficient influence to arrange approval of private-sector proposals to develop private prisons and continue their use in the local jurisdictions. The "rain" refers to monetary gain to the provider of private prisons and can also apply to personal political contributions by private-sector providers to the election of candidates friendly to the providers.

Recidivism. Continued criminal activity following initial law-violating behavior.

RECLAIM. Ohio initiative designed to reduce admissions to the state's juvenile institutions through grants to local governments to underwrite such diversion.

Reclassification. The process by which inmate control and programming are changed.

Reentry. Process of inmates' return to the community and their adjustment to society ("free world").

Reentry courts. Specialized courts designed to reduce recidivism and improve public safety through judicial oversight of those offenders released from prison.

Reformatory. An institution for younger offenders that requires education and training, conditional release, and potential revocation of parole.

Reformatory movement. Offenders are unfortunate persons whose education, training, and discipline are inadequate; offenders should be sent to an educational penal institution for reform.

Regional offices. Second-tier management level of the Federal Bureau of Prisons.

Registration of criminals. Requirement imposed by government that all offenders be registered with local law enforcement agencies.

Rehabilitation ideology. Crime prevention through treatment of offenders and inmates to rehabilitate such offenders.

Rehabilitation model. Literally means using treatment to restore an offender to levels of social functioning not yet attained; seeks a change in behavior produced by providing treatment and services.

Reintegration. The planned transition of an inmate from prison to the community.

Reintegration model. A treatment approach to prevent relapse and recidivism by use of existing community services, often bundled into a reentry plan to lower recidivism; doctrine that assumes that crimes are caused by the community, with the assumption that community resources should be garnered and provided by local agencies to prevent recidivism.

Release on parole. Release of an inmate from confinement to expiration of sentence on condition of good behavior and supervision in the community.

Remand. To send a case back to the trier of fact for considerations not contrary to the appeal court's order.

Reprieve. A reduction in sentencing severity; sometimes used in death penalty cases, when execution of the offender is at least temporarily stopped.

Residential treatment center (RTC). A community-based facility for offenders that offers a wide range of programs and services, including housing. RTCs can include halfway houses, community-based correctional facilities, and group homes (for juveniles).

Restitution order. Requirement that the offender repay the victim.

Restorative justice. Punishment or sanctions intended to repair the damages done by the offender's crimes against the victim and the community. Restorative justice can include community service, restitution, sentencing circles, and mediation.

Retaliation. Act designed to repay (as an injury) in kind, or to return like for like, *especially* "to get revenge."

Retentionist. Person seeking to retain the death penalty.

Retribution. Getting even with the offender who has violated the rights of others and deserves to be punished.

Revenge. Seeking retribution for a harm inflicted.

Reverse. Appeal court's order to cease acting, operating, or arranging in a manner contrary to the usual.

Right of sanctuary. Privilege to avoid punishment by the offender's relocation to a sacred city or location.

Risk and needs assessments. Instruments used to determine the probability of recidivism or future criminal behavior.

Risk management. Strategies designed to provide increased supervision and surveillance for higher-risk offenders and less restrictive options for those of lower risk.

Roper v. Simmons. A U.S. Supreme Court decision that made it unconstitutional to impose capital punishment for a crime committed while under the age of 18.

Ruiz v. Estellez. U.S. Supreme Court decision that prisons must provide treatment to the developmentally challenged, assessing the conditions in the Texas Department of Corrections.

Sally port. Double-gated entry or exit point that restricts movement between the free world and prison.

Sanctuary. Asylum that placed the wrongdoer in seclusion or arrest in cities.

Sanford Bates. First director of the U.S. Bureau of Prisons.

"Screws". Inmate term for correctional officers.

Section 1983. Legal statute for seeking redress regarding deprivation of legal rights of prisoners.

Secure housing unit (SHU). "Control unit" within prisons, including single-cell and cell confinement practices to lessen directives by inmates to outside criminal organizations.

Security threat group (STG). Any organization or group of three or more persons having as one of its primary activities the commission of one or more criminal acts within the prison setting; prison gangs; a criminal enterprise having an organizational structure and internal leadership, acting as an ongoing criminal conspiracy that uses violence and other criminal activity to continue.

Selective incapacitation. Incapacitating high-risk offenders believed to pose substantial probability of additional crime, usually through imprisonment.

Self-efficacy. Ability of offenders to assume direction of their lives.

Self-insured. Government unit whose operations are not covered by external insurers.

Sentencing disparity. Difference between both the types and the length of sentences imposed for the same crime or seriousness of crimes when there is no legal basis that can be identified to explain this difference.

Sentencing guidelines. System of sentencing that imposes a predefined sentence length based on prior criminal history and crime severity that allows judges to depart from the guidelines if warranted by the circumstances.

Sex offender file. Official documents containing information on sex offenders and their previous crimes.

Sex offense. A violation of laws that control sexual intercourse or crimes of a carnal nature, including attempts at such crimes.

Sexual victimization. An umbrella term that includes any nonconsensual sexual activity that is committed by force or fear or mental or physical incapacitation, including through the use of alcohol or drugs.

Shakedown. Cell search to detect and control contraband.

Shock probation. Designed to give offenders a short "taste of the bars" followed by a period of supervised probation.

Shot caller. A group leader with authority to order events or changes, such as assault on a member of another prison gang.

Sick call. Opportunity for inmates to seek medical treatment.

Silence. Absence of speech between inmates within early prisons.

Single-sex experience. Inmate behavior involving other persons of the same sex in either a homogenital or homosocial relationship.

Slaves of the master. Inmates who are compelled to obey correctional managers and their staff.

Social stigma. Mark of dishonor or shame.

Societal protection argument. The argument that once executed, the offender cannot commit another crime, thus protecting society.

Sodomy. Anal or oral copulation with a member of the same or opposite sex or copulation with an animal; the U.S. Supreme Court recently struck down sodomy law application to consenting adults in private.

Solitary confinement. A punishment program requiring isolation of an inmate in a cell, also known as a "prison within a prison."

Special conditions of probation. Additional punishments ordered by the courts to probationers, such as fines, electronic monitoring, and house arrest.

Specific deterrence. Punishing individual offenders to prevent their further criminal behavior.

Status offenders. Juveniles who have committed acts that are law violations by virtue of the child's age but would not be criminal if committed by an adult (such as running away, incorrigibility, defiance).

Statutory exclusion. Principle that requires a category juvenile offender to be bound over as an adult, based on the type of offense committed. All such juveniles committing an identified offense must be transferred to adult court.

Step-down program. A prison practice designed to encourage inmates to earn release from a secure housing unit, earn more privileges and get out of isolation units faster if they stop engaging in gang activities, and participate in anger management and drug rehabilitation programs.

Stigma. A mark of shame and disgrace attached to the offender by virtue of his or her having committed an offense; mark of dishonor or shame attached to a person based on crime or criminal status and behavior.

Stigma of conviction. Effect of labeling, interference with ordinary social functioning, and resulting diminishment of offender.

Street gang. Criminal street gang means any ongoing organization, association, or group of three or more persons, whether formal or informal, having as one of its primary activities the commission of one or more of the criminal acts, having a common name or common identifying sign or symbol, and whose members individually or collectively engage in or have engaged in a pattern of criminal gang activity.

Strip search. Process of detecting inmate contraband by visual inspection of the bodies of inmates.

Supermax prison. A freestanding prison or designated area within a prison that functions to control and contain dangerous, violent, disruptive, and other serious behavior in a prison facility.

Super-predator. Aggressive juvenile offender believed to engage in frequent and dangerous behaviors.

Sursis. A suspended sentence in European countries requiring no future punishment provided the offender remains crime free during a specified time period.

Suspended sentence. Court determination to stop some formal processing of an offender, primarily stopping prosecution, not pronouncing a determination of guilt, or not requiring a sentence.

Technical probation violation. Probation sentence change due to charges that the offender violated the rules imposed by the court but not by committing a new crime.

Technical violation. A violation of the conditions of release other than the conviction for a new crime that can result in the offender being returned to prison.

Technologies for surveillance. Application of electronic and other programs designed to allow for the identification of locations of offenders.

Teen court. Courts staffed by juveniles who adjudicate juvenile problems and have the authority to enforce those adjudications.

Texas Syndicate. A prison gang operating in Texas that is primarily a Hispanic group that occasionally accepts Caucasian members.

The 211 Crew. A security threat group prison gang formed in 1995 in the Denver County Jail by Benjamin Davis, now serving the remainder of his 108-year sentence for the crimes of racketeering, conspiracy, and solicitation to commit assault. It is now headquartered in the Buena Vista Correctional Facility in Colorado.

The Great Law. Body of laws of the Quakers that saw hard labor as a more effective punishment than death for crimes and one that demanded compensation to victims.

Theory of disablement. Preventing offenders from commission of more crime through isolation, death, banishment, or mutilation.

Therapeutic community. A term applied to a participative, group-based approach to treating criminal behavior and drug addiction.

Ticket-of-leave. Certificate that is issued by the warden certifying that the offender has permission to leave the facility but that does not represent parole.

Total institution. Term describing institutional control over inmates and prison operations.

Tourniquet sentencing. When a judge increases the sanctions and conditions imposed on an offender.

"Traditional" female crimes. Those criminal offenses particular to the female gender (prostitution and infanticide, for example).

Training school for youth. A secure correctional institution for the custody, control, and reeducation of juvenile delinquents, usually housing more serious offenders sentenced to incarceration.

Transgender inmate. An inmate having a gender identity that is different from the assigned sex at birth.

Transincarceration. Movement of offenders diverted from mental health institutions to prisons.

Transinstitutionalism. Process referring to the transfer of the mentally ill to the justice system facilities, particularly jails and prisons.

Transportation. Legal sentence requiring the banishment of the offender to a different location; the act of transporting that offender to another country.

Treadmills. A mill worked by inmates treading on the periphery of a wide wheel having a horizontal axis and used in prison as a punishment.

Treatment in lieu of conviction. Diversion offered to offenders in which successful completion of probation allows the prosecutor or judge to cease prosecution if treatment program results in no conviction.

Treatment services. Any in-prison program designed to meet an inmate's needs and lower recidivism.

Truth-in-sentencing movement. Begun in the 1990s, this movement required inmates to serve a significant portion of their sentences before consideration for release.

UNICOR. A wholly owned federal subsidiary that supports the Federal Bureau of Prisons through the gainful employment of inmates across a variety of work programs.

Unionization. Organization of correctional officers for purposes of improved work conditions or salaries.

Unit team management. Control scheme uniting all staff into a coherent and unified force to attain prison objectives.

U.S. Corrections Corporation (USCC). A private-sector correctional provider.

U.S. Office of Juvenile Justice and Delinquency Prevention (OJJDP). A branch of the U.S. Department of Justice that seeks to improve knowledge about juvenile offenders and evaluate both exploratory and prevention research and that is capable of providing grants to researchers and administrators who would focus on solution of a major juvenile offense.

U.S. penitentiary. A correctional facility in which offenders are incarcerated to keep them from society and from each other so they can reflect on their crimes, repent, and be rehabilitated.

"Victimless" crimes. Offenses in which the victim does not seem to appear, or is equaled to the offender (prostitution and drug abuse, for example).

Vocational training. Any training program designed to increase job readiness and skills for inmates.

Walnut Street Jail. First penitentiary created in Philadelphia by the Quakers.

War on Drugs. A criminal justice program focusing on reducing the manufacture, use, sale, or trafficking of drugs.

Ward. A minor subject to wardship or protection by the state; may also refer to other persons protected by court order or legal status.

Weekender. A jail inmate who is allowed to live at home during the week (usually to work) and who must report to jail to serve his or her sentence on weekends.

Wergeld. The European word denoting *lex salica.*

White supremacist soldier. A low-ranking member of a prison gang who acts on the orders of a higher gang officer.

Women's liberation movement. A series of social movements intended to narrow the gaps between rights and privileges accorded to males and to free females from oppressive minority status.

Work camp. A low-security facility organized around work on the exterior of the prison facility.

Work release. A program in which inmates are allowed to work in the community with minimal restrictions but must return to confinement during nonworking hours.

Workhouse. A house of correction for persons guilty of minor law violations; sometimes referred to as a "poorhouse."

Writ of habeas corpus. A judicial order demanding that another person holding an inmate to produce the same in court and to justify continued imprisonment.

Writ of mandamus. A judicial order requiring the recipient to conform to the court's decision.

"Yellow card". European identification card, yellow in color, that signifies the carrier has been convicted of a crime.

Youth gang. A continuing criminal enterprise by juveniles and young adults that commits violence and other criminal acts to sustain itself.

author index

Note: References including the letter "n" refer to the note number indicated on the specified page. For example, 240n5 means the author is cited in note 5 on page 240.

a

C

d

f

g

h

i

j

l

m

n

o

p

r

s

V

W

Z

subject index

a

b

c

d

e

f

g

h

i

j

l

m

n

o

p

q

r

S

t

u

V

W

Z